Handbook of Complex Occupational Disability Claims

Early Risk Identification, Intervention, and Prevention

D1716505

Handbook of Complex Occupational Disability Claims

Early Risk Identification, Intervention, and Prevention

Edited by

Izabela Z. Schultz
The University of British Columbia
Vancouver, British Columbia, Canada

WITHDRAWN

and

Robert J. Gatchel
The University of Texas at Arlington
Arlington, Texas

TOURO COLLEGE LIBRARY
Kings Hwy

KH

Editors
Izabela Z. Schultz
University of British Columbia
Department of Education, Counselling Psychology & Special Education
2125 Main Hall
Vancouver, BC V6T 1Z4
Canada
ischultz@telus.net

Robert J. Gatchel
University of Texas
Southwestern Medical Center
5323 Harry Hines Blvd.
Dallas, TX 75235
USA
robert.gatchel@utsouthwestern.edu

ISBN: 978-0-387-22451-0 (hardcover) e-ISBN: 978-0-387-28919-9
ISBN: 978-0-387-89383-9 (softcover)
DOI: 10.1007/978-0-387-28919-9

Library of Congress Control Number: 2005926893

© 2005 Springer Science+Business Media, LLC, First softcover printing 2009
All rights reserved. This work may not be translated or copied in whole or in part without the written permission of the publisher (Springer Science+Business Media, LLC, 233 Spring Street, New York, NY 10013, USA), except for brief excerpts in connection with reviews or scholarly analysis. Use in connection with any form of information storage and retrieval, electronic adaptation, computer software, or by similar or dissimilar methodology now known or hereafter developed is forbidden.
The use in this publication of trade names, trademarks, service marks and similar terms, even if they are not identified as such, is not to be taken as an expression of opinion as to whether or not they are subject to proprietary rights.

Printed on acid-free paper

springer.com

4/15/13

Contributors

Jonathan Borkum, Ph.D.
Health Psych Maine
Waterville, Maine

Marilyn L. Bowman, Ph.D.
Department of Psychology
Simon Fraser University
Vancouver/Burnaby, Canada

Nancy Canning, Psy.D.
Alta Bates/Summit
Medical Center–Henrick
Campus Berkeley, California

Joan Crook, Ph.D.
School of Nursing
Faculty of Health Science
McMaster University
Hamilton, Ontario, Canada

Jeffrey Dersh, Ph.D.
Productive Rehabilitation Institute of
Dallas for Ergonomics (PRIDE)
Dallas, Texas

Marie-José Durand, Ph.D.
Disability Research and
Training Center
Department of Community Health
Sciences
Université de Sherbrooke
Quebec, Ontario, Canada

Renée-Louise Franche, Ph.D.
Institute for Work and Health
Public Health Sciences
University of Toronto
Toronto, Ontario, Canada

John Frank, M.D., CCFP, M.Sc., FRCP(C)
Institute for Work and Health
Public Health Sciences
University of Toronto
Toronto, Canada

Gary M. Franklin, M.D., M.P.H.
School of Public Health and
Community Medicine
University of Washington
Seattle, Washington
University of British Columbia
Vancouver, British Columbia, Canada

Niklas Krause, M.D. M.P.H. Ph.D.
Division of Occupational and
Environmental Medicine
Occupational Epidemiology Program
University of California
at San Francisco
San Francisco, California

Jacob Lazarovic, M.D.
Vice President and Chief Medical
Officer
Broadspire Services, Inc.
Plantation, Florida

Gordon Leeman, M.S.
Productive Rehabilitation Institute of Dallas for Ergonomics (PRIDE)
Dallas, Texas

Steven James Linton, Ph.D.
Department of Occupational and Environmental Medicine
Örebro University Hospital and Department of Behavioral, Social and Legal Sciences—Psychology
Örebro University, Örebro, Sweden

Patrick Loisel, M.D.
Disability Research and Training Center
Department of Surgery (Division of Orthopaedics
Université de Sherbrooke
Quebec, Ontario, Canada

Chris J. Main, Ph.D.
Department of Behavioural Medicine
Hope Hospital, Salford Royal Hospitals NHS Trust and
Honorary Professor (Faculty of Medicine)
University of Manchester
United Kingdom

Donald D. McGeary, Ph.D.
Clinical Health Psychology
Wilford Hall Medical Center
59th MDOS/MMCPH
San Entario, Texas

J. Mark Melhorn M.D.
Section of Orthopaedics, Department of Surgery
University of Kansas School of Medicine
Wichita, Kansas

Akiko Okifuji, Ph.D.
Pain Research and Management Center
Department of Anesthesiology
University of Utah

Thomas M. Pendergrass, RN, Ph.D.
UnumProvident
Chattanooga, Tennessee

Ceri J. Phillips, Ph.D.
Centre for Health Economics and Policy Studies
School of Health Sciences
University of Wales Swansea
Wales, United Kingdom

Peter Polatin, M.D.
Departments of Psychiatry and Anesthesiology and Pain Management
The University of Texas Southwestern Medical Center at Dallas
Dallas, Texas

Richard C. Robinson, Ph.D.
Departments of Psychiatry and Anesthesiology and Pain Management
The University of Texas Southwestern Medical Center at Dallas
Dallas, Texas

Wanda K. Roehl, C.S.P.
Manager of Workforce Placement
Raytheon Aircraft Company
Wichita, Kansas

Ronald M. Ruff, Ph.D.
St. Mary's Hospital and Medical Center Department of Neurosurgery
University of California, San Francisco San Francisco Clinical Neurosciences
San Francisco, California

Joti Samra, Ph.D.
Private Practice
Vancouver, British Columbia, Canada

Robert J. Sbordone, Ph.D., A.B.P.P
Private Practice
Laguna Hills, California

Jerome A. Schofferman, M.D.
The San Francisco Spine Institute
SpineCare Medical Group
San Francisco, California

Izabela Z. Schultz, Ph.D., ABPP, ABVE
Department of Educational and Counseling Psychology and Special Education
The University of British Columbia
Vancouver, British Columbia, Canada

Alan M. Strizak, M.D.
College of Medicine
University of California
Irvine, California

Dennis C. Turk, Ph.D.
Department of Anesthesiology
University of Washington
School of Medicine
Seattle, Washington

Judith A. Turner, Ph.D.
Department of Psychiatry and Behavioral Sciences
University of Washington
Seattle, Washington

Paul Watson, Ph.D., M.Sc., Bask (Hones), MCSP
Department of Anesthesia, Critical Care and Pain Management
Leicester-Warwick Medical School
Leicester, United Kingdom

Travis Whitfill, B.A.
Department of Anesthesiology and Pain Management
The University of Texas Southwestern Medical Center at Dallas
Dallas, Texas

Alanna Winter, M.A.
Department of Educational and Counseling Psychology and Special Education
University of British Columbia
Vancouver, British Columbia Canada

Larry K. Wilkinson M.D.
Pro-Med Physician Services
Wichita, Kansas

Anna Wright Stowell, Ph.D.
Department of Psychiatry and Anesthesiology and Pain Management
The University of Texas Southwestern Medical Center at Dallas
Dallas, Texas

Preface

The health care, compensation, insurance and legal systems, together with employers, in the Western world are challenged by a "new generation" of complex and multifaceted, yet still inadequately understood, clinical conditions with major occupational impact. These conditions include chronic pain (such as headache, back pain, neck pain and fibromyalgia), repetitive strain injuries, mild traumatic brain injuries, depression, anxiety and specific posttraumatic stress disorders. The resulting wave of occupational disabilities brought on by these conditions defies traditional but outdated biomedical reductionistic models of identification, rehabilitation and management. These occupational disabilities, which we conceptualize and term in this Handbook as "*biopsychosocial*," have been expanding more rapidly than medically based disabilities. They have now reached the very top rankings in the hierarchy of occupational disabilities in industrialized countries, and are accompanied by spiraling costs from associated health care, compensation, rehabilitation, litigation, and productivity losses.

The last two decades have seen a proliferation of basic science and clinically based research on these conditions. Despite these efforts, the knowledge generated by this research has not yet been integrated and translated into clinical and case management practice, policy and new paradigms of service delivery. There is no overarching conceptual framework for diagnosis, risk identification, early intervention, return to work and prevention. Rehabilitation and compensation systems, and professionals working within them, together with employers, are challenged by the pressing need to develop effective clinical and occupational interventions, as well as management and prevention approaches for these complex yet still elusive disabilities. Unfortunately, these professionals still have no access to a systematic and integrated body of knowledge that would provide them with conceptual and research support for evidence-based effective practices and policies in this expanding field. This urgent need stimulated the development of the present Handbook.

Likewise, the managed care systems, insurance industry, workers' compensation systems, health care and rehabilitation systems, as well as our legal system, continue to struggle with the onslaught of these complex, chronic, labor-intensive, poorly understood and costly claims. The absence of evidence-informed paradigms, guidelines and strategies for early identification, intervention and management of these claims (for use in compensation, occupational and clinical settings) results in multi-billion dollar disability-related economic losses across industrialized countries. These losses are already estimated at several percent of the gross national product in those countries, and they are continuing to rise. Moreover, for more than a decade, the system "stakeholders" delineated above have not been able to effectively deal with secondary prevention of occupational disabilities that require a biopsychosocial diagnostic and intervention framework. Their mandate to facilitate the recovery and return to work of persons with biopsychosocial disabilities (and thereby reducing disability costs) has therefore been seriously compromised.

The problem continues to escalate despite the proliferation of thousands of studies on predictors and early intervention programs for individuals at high risk for chronic occupational disability. The role of psychosocial factors in the development or maintenance of occupational disability is frequently raised, though still poorly understood. Explanations of disability as solely, or primarily, motivated by secondary gain or preexisting psychology abound in the medico-legal context. Yet, no systematic and legally defensible ways of identifying those at risk for disability and then intervening with them early before disability sets in, have been implemented in such contexts. This is the current status in the field, in spite of the consistently promising outcome data on the use of an interdisciplinary model of early intervention, coupled with the effectiveness of cognitive-behavioral approaches.

A mismatch and a chasm between the traditional biomedical model, upon which health care, compensation and legal systems have been historically constructed, and the new paradigm required for the effective management of biopsychosocial disabilities, have been largely responsible for the escalation of this problem. At the same time, the current clinical literature has few examples of attempts at the integration of research evidence on the seemingly disparate clinical conditions (e.g., non-specific chronic pain, repetitive strain injury and posttraumatic psychological and neuropsychological conditions) for which the biomedical model has failed in both research and practice. The major aim of this interdisciplinary Handbook, therefore, is to bridge the gap between new developments in the science of biopsychosocial disabilities, with particular emphasis on medicine and psychology, and the clinical, occupational, organizational, compensation, and case management practices in what is widely understood as the "disability industry". This has been accomplished using an integrative biopsychosocial paradigm, as opposed to the traditional but outdated unidisciplinary biomedical model following the anachronistic Cartesian mind-body distinction. The Handbook focuses on the translation of the science of prediction of work disability from early markers to new research and clinical practice models including the clinical, rehabilitation, occupational, case management and compensation approaches in the area of high risk, costly and complex disabilities. Being cognizant of the evidence that only a minority of individuals with biopsychosocial disability go on to develop chronicity and fail to return to work, identification of these individuals who are at highest risk for such disability becomes critically important.

Our Handbook has been envisioned as a "transfer of knowledge" project that contributes an integration of the best, state-of-the-art research on the identification of high risk for disability, prediction of occupational disability, and early intervention with those who are at risk of failing to return to work following trauma and injury. Those individuals are most likely to become the insurance and rehabilitation industry's "complex claims": poorly understood, traditionally treatment-resistant, contentious, litigious and expensive. They are also likely to become employers' most significant human resource, productivity and "bottom line" economic challenges with respect to prevention, disability management and job accommodation. The incurring disability costs may potentially threaten their company's economic viability. And, last but not least, they are most likely to become an object of litigation involving employment law, personal injury, workers' compensation, and long-term disability entitlement.

These adverse scenarios are not yet fully preventable in the current social, political, legal, policy and economic contexts. However, major changes in systems, policies and practices applied with these disabilities can be effected if new integrated evidence-based approaches to prediction, risk identification, early clinical, case management and occupational interventions are applied. Our Handbook constitutes a state-of-the-art, integrated research-based resource to facilitate the transfer of knowledge and the development of new clinical and occupational practices in healthcare, rehabilitation, insurance and workers' compensation industries. This Handbook also synthesizes and critically reviews the current research on biopsychosocial conditions, and provides an etiological and epidemiological synopsis with implications for early diagnosis, risk identification, intervention, case management and disability prevention. It focuses on the functional and occupational impact of these conditions, as well as the most effective intervention approaches in clinical, workplace and compensation environments. The conceptual and methodological issues and controversies, together with directions for future research and practice, are also highlighted. Not only will the reader be provided with knowledge of concepts and the empirical evidence gathered to date, in order to guide their practice, but also the necessary key components of a "how-to" toolbox for their everyday work and for future advances.

ACKNOWLEDGMENTS

We would like to thank all of the authors for their valuable state-of-the-art contributions, and for making this first integrative Handbook on a biopsychosocial approach to early detection and intervention with occupational disabilities come to fruition. We would also like to acknowledge the support and assistance of many colleagues on both the research and clinical sides of occupational disability through discussion, exchange of information and suggestions. In addition, we would like to thank Sharon Panulla, Malcolm Crystal, and Herman Makler of Springer, who supported the vision of this Handbook and encouraged its timely completion. We are also indebted to Alanna Winter, Research Coordinator at the University of British Columbia, for her technical and research contributions to the development of this book. We also thank the numerous consultants who helped with different aspects of this multifaceted project, including physicians, psychologists, vocational rehabilitation experts, occupational health nurses, researchers, and compensation/insurance specialists spanning the North American continent.

Izabela Z. Schultz
Robert J. Gatchel

Contents

II. PREDICTION OF DISABILITY IN PAIN-RELATED AND PSYCHOLOGICAL CONDITIONS

A. PREDICTION OF CHRONIC PAIN DISABILITY

B. PREDICTION OF DISABILITY AFTER HEAD INJURY

C. PREDICTION OF DISABILITY AFTER PSYCHOLOGICAL TRAUMA

Introduction

Izabela Z. Schultz and Robert J. Gatchel

Our Handbook constitutes a state-of-the-art, integrated research-based resource to facilitate the transfer of knowledge and the development of new clinical and occupational practices in healthcare, rehabilitation, disability insurance and workers' compensation industries. This Handbook also synthesizes and critically reviews the current research on biopsychosocial conditions, and provides an etiological and epidemiological synopsis with implications for early diagnosis, risk identification, intervention, case management and disability prevention. It focuses on the functional and occupational impact of these conditions, as well as the most effective intervention approaches in clinical, workplace and compensation environments. The conceptual and methodological issues and controversies, together with directions for future research and practice, are also highlighted. Not only will the reader be provided with knowledge of concepts and the empirical evidence gathered to date, in order to guide their practice, but also the necessary key components of a "how-to" toolbox for their everyday work and for future advances.

This Handbook has been written by distinguished researchers and clinicians, all recognized experts in the fields of occupational rehabilitation, medicine, psychology and neuropsychology, to provide the most "cutting edge" account of the key discussed conditions. Implications for best evidence-informed practices in clinical and vocational rehabilitation, case management, healthcare and compensation are drawn from the body of knowledge of each one of the biopsychosocial conditions, and from integrative themes cutting across these seemingly disparate conditions.

The Handbook consists of five major parts. Part I, "Conceptual and Methodological Issues in Prediction of Disability," provides an overview, critical analysis and integration of emerging conceptual models guiding theory, research and practice in the areas of diagnosis, risk identification, early intervention and prevention of biopsychosocial disabilities. The epidemiological rationale for the development of new paradigms of early identification and intervention is presented, highlighting the evidence for "disability epidemics" in industrialized countries and the likely contributors to the spiraling human and economic impact of disability costs. The conceptual quagmire associated with the relationship between impairment and disability is also discussed. Key conceptual models, factors and outcomes implicated in prediction of disability are discussed. A Three Stage Continuum Model from cause to disability to decision is also proposed to guide research and practice in predicting and intervening with occupational disability. This part addresses the key methodological issues identified in the literature. Factors that particularly hamper research and practice are critically reviewed, and solutions to some of the problems suggested. Integrative approaches to the expanding research data and current systematic reviews of the literature on predictors of disability are also presented. In addition, methodological issues associated with outcome measures in occupational disability are highlighted. Concluding this part is a discussion of key issues associated with outcome measures in occupational disability.

Part II, "Prediction of Disability in Pain-Related and Psychological Conditions," provides state-of-the-art critical reviews of evidence on specific disabilities which are best understood using a biopsychosocial approach. The conditions discussed in this section are (1) pain-related conditions: back pain, neck pain, whiplash, fibromyalgia, headache and repetitive strain injury; (2) brain injury, with a specific focus on mild traumatic brain injury; (3) posttraumatic stress disorder; and (4) depression and anxiety in the workplace. Critical conceptual, evidentiary and clinical issues associated with these conditions (including diagnoses, causality, risk identification, impact on work function and intervention directions) are highlighted in this part. Controversies around the "objective" versus "subjective" aspects of these disabilities are also addressed using current scientific and clinical evidence.

Part III, "Application of Disability Prediction in Compensation, Health Care and Occupational Contexts," bridges the research and clinical evidence discussed in previous chapters with clinical and occupational practices in secondary prevention, early detection and intervention with biopsychosocial disabilities. Risk for disability flagging systems are reviewed and implications for practice drawn. The medico-legal aspects of clinical practices with these disabilities, in the private disability insurance contexts, and applicable in other compensation environments (such as workers' compensation), are discussed, and best practices for clinicians suggested. Controversies around the identification of secondary gains and losses in the medico-legal context are addressed using current research evidence. Finally, evidence-informed practices for early intervention with injured workers at high risk for disability at the subacute stage in the workers' compensation environment are drawn from a systematic review of the current literature.

Part IV, "Early Intervention with At-Risk Groups," provides an overview of the specific early intervention programs for persons at risk for disability that show evidence of effectiveness. The following approaches are discussed: (1) an early interdisciplinary clinical team approach (the Dallas model); (2) an integrative clinical and occupational approach (the Sherbrooke model); (3) a cognitive-behavioral approach (the Swedish model); and (4) the Ctd MAP Intervention Program for Musculoskeletal Disorders.

Finally, Part V, "Where Are We Now and Where Are We Heading," discusses the common and emerging themes that guide the research and practice of risk identification and early intervention across various conditions, integrating the critical "what we know" and "what we don't know" with respect to the application of knowledge in clinical and case management and occupational practice. Current and future research, policy and practice directions emerge from this overview. The evidence is converging that we are currently on the brink of solving the complex problem of biopsychosocial disabilities!

It is likely that the reader of this Handbook will find some of the chapters controversial or offering disparate explanations. This would not be surprising in a field which has been historically polarized and politicized. In a larger socio-political context, this polarization likely reflects the continuing disagreement between those advocating purely biomedical (the body), purely psychological (the mind), or purely systemic (the workplace, the medico-legal system or society at large) explanations and solutions to the problem of biopsychosocial disability. Our Handbook attempts to cut through this politicization and polarization with current scientific evidence in order to impact the best practices in a balanced way, without attributing blame either to the individual or the system. Just like any human behavior, occupational disability is a function of individual differences and the environmental and personal context in which an individual's motivations and actions are formed and executed. Last, but not least, the Editors wish to note that this Handbook was expanded beyond the current original author contributions to the field, by the addition of several recently published leading or seminal papers, to which chapter contributors made frequent references.

I

CONCEPTUAL AND METHODOLOGICAL ISSUES IN PREDICTION OF DISABILITY

1

Do We Have a Disability Epidemic?

J. Mark Melhorn, Jacob Lazarovic, and Wanda K. Roehl

Disability is a subject you may read about in the newspaper, but not think of as something that might actually happen to you. However, the chances of becoming disabled are probably greater than you realize. Studies show that a 20-year-old worker has a 3-in-10 chance of becoming disabled before reaching retirement age (Social Security Administration, 2003). In 1997, 52.6 million people or 19.7 percent of the population had some level of disability and 33.0 million or 12.3 percent had a severe disability (McHeil, 2001).

In the United States, there are three major types of disability insurance: A federal program (which has three parts: Disability Insurance (DI), Supplemental Security Income (SSI), and Veteran's Administration (VA) disability; a state or federally regulated program (Workers' Compensation Insurance); and commercial insurance programs (private long-term disability insurance). Recent years have seen a greater demand for private long-term disability insurance, as the trend increases toward less than total reliance on public programs to support disabled workers (Snook & Webster, 1987). In 2001, DI, SSI and VA provided over $89.7 billion in cash benefits to 10.2 million adults (Social Security Administration, 2003). However, insurance costs are only part of the total cost because not everyone is covered by insurance, and insurance does not cover all disabilities. Disability can never be totally prevented or eliminated, but disability and its costs can be substantially reduced through more effective treatment and rehabilitation, including patient education, vocational rehabilitation and improved criteria reflecting medical and technological advances, changes in the labor market that affect the skills needed to perform work and work settings. If these federal disability programs do not update scientific and labor market information, they risk overestimating the limiting nature of some disabilities while underestimating others.

INTRODUCTION: EMERGING TRENDS IN DISABILITY

Musculoskeletal pain is the most common cause of short-term and long-term workplace disability (Chaplin, 1991). Musculoskeletal pain, however, is a natural part of everyone's life (Hadler, 1992). The term disability has historically referred to a

DOI: 10.1007/978-0-387-28919-9_1, © 2009 Springer Science+Business Media, LLC

broad category of individuals with diverse limitations in their ability to meet social or occupational demands. Disability is an ambiguous demographic, but one that is unambiguously increasing (Aarts, Burkhauser, & de Jong, 1992). Socioeconomic trends such as aging, employment, family support, and changing legislative criteria have contributed to the growth of the population categorized as disabled, making disability an important issue for policymakers, even though its definition is often a point of contention. In an effort to control this epidemic, several organizations are moving away from the term disability and instead are referring to specific activity limitations (Barnhart, 2002). This is to encourage an emphasis on the specific activities the individual can perform relative to the environmental conditions in which the activities are to be performed. This implies that disability is context specific, not inherent in the individual, but a function of the interaction of the individual and the environment.

Thus, the definitions of disability expand and contract more along political and ideological lines than according to any clear physical determinations. Depending upon one's definition of disability, between 35 and 46 million Americans can be labeled as disabled (Demeter, Andersson, & Smith, 2001). Unlike other human conditions such as poverty, gender, childhood, old age, and race, the definition of disability and the determination of who is disabled continues to challenge governments and adjudicating bodies. Since no standardized or generally accepted definition exists, calculating the cost of disability is even more difficult. If the cost of exclusion from the workplace, medical care, legal services, and earning replacements are summed, the 1980 estimate was $177 billion or approximately 6.5% of the gross domestic product (Demeter et al., 2001).

Obviously, disability management represents an area of medicine that has a large financial impact upon society (Melhorn, 2000e). It is only in recent times that disability and impairment have been accorded legal status. Despite the large expenditures of money, time, personnel, and resources there exists no single comprehensive compendium of information on disability, the role of physicians in diagnosing and quantifying impairment, the role of lay professionals (most notable lawyers) in translating medically derived impairment into legally allowable disability for financial reimbursements, and an analysis of the social and legal constructs upon which disability determination is to be based (Melhorn, 2001b). Impairment and disability evaluations encompass medical and nonmedical aspects of injuries and illnesses and are effectively accomplished only when both components are properly managed. These evaluations are often completed by a physician not involved in the patient's care through a process called an independent medical evaluation or IME (Melhorn, 2001a; Melhorn, Zeppieri, & Wilkinson, 2000).

Physicians are trained to assemble and analyze medical information and communicate with each other within a framework of established medical diagnostic criteria and generally accepted medical principles and practice. This highly technical and specialized medical language must be translated for communication with nonmedical users of medical information. In addition, the legal system has its own highly specialized language. Definitions of the same word may be different for each party. Therefore, physicians must become more than casually acquainted with the specific provisions and procedures of the employment and workers' compensation laws and regulations in the states where they practice, the Social Security Act, the Americans with Disabilities Act, the Family and Medical Leave Act, and the regulations published by the federal agencies administering these statutes.

Physicians are often asked to provide a report describing the functional loss an individual developed as a result of personal injury or industrial accident. A paradox is created by this legal request because the rating of functional impairment is, at best, an inexact science (Gloss & Wardle, 1982; Rondinelli et al., 1997; McCarthy et al., 1998). Further, the *AMA Guides* 5th edition (AMA, 2000) states that "the *Guides* are not intended to be used for direct estimates of work disability." Impairment percentages derived according to the *Guides* criteria do not measure work disabilities. Therefore, it is inappropriate to use the *Guides'* criteria or ratings to make direct estimates of work disability. Yet, often the impairment of function or rating is used by the legal system to provide a monetary award for the patient based on a perceived disability. Therefore, disability evaluations encompass both medical and nonmedical aspects of functional loss and are only effectively defined when all components are properly managed and considered. Unfortunately, this conversion of impairment to work disability can lead to an adversarial situation with potential for abuse and possible physician exploitation. Litigation may be encouraged by attempts to increase the rating and the physician "gatekeeper" may be drawn unwittingly into the fray between the warring adversaries. It is essential that physicians understand the principles and process of impairment evaluation if they are to be effective in providing assessment services which will play a role in determining a financial award to a claimant. In an effort to provide a uniform approach, based on the current science and medical consensus, the *AMA Guides* is used worldwide to estimate adult permanent impairment. A survey completed in 1999 indicates that 40 of 51 jurisdictions in the United States (the 50 states and the District of Columbia) currently use or reference the *AMA Guides* as their standard in workers' compensation (AMA, 2000).

DEFINITION OF EPIDEMIC

Outbreak: Webster's Dictionary (Mish & Gilman, 1991) defines outbreak (1602) as a sudden or violent increase in activity or currency, a sudden rise in the incidence of a disease, a sudden increase in numbers of a harmful organism and especially an insect within a particular area.

Epidemic: Webster's Dictionary (Mish et al., 1991) defines epidemic (1603) from the French épidémique from Late Latin epidemia, from Greek epidEmia visit, epidemic, from epidEmos visiting, epidemic, from epi- + dEmos people as affecting or tending to affect a disproportionately large number of individuals within a population, community, or region at the same time, excessively prevalent, or contagious.

Contagious: Webster's Dictionary (Mish et al., 1991) defines contagious (14th century) as communicable by contact, catching, or exciting similar emotions or conduct in others.

A health epidemic (American Academy of Orthopaedic Surgeons, 1996; Greenberg, Daniels, Flanders, Eley, & Boring, 1993; Fraumeni & Hoover, 1985) requires the following five criteria:

1. *An outbreak*: Large number of individuals affected
2. *Transmission*: source, vehicle, mode of transmission, and method of propagation
3. *Causation*: time factors, location, and risk factors

4. *Links*: observed association between a risk factor and affected individual
5. *Diagnosis*: What is the disease?

How do these five criteria impact the disability epidemic?

5. *Diagnosis*: An individual is often considered disabled if they have a decrease in, or the loss or absence of, the capacity to meet personal, social, or occupational demands, or to meet statutory or regulatory requirements (AMA, 1993). Additional definitions can be found in this chapter. Figure 1 shows the percentage distribution by organ system.

4. *Links*: The current literature indicates that the growth in disability from musculoskeletal discomfort is somewhat unique to modern western culture (Colledge & Johnson, 2000). Studies of third world countries show similar prevalence of discomfort (approximately 44%), but disability is virtually nonexistent (Anderson, 1984; Waddell, 1998). Pain and discomfort is seen as an acceptable part of living. Interestingly, however, as western medicine becomes more prevalent in these countries, disability increases (Waddell, 1998). Historically, those who did the manual labor required in developing our modern society likely suffered musculoskeletal discomfort over the years, yet the record is mostly silent about disability. As with today's less-developed cultures, if they had pain and discomfort it appears they simply accepted it and made necessary adjustments in their lives. The Menninger study on disabled workers based on wage replacement in the 80's showed a marked increase in absenteeism based on wage replacement when disabled (Drury, 1990). About 16% remained disabled when the wage replacement was 25% or less and about 75% remained disabled when the wage replacement was over 75%. This was independent of the severity of the injuries. All statistics show this trend. As well there is greater disability in those who are represented by an attorney. The number of individuals considered disabled and disability payments increases as the jobless rate increases (Unchitelle, 2002).

3. *Causation*: Factors associated with increasing disability include specific individual demographics, socioeconomic concerns, healthcare trends, and legislation. An overview is presented here with details provided later in the chapter. The impact of an aging population on disability prevalence is straightforward. Nearly three out of four Americans over the age of 80 had a disability in the form of a limitation on a basic functional activity in 1997 (Drury, 1990). As both a consequence and cause, poverty

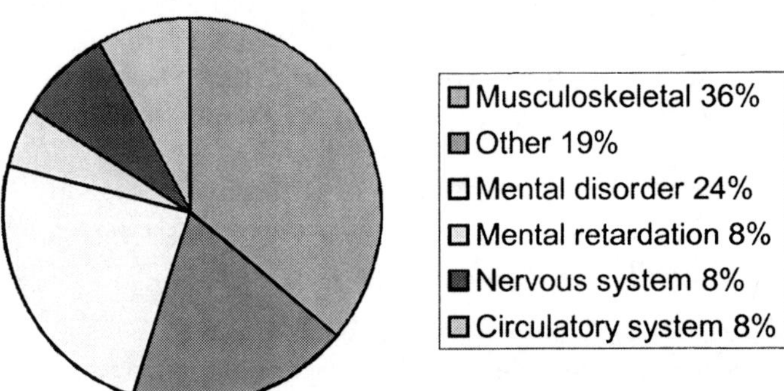

Figure 1. Percentage Distribution of Disabled Workers.

has long been linked to disability (McHeil, 2001). In the 1997 Survey of Income and Program Participation (SIPP), 28 percent of adults ages 25 to 64 with a severe disability lived in poverty, compared with 8.3 percent for the general population; poverty rates under the National Health Interview Survey (NHIS) were 27 percent with an additional 19 percent of disabled Americans considered "near poor" (with incomes up to twice the official poverty cutoff). Americans with a disability are at a substantial disadvantage in employment, access to private health insurance, and levels of educational achievement. Survival across a wide spectrum of diseases and traumas has improved due to medical advances.

Many individuals have a continual presence of discomfort in their lives. A recent study of 3000 randomly selected individuals showed that 14.4% of a general population experience carpal tunnel-like symptoms as a part of daily living (Atroshi et al., 1999). Back pain shows a yearly prevalence in the United States population of 15–20% (Andersson, 1995). Among working-age people surveyed, 50% admit to back symptoms each year (Sternbach, 1986; Vallfors, 1985). Most of these common ailments are benign, and recovery time is minimal. However, a small number recover much more slowly than expected and generate a considerably greater cost. A 1992 review of 106,961 workers' compensation low back injury cases found that approximately 86% of the costs were incurred by 10% of the injured workers (Hashemi, Webster, Lancey, & Volinn, 1997). A similar study of 21,338 work-related upper extremities injuries found that 25% of the claims accounted for 89% of the costs (Hashemi, Webster, Clancy, & Courtney, 1998). A State of Washington study found that 5% of their compensation claims (accounting for 84% of the costs) are from individuals with nonverifiable muscle and back complaints (Cheadle et al., 1994). Nationally, injured workers with skeletal fractures incur an average of 21 days off work, and those with amputations incur 18 lost days (Bureau of Labor and Statistics, 2003). Yet patients with carpal tunnel syndrome complaints average 25 days away from work (Bureau of Labor and Statistics, 2003). Similar studies have demonstrated that compensated injuries have delayed recovery (Vallfors, 1985; Hunter, Shaha, Flint, & Tracy, 1998; Sander & Meyers, 1986), increased disability (Guest & Drummond, 1992; Jamison, Matt, & Parris, 1988; Leavitt, 1992; Milhous et al., 1989), and decreased return to work rates (Trief & Donelson, 1995; Bednar, Baesher-Griffith, & Osterman, 1998; Milhous et al., 1989; Guck, Meilman, Skultety, & Dowd, 1986).

At any given time, up to 45% of currently employed workers could file work related injury or disability claims, but most do not, choosing instead to carry out their job responsibilities, accepting some discomfort as part of living (Biddle, Roberts, Rosenman, & Welch, 1998).

A major international report from 15 centers in Asia, Africa, Europe, and the Americas reviewed 5,438 adults coming to health clinics with persistent pain during a period of 6 months or more during the prior year (Gureje, von Korff, Simon, & Gater, 1998; Gureje, Simon, & von Korff, 2001). Participants, who were interviewed and given psychological testing, were found to have rates of anxiety and/or depression four times higher than the normal population. Of these, 48% had complaints of back pain, 42% joint pain, and 34% arm or leg pain. These results imply, as other studies have done, that psychological or social distress can be manifest as physical complaints that create a perceived need for professional health care (Ciccone, Just, & Bandilla, 1996). In the workplace, psychosocial stress added to work activities can make even the normal discomfort levels associated with a particular job intolerable and result in a disability claim. Often these complaints can have minimal or only coincidental relationship to the actual job tasks. After becoming disability claimants, these individuals can, by maintaining their symptoms, exert a level of control over their psychosocial stressors. With a medically acceptable physical diagnosis, the psychosocial concerns are legitimized, pride is maintained, and an unpleasant environment now becomes more socially acceptable (Aronoff, 1991).

Jurisdictional rules, social economics, and legislative guides impact the causation of disability.The Veterans Administration was established as an independent agency on July 21, 1930 by Executive Order 5398 and later became the Department of Veterans Affairs (VA). The Social Security Act was passed into law by President Franklin D. Roosevelt on August 14, 1935. In 1980, President Carter signed PL 96-265, requiring that the Social Security Administration commence periodic reviews of the validity of the disability claims. The intent was to purge the rolls of those who could work. PL 96-265, enacted a century after the birth of social reform, produced one of the bleakest chapters in the annals of the disabled. Many did not meet impairment criteria. These claimants ascribed their disability to symptoms, particularly the symptom of pain, and were victims of a legal system that simultaneously certifies people as totally disabled and at the same time seeks to rehabilitate. The healthcare system shared concerns that labeling a person as disabled could weaken motivation for recovery, income awards based on disability would provide a financial disincentive to rehabilitation, and certifying a patient's disability for a government program would be in conflict with the physician's therapeutic relationship. The Occupational Safety and Health Act of 1970, 29 USC 651, Public Law 91-596 developed the concept of disability starting at more than 30 days away from work. In January of 1990, the Americans with Disabilities Act (ADA) redefined disabilities and subsequently impacted the disabled. The Government Accounting Office authored two reports, the first (GAO-01-367) : Workers' Compensation: Action needed to reduce payment errors in SSA disability and other programs (McMullin, 2001), the second (GAO-02-597) or SSA and VA disability programs. Re-examination of disability criteria is needed to help ensure program integrity (Barnhart, 2002). Their conclusions were that over time, progress in the fields of medicine and technology has provided a better understanding of how disease and injury affect the ability to work. Likewise, changes in the labor market have affected the skills needed to perform work and the settings in which work occurs. Together, scientific advances and labor market changes redefine the extent that physical or mental conditions affect the ability of people with disabilities to work. Not keeping abreast of scientific and labor market information puts federal programs at risk of undermining their efforts to help some persons with disabilities achieve economic independence or work to their full potential.

Employer practices have changed in response to the Americans With Disabilities Act and the Equal Employment Opportunity Commission who have responded with the stated goal "to provide a clear and comprehensive national mandate for the elimination of discrimination against individuals with disabilities" (Equal Employment Opportunity Commission, 1997; Equal Employment Opportunity Commission: 2001). The ADA establishes that individuals cannot be excluded from opportunities unless they are actually unable to do the job with reasonable accommodation by the employer. Therefore, any system an employer might choose should meet three standards: integration of individual and departmental responsibilities; documentation, quantification and measurement of individual demands and each worker's abilities; and annual follow-up and re-testing (Smith, 1996).

2. *Transmission*: Variations in the size of the population receiving disability payments across countries cannot be explained by simple differences in health. Rather, the process to disability is shaped by both social and medical factors. When governments ignore this reality, a policy-generated disability epidemic is possible. Aarts et al (Aarts et al., 1992; Aarts, Burkhauser, & Jong, 1996) found that the extraordinary increase in Dutch disability rolls in the 1970s was caused by a general government policy to reduce official unemployment, and that by the end of the 1980s, this policy had left Holland with a hidden unemployment rate that was twice its official rate and three times the unemployment rates in the United States and Germany. A similar effect as noted above with the 1980, PL 96-265, requiring that the Social Security Administration commence periodic reviews of the validity of disability claims.

1. *Outbreak*: Although the number of individuals considered disabled continues to increase slowly, the costs associated with those individual's have increased exponentially (McHeil, 2001). Therefore we have an outbreak and if adequate controls are not developed we could have a disability epidemic.

DEFINITION OF DISABILITY

The American Medical Association Guides to the Evaluation of Permanent Impairment, 5th Edition (AMA, 2000) defines disability as an alteration of an individual's capacity to meet personal, social, or occupational demands or statutory or regulatory requirements because of impairment. Disability is a relational outcome, contingent on the environmental conditions in which activities are performed. Therefore, an individual can have a disability in performing a specific work activity but not have a disability in any other social role (AMA, 1988).

The impairment evaluation, however, is only one aspect of disability determination. A disability determination also includes information about the individual's skills, education, job history, adaptability, age, and environment requirements and modification (Berkowitz & Burton, Jr., 1987). Assessing these factors can provide a more realistic picture of the effects of the impairment on the ability to perform complex work and social activities. If adaptations can be made to the environment, the individual may not be disabled from performing that activity.

The term *disability* has historically referred to a broad category of individuals with diverse limitation in the ability to meet social or occupational demands. However, it is more accurate to refer to the specific activity or role the "disabled" individual is unable to perform. According to a 1977 Institute of Medicine Report, "disability is a relational outcome, reflecting the individual's capacity to perform a specific task or activity, contingent on the environment conditions in which they are to be performed" (Brandit Jr. & Pope, 1997). Disability is context-specific, not inherent in the individual, but a function of the interaction of the individual and the environment (Melhorn, Andersson, & Mandell, 2001).

The World Health Organization (WHO) is revising its 1980 International Classification of Impairments, Disabilities and Handicaps and has released a draft document, The International Classification of Impairments, Activities and Participation (ICIDH-2) (World Health Organization, 2001). The term disability has been replaced by a neutral term, activity, and limits in ability are described as activity limitations. The change in terminology arose for several reasons: to choose terminology without an associated stigma, to avoid labeling, and to emphasize the person's residual ability.

Disability: The Americans with Disabilities Act (United States Equal Employment Opportunity Commission, 1992) provides only a legal definition and does not require a medical evaluation. An individual with a disability is defined by the ADA (28 CFR 35.104) as a person who has a physical or mental impairment that substantially limits one or more major life activities, a person who has a history or record of such an impairment, or a person who is perceived by others as having such an impairment. The ADA does not specifically name all of the impairments that are covered. Further, whether a person has a disability is assessed without regard to the availability of mitigating measures, such as reasonable modifications, auxiliary aids and services, services and devices of a personal nature, or medication.

Impairment: The American Medical Association Guides to the Evaluation of Permanent Impairment, 5th Edition (AMA, 2000) defines impairment as a loss, loss of use, or derangement of any body part, organ system, or organ function.

When considering disability under the workers' compensation system, disability is often divided into two types: temporary or permanent (Melhorn, 2000a; Melhorn, 1997a). Each can be further divided into partial or total. Temporary partial disability or TPD is considered for those employees who work part-time or at a lesser amount of pay, while temporary total disability or TTD is for those employees who are unable to perform any and all jobs for a set period. Temporary total disability benefits, the most frequently occurring type, are paid during the period when an injured employee is unable to work and end when the injured employee returns to work. It is considered temporary because the medical condition that is responsible for the disability is not fixed.

Permanent partial disability or PPD occurs when the employee's medical condition is stable and unlikely to change but does not prevent the employee from returning to gainful employment. Permanent partial disability benefits are paid to compensate workers when they incur some type of permanent impairment that does not preclude a future return to work. These benefits can either be a preestablished amount for specific impairments (loss of eye, hand, toe, etc.) or a defined range of payments over a set period of time if an amount has not been preestablished for a particular impairment. Permanent total disability or PTD occurs when the employee's medical condition is stable and the employee is unable to return to any and all jobs permanently. Permanent total disability benefits are paid when employees incur serious permanent impairments that make them unable to return to work. Permanent total benefits are usually payable for the duration of the disability, except in some states like Kansas where it is capped at $125,000.

These arbitrary divisions are important when considering the financial reimbursements or payments that the injured worker will receive while unable to be paid for working. Each state and often each employer will have specific requirements for time off work before payments will begin. The usual payment is two-thirds of the employee's week earnings at the time of the injury and programs have caps on the maximum benefits based on the average wages in a state. Additionally, maximum limits are set for total indemnity costs to employer per injury in some states. Workers' compensation cash benefits are typically periodic payments. However, most workers' compensation programs allow benefits to be paid all at once in a lump sum, a method of payment commonly used to resolve disputes in workers' compensation cases involving permanent impairments. The disputes most often arise in permanent partial impairment cases when evidence conflicts about the cause of the injury or opinions differ about whether the injury precludes an employee from returning to work. Rather than face the delays and risks inherent in litigation, insurers and injured employees may choose to compromise and set specific terms in settlement agreements.

Another consideration is the final payment. The final payment is often reduced by an offset for some of the amounts paid during the partial or total temporary disability phase. It is therefore possible that an injured worker may receive no additional funds if their temporary disability payments exceed their final payment which is based on their permanent physical impairment. The permanent physical impairment is usually based on a physician's evaluation and may be a scheduled injury or a non scheduled injury. Scheduled injuries are established by the appropriate state specific workers' compensation legislation. An example, an amputation at the level of the distal phalangeal joint is equal to 50 percent of the finger. Non scheduled injuries might include bilateral carpal tunnel syndrome. In this case the *AMA Guides* are used to establish a percentage of functional loss, which is then converted by the states specific legislation into a dollar award settlement. In some states (Kansas is one), the process of final settlement has been modified to include the concept of job loss or task loss. In Kansas, job loss or task loss has a two-prong test: task loss and wage loss. Task loss is calculated by a list of all previous jobs over the last fifteen years (amount of time state specific). Based on the work guides, the physician reviews the tasks and determines which activities cannot be performed. The total tasks loss is divided by the total nonduplicated task and a task loss percentage is derived. This total task loss can then be used to calculate a final dollar award settlement. The wage loss is based on income at the time of the injury. If the employee returns back to work, but is paid $15 per hour but was earning $20 per hour before the work injury, the employer must pay the additional $5 per hour. A twist, if the employee is laid off unrelated to the injury, the employee has a 100% wage loss. The method selected is that in which the largest final dollar award is given to the employee.

THE COST OF DISABILITY

The Employer's Point of View

Denniston (2003) reported a new disability benchmarking report based on data from the Centers for Disease Control & Prevention (CDC) which quantifies the total cost of disability in the workforce. For United States employers in 2000 it shows that, for all conditions together, direct disability lost-time costs were $91,360 per 100 workers, total disability lost-time costs (including indirect costs) were $458,150 per 100 workers, and medical costs were $268,539 per 100 workers. In a 2002 survey (Taub, 2003) time-off and disability program costs averaged 15 percent of payroll in 2001, up from 14.6 percent in 2000, or an employee earning $40,000 annually is paid $6,000 for time away from work. This cost translates into 39 days of absence per employee per year—27 scheduled days and 12 unscheduled days.

Another survey (Marsh Home Page accessed at http://www.marsh.com/MarshPortal/PortalMain on July 7, 2003) found that workers' compensation costs, on average, increased by 20 percent during 2001, rising to $1.80 per $100 of payroll from $1.50 a year earlier, while workers compensation protection accounts for 62 cents of every dollar American industry spends to manage its casualty exposures. Additionally, that survey found that small employers pay 11 times more than the largest companies, while most companies, on average, shell out $2.45 for every $1,000 of revenues. This is especially ominous, since the findings do not fully reflect the sharp rise in insurance costs that began at the end of 2000. A recent report by the United State Chamber of Commerce reported total employee benefit costs averaged 39 percent of total payroll costs in 2001, up from 37.5 percent the prior year (United States Chamber of Commerce Home Page http://www.uschamber.com/default accessed on July 7, 2003).

The Government's Point of View

The Government Accounting Office (GAO) (McMullin, 2001) reported that musculoskeletal injuries represent 36 percent of all short-term disability (STD) claims with a typical working population generating 100 STD claims for every 1000 covered lives. Musculoskeletal injuries represent 34 percent of all LTD claims with a typical working population generating 4 LTD claims for every 1000 covered lives. The Government Accounting Office (GAO) reported that in 1991 the Social Security Administration (SSA) spent about $32.3 billion of disability benefits compared to $54.2 billion to 5.3 million disabled workers in 2001 resulting in a 69 percent increase. This does not include the $19 billion SSA spent on 3.7 million Supplemental Security Income benefits (SSI) recipients and the $16.5 billion the Veteran's Administration spent on 2.3 million veterans with service connected disabilities. Add in the $52.1 billion in 1998 by State workers' compensation programs and the $6 billion in long term disability benefits by private insurers and you have a total of $147.8 billion, or about $647.00 per year, for every man, woman and child in the United States (Walker, 2002; McMullin, 2001).

In 2001, the GAO (Barnhart, 2002) recommended a change in the relationship between SSA's and workers' compensation payment. The GAO found that in addition to overpayments, a 1998 Office of the Inspector General (OIG) report showed that voluntary reporting of workers' compensation benefits also leads to the underpayment of disability insurance (DI) benefits. The OIG reported that it had found underpayment and overpayment errors in 82 percent of the 50 workers' compensation offset cases it reviewed from a sample of 100 cases, and projected that they totaled about $527 million ($385 million in overpayments and $142 million in underpayments). The most significant payment errors occurred because SSA relied on beneficiaries to file timely reports on the status of their workers' compensation benefits. When SSA is unaware of benefit changes, such as the termination of workers' compensation benefits, it continues to offset DI benefits at the same rate, resulting in underpayments. In 1980, Chirikos (1989) used the prevalence approach and placed the aggregate costs of disability in 1980 at $177 billion or about 6.5% of gross domestic product for that year with healthcare represented 51%, lost earnings 39%, and administrative costs 10%. Hill (1991) reported the direct costs of disability in 1984 to be $145 billion using a different set of assumptions and limiting the disability group to age 18 to 64. These estimates do not include the costs of pain and suffering which are real costs that the courts and juries are frequently called upon to consider. Because pain and suffering are so difficult to evaluate and because there are economic incentives to embellish or to diminish their scope, it is understandable that substantial suspicion surrounds claims for damages.

The Injured Worker's Point of View

The injured worker suffers a financial and social loss. It is often difficult to place a value on this loss. Disabilities are but a part of the workers' compensation system and often receives a disproportional amount of the lay public's attention. Although important to the resolution of the work compensable injury, disability payments do not provide as much benefit to the individual as appropriate health care for the injury (Melhorn, 2001b; jmm & Mandell, 2000) and early return to work (Melhorn, 2000e; Melhorn, 2000c).

Ambiguity in definition notwithstanding, a significant number of Americans live with a disability. In 1997, the prevalence of disability as measured by the National Health Interview Survey (NHIS) was 13 percent of the noninstitutionalized United States population, or 35 million people (National Center for Health Statistics, 2003). Under the broader, functional limits conception of the Survey of Income and Program Participation (SIPP), the 1997 rate was close to 20 percent, or approximately 53 million people (United States Census Bureau, 2003). About half of the disabled are severely limited and unable to work regularly. Musculoskeletal disorders are the most frequent type of disability. In 1993, sociologist Irving Zola (1993) described the futility of pinpointing the exact size of the population with disability, noting that disability represents "a set of characteristics everyone shares to varying degrees." There is dynamism in disability status both because of the transitory character of health and because the connection between a person's impairment and subsequent loss of function is often determined by barriers in his or her physical environment. The legal skirmishes over the definition of disability under the Americans with Disability Act (ADA) underscore this dynamism, making disability less a concern of medicine and more the province of broadly based civil rights protections.

CONCLUSIONS AND SUGGESTIONS

Disability is multifactorial, therefore, there is no simple cure for the prevalence or associated costs. Certainly the context in which individuals generate disability claims, both occupational and non-occupational must be understood and addressed. It is well known that in difficult economic times, with reductions in workforces, either actual or anticipated, claims increase substantially. This phenomenon is so predictable that insurance carriers typically recruit additional claims handlers in advance of major layoffs for a client's account. Alternative strategies to reduce the impact of such events would reduce the incidence of disability claims, which constitute a very cost-ineffective compensatory mechanism to restore security which is being lost because of a turbulent work environment. Managed care techniques applied to workers' compensation programs are controversial, but the weight of evidence demonstrates that various approaches can be productive and cost-effective (Boseman, 2001; Burton & Conti, 2000; Melhorn, 1999). Utilization management is commonly used to ensure that treatment rendered is medically necessary and appropriate. However, the process can be cumbersome and resource-intensive and needs to be applied when there is clear benefit. Case management offers the opportunity for coordination of care, rehabilitation and return to work planning, ensuring that a focal point is established to integrate the efforts of all parties (employer, physician, claimant). It is critical to ensure that case managers receive the full and timely cooperation of all those involved in the process. The use of preferred provider networks has been shown to reduce medical costs through favorable contract terms and the selection of providers who have particular expertise in the treatment of occupational injuries, and are knowledgeable about, and compliant with, the complex regulatory aspects of the workers' compensation system. This is accomplished most successfully when states permit injured employees to be directed into networks, with complete or partial restriction of the claimant's freedom of physician choice. In such circumstances, it is necessary for sanctions and/or penalties to be applied when claimants obtain care from unauthorized providers. However, understandably, this is perceived by some as an unacceptable restriction of choice, and a threat to high-quality care.

Most insurance carriers recognize that a rigid focus on utilization management may create a barrier to the definitive treatment of a claimant, prolonging the recovery period, and delaying an early return to work. They are increasingly attuned to the fact that "doing the right thing" in a timely way will ultimately reduce both medical and indemnity costs. State fee schedules for workers' compensation services continue to be a restraining influence on escalating costs. However, many states have been slow to recognize the shift of medical site of care from the inpatient to the outpatient sector. Consequently, several jurisdictions still fail to define fee schedules for hospital outpatient and ambulatory surgery centers, resulting in unregulated and explosive inflation in the costs of these services. Other gaps in fee schedule regulation should also be addressed. Similarly, pharmacy expenses continue to soar at double-digit rates each year. Only recently have workers' compensation carriers turned to third party pharmacy benefit managers to assist in the control of drug costs through preferred pharmacy networks, contract reductions, and utilization review. On the other hand, several states with excessively low fee schedules, such as Florida, have recognized the need to increase their physician fee schedules in order to maintain access to high-quality care for workers' compensation claimants; reimbursement below Medicare levels has not been attractive to providers.

Clearly, a balanced approach to reimbursement must be sought so that all parties are comfortable that their critical needs are satisfied. Physicians need to assume the responsibility of reporting information to insurance carriers and other applicable parties in a manner that is objective and accurate. Studies have revealed that some physicians, to a significant extent, believe that it is proper to skew responses concerning their patients such that the patients' benefits are maximized (Malleson, 2002; Loeser & Sullivan, 1997; Florence, 1979; Hadler, 1986; Chaplin, 1991; Nachemson, 1994). Additionally, physician training in the science of disability evaluation would do much to enhance the value of their contributions to the process. As discussed earlier in this chapter, the conceptual framework of impairment and disability must be understood, as well as the technical aspects of impairment evaluating and rating, the fundamentals of a comprehensive independent medical examination, and the interpretation of functional capacity evaluations. Local knowledge of workers' compensation regulations and procedures is highly desirable. All clinicians involved in the disability process should be aware of the contributions of "evidence-based medicine" and outcomes measurement, and the guidelines and criteria that are generated through this rigorous, systematic and consensual approach to therapy. This base of knowledge can be applied to the diagnoses and treatments commonly encountered in the disability arena. Some states have mandated the use of designated treatment guidelines which may be too generic to be of practical value. One test of any program or system is its ability to develop consistent and minimally contentious regulations and procedures. Additionally, there needs to be mechanisms for dispute resolution that are timely, efficient, and inexpensive. Using this benchmark, disability determinations, whether occupational or non-occupational, fail in several respects. Workers' compensation systems suffer from a lack of standardization, since each state establishes its own distinct rules. Further effort to create national standards for workers' compensation claims handling is warranted. Each state Department of Insurance drafts its own policies, despite the availability of model standards promulgated by the National Association of Insurance Commissioners (NAIC). Litigation is excessive; there is insufficient reliance on mediation and arbitration and expert medical review panels; and political manipulation by interest groups is persistent. Caps and other restrictions of excessive attorney fees are useful where they have been implemented. In the non-occupational disability arena, there is a general consensus that group disability programs, which are comprehensively regulated on a federal level through Employee Retirement Income Security Act (ERISA), (United States Department of Labor, 2003) successfully prevent abuse through explicit claims processing guidelines and caps on damages. On the other hand, individual disability policies are governed by state law, without benefit of ERISA protections, and without limitations on punitive or extra-contractual damages.

The solution will likely require the following steps:

- *Communication*: For that thought or idea to be properly interpreted by the receiver, both sender and receiver must have a common frame of reference or speak the same language. Communication is the successful flow each way of this information in an understandable, supportable, reasonable, and useful format (Melhorn, 2001b).
- *Role awareness*: Physicians are the primary decision makers in traditional healthcare. In the disability field, the physician's role as primary decision maker is yielded to other participants. This can often lead to frustration or confusion on the physician's part, particularly when every word is being challenged in an adversarial format common in court testimony (Melhorn, 2001b).
- *Ground rules*: Physicians must become more than casually acquainted with the specific provisions and procedures of the employment and workers' compensations laws and regulations in the states where they practice, the Social Security Act, the Americans with Disabilities Act, the Family and Medical Leave Act, and the regulations published by the federal agencies administering these statutes.
- *Legal Construct of Impairment/Disability*: The definitions of disability change more along political and ideological lines than according to any clear clinical determinations. This has resulted in a mismatch between impairment and disability, since impairment is associated with disability only insofar as it is a necessary and contributory factor; in itself it is not sufficient to cause disability (Melhorn, 2001b).

- *Medical—legal interface*: The interface between physicians and the legal world is not always an easy one. Confusion between the professions requires that care must be taken anytime the law and medicine interface. Both are complex fields, with many important decisions being made, and neither field is an exact science (Melhorn, 2001b).
- *Legislative—Administrative*: Rules and regulations must keep current with the changes in the medical field and realize that disability is context specific, not inherit in the individual, but a function of the interaction of the individual and the environment (Melhorn, 2001b).

  The SPICE (Colledge et al., 2000) system is a proven approach to reducing unnecessary work disability and consists of five steps:
  - *Simplicity*: The concept that simple, benign conditions, treated in a complicated fashion become complicated.
  - *Proximity*: The need to keep the worker associated with the workplace by building morale and support of employees.
  - *Immediacy*: The need to deal with industrial claims in a timely manner.
  - *Centrality*: All parties involved with workers share a common philosophy and ultimate goal of returning the individual back to gainful employment as quickly as possible.
  - *Expectancy:* The concept that individuals often fulfill the expectations placed on them.

REFERENCES

Marsh Home Page (2003a). Charlotte, NC: Marsh & McLennan Companies.

The United States Chamber of Commerce Home Page (2003b). Washington, DC: United States Chamber of Commerce.

Aarts, L., Burkhauser, R. V., & de Jong, P. (1992). *A cautionary tale of European disability policies: Lessons for the United States.* Syracuse, NY: Maxwell School, Syracuse University.

Aarts, L., Burkhauser, R. V., & Jong, P. R. (1996). *Curing the Dutch disease an international perspective on disability policy reform.* Aldershot: Brookfield, Vt., USA.

AMA (1988). *Guides to the evaluation of permanent impairment.* (3rd ed.) Chicago: AMA.

AMA (1993). *Guides to the evaluation of permanent impairment.* (4th ed.) Chicago: American Medical Association.

AMA (2000). Philosophy, Purpose, and Appropriate Use of the *Guides.* In L.Cocchiarella & G. B. J. Andersson (Eds.), *Guides to the Evaluation of Permanent Impairment* (5th ed., pp. 1–16). Chicago, IL: American Medical Press.

American Academy of Orthopaedic Surgeons (1996). Clinical epidemiology. In J.R.Kasser (Ed.), *Orthopaedic knowledge update 5* (5 ed., pp. 71–80). Rosemont, IL: American Academy of Orthopaedic Surgeons.

Anderson, R. T. (1984). An orthopedic ethnography in rural Nepal. *Med Anthropol, 8,* 46–59.

Andersson, G. B. J. (1995). Epidemiology of occupational neck and shoulder disorders. In *Repetitive motion disorders of the upper extremity* (pp. 31–42). Rosemont, IL: American Academy of Orthopaedic Surgeons.

Aronoff, G. M. (1991). Chronic pain and the disability epidemic. *Clin J Pain, 7,* 330–338.

Atroshi, I., Gummesson, C., Johnsson, R., Ornstein, E., Ranstam, J., & Rosen, I. (1999). Prevalence of carpal tunnel syndrome in a general population. *JAMA, 282,* 153–158.

Barnhart, J. B. (2002). *SSA and VA disability programs. Re-examination of disability criteria needed to help ensure program integrity.* (vols. GAO-02–597) Washington, DC: United States General Accounting Office.

Bednar, J. M., Baesher-Griffith, P., & Osterman, A. L. (1998). Workers' compensation effect of state law on treatment cost and work status. *Clin Orthop, 351,* 74–77.

Berkowitz, M. & Burton, J. F., Jr. (1987). *Permanent Disability Benefits in Workers' Compensation.* Kalamazoo, MI: Upjohn Institute for Employment Research.

Biddle, J., Roberts, K., Rosenman, K. D., & Welch, E. M. (1998). What percentage of workers with work-related illnesses receive workers' compensation benefits? *J Occup Environ Med, 40,* 325–331.

Boseman, J. (2001). Disability management. Application of a nurse based model in a large corporation. *American Association Occupational Health Nursing Journal, 49,* 176–186.

Brandit Jr., E. N. & Pope, A. M. (1997). *Enabling America: Assessing the Role of Rehabilitation Science and Engineering.* Washington, DC: National Academy Press.

Bureau of Labor and Statistics (2003). *2001 Bureau of Labor Statistics Annual Survey of Workplace Injuries and Illnesses.* Washington, DC: United States Department of Labor.

Burton, W. N. & Conti, D. J. (2000). Disability management: corporate medical department management of employee health and productivity. *J Occup Environ Med, 42,* 1006–1012.

Chaplin, E. R. (1991). Chronic pain and the injured worker: A sociobiological problem. In M.L.Kasdan (Ed.), *Occupational Hand & Upper Extremity Injuries & Diseases* (pp. 13–46). Philadelphia: Hanley & Belfus.

Cheadle, A., Franklin, G. M., Wolfhagen, C., Savarino, J., Liu, P. Y., Salley, C. et al. (1994). Factors influencing the duration of work-related disability: A population-based study of Washington state workers' compensation. *Am J Public Health, 84,* 190–196.

Chirikos, T. N. (1989). Aggregate economic losses from disability in the United States: Preliminary assay. *Milbank, 67,* 59–91.

Ciccone, D. S., Just, N., & Bandilla, E. B. (1996). Non-organic symptom reporting in patients with chronic non-malignant pain. *Pain, 68,* 329–341.

Colledge, A. L. & Johnson, H. I. (2000). S.P.I.C.E.—a model for reducing the incidence and costs of occupationally entitled claims. *Occup Med, 15,* 695–722, iii.

Demeter, S. L., Andersson, G. B. J., & Smith, G. M. (2001). *Disability Evaluation.* St. Louis, MO: Mosby.

Denniston, P. (2003). *Workers' compensation disability costs for 2000.* Corpus Christi, TX: Work Loss Data Institute.

Drury, D. (1990). *Workers with disabilities in large and small firms: Profiles from the SIPP (the survey of income and program participation).* Topeka, KS: Menninger Foundation.

Equal Employment Opportunity Commission (1997). *The Americans with Disabilities Act. Your Responsibilities as an Employer from the Equal Employment Opportunity Commission.* (1 ed.) Topeka, KS: Kansas Department of Human Resources.

Equal Employment Opportunity Commission: (2001). *Laws Enforced by the United State Equal Employment Opportunity Commission (Equal Employment Opportunity Commission).* Washington, DC: Equal Employment Opportunity Commission.

Florence, D. W. (1979). Diary of a work-related disability. *Legal Aspects of Medical Practice, 8,* 5–10.

Fraumeni, J. F. & Hoover, R. N. (1985). Epidemiology: Principles and methods. *Fed Register Part II,* 58–64.

Gloss, D. S. & Wardle, M. G. (1982). Reliability and validity of American Medical Association's Guide to Ratings and Permanent Impairment. *JAMA, 248,* 2292–2296.

Greenberg, R. S., Daniels, S. R., Flanders, D., Eley, J. W., & Boring, J. R. (1993). *Medical epidemiology* . Norwalk: Appletion & Lange.

Guck, T. P., Meilman, P. W., Skultety, F. M., & Dowd, E. T. (1986). Prediction of long-term outcome of multidisciplinary pain treatment. *Arch Phys Med Rehabil, 67,* 293–296.

Guest, G. H. & Drummond, P. D. (1992). Effect of compensation on emotional state and disability in chronic back pain. *Pain, 48,* 125–130.

Gureje, O., Simon, G. E., & von Korff, M. (2001). A cross-national study of the course of persistent pain in primary care. *Pain, 92,* 195–200.

Gureje, O., von Korff, M., Simon, G. E., & Gater, R. (1998). Persistent pain and well-being: a World Health Organization Study in Primary Care. *JAMA, 280,* 147–151.

Hadler, N. M. (1986). Criteria for screening workers for the establishment of disability. *J Occup Environ Med, 28,* 940–945.

Hadler, N. M. (1992). Arm pain in the workplace. A small area analysis. *J Occup Environ Med, 34,* 113–119.

Hashemi, L., Webster, B. S., Lancey, E. A., & Volinn, E. (1997). Length of disability and cost of workers' compensation low back pain claims. *J Occup Environ Med, 39,* 937–945.

Hashemi, L., Webster, B. S., Clancy, E. A., & Courtney, T. K. (1998). Length of disability and cost of work-related musculoskeletal disorders of the upper extremity. *J Occup Environ Med, 40,* 261–269.

Hill, M. A. (1991). The economics of disability. In S.Thompson-Hoffman & I. F. Storck (Eds.), *Disability in the U.S.: A portrait from national data* (pp. 1–255). New York, NY: Springer.

Hunter, S. J., Shaha, S., Flint, D., & Tracy, D. M. (1998). Predicting return to work. A long-term follow-up study of railroad workers after low back injuries. *Spine, 23,* 2319–2328.

jmm & Mandell, P. J. (2000). or 3992 Impairment and Disability. In *aaos wc primer* (Rosemont, IL: American Academy of Orthopaedic Surgeons).

Leavitt, F. (1992). The physical exertion factor in compensable work injuries: a hidden flaw in previous research. *Spine, 17,* 307–310.

Loeser, J. D. & Sullivan, M. (1997). Doctors, diagnosis, and disability: a disastrous diversion. *Clin Orthop,* 61–66.

Malleson, A. (2002). *Whiplash and Other Useful Illnessess.* Montreal, Canada: McGill-Queen's University Press.

McCarthy, M. L., McAndrew, M. P., Mackenzie, E. J., Burgess, A. R., Cushing, B. M., Delateur, B. J. et al. (1998). Correlation between the measures of impairment, according to the modified system of the American Medical Association, and function [see comments]. *J Bone Joint Surg, 80A,* 1034–1042.

McHeil, M. (2001). *Americans with disabilities. Household economic studies.* (vols. P70–73) Washington, DC: United States Department of Commerce.

McMullin, M. (2001). *Workers' compensation: Action needed to reduce payment errors in SSA disability and other programs.* Washington, DC: United States General Accounting Office.

Melhorn, J. M. (1996a). A prospective study for upper-extremity cumulative trauma disorders of workers in aircraft manufacturing. *J Occup Environ Med, 38,* 1264–1271.

Melhorn, J. M. (1996b). Cumulative trauma disorders: How to assess the risks. *J Workers Compensation, 5,* 19–33.

Melhorn, J. M. (1997a). CTD in the Workplace: Treatment Outcomes. In *Seventeenth Annual Workers' Compensation and Occupational Medicine Seminar* (pp. 168–178). Boston, MA: Seak, Inc.

Melhorn, J. M. (1997b). CTD Solutions for the 90's: Prevention. In *Seventeenth Annual Workers' Compensation and Occupational Medicine Seminar* (17 ed., pp. 234–245). Boston, MA: Seak, Inc.

Melhorn, J. M. (1997c). Identification of Individuals at Risk for Developing CTD. In D.M.Spengler & J. P. Zeppieri (Eds.), *Workers' Compensation Case Management: A Multidisciplinary Perspective* (pp. 41–51). Rosemont, IL: American Academy of Orthopaedic Surgeons.

Melhorn, J. M. (1997d). Physician Support and Employer Options for Reducing Risk of CTD. In D.M.Spengler & J. P. Zeppieri (Eds.), *Workers' Compensation Case Management: A Multidisciplinary Perspective* (pp. 26–34). Rosemont, IL: American Academy of Orthopaedic Surgeons.

Melhorn, J. M. (1998a). Cumulative trauma disorders and repetitive strain injuries. The future. *Clin Orthop, 351,* 107–126.

Melhorn, J. M. (1998b). Pain responses in patients with upper-extremity disorders. [Letter]. *J Hand Surg, 23A,* 954–955.

Melhorn, J. M. (1998c). Prevention of CTD in the Workplace. In *Workers' Comp Update 1998* (pp. 101–124). Walnut Creek, CA: Council on Education in Management.

Melhorn, J. M. (1998d). Understanding the types of carpal tunnel syndrome. *J Workers Compensation, 7,* 52–73.

Melhorn, J. M. (1998e). Upper-extremity cumulative trauma disorders on workers in aircraft manufacturing [Letter, Response] Upper extremities cumulative trauma disorders. *J Occup Environ Med, 40,* 12–15.

Melhorn, J. M. (1999). *Disability Case Management.* Wichita, KS: The Hand Center.

Melhorn, J. M. (2000a). Cost Effective Management of Musculoskeletal Disorders. In *The 24th Annual Carroll P Hungate Postgraduate Seminar on Occupational and Environment Health* (pp. 1–45). Overland Park, KS: Great Plains College of Occupational and Environment Medicine.

Melhorn, J. M. (2000b). Occupational orthopaedics. *J Bone Joint Surg, 82A,* 902–904.

Melhorn, J. M. (2000c). The benefits of returning the injured worker to work early: A review of the research. *J Workers Compensation, 10,* 60–75.

Melhorn, J. M. (2000d). Treating More Than the Injury—Reducing Disability with Early Return to Work. In P.J.Mandell (Ed.), *Occupational Health at the Dawn of the New Millennium* (pp. 1–15). Sacramento, CA: California Orthopaedic Association.

Melhorn, J. M. (2000e). Workers' compensation: Avoiding the work-related disability. *J Bone Joint Surg, 82A,* 1490–1493.

Melhorn, J. M. (2001a). Foward. In T.G.Grace (Ed.), *Independent Medical Evaluations* (pp. vii–viii). Rosemont, IL: American Academy of Orthopaedic Surgeons.

Melhorn, J. M. (2001b). Impairment and disability evaluations: Understanding the process. *J Bone Joint Surg, 83A,* 1905–1911.

Melhorn, J. M. (2002). CTD's: Assessment of Risk (Risk Assessment Applications in the Workplace). In J.Williams (Ed.), *Proceedings of McPherson College Science Symposium April 26–27, 1996* (pp. 161–166). McPherson, KS: McPherson College.

Melhorn, J. M. (2003). Worker's Disability: Case Management and Voc Rehab. In J.M.Melhorn & D. M. Spengler (Eds.), *Occupational Orthopaedics and Workers' Compensation: A Multidisciplinary Perspective* (Rosemont, IL: American Academy of Orthopaedic Surgeons.

Melhorn, J. M., Andersson, G. B. J., & Mandell, P. J. (2001). Determining Impairment and Disability. In J.M.Melhorn (Ed.), *The Fundamentals of Workers' Compensation* (pp. 13–21). Rosemont, IL: American Academy of Orthopaedic Surgeons.

Melhorn, J. M. & Wilkinson, L. K. (1996). *CTD Solutions for the 90's: A Comprehensive Guide to Managing CTD in the Workplace.* Wichita, KS: Via Christi Health Systems.

Melhorn, J. M., Wilkinson, L. K., Gardner, P., Horst, W. D., & Silkey, B. (1999). An outcomes study of an occupational medicine intervention program for the reduction of musculoskeletal disorders and cumulative trauma disorders in the workplace. *J Occup Environ Med, 41,* 833–846.

Melhorn, J. M., Zeppieri, J. P., & Wilkinson, L. K. (2000). Impairment Evaluations for the Upper Extremities Using the AMA Guides. In J.M.Melhorn (Ed.), *Case WorkBook for Physicial Impairments AAOS 2000* Rosemont, Ill: American Academy of Orthopaedic Surgeons.

Milhous, R. L., Haugh, L. D., Frymoyer, J. W., Ruess, J. M., Gallagher, R. M., Wilder, D. G. et al. (1989). Determinants of vocational disability in patients with low back pain. *Arch Phys Med Rehabil, 70,* 589–593.

Mish, F. C. & Gilman, E. W. (1991). *Webster's ninth new collegiate dictionary.* (9th ed.) Springfield: Merriam-Webster Inc.

Nachemson, A. L. (1994). Chronic pain—the end of the welfare state? *Quality of Life Research, 3,* S11–S17.

National Center for Health Statistics (2003). *National health interview survey.* Washington, DC: Center for Disease Control.

Rondinelli, R. D., Dunn, W., Hassanein, K., Keesling, C. A., Meredith, S. C., Schulz, T. L. et al. (1997). Simulation of hand impairments: Effects on upper extremity function and implications toward medical impairment rating and disability determination. *Arch Phy Med Rehabil, 78,* 1358–1563.

Sander, R. A. & Meyers, J. E. (1986). The relationship of disability to compensation status in railroad workers. *Spine, 11,* 141–143.

Smith, R. J. (1996). Physical ability profiling for work and return-to-work. *J Workers Compensation, Spring,* 31–37.

Snook, S. H. & Webster, B. S. (1987). The cost of disability. *Clin Orthop,* 77–84.

Social Security Administration (2003). *Social Security Administration OnLine.* Washington, DC: Social Security Administration.

Sternbach, R. A. (1986). Pain and 'hassles' in the United States: findings of the Nuprin pain report. *Pain, 27,* 69–80.

Taub, S. (2003). The Great Depression. *CFO.com, February 26, 2003,* 1–2.

Trief, P. M. & Donelson, R. G. (1995). The Potential Impact of the Workers' Compesation System on Quality of Life Outcomes: A clinical Analysis. *J Occup Rehabil,* 185–193.

Unchitelle, L. (2002). Jobless increasingly claim disability pay. *The Wichita Eagle, September 2, 2002,* 2–3.

United States Census Bureau (2003). *Survey of income and program participation.* Washington, DC: United States Census Bureau.

United States Department of Labor (2003). Employee Retirement Income Security Act (ERISA). In *Employee Retirement Income Security Program* (Washington, DC: United States.

United States Equal Employment Opportunity Commission (1992). *A Technical Assistance Manual on the Employment Provision (Title I) of the Americans with Disabilities Act.* Washington, DC: United States Government Printing Office.

Vallfors, B. (1985). Acute, subacute and chronic low back pain: clinical symptoms, absenteeism and working environment. *Scand J Rehabil Med Suppl, 11,* 1–98.

Waddell, G. (1998). *The back pain revolution.* Edinburgh London New York Philadelphia Sydney Toronoto: Churchill Livingstone.

Walker, D. M. (2002). *Government Accounting Office Home Page.* Washington, DC: GAO Printing Office.

World Health Organization (2001). *ICIDH: International Classification of Impariments, Activities and Participation: A Manual of Dimensions of Disablement and Health.* New York, NY: World Health Assembly.

Zola, I. K. (1993). Self, identity and the naming question: reflections on the language of disability. *Soc Sci Med, 36,* 167–173.

2

Impairment and Occupational Disability in Research and Practice

Izabela Z. Schultz

INTRODUCTION

Central to the development of an effective model of occupational disability prediction in research and practice is the issue of the relationship between impairment and disability. To what degree, when and how does low back pain affect work performance and employability? Under what conditions can persons with mild traumatic brain injuries work? Can posttraumatic stress disorder be disabling from work at all? None of these questions can be answered unequivocally on the basis of current research evidence. Ambiguity and a multiplicity of definitions for both of the foundational concepts constitute major barriers to the development of the empirical evidence needed by healthcare, compensation systems and employers, and for its applications for prevention and reduction of work disability.

This chapter focuses on dissecting the controversial issues and conceptual quagmires adversely affecting the establishment of effective research and clinical methodology in this field. The multiplicity of factors affecting work disability, determination and prediction of work disability, and knowledge transfer to clinical practice will be discussed. Issues which require addressing and clarification in research and practice related to the relationship between impairment and work disability will be highlighted. A need for an integrated biopsychosocial model in determination of occupational disability, regardless of the clinical nature of disability, will be identified as one of the solutions to the quagmire.

DEFINITIONS OF DISABILITY

In the literature, definitions of impairment are usually embedded within definitions and models of disability. Historically, three major theoretical schools affected the development of models and definitions of disability: social contruction, the biomedical approach, and the biopsychosocial approach (Bickenbach, Chatterji, Badley

DOI: 10.1007/978-0-387-28919-9_2, © 2009 Springer Science+Business Media, LLC

and Ustin, 1999). According to the social construction theory, disability is not just an attribute of an individual but rather a complex set of conditions, activities and relationships, which have been to a significant degree produced by the social environment of the person (Bickenbach et al., 1999, Tate and Pledger, 2003 and Olkin and Pledger, 2003). In the biomedical model, disability is understood as an observable deviation from biomedical norms of structure or function that is directly produced by a medical condition (Boorse, 1975,1977, Bickenbach et al., 1999, Schultz et al., 2000). The biopsychosocial model integrates clinical impairment into a system-based approach. The classic work of Engel advocated for an approach that combines the micro (interactional), mezo (community or organizational), and macro (structural) social ecological levels as predictors of clinical and social outcomes (Engel, 1977, Tate and Pledger, 2003). Recent biopsychosocial models emphasize the multifactorial nature of disability, with the inclusion of both personal and environmental characteristics (Fine and Asch, 1988; Meyerson, 1988) and an important role played by psychological factors (Tate and Pledger, 2003, Schultz et al., 2000). In addition, Verbrugge and Jette (1994) postulated that disability is situational and functional limitations can be altered by social and environmental factors.

The biopsychosocial model of disability and the relationship between impairment and disability, a synthesis of medical and social models, has been espoused in the World Health Organization's International Classification of Impairments, Disabilities and Handicaps (1999; Bickenbach et al., 1999). Disablement is conceptualized as a universal variation of human functioning, with its three equally important key dimensions being impairments, activity limitations and participation restrictions. Bickenbach et al. (1999) described the implications of the model for clinical and systemic interventions in the following way:

> At the level of impairment, medical or rehabilitative responses are the most appropriate, and in this sense, the medical model is an accurate representation of disablement, in that manifestation. At the person level of activity limitations, identified by evaluating a person's performance against a set or standardized environment, the appropriate responses are either those that strive to correct or extend the range of the person's own capabilities through rehabilitation or those that provide assistive devices to compensate for activity limitations. Finally, at the level of individual's participation, in which the person's actual social and physical environment is taken into account, the primary interventions envisaged are those that either remove environmental barriers to full participation or put into place environmental facilitators (p. 1184).

Biomedical, social construction and biopsychosocial theoretical constructs of disability are reflected, in varying degrees and interactions, in three different applied perspectives on disability: (1) legal and administrative, (2) clinical and (3) scholarly research (Altman, 2001).

Due to the legal ramifications of the concept of disability, involving rights, benefits and responsibilities, various administrative and programmatic bodies, public and private, form their own definitions of disability. Most often, disability is defined as "situations associated with injury, health, or physical conditions that create specific limitations that have lasted (or are expected to last) for a named period of time" (Altman, 2001, p. 98). In the public arena broad definitions of disability, such as the one contained in the Americans with Disabilities Act (ADA, 1990) have been gradually replacing narrower, function-specific disabilities. ADA defines disability as the following: (1) a physical or mental impairment that substantially limits one or more of the major life activities of such individuals; (2) a record of such impairment, or (3) being regarded as having such an impairment (Sec. 3 (2), 42 U.S.C. 12102, 1990).

Disability compensation systems, however, including workers' compensation and long-term disability insurance companies, have historically preferred more narrow and specifically functionally focused definitions, with emphasis on "objective proof" of impairment leading to work disability. At this time, these two opposing definitional trends, to broaden the scope of definition to ensure equal rights for persons with disability, and to narrow down the scope to make compensability objectively verifiable and financially viable for the institutions granting disability status, have not shown signs of convergence.

Clinical definitions of disability have focused on the identification, qualification and quantification of pathology, used by medical practitioners for the prediction (prognosis) of future function. The type of condition and the individual characteristics of the patient are the basis of such predictions. Since 1958, guidelines for the evaluation of permanent impairment have been developed and disseminated by the American Medical Association to make the impairment determination process best practice-based and standardized. The most recent *Guides to the Evaluation of Permanent Impairment*, Fifth Edition (2001) have retained the earlier definition of impairment as "a loss, loss of use, or derangement of any body part, organ system, or organ function" (p. 2). Disability continues to be defined as "an alteration of an individual's capacity to meet personal, social, or occupational demands or statutory or regulatory requirements because of an impairment" (p. 8). Disability is conceptualized as "a relational outcome", reflecting the individual's capacity to perform a specific task or activity, contingent on the environmental conditions in which they are to be performed (Brandt & Pope, 1997). Disability, therefore, constitutes a contextualization of impairment.

Notably, the World Health Organization (WHO) has replaced the term "disability" by the neutral term activity, thus disability is understood as "activity limitations" (WHO, 1999). The AMA Guides, Fifth Edition (2001) described the relationships among the concepts of normal health, impairment, functional limitation and activity disability (performance limitation) in a non-linear and interactive fashion.

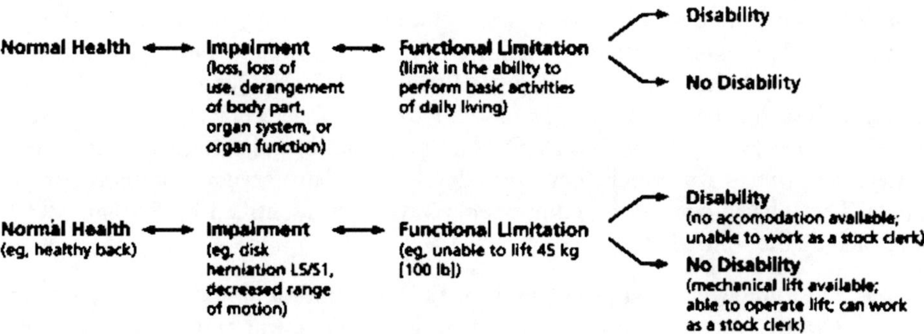

Figure 1. The Relation among the Concepts of Normal Health, Impairment, Function Limitation, and Activity Disability (Performance Limitation). (*Source*: *AMA Guides*, Fifth Edition (2001)

The clinical definitions of impairment and disability, unlike legal and administrative definitions, must adhere to methodological standards of measurability, reliability and validity of the evaluative approach. However, the actual research measurement properties of AMA Guide-developed procedures, particularly in the area of complex conditions such as pain or psychiatric disability, are in their infancy. In the low back pain condition, the most common work disability, serious doubts were raised with respect to the reliability of the AMA-based physical examination of range of motion (Zuberbier et al., 2001).

Research definitions of disability, particularly occupational disability, are even more diverse than the legal and clinical definitions. Definitions of work disability encountered in the rehabilitation outcome literature are either clinically or economically-derived and tend to fall into one of the following categories:

1. Self-report of disability by an individual with disability (e.g. as measured by Sickness Impact Profile or various Disability Indices)
2. Report of disability by a clinician and/or significant other
3. Return to work and/or employability
4. Duration of disability
5. Health-care and wage-loss based costs of disability
6. Health-care utilization.

Due to this multiplicity of definitions and related methodological approaches, research on the relationship between impairment and disability has been difficult to integrate.

However, the accumulation of a substantial body of research evidence is essential for legal and clinical definitions and related disability determination methodologies to have relevance, reliability and validity, thus allowing their fair applications to persons with disabilities. At this time, the largely market-driven disability determination industry has been expanding exponentially without consideration to measurement properties, and particularly, validity evidence. Likewise, prediction of disability, early identification of high risk individuals and prevention of disability, has been hampered, in research, clinical and administrative applications.

DISSECTING AND INTEGRATING CONCEPTS OF DISABILITY

The best known definitions of disability, including those from the World Health Organization (1980 and 1999), the Institute of Medicine at the National Institute of Medicine (Brandt & Pope, 1997; Pope & Tarlov, 1991), the Quebec model (Fougeyrollas & Beauregard, 2001), Nagi's model (1965, 1976, 1991) and Verbrugge and Jette's model (1993), despite conceptual and terminological differences, as well as different purposes for which they were developed, share several common components. These basic conceptual components have been identified by Altman (2001) and include the following:

1. *Pathology:* Understood variably as the interruption in body processes which requires restoration, medically identified biochemical and physiological abnormalities or a key aspect of disease which also incorporates etiology and manifestation;

2. *Impairment.* Conceptualized as anatomical or physiological abnormalities and losses, dysfunctions and significant structural abnormalities in specific body systems, loss or abnormality of mental, physical or biochemical function or structure, or generally as problems in body function and structure.
3. *Functional limitations.* Defined implicitly or explicitly as physical or mental restrictions that the impairments pose on performance of tasks and obligations of daily function and/or fulfillment of social roles, the newly used term "activity limitations" (WHO, 1999) denoting functional limitations since the concept of impairment was divided into "impairment of structure" and "impairment" of functions, and the blurred boundaries between definitions of impairment and disability were clarified;
4. *Outcomes.* Conceptualized as a "pattern of behavior that evolves in situations of long term or continued impairments that are associated with functional limitations" (Nagi, 1965, p. 103), as "the expression of a physical or mental limitation in a social context- the gap between a person's capabilities and the demands of the environment" (Pope & Tarlov, 1991, p. 81), difficulty performing life activities due to physical problems (Verbrugge & Jette, 1993) or an "individual's involvement in life situations in relation to health conditions, body functions and structures, activities and contextual factors (WHO, 1999, p. 19);
5. *Contextual factors.* Related to personal background and environmental factors and demands, stipulated in WHO (1999) model and in the AMA Guides' Model (1994, 2001).

Several integrative models of the relationship between impairment and disability have been postulated in the literature. Altman (2001) argued that the classic model by Nagi (1965) had been misunderstood in the literature as implying a linear relationship between impairment and disability mediated by functional impairment. In the adopted model, the relationship between impairment and disability is non-linear and mediated by the interaction between (1) pathology and functional limitations, (2) impairments and functional limitations, and (3) the functional limitations and impairments and role restrictions; as shown in Figure 2.

Complexities of interactions in the multidimensional models of the relationship between impairment and disability are underscored in the most recent (1999) WHO Model. It is shown in Figure 3.

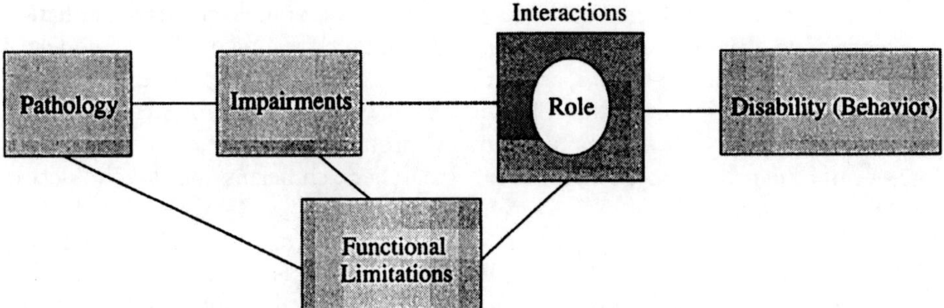

Figure 2. Nagi Model: Symbolic Representation. (*Source:* Adapted from [Nagi, 1965] by Altman [2001].)

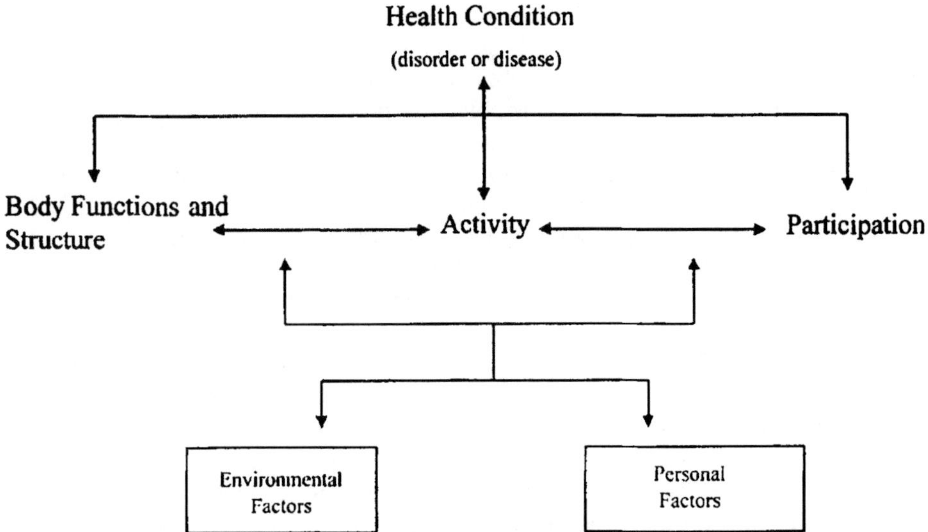

Figure 3. World Health Organization Model—ICIDH-2. (*Source:* World Health Organization [1999]).

In the WHO Model, impairment is conceptualized as reflecting a reciprocal relationship with activity. Activity, in turn, is a component of the reciprocal interaction with participation. Contextual factors, including both environmental and personal factors, are conceptualized as mediating the relationship between impairment and disability. A review of current conceptual models of the relationship between impairment and disability underscores difficulties in applying these models to research and practice. Most importantly the models, in their current form, are, due to their multidimensional and interactive nature and imprecise definitions, difficult at this stage to operationalize in research and practice. Multiple definitions exist for each one of the components and each one can be broken down to even more specific components. As a result, the chasm between theory and empirical-observational investigation is too significant to be easily bridged. Moreover, current studies capturing the relationship between impairment and disability are largely atheoretical and collect evidence on specific clinical conditions to expand knowledge of the condition and its functional impact, rather than contribute to validation of any particular conceptual model.

This context certainly makes the development of integrative models of prediction of occupational disability difficult even though similarity among predictive models of disability for different conditions, are likely present. Thus the development of biopsychosocial predictive models of disability, and early intervention approaches based on empirically supported theory, though showing promising advances, continue to be a long-term, rather than short-term goal for researchers, clinicians and stakeholders in disability prevention.

At present, research studies pay particularly limited attention to contextual components of disability in general and of work disability specifically. Contextual factors mediating the relationship between impairment and disability such as interaction between individual (personal) characteristics on one side and systemic factors arising from health care, compensation and other social systems on the other side are frequently neglected. The traditional clinical model implying linear relationships between impairment and disability is gradually giving way to a multidimensional biopsychosocial model in both research and practice, but not necessarily so in medico-legal applications such as those arising in disability compensation settings.

COMMON MISCONCEPTIONS IN CLINICAL MODELS OF THE RELATIONSHIP BETWEEN IMPAIRMENT AND OCCUPATIONAL DISABILITY

Despite recent theoretical, research, and clinical practice advances in the determination of the relationship between impairment and occupational disability, misconceptions abound that limit progress in this field.

Confusing Impairment and Disability

The concepts of impairment and disability are frequently used interchangeably in research and clinical literature and in practice. Clinicians are frequently rendering opinions of disability, instead of focusing on measurement and determination of impairment, and of the impact such impairment has on the individual's work performance, currently and in the future. Of particular concern in medico-legal contexts, are opinions about employability rather than impact on work performance often expected of clinicians by referring sources requesting independent medical examinations (Schultz, 2003). Such opinions should be reserved, at a professional level, to vocational experts, who are qualified to evaluate the context in which impairment occurs, i.e., labor market, availability of jobs in the area and work accommodation options, and therefore to contribute, based on clinical impairment and contextual findings, directly to disability determination. However, ultimately, the decisions regarding entitlement to disability status are reserved to triers of fact in the legal system including judges and adjudicators of such disability status.

Clinical practices in which impairment and disability are confused have likely been stemming from the interchangeable use of both terms in various legal statutes underlying disability determination systems such as workers' compensation or long-term disability or social security insurance systems. Lack of clarity in legal statutes and policies has resulted in terminological confusion in clinical practice and research.

Notably, the single most influential definitions of impairment and disability for clinical purposes, published by the AMA Guides for the Evaluation of medical impairment (1993, 2001), still blur impairment and disability. The AMA Guides include "organ function" (in absence of its definition) in their definition of impairment, despite an attempt to discriminate between "anatomic" and "functional" losses. The AMA Guides impairment measurement approach, focusing on functional limitations, becomes particularly blurred with disability determination in cases where a biopsychosocial rather than a biomedical approach applies, i.e., in the evaluation of psychiatric, neuropsychiatric and pain-related disorders. In those conditions, the functional focus in impairment evaluation becomes frequently inseparable from the evaluation of the capacity to meet personal, social and occupational demands, i.e., disability.

In the evaluation of psychiatric impairments the requirement to evaluate daily functions, concentration, persistence, pace, social functioning and adaptability to stressful circumstances in the work context (i.e., work setting) are not sufficiently defined to allow for reliable and valid determination of disability. Likewise, AMA Guides-recommended determination of pain-related impairment is similarly functionally-oriented, with respect to activities of daily living and a focus on activity limitations. The recommended method also incorporates the assessment of a person's credibility, an area for which valid and reliable clinical assessment instruments do not yet exist, and the assessment of emotional status, typically not a domain of physical examination. This likely compounds the conceptual and methodological problems arising from this proposed approach to impairment determination.

To complicate the matter, clinically-estimated impairment ratings are often used in compensation systems as a proxy for disability, without considering work-related contextual demands, and without performing employability assessments. Such practice reflects the lack of evidence-supported decision-making systems for the translation of impairment into an occupational disability determination, and into ratings completed by compensation systems for entitlement purposes (Schultz, 2003).

Assumption of the Linear Relationship between Impairment and Disability

Even though the current body of evidence supports the multidimensional and biopsychosocial model of the relationship between impairment and disability, both clinical practice and research appear to assume a linear relationship, at times despite professed assurances to the contrary. The assumption of a linear relationship between impairment and disability are the cornerstones of biomedical and forensic (insurance) models of disability (Schultz, et al., 2000). They continue to adversely affect practices in disability determination, prediction and interventions, particularly with those highly prevalent and work-disabling conditions which require a biopsychosocial approach such as psychological, neuropsychological and musculoskeletal pain conditions.

Notably, the influential AMA Guides (2001), as seen in figure 1 in this chapter, also appears to assume a linear relationship between impairment and disability mediated by functional limitations. The contextual factors in this model are limited to specific task functions and job accommodation available at work.

Excessive Reliance on Impairment Evaluation While Neglecting Workplace Environment

Lack of discrimination between impairment and occupational disability encountered in both research and practice in disability determination and prediction is often associated with an excessive reliance on impairment in the absence of its contextualization. In particular, the compensation systems and courts in charge of legal disability determination often rely excessively on medical and psychological descriptions and ratings of impairment. This reliance is often to the detriment of factoring in the employment-related context including the labor market, availability of jobs, job accommodation, transitional return to work programs, and specific work duties and responsibilities.

Work characteristics that have been identified as important in the determination of the impact of impairment on work are rarely systematically investigated in work disability prediction models. Such characteristics include physical, emotional, social, cognitive and language demands, speed and productivity demands, degree of structure and support, flexibility in scheduling tasks and activities, availability and type of supervision and performance coaching, skill discretion, availability of breaks, shift-work and access to physical and psychological job accommodation (Schultz, 2003). Moreover, the outcomes of vocational rehabilitation are not commonly built-in to the disability prediction models in research and practice.

Key questions that assist in bridging the chasm between impairment and work disability are not often asked in clinical assessments. These include questions as to what degree impairment actually affects current or future work capacity, whether there is a significant risk of deterioration after return to work and if a job change, modification or accommodation can attenuate or eliminate disability, or even impairment. Generally, at this time, in the field of impairment and disability determination, theory research and practice still continue on divergent paths. Impairment evaluation procedures, largely driven by the methodology of the AMA Guides for the Evaluation of Permanent Impairment has been expanding within the scientist-practitioner inquiry model. This model has been clearly moving towards recognition of standardization, norms, reliability and validity factors in evaluation and importance of evidentiary support. At the same time, however, disability determination models, despite the proliferation of quantitative studies on predictors of disability with emerging actuarial approaches to return to work prediction, have not yet led to development of work disability determination models validated for various clinical, case management and legal applications. This divergence serves to fuel litigation and costs of disability for personal injury, long-term disability and workers' compensation systems.

Multiple Definitions of Occupational Disability

Determination of the relationship between impairment and disability, in both research and practice, is adversely affected not only by the lack of a single universally accepted concept of such a relationship but also by multiple operational definitions of disability (Schultz, 2003). Definitions of work disability include loss of earning capacity, duration of disability (or absence from work), employability, return to pre-injury versus new employment, impaired work performance or perception of disability by self or others. The diversity of definitions of disability in research complicates both predictive and outcome studies of disability, limits the generalizability of findings, the development of integrative models and the transfer of knowledge to practice.

Moreover, it is not clear how to qualify disability outcomes such as the ability to work with significant job modifications and accommodations, which attenuate manifestations of disability in the presence of ongoing impairment. Inclusions of such outcomes in research is rare due to the paucity of their operational definitions, yet essential in medico-legal applications in which decisions on disability determination, entitlement and reasonable job accommodations are made.

In clinical applications, occupational disability is often confused with general disability, which includes the inability to meet personal, daily living, social and recreational demands, in addition to work demands. The AMA Guides for the Evaluation of Permanent Impairment (1993, 2001), clearly caution against the indiscriminate use of impairment ratings as work disability ratings:

> Impairment percentages estimate the extent of the impairment on whole person functioning and account for basic activities of daily living, not including work. The complexity of work activities requires individual analyses. Impairment assessment is a necessary *first step* for determining disability (AMA Guides, 2001, p.13).

Notably, since impairment and disability are often erroneously equated, in law and in practice, AMA Guides-derived general impairment ratings are contrary to their intent, as a proxy, or major contributor to work disability, in the absence of clear empirically-supported evidence of how the two outcomes are related. More often in clinical rather than in forensic disability determination settings, assessed individuals are referred to as "disabled" or "totally disabled", in absence of evidence of the impact of impairment on work ability and on performance in general, and without factoring in specific workplace contextual characteristics.

IMPAIRMENT AND WORK DISABILITY IN CONTEXT: BRIDGING THE GAP

The literature converges in pointing out that the relationship between impairment and occupational disability is not linear. Two groups of factors emerge as mediating the relationship: (1) individual resources including residual work capacity, coping and motivation, and (2) characteristics of the workplace and/or job to which an individual is expected to return (Schultz, 2003).

Individual resources identified in research on the prediction of disability include sociodemographic factors, emotional factors, attitudes and beliefs, and general and specific health factors (Krause, Frank, Dasinger, Sullivan and Sinclair, 2001). Biopsychosocial models of disability particularly emphasize the role of cognitions such as perception, beliefs and expectations, as well as ways of coping, in the prediction of disability (Crook et al., 2002; Jensen, 1999; Linton, 2000; Schultz et al., 2002; Schultz et al., 2004; Sullivan, 1998; Turk, 2002).

Motivation to return to work is closely related to expectations of outcome, postulated, together with expectations of efficacy, in Bandura's social learning theory (1986). According to the instrumental theory of motivation: "action results when an outcome, i.e., returning to work, is perceived as both probable and beneficial to the individual" (Roessler, 1989, p. 14). Further, motivation can be conceptualized as a function of expectations, which are understood as a person's chances of achieving a desirable outcome and the value of the outcome divided by the costs of performing such action (McDaniels, 1976).

In application to occupational disability, it is likely that a person's motivation to return to work with residual impairment or symptoms may be a function of their expectations of recovery and the value of the work balanced by the personal costs associated with coping with impairment (Schultz et al., 2004). This concept of motivation to return to work, though promising, does require further validation research. Generally, the construct of "work motivation" has not received much attention in research of occupational disability, likely due to operationalization and measurement difficulties. It has been largely replaced by the more widely used term "coping".

In addition to individual resources, work and workplace-related characteristics also mediate between impairment and disability. Both individual task-level physical and psychosocial job characteristics and organizational, mezo-level employer factors predictive of duration of disability have been widely investigated. Physical job characteristics with a link to prolonged disability have been found to include heavy physical work, repetitive or continuous strain, musculoskeletal strain, uncomfortable working position, crouching, noise exposure, bending, twisting, or fixed positions, more daily hours of physical labor, construction work, interaction of physical demands with physical limitations, and interaction of physical demands and place of residence (Krause et al., 2001). Psychosocial job characteristics included exposure to more than one of the following: piece work, time pressure, shift work, heavy physical labor, high job strain or stress, low job control, high psychological job demands, monotonous work, long work hours, low job seniority and job dissatisfaction (Krause et al., 2001).

At the organizational level, the following factors have been linked to *shortened* duration of disability: people-oriented culture (Amick III et al., 2000; Hunt & Habeck, 1993), proactive return to work program (Amick III et al., 2000; Hunt & Habeck, 1993), positive safety climate (Amick III et al., 2000; Hunt & Habeck, 1993), ergonomic job design practices (Amick III et al., 2000) and public employer (Infante-Rivard & Lortie, 1996).

Societal level, social policy and macroeconomic contextual factors affecting the duration of disability have also been investigated producing disparate results. Litigation, complexity of the compensation system and dismissal during sick leave have led to prolonged disability whereas a high number of job benefits tended to shorten disability (Krause et al., 2001).

The transfer of the knowledge of researched predictors of disability to the practice of disability determination in medico-legal contexts is in its early stage. This reflects the absence of integrative, empirically supported models of disability prediction for both medico legal and clinical (prevention, case-management, and rehabilitation) applications, and the prevalence of outdated biomedical and forensic models of disability determination in compensation and legal settings. Before any compensation-related analyses are completed, decisions on the severity of occupational disability must be made. Yet, such decisions, whether made by a vocational expert, a judge, jury, or compensation specialist, are extremely complex requiring the bridging of impairment and disability via contextual, individual and work-related factors. To date, no established methodology or algorithm for such decisions has been described in the literature (Beck & Schultz, 2000).

A recent qualitative exploration of the implicit decision-making criteria utilized in determining occupational disability in psychological injury cases in the workers' compensation system (Beck & Schultz, 2000) allowed for formulation of a preliminary decision-making tree using Gladwin's ethnographic decision-making model (Gladwin, 1989). Table 1 outlines the questions implicated in the subsequent steps of decision-making regarding severity of occupational disability.

This is an example of a qualitatively determined algorithm for use in decision-making for occupational disability determination in a compensation setting to be used for future validation research. Notably, existing predictive actuarial formulas

TABLE 1. Decision-making steps in determining occupational disability due to psychological disability

1. Are the symptoms of diagnosable psychological impairment present?
2. Is there a pre-existing psychological impairment?
3. Is there a portion of the psychological impairment which arises from injury at claim?
4. Does the psychological impairment affect current work capacity?
5. Is the person able to return to their pre-injury employment?
6. If so, is there a significant risk for deterioration and/or of residual symptoms after return to work?
7. Can a job change attenuate or eliminate the psychological impairment?
8. Does the person have work capacity in a competitive environment?
9. Is the person able, or expected, to adapt adequately, with or without job accommodation, despite the psychological impairment?
10. Is the person able to perform most activities of daily living despite the psychological impairment?
11. Is there significant executive dysfunction and/or significant lack of adaptability to change and stress?

Source: *Psychological Injuries at Trial* (2003). Washington, DC., American Bar Association. Reprinted by permission.

and research-supported models of occupational disability are group based and do not yet allow for individual decision-making in individual medico-legal cases due to problems with such aspects of validity as sensitivity and specificity (Schultz et al., 2004) and insufficient validation of the model for such applications.

Such models, at the current state of development and validation, are likely better used to serve in identifying individuals at elevated risk for disability, and to apply early intervention and secondary prevention, than to aid in the determination of disability in medico-legal settings.

TRANSFER OF KNOWLEDGE: FROM THEORY TO RESEARCH AND FROM RESEARCH TO PRACTICE

The relationship between impairment and occupational disability, at research and clinical levels, is at the core of the identification of individuals at risk for chronic disability, early intervention, secondary prevention and the legal determination of entitlement and disability benefits. Multiple issues arise in the process of transferring knowledge from theoretical models to research and from research to clinical and administrative practice. Questions typically cluster around two areas: is knowledge ready to be transferred? Is practice ready for knowledge?

Current problems with the transfer of knowledge in the area of impairment and occupational disability arise from the difficulty of integrating the research data collected on diverse clinical conditions. Studies on impairment and work disability span physical, pain-related and psychosocial conditions and follow different conceptual models, methodologies and questions. This book constitutes an attempt to capture the integrative themes, conclusions and recommendations pertaining to most common occupational disabilities.

At this time, the transfer of knowledge regarding the relationship of impairment and occupational disability to practice is limited to *specific conditions* (with musculoskeletal pain having received most of the research attention), the *specific stage of disability* (Krause et al., 2001), the *specific context* including primary health care, rehabilitation settings, and/or compensation (workers' compensation or insurance system) context, the *specific region or sociodemographic profile of individuals* and *specific applications*, including risk identification, early intervention and disability determination for medico-legal purposes. Due to problems with the generalizability of studies, any knowledge transfer is limited to the specific applications for which the determination of the relationship between impairment and disability has been validated. For example, a predictive model of work disability for workers with low back pain in the subacute stage in the Canadian province of British Columbia, will not likely translate to chronic musculoskeletal disability determination practices in the state of Ohio, as the original model was not validated for such an application.

As discussed in this chapter, despite conceptual convergence of some of the main tenets of key models of disability and the diversity of specific operational definitions, including the terms impairment and disability, it is difficult to integrate the research in the literature and develop empirically supported models of the relationship between impairment and disability. In addition, some of the critical explanatory concepts related to mediation of the relationship between impairment and disability are ill defined, substituted by other concepts or not defined. The concept of motivation and coping, an issue critical to the understanding of why some individuals with severe impairments continue to work and others, with medically mild impairments become totally disabled, have not been clarified. Particularly the concept of work motivation, derived from organizational psychology (Kanfer, 1990; Locke, 1999; Pinder, 1984, 1998, 2000) and social learning theory (Bandura, 1986; McDaniel, 1976; Roessler, 1989), has not yet been conceptualized and operationalized in rehabilitation and disability studies.

The emerging studies on suboptimal motivation (e.g., Fishbain, 2003) are largely atheoretical and contribute to the improvement of the assessment of impairment in medico-legal settings but not to learning why some people are motivated to cope with impairment and return to work and others have difficulties. This knowledge is of critical importance in designing effective return to work programs.

In addition, the other complementary contextual factors mediating between impairment and disability are the workplace and job-related factors. These factors have not received as much research attention as individual factors have. The knowledge to be transferred into practice in the workplace area is limited in scope and focused primarily on what helps people return to work rather than what does not. Workplace organizational factors which are most clearly associated with occupational stress and musculoskeletal disability include high demand and low control, time pressure-monotonous work, lack of job satisfaction, unsupportive management style, low practical support from peers and high perceived load (Main, 2000; Krause et al., 2000). In addition, job accommodation and transitional work programs have been linked to improved return to work outcomes (Krause et al., 2000; Crook et al., 2002) but not necessarily incorporated into integrated models of disability prediction. It is however, unclear how various impairments and workplace/job characteristics interact with individual characteristics in contributing to and maintaining work disability.

Moreover, despite advances made in the measurement of impairment, the assessment of pain-related and psychological impairment continues to lag behind the measurement of physical impairment. The need for the application of an interdisciplinary model of assessment likely complicates measurement of these conditions in research and practice. Importantly, the most influential guide to determination of medical impairment, the AMA Guides (2001), admits that

> Research is limited on the reproductibility and validity of the *Guides*. Anecdotal reports indicate that adoption of the *Guides* results in a more standardized impairment process. As relevant research becomes available, subsequent editions of the *Guides* will incorporate these evidence-based studies to improve the *Guides*' reliability and validity (p.10).

Notably, in the absence of reliability data, studies on validity are unlikely to be contributory.

Last, but not least, clinical and legal/administrative practices in the translation of impairment into occupational disability also face barriers and limitations in using new knowledge. A health care or compensation system needs to be aware whether the model of determination of the disability of interest (e.g., a disability risk identification system) has been validated in a similar setting and for a similar application. If the answer is yes, further potential barriers emerge. The new model may be inconsistent with current practices, particularly if these practices are based on a biomedical or forensic concept of impairment and disability (Schultz et al., 2000). The recognition of the importance and systematic collection of both psychosocial and workplace data may prove too foreign to such systems. The new practices and information collected in the process must meet legal standards for admissibility of evidence accepted in a given system.

Data collection issues inherent in administrative databases involved in disability determination systems usually do not meet requirements of completeness, standardization, reliability and validity (Schultz et al., 2002) and effectively hamper development of risk identification and early intervention systems in practice. Staff training to collect data in standardized fashion and need for periodic re-calibration of skills must be recognized by the administration of the system (Schultz et al., 2002). Also, the need to change and update the system as the new knowledge becomes available can be cumbersome and costly to the system.

CONCLUSIONS

In the context of epidemiological trends demonstrating an increased and increasing incidence and/or duration of musculoskeletal, pain-related, psychological and neuropsychological disabilities a biomedical model of disability should give way to the implementation of a biopsychosocial model. The determination of disability from impairment becomes, under such a model, an interdisciplinary task.

The evaluation of the relationship between impairment and disability is at the core of the identification of individuals at risk for disability, early intervention, disability prevention, and disability determination, in both clinical and legal contexts.

The relationship between impairment and work disability is not linear but multidimensional and interactive. The key factors mediating this relationship are related to the individual and the workplace context in which impairment occurs. An understanding of the individual factors critical for prediction of disability including sociodemographic factors, physical factors, and psychosocial factors, such as beliefs, perceptions, expectations, coping and motivation using a cognitive behavioral conceptualization, workplace and job factors as well as with the limitations posed by impairment, is critical in both research and practice applications.

Workplace and job factors have not been researched as well as individual factors, and have only recently been incorporated into integrative predictive models. The workplace factors can be seen from a mezo-level perspective of organizational characteristics of the workplace such as company climate, culture or job design and return to work practices. At the same time, specific job characteristics usually conceptualized using a control-demand model (Karasek & Theorell, 1990) augmented by social support factors and job accommodation (Krause et al., 2001), were identified as linked to prevalence and/or duration of occupational disability.

Gradual replacement of judgement-based decision-making models of translation of impairment into disability and identification of individuals at risk for disability, by actuarial predictive formulae and algorithms for decision making continues to be an aspirational goal. At this time however, numerous conceptual, methodological and system-based barriers impede direct transfer of knowledge in the area.

Specifically, the multiplicity of research studies on various clinical conditions, with discrepancies in conceptual models, operational definitions of impairment and disability, methodological approaches, applications and outcomes, constitute the most significant barriers. The existing research-based models of prediction of work disability are not easily transferable to practice. This is due to generalizability problems secondary to different sociodemographic and clinical sample characteristics and stages of disability, regional and system based differences, disparate outcome definitions and measures, different methodological designs, intended applications of models and specificity and sensitivity of the prediction formulae. In addition, disability prediction studies lack an overarching conceptual model, despite the preference of biopsychosocial over forensic or biomedical approaches.

An actual impairment measurement, despite attempts at the standardization of an evaluative approach by the AMA Guides for the Evaluation of Permanent Impairment, continues to require reliability and validity research. With the absence of evidence for the reliability of impairment evaluation, any need for evidence of validity becomes a moot point.

The issue of motivation, particularly measurement of suboptimal motivation, is implicated in evaluation of both impairment and disability. Current attempts at measuring motivation are largely atheoretical. In studies of the prediction of disability, the construct of motivation was replaced by the construct of coping. Yet, social learning theory of work motivation (Bandura, 1986; Roessler, 1989; McDaniel, 1976) appears to have gained research support. It is likely that a person's motivation to return to work may be a function of expectations of recovery (beliefs and/or perceptions) and value of work balanced by personal costs associated with coping with impairment.

System-based barriers inherent in medico-legal contexts, in which the determination of disability from impairment occurs, such as workers' compensation or long-term disability insurance, include systemic preference for biomedical and forensic models of disability, methodological problems associated with the use, relevance, standardization, reliability and validity of administrative data-bases involved in the process of risk for disability and work disability identification.

Despite all of these barriers, the systems mandated with identification, management, prevention and compensation for disability, can already benefit from evidentiary support to date that would inform and guide their best practices, and improve both clinical and economic disability outcomes.

REFERENCES

Altman, B. (2001). Disability definitions, models, classification schemes, and applications. In G.L. Albrecht, K.D. Seelman & M. Bury (Eds.) *Handbook of Disability Studies.* Thousand Oaks, CA: Sage Publications.

Americans With Disabilities Act of 1990, *42 U.S.C.A. § 12101 et seq.* (West 1993).

American Medical Association (2001). *Guides for the evaluation of permanent impairment* (5th ed.). Chicago: AMA Press.

American Medical Association (1993). *Guides for the evaluation of permanent impairment* (4th ed.). Chicago: AMA Press.

Amick B. C., Habeck, R. V., Hunt, A., Fossel, A. H., Chapin, A., Keller, R. B., & Katz, J. N. (2000). Measuring the impact of organizational behaviors on work disability prevention and management. *Journal of Occupational Rehabilitation, 10*(1), 21–38.

Bandura, A. (1986). *Social foundations of thought and action.* Englewood Cliffs, NJ: Prentice-Hall.

Beck, K., A., & Schultz, I. Z. (2000). *Translating psychological impairment into occupational disability ratings: A decision making model* (Research report). Vancouver, British Columbia: Workers' Compensation Board of British Columbia.

Bickenbach, J.E., Chatterji, S., Badley, E.M., & Ustin, T.B. (1999). Models of disablement, universalism and the international classification of impairments, disabilities and handicaps. *Social Science and Medicine, 48,* 1173–1187.

Boorse, C. (1975). On the distinction between disease and illness. *Philosophy and Public Affairs, 5,* 49.

Boorse, C. (1977). Health as a theoretical concept. *Philosophy and Science, 44,* 542.

Brandt, E.N. & Pope, A.M. (Eds.) (1997). *Enabling America: Assessing the Role of Rehabilitation Science and Engineering.* Washington, DC: National Academy Press.

Crook, J., Milner, R., Schultz, I. Z., & Stringer, B. (2002). Determinants of occupational disability following a low back injury: A critical review of the literature. *Journal of Occupational Rehabilitation, 12*(4), 277–295.

Engel, G. (1977). The need for a new medical model: A challenge in biomedicine. *Science, 196,* 129–136.

Fine, M., & Asch, A. (1988). Disability beyond stigma: Social interaction, discrimination, and activism. *Journal of Social Issues, 44,* 3–21.

Fishbain, D.A., Cutler, R., Rosomoff, H.L., & Rosomoff, R.S. (2003). Chronic pain disability exaggeration/malingering and submaximal effort research. In I. Z. Schultz, & D. O. Brady (Eds.), *Psychological Injuries at Trial.* Chicago: American Bar Association.

Fougeyrollas, P., & Beauregard, L. (2001). An interactive person-environment social creation. In G.L. Albrecht, K.D. Seelman & M. Bury (Eds.) *Handbook of Disability Studies.* Thousand Oaks, CA: Sage Publications.

Gladwin, C.H. (1989). *Ethnographic decision tree modeling.* Newbury Park, CA: Sage Publications.

Hunt, H.A., Habeck, R.V., VanTol, B. & Scully, S. (1993). *Disability prevention among Michigan employers (Upjohn Institute Technical Report No. 93–004).* W.E. Upjohn Institute for Employment Research, Kalamazoo, MI.

Infante-Rivard, C., & Lortie, M. (1996). Prognostic factors for return to work after a first compensated episode of back pain. *Occupational and Environmental Medicine, 53,* 499–494.

Jensen, M.P., Romano, J.M., Turner, J. A., Good, A.B., & Wald, L.H. (1999). Patient beliefs predict patient functioning: Further support for a cognitive-behavioural model of chronic pain. *Pain, 81,* 95–104.

Kanfer, R. (1990). *Motivation theory in industrial/organizational psychology* (2nd ed., Vol. 1). Palo Alto, CA: Consulting Psychologists Press.

Karasek R., & Theorell, T. (1990). *Healthy work—stress, productivity and the reconstruction of working life.* New York: Basic Books, Inc.

Krause, N., Ragland, D.R., Greiner, B.A., Syme, L., Fisher, J. M. (1997). Psychosocial job factors associated with back and neck pain in public transit operators. *Scandinavian Journal of Work and Environmental Health, 23,* 179–186.

Krause, N., Dasinger L.K., Deegan, L.J., Rudolph, L., Brand, R.J. (2001). Psychosocial job factors and return-to-work after compensated low back injury: A disability phase-specific analysis. *American Journal of Industrial Medicine, 40,* 374–392.

Krause, N., Frank, J.W., Sullivan, T.J., Dasinger, L.K., & Sinclair, S.J. (2001b). Determinants of duration of disability and return to work after work-related injury and illness: Challenges for future research. Invited Paper for Special Issue of *American Journal of Industrial Medicine, 40,* 464–484.

Linton, S.J. (2000). A review of psychological risk factors in back and neck pain. *Spine, 25*, 1148–1156.

Locke, E. A. (1999). The motivation to work: What we know. In P. Pintrich & M. Maehr (Eds.), *Advances in motivation and achievement* (Vol. 10). Greenwich, CT: JAI Press.

Main, C.J., Spanswick, C.C. (2000). *Pain Management: An interdisciplinary approach.* Edinburgh: Churchill Livingstone.

McDaniel, J. (1976). *Physical disability and human behavior.* New York: Pergamon.

Meyerson, L. (1988). The social psychology of disability: 1948 and 1988. *Journal of Social Issues, 44*, 173.

Nagi, S.Z. (1965). Some conceptual issues in disability and rehabilitation. In M. Sussman (Ed.) *Sociology and Rehabilitation.* Washington, DC: American Sociological Association.

Nagi, S.Z. (1977). The disabled and rehabilitation services: A national overview. *American Rehabilitation,* 2(5), 26–33.

Nagi, S.Z. (1991). Disability concepts revisited: Implications for prevention. In A.M. Pope & A.R. Tarlov (Eds.) *Disability in America: Toward a National Agenda for Prevention.* Washington, DC: National Academy Press.

Olkin, R., & Pledger, C. (2003). Can disability studies and psychology join hands? *American Psychologist, 58*(4), 296–304.

Pinder, C. C. (2000, October). *Work motivation theory at the start of the new millennium.* Presented to American Board of Vocational Experts, Vancouver, British Columbia.

Pinder, C. C. (1998). *Work motivation in organizational behavior.* Upper Saddle River, NJ: Prentice Hall.

Pinder, C. C. (1984). *Work motivation: theory, issues, and applications.* Glenview, IL: Scott, Foreman.

Pope, A.M. & Tarlov, A.R. (1991). *Disability in America: Toward a National Agenda for Prevention.* Washington, DC: National Academy Press.

Roessler, R.T. (1988). A conceptual basis for return to work interventions. *Rehabilitation Counselling Bulletin, 32*, 99–107.

Schultz, I. Z. (2000). *Translating psychological impairment into occupational disability* (Research report). Vancouver, British Columbia: Workers' Compensation Board of British Columbia.

Schultz, I. Z. (2003). The relationship between psychological impairment and occupational disability. In I. Z. Schultz, & D. O. Brady (Eds.), *Psychological Injuries at Trial.* Chicago: American Bar Association.

Schultz, I. Z., Crook, J., Fraser, K., & Joy, P. W. (2000). Models of diagnosis and rehabilitation in musculoskeletal pain-related occupational disability. *Journal of Occupational Rehabilitation, 10*(4), 271–293.

Schultz, I. Z., Crook, J., Meloche, G. R., Berkowitz, J., Milner, R., Zuberbier, O. A., Meloche, W. (2004). Psychosocial factors predictive of occupational low back disability: Towards development of a return to work model. *Pain, 107*, 77–85.

Schultz, I., Crook, J., Milner, R., Berkowitz, J., Meloche, G. (2002). Use of Administrative Databases for the Multivariate Prediction of Occupational Disability: A feasibility assessment. *The Journal of Workers Compensation, 12*(1), 43–55.

Sullivan, M.J.L., Stanish,W., Waite, H., Sullivan, M., Tripp, D.A. (1998). Catastrophizing, pain, and disability in patients with soft-tissue injuries. *Pain, 77*, 253–260.

Tate, D.G., & Pledger, C. (2003). An integrative conceptual framework of disability: New directions for research. *American Psychologist, 58*(4), 289–295.

Turk, D.C. (2002). A diathesis-stress model of chronic pain and disability following traumatic injury. *Pain Research Management, 7*, 9–19.

Verbrugge, L.M. & Jette, A.M. (1993). The disablement process. *Social Science and Medicine, 6*(1), 1–14.

World Health Organization (WHO) (1980). *International Classification of Impairments, Disabilities, and Handicaps: A Manual of Classification Relating to the Consequences of Disease. Geneva: Author.*

World Health Organization (WHO) (1999). *ICIDH-2 International Classification of Functioning and Disability.* Beta-2 draft, full version. Geneva: Author.

Zuberbier, O. A., Hunt, D. G., Kozlowski, A., Berkowitz, J., Schultz, I.Z, Crook, J. M., & Milner, R. A. (2001). Commentary on the AMA guides lumbar impairment validity checks. *Spine, 26*(24), 2735–2737.

3

Models of Diagnosis and Rehabilitation in Musculoskeletal Pain-Related Occupational Disability

Izabela Z. Schultz, Peter W. Joy, Joan Crook, and Kerri Fraser

Musculoskeletal, pain-related occupational injuries are among the most common and disabling impairments in the working population and pose a formidable health care problem for industry. Annually, 2% of the national work force incurs industrial-related back injuries, with approximately 1.4% of these resulting in a period of work absence (1). Despite the good prognosis for most episodes, musculoskeletal injuries consume considerable resources in medical care, absence from work, productivity losses and compensation benefits. Spitzer (1) found that about three-quarters of work-injured employees return to work in two to three weeks. Only about 7% had not returned by six months; however, these few accounted for about 75% of costs to the compensation system in lost hours, indemnities, and utilization of health services.

Difficulties inherent in the diagnosis and treatment of pain-related occupational injury are compounded by problems in determining disability and entitlement to compensation. The escalating personal, societal, health care and industrial costs of pain-related occupational injury have led to considerable need to integrate conceptual models for the organization of knowledge on injury, pain and disability.

The purpose of this chapter is to describe, compare and critique five models of diagnosis and rehabilitation in pain-related occupational disability. The five models, derived from the multidisciplinary literature and chosen for review were the biomedical model, the psychiatric model, the forensic/insurance model, the labor relations model, and the biopsychosocial model. The characteristics, tenets, values, scope of applicability and practical applications associated with each model are presented. Major limitations associated with each model and recommendations for the applicability for health care and compensation are discussed.

This chapter originally appeared in *Journal of Occupational Rehabilitation, 10* (4), 271–293 (2001) and is reprinted by permission.

DOI: 10.1007/978-0-387-28919-9_3, © 2009 Springer Science+Business Media, LLC

In order to search for relevant publications, electronic databases, MEDLINE and PsychINFO, were searched from 1985 to 1999. Key words included models in the following areas: chronic pain, diagnosis, rehabilitation, disability management and psychosocial rehabilitation. The retrieved articles were hand-searched for bibliographic information that may have been missed by the computer searches. Experts in the medicine, psychology, disability management, compensation and law fields were consulted for other articles that might have been omitted.

THE BIOMEDICAL MODEL

Tenets and Values

The biomedical model is the predominant framework for a sizeable group of health care professionals. The core tenet of the model is the belief that illness is due to biological pathology (2,3). The literature reveals two slightly different articulations of this principal belief: the mechanical and the linear view of disease. Bravo et al. (4) described the mechanical perspective as a conception of the human organism as a biological machine that can be analyzed in terms of its parts, whose mechanism is understood from the point of view of cellular or molecular biology. Illness is considered a consequence of the ill functioning of the machine. In linear terms of the basic belief that problems lie wholly within the biological nature of the individual (2), disease is described as a linear sequence from causal factor, to pathology, to symptoms or manifestations, (5). The second tenet of the biomedical model holds that symptoms and disability are directly related to, and proportionate to, biological pathology (5,6) therefore, elimination of pathological causes will result in cure or improvement.

In the biomedical model, mind and body are separate entities (5,7,8). Psychological, social and behavioral dimensions are relatively unimportant or secondary to the physical disorder, or pejoratively identified as "functional overlay". Lastly, fundamental to the biomedical model is the belief that the physician is responsible for the control and, ideally, the relief of pain (9); that patients, the service recipients, are dependent on their physicians in their capacity to help themselves.

The espoused core value of the biomedical model is scientific truth, based on scientific evidence. The scientific method involves careful observation, the systematic collection of information, and objectivity. Medicine is judged to be scientific only when dealing with bodily processes (7,9). In addition, when discrepancies occur between physical findings and patient self-reports, the "objective" data, such as radiographs, laboratory tests, and observable physical findings, are given more credence and weighted more heavily (10).

Implications for Diagnosis, Treatment, and Compensation

A focus on clinical recognition and diagnosis of the underlying organic pathology is a key implication of the biomedical model. Diagnostic procedures are used to establish the extent of tissue damage that induces patients to report pain (10). A sequential diagnostic approach is adopted. Under the model, physicians seek to identify symptoms and/or syndromes, then pathology. The model also leads to an emphasis on history taking and medical/neurological testing such as radiography, laboratory tests and physical examinations (2). The biomedical model has significant influence over treatment decisions. First, the model tends to lead to a cure-oriented approach to treatment typical of acute health care settings. Second, the model promotes the use of physical treatment modalities (e.g., physiotherapy, surgery, and pharmacotherapy) directed towards the underlying physical disorder (2,6,11).

The biomedical model lends theoretical support for restrictive compensation of occupational pain-related injury. Under the model, it is likely that only patho-anatomical defects, demonstrated or inferred, would be compensated (5,12).

Clinical Limitations and Their Relationship to Compensation

The biomedical model continues to be the dominant model of illness today. The model is, however, limited in several ways. Engel (7) notes that one of the most constraining and limiting features of the model is its "...adherence to a seventeenth century paradigm predicated on the mechanism, reductionism, determinism and dualism of Newton and Descartes . . .[This adherence] . . . automatically excludes what is distinctly human from the realm of science and the scientific". Considering the complex nature of pain, a sole focus on biomedical pathology results in a lack of consideration of the multidimensional nature of the phenomenon, the variety of reactions to pain, and the changing nature of injury and pain over time. Further, this exclusive attention on objectively identified pathology negates the importance of patient-centered measures of pain, symptoms and disability (3,11). Ironically, "objective" measures of pathology have not been shown to predict disability, and a pathophysiological explanation cannot be offered in more than 85% of occupational injury cases of low back pain (1,5).

Scope of Applicability

The biomedical model purports to offer a systematic, scientific approach to the evaluation of treatment effectiveness. The model is, accordingly, most relevant in relation to medical decision-making, particularly in regards to uncomplicated, physical injuries (5) and/or pain in its acute stages (11). The model has also proven applicable in the identification of medical "red flags"; that is, the ruling out of serious medical conditions, such as tumors, infections and fractures (13).

PSYCHIATRIC MODEL

Tenets and Values

The traditional medical/psychiatric model holds three fundamental beliefs. First, proponents of the model believe that pain is either organic or psychological in origin (14–17). In this assumption, therefore, the model perpetuates traditional dualistic thinking typified by the biomedical model (15,16). Second, underlying the model, is the belief that pain that cannot be attributed to physical causes must be psychological in origin (16). Gamsa (15) pointed out that according to the psychoanalytical views "intractable pain which defies organic explanation is a defense against unconscious psychic conflict". Third, the model is founded on the belief that patients with undiagnosed, intractable pain are a psychologically homogeneous group (16).

Another principal tenet of the psychiatric model is that patients' reactions to pain are either "normal" or "abnormal", and abnormal responses invariably constitute a mental disorder. Abnormal reactions are considered to be those which are "grossly"

TABLE 1. Comparison of models of diagnosis and rehabilitation in musculoskeletal pain-related disability

	Biomedical Model	Psychiatric Model	Insurance Model	Labor Relations Model	Biopsychosocial Model
Main Tenets	• Illness is due to physical pathology • Symptoms and disability are directly proportionate to physical pathology • Mind and body are separate • Physicians in control of diagnosis and treatment direction	• If there is no physical explanation of symptoms, the problem is likely psychiatric • Person's reaction to injury is either: a) proportionate to tissue damage (normal); or b) abnormal • Abnormal reactions to injury constitute a mental disorder	• People who anticipate secondary gains are likely to be dishonest about their symptoms • Objective proof of impairment and disability must be provided • It is paramount to clearly discriminate between "honest" and "dishonest" clients	• Work injury understood and managed within the socio-political context of the workplace • The needs of the workers and the employers can be complementary • Systemic responsibility for outcomes • Workplace environment and labor relations significantly influence injury sequelae/recovery and rehabilitation • Employer has a key role in return to work and needs incentives to assist injured workers. Systemic changes necessary to accommodate Return to Work (RTW) needs of injured worker • Multidisciplinary approach • Proactive; early intervention in the workplace • Service recipient seen as a worker	• Response to injury considered to be multidimensional • Organic impairment does not reliably predict disability and symptoms. Psychosocial factors mediate one's reaction to injury • Interdisciplinary/whole person approach • Focus on self-responsibility of the worker
Underlying Values	• Scientific evidence and objectivity	• Detection and identification of mental disorders	• Scientific truth • Protection of the system from abuse and dishonesty • Cost limitation	• Integration of prevention and rehabilitation • Harmonious labor relations/well-functioning system • Protection of injured worker from exploitation • Cost containment	• Client and his/her well-being • Outcome = improved function • Chronicity prevention

Implications for Diagnosis	• Focus on uncovering organic pathology • Sequential diagnostic approach	• Focus on psychiatric diagnosis as stipulated in DSM* • Inability to identify individuals who do not fit DSM	• Exhaustive assessment using special forensic methods aimed at detection of inconsistencies and deception • Interdisciplinary model may be utilized • Individuals showing inconsistencies in testing identified as "illegitimate", "malingerers", "symptom magnifiers" and/or motivated by secondary gain • Adversarial service climate	• Focus on the assessment of functional work capacity • Analyze the impact of work organization, climate and labor relations on the clinical profile of injured workers • Importance of correct clinical diagnosis is secondary	• Multi-dimensional/ interdisciplinary diagnosis • Acknowlegement of limitations of diagnosis • Functional focus on diagnosis • Treatment-oriented assessment
Implications for Treatment	• Cure-orientation rather than coping-orientation • Need to relate physical treatment to underlying pathology • Focus on physical treatment modalities	• Psychiatric treatment/medication for the diagnosed • No treatment for workers who do not fit the criteria	• Wide range of treatment options for clients identified as "honest" only • No treatment for clients identified as "dishonest"	• Disability management in the workplace • Treatment integrated with return to work process • Work return transition programs • Case management approach	• Rehabilitation and return to work more important than diagnosis • Coping is a desirable outcome if cure not possible • Worker as an active participant in the process and responsible for the outcome • Coordinated team and case management approach • Linkeages with the environment the worker returns to (employer, family) • Time-based intervention approach with early intervention

(*cont.*)

TABLE 1. (*Continued*)

	Biomedical Model	Psychiatric Model	Insurance Model	Labor Relations Model	Biopsychosocial Model
Implications for Compensation	• Compensation for impairments with clearly identified organic causes • Lack of specific built-in financial incentives for coping and well behaviour	• Compensation for all diagnosable mental disorders arising from the injury: e.g., somatoform/pain disorders	• Compensation for "honest" clients only • Appears an attractive option due to simplicity • Long term costs due to: a) chronicity in incorrectly identified clients b) multiple systemic safeguards necessary to detect malingering causing service inefficiencies	• Anticipated reduction in disability costs, long-term • Costs partly shifted to the specific accident employer	• Clear guidelines required for compensability if exact etiology unknown or interactive • Higher rehabilitation, lower compensation costs • Compensability primarily for treatment failures and permanent impairment • Compensation used as an incentive for rehabilitation/return to work
Scope of Applicability	• Uncomplicated physical injuries occurring to adaptable people • Early/acute stages of physical injury • Identification of red flags	• Persons with diagnosed psychiatric disorders	• Individuals with clear objective finding • Confirmed malingerers	• Individuals with attachment to the workplace • Wide range of post-acute clinical problems • Prevention—workplace based educational programs	• Wide range of clinical problems • Individuals willing to participate in treatment • Prevention—workplace based programs addressing both physical and psychosocial aspects of injury prevention

Potential Limitations	• Organic etiology may not be detectable given present state of knowledge • In complex cases prolongs diagnostic process endlessly – promotes chronicity • Ignores multidimensional nature of reaction to injury and psychosocial factors • Can increase human suffering and drive up cost of compensation	• Misses most of the population due to low prevalence of psychiatric diagnoses • Overpathologizes normal people • Unknown applicability of DSM outside clinical and research settings and to non-Western cultures • Poor interrater reliability due to inability to identify the "norm" • Diagnosis of "mental disorder" according to DSM does not imply disability • Drives up costs	• No single scientific method can reliably and accurately discriminate between "honest" and "dishonest" clients • False-positives and negatives • No objective method measuring human motivation and intentionality • Concept of "secondary losses" not addressed • Potential for abuse by poorly trained clinicians and administrative staff • Lack of scientific and clinical research consensus on the issue of malingering, secondary gain, symptom magnification and illness behaviour • can increase human suffering, chronicity and compensation costs in the long run • No link to prevention	• Clinically complex and acute cases cannot be addressed • Loss of privacy/confidentiality for the worker • Small employers unable to implement the model • High organizational complexity of the undertaking, "seamless" cooperation of all parties required • Requires incentives for employers as considerable resources and commitment are necessary • Strongly affected by economy and politics	• Too "luxurious" a model for simple physical injuries occuring to good copers • Organizational structure requires changes to promote team approach • Rehabilitation must be empirically validated and cost effective • Low acceptance level among some health professionals • Treatment may be unnecessarily extended to people who are not likely to benefit from it • Time consuming and labor-intensive approach

Dsm—*Diagnostic and Statistical Manual of Mental Disorders*, Forth edition, Washington, DC, 1994. American Republicatin Association.

out of proportion to the underlying organic pathology, even when there is no positive evidence for psychopathology other than this "discrepancy" (14,15).

The literature informing the psychiatric model focuses on the importance of psychiatric diagnosis, as exemplified by the Diagnostic and Statistical Manual of Mental Disorders (DSM) (18). The DSM is based on the application of the medical paradigm to psychopathology and the application of the scientific method to "the elucidation and classification into discrete entities of disease" (9). The DSM considers the problems of pain (19) through the conceptualization of Pain Disorder as associated with either psychological or physical factors.

Implications for Diagnosis, Treatment, and Compensation

As in the biomedical model, the diagnosis of a mental disorder is made on the basis of history, signs and symptoms. The differential diagnosis of chronic pain historically has included several DSM diagnoses, such as somatoform pain disorders, hypochondriases, somatization disorders, factitious disorders with physical symptoms, substance abuse disorders, malingering, and conversion disorder (14,19). The latest DSM (IV) has attempted to respond to the problem of questionable reliability of the diagnostic labels by tightening the diagnostic criteria (19). However, some would still argue that an individual may have a mental or behavioral problem without meeting the criteria specified in DSM. Others would argue that psychologic factors are not usually etiologic of pain and that chronic pain does not constitute a "mental disorder" per se and under most circumstances should not be conceptualized as such. Nevertheless, both camps would agree that early identification and timely treatment of diagnosed emotional disorders are likely to reduce recurrences, improve overall prognosis and be cost effective (14).

Receiving a diagnosis of a mental disorder recognized by the DSM can entitle a patient to services and benefits that might not otherwise have been available, or that might not have been paid for by a third party payer. Under the psychiatric model, compensation would be available for all diagnosable mental disorders arising from the injury, including Pain Disorder. This constitutes a controversial implication of the psychiatric model as it is derived from an anachronistic dualistic model of pain. The psychiatric framework for pain has proven rehabilitatively ineffective and diagnostically misguiding.

Clinical Limitations and Their Relationship to Compensation

Given the relatively low prevalence of psychiatric diagnoses, there is a real likelihood of over-investigation, over-diagnosis and over-pathologizing of "normal" people (15,16,20). Workers with prolonged pain syndromes are not necessarily psychologically abnormal, although they often become depressed and develop other co-morbidity; yet, under the model, these workers would likely receive a DSM "label" (21). These labels may often be unduly damaging and harmful to workers due to stigmatization.

The argument that pain is caused by a psychopathological mechanism is based on inference and questionable research (15,16). Considering the complex natural history of chronic pain development in back pain patients receiving compensation payments, the use of the simplistic and victim-blaming terms, such as "compensation neurosis", contributes little to recovery and, one may speculate, may in fact contribute to chronicity (22). Further, a diagnosis of a "mental disorder" under the DSM does not imply disability and does not necessarily equate with an inability to work (20). Reliance on labels, therefore, may lead to inappropriate case management decisions and, as a result, lost opportunities to preserve patient role functioning.

Scope of Applicability

The psychiatric model is relevant for persons with diagnosed psychiatric disorders, but its applicability to chronic pain conditions *not* accompanied by psychiatric disorder is questionable and limited due to diagnostic validity and reliability problems. Moreover, the DSM was not designed for forensic purposes and is not suited for legal determinations: "...the concept of diagnosis, which refers to mental disorder, and the concept of disability, which refers to functional capacity, are not interchangeable and should not be confused" (23). The translation of diagnosis from a general clinical assessment to disability compensation, accordingly, poses a formidable challenge in the absence of empirically supported data and guidelines. In sum, therefore, the DSM, despite its popularity and recent advances on definitional clarity, is still limited both in its generalizability and in its scope of applicability to pain-related conditions.

INSURANCE MODEL

Tenets and Values

The insurance model is variously called the forensic, compensation, and the "perverse incentives" model (21). The major tenet of this model is that claimants who anticipate financial benefits through compensation, pending litigation, special services or considerations, such as job transfer or reduced workload, are likely to be dishonest about their symptoms. This dishonesty implies a purely conscious intention to deceive, an intentional attempt at "freeloading", and an attempt to live off the avails of others by faking pain (24). In this model, financial incentives are correlated with prolongation and exacerbation of physical or psychological symptoms (25). A plethora of usually derogatory terms and "diagnoses" have been used to describe such claimants including malingering, compensation neurosis, accident neurosis, functional overlay, green back neurosis and compensationitis, to name but a few. Workers on compensation are "role-cast as sly, devious, neurotics and malingerers who are faking their pain to win or maintain comfortable financial compensation for the rest of their lives" (24). A second tenet that may be discerned is the "etiologic" role law and its application play in perpetuating malingering. This is captured in the oft-quoted definition of compensation neurosis as, "a state of mind, borne out of fear, kept alive by avarice, stimulated by lawyers, and cured by a verdict" (26). The compensation system itself is seen as "etiologic": "there are no malingerers in countries where there is no Workmens' Compensation Act" (27).

There is a strong moralistic element in this model where it is necessary to clearly differentiate between "honest" and "dishonest" claimants. The insurance model nurtures a climate wherein the claimant must vigorously prove and re-prove his or her disability with objective, verifiable, repeatable medical evidence of impairment (28).

The insurance model shares one value with the biomedical model, that is, the need for objective evidence of biopathology for the determination of a legitimate claim. The effect of this value is to separate those with a legitimate claim from those who may be providing, consciously, an inaccurate self-report. The latter are not entitled to benefits: "... malingering constitutes fraud; if it can be proved, the claimant is not entitled to any payment for the alleged condition" (29). The proponents of the insurance model also espouse a higher level societal value. They are concerned with protecting the system from abuse and dishonesty. This value purports to reduce and limit costs by "weeding out" dishonest malingerers and symptom magnifiers.

Implications for Diagnosis, Treatment, and Compensation

There are several implications of this model in relation to diagnosis and treatment. First, there is a need for objective findings of biopathology and a determination of the consistency among the severity of the injury, the physical findings, the symptoms, and the disability. Second, there is a need for an evaluation of malingering and deception. Diagnosis, therefore, demands a thorough and exhaustive assessment by many disciplines using not only physical diagnostic methods but also special forensic methods aimed at the detection of inconsistencies and deception. The assessment methods include clinical impressions of the credibility of the account of symptoms; clinical impressions of exaggerated claims; clinical impressions of inappropriate responses to examination and scores on non-organic signs; examiner impressions of apparent honesty, openness, truthfulness, reliability, candor or resistance, hostility, suspiciousness, guardedness, or defensiveness, and; reviews of specialist reports for evidence of inconsistencies among them. Failure to improve or return to work may heighten "blame" of the claimant and suspicions of malingering. In addition, certain scale test patterns and profiles on tests developed for other purposes for example, MMPI, neuropsychological tests, IQ tests, and tests specifically designed for the detection of malingering are applied (15,16,30–32). Claimants showing inconsistencies in testing and examination are identified as "illegitimate", "malingerers" or "symptom magnifiers". They are thought to be motivated by secondary gain, even though there may be alternative clinically plausible explanations of observed inconsistencies such as mood and pain fluctuations, fatigue, boredom or attentional difficulties. Consequently, an adversarial and suspicion-laden service climate results from the basic tenets of the model and the "deceptive measures" that are used to identify dishonesty and malingering.

According to this model there would be a wide range of treatment options available for claimants with "legitimate" painful injuries and no treatment for claimants identified as malingerers or magnifiers (28). Advocates of the insurance model have argued that claimants receiving Workers' Compensation benefits, as compared to their non-compensated counterparts, show a lack of cooperation with the diagnostic evaluation, poorer compliance, poorer motivation for rehabilitation, prolonged recovery, and poorer treatment outcomes (5, 27–30).

Several approaches to reduce financial incentives and limit financial liabilities for disability compensation systems have been proposed under this model: (i) deny compensation and treatment claims for those whose pain persists longer than six weeks, that is not surgically correctable or has not improved (5); (ii) deny claims of "symptom magnifiers", those showing inconsistencies in testing and "malingerers", and; (iii) "across the board" reductions in compensation benefits. The insurance model is attractive due to its apparent simplicity and its emphasis on business outcomes of cost containment and cost reduction. It appeals to the widely held societal values of truth and honesty. Application of the model likely offers considerable short-term cost-savings in terms of reduced compensation benefit levels. In the long term, however, the economic benefits of the model for compensation systems are dubious. The multiple system safeguards and exhaustive testing necessary to detect malingering may cause service inefficiencies. Adversarial claim climate coupled with unknown validity and reliability of so-called malingering tests and other methods for detection of deception are a fertile ground for appeals, litigation and promotion of chronicity. At the same time, low base rates make across-the-board, case-by-case investigations of malingering by compensation systems not cost-effective. In addition, a potential for chronicity rises particularly in those claimants incorrectly identified as malingerers and consequently denied funds for treatment (24).

Clinical Limitations and Their Relationship to Compensation

Clinical application of the insurance model to clinical practice is not intuitively obvious. The Hippocratic oath speaks to a patient-centered focus and concern; yet, the model, as evidenced by clinicians' increasing use of such "diagnoses" as "secondary gain" and "malingering", has found adherents within the health care system. The most important and obvious limitation of the insurance model is its lack of a scientific methodology to reliably and accurately discriminate between "honest" and "dishonest" clients. First, as there is no gold standard, there is no validity to measurement instruments used by clinicians under the model. Second, there are no reliable, foolproof methods for detecting malingering (25,30,31,33,34). It follows, therefore, that if standardized measures cannot accurately discriminate between "malingerers" and "honest" clients, then impressions gleaned from unstructured clinical interviews and physical exams also will not provide an accurate identification of malingering (35). Additionally, even if a reliable and valid assessment instrument for malingering were to exist, the prevalence rate of malingering would affect the usefulness of any test; that is to say, if prevalence were low, as is suspected, the positive predictive value of the test would be low. Most malingering research has relied exclusively on simulation designs (31). While there is questionable generalizability from simulators to malingerers, the prevalence rate for "faking" is also set artificially high, usually at 50%. Such a high prevalence rate can make any test look good.

The insurance model has a high potential for increasing claimants' suffering and compensation costs in the long run. This potential abuse by the system was recognized by a landmark decision in Ontario. The Workers' Compensation Appeal Tribunal (Decision No. 50:8, April 1986) stated: " it must be appreciated that... (non-organic chronic pain cases)... have not only a high potential for claimants abusing the system but also high potential for the system inflicting grave injustices on claimants" (36). Without a scientific approach to the identification and treatment of occupation-related injury and pain, there can be no reliable and accurate discrimination between "honest" and "dishonest" clients, merely groundless bias.

Scope of Applicability

Clearly, the insurance model works best for claimants with clear objective findings of organic pathology (15,16,37). However, it is important to note that a clear pathogenic explanation cannot be offered in many pain syndromes (1). Conspicuously, the followers of the insurance model fail to balance out their focus on the secondary gain with the complementary recognition of secondary losses the individual suffered as a result of injury. The secondary losses, rarely attended to within the forensic model, include the loss of social, family and financial status (38,39).

THE LABOR RELATIONS MODEL

Tenets and Values

Work injury, as characterized in the labor relations model, a systems-based model, is understood and managed within the socio-political context of the workplace. Habeck (40) asserts: "(we) must come to understand work disability in an employment context versus a medical process alone and maintain the employment situation as the focus and goal of activity". In this model, preventative and post-injury interventions are directed towards the entire work system including the worker, the work demands, the work organization and environment (41–44). The proponents of the labor relations model hold the belief that this approach results in a mutually beneficial situation in which both economic and humanistic ends are achieved. The assumptions are made that workers hold an attachment to the workplace and that the needs of the worker and the employer are complementary (40,45). It is argued that the personal, economic, physical, psychological, social and domestic losses related to work disruptions caused by injury are minimized for the employee, even as the bottom line improves for the employer (43). The second fundamental tenet of the model is the importance of work. Proponents of the labor relations model view work and the maintenance of the employment relationship as critical as work gives men and women a sense of identity, purpose, daily structure and meaningful existence. It follows that the loss of occupational status will threaten the emotional, psychological, financial and social well being of the individual, and must, therefore, be avoided. The third principal characteristic of the labor relations model is the belief that the employer is primarily responsible for the success or failure of return to work and the long-term maintenance of the employment relationship (41,45–49). Successful work accommodation often requires a wide range of experts, management-labor and multi-departmental collaboration (43,48). Proponents, therefore, also advocate a multifaceted, workplace-based team approach to the management, resolution and prevention of disability problems.

A primary value underlying the labor relations model is harmonious and collaborative employer-employee relations, wherein both parties assume an active role in the prevention and management of workplace injury and both make a contribution toward the attainment of the other party's goals (49). Both labor and management have vested interests in controlling the personal and economic costs of injury and disability: "Labor unions want to protect the employability and safety of the workers they represent. Management wants to retain productive, reliable and experienced employees" (49). Attitudes, policies and procedures jointly promulgated and supported by labor and management are seen as critical to the success of an effective disability management program (45).

The labor relations model holds the workplace system primarily responsible for return to work outcomes. This characteristic is an expression of the model's fundamental underlying values of job security and continued employability. Third, the model emphasizes the development and implementation of fair, equitable and proactive workplace-based health and safety policies and programs. Expressions of this core value include health promotion, prevention, safety, return-to-work and disability management programs, all of which are viewed as cost effective by employers.

Implications for Diagnosis, Treatment, and Compensation

The labor relations model's emphasis on the workplace and the employer-employee relationship sets the tone for the response to disability and significantly influences injury sequelae, recovery and rehabilitation. The focus for assessment is on employee functional work capacity and work tolerance. The assessment is completed in the context of specific organizational culture and health and safety policies. The purpose of the assessment is to explore the match between the employee's capabilities and limitations and the occupation's demands. With a functional, workplace-oriented assessment as the primary tool, it follows that the actual medical diagnosis is secondary. It is argued that a comprehensive assessment should be conducted at the work site with real life work demands and use a team approach to assist injured workers with realizing their optimal physical functioning levels and the necessary coping strategies to sustain optimal levels in spite of symptomatology (41,50).

The workplace is also a therapeutic medium for the injured worker. Workplace rehabilitation services to accommodate or retrain injured workers are based on the recognition of the therapeutic value of the physical, psychological, social and environmental dimensions of the workplace (43). The primary goals of employer-based disability management programs are to prevent unnecessary work disruptions, ensure a safe and timely return to work, and protect the employability of workers (45). Flexible work return programs are based on a gradual assumption of work tasks, job site redesign, reasonable accommodation, and job restructuring for the injured worker. It may of necessity involve permanent job reassignment, retraining, out-placement services, litigation/case closure services, or award of disability benefits (41,45).

Clinical Limitations and Their Relationship to Compensation

There are two chief implications of the labor relations model for compensation systems. First, the model lends support for the introduction of incentives and disincentives for prolonged disability for both employer and employee. Reardon and Whelan (48), for example, propose that a balanced incentive program can be achieved "... by providing a benefits structure and support system that encourages a return to work... (and)... by removing a major disincentive to return to work, the 'common law' payout." Second, the model encourages shifting of the costs toward the employer(e.g., compensation experience ratings and legislative requirements that employers bear reasonable costs of accommodation), and, also, a proliferation of the services employers must provide injured workers (46).

There are several limitations to the labor relations model. The primary difficulty is that small employers are unable to easily implement the model. Also, the model requires incentives for employers as considerable workplace resources and a substantial commitment are necessary. Success in managing disability in the workplace is achieved through top-level management commitment, the integration of medical and disability benefits and services, supportive policies and procedures, effective communication at and across all levels of the organization, and a skilled labor-management-rehabilitation team (40,43,46).

The labor relations model is strongly affected by the economy and politics: "... the worker with a disability, employer, insurer, family, rehabilitation professional and others are subject to powerful social and economic forces, including health and labor force economics, public and private sector policies and provider initiatives" (51). To justify the expense of initiating employee support services, the benefits to employers clearly must outweigh the costs. For those who become disabled at the workplace, the ability to remain on the job is affected by the local employment context, whether the employer is hiring or laying off, and whether the disabled employee is considered valuable to the organization.

The final major limitation of the labor relations model is that there are still too few empirically based studies on the effectiveness and costs/benefits of work site health promotion programs or workplace disability management strategies. While the model holds promise, it has not yet experienced widespread acceptance (43,51) among rehabilitation researchers, clinicians and the public stakeholders.

Scope of Applicability

The labor relations model applies to employment relationships. Workers who do not have a job to return to or those without stable work histories are outside of the model's scope of applicability. In its application, the model focuses on the prevention of disability by encouraging health promotion practices and decreasing physical and mental strains experienced by employees at the work site. A wide range of post-acute clinical problems (e.g., post-injury pain, post-cardiac conditions, alcoholism) have the potential to be considered under the labor relations model. Education programs related to potential occupational hazards and demands that are specific to the job (e.g., back care, lifting and handling) and general prevention programs, such as control of alcohol, stress management, harassment and violence prevention programs, fall within the scope of this model (52).

THE BIOPSYCHOSOCIAL MODEL

Tenets and Values

The biopsychosocial model espouses an integrated, multifactorial understanding of pain. The model recognizes that the relationship between pain, physical and psychological impairment, functional and social disability is far from simple: pain and response to injury are complex and interactive phenomena (3,38,53,54). Work disability due to pain has been conceptualized as a function of interactions among medical status, physical capacity, and work tolerances in the context of work demands and individual psychosocial factors (53). Worklessness has been seen as a major contributor to long term disability through the psychological, occupational, social and iatrogenic problems it produces (54). The overall model is, therefore, comprehensive and multidimensional, incorporating and organizing much of the current thought and research on the subject of pain (3,55).

The conceptual roots of this more comprehensive view of health may be traced back 50 years to when the World Health Organization (WHO) defined health as "a state of complete physical, mental and social well-being and not merely the absence of disease..." (56). The biopsychosocial model, in its present state, is a scientific paradigm that views the experience of the person as integrated into a hierarchy of dynamically related natural systems from small, less complex systems to larger, more complex systems (7,9). Under this model, pain is comprised of: (i) a biological component, which includes physiologic and neurologic functioning at the level of cells, organs and organ systems; (ii) a physical functioning component, which includes the ability to accomplish activities of daily living at the level of the individual; (iii) a psychological component, which consists of cognitive and emotional processes such as anxiety, anticipation, mood and beliefs about the future; (iv) a social functioning component, which involves the interaction of the individual at the complex societal level and includes the carrying out of social roles (e.g., work, interpersonal relationships, and vocational activities) within a certain socio-cultural environment (5).

The principal tenet of the model is the recognition of the complexity of the human organism and the complexity of the phenomenon of pain within humans. In the biopsychosocial model, the various natural systems of the human "domain" are seen as interactive, interconnected and interdependent (7,9,57). Pain is understood as a result of the interaction among these systems. The second tenet of the model involves a conceptual distinction between impairment and disability. Impairment has been defined as "the loss of use of, or derangement of any body part, system or function" whereas disability has been conceptualized as contextualization of impairment. Disability has been described as the decrease in an individual's capacity to meet personal, social or occupational demands, or to meet statutory or regulatory requirements (58). The third major tenet is that organic pathology does not reliably predict impairment and disability (59,60). Psychological and socio-cultural factors play a major role in defining pain and mediating the client's reaction to injury and subsequent disability (7,9,61). No single dimension is adequate to understand chronic pain. Further, proper understanding requires an appreciation of the clinical course of pain over time, as well as the interaction of biological, psychological and social factors (62).

Another feature of the model is the importance proponents ascribe to the affected individual. The injured individual is seen a collaborator and a co-manager of his/her rehabilitation. Injured individuals are encouraged to take responsibility for their own health management and participate actively in treatment (4,63).

In the biopsychosocial model, the "whole" person becomes the focal point in a comprehensive, integrated, therapeutic process. The anticipated client outcomes are the preservation and optimization of client health, increased independence, economic productivity and an improved quality of life (5,28,59). The emphasis is on helping the client obtain optimal functioning, despite residual disability, and to improve and restore his or her level of occupational, social and familial role functioning.

The biopsychosocial model is client-focused; it values, above all else, the preservation and optimization of health, the improvement of quality of life, the improvement of physical and role functioning, and the reduction of disability. The therapeutic focus of proponents, accordingly, is the restoration of full function, not symptom removal or "cure", and full function is understood as encompassing not only physical strength and functional status, but also the level of function in social and familial, household and occupational roles. The chief goal of adherents of the model is to prevent chronicity and disability.

Implications for Diagnosis, Treatment, and Compensation

The biopsychosocial model influences clinical practice in a number of ways. With its emphasis on comprehensive, multidimensional assessment, the model encourages the involvement of professionals from many disciplines and the collection, integration and interpretation of a variety of data, including the biological, psychological, functional, social and vocational. The diagnostic focus of clinicians, under the model, shifts from the etiological concerns of the medical, psychiatric and insurance models to more performance-based grounds; that is, to "... deficiencies in previously held adaptive patterns of functioning... " (64).

The restoration of employment status with minimal delay is one of the major goals of treatment. Early intervention designed to restore physical and role function, increase activity levels, achieve work maintenance or work re-entry is thought to expedite the return-to-work process (5, 28, 37). Comprehensive rehabilitative treatment is outcome oriented. If cure or relief of pain is not possible, rehabilitation focuses on helping the client develop a variety of coping strategies and skills to deal with the pain and circumstances surrounding the pain (62,65).

In the biopsychosocial model, the client is an active participant in the rehabilitation process. The rehabilitation team only facilitates the process; it helps the client achieve his/her rehabilitation goals (66). Case management is essential: a client's treatment must be coordinated, planned and monitored under this model. A case manager would establish linkages, as the client's coach and mentor, not only with the client but also with his/her familial, social and work environment. The biopsychosocial model encourages early rehabilitation intervention. This emphasis flows from the belief that the longer pain and disability persist, the more difficult they are to treat. Identification of those factors that predict poor prognosis for continued disability and identification of those workers at high risk for continued work disability is an important component of early intervention.

The biopsychosocial model demands a conceptual shift from the linear thinking of the medical and psychiatric models to an open system perspective. Further, the model appears to demand a shift in the value to which clinicians and compensation systems are willing to place on client self-reports. By giving explicit attention to "humanness", the biopsychosocial model casts a "broader net", including a far greater proportion of claimants and compensable conditions (67). Where the exact pathological etiology is unknown, clear clinical and compensability guidelines would be instituted under the model and be used to establish the presence of disability for the purposes of compensation. Such interdisciplinary guidelines would address the interaction between individual factors such as medical status, physical capacity and work-tolerances with physical and psychological work demands in the context of the individual's psychological functioning and coping ability.

Clinical Limitations and Their Relationship to Compensation

Compensation under the model would primarily be required for those who, after a period of comprehensive rehabilitation, remain chronically disabled from work. However, the possibility of change in the injured worker and his/her environment is recognized. Therefore, continuing entitlement to benefits should be reviewed periodically to ensure that only those who continue to meet the eligibility requirements receive benefits; that is, once workers' disability improves to the point where substantial gainful activity is again possible their disability benefits ought to be terminated. The biopsychosocial model encourages the use of compensation as an incentive for rehabilitation and return to work. Incentives could include ease of re-entitlement, extended period of eligibility, provisions for residual earning capacity for claimants to work part-time and incentives to employers who provide temporary modified work for injured workers (37). It has been postulated that using the model would produce lower medical costs and lower wage replacement costs, but, at the same time, higher rehabilitation costs.

The best examples of the biopsychosocial model in action are Multidisciplinary Pain Treatment Centers for chronic back or heterogeneous pain problems (68). The multimodal treatments offered at the centers include a combination of psychological interventions, medical treatments and physical and occupational therapy conducted by multidisciplinary treatment teams in an individual and group format. Many questions have been raised as to the relative efficacy and cost-effectiveness of these clinics, although a number of reviews have generally supported multidisciplinary pain treatment (3,69). Clearly, not all injured workers require pain clinic treatment. It is estimated that two to ten percent of injured workers who have persistent problems with pain will benefit from this multidisciplinary treatment approach (1). Predicting who will benefit at an early point after injury is the major issue. Consequently, there is a concern among rehabilitation and compensation professionals that treatment may be unnecessarily extended to workers who are not likely to benefit from it, with the resulting increase in costs.

Scope of Applicability

The biopsychosocial model can be applied to a wide range of clinical problems. The model can also incorporate within its framework a wide range of clinical and nonclinical activities, including prevention and health promotion programs. In the area of pain-related injury and disability, workplace programs are implemented to include the identification and correction of ergonomic risk factors, back education programs in both the prevention and rehabilitation context, job stress-oriented interventions and health promotion programs combined with training directed at supervisors and other employees about the nature of the worker's disability.

DISCUSSION

None of the models of diagnosis and rehabilitation in pain-related disability has proven to be of no benefit in conceptualizing and planning care for individuals with pain. Conversely, all these models possess their unique applications and limitations.

As compensation policies and practices are vulnerable to sociopolitical and economic pressures, the core issue facing health care planners and compensations systems is the selection of the right model for the right service recipient at the right time.

The concepts and propositions of five conceptual models of pain-related occupational disability have been canvassed in this paper. Like their counterparts in other domains of inquiry, these conceptual models influence theory, practice and research. Unfortunately, much of the published research in the area of occupational pain fails to explicitly identify and summarize the conceptual model upon which the study was based.

The five conceptual models exert considerable influence over clinical rehabilitation practice. The models outline what to do, how to do it and why to do it. Consumers, policy makers, administrators and compensation systems stakeholders, as well as health care professionals, are increasingly concerned with results, costs and a rationale for practice and policy. Conceptual models provide the rationale and the basis upon which clinicians can explain the benefits of their assessment and treatment decisions, recommendations and plans. The practical utility of a model may be assessed by the ease with which clinicians are able to transfer the concepts and principles into assessment and treatment practice, and the effectiveness of these clinical decisions.

Most health care systems in the world are still based on a purely biomedical model of illness and injury. Pain-related disabilities constitute a significant mismatch and challenge for these systems. First of all, organic etiology sought by the biomedical model is often not detectable given the present state of knowledge and practice in the area of pain. Therefore, a search for an elusive "medical explanation" of pain in most cases prolongs the diagnostic process endlessly. An effective treatment cannot be applied, since the multidimensional nature of reaction to injury and the role of psychosocial factors in onset, maintenance and recovery from pain-related disability are ignored. As a result, this model, when applied to nonspecific pain conditions, can increase chronicity and human suffering and take its financial toll on health care and compensation systems.

A similar mismatch can be identified in attempts to apply a psychiatric model to pain-related disability. By sheer inclusion of "Pain Disorder" in the most popular reference manual of mental disorders, the DSM (18), the health care system and its stakeholders have been informed that pain conditions constitute a mental disorder and can, or should, be treated as such. This notion represents an anachronistic mind-body dualism and stigmatizes the recipient of the label. Limitations inherent in the use of DSM, identified infra, could also apply, particularly, a lack of correspondence between DSM-diagnosable mental disorders and disability. Moreover, the majority of the chronic pain population cannot be diagnosed and treated within the psychiatric model.

The insurance model of pain-related disability tends to be a model of choice for most disability compensation and insurance systems in the Western world. Given this model's focus on detection of secondary gains and symptom exaggeration or malingering, all scientific and clinical problems associated with this function apply. Firstly, no single scientific method can reliably and accurately discriminate between "honest" and "dishonest" individuals without incurring false-positives and false-negatives. Moreover, there currently exists no objective method measuring human motivation and intentionality of behavior. Therefore, the model has created a significant potential for abuse of power by poorly trained clinicians and administrative staff of insurance and compensation systems.

Importantly, the twin concept of "secondary losses" including loss of work, social, family and financial status due to disability is systematically omitted in the insurance model. This produces an unbalanced, and highly biased portrayal of the pain condition as one highly, or even primarily, motivated by financial gains and lack of desire to work. This erroneous notion, if applied to the entire chronic pain population served by compensation systems, results not only in a hostile or adversarial service climate and secondary psychological problems such as anger, depression and anxiety arising from such climate, but also in increased human suffering, lack of access to appropriate health care services, chronicity and growing compensation costs. The absence of any link to injury and disability prevention activities should also be noted when evaluating the insurance model.

The problem lies within the individual injured worker in the biomedical, psychiatric and insurance models. In the labor relations model, the focus shifts to the workplace. In the first three models, the problem is an individual one, wherein the worker is identified as "ill", "mad", or "bad", and is responsible for his/her own "lot in life". The focus on the individual injured worker may have the unfortunate consequence of diverting attention from other factors in the pre-injury and injury sequelae, defects in the work environment and subsequently other possible solutions to the disability dilemma (70). The labor relations model offers redress to this deficit. It directs attention to the "system", in this instance, the workplace where it is assumed that the employer is largely responsible for the success or failure of the injured worker's return to work. The focus is, therefore, on issues such as workplace safety and work accommodation.

The labor relations model tends to apply to large, resource-endowed and well organized employers who have a commitment to the health and safety of their employees. The implementation of the model is characterized by a high organizational complexity since seamless cooperation of all parties is required. Employers must obtain incentives of a financial nature as well as have considerable resources and commitment to the implementation of the model. Under difficult economic and political conditions such incentives may not be available as the model likely brings long-term rather than short-term outcomes. From a rehabilitation perspective, clinically complex and acute cases are not likely to be effectively addressed in the workplace in the absence of an appropriate health care setting to provide expert resources and worker privacy.

The biopsychosocial model, with its emphasis on multidimensional interdisciplinary assessment and treatment, tends to be labor intensive, time consuming and expensive, requiring an organizational structure which supports teamwork, and high treatment motivation on the part of the individual with the pain condition. Overall, the biopsychosocial model appears to constitute too luxurious a model for simple injuries with an acute pain component that occurs to adaptable people who possess well-developed coping skills. The application of the model to such individuals would not be a medical necessity and would cause the costs of care and disability to further accelerate out of control.

In conclusion, it is evident that the applicability of a given model of rehabilitation of pain-related occupational disability depends largely on two factors: firstly, time since injury, and secondly, the clinical complexity of the case as determined by the interaction of pain presentation, functional tolerances, co-morbid conditions, preexisting factors, current environmental stressors, workplace demands and resources, and individual coping skills and adaptability.

Where the biomedical model is largely applicable to individuals with uncomplicated psychological profiles in early stages post injury, the labor relations and biopsychosocial models become models of choice as the time since injury progresses and in cases where there exists complicating psychosocial and other clinical factors. Notably, the latter could have been preexisting, co-existing or could have developed as a reaction to injury.

The insurance model applies best to those cases where marked risk factors for symptom magnification of malingering specifically exist. An indiscriminate application of this model to a general pain population is likely to be clinically, socially and economically erroneous and will result in a further acceleration of a "pain epidemic" in the Western world, despite societal intentions to the contrary.

Given particular promise demonstrated by the biopsychosocial model in diagnosis and treatment of pain-related disability, attention should be drawn to factors potentially limiting its applicability. The need for further research arises out of this review of models of diagnosis and rehabilitation. The most obvious need is for clinical trials to determine the effectiveness of model-based intervention. We must determine not only if a model-based intervention works, but for whom? at what time during the course of disability? on what outcome? and at what cost? Researchers need to compare model-based interventions between different systems using appropriate non-biased control groups. As each model lends itself to a focus on different outcomes, for example, pain relief, disability, return to work, or costs of care and disability benefits, researchers need to evaluate a variety of outcomes under the different models. The development of an empirically based and theoretically sound predictive model for pain-related disability is imperative. Such a model could identify groups or clusters of individuals as well as systemic risk factors of a medical, psychosocial and employment-related variety, which are interactively responsible for potential chronicity. A predictive model of pain-related disability would allow for matching the individuals in early stages of pain condition to appropriate intervention modalities and their respective combinations. Despite promising attempts, such a comprehensive, integrated and multidimensional model, rooted in the biopsychosocial view of disability, remains largely unarticulated, let alone empirically supported.

The identification of key tenets, limitations and applicability of models of diagnosis and rehabilitation of occupational pain-related disability leads to critically overdue policy and health care organization recommendations. In the area of occupational rehabilitation and disability management, there is a need to shift from biomedical, psychiatric and insurance models of service delivery as early as possible in the postacute stages of disability to labor relations and biopsychosocial models. Such a shift should be accompanied by the enhancement of interdisciplinary, functionally-oriented assessment with identification of return to work barriers; and a time-sensitive, clinical and workplace-based, multi-specialty intervention approach well before chronicity sets in.

Compensation systems usually attempt to stop the disability epidemic and spiralling costs of disability by strict enforcement of insurance or biomedical models in entitlement determination accompanied by a proliferation of forensically-oriented medical assessments usually in late disability stages. However, compensation systems would most benefit from shifting their policies towards biopsychosocial and labor relations models and forming collaborative partnerships with health care service delivery systems specializing in assessment, early active pain rehabilitation, pain education, interdisciplinary pain program delivery and disability management on one hand and the effective linkages with the employers on the other hand. Similarly, disability prevention in the workplace can be best effected by policies espousing the main tenets of dovetailing biopsychosocial and labor relations models.

REFERENCES

1. Spitzer WO, LeBlanc FE, Dupuis M. Scientific approach to the assessment and management of activity-related spinal disorders: A monograph for clinicians. Report of the Quebec Task Force on spinal disorders. *Spine* 1987; 12: S1–S59.
2. Leibowitz G. Organic and biophysical theories of behavior. *J Dev Phys Disabil* 1991; 3: 201–43.
3. Turk DC. Biopsychosocial perspective on chronic pain. In: Gatchel RJ, Turk DC, (eds.). *Psychological approaches to pain management: A practitioner's handbook*. New York: Guilford Press, 1996: 3–32.
4. Bravo M, Serrano-García I, Bernal G. La perspectiva biopsicosocial de la salud *vis a vis* la biomedica como esquema teorico para enmarcar el proceso de estres. *Intam J Psychol* 1991; 25: 35–52.
5. Fordyce WE. *Back pain in the workplace: Management of disability in nonspecific conditions*. Seattle: IASP Press, 1995.
6. Waddell G. Biopsychosocial analysis of low back pain. *Baillière's Clinical Rheumatology* 1992; 6: 523–57.
7. Engel GL. How much longer must medicine's science be bound by a seventeenth century world view? *Fam Syst Med* 1992; 10: 333–46.
8. Novy DM, Nelson DV, Francis DJ, Turk DC. Perspectives of chronic pain: An evaluative comparison of restrictive and comprehensive models. *Psychol Bull* 1995; 118: 238–47.
9. Engel GL. The need for a new medical model: A challenge for biomedicine. *Fam Syst Med* 1992; 10: 317–31.
10. Turk DC. Evaluation of pain and dysfunction. *J Disabil* 1991; 2: 24–43.
11. Vasudevan SV. The relationship between pain and disability: An overview of the problem. *J Disabil* 1991; 2: 43–53.
12. Teasell RW, Merskey H. Chronic pain disability in the workplace. *Pain For* 1997; 6: 228–38.
13. Bigos S, Bowyer O, Braen G, et al. *Acute low back problems in adults.* Clinical Practice Guideline, Quick Reference Guide Number 14. Rockville, MD: U.S. Department of Health and Human Service, Agency for Health Care Policy and Research, AHCPR Pub. No 95–0643, 1994.
14. Becker GE. Chronic pain, depression and the injured worker. *Psychiatr Ann* 1991; 21: 23–26.
15. Gamsa A. The role of psychological factors in chronic pain. I. A half century of study. *Pain* 1994; 57: 5–15.
16. Gamsa A. The role of psychological factors in chronic pain. II. A critical appraisal. *Pain* 1994; 57: 17–29.
17. Merskey H. Psychiatry and chronic pain. *Can J Psychiatry* 1989; 34: 329–36.
18. American Psychiatric Association. *Diagnostic and statistical manual of mental disorders.* (4th ed.). Washington, DC: American Psychiatric Association, 1994.
19. King SA. Review: DSM-IV and pain. *Clin J Pain* 1995; 11: 171–76.
20. Fishbain DA. DSM-IV: Implications and issues for the pain clinician. *Am Pain Soc Bul* 1995; March/April: 6–18.
21. Frank JW, Pulcins IR, Kerr MS, Shannon HS, Stansfeld SA. Occupational back pain—an unhelpful polemic. *Scand J Work Environ Health* 1995; 21: 3–14.
22. Niemeyer LO. Social labelling, stereotyping and observer bias in workers' compensation: The impact of provider-patient intervention on outcome. J Occup Rehab 1991; 1: 251–59.
23. Whyman AD, Underwood RJ. The psychiatric examination in workers' compensation. *Psychiatr Ann* 1991; 21: 36–52.
24. Melzack R, Katz J, Jeans ME. The role of compensation in chronic pain: Analysis using a new method of scoring the McGill Pain Questionnaire. *Pain* 1985; 23: 101–12.

25. Butcher JN, Harlow TC. Personality assessment in personal injury cases. In: Hess A, Weiner I, (eds.). *Handbook of forensic psychology*. New York: John Wiley, 1987: 128–54.
26. Kennedy F. The mind of the injured worker: Its effect on disability. *Comp Med* 1946; 1: 19–24.
27. Mendelson G. Chronic pain and compensation issues. In: Wall PD, Melzack R, (eds.). *Textbook of pain* (3rd ed.). New York: Churchill Livingston, 1994: 1387–400.
28. Aronoff GM. Chronic pain and the disability epidemic. *Clin J Pain* 1991; 7: 330–338.
29. Resnick PJ. Malingering of posttraumatic disorders. In: Rogers E, (ed.). *Clinical assessment of malingering and deception*. New York: Guilford Press, 1988: 85–103.
30. Chapman SL, Brena SF. Patterns of conscious failure to provide accurate self-report data in patients with low back pain. *Clin J Pain* 1990; 6: 178–90.
31. Rogers R. Development of a new classificatory model of malingering. *Bul Am Acad Psy and Law* 1990; 18: 323–33.
32. Weissman HN. Distortions and deceptions in self presentation: Effects of protracted litigation in personal injury cases. *Behav Sci Law* 1990; 8: 67–74.
33. Ogloff JRP. The admissibility of expert testimony regarding malingering and deception. *Behav Sci Law* 1990; 8: 27–43.
34. Yelin E. The myth of malingering: Why individuals withdraw from work in the presence of illness. *Milbank Q* 1986; 64: 622–49.
35. Ziskin J, Faust D. *Coping with psychiatric and psychological testimony*. Los Angeles: Law and Psychology Press, 1983.
36. Dee G, McCombie N, Newhouse G. *Workers' compensation in Ontario*. Toronto: Butterworths, 1987.
37. Wyman ET, Cats-Baril WL. Working it out: Recommendations from a multidisciplinary national consensus panel on medical problems in workers' compensation. *J Occup Med* 1994; 36: 144–54.
38. Gatchel RJ. Psychological disorders and chronic pain: Cause-and-effect relationships. In: Gatchel RJ, Turk DC, (eds.). *Psychological approaches to pain management: A practitioner's handbook*. New York: The Guildford Press, 1996: 33–52.
39. Schultz IZ. *Psychological causality determination in personal injury and workers' compensation context*. In Schultz IZ, Brady DO, Carella S. (eds.). 2003. Chicago: American Bar Association.
40. Habeck RV. Managing disability in industry. *Disability management interventions for the industrially injured worker*. London, Ontario: London Disability Management Research Group, 1993: 13–18.
41. Lacerte M, Wright GR. Return to work determination. *Phys Med Rehab: State Art Rev* 1992; 6: 283–302.
42. Shrey DE. Worksite disability management and industrial rehabilitation: An overview. In: Shrey DE, Lacerte M, (eds.). *Principles and practices of disability management in industry*. Winter Park, Florida: GR Press, Inc., 1995: 3–53.
43. Shrey DE, Olsheski JA. Disability management and industry-based work return transition programs. *Phys Med Rehab: State Art Rev* 1992; 6: 303–14.
44. Amick BC, III, Habeck RV, Hunt A, Fossel AH, Chapin A, Keller RB et al. Measuring the impact of organizational behaviors on work disability prevention and management. *J Occup Rehab* 2000; 10: 21–38.
45. Bruyère SM, Shrey DE. Disability management in industry: A joint labor-management process. *Rehab Coun Bul* 1991; 34: 227–42.
46. Galvin DE. Implementing a successful disability management program. *Occupational Disability Management*. Canada: Disabled Forestry Workers Foundation of Canada, 1992.
47. Morrison MH. Injury management: A four-country perspective. *Rehab Int* 1993; Fall: 22–25.
48. Reardon GR, Whelan D. Success in disability management. *Occupational Disability Management*. Canada: Disabled Forestry Workers Foundation of Canada, 1992.
49. Shrey DE. *Disability management, occupational bonding & the industrially injured worker*. Presented at Work Injury Management 1991—Industry and Healthcare: Building a Coalition; San Antonio, Texas, 1991.
50. Deutsch PM, Sawyer HW. Work capacity evaluation and work hardening: Process and applications in private sector rehabilitation. *A guide to rehabilitation*. New York: Matthew Bender & Co., Inc., 1994.
51. Schwartz GE, Watson SD, Galvin DE, Lipoff, E. *The disability management sourcebook*. Washington, DC: Washington Business Group on Health/Institute for Rehabilitation and Disability Management, 1989.

52. Shrey DE, Lacerte M. *Principles and practices of disability management in industry.* Winter Park, Florida: GR Press, Inc., 1995.
53. Feuerstein M, Thebarge RW. Perceptions of disability and occupational stress as discriminatory of work disability in patients with chronic pain. *J Occup Rehab* 1991; 1: 185–95.
54. Schulman BM. Worklessness and disability: Expansion of the biopsychosocial perspective. *J Occup Rehab* 1994; 4: 113–22.
55. Melzack R, Wall PD. Evolution of pain theories. *Int Anesthesiol Clin* 1970; 8: 3–34.
56. Badley EM. An introduction to the concepts and classifications of the international classification of impairments, disabilities, and handicaps. *Disabil Rehabil* 1993; 15: 161–78.
57. Levi L. A biopsychosocial approach to etiology and pathogenesis. *Acta Physiol Scand Suppl.* 1997; 640: 103–6.
58. American Medical Association. *Guides to the evaluation of permanent impairment.* (4th ed.). Chicago: American Medical Association, 1993.
59. Hazard RG, Haugh LD, Green PA, Jones PL. Chronic low back pain: The relationship between patient satisfaction and pain, impairment, and disability outcomes. *Spine* 1994; 19: 881–87.
60. Hollenbeck JR, Ilgen DR, Crampton SM. Low back disability in occupational settings: A review of the literature from a human resource management view. *Pers Psych* 1992; 45: 247–78.
61. Bongers PM, de Winter CR, Kompier MAJ, Hildebrandt VH. Psychosocial factors at work and musculoskeletal disease. *Scand J Work Environ Health* 1993; 19: 297–312.
62. Wall PD, Melzack R. *Textbook of pain* (3rd ed.). Edinburgh: Churchill Livingstone, 1994.
63. Nelems, B. *The infectious disease model vs the chronic disease model.* An address delivered to the 35th annual reunion of the Asociacion de Medicos del Instituto Nacional de la Nutricion "Salvador Zubiran", Veracruz, Mexico, October, 1993.
64. Livneh H. Person-environment congruence: A rehabilitation perspective. *Int J Rehabil Res* 1987; 10: 3–19.
65. Gatchel RJ, Turk DC. *Psychological approaches to pain management: A practitioner's handbook.* New York: The Guildford Press, 1996.
66. Livneh H. Rehabilitation intervention strategies: Their integration and classification. *J Rehab* 1989; 55: 21–30.
67. Engel GL. From biomedical to biopsychosocial: 1. Being scientific in the human domain. *Psychother Psychosom* 1997; 66: 57–62.
68. Talo S, Rytökoski U, Puukka P, Alanen E, Niitsuo L, Hämäläinen A et al. An empirical investigation of the 'Biopsychosocial Disease Consequence Model': Psychological impairment, disability and handicap in chronic pain patients. *Disabil Rehabil* 1995; 17: 281–92.
69. Malone M, Strube M. Meta-analysis of non-medical treatments for chronic pain. *Pain* 1988; 4: 231–44.
70. Marks D. Models of disability. *Disabil Rehabil* 1997; 19: 85–91.

4

Readiness for Return to Work Following Injury or Illness

Conceptualizing the Interpersonal Impact of Health Care, Workplace, and Insurance Factors

Renée-Louise Franche and Niklas Krause

INTRODUCTION

Disability and return to work following an injury or illness has been recognized as a process influenced by a variety of social, psychological, and economic factors (1–6). The epidemiological and economic literature shows that characteristics of the work environment, health care, and the insurance system all have a significant influence on return-to-work outcomes independently of the underlying medical condition and other risk factors. The employee's psychological processes initiating and sustaining return to work cannot be considered in isolation of these factors. Nevertheless, the employee remains the ultimate agent of change in the return-to-work process in that only he or she takes the final decision of going in for a day's work.

A recent review of the literature cites the lack of a comprehensive theoretical frame-work as a major challenge for research on occupational disability and return to work (2). This paper addresses the need for a conceptual framework to understand the work-disabled employee's decision-making and behavior change processes regarding return to work, and how employers, coworkers, health care providers, and insurance companies can assist in these processes in order to facilitate a timely and safe return-to-work. The development of a comprehensive theory of the disablement and return-to-work process requires the understanding and integration of different theories from various disciplines. While there are some excellent general theories of disablement (6–8) which emphasize the importance of the social environment, these make only passing reference to work disability specifically or to the various stakeholders in

This chapter originally appeared in *Journal of Occupational Rehabilitation, 12* (4): 233–256 (2002) and is reprinted by permission.

DOI: 10.1007/978-0-387-28919-9_4, © 2009 Springer Science+Business Media, LLC

the return-to-work process. Furthermore, extant general models of disability tend to focus on risk factors influencing the pathways from disease to impairment, to functional limitation, and to disability, i.e., up to the point where disability is first recognized. Much less emphasis has been placed on the processes and interventions which sustain return-to-work and participation in the work force. This paper focuses on this part of the disablement process and, specifically, on the interpersonal aspects of work disability and the return-to-work process for employees sustaining a work-related injury or illness.

We propose a heuristic model with which the interpersonal context of the work-disabled employee can be understood. The model proposed would capture both the primary agency of the employee as well as the determining impact of interactions with the health care system, the workplace, and the insurance system. It would also be compatible with and complement sociomedical models of occupational disability. Two theoretical models are considered jointly in this chapter: 1) The Phase Model of Occupational Disability (3) providing a conceptual and analytical framework for work disability taking into account the temporal aspects and developmental nature of the disabling process and its reversal during recovery and return to work and 2) The Readiness for Change Model (9–11) providing a conceptual model of the development of motivation for behavior change within a social context, here specifically and for the first time applied to the disabled employee's motivation to return to work. Both models allow for a timing of interventions in the return-to-work process, the first based on duration of work disability and the second on the motivational state of the employee. We propose that the combination of these models may be useful for guiding future research and for choosing and timing specific interventions aimed at preventing occupational disability and facilitating return to work. It will also provide guidance in concept development, measurement development, study designs, as well as facilitate communication among professionals and researchers across disciplines.

Two phase models of disability emerge in the literature, which recognize the developmental character of disability (3,12): an 8-phase Occupational Disability Model (3) and a 3-phase model of low back pain (13,14). The 8-phase model encompasses two pre-disability phases—the occurrence of symptoms and the formal report of an injury or illness—and six disability phases. The latter are defined socially by duration of work disability (12). The low back pain phase models delineate three disease phases clinically defined by duration of pain (13,14). Recent empirical studies building on both models distinguish three disability phases defined by the number of days off work: acute (up to 1 month), subacute (2–3 months), and chronic (more than 3 months) (12,15,16). Although both models differ in the way they define duration of disability and in the degree to which they integrate medical and social aspects of occupational disability, they share important principles: Both models highlight the phase specificity of risk factors, of interactions with the social environment, and of interventions. They address the importance of matching occupational and clinical interventions to the appropriate phase of disability.

There is increasing evidence for the phase-specificity of risk factors (2). It has been suggested that physical and injury factors are determining predictors of disability in the acute phase, whereas psychosocial factors have stronger predictive value in the subacute and chronic phases of disability (17). The evidence for such a clear-cut distinction of the impact of physical and psychosocial factors is mixed. While the impact of severity of injury has been supported in the acute phase (12,15,18–20), it continues to be a significant factor for return-to-work outcomes throughout the subacute and chronic phases, albeit to a lesser degree (12,15). The phase-specificity of health care provider recommendation for return to work, and of psychosocial job factors in the subacute/chronic phase (12,15) has been supported empirically. Several recent cohort studies employing phase-specific analyses show that high physical workplace demands are significant predictors of disability throughout all phases (15,21), even after controlling for injury severity and psychosocial job factors (12). Overall, there is convincing empirical evidence to support that adopting a phase-specific analytic approach leads to a better understanding of the return-to-work process.

The Readiness for Change Model (9–11) addresses the motivational factors contributing to and maintaining behavior change, and its application to returning to work is considered in this paper. Returning to work can be conceptualized as a complex human behavior change, involving physical recovery, motivation, behavior, and interaction with a number of parties. The Readiness for Change Model offers a promising conceptual framework to facilitate the integration of individual and interpersonal aspects of the behavior of returning to work.

The Readiness for Change Model proposes that relative to a given behavior change, individuals will be in one of five motivational stages, as determined by their self-efficacy, decisional balance, and change processes (9–11). More details on the assumptions and mechanisms of the model are found in the following section. The model has received strong empirical support relative to the behaviors of smoking cessation, weight control, delinquency, condom use, sunscreen use, exercise acquisition, mammography screening, physicians' preventive practices with smokers (22–24). The model also has excellent predictive validity, particularly with regard to smoking cessation behavior (25). As well, the proposed change processes have been supported by factor analysis of 770 participants followed-up for 6 months relative to the behavior of smoking cessation (26). This evidence-based model can facilitate communication amongst individuals from various disciplines. It also prescribes stage-based interventions, in that the intervention of choice for a given individual is tailored to reinforce stage-specific factors that mediate progression towards behavior change.

The Phase Models of Disability and the Readiness for Change Model are compatible in their approach to the issue of return-to-work. They both highlight the dynamic and evolving nature of the disability process, and conversely of recovery. They acknowledge the interactive process taking place between employee, employer, insurer, and health care provider and its interaction with time since the injury or illness.

By placing emphasis on the impact of the interactions with various parties involved in the recovery and return-to-work process on the employee's psychological state, we intend to recognize the highly interpersonal nature of the return-to-work process and give attention to the role of psychological factors within a wider interpersonal context. The consideration of individual psychological factors as determinants of return-to-work is often met with criticisms invoking that such an approach leads to blaming the employee for unsuccessful return-to-work outcomes. However, there exists an impressive body of evidence supporting psychosocial and psychological factors as crucial determining elements in the return-to-work process either in conjunction with physical or pain status (17,27–30), or when physical/pain status is controlled for (31). Moreover, if psychological and interpersonal factors are not systematically examined, research in this area will be of limited assistance to the psychologically distressed employee.

APPLYING THE READINESS FOR CHANGE MODEL TO THE BEHAVIOR OF RETURNING TO WORK

The Readiness for Change Model suggests that individuals will progress from one stage to the other; however, they can "relapse back" to a previous stage at any point. The five stages are described below as they would apply to return to work:

Precontemplation

In this stage, the work-disabled employee is not thinking about initiating behaviors that support adaptive adjustment to his/her return to work. For a severe injury or illness, it may be appropriate for the individual to temporarily put work issues aside in order to focus exclusively on the recovery process.

Contemplation

The employee is beginning to consider returning to work in the foreseeable future. Although employees are typically engaged in thinking about pros and cons of returning to work, they are not actively engaged in making concrete plans to do so. The most defining characteristic of this stage is ambivalence, where employees are unable to initiate change because they are stuck in the view that positive benefits of a return to work fail to outweigh negative experiences or outcomes that are also implicated.

Preparation for Action

The employee is making plans to return to work in the near future. Employees are actively seeking information regarding a return to work, testing their abilities to do so, and making a concrete plan to return to work. In this stage, employees will be very responsive to help from external sources in order to create a return-to-work schedule.

Action

In this stage, the employee is putting the plan into action and going back to work in some capacity. The employee will continue to be responsive to help from external sources, and motivated to initiate and follow through on targeted behavioral changes. In this stage individuals are at high risk for relapse as they attempt to negotiate their way around potential obstacles. To the extent that they perceive themselves as being successful in returning to work, they will increase their sense of self-efficacy.

Maintenance

In this stage, employees will use specific skills to identify and face high-risk situations that can trigger a relapse back to behaviors that interfere with successful return to

TABLE 1. Summary of Dimensions of Stages of Change

	Stages of Change				
Dimension	Precontemplation	Contemplation	Preparation for Action	Action	Maintenance
Decisional balance	Cons > Pros	Cons = Pros	Pros > Cons	Pros > Cons	Pros > Cons
Self-efficacy	Low	Low	Moderate	Moderate to high	High
Change processes	Minimal	Experiential	Experiential	Behavioral	Behavioral
General motivational state	Unaware, uninterested	Ambivalent	Committed and motivated to change	Confident internalizing new behaviors	Internalized behaviors relapse risk

work. They will also need to maintain preventive strategies such as stretching and strengthening exercises for musculoskeletal problems, safety practices, etc.

It is important to note that the Readiness for Change Model proposes certain time frames which need to be considered when determining one's stage. For example, to be in the Contemplation phase, one has to consider doing the targeted behavioral change in the next 6 months. The applicability of such time frames, which were originally developed to apply to health-risk behaviors, remains to be determined for the return-to-work behavior. Severity of injury may have a determining impact on these time frames—for example, it may be appropriate for a severely injured employee in the Preparation for Action phase to consider returning to work in 3 months, while for a mildly injured employee to consider returning to work in the next week.

Three dimensions are involved in mediating progression from Precontemplation to Maintenance regarding behavioral change: the decisional balance, self-efficacy, and change processes (see Table 1). The decisional balance reflects the cognitive process of weighing the pros and cons of returning to work. As an individual progresses from Precontemplation to Maintenance, the decisional balance scale tips as the saliency of the cons of the behavior decreases and the saliency of the pros of the behavior increases. Self-efficacy refers to one's confidence in engaging in return to work and the activities maintaining return to work. It becomes an important factor in Preparation for Action, Action, and Maintenance stages as individuals test their abilities and obtain feedback on their actual ability to return to work. Several studies support the determining role of self-efficacy with regard to return to work as a crucial determinant of the likelihood of return to work (31,32). Two categories of processes of change have been described: experiential and behavioral. Experiential processes of change involve change in thoughts, feelings, and attitudes which increase awareness and the perceived need to change, as well as communication with others about the intention or desire to change. These experiential processes are more prominent in the Precontemplation and Contemplation stages. Behavioral processes involve actual change in behavior such as increased levels of activity or contacting one's employer, and are more prominent in later stages of the model. Before one engages in behavior changes, one's thoughts, feelings, and attitudes have to be aligned towards return to work.

The innovative aspects and the strengths of the Readiness for Change Model are the following. The model recognizes the contribution of life events as determinants of behavior change, as opposed to relying solely on interventions. Indeed, events such as having children or becoming unemployed can create an emotional arousal conducive to self-reevaluation and behavioral change. The model generalizes to various behaviors (addictive and nonaddictive, socially acceptable and not, legal and illegal, frequent and not frequent) and, as mentioned before, it is particularly well-validated in the area of health-risk behaviors (22–26).

Limitations of the model most pertinent to the area of return-to-work are the following. First, the model has not been sufficiently validated with nonaddictive behaviors (33). Second, the number of discrete stages of readiness has undergone modification through the development of the Readiness for Change Model, and studies do not consistently support the presence of five distinct stages. For instance, in a factor analysis relative to pain management behavior, the stage of Preparation for Action was combined in one factor with the Contemplation stage (24). Third, the model poorly addresses the impact of sociodemographic factors, such as age, income, and education, on behavior change which, in the area of return-to-work, is of prime importance (33,34).

We will review how interactions occurring between the injured/ill employee and various parties of the recovery/return-to-work process impact on the three dimensions of change—the decisional balance, self-efficacy, and change processes. Although the evidence for the model is strong regarding health-risk behaviors, no empirical work has been conducted yet examining the Readiness for Change Model with regard to the behavior of returning to work. For that reason, it appears premature to examine in a detailed fashion how the proposed five stages apply to the return-to-work behavior at this point. Instead, we will focus on the three dimensions of change which offer a promising model with which to conceptualize the interpersonal impact of the health care provider, the workplace, and the insurer on the work-disabled employee.

THE HEALTH CARE PROVIDER

Health care providers can foster realistic or unrealistic expectations in an employee regarding the course, nature, and speed of recovery and their ability to return to work. The impact of the health care provider on the employee's readiness for change needs to be considered within the framework of the developmental models of disability.

Direct physician advice to return to work has an impact on return-to-work rates. A retrospective study of 325 claimants in California with a 3.7 years follow-up period supports the important role of doctor's recommendation to return to work in a phase-specific way: The positive recommendation for readiness for return to work was associated with a 39% higher return-to-work rate during the acute disability phase and a 67% higher return-to-work rate during the subacute and chronic phases (20). After adjustment for possible confounders, including patient demographics, injury severity, previous injuries, physical and psychosocial job factors, and employment factors, such as length of time at the preinjury job and employer size, the effect of the doctor's advice to return to work was attenuated to a statistically nonsignificant 24% increase in return-to-work rates during the acute phase and an only marginally statistically significant but still substantial increase of 42% during the subacute/chronic disability phase. The smaller effect in the acute phase of the recovery suggests that severity of injury, physical job demands, and psychosocial job characteristics may dominate one's ability to return to work during the acute phase and limit the doctor's direct influence on duration of work disability.

In patients having suffered an uncomplicated myocardial infarction, receiving a specific recommendation by a physician to return to work early resulted in earlier return to work, lower perception of disability, and increased productivity at 6-month postcardiac event, as opposed to a group who did not receive this intervention. At the 1-year follow-up, return-to-work rates and hours worked per week were however similar (35).

The conclusions one can make based on the above studies are restricted by their methodological limitations. The retrospective nature of the cohort study (20) imposes caution when interpreting results based on the recollection of employees' interaction with their physicians. The intervention study (35), although prospective, did not control for all confounding factors included in the cohort study and comprised a 1-year follow-up period only. Overall, evidence from this research suggests that direct advice from a health care provider can have an impact on return-to-work rates, but that it needs to be examined within the larger context of severity of injury, sociodemographic factors, and workplace factors.

Decisional Balance

Interactions with health care providers may be particularly potent as determinants of pros and cons of return to work. Messages of health care providers concerning factors influencing one's state of health, including return to work, work environment, and type of work offered, will bear considerable weight in one's decisional balance. For instance, if work is perceived as a threat to one's health, clearly this will weigh heavily in weighing the pros and cons of returning to work.

More intense pain is associated with lower rates of return-to-work (16,19, 36,37). The health care provider is therefore critical in supporting pain management strategies and in providing reassurance regarding what type of pain is normal.

Fear and avoidance of work and pain will clearly weigh heavily in one's decisional balance regarding return-to-work. Fear/avoidance constructs have been examined as they relate to physical activity and work—that is the degree to which an individual fears and/or avoids physical activity and/or work as a result of being concerned about the impact of physical activity/work on symptoms. In one study of 63 individuals with low back pain, anticipation of pain and fear–avoidance beliefs about physical activities were the strongest predictors of variations in physical performance (38). Anxiety about potentially negative effects of working may not disappear completely when one returns to work and may be related to injury-related work absences.

Only a few studies have included fear and avoidance as predictors of return to work. Fear of starting to work again is associated with a higher likelihood of not being back at work or in retraining 1 year postinjury event, and a higher likelihood of being sick-listed for more than 6 months, 4 years postinjury for individuals with low back pain (32). In a cross-sectional study of 184 patients with low back pain or sciatica, fear–avoidance belief about work accounted for 26% of the variance for work loss days, and 23% of the variance of disability in activities of daily living, even after controlling for severity of pain (39).

Self-Efficacy

Return-to-work self-efficacy and expectations regarding recovery have a significant impact on rates of return-to-work. In patients having suffered a cardiac event, return-to-work self-efficacy measured early in the recovery process was the strongest predictor of 6 month self-reported full-time or part-time return-to-work, independent of disease severity, age, job classification, and gender (31). This underscores the importance of increasing the employee's self-efficacy early on in the recovery process.

A recent review of 16 high-quality studies examining the impact of expectations about recovery from physical and psychiatric conditions (40) supports the important role of patient expectations on outcomes such as subsequent subjective well-being after minor surgery (41), physical functional ability after a cardiac event (42–45), and psychological adjustment following surgery (46). Regarding the outcome of return to work, the review found that in patients having had a myocardial infarction, recovery expectations were predictive of their return-to-work rates at 6 weeks (44), 6 months (47), and 1 year postcardiac event (43). In employees with occupational musculoskeletal disorders, while one study did not support the predictive value of initial return-to-work expectations (48), another study involving a small sample of patients with low back pain found that the expectation of not being able to "manage" returning to work was associated with a higher likelihood of not being back at work or in retraining 1 year postinjury event, and a higher likelihood of being "sick-listed" for more than 6 months, 4 years postinjury (32).

One of the most compelling studies on the impact of expectations regarding recovery and return to work is a Canadian study involving 1332 employees from the province of Ontario who had filed a lost-time claim following an injury (49). Based on assessments made within 3 weeks of injury regarding four dimensions of recovery/return-to-work expectations, it was found that progressing worse than expected, uncertainty about recovery or expectation of slower recovery, and expectations of longer time to return to usual activities were associated with longer periods receiving benefits within the first year following injury. Results were statistically significant after controlling for pain level, quality of life, functional status, comorbidities, sex, income, marital status, age, job demands, and workplace accommodations. Surprisingly, the variable assessing expected time for return to work was not kept in the final model. This finding may suggest that individuals are operating at a precontemplative level regarding the behavior of returning to work in the initial phases of recovery. Correlations between the four measures of recovery were low. Overall, this study points to the determining impact of early expectations about recovery on duration of work disability held during the acute phase of disability. The absence of an effect for return-to-work expectations in the acute phase suggests two scenarios: 1) that recovery expectations are consistently better predictors of return-to-work than expectations specific to work during the entire course of recovery, possibly because they would be more closely associated with one's perceived health and 2) that return-to-work expectations gain more importance for individuals remaining work-disabled in the subacute and chronic phases when they are more likely to have moved out of the Precontemplation stage.

Self-efficacy may be affected by other factors mediated by the health care provider. Prescriptive advice, such as prescribed paced, gradual, mild to moderate activities vs prescribed prolonged bedrest, will have very different impacts on one's self-efficacy. Successful engagement in work for a short period of time (1–2 h/day) will increase one's sense of self-efficacy relative to working for a more sustained period of time—in that sense reduced hours of work can be conceptualized as a proximal subgoal leading to a larger and more distal goal of returning to work at same number of hours as preinjury (50).

Depressive symptomatology has a significant impact on self-efficacy in general (51) and on return-to-work rates. The impact of depression mediated by self-efficacy, may decrease the likelihood of engaging in successful change processes regarding return-to-work. The evidence supporting the impact of depressive symptomatology on return-to-work outcomes is substantial. In a prospective study of 46 patients with lumbar discectomy, return to work 2 years postsurgery was predicted by depression and occupational mental stress and not by clinical findings or MR-identified morphological alterations (30). Similarly, injured employees on compensation with moderate to severe depressive symptomatology were significantly less likely to return to work following vocational rehabilitation than individuals with lower depressive score (52). In a sample of 7462 individuals with whiplash who were followed prospectively over 1 year, presence of depressive symptomatology was associated with a 37% reduction of claim-closure rate under a tort system, and a 36% reduction under a no-fault system (27).

While effective treatment for depression is available, it is now well recognized that depression is underdiagnosed in primary care settings: 35–70% of primary care patients with depression do not receive a diagnosis or receive inadequate treatment (53–55). The extent to which the underdiagnosis and undertreatment is occurring in work-disabled individuals remains unknown and calls for research in the role of the health care provider in that regard.

Change Processes

If a person enters the long-term disability phase, as defined by the Phase Model of Disability (3), around 8 weeks postinjury, the health care provider will again play a determining role in coordinating clinical interventions (56). More intense rehabilitation efforts, such as physiotherapy, use of medication, or gradual exercise program, may be beneficial at that point and iatrogenic effects are less likely to occur as compared to the acute phase of disability (57). In addition to coordinating therapeutic interventions, the health care provider plays a key role in the decision about the employee's readiness to return to work.

One recent, well-designed study, highlights the importance of integrating both the health care provider care and the workplace accommodation process (58): In the city of Sherbrooke in Canada, 130 employees from 31 workplaces who had been absent from work for more than 4 weeks for back pain, were randomized, based on their workplace, in one of four treatment groups: usual care, multidisciplinary clinical intervention, ergonomic intervention, and full intervention (a combination of the last two). All interventions started between 6 and 13 weeks after injury, in the long-term disability phase. The full intervention group returned to regular work 2.41 times faster than the usual care intervention group, supporting the benefits of integrating both clinical and ergonomic interventions. Clinical intervention alone had no statistically significant incremental effects over usual care. The ergonomic intervention was responsible for most of the beneficial effects observed in the combined approach: the group receiving this treatment component alone was 1.91 times faster to return to work than groups without it.

The health care provider can act as a facilitator for return to work. A recent study examined employees' recollection of their interaction with their doctor in terms of the doctor's proactive efforts to provide information about work restrictions and modifications, and employee behavior facilitating recovery and prevention of future injury (20). While doctor's proactive communication regarding return to work was associated with a 39% higher likelihood to return to work in the acute phase of recovery, this effect was reduced by half and was no longer statistically significant when physical and psychosocial workload factors were added in the statistical model. There was no effect of doctor's proactive communication in the subacute and chronic phases. These results suggest that the phase-specific impact of the health care provider as a facilitator of return to work remains limited if it does not translate into actual changes in the physical and psychosocial workload of the employee. It points to the importance of the health care provider not solely conveying work-related information to the employee but also liaising with the workplace to ensure that appropriate work accommodations are in fact available. The Sherbrooke study discussed earlier (58) further points to the importance of coordinating workplace and health care interventions to achieve a consensus on how the return-to-work process should take place. The latter study was conducted in Canada where the parties involved in the return-to-work process are relatively independent from each other. The degree to which health care providers act as independent parties in the return-to-work process varies immensely from country to country. In some states of the United States, the employee's physician will be chosen by the employer or insurer in the initial period following an injury. In such a situation, the health care provider's practice may be influenced by the nature of their contract with the employer and/or insurer. Clearly, the level of independence of the health care provider from the insurer and employer will impact on the relationship between health care provider and employee.

THE WORKPLACE

Workplace disability management strategies are repeatedly found to be critical and determining factors of return-to-work outcomes (59–61). Disability management can be described as a proactive, employer-based approach developed to (a) prevent the occurrence of accidents and disability, (b) provide early intervention services for health and disability risk factors, and (c) foster coordinated administrative and rehabilitative strategies to promote cost-effective restoration and return to work (62). We will focus primarily on return-to-work strategies and will differentiate structure from process of disability management.

We define structure as referring to the components of disability management, as opposed to process which refers to the manner in which these components are offered. Initial studies in the area of return-to-work tended to focus on the presence or absence of structure of disability management (63). These studies examined how strategies such as having a return-to-work coordinator, provision of work accommodations, or monitoring of outcomes impacted on return-to-work outcomes such as claim rates. During the last few years, more attention has been devoted to the process of return-to-work. The importance of interactional factors in the process of return-to-work programs has repeatedly been highlighted in both qualitative (64,65) and empirical studies (19). The following section will focus on interpersonal aspects of the workplace as prognostic factors of return-to-work after the occurrence of an injury.

Decisional Balance

Interactions within the worksite may affect one's decisional balance of the pros and cons of returning to work. Various factors will weigh in the decisional balance: employer's and coworkers' responses, legitimacy issues, workplace culture.

Qualitative studies of injured employees suggest that a nonconfrontational and non-judgmental approach from the workplace is considered to be essential to successful return to work (64,65). The importance of a supportive supervisor response has been raised in qualitative studies (66) and in quantitative studies (2,12,36,67). In a study of employees with work-related upper extremity disorders, employees who were work-disabled indicated being significantly more angry towards their employer as compared to employees who returned to work or never left work following the injury (68). In a study of 120 Dutch workers with work absences of 10 days or more because of low back pain, problematic relations with colleagues was one of four predictive factors of time off work (19). In a study of 434 employees with low back pain, low supervisor support reduced return to-work rates by 21% (12).

Studies of the role of coworker support have provided mixed results. In one study, it was found to be associated with longer duration of work disability (36), while in other studies it had no effect (12,69). The inconsistency of results may be related to the various forms of "coworker support": coworkers may provide support by cooperating with the injured employee in their modified work programs, or they may also support the injured employee in their pain/limited behavior by suggesting that the injured employee take more time off or waits until he/she is 100% better, out of concern for the injured employee. The absence of a consistent effect for coworker support may be explained by the variation in the amount of contact with coworkers an employee has as a function of the type of work he/she does (12). Gender also affects the impact of relationships with coworkers: in one British study, a trend for greater effects of coworker support in women than in men was found (70).

One concept which has received increased attention is the one of legitimacy (71–73). Legitimacy refers to the degree to which an injured employee feels believed by others regarding the authenticity of their injury and of their symptoms. It is of particular relevance to injuries and illnesses which involve work absences and to injuries/illnesses which are "invisible." In a sample of Canadian claimants with musculoskeletal disorders, decreased legitimacy was a significant predictor of longer duration on benefits (74). The mechanisms underlying the association between legitimacy and return-to-work outcomes remain speculative. If an employee feels that workplace staff question the legitimacy of their symptoms, the worker may develop negative feelings towards the workplace, which will certainly weigh against returning to work in their decisional balance. Alternatively, the perceived expression of disbelief of one's symptoms and complaints may bring an employee to invest energy in "proving" that their injury and pain are real by not returning to work.

Certain aspects of work accommodation programs have been highlighted as being critical to the success of these programs in qualitative studies (75). The meaningfulness of the proposed work, whether or not the employee returns in a setting with which he/she is familiar or comfortable, and the degree of control experienced by employees over various facets of their work will factor in the employee's decisional balance. When employees report a greater degree of control over their work and rest periods, they are about 30% more likely to return to work during the subacute and chronic disability phases than workers with low job control even after physical job demands and severity of injury are controlled for (12).

Workplace culture, which refers to a general interpersonal and value-focused atmosphere, is also associated with return-to-work outcomes (59). In one prospective study of 198 employees with carpal tunnel syndrome, an increased level of people-oriented culture was associated with higher return-to-work rates 6 months after being identified in community medical practices, when age, gender, and baseline carpal tunnel syndrome symptom severity were controlled for (76). People-oriented culture was a factorially derived dimension defined as "the extent to which the company involves employees in meaningful decisionmaking, where there is trust between management and employees, and openness to share information in a cooperative work environment" (76, p. 30).

Self-Efficacy and Change Processes

Self-efficacy is increased by the successful engagement in the behavior of interest. Increased self-efficacy can be seen whether the behavior is partially or fully engaged in. Returning to work gradually in terms of hours worked, or type of work done can have a significant impact on one's self-efficacy regarding ability to return to original work. Through the mediation of increased self-efficacy, the offer and acceptance of a modified work accommodation may represent the decisive change process for successful return-to-work (59,61).

In a systematic review of the scientific literature on modified work from 1975 to 1997, Krause and colleagues identified 13 high-quality studies out of 29 empirical studies (61). Based on the high-quality studies, it was found that injured employees who are offered modified work are twice as likely to return to work than those who are not offered such an arrangement. As well, modified work reduces by half the number of lost days (60,61,77). Satisfactory work accommodations have been shown to significantly decrease injured employees' anxiety about returning to work (78). Offers of modified work also reduce duration receiving compensation, and reduce the incidence of injuries (76,79,80). The reduction of new injuries can possibly be explained by the fact that redesign of one's job tasks will often lead to positive change in the job tasks of other employees doing the same type of work.

Paradoxically, while the majority of studies show beneficial effects of work accommodations, one study actually shows an increase in incidence of injuries following the implementation of programs which include work accommodations (81). Increases in injury reports could be attributed to an increase in previously unreported injuries, if, as part of the program, reporting of injuries was encouraged (81).

However, it also brings attention to the danger of returning the employee to work too early through work accommodation. The physician who wishes to avoid the vicious cycle of inactivity and deconditioning may in fact return an employee too soon. The employee may still not have the physical strength to sustain the proposed work program. It is generally accepted that an employee does not need to wait until he or she is "100%" to initiate a return to work. But what is too soon? How can it be determined? These questions remain some of the most interesting and relevant ones in the field of rehabilitation.

Of concern is the realization that the interpersonal processes surrounding the presence or absence of a modified work offer are less than optimal. Indeed, in the Canadian study of claimants (60), 74% of the sample interviewed within 3 weeks after an accepted claim reported negative supervisor response to their injury. In that same cohort, 73% reported that there had not been any offers of modified work. Coworkers' concerns need to be considered as well when planning a modified work arrangement: coworkers whose safety is put at risk, or who experience an increase in workload as a result of a modified work accommodation may not welcome or facilitate the arrangement.

Self-efficacy is not only determined by one's ability to be successful at the given modified work but also by one's sense of value derived from the modified work. Clinicians and researchers are becoming acutely aware that meaningless and devaluing modified work, which does not contribute to the overall functioning of one's workplace, can actually do more harm than good in the return-to-work process (64). Coworkers who perceive modified work to be worthless or devaluing will have an impact on the injured employee's self-efficacy.

Other factors impacting on the probability of success of a modified work accommodation and on self-efficacy deserve mention although they are less interpersonal in nature. The pace and nature of modified work, the ergonomic aspects of work (15,76,82–85), have a significant impact on return-to-work outcomes. Physical demands of work are associated with the development of musculoskeletal disorders (86). Size (15,62,63,87,88) and sector of workplaces (62) will also impact on the range of modified work accommodations available as well as on the general culture of workplaces.

Overall, a collaborative and respectful approach from workplace parties will clearly lead to a climate of trust much more conducive to reducing one's anxieties about returning to work and to shifting the decisional balance towards being ready for a return-to-work attempt. Attention to coworkers' safety, workload, and understanding of modified work will set the stage for a modified work accommodation conducive to increased self-efficacy and success.

THE INSURER AND ECONOMIC CONSIDERATIONS

Available evidence suggests that the majority of appeals of disability claims are brought on by the consequences of the disability, rather than the appeal process contributing to the development of disability. Indeed, an American study (89) found that appeals of disability claims were consistently made long after the date of injury—none were made within the first 90 days, and only one fourth were made within the first year postinjury. With regards to establishing the direction of causality, this study strongly suggests that it is the disability and the experience of the claims handling process which brings individuals to resort to legal procedures.

The impact of the insurance provider and of types of compensation available on return-to-work has been the focus of ample discussion and controversy. Most of the literature has focused on the financial aspects of available compensation and on the impact of litigation. Compensation and litigation are closely linked—the provision of compensation perceived to be fair and adequate by an employee gives the employee social legitimacy (90) and consequently decreases the motivation for the employee to engage in litigation. For those reasons, select aspects of both the insurance and the legal systems are discussed in this section.

Decisional Balance

Before one considers the impact of compensation on return to work, it is important to step back and appreciate the fundamental purpose of disability compensation systems. "The primary purpose of workers' compensation is to help employees who sustain on-the-job injuries recover and return to work and/or be compensated by any resulting permanent disability" (90, p. 28). The refusal of such needed financial assistance can result in the denial of social legitimacy (90), which in turn can lead to anxiety and depressive effect (91). The profound negative consequences for the employee of a wrongfully denied claim have been recognized in cases where compensation was granted not just for the initial work injury but for the disability (most often depression) related to the compensation process itself in Canada (92) and the United States (93).

There is substantial controversy over the effect of compensation on the decisional balance regarding return to work. While some studies found no effect of compensation on return-to-work rates (94,95), other studies found that increases in compensation are associated with increases in frequency and duration of claims (96–101). These studies are limited in that they do not focus on actual return to work, but on duration of claims only. Two studies of Canadian workers from the province of Ontario did focus on actual return to work and found that higher benefit rates were associated with lower rates of return to work (34,102).

Other studies have considered the impact of compensation on employees' return-to-work rates as it interacts with other factors. These studies generally point to a more complex situation, in which compensation does not unequivocally translate in lower return-to-work rates. One multinational prospective study, the Work Incapacity and Reintegration Project (103), compared the effectiveness of different return-to-work interventions used by social security systems and health care providers in six countries (Denmark, Germany, Israel, The Netherlands, Sweden, USA). Employees who were work-disabled for at least 3 months because of low back disorders were followed over a 2-year period. The association between wage replacement and duration of disability was dependent on the degree of job security. The combination of extensive compensation with strong job protection predicted early return to work, while weak job protection combined with extensive compensation did not improve return to work. Shorter disability periods were seen for low levels of job protection combined with low levels of compensation, but mainly for new employees.

Clearly, individuals weigh the pros and cons associated with their levels of wage replacement and job security. The goal adopted in the area of return-to-work is generally to achieve an early and safe return to work, and risk factors contributing to a premature and unsafe return to work are seldom considered. It is important to consider that fear of losing one's job and financial strain will weigh in one's decisional balance and can contribute to the decision of going back to work too soon, increasing risk of reinjury and ill health (78).

The explicit purpose of wage replacement benefits is to allow injured employees to stay off work to allow the injury to heal. In the early phases postinjury, compensation should therefore be associated with longer duration off work. In an American study of 312 individuals with severe lower extremity fractures followed for 12 months postinjury, receiving disability compensation was associated with longer duration of work disability during the initial 6 months postinjury only (21). While this study points to the impact of compensation, it also points to its complexities. It suggests that individuals receiving no compensation may return to work too soon because of financial pressures.

The role of the family in the decisional balance needs to be discussed both in terms of its impact on financial needs and on social role perceptions. Each family member is either a dependent, an income provider, or both. As such, they represent a stressor or buffer on financial strain. One American study found an interaction between wage replacement and number of children combined with marital status, with length of work disability as the outcome (89): Given equal wage compensation ratios, widowed and divorced individuals were twice as likely as single individuals to be work-disabled for 90 days or more. This effect was lessened by the presence of children for widowed and divorced individuals. As well, when one considers significant predictors of disability retirement in a Finnish population, increased number of family members working and fewer unemployed family members are associated with increased likelihood of a disability retirement (67).

The value given to the working role in society will also weigh heavily in the decisional balance. More traditional families may foster the belief that a man's primary role is as a financial provider, and that a woman is expected to continue to attend to other family members' needs even when in recovery. In that sense, multiple role strain, associated with caregiving for family members, may hinder recovery and return to work in women, as is suggested in the cardiac rehabilitation area (104–109). Little work has been conducted on the impact of family and social contacts on return-to-work outcomes. These interpersonal contacts may be quite powerful in terms of shaping an individual's goals and expectations. Important messages about health and work are conveyed by these individuals despite their informality.

Overall, when assessing the weight of compensation, the above studies highlight the importance of analyzing it in conjunction with other factors, such as job security, ratio of income replacement to previous earnings, amount of regular income, number of dependents, financial pressure to return to work, gender, and societal roles. When one does take these factors into account, the impact of compensation in the decisional balance is less absolute and unvariable, as was once believed.

The manner in which compensation is administered will also factor in the decisional balance. If workers are concerned about their ability to perform full-time work and face the prospect of losing all compensation if they return only part-time, despite their desire to return to work they may opt to delay the return to work (110). This points to a major weakness in most compensation programs, that is, the dichotomization of employability. Individuals are categorized as employable or not employable, which has a direct impact on their eligibility for compensation. This polarized view of employability does not acknowledge that some individuals may be able to work only with accommodations, removal of barriers, adapted transportation, or on a part-time basis only.

Self-Efficacy

The employee's self-efficacy regarding return-to-work can be affected by compensation and litigation issues in an indirect way. Facing the denial of a claim, the sense that the legitimacy of one's complaints and symptoms is questioned, and the belief that one has not been treated fairly can foster depression and anxiety. The negative impact of depression and anxiety on return-to-work is well documented and was discussed earlier in this paper. Moreover, the long delays in legal and compensation procedures keep the employee immersed in details associated with the injury/illness, and focused on the consequences of their limitations. As a consequence, it may not only delay the rehabilitation process but affect negatively the permanent outcome of such rehabilitation (91).

Change Processes

The impact of the compensation and litigation on the necessary change processes supporting behavioral change regarding returning to work is not direct. However, it is well recognized that being involved in litigation is a process which can consume one's energies in an encompassing way. Similarly, if application for compensation involves a complicated bureaucratic, medico-legal, or even adversarial process, then being involved in compensation or litigation competes with the resources and energy necessary to support the change processes necessary to recovery, rehabilitation, and return to work.

THE READINESS FOR RETURN-TO-WORK MODEL AND THE PHASE MODEL OF OCCUPATIONAL DISABILITY: LIMITATIONS AND STRENGTHS

There is growing evidence for the phase-specificity of predictors of work disability after occupational injury or illness. Epidemiological studies have identified specific predictors of disability during the acute, subacute, and—to a lesser extent—the chronic phases of disability. The Phase Model of Occupational Disability provides the conceptual and analytical framework for epidemiological research that takes into account the developmental nature of the disabling process and its reversal during recovery and return to work. The model is instrumental in identifying and discriminating predictors of disability that are influential only in certain phases of disability, throughout all phases of disability, or change their impact across disability phases. It is important to note that effect estimates of these phase-specific predictors reflect the average experience of all individuals in the underlying population and do not clarify at which exact time an intervention should be offered to any specific individual within each disability phase. The Readiness for Return-to-Work Model has the ability to account for individual variation in optimal timing of interventions based on an individual's readiness for return to work. The model therefore complements the Phase Model of

Disability by allowing for an individual-level staging of the disability and recovery process within the broader group-level-derived framework of occupational disability phases.

The proposed Readiness for Return-to-work Model places the injured/ill employee as the primary agent of change, as he or she interacts with various parties in the return-to-work process. As such it does not comment on the interpersonal impact of the employee on the employer, health care provider, and insurer, but focuses solely on the unidirectional impact of the latter parties on the employee. This model provides a solid framework for the first step in the study of the interpersonal aspects of the return-to-work process, but to fully capture its dynamic process, one would need to go one step further and consider the impact of the employee on other parties.

The original Readiness for Change Model posits specific time frames to consider when attempting to "stage" a person (determining in which stage a person is in). These time frames may not apply to the behavior of returning to work following an injury, and may vary depending on the degree of severity and the type of injury or illness. The more severe the impairment, the longer one would be expected to remain in the Precontemplation and Contemplation stages regarding return-to-work, as one's energies are focused on physical recovery. Future research will clarify appropriate time frames for each stage, taking into account the type and severity of injury (111).

The Readiness for Change Model posits that, depending on the stage of change of an individual, the effectiveness of offered interventions will vary. In that sense, prescribed interventions are stage-based, targeting the dimensions of readiness most likely to be modified. This approach offers a good fit with recent modeling of optimal return-to-work interventions which emphasize stage-specificity of risk factors and interventions (3,56,58).

DIRECTIONS FOR FUTURE RESEARCH

The Interface of the Phase Model of Disability and the Readiness for Return-to-Work

The key features of the Phase Model of Disability and the Readiness for Return-to-Work Model are summarized in Table 2. The two models emerged from different disciplines, were originally constructed for different purposes, and differ in their emphasis of psychological or social factors as well as in their previous research applications. We propose that the combination of both models will facilitate the integration of the developmental, interpersonal, behavioral, and social aspects of the return-to-work process in future research. The interface of the two models still needs to be explored empirically. In the following we provide some suggestions for this scientific inquiry.

Research is required to achieve a better understanding of how the two models interface with one another. One possible step is to assess the distribution of stages of individuals within phases of disability. For instance, for individuals in the subacute phase of disability, how many are still in the Precontemplation stage, the Contemplation phase, or have moved to the Preparation phase or Action phase? Another important application of the Readiness for Return-to-work Model will be to use the staging of individuals as predictors of their progression or absence of progression to

TABLE 2. Summary of Characteristics of the Phase Model of Disability and the Readiness for Return-to-Work Model

Dimensions	Phase Model of Disability	Readiness for Return-to-Work Model
Original purpose	Interdisciplinary classification of occupational disability due to low back pain	Psychological modeling of motivation for individual health behavior change
Proposed expansions	Application to other musculoskeletal disorders and to nonoccupational illnesses	Application to resumption of occupational role after injury or illness
Categories of change	Two predisability phases Occurrence of symptoms Formal report of injury	Five stages Precontemplation Contemplation Prepared for action Action Maintenance
	Three disability phases Acute (<30 days) Subacute (30–90 days) Chronic (>90 days) Or six disability phases Short-term disability (<1 week) Timely intervention (1–7 weeks) Long-term disability (7–12 weeks) Late rehabilitation (3–6 months) Chronic disability (6–18 months) Permanent disability (>18 months)	
Primary defining dimensions	Time off work Time since injury	Decisional balance Self-efficacy Change processes Occupational behavior
Secondary defining dimensions	Medical diagnosis and severity of condition Type of medical treatment Legal status	
Progression through categories	Forward, but recurrences of disability episodes exist	Forward, but relapses back into stages are expected
Risk factor domains	Occupational and nonoccupational social environment Compensation system Social security system Health care system Legal, political, economic context Individual	Occupational and nonoccupational social environment Compensation system Social security system Health care system Individual
	Focus is on social factors and to a lesser degree on psychological ones	Focus is on psychological factors, and to a lesser degree on social ones
Changes associated with movement through phases of stages	Change in epidemiologic risk factor profiles and size or sign of risk estimates (biological, psychological, and social factors)	Proposed changes in motivational states and in return-to-work behavior require future investigation
Measurement	Duration of work disability Administrative records Self-report	Decisional balance, self-efficacy, change processes Psychometric assessment of above dimensions which require future development

TABLE 2. (*cont.*)

	Medical diagnosis/treatment Medical records	Occupational status Self-report of whether they are working or not
	Legal status Workers' compensation status Insurance records Self-reports	
Implications for intervention	Efficacy of intervention is considered using a phase-specific analysis	Proportion of individuals in each stage needs to be assessed when considering efficacy of interventions
Population with which model has been validated	Individuals with disabling occupational low-back pain	Model validated primarily as it applies to health-risk behaviors
		No studies available on any work-disabled individuals
Discipline of origin	Epidemiology Rehabilitation	Psychology Health promotion

the subacute and chronic phases of disability. It is possible that only individuals who are precontemplators and contemplators during the acute phase of disability progress to the subacute phase, while those in the Prepared for Action or Action stage never progress beyond the acute phase.

Validation and Measurement of the Readiness for Return-to-Work

Although the Readiness for Change model is solidly evidence-based regarding healthrisk behaviors, it remains a heuristic theoretical model regarding its application for return-to-work behavior. The first step in the application of the Readiness for Change Model to a specific behavior is the development of a staging algorithm, followed by behavior-specific scales of the three dimensions of change—decisional balance, self-efficacy, and change processes (112).

There are specific temporal relationships between the stages and the three dimensions of change which are specified by the Readiness for Change Model, as was outlined in Table I. For instance, the decisional balance shows a shift from higher saliency of the cons of the behavior to higher saliency of the pros of the behavior as an individual progresses from Precontemplation to Maintenance. As well, self-efficacy is hypothesized to increase. These stage-specific relationships among constructs can be examined with a cross-sectional design. However, only a longitudinal design would allow examination of the hypothesized changes over time.

Impact on Intervention and Risk Factor Studies

It is important to adopt both the Phase Disability and the Readiness for Return-to-work analytic approaches when designing intervention and risk factor studies, both in terms of the nature of interventions to be developed and the design of the studies to examine them. The phase-specific efficacy of certain types of interventions, such as physician advice to return to work (20) or clinical interventions (58), is increasingly being recognized. The Readiness for Change Model highlights the importance of stage-specific interventions. For instance, the individual in Contemplation stage who is highly ambivalent about returning to work may benefit from a discussion with his health care provider about the pros and cons of returning to work, while the individual in Prepared for Action stage may profit from a structured plan regarding gradual increase in work hours and new ergonomic aids. The model also draws attention to the need for development of interventions tailored to the precontemplative and contemplative individual since most interventions available target the Preparation for Action and Action stages.

The Phase Disability analytic strategy needs to be applied as one examines outcomes such as functional ability and pain severity, which are clearly related to time elapsed since time of injury, as well as the outcome of return-to-work behavior. The Readiness for Return-to-Work analytic approach is relevant when considering the efficacy of interventions regarding the motivation for and behavior of return-to-work: One needs to examine the proportion of individuals in each stage in groups receiving interventions since it may have a significant impact on the efficacy of the intervention, as is known to be the case in health-risk behavior modification programs (113). Indeed, in smoking interventions, the rates of quitting and of relapse during the follow-up period vary widely depending on the stage of individuals during the intervention. In a parallel fashion, one can examine whether staging of individuals at the beginning of a return-to-work intervention can predict both return-to-work rates and sustainability of return to work.

The impact of the Phase Disability model on risk factor studies has received attention in the literature (2) and is now being incorporated in most studies of return-to-work behavior, following a pain-related occupational injury. Phase of disability needs to be considered when examining the impact of physical risk factors such as severity of injury or physical demands of the workplace (20). The impact of the Readiness for Return-to-Work on risk factor studies is less well-understood and needs exploration. The relevance of the latter model as it relates to return-to-work behavior may apply to psychosocial risk factors: Having had a previous episode of depression may affect the individual's progress throughout the stages of changes by limiting the increment in self-efficacy, while having an uncollaborative work environment may have an impact only when the individual in Preparation for Action and Action stages is in need of behavioral change processes.

The above future research directions regarding the applicability and predictive power of the Readiness for Return-to-Work Model need to be considered within the context of the Phase Disability Model in injured and ill work-disabled employees. The empirical testing of the model could first be examined in individuals with pain-related occupational injuries, firstly because this appears to be the most studied group of work-disabled individuals, and secondly, because it would allow integration with the Phase Disability Model. Future steps could involve extending both models to the population of ill employees.

REFERENCES

1. Frank JW, Brooker AS, DeMaio S, Kerr MS, Maetzel A, Shannon HS, Sullivan TJ, Norman RW, Wells R. Disability resulting from occupational low back pain part II: What do we know about secondary prevention? A review of the scientific evidence on prevention after disability begins. *Spine* 1996; 21(24): 2918–2929.

2. Krause N, Frank JW, Dasinger LK, Sullivan T, Sinclair SJ. Determinants of duration of disability and return to work after work-related injury and illness: Challenges for future research. *Am J Industr Med* 2001; 40: 464–484.
3. Krause N, Ragland DR. Occupational disability due to low back pain: A new interdisciplinary classification based on a phase model of disability. *Spine* 1994; 19(9): 1011–1020.
4. Lawrence RH, Jette AM. Disentangling the disablement process. *J Gerontol Soc Sci* 1996; 51B(4): S173–S182.
5. Committee on a National Agenda for the Prevention of Disabilities, Division of Health Promotion and Disease Prevention and Institute of Medicine. *Disability in America. Toward a national agenda for prevention.* Washington, DC: National Academy Press, 1991.
6. Verbrugge LM, Jette AM. The disablement process. *Soc Sci Med* 1994; 38(1): 1–14.
7. Nagi SZ. *Some conceptual issues in disability and rehabilitation. Sociology and rehabilitation.* Washington, DC: American Sociological Association, 1965, pp. 100–113.
8. Stone DA. *The disabled state.* Philadelphia: Temple University Press, 1984.
9. Prochaska JO, Diclemente CC. Stages and processes of self-change of smoking: Toward an integrative model of change. *J Consult Clin Psychol* 1983; 51(3): 390–395.
10. Prochaska JO, Diclemente CC, Velicer WF, Ginpil S, Norcross JC. Predicting change in smoking status for self-changers. *Addict Behav* 1985; 10(4): 395–406.
11. Prochaska JO, Diclemente CC, Norcross JC. In search of how people change. Applications to addictive behaviors. *Am Psychol* 1992; 47(9): 1102–1114.
12. Krause N, Dasinger LK, Deegan LJ, Rudolph L, Brand RJ. Psychosocial job factors and return to work after low back injury: A disability phase-specific analysis. *Am J Industr Med* 2001; 40: 374–392.
13. Frank J, Sinclair S, Hogg-Johnson S, Shannon H, Bombardier C, Beaton D, Cole D. Preventing disability from work-related low-back pain: New evidence gives new hope—If we can just get all the players on onside. *CMAJ* 1998; 158(12): 1625–1631.
14. Spitzer WO, LeBlanc FE, Dupuis M, Abenhaim L, Bélanger AY, Bloch R, Bombardier C, Cruess RL, Drouin G, Duval-Hesler N, Laflamme J, Lamoureux G, Nachemson AL, Page JJ, Rossignol M, Salmi LR, Salois-Arsenault S, Suissa S, Wood-Dauphinee S. Scientific approach to the assessment and management of activity-related spinal disorders: A monograph for clinicians. Report of the Quebec task force on spinal disorders. *Spine* 1987; 12(7S): S4–S55.
15. Dasinger LK, Krause N, Deegan LJ, Brand RJ, Rudolph L. Physical workplace factors and return to work after compensated low back injury: A disability phase-specific analysis. *J Occup Environ Med* 2000; 42(3): 323–333.
16. McIntosh G, Frank J, Hogg-Johnson S, Bombardier C, Hall H. Prognostic factors for time receiving workers' compensation benefits in a cohort of patients with low back pain. *Spine* 2000; 25(2): 147–157.
17. Shanfield SB. Return to work after an acute myocardial infarction: A review. *Heart Lung J Crit Care* 1990; 19(2): 109–117.
18. Hogg-Johnson S, Frank JW, Rael EGS. *Prognostic risk factor models for low back pain: Why they have failed and a new hypothesis.* Toronto, Canada: OWCI, 1994.
19. van der Weide WE, Verbeek JHAM, Salle HJA, van Dijk FJH. Prognostic factors for chronic disability from acute low-back pain in occupational health care. *Scand J Work Environ Health* 1999; 25(1): 50–56.
20. Dasinger LK, Krause N, Thompson PJ, Brand RJ, Rudolph L. Doctor proactive communication, return to work recommendation, and duration of disability after a workers' compensation low back injury. *J Occup Environ Med* 2001; 43(6): 515–525.
21. MacKenzie EJ, Morris JA, Jurkovich GJ, Yasui Y, Cushing BM, Burgess AR, DeLateur BJ, McAndrew MP, Swiontkowski MF. Return to work following injury: The role of economic, social and job-related factors. *Am J Public Health* 1998; 88(11): 1630–1637.
22. Prochaska JO, Velicer WF, Rossi JS, Goldstein MG, Marcus BH, Rakowski W, Fiore C, Harlow LL, Redding CA, Rosenbloom D. Stages of change and decisional balance for 12 problem behaviors. *Health Psychol* 1994; 13(1) :39–46.
23. Gallagher RM. Treating depression in patients with co-morbid pain: Part I. *Health Psychol* 1998; 18(1): 81–97.
24. Kerns RD, Rosenberg R, Jamison RN, Caudill MA, Haythornthwaite J. Readiness to adopt a self-management approach to chronic pain: The Pain Stages of Change Questionnaire (PSOCQ). *Pain* 1997; 72: 227–234.

25. Velicer WF, Norman GJ, Fava JL, Prochaska JO. Testing 40 predictions from the transtheoretical model. *Addict Behav* 1999; 24(4): 455–469.
26. Prochaska JO, Velicer WF, Diclemente CC, Fava J. Measuring processes of change: Applications to the cessation of smoking. *J Consult Clin Psychol* 1988; 56(4): 520–528.
27. Côte P, Hogg-Johnson S, Cassidy JD, Carroll L, Frank JW. The association between neck pain intensity, physical functioning, depressive symptomatology and time-to-claim-closure after whiplash. *J Clin Epidemiol* 2001; 54: 275–286.
28. Hlatky M, Haney T, Barefoot J, Califf R, Mark D, Pryor D, Williams R. Medical, psychological and social correlates of work disability among men with coronary artery disease. *Am J Cardiol* 1986; 58(10): 911–915.
29. Linton SJ. A review of psychological risk factors in back and neck pain. *Spine* 2001; 25(9): 1148–1156.
30. Schade B, Semmer N, Main CJ, Hora J, Boos N. The impact of clinical, morphological, psychosocial and work-related factors on the outcome of lumbar discectomy. *Pain* 1999; 80: 239–249.
31. Fitzgerald S, Becker D, Celentano D, Swank R, Brinker J. Return to work after percutaneous transluminal coronary angioplasty. *Am J Cardiol* 1989; 68(18): 1108–1112.
32. Sandstrom J, Esbjornsson E. Return to work after rehabilitation. The significance of the patient's own prediction. *Scand J Rehab Med* 1986; 18: 29–33.
33. Joseph J, Breslin C, Skinner H. Critical perspectives on the transtheoretical model and stages of change. In: Tucker JA, Donovan DM, Marlatt GA. eds. *Changing addictive behaviors—Bridging clinical and public health strategies.* New York: Guilford Press, 1999, pp. 161–190.
34. Butler RJ, Johnson WG, Baldwin M. Managing work disability: Why first return to work is not a measure of success. *Industr Labor Relat Rev* 1995; 48(3): 452–469.
35. Dennis C, Houston-Miller N, Schwartz RG, Ahn DK, Kraemer HC, Gossard D, Juneau M, Taylor CB, DeBusk RF. Early return to work after uncomplicated myocardial infarction. *JAMA* 1988; 260: 214–220.
36. Bergquist-Ullman M, Larsson U. Acute low back pain in industry. A controlled prospective study with special reference to therapy and confounding factors. *Acta Orthop Scand* 1977; 170(Suppl): 1–117.
37. Coste J, Delecoeuillerie G, Cohen de Lara A, Le Parc JM, Paolaggi J. Clinical course and prognostic factors in acute low back pain: An inception cohort study in primary care practice. *BMJ* 1994; 308: 577–580.
38. Al-Obaidi SM, Nelson RM, Al-Awadhi S, Al-Shuwaie N. The role of anticipation and fear of pain in the persistence of avoidance behavior in patients with chronic low back pain. *Spine* 2001; 25(9): 1126–1131.
39. Waddell G, Newton M, Henderson I, Somerville D, Main CJ. A Fear-Avoidance Beliefs Questionnaire (FABQ) and the role of fear-avoidance beliefs in chronic low back pain and disability. *Pain* 1993; 52: 157–168.
40. Mondloch MV, Cole DC, Frank JW. Does how you do depend on how you think you'll do? A systematic review of the evidence for a relation between patients' recovery expectations and health outcomes. *CMAJ* 2001; 165(2): 174–179.
41. Flood AB, Lorence DP, Ding J, McPherson K, Black NA. The role of expectations in patients' reports of post-operative outcomes and improvement following therapy. *Med Care* 1993; 31: 1043–1056.
42. Allen JK, Becker DM, Swank RT. Factors related to functional status after coronary artery bypass surgery. *Heart Lung* 1990; 19(4): 337–343.
43. Diederiks JPM, van der Sluijs H, Weeda HWH, Schobre MG. Predictors of physical activity one year after myocardial infarction. *Scand J Rehab Med* 1983; 15(2): 103–107.
44. Petrie K, Weinman J, Sharpe N. Role of patients' view of their illness in predicting return to work and functioning after myocardial infarction: Longitudinal study. *BMJ* 1996; 312(7040): 1191–1194.
45. Ruiz BA, Dibble SL, Gilliss CL, Gortner SR. Predictors of general activity 8 weeks after cardiac surgery. *Appl Nurs* 1992; 5: 59–65.
46. Jamison RN, Parris WC, Maxson WS. Psychological factors influencing recovery from outpatient surgery. *Behav Res Ther* 1987; 25(1): 31–37.
47. Maeland JG, Havik OE. Psychological predictors for return to work after a myocardial infarction. *J Psychosom Res* 1987; 31(4): 471–481.
48. Pransky G, Benjamin, K, Himmelstein J, Mundt K, Morgan W, Feuerstein M, Koyamatsu K, Hill-Fotouchi C. Work-related upper-extremity disorders: Prospective evaluation of clinical and functional outcomes. *JOEM* 1999; 41(10): 884–892.

49. Cole DC, Mondloch MV, ECC Prognostic Modelling Group. Listening to workers: How recovery expectations predict outcomes? *Can Med Assoc J* 2002; 166: 749–754.
50. Bandura A. Self-efficacy: Toward a unifying theory of behavioral change. *Psychol Rev* 1977; 84(2): 191–215.
51. Norman G, Fava JL, Levesque DA, Redding CA, Johnson S, Evers K, Reich T. An inventory for measuring confidence to manage stress. *Ann Behav Med* 1997; 19(Suppl): 78.
52. Ash P, Goldstein SI. Predictor of returning to work. *Bull Am Acad Psychiatry Law* 1995; 23(2): 205–210.
53. Depression Guideline Panel—U.S. Department of Health and Human Services, Public Health Service Agency for Health Care Policy and Research. Depression in primary care, Vol 1: Detection and diagnosis. Clinical Practice Guideline, No. 5. Rockville, MD: U.S. Department of Health and Human services, 1993. (AHCPR Publication No. 93–0550).
54. Coyne JC, Fechner-Bates S, Schwenk TL. Prevalence, nature, and comorbidity of depressive disorders in primary care, *Gen Hosp Psychiatry* 1994; 16: 267–276.
55. Hirschfeld RM, Keller MB, Panico S, Arons BS, Barlow D, Davidoff F, Endicott J, Froom J, Goldstein M, Gorman JM, Marek RG, Maurer TA, Meyer R, Phillips K, Ross J, Schwenk TL, Sharfstein SS, Thase ME, Wyatt. The national depressive and manic-depressive association consensus statement on the undertreatment of depression. *JAMA* 1997; 277: 333–340.
56. Loisel P, Durand P, Abenhaim L, Gosselin L, Simard R, Turcotte J, Esdaile JM. Management of occupational back pain: The Sherbrooke model. Results of a pilot and feasibility study. *Occup Environ Med* 1994; 51: 597–602.
57. Sinclair SJ, Hogg-Johnson SA, Mondloch MV, Shields SA. The effectiveness of an early active intervention program for workers with soft tissue injuries: The early claimant cohort study. *Spine* 1997; 22(24): 2919–2931.
58. Loisel P, Abenhaim L, Durand P, Esdaile JM, Suissa S, Gosselin L, Simard R, Turcotte J, Lemaire J. A population-based, randomized clinical trial on back pain management. *Spine* 1997; 22(24): 2911–2918.
59. Hunt HA, Habeck RV, Van Tol B, Scully SM. *Disability prevention among Michigan employers, 1988–1993.* Kalamazoo MI: WE. Upjohn Institute for Employment Research, 1993.
60. Hogg-Johnson S, Cole DC. Early prognostic factors for duration on benefits among workers with compensated occupational soft tissue injuries. *Occupational and Environmental Medicine* 2003;60:244–252.
61. Krause N, Dasinger LK, Neuhauser F. Modified work and return to work: A review of the literature. *J Occup Rehab* 1998; 8(2): 113–139.
62. Habeck R, Leahy MJ, Hunt HA, Chan F, Welch EM. Employer factors related to workers' compensation claims and disability management. *Rehab Counsell Bull* 1991; 34: 210–226.
63. Hunt HA, Habeck RV. *The Michigan disability prevention study*. Kalamazoo, MI: W. E. Upjohn Institute for Employment Research, 1993.
64. Clarke J, Cole D, Ferrier S. Return to work after a soft tissue injury: A qualitative exploration (Working Paper # 127). Institute for Work and Health, unpublished manuscript, 2000.
65. Cote P, Clarke J, Deguire S, Frank JW, Yassi A. A report on chiropractors and return-to-work: The experiences of three canadian focus groups. *J Manipulat Physiol Therapeut* in press.
66. Frank JW, Guzman J. *Facilitation of return to work after a soft tissue injury: Synthesizing the evidence and experience. A HEALNet report on the findings of the Work-Ready projectHEALNet.* Toronto, Ontario, Canada, 1999.
67. Krause N, Lynch J, Kaplan GA, Cohen RD, Goldberg DE, Salonen JT. Predictors of disability retirement. *Scand J Work, Environ Health* 1997; 23(6): 403–413.
68. Himmelstein JS, Feuerstein M, Stanek EJ, III, Koyamatsu K, Pransky GS, Morgan W, Anderson KO. Work-related upper-extremity disorders and work disability: Clinical and psychosocial presentation. *JOEM* 1995; 35(11): 1278–1286.
69. Krause N, Ragland DR, Fisher JM, Syme SL. Psychosocial job factors, physical workload and incidence of work-related spinal injury: A 5-Year prospective study of urban transit operators. *Spine* 1998; 23(23): 2507–2516.
70. Papageorgiou AC, Macfarlane GJ, Thomas E, Croft PR, Jayson MIV, Silman AJ. Psychosocial factors in the workplace: Do they predict new episodes of low back pain? Evidence from the South Manchester back pain study. *Spine* 1997; 22(10): 1137–1142.

71. Tarasuk V, Eakin JM. The problem of Legitimacy in the experience of work-related back injury. *Qual Health Res* 1995; 5(2): 204–221.
72. Tarasuk V, Eakin JM. "Back Problems Are for Life": Perceived vulnerability and its implications for chronic disability. *J Occup Rehab* 1994; 4(1): 55–64.
73. Smith JM, Tarasuk V, Shannon H, Ferrier S, ECC Prognosis Modelling Group. *Prognosis of musculoskeletal disorders: Effects of legitimacy and job vulnerability* (IWH Working Paper # 67 ed). Toronto, Canada: Institute for Work & Health, 1998.
74. Smith J, Tarasuk V, Ferrier S, Shannon H. Relationship between workers' reports of problems and legiti-macy and vulnerability in the workplace a duration of benefits for lost-time musculoskeletal injuries. *Am J Epidemiol* 1996; 143(11): S17.
75. Clarke JA, Cole DC, Ferrier SE. *Work-ready 1: Report of qualitative component from Ontario,* unpublished manuscript, 1999.
76. Amick BC, Habeck RV, Hunt A, Fossel AH, Chapin A, Keller RB, Katz JN. Measuring the impact of organizational behaviors on work disability prevention and management. *J Occup Rehab* 2000; 10(1): 21–38.
77. Bernacki EJ, Guidera JA, Schaefer JA, Tsai S. A facilitated early return to work program at a large urban medical center. *J Occup Environ Health* 2000; 42(12): 1172–1177.
78. Pransky G, Benjamin K, Hill-Fotouhi C, Himmelstein J, Fletcher KE, Katz JN, Johnson WG. Outcomes in work-related upper extremity and low back injuries: Results of a retrospective study. *Am J Indust Med* 2000; 37(4): 400–409.
79. Gice JH, Tompkins K. Return to work in a hospital setting. *J Bus Psych* 1989; 4: 237–243.
80. Yassi A, Tate R, Cooper JE, Snow C, Vallentyne S, Khokhar JB. Early intervention for back-injured nurses at a large Canadian tertiary care hospital: An evaluation of the effectiveness and cost benefits of a two-year pilot project. *Occup Med* 1995; 45(4): 209–214.
81. Fitzler SL, Berger RA. Chelsea back program: One year later. *OH&S Canada* 1983; 52(7): 52–54.
82. Adams ML, Franklin GM, Barnhart S. Outcome of carpal tunnel surgery in Washington state workers' compensation. *Am J Industr Med* 1994; 25(4): 527–536.
83. National Institute for Occupational Safety and Health. *Musculoskeletal disorders and workplace factors. A critical review of epidemiologic evidence for work-related musculoskeletal disorders of the neck, upper extremity, and low back.* Baltimore: U.S. Department of Health and Human Services, 1997.
84. Nachemson AL. Work for all: For those with low back pain as well. *Clin Orthop* 1983; 179: 77–85.
85. Ranney D, *Chronic musculoskeletal injuries in the workplace.* Philadelphia: W.B. Saunders, 1997.
86. National Research Council and Institute of Medicine. *Musculoskeletal disorders and the workplace; low back and upper Extremities.* Washington, DC: National Academy Press, 2001.
87. Eakin JM, Lamm F, Limborg HJ. International perspective on the promotion of health and safety in small workplaces. In: Frick K, Jensen PL, Quinlan M, Wilthagen T, eds. *Systematic occupational health and safety management.* New York: Pergamon, 2000, pp. 227–247.
88. Cheadle A, Franklin G, Wolfhagen C, Savarino J, Liu PY, Salley C, Weaver M. Factors influencing the duration of work-related disability: A population-based study of Washington state workers' compensation. *Am J Public Health* 1994; 84(2): 190–196.
89. Volinn E, Van Koevering D, Loeser JD. Back sprain in industry: The role of socioeconomic factors in chronicity. *Spine* 1991; 16(5): 542–548.
90. Wilkinson WE. Therapeutic jurisprudence and workers' compensation. *Ariz Attorn* 1994; 30(8): 28–33.
91. Ison TG. The therapeutic significance of compensation structures. *Can Bar Rev* 1986; 64(4): 605–637.
92. Lippel K. Therapeutic and anti-therapeutic consequences of workers' compensation. *Int J Law Psychiatry* 1999; 22(5/6): 521–546.
93. Kornblum GO. The role of the life, health and accident insurer's medical director in extra-contract claims litigation. *Transact Assoc Life, Ins Med Direct Am* 1979; 62:61.
94. Hogelund J. *Bringing the sick back to work: Labor market reintegration of the long-term sicklisted in the Netherlands and Denmark.* Denmark: Danish National Institute of Social Research, Roskilede University, Copenhagen, 2000.
95. Yelin EH. The myth of malingering: Why individuals withdraw from work in the presence of illness. *Milbank Mem Fund Q Health Soc* 1986; 64(40): 622–647.

96. Fortin B, Lanoie P. Substitution between unemployment insurance and workers' compensation: An analysis applied to the risk of workplace accidents. *J Public Econ* 1992; 49: 287–312.
97. Lanoie P. The impact of occupational safety and health regulation on the risk of workplace accidents: Quebec, 1983–87. *J Hum Resour* 1992; 27(4): 643–660.
98. Dionne C, Koepsell TD, Von Korff M, Deyo RA, Barlow WE, Checkoway H. Formal education and back related disability: In search of an explanation. *Spine* 1995; 20(24): 2721–2730.
99. Kralj B. Experience rating of workers' compensation insurance premiums and the duration of workplace injuries. In: Thomason T, Chaykowski R, eds. *Research in Canadian workers compensation.* Kingston, Canada: IRC Press, 1995, pp. 106–121.
100. Johnson WG, Butler RJ, Baldwin M. First spells of work absences among Ontario workers. In: Thomason T, Chaykowski RP, eds. *Research in Canadian workers' compensation.* Kingston, Canada: IRC Press, 1995, pp. 73–84.
101. Thomason T, Pozzebon S. The effect of worker's compensation benefits on claims incidence in Canada. In: Thomason T. Chaykowski R, eds. *Research in Canadian workers' compensation.* Kingston, Canada: IRC Press, 1995, pp. 53–69.
102. Hyatt D. Work disincentives of workers' compensation permanent partial disability benefits: Evidence for Canada. *Can J Econ* 1996: 29(2): 289–308.
103. Bloch FS, Prins R. *Who returns to work and why?* New Burnswick, NJ: International Social Security Association and Transaction Publishers, 2001. (International Social Security Series, 5).
104. Hawthorne MH. Women recovering from coronary artery bypass surgery. *Schol Inquiry Nurs Pract Int J* 1993; 7(4): 223–252.
105. Lacharity L.A. The experiences of younger women with coronary artery disease. *J Women's Health Gender Based Med* 1999; 8(6): 773–785.
106. Boogaard MA. Rehabilitation of the female patient after myocardial infarction. *Nurs Clin N Am* 1984; 19: 433–440.
107. Benson G. Arthur H, Rideout E. Women and heart attack: A study of women's experiences. *Can J Cardiovaseul Nars* 1997; 8(3): 16–23.
108. Johnson JL, Morse JM. Regaining control: The process of adjustment after myocardial infarction. *Heart Lung* 1990; 19(2): 126–135.
109. King KM, Jensen L. Preserving the self: Women having cardiac surgery. *Heart Lung* 1994; 23(2): 99–105.
110. Ferrier S, Lavis J. *With health comes work?* Toronto, Canada: Institute for Work and Health, 2001.
111. Menard MR. Comparison of disability behavior after different sites and types of injury in a workers' compensation population. *JOEM* 1996; 38(11): 1161–1170.
112. Velicer WF, Prochaska JO, Fava JL, Norman GJ, Redding CA. Smoking cessation and stress management: Applications of the transtheoretical model of behavior change. *Homeostasis* 1998; 38(5/6): 216–232.
113. Prochaska JO. Why do we behave the way we do? [Review]. *Can J Cardiol* 1995; 11(Suppl. A): 20A–25A.

5

Prediction of Occupational Disability

Models, Factors, and Outcomes

Renée-Louise Franche, John Frank, and Niklas Krause

INTRODUCTION

Safe and timely return to work (RTW) reduces the risk of development of chronicity of work disability. By 6 months post-injury, if a worker has not yet returned to work, the likelihood of developing chronic disability is substantial (Abenhaim & Suissa, 1987). Returning to work when one is ready can reduce the risk of entering a cycle of deconditioning, decreased self-efficacy about RTW, and increased habituation to being work disabled. Conversely, it should be noted that returning to work too early or in inappropriate conditions can also have deleterious effects (Pransky et al., 2001). Consequently, it is important to identify the factors facilitating safe RTW in the early phases of recovery.

This chapter will first provide a brief overview of the operative conceptual models of occupational disability, as they apply to predictive factors of occupational disability. We wish to distinguish conceptual models from statistical models—the conceptual models we will discuss may or may not be supported by statistical modeling, however they all involve constructs which provide a framework with which to organize the relationships between various predictive factors, interpret statistical results, and lead to hypotheses testing. An overview of predictive factors of occupational disability will be presented, which will not involve a review of clinical interventions for occupational injuries, as such a task would need to be overly detailed and remain beyond the intended scope of the chapter. This will be followed by a discussion of the challenges associated with measuring RTW outcomes.

The main focus of this chapter is on physical conditions as the primary condition resulting from occupational injury. This does not reflect the view that work conditions can not cause or magnify mental conditions. However, addressing the issue of work disability associated with mental conditions would require enlarging the discussion to additional conceptual frameworks, as mental conditions encompass a new set of

DOI: 10.1007/978-0-387-28919-9_5, © 2009 Springer Science+Business Media, LLC

issues and social circumstances. Our literature review reflects the fact that most of the current research on work disability involves the study of musculoskeletal (MSK) conditions since they represent the majority of worker's compensation claims for lost-time.

THE DEPARTURE FROM THE MEDICAL MODEL

The essential and necessary initiating element of occupational disability is an occupational injury. For that reason, it is only natural that the first conceptual model applied to what is initially understood as a physical event was the biomedical model. The biomedical model espoused etiological and treatment approaches heavily laden with illness and physical factors. While it remains important in the area of occupational disability to not lose sight of the physical realities of disability, the biomedical model, due to its narrow focus, soon became insufficient to explain occupational disability, a phenomenon involving complex social and psychological elements. As Krause and Ragland described: "It is impossible to adequately describe disability exclusively in medical categories. Although a medical condition is necessary for a disability to develop, disability (especially of long duration) is never solely the result of pathology or functional limitation; it is essentially a social phenomenon" (Krause & Ragland, 1994).

In an initial response to a growing dissatisfaction with the medical model, researchers began to identify the multiple players involved in the process of occupational disability (Frank et al., 1998; Krause et al., 1994; Schultz, Crook, Fraser, & Joy, 2000). This descriptive approach was critical in mapping out the components which led to a recognition of the multifactorial nature of occupational disability, and went beyond the narrow biomedical focus. Krause and Ragland (1994) identified seven major systems which interact with each other and affect disability outcomes: 1) the individual 2) the non-occupational social environment 3) the occupational environment 4) the compensation and disability insurance systems 5) the social security and welfare system 6) the healthcare or medical system 7) the legal, political and economic context. Frank and colleagues (Frank et al., 1998) characterize the main players involved in the RTW process as being the employer/workplace, the healthcare provider, the insurer, and the employee. They highlight how coordination of these main players (Frank et al., 1996; Frank et al., 1998) is of critical importance to achieve optimal RTW and to decrease risk of chronicity. Similarly, in their review of the main operating models in the area of occupational disability, Schultz and colleagues (Schultz et al., 2000) describe the strengths, limitations, fundamental principles and practical implications of the biomedical, the psychiatric, the insurance, and the labor relations models, again highlighting the various stakeholders' view on occupational disability. The descriptive model of occupational disability was further specified by Friesen and colleagues (2001) who structured factors associated with RTW by situating them in the micro-system (worker factors) and meso-systems (workplace, health, and insurer factors) and who added the macro-system of economic, social and legislative factors, such as physician reimbursement policies, and downsizing (Friesen, Yassi, & Cooper, 2001).

In parallel to the structural description of occupational disability, the temporal aspect of occupational disability has also been incorporated in models of disability.

The phase-specificity model of occupational disability addresses the developmental character of the chronicity of disability (Krause et al., 1994; Spitzer et al., 1987). Two main models emerge in the literature: the eight phase Occupational Disability Model (Krause et al., 1994) and the Acute/Subacute/Chronic Phases models of low back pain (Spitzer et al., 1987). Although the models differ in the number of phases they propose, their main principles are similar: both models highlight the phase specificity of risk factors, of interactions with the social environment, and of interventions. Each phase of disability is hypothesized to be associated with specific risk factors, sensitivity to physical and psychosocial factors, and consequently with specific response patterns to occupational and clinical interventions. Although both models differ regarding the timing of the beginning of the chronic phase of disability, by six months post-injury, chronicity of work disability is established. The phase-specificity model proposes three phases of disability - the acute, subacute, and chronic phases. The use of the phase-specificity model provides an analytical strategy which can be applied to understanding prognostic factors occurring in the workplace/healthcare/insurer/psychological domains during phases of recovery.

More recent and exploratory conceptual work in the area of occupational disability show a shift back to "worker-centered" models. While a focus on individual factors has been criticized as "blaming the worker", two recent models in fact integrate workplace, healthcare, and insurer factors as they impact on the worker, and recognize the centrality of the worker in the process. The first model, the biopsychosocial predictive model of occupational low back disability (Gatchel & Gardea, 1999; Schultz et al., 2000) integrates the physiological component, the physical functioning component, the psychological components of cognition and emotion, and the social functioning components of disability. Initial empirical support for this model has highlighted the importance of disability-related cognitions (Schultz et al., 2002). These findings point to the importance of incorporating cognitive-behavioral strategies in RTW interventions.

The second model, the Readiness for RTW model (Franche & Krause, 2002) (Franche & Krause, 2003) considers two theoretical models as they apply to the behavior of returning to work: 1) the Readiness for Change Model originating from the field of health promotion (Prochaska & Di Clemente, 1992; Velicer, Norman, Fava, & Prochaska, 1999; Prochaska et al., 1994) and 2) the phase-specificity models of occupational disability (Krause et al., 1994; Spitzer et al., 1987). Employee interactions with the workplace, the healthcare, and insurance systems are considered as they impact on motivational dimensions of behavior. The model complements the phase-specificity model of disability by allowing for an individual-level staging of the disability and recovery process within the broader group-level-derived framework of occupational disability phases. The model requires future empirical validation but remains interesting due to its potential to integrate the impact of various systems on the worker with the well-validated motivational model of Readiness for Change.

One of the critical steps of empirical validation of a model remains its predictive value and relevance when tested within an intervention study. When examined in randomized trials, interventions promoting integration of the workplace and healthcare systems have indeed been more successful in returning workers to work than standard care (Lindstrom et al., 1992; Loisel et al., 2001; Loisel et al., 2002a). Although evidence is not conclusive, it appears that interventions offered in the subacute phase of disability are most successful, suggesting that the subacute phase may prove to be the "golden hour" for RTW interventions (Loisel et al., 2001; Loisel et al., 2002a) and offering further validation to phase-specificity models. These intervention trials provide the evidenced-based support for the growing consensus regarding the multifactorial nature of occupational disability and offer grounds for investing into a disability management practice which would address all possible factors.

PREDICTING CHRONICITY OF WORK DISABILITY

The following section describes select predictive factors of safe and timely RTW which are 1) most amenable to change or 2) most relevant to stakeholders and parties in the RTW process or 3) most likely to have a significant impact on RTW outcomes.

The Workplace

Disability Management Practices

The early work of Hunt and Habeck (1991), brought attention to the importance of disability management strategies to reduce the burden of work disability. Their study involved a survey of 220 employers in 7 industries with a response rate of 46% (Hunt, Habeck, & Leahy, 1993) and a survey of 124 firms in Michigan with a response rate of 43.7% (Habeck, Leahy, Hunt, Chan, & Welch, 1991). They presented unadjusted effects of organizational level variables and supported the univariate impact of the following variables on duration of work disability—active safety leadership, presence of an in-house organized RTW program, people-oriented culture, safety education of employees, incentives to encourage participation of employees and of supervisors to participate in safety and disability management, early contact of employer representative with the worker after injury/illness, ongoing monitoring of disability cases, top management commitment to safety and disability management issues, and work accommodation offers. These factors were related to the rate of closed disability compensation claims in the firms surveyed. The studies provide some evidence for an association between organizational policies and practices and RTW. However, the absence of control for work sites exposures to certain job conditions, or for sociodemographic characteristics does warrant caution about the conclusions which can be drawn from this early, but leading, work.

Work Accommodation

The offer of a work accommodation or modified work is the pivotal stepping stone in disability management. It refers to the process by which a work-disabled employee returns to work with a gradual reinsertion in his/her previous tasks, with modified tasks, or with a combination of both. A systematic review of 13 high quality studies (Krause, Dasinger, & Neuhauser, 1998) showed that 1) injured employees who are offered modified work are twice as likely to return to work than those who are not and 2) modified work reduces by half the number of lost days. Subsequent studies provided further confirmation that offers of work accommodation significantly increase the likelihood of returning to work (Bernacki, Guidera, Schaefer, & Tsai, 2000;

Bloch & Prins, 2001; Franche et al., 2003; Manno & Hogg-Johnson, 2000; Sinclair, Hogg-Johnson, et al. 1997), however, one recent retrospective study of workers with back pain-related sickness absence (Hiebert, Skovron, Nordin, & Crane, 2003) found no association between a prescription of work restrictions and length of work absence, using a one year follow-up period. It should be noted that only prescriptions of work accommodations were examined, and not if they were implemented, or how they were implemented. Moreover, in that same study, no information on severity of back injury was available, and work restrictions may have been more frequently prescribed for more serious injuries. The impact of this important confounding variable, which was not controlled or measured, may explain the discrepancy between results of the latter study with those of the vast majority of previous studies examining the influence of work accommodation in the RTW process.

Interestingly, one study of claimants with musculoskeletal (MSK) disorders showed that the positive effects of work accommodation are more pronounced for workers with poorer physical and psychological health (Hogg-Johnson & Cole, 2003). Indeed, work accommodation seemed to make a difference for workers in the worse circumstances. For workers who were optimistic about recovering and who reported less pain/functional limitation, the work accommodation offer made little difference in their RTW rates. However, in the case of workers with the opposite circumstances, the offer of work accommodation was key, resulting in the median of days on benefits dropping from 112 days (with no offer of accommodation) to 32 days (with an offer of accommodation).

There are a number of benefits to offering work accommodations. Satisfactory work accommodations have been shown to significantly decrease injured employees' anxiety about returning to work (Pransky et al., 2000). As well, offers of modified work are associated with a reduction in incidence of injuries (Gice & Tompkins, 1989; Yassi et al., 1995b; Amick et al., 2000a; Yassi et al., 1995a). The reduction of new injuries can possibly be explained by the fact that redesign of one's job tasks will often lead to positive change in the job tasks of other employees doing the same type of work.

Paradoxically, while the majority of studies show beneficial effects of work accommodation, some studies actually show an increase in incidence of injuries following the implementation of programs which include work accommodations (Fitzler & Berger, 1983) or an increase in re-injury rates in employees with low back injuries following their involvement in work accommodations (Pransky et al., 2002). Increases in injury reports could be attributed to an increase in previously unreported injuries, if, as part of the program, reporting of injuries was encouraged (Fitzler et al., 1983). It should be noted that in the case of the Fitzler study, the additional reported injuries were much less severe and less costly than those which were prevented. However, increases in re-injuries can suggest that although modified work can accelerate RTW, insufficient attention to risk factors may lead to re-injury (Pransky et al., 2001). These studies bring attention to the danger of returning the employee to work too early.

Offering an adequate work accommodation can be challenging, particularly in small workplaces where there are fewer work options. As well, clinicians and researchers are becoming acutely aware that meaningless and devaluing modified work, which does not contribute to the overall functioning of one's workplace, can actually do more harm than good in the return-to-work process (Clarke & Cole, 2000). A work accommodation most likely to lead to a continued return to work will be one which returns the employee to a similar setting than the pre-injury job, with same or similar co-workers, and which provides a sense of accomplishment .

Job Characteristics

The decision of employees to return to work, and their judgement about their ability subsequently to stay at work, will depend in part on the actual job demands and job conditions they face, both psychosocial and physical.

Regarding psychosocial job characteristics, the following factors have been associated with prolonged work disability: low worker control over the job (Melchior, Niedhammer, Berkman, & Goldberg, 2003; Krause, Dasinger, Deegan, Rudolph, & Brand, 2001a; Marklund, 1995; Yelin, Henke, & Epstein, 1986b) and, especially, over the work and rest schedule (Infante-Rivard & Lortie, 1996; Krause et al., 2001a; Kristensen, 1991); long work hours (Krause, Ragland, Greiner, Syme, & Fisher, 1997b); high psychological job demands (Krause et al., 2001a; Krause et al., 1997b; Marklund, 1995); monotonous work (Kristensen, 1991); low skill discretion (Lund, 2001), and high job stress or job strain (Krause et al., 2001a; Marklund, 1995; Theorell, Harms-Ringdahl, Ahlberg-Hulten, & Westin, 1991; Yelin et al., 1986b).

Supervisor and co-worker response are a key element in the RTW process. The importance of a non-confrontational and non-judgmental approach has repeatedly been highlighted in both qualitative (Clarke & Cote, 2000; Cote, Clarke, Deguire, Frank, & Yassi, 2000; Frank & Guzman, 1999) and empirical studies (Bergquist-Ullman & Larsson, 1977b; Himmelstein et al., 1995; Krause, Frank, Dasinger, Sullivan, & Sinclair, 2001a; Krause et al., 1997a; Krause, Dasinger, et al. 2001; Melchior, Berkman, Niedhammer, Chea, & Goldberg, 2003; van der Weide, Verbeek, Salle, & van Dijk, 1999b). However, inconsistent findings are reported for social support at work: some studies linked low supervisor support (Krause et al., 2001a; Krause et al., 1997b) or low co-worker support (Bergquist-Ullman & Larsson, 1977; van der Weide, Verbeek, Salle, & van Dijk, 1999a) to prolonged disability, other studies reported no effect (Marklund, 1995). In a retrospective cohort study of low back pain claimants with 1–4 years of follow-up, low supervisor support reduced RTW rates by up to 21 percent even after adjustment for injury severity, physical workload, and other confounding factors, but no significant effect was seen for coworker support (Krause et al., 2001a). Mixed results regarding co-worker support may be due to various forms of "co-worker support": Co-workers may provide support by cooperating with the injured employee in their modified work program, or they may also support the injured employee by suggesting to stay off work until they are "100 percent recovered." Variation in the amount of contact with co-workers as a function of the type of work may also contribute to null findings regarding co-worker support.

One concept which is closely linked to the social climate of work is legitimacy (Tarasuk & Eakin, 1995; Tarasuk & Eakin, 1994; Smith, Tarasuk, Shannon, Ferrier, & ECC Prognosis Modelling Group, 1998). Legitimacy refers to the degree to which an injured employee feels that others believe the authenticity of their injury and of their symptoms. It is of particular relevance to injuries and illnesses which involve work absences and to injuries/illnesses which are "invisible". Legitimacy has been found to be a significant predictor of duration on benefits (Smith, Tarasuk, Ferrier, & Shannon, 1996).

Although there are multiple workplace psychosocial factors of crucial importance in the RTW process, the importance of job physical demands cannot be understated. When physical demands are considered indiscriminately, with various types of demands and types of conditions grouped together, there is conflicting evidence regarding their role as predictors of long-term work disability (Waddell, Burton, & Main, 2003). However, when physical demands are examined in a more detailed fashion, more intense physical demands are repeatedly found to be associated with less favorable RTW outcomes. In individuals with low back pain, the following characteristics have been associated with prolonged work disability for individuals: bending (Bergquist-Ullman et al., 1977a; Dasinger, Krause, Deegan, Brand, & Rudolph, 2000), twisting (Bergquist-Ullman et al., 1977), fixed positions (Bergquist-Ullman et al., 1977a), repetitive or continuous strain (Bergquist-Ullman et al., 1977), heavy physical work (Dasinger et al., 2000), lifting (Dasinger et al., 2000), pushing (Dasinger et al., 2000), and pulling (Dasinger et al., 2000). Regarding job physical demand effects on duration of work disablity specific to upper extremity MSK disorders, little information is available. However, an extensive review of 43 studies (National Research Council, Panel on Musculoskeletal Disorders and the Workplace, Commission on Behavioral and Social Sciences and Education, & Institute of Medicine, 2001) found the following physical work factors to be consistently associated with the occurrence of upper extremity MSK disorders: repetitive tasks, forceful tasks, repetition and force, repetition and cold, and vibration. Job physical demands do not explain all of the variance in RTW outcomes, however, they can be thought of as defining the parameters or the range of possibilities of RTW.

Only a few studies investigated the phase-specificity of these risk factors, and all of them for duration of disability after low back pain (Dasinger et al., 2000; Krause et al., 2001a; MacKenzie et al., 1998). Both high physical and psychological job demands appear as independent barriers to RTW during the acute and sub-acute/chronic disability phases, while supervisor support, low job control, and low control over the work and rest schedule seem to be especially strong predictors during the sub-acute/chronic disability phase (Krause et al., 2001a).

Organizational Factors

More attention has recently been given to the role of organizational aspects of the workplace in relation to RTW (Amick et al., 2000; Hunt, Habeck, VanTol, & Scully, 1993). Organizational aspects are closely tied to job characteristics in that organizational aspects become operationalized or "translated" into practices impacting on job characteristics, such as ergonomic factors, supervisor support, disability management practices. However, organizational aspects and job characteristics remain distinct constructs in that organizational factors are a higher-order phenomenon, which can be measured independently from job characteristics. As well, the same type of organizational climate may result in different practices, depending on the nature of the sector, size, geography of a specific workplace.

Workplace culture, which refers to a general interpersonal and value-focused atmosphere, is also associated with RTW outcomes. In one prospective study of 198 employees with carpal tunnel syndrome (Amick et al., 2000), an increased level

TOURO COLLEGE LIBRARY

of people-oriented culture, improved safety climate, presence of disability management programs, and ergonomics practices were all associated with higher RTW rates 6 months after being identified in community medical practices, when age, gender and baseline carpal tunnel syndrome symptom severity were controlled for (Amick et al., 2000). People-oriented culture is defined as "the extent to which the company involves employees in meaningful decision-making, where there is trust between management and employees, and openness to share information in a cooperative work environment." (Amick et al., 2000, p. 30). Such a culture is typically expressed in the provision of worker training programs in safe job practices, company policies aiming at reducing the biomechanical workload (heavy lifting and repetitive movements), and policies and practices stressing early intervention, communication and co-ordination in disability case management along with a proactive RTW policy (education and accommodation of employees returning to work after disability). Closely linked to a people-oriented culture, is safety climate, which refers to the shared perceptions of an organization with respect to policies, procedures and practices regarding safety.

It should be noted that none of the studies addressing organizational policies and practices simultaneously addressed the effects of work site exposures occurring at the individual level. It remains important to estimate simultaneously the effects of organizational level and individual task level exposures, in order to address the mediating pathways of these two levels of factors impacting on disability duration.

Firm size

Larger firm size has consistently been associated with improved RTW rates when indexed by time on benefits (Cheadle et al., 1994; Manno & Hogg-Johnson, 2000; Sinclair, Hogg-Johnson, Mondloch, & Shields, 1997; Oleinick, Gluck, & Guire, 1996) and by self-reported RTW (Franche et al., 2003; Oleinick, Gluck, & Guire, 1996). However, one study which examined the impact of firm size using a phase-specific analytical framework (Boden & Galizzi, 1999) found phase-specific effects for size of firm: for employees with periods of disability less than 30 days, time to first RTW was shorter if the employer was small (less than 50 employees), whereas the opposite was the case if the disability period exceeded 30 days in that small employer size lengthened time to first RTW as opposed to large employer size (more than 1,000 employees). The positive effects on RTW of large employer size for long-term disabled workers may be related to the better opportunities of the larger organization to find alternative work for a disabled employee. There is also preliminary evidence that larger firm size is associated with a decreased likelihood of returning on benefits after a first RTW in the first year post-injury (Manno et al., 2000). The mechanisms underlying the association between larger firm size and improved RTW outcomes deserve some attention. Larger workplaces are more likely to have coordinated disability management strategies available (Brooker, Cole, Hogg-Johnson, Smith, & Frank, 2001), as described by Habeck et al. (Habeck et al., 1991) and NIDMAR (National Institute of Disability Management and Research, 2000). Clearly, the size of a firm is not modifiable, however, disability management strategies and other correlates of large firms are. It is still unclear which disability management strategies (e.g. early contact with worker) are most conducive to improved RTW and which ones should be promoted in small and medium workplaces.

TOURO COLLEGE LIBRARY

BOX 5.1. Workplace Factors Predictive of Improved RTW Outcomes

- Work accommodation offer
- Increased job control and decreased job demands
- Decreased physical demands
- Non-confrontational approach from supervisor
- Sense of legitimacy of injury and symptoms
- People-oriented workplace culture

The Healthcare Provider

The healthcare provider is often the first RTW player the employee encounters, and remains involved in the acute and subacute phases of recovery. The healthcare provider not only has a role in the treatment of workplace injury but is often expected to provide information and make judgment on the cause of injury, disability level, readiness to return to work and even the authenticity of an injury (Carey & Hadler, 1986; Dobyns, 1987). In the case of multi-causal injuries or injuries with symptoms not obviously visible (such as musculoskeletal injuries), the healthcare provider's role may be challenging.

Communication between the healthcare provider and patient was examined by Dasinger and colleagues (Dasinger, Krause, Thompson, Brand, & Rudolph, 2001). Communication which involved a positive recommendation to return to work was associated with a 60% greater RTW rate for patients with a low back injury lasting more than 30 days even after adjusting for sex, age, injury factors and physical/psychosocial workload (Dasinger et al., 2001) In addition, proactive communication, defined as the gathering and imparting of information to the patient about his or her job, prevention of injury, and return to modified work, was also associated with a greater likelihood of RTW in the acute phase of disability. However, this association ceased to be statistically significant when injury and workplace characteristics were taken into consideration, suggesting that the latter factors remain critical in the acute phase of disability. Taken together, this study suggests that doctor-patient communication may have more impact on RTW in the subacute phase as opposed to the acute phase, as severity of injury and job characteristics may dominate one's ability to return to work during the acute phase.

Direct communication with the workplace may provide the healthcare provider with a more complete perspective on the kind of work conditions an injured employee will return to. In response to a patient's physical limitations, physicians and chiropractors may communicate directly with the workplace to recommend work modifications. It seems that when recommendations for ergonomic or job changes are made by physicians to employers, employers tend to listen. One study (Keogh, Gucer, Gordon, & Nuwayhid, 2000) found that although 48% of employers took no action in response to a worker's repetitive strain injury, a physician's recommendation for change doubled the likelihood of a response.

Paradoxically, it is also important to note that direct communication with a workplace or a patient about their job may delay return to work precisely because the healthcare provider may feel that the job will not be changed sufficiently to accommodate the worker and the worker may be at risk for greater injury. However, such an approach may lead to fewer recurrences of work disability.

Treatment of an injured worker requires a balanced approach that moves beyond the biomedical model. Healthcare providers must not dismiss patients because they do not readily see an objective basis for the patient's pain. On the other hand, overly aggressive treatment (early referrals to specialists and tests) may only reinforce illness behaviour and delay recovery. Abenhaim and colleagues (Abenhaim et al., 1995) found that when a physician made an initial specific diagnosis of back pain (such as sciatica or lesions of the vertebrae), patients' back pain was much more likely to develop into a chronic condition than when a physician made a non-specific diagnosis of low back pain. The authors suggest that one consequence of a specific diagnosis is that patients then focus less on pain management and more on a treatment and cures which tend to be only marginally successful. However, the latter study did not control for severity of injury suggesting that certain conditions which are associated with specific diagnoses, i.e. sciatica, may have a natural history with poorer outcome. There is consensus that healthcare provider communication with patients suffering from back pain should incorporate reassuring information about the high likelihood that the pain will resolve over time and that the patient should remain as active as possible i.e., refrain from bed rest (Agency for Health care Policy and Research, 1994; Loisel et al., 2001).

There is some evidence that increased delay between injury and treatment increases time on benefits, especially for the acute and subacute phases of injury (McIntosh, Frank, et al., 2000). A delay in treatment may increase fear of returning to work prior to the treatment, increase anxiety about an individual injury and prognosis, and promote a decrease in activity level. Increased waiting times between a referral for a test or specialist appointment may also delay RTW since the healthcare provider and the patient may postpone making a decision about RTW until they receive results or a specialist's opinion about the severity of the injury. Although, this sort of caution may be warranted, when waiting times are long, a patient's return to work may be unnecessarily delayed. It is interesting to note that a recent study (Sinnott, 2003) found that patients with low back pain with less experienced healthcare providers were 3 times more likely to have a work disability episode longer than 90 days than patients with more experienced healthcare providers. It is possible that less experienced healthcare providers are generally more cautious with patients facing RTW issues, and tend to err on the more conservative management of these cases.

The Worker: Physical and Psychological Factors

Physical Factors

Functional impairment (Galizzi & Boden, 1996; MacKenzie et al., 1998; Hogg-Johnson, Frank, & Rael, 1994; Hogg-Johnson & Cole, 2003) and poor general health (van der Giezen, Bouter, & Nijhuis, 2000; Yelin, Henke, & Epstein, 1986a) are predictive of prolonged work disability, as is more intense pain (Bergquist-Ullman et al., 1977; Coste, Delecoeuillerie, Cohen, Le Parc, & Paolaggi, 1994; Reiso et al., 2003; Sinclair et al., 1997; van der Weide et al., 1999a). For low back pain, pain

BOX 5.2. Healthcare Provider-Related Predictors of Improved RTW Outcomes

- Positive recommendation for RTW to patient
- Proactive communication with patient addressing workplace factors
- Reassurance regarding prognosis and encouragement of maintenance of activities to patient
- Decreased delays to diagnostic tests and specialist consultation, if they are needed

radiating below the knee has been associated with prolonged work disability in some studies (Loisel et al., 2002b; van der Weide et al., 1999) and with increased pain (Loisel et al., 2002b), but not in others (Reiso et al., 2003). Radiating pain is also associated with decreased functional status (Loisel et al., 2002b), increased medication use (Selim et al., 1998), and surgery (Selim et al., 1998). Few studies have addressed the role of co-morbidities. A recent study showed that workers with LBP and comorbidities were 1.31 (C.I.=1.12–1.52) more likely to stay work disabled than those without co-morbidities, with MSK comorbidities having the strongest associations (Nordin et al., 2002). The review of reviews section of a recent conceptual and scientific review of predictors of long-term work disability found strong evidence for pain intensity and functional status to be strong predictors of chronic work disability (Waddell et al., 2003).

Psychological Factors

The relation between physical and mental well-being seems critical, yet the role of psychological factors has received relatively less attention than physical factors. In the recent review by Waddell and colleagues, strong evidence was reported for the role of the following psychological factors as strong predictors of chronic work disability: general psychological distress, expectations about RTW, depression, fear avoidance, and catastrophizing (Waddell, 2003). The role of individual expectations, depressive symptomatology, fear-avoidance and catastrophization will now be discussed.

Individual expectations about recovery and RTW are important predictors of RTW behavior. A recent review of 16 high-quality studies examining the impact of expectations about recovery from a wide variety of physical and psychiatric conditions (Mondloch, Cole, & Frank, 2001) supports the important role of patient expectations on outcomes such as subsequent subjective well-being after minor surgery (Flood, Lorence, Ding, McPherson, & Black, 1993), physical functional ability after a cardiac event (Allen, Becker, & Swank, 1990; Diederiks, van der Sluijs, Weeda, & Schobre, 1983), and psychological adjustment following surgery (Jamison, Parris, & Maxson, 1987). Regarding the specific outcome of RTW following an occupational injury, while one study did not support the predictive value of initial RTW expectations in a small sample of patients with low back pain (Pransky et al., 1999) , the expectation of not being able to " manage" returning to work was associated with a higher likelihood of not being back at work or in retraining 1 year post-injury, and a higher likelihood of being "sick-listed" for more than 6 months 4 years post-injury (Sandstrom & Esbjornsson, 1986) In addition, in a prospective study involving 1332 Canadian employees with lost-time claims following an injury (Cole, Mondloch & Hogg-Johnson, 2002), expectations about recovery measured within 3 weeks of their reported injury were significantly associated with longer periods receiving benefits within the first year following injury, even when controlling for pain level, quality of life, functional status, comorbidities, sex, income, marital status, age, job demands, and workplace accommodations.

Expectations about recovery and RTW may go hand in hand with self-efficacy. Self-efficacy refers to one's confidence about being able to achieve or complete successfully a given behavior (Bandura, 1977). It is quite likely that increased self-efficacy about one's ability to RTW would be closely linked to their expectations about their RTW behavior. Injured workers' increased self-efficacy about their ability to manage their pain and to function well in their job given their health was associated with a greater likelihood of being back at work 12 months later (Pransky, Katz, Benjamin, & Himmelstein, 2002) . As well, workers with back pain-related work absence reporting low self-assessed work ability had longer durations of work disability (Reiso et al., 2003).

Depressive symptomatology has an important impact on RTW outcomes. In prospective studies, depressive symptoms predict RTW in clinical patients (Schade, Semmer, Main, Hora, & Boos, 1999; Dozois, Dobson, Wong, Hughes, & Long, 1995) and claimants (Ash & Goldstein, 1995); in individuals with motor vehicule accidents, they are associated with reductions of claim-closure rates (Côté, Hogg-Johnson, Cassidy, Carroll, & Frank, 2001). Despite the high cost of untreated depressive disorders, primary care physicians detect only 24% to 64% of patients with major depression (Simon, Ormel, VonKorff, & Barlow, 1995; Coyne & Schwenk, 1995; Kirmayer, Robbins, Dworkind, & Yaffe, 1993; Perez-Stable, Miranda, Munoz, & Ying, 1990; Ormel et al., 1999; Wells et al., 1989). While the prevalence of depression is known to be high among patients with chronic work-related MSK pain (48.5%) (Dersh, Gatchel, Polatin, & Mayer, 2002) and treatment rates are low, the prevalence and treatment rates among workers' compensation claimants are still to be determined.

A review of the relationship between pain and depression based on epidemiological studies of the well-known pain-depression comorbidity in primary care and population samples shows that pain is as strongly associated with anxiety as with depressive disorders (Von Korff & Simon, 1996). A fear-avoidance model of exaggerated pain perceptions has recently been developed, which highlights the importance of the maladaptive coping mechanism of catastrophizing, which leads to fear of pain, which in turns leads to avoidance behavior contributing to work disability (Vlaeyen & Linton, 2000). Fear/avoidance constructs have been examined as they relate to both physical activity and work—that is the degree to which an individual fears and/or avoids physical activity and/or work as a result of being concerned about the impact of physical activity/work on symptoms. In individuals with low back pain, fear/avoidance of work as a result of fear of pain has been associated with a higher likelihood of not being back at work or in retraining 1 year post-injury, and a higher likelihood of being " sick-listed" for more than 6 months 4 years post-injury (Sandstrom & Esbjornsson, 1986). After controlling for severity of pain, fear/ avoidance of work (Waddell, Newton, Henderson, Somerville, & Main, 1993) as well as catastrophizing coping strategies (Sullivan, Stanish, Waite, Sullivan, & Tripp, 1998) are found to be significantly associated with work disability.

It remains to be examined if the impact of symptoms of depressed mood and fear/avoidance impact directly on RTW or through their effect on perceived disability status (Feuerstein & Thebarge, 1991) or expectations. A major challenge remains to assess the directionality of causality between psychological factors and development of chronicity: psychological distress could amplify physical sensation of pain, or pain and associated inactivity could induce or exacerbate psychological distress (Von Korff et al., 1996). Both an increase in pain and distress could easily lead to fear of working. The available data in the area of chronic pain suggests that depression does not predate and cause chronicity in pain patients, but rather that certain individuals may be vulnerable to the stressor of the injury and subsequently develop pain concomitantly with depression (Gatchel, Polatin, & Mayer, 1995). It remains to be determined if the same type of vulnerability model would apply to the relationship between depressive symptoms or fear avoidance with the development of work disability.

BOX 5.3. Individual Factors Predictive of Improved RTW Outcomes

- Positive expectations and increased self-efficacy about RTW
- Low levels of depressive symptomatology
- Low levels of fear-avoidance of work

The Insurer

Receiving disability benefits for lost time may play a role in the RTW process. There is substantial controversy over the magnitude and even the existence of the impact of such factors on RTW decisions. While some studies find no effect of compensation on RTW rates (Hogelund, 2000; Waehrer, Miller, Ruser, & Leigh, 1998; Yelin, 1986), other studies find that higher wage replacement is associated with increases in frequency and duration of claims (Dionne et al., 1995; Fortin & Lanoie, 1992; Johnson, Butler, & Baldwin, 1995; Kralj, 1995; Lanoie, 1992; Thomason & Pozzebon, 1995). These studies are limited in that they do not focus on actual RTW, but on duration of claims only. Two studies of Canadian workers from the province of Ontario did focus on actual RTW and found that higher benefit rates were associated with lower rates of RTW (Butler, Johnson, & Baldwin, 1995; Association of Workers' Compensation Boards of Canada, 2001).

Other studies have considered the impact of compensation on employees' RTW rates as it interacts with other factors. These studies generally point to a more complex situation, in which compensation does not unequivocally translate to lower RTW rates. For instance, the association between wage replacement benefits and duration of disability seems to be dependent on the degree of job security. In one multinational prospective (Bloch et al., 2001), the combination of extensive benefits with strong job protection predicted early RTW, while weak job protection combined with extensive benefits did not improve RTW. Shorter disability periods were seen for low levels of job protection combined with low levels of benefits, but mainly for new employees.

In the work of Yelin (Yelin, Nevitt, & Epstein, 1980; Yelin, 1986), when psychosocial job and physical work factors were controlled for, wage replacement ratio did not exert an effect on workforce participation for individuals with disabilities.

Overall, when assessing the influence of compensation on RTW, current studies highlight the importance of analyzing it in conjunction with other factors, such as job security, ratio of income replacement to previous earnings, amount of regular income, number of dependents, and financial pressure to return to work. When these factors are taken into account, the impact of compensation is less absolute than was once believed.

Recent studies have focused on the nature of the processing of the claim of injured workers, both in terms of their interactions with compensation staff and in terms of the procedural aspects of the processing of the claim. Injured workers develop perceptions of the fairness of their interactions with their workers' compensation system which can impact on the RTW process (Injured Workers' Participatory Research Project, 2001). A recent study of 100,000 cases of occupational low-back pain (Sinnott, 2003) showed that delay between first day of time loss and first compensation cheque was associated with an increased probability of chronicity of work disability (defined as still being off work 91 days post-injury). Time-dependent effects were reported in that the negative impact of delay in the issuing of a compensation cheque was stronger when it occurred in the first 14 to 28 days in the claim processing, weaker in the second and third month, and again strong when occurring after 90 days post-injury. More specifically, for the least severe cases, the probability of becoming chronic increased by approximately 28% for delays occurring between 2 and 4 weeks, by 6% in the change from 2 to 3 months, and by 60% in the change from 14 days to 91 days. It should be noted that delays of over 90 days in cheque issuing may have been associated with a denial status, making it necessary for the claimant to invest more energy in their claim process. This also suggests that the denial of a claim has even stronger negative impact than delay in processing.

BOX 5.4. Insurer Factors Predictive of RTW Outcomes

- The impact of insurer factors interact with other factors such as job security, previous earnings, tenure, and number of dependents.
- A higher rate of compensation does not necessarily translate into longer time on benefits.
- Delays in the processing of claims can have a strong impact on the probability chronic work disability.

DEFINING RETURN-TO-WORK OUTCOMES

Levels of Return-to-Work

It is important to recognize that different meanings are given to the word "return-to-work". Return to work can be considered along a number of dimensions: Has the worker returned to 1) the same employer? 2) the same unit or work team? 3) the same job? 4) the same number of hours? These aspects have important implications for the worker's status with the compensation agency, income level, as well as occupational identity.

Methodological Aspects of Administrative Database and Self-Report

The most frequently used measure of RTW has been duration of time on benefits extracted from workers' compensation administrative databases. Despite its benefits of economical precision and wide accessibility, there is a consensus about the fact that cessation of benefits is not an adequate reflection of actual RTW (Baldwin, Johnson, & Butler, 1996; Butler & Worrall, 1985; Krause, Frank, Dasinger, Sullivan, & Sinclair, 2001b; Dasinger, Krause, Deegan, Brand, & Rudolph, 1999). In one study of California claimants, the difference between administrative measures and self-reported measures of first RTW had a mean of 142 days (C.I. 101–177) over a period of 3.7 years (Dasinger et al., 1999). Individuals may not return to work even if their benefits are terminated, and the reverse can occur as well (receiving benefits when back at work). Discrepancies between administrative data and self-report data of RTW also increase as time since injury increases (Dasinger et al., 1999).

Self-reports of RTW offer the advantage of capturing non-compensated time off work due to poor health, such as sick leave, unpaid leave, personal days, vacation days used when sick/injured, and to capture time off work when the claim has been denied by the compensation system or abandoned.

The Challenge of Sustainability of Return-to-Work

The natural history of low back pain, and possibly of other MSK disorders, is marked by recurrences of symptoms and its course can be characterized as chronic-recurrent (Pengel, Herbert, Maher, & Refshauge, 2003; Von Korff, Barlow, Cherkin, & Deyo, 1994; Von Korff, 1994). A similar pattern is observed when examining MSK related work disability as an outcome: a first RTW is frequently followed by one or more recurrences of work disability, making a focus on first RTW an overly limited, and potentially misguiding index of RTW outcomes, and one that does not address the important issue of sustainability of RTW (Krause et al., 2001b; Butler et al., 1995). Recurrence rates of work disability vary between 20% and 44% at 1 year post-injury in workers with low back pain (Bergquist-Ullman et al., 1977; Nachemson, 1991; Abenhaim, Suissa, & Rossignol, 1988; Rossignol, Suissa, & Abenhaim, 1988; Troup, Martin, & Lloyd, 1981) , are 14% in workers with general work-related MSK disorders (Manno et al., 2000), and are as high as 36.3% 3 years after the inception low back pain episode (Abenhaim et al., 1988; Rossignol et al., 1988; Rossignol, Suissa, & Abenhaim, 1992). The number and duration of work disability episodes subsequent to the first episode following an injury is a critical outcome for the assessment of sustainability of RTW. For that reason, it is important to evaluate the impact of RTW interventions and strategies with a follow-up of sufficient duration in order to assess the sustainability of the first RTW.

The follow-up period of prospective studies to date is typically insufficient to allow full understanding of the risk factors for chronic and recurrent work disability (Krause et al., 2001b). Researchers advocate a follow-up period ranging between

2 and 5 years (Krause et al., 2001b; Nachemson & Andersson, 1982; Troup et al., 1981).

Defining Recurrences of Work Disability

Various definitions of "recurrence" can apply, with varying levels of inclusiveness. A recurrence can capture work disability due to the original MSK injury, due to a new MSK injury, due to other types of injuries, or to a combination of the 3 categories. Criterion duration of episodes and duration between episodes can also vary. One study (Wang, 2000) examined workers' compensation data from 5,346 employees with lost-time claims of soft tissue injuries (STI) over a 6 year follow-up. Within the 6 year period, 21.8% of claimants re-opened their original claim or had a new STI claim in same part of body, and an additional 15.2% had a new STI claim in another part of body for a total of 37%. When claims due to injuries other than STIs were included, number of recurrences increased dramatically to 47.8%.

The large number of recurrences due to injuries other than the original injury raises the possibility that a person with an MSK disorder is at risk of suffering from other MSK and other physical problems. This "cascading effect" points to the possibility of an increased vulnerability, which could have various underlying mechanisms. One possible mechanism is through direct physiological mediation, such as compensatory overuse of an originally not afflicted body part and/or due to concurrent problems in job and workstation design. Another mechanism is indirect mediation through the physiological impacts of psychological distress (Cassel, 1976; Geiss, Varadi, Steinbach, Bauer, & Anton, 1997; Lundberg & Melin, 2002; Melzack, 1999) and social stressors.

Expanding Return-to-Work Outcomes

The total burden of work-disability exceeds traditional measures of RTW such as time on benefits. Recent data suggest that indirect costs of disability are double those of direct costs (Leigh, Cone & Harrison, 2001).

It is important to examine the relationship between worker, insurer, and employer outcomes. Although these players may seem to have conflicting agendas, research which considers the outcomes concurrently can show that RTW can be a mutually beneficial situation. For instance, Lerner (Lerner et al., 2003) showed that for every 10% increase in work limitations associated with an unspecified cause, there was an 4 to 5% decrease in productivity. As well, a randomized controlled trial of three workplace-based RTW interventions (occupational only, clinical only, occupational and clinical combined) primarily targeting the subacute phase of disability showed that when compared to standard care, over a six year follow-up period, the three interventions all reduced insurer costs, and also benefitted workers in that they were work disabled for significantly less time (Loisel et al., 2002a). These effects were most pronounced for the intervention which combined both clinical and occupational components. It should be noted that the cost-beneficial effects of the clinical and combined clinical/occupational interventions were not yet apparent in the first year of follow-up but emerged over the course of the six year follow-up. These results speak to the importance of incorporating longer follow-up periods in research design to address the issue of sustainability of RTW and of cost reduction.

There is also a need to include quality of life outcomes, which are neither part of direct or indirect costs. These include reduced role participation in family and social roles, reduced quality of work life, and increased pain and suffering.

FUTURE PRIORITIES FOR RESEARCH IN WORK DISABILITY

Several areas of work disability remain underdeveloped. While we know that the provision of work accommodation is a critical component of effective disability management, we remain poorly informed about the most effective process by which a work accommodation offer should be developed and offered in order to facilitate its acceptance and its contribution to a sustainable RTW. The role of the healthcare provider in the development of a realistic work accommodation deserves further consideration as well. With respect to insurance factors, most of the research conducted has focused on the impact of the rate of compensation. It is now clear that rate of compensation should be considered with rigorous research designs which include the control for confounding variables such as job security, previous earnings, number of dependents. Qualitative research suggests that the type of interactions injured workers have with representatives of their insurance companies may influence the course of their work disability. Future research should focus on understanding the impact of interaction patterns with insurance representatives and of the processing of claims on work disability.

Given the multifactorial nature of the development of work disability, special attention should be given to the careful consideration and control of confounding variables. In addition, outcomes of research should be expanded to consider general quality of life and quality of work life. Research designs should address the issue of phase-specificity by measuring time since injury. Given the recurring nature of MSK disorders, as well as of other physical conditions, the additional expense associated with longer duration of follow-up is warranted.

CONCLUSIONS

This chapter has focused on modifiable determinant factors in the development of work disability. Four domains of factors have been considered, using a phase-specific framework when possible: the individual, the workplace, the healthcare provider, and the insurer.

When considering the specific nature of the factors, it becomes apparent that an array of strategies are necessary to fully address the problem of work disability. At the individual level, functional ability, pain, coexisting medical conditions and psychological distress may most efficiently be addressed with clinical interventions. The workplace factors involve disability management strategies, provision of work accommodation, physical and psychosocial work conditions, and higher-level organizational factors. The diverse nature of workplace factors affecting RTW and its sustainability suggest that a multi-level approach to changing the workplace may be most judicious. Indeed, the literature on workplace interventions suggests that a gradual and multi-level approach (e.g. approaching ergonomic aspects, supervisory aspects and top management messages) appears to yield the best results (Kristensen,

2000). Regarding the healthcare system, healthcare providers would benefit from obtaining more education regarding work disability in order to increase their likelihood of and their comfort in addressing workplace factors with their patients. A more expedient access to necessary diagnostic tests and treatment would also prevent patients from entering the "deconditioning" cycle and developing negative expectations about their RTW.

Given the paucity of research on insurance factors other than compensation rates, it is not yet clear what kind of changes within insurance systems should occur in order to promote safe and sustainable RTW. However, there is now strong evidence available (Sinnott, 2003) that more expedient processing of claims and reduction of unwarranted denial of claims may reduce the risk of chronic work disability. Policy changes addressing the overall compensation system functioning as well as internal functioning will most likely be effective modes of meaningful change. Finally, for researchers, clinicians, workplace representatives, and insurance representatives, it is important to recognize the recurring nature of many occupational disorders, most notably MSK disorders. This will have repercussions on the development of research designs, on interventions, and on developing realistic expectations regarding outcomes.

REFERENCES

Abenhaim, L., Rossignol, M., Gobeille, D., Bonvalot, Y., Fines, P., & Scott, S. (1995). The prognostic consequences in the making of the initial medical diagnosis of work-related back injuries. *Spine, 20,* 791–795.

Abenhaim, L. & Suissa, S. (1987). Importance and economic burden of occupational back pain: a study of 2,500 cases representative of Quebec. *Journal of Occupational Medicine, 29(8),* 670–674.

Abenhaim, L., Suissa, S., & Rossignol, M. (1988). Risk of recurrence of occupational back pain over three year follow up. *British Journal of Industrial Medicine, 45,* 829–833.

Agency for Health care Policy and Research (1994). *Clinical practice guideline: Acute low back problems in adults.* (Rep. No. 14). Rockville: US: Department of Health and Human Services.

Allen, J. K., Becker, D. M., & Swank, R. T. (1990). Factors related to functional status after coronary artery bypass surgery. *Heart & Lung, 19,* 337–343.

Amick III, B. C., Habeck, R. V., Hunt, A., Fossel, A. H., Chapin, A., Keller, R. B. et al. (2000). Measuring the impact of Organizational Behaviors on work disability prevention and management. *Journal of Occupational Rehabilitation, 10,* 21–38.

Ash, P. & Goldstein, S. I. (1995). Predictor of returning to work. *Bulletin of American Academy of Psychiatry Law, 23,* 205–210.

Association of Workers' Compensation Boards of Canada (2001). *Work injuries and disease, 1998–2000.*

Baldwin, M. L., Johnson, W. G., & Butler, R. J. (1996). The error of using returns-to-work to measure the outcomes of health care. *American Journal of Industrial Medicine, 29,* 632–641.

Bandura, A. (1977). Self-efficacy: toward a unifying theory of behavioral change. *Psychol Rev, 84,* 191–215.

Bergquist-Ullman, M. & Larsson, U. (1977). Acute low back pain in industry. A controlled prospective study with special reference to therapy and confounding factors. *Acta Orthopaedica Scandinavia (Suppl), 170,* 1–117.

Bernacki, E. J., Guidera, J. A., Schaefer, J. A., & Tsai, S. (2000). A facilitated early return to work program at a large urban medical center. *Journal of Occupational & Environmental Medicine, 42,* 1172–1177.

Bloch, F. S. & Prins, R. (2001). *Who returns to work and why? A six-country study on work incapacity and reintegration* . New Brunswick, New Jersey: Transaction Publishers.

Boden, L. I. & Galizzi, M. (1999). Economic consequences of workplace injuries and illnesses: lost earnings and benefit adequacy. *American Journal of Industrial Medicine, 36,* 487–503.

Brooker, A.-S., Cole, D. C., Hogg-Johnson, S., Smith, J., & Frank, J. W. (2001). Modified work: prevalence and characteristics in a sample of workers with soft-tissue injuries. *Journal of Occupational & Environmental Medicine, 43*, 276–284.

Butler, R. J., Johnson, W. G., & Baldwin, M. (1995). Managing work disability: Why first return to work is not a measure of success. *Industrial and Labor Relations Review, 48*, 452–469.

Butler, R. J. & Worrall, J. D. (1985). Work injury compensation and the duration of nonwork spells. *Economic Journal, The, 95(379)*, 714–724.

Cassel, J. (1976). The contribution of the social environment to host resistance. *American Journal of Epidemiology, 104*, 107–123.

Cheadle, A., Franklin, G., Wolfhagen, C., Savarino, J., Liu, P. Y., Salley, C. et al. (1994). Factors influencing the duration of work-related disability: a population-based study of Washington State workers' compensation. *American Journal of Public Health, 84*, 190–196.

Clarke, J. & Cole, D. F. S. (2000). Return to work after a soft tissue injury: A qualitative exploration. Working Paper # 127. Institute for Work & Health.

Clarke, J. & Cote, P. (2000). Work-ready: return-to-work approaches for people with soft-tissue injuries. Toronto, IWH/WSIB. Clinical Grand Rounds.

Cole, D. C., Mondloch, M. V., & Hogg-Johnson, S. (2002). Listening to injured workers: how recovery expectations predict outcomes—a prospective study. *CMAJ, 166*, 749–754.

Coste, J., Delecoeuillerie, G., Cohen, D. L., Le Parc, J. M., & Paolaggi, J. B. (1994). Clinical course and prognostic factors in acute low back pain: an inception cohort study in primary care practice. *British Medical Journal, 308*, 577–580.

Côté, P., Clarke, J., Deguire, S., Frank, J. W., & Yassi, A. (2000). *Chiropractors and return-to-work: the experiences of three Canadian focus groups*. Toronto: Institute for Work & Health.

Côté, P., Hogg-Johnson, S., Cassidy, D., Carroll, L., & Frank, J. W. (2001). The association between neck pain intensity, physical functioning, depressive symptomatology and time-to-claim closure after whiplash. *Journal of Clinical Epidemiology, 54*, 275–286.

Coyne, J. C. & Schwenk, T. L. (1995). Nondetection of depression by primary care physicians reconsidered. *General Hospital Psychiatry, 17*, 3–12.

Dasinger, L. K., Krause, N., Deegan, L. J., Brand, R. J., & Rudolph, L. (1999). Duration of work disability after low back injury: a comparison of administrative and self-reported outcomes. *American Journal of Industrial Medicine, 35*, 619–631.

Dasinger, L. K., Krause, N., Deegan, L. J., Brand, R. J., & Rudolph, L. (2000). Physical workplace factors and return to work after compensated low back injury: a disability phase-specific analysis. *J Occup Environ Med, 42*, 323–333.

Dasinger, L. K., Krause, N., Thompson, P. J., Brand, R. J., & Rudolph, L. (2001). Doctor proactive communication, return-to-work recommendation, and duration of disability after a workers' compensation low back injury. *J Occup. Environ. Med., 43*, 515–525.

Dersh, J., Gatchel, R. J., Polatin, P., & Mayer, T. (2002). Prevalence of psychiatric disorders in patients with chronic work-related musculoskeletal pain disability. *J Occup Environ Med, 44*, 459–468.

Diederiks, J. P. M., van der Sluijs, H., Weeda, H. W. H., & Schobre, M. G. (1983). Predictors of physical activity one year after myocardial infarction. *Scand J Rehab Med, 15*, 103–107.

Dionne, C., Koepsell, T. D., Von Korff, M., Deyo, R. A., Barlow, W. E., & Checkoway, H. (1995). Formal education and back-related disability: in search of an explantion. *Spine, 20*, 2721–2730.

Dozois, D. J. A., Dobson, K. S., Wong, M., Hughes, D., & Long, A. (1995). Factors associated with rehabilitation outcome in patients with low back pain (LBP): prediction of employment outcome at 9-month follow-up. *Rehabilitation Psychology, 40*, 243–259.

Feuerstein, M. & Thebarge, R. W. (1991). Perceptions of disability and occupational stress as discriminators of work disability in patients with chronic pain. *Journal of Occupational Rehabilitation, 1*, 135–195.

Fitzler, S. L. & Berger, R. A. (1983). Chelsea back program: one year later. *OH & S Canada, 52(7)*, 52–54.

Flood, A. B., Lorence, D. P., Ding, J., McPherson, K., & Black, N. A. (1993). The role of expectations in patients' reports of post-operative outcomes and improvement following therapy. *Medical Care, 31*, 1043–1056.

Fortin, B. & Lanoie, P. (1992). Substitution between unemployment insurance and workers' compensation: an analysis applied to the risk of workplace accidents. *Journal of Public Economics, 49*, 287–312.

Franche, R.-L. & Krause, N. (2003). Critical factors in recovery and return to work. In T.Sullivan & J. Frank (Eds.), *Preventing & Managing Disabling Injury at Work* (pp. 33–55). New York, U.S.A.: Taylor & Francis.

Franche, R. L. & Krause, N. (2002). Readiness for return to work following injury or illness: conceptualizing the interpersonal impact of health care, workplace, and insurance factors. *J Occup Rehabil, 12,* 233–256.

Franche, R. L., Mustard, C., Krause, N., Hepburn, G., Breslin, C., Kosny, A. et al. (2003). Summary of the return-to-work pilot study. Toronto: Institute for Work & Health.

Frank, J., Sinclair, S., Hogg-Johnson, S., Shannon, H., Bombardier, C., Beaton, D. et al. (1998). Preventing disability from work-related low-back pain: new evidence gives new hope—if we can just get all the players onside. *CMAJ, 158,* 1625–1631.

Frank, J. W., Brooker, AS., DeMaio, S., Kerr, M. S., Maetzel, A., Shannon, H. S. et al. (1996). Disability resulting from occupational low back pain part II: What do we know about secondary prevention? A review of the scientific evidence on prevention after disability begins. *Spine, 21,* 2918–2929.

Frank, J. W. & Guzman, J. (1999). *Facilitation of return to work after a soft tissue injury: synthesizing the evidence and experience: A HEALNet report on the findings of the Work-Ready project.* HEALNet.

Friesen, M. N., Yassi, A., & Cooper, J. (2001). Return-to-work: The importance of human interactions and organizational structures. *Work, 17,* 11–22.

Galizzi, M. & Boden, L. I. (1996). *What are the most important factors shaping return to work? Evidence from Wisconsin.* Workers Compensation Research Institute.

Gatchel, R. J. & Gardea, M. A. (1999). Psychosocial issues: their importance in predicting disability, response to treatment, and search for compensation. *Neurologic Clinics, 17,* 149–166.

Gatchel, R. J., Polatin, P. B., & Mayer, T. G. (1995). The dominant role of psychosocial risk factors in the development of chronic low back pain disability. *Spine, 20,* 2702–2709.

Geiss, A., Varadi, E., Steinbach, K., Bauer, H. W., & Anton, F. (1997). Psychoneuroimmunological correlates of persisting sciatic pain in patients who underwent discectomy. *Neuroscience. Letters, 237,* 65–68.

Gice, J. H. & Tompkins, K. (1989). Return to work in a hospital setting. *Journal of Business and Psychology, 4,* 237–243.

Habeck, R. V., Leahy, M. J., Hunt, H. A., Chan, F., & Welch, E. M. (1991). Employer factors related to workers' compensation claims and disability management. *Rehabilitation Counselling Bulletin, 34(3),* 210–226.

Hiebert, R., Skovron, M. L., Nordin, M., & Crane, M. (2003). Work restrictions and outcome of nonspecific low back pain. *Spine, 28,* 722–728.

Himmelstein, J. S., Feuerstein, M., Stanek, E. J. I., Koyamatsu, K., Pransky, G. S., Morgan, W. et al. (1995). Work-related upper-extremity disorders and work disability: clinical and psychosocial presentation. *Journal of Occupational and Environmental Medicine, 35,* 1278–1286.

Hogelund, J. (2000). *Bringing the sick back to work: Labor market reintegration of the long-term sicklisted in the Netherlands and Denmark.* Danish national Institute of Social Research. Roskilede University, Copenhagen.

Hogg-Johnson, S. & Cole, D. C. (2003). Early prognostic factors for duration on temporary total benefits in the first year among workers with compensated occupational soft tissue injuries. *Occupational and Environmental Medicine, 60,* 244–253.

Hogg-Johnson, S., Frank, J. W., & Rael, E. G. S. (1994). *Prognostic risk factor models for low back pain: why they have failed and a new hypothesis.* Toronto: OWCI.

Hunt, H. A., Habeck, R. V., & Leahy, M. J. (1993). Firm characteristics and workers' compensation claims incidence. In D. Durbin & P. S. Borba (Eds.), *Workers' compensation insurance: claim costs, prices, and regulation.* (pp. 243–292). Boston: Kluwer Academic Publishers.

Hunt, H. A., Habeck, R. V., VanTol, B., & Scully, S. M. (1993). *Disability prevention among Michigan employers, 1988–1993.* Michigan: W.E. Upjohn Institute for Employment Research.

Infante-Rivard, C. & Lortie, M. (1996). Prognostic factors for return to work after a first compensated episode of back pain. *Occupational and Environmental Medicine, 53,* 488–494.

Injured Workers' Participatory Research Project. (2001). *Making the System Better: Injured Workers Speak Out on the Compensation System and Return to Work Issues in Ontario.* Toronto, Ontario..

Jamison, R. N., Parris, W. C., & Maxson, W. S. (1987). Psychological factors influencing recovery from outpatient surgery. *Behavior, Research and Therapy, 25,* 31–37.

Johnson, W. G., Butler, R. J., & Baldwin M (1995). First spells of work absences among Ontario workers. In T. Thomason & R. P. Chaykowski (Eds.), *Research in Canadian workers' compensation.* (pp. 73–84). Kingston: IRC Press.

Keogh, J. P., Gucer, P., Gordon, J. L., & Nuwayhid, I. (2000). Patterns and predictors of Employer Risk-Reduction Activities (ERRAs) in response to a work-related Upper Extremity Cumulative Trauma Disorder (UECTD): reports from workers' compensation claimants. *American Journal of Industrial Medicine, 38,* 489–497.

Kirmayer, L. J., Robbins, J. M., Dworkind, M., & Yaffe, M. J. (1993). Somatization and the recognition of depression and anxiety in primary care. *American Journal of Psychiatry, 150,* 734–741.

Kralj B. (1995). Experience rating of workers' compensation insurance premiums and the duration of workplace injuries. In Thomason T. & R. Chaykowski (Eds.), *Research in Canadian Workers' Compensation* (pp. 106–121). Kingston: IRC Press.

Krause, N., Dasinger, L. K., Deegan, L. J., Rudolph, L., & Brand, R. J. (2001a). Psychosocial job factors and return-to-work after compensated low back injury: a disability phase-specific analysis. *American Journal of Industrial Medicine, 40,* 374–392.

Krause, N., Dasinger, L. K., & Neuhauser, F. (1998). Modified work and return to work: a review of the literature. *Journal of Occupational Rehabilitation, 8,* 113–139.

Krause, N., Frank, J. W., Dasinger, L. K., Sullivan, T., & Sinclair, S. J. (2001). Determinants of duration of disability and return to work after work-related injury and illness: Challenges for future research. *American Journal of Industrial Medicine, 40,* 464-484.

Krause, N., Lynch, J., Kaplan, G. A., Cohen, R. D., Goldberg, D. E., & Salonen, J. T. (1997a). Predictors of disability retirement. *Scandinavian Journal of Work, Environment and Health, 23,* 403–413.

Krause, N. & Ragland, D. R. (1994). Occupational disability due to low back pain: a new interdisciplinary classification based on a phase model of disability. *Spine, 19,* 1011–1020.

Krause, N., Ragland, D. R., Greiner, B. A., Syme, S. L., & Fisher, J. M. (1997b). Psychosocial job factors associated with back and neck pain in public transit operators. *Scandinavian Journal of Work, Environment and Health, 23,* 179–186.

Kristensen, T. S. (1991). Sickness absence and work strain among Danish slaughterhouse workers: an analysis of absence from work regarded as coping behaviour. *Social Science and Medicine, 32,* 15–27.

Kristensen, T. S. (2000). Workplace interventions studies. *Occupational Medicine: State of the Art Reviews, 15,* 293–305.

Lanoie, P. (1992). The impact of occupational safety and health regulation on the risk of workplace accidents: Quebec, 1983–87. *Journal of Human Resources, 27(4),* 643–660.

Leigh, J. P., Cone, J. E., & Harrison, R. (2001). Costs of occupational injuries and illnesses in California. *Preventive Medicine, 32,* 393–406.

Lerner, D., Amick, B. C., III, Lee, J. C., Rooney, T., Rogers, W. H., Chang, H. et al. (2003). Relationship of employee-reported work limitations to work productivity. *Medical Care, 41,* 649–659.

Lindstrom, I., Ohlund, C., Eek, C., Wallin, L., Peterson, L. E., Fordyce, W. E. et al. (1992). The effect of graded activity on patients with subacute low back pain: a randomized prospective clinical study with an operant-conditioning behavioral approach. *Physical Therapy, 72(4),* 279–293.

Loisel, P., Durand, M.-J., Berthelette, D., Vezina, N., Baril, R., Gagnon, D. et al. (2001). Disability prevention: New paradigm for the management of occupational back pain. *Disease Management & Health Outcomes, 9,* 351–360.

Loisel, P., Lemaire, J., Poitras, S., Durand, M.-J., Champagne, F., Stock, S. et al. (2002a). Cost-benefit and cost-effectiveness analysis of a disability prevention model for back pain management: a six year follow up study. *Occupational & Environmental Medicine, 59,* 807–815.

Loisel, P., Vachon, B., Lemaire, J., Durand, M. J., Poitras, S., Stock, S. et al. (2002b). Discriminative and predictive validity assessment of the Quebec task force classification. *Spine, 27,* 851–857.

Lund, T. (2001). *Associations between health and work disability.* University of Copenhagen.

Lundberg, U. & Melin, B. (2002). Stress in the development of musculoskeletal pain. In S. J. Linton (Ed.), *New Avenues for the Prevention of Chronic Musculoskeletal Pain and Disability* (pp. 165–182). Amsterdam: Elsevier.

MacKenzie, E. J., Morris, J. A., Jurkovich, G. J., Yasui, Y., Cushing, B. M., Burgess, A. R. et al. (1998). Return to work following injury: The role of economic, social and job-related factors. *American Journal of Public Health, 88,* 1630–1637.

Manno M. & Hogg-Johnson, S. (2000). *Multistate Hazard Models for Analyzing Recurrences of Soft-tissue Injuries* (Rep. No. Working Paper #88.). Institute for Work & Health.

Marklund, S. (1995). Rehabilitering i ett samhallsperspektiv.

Melchior, M., Berkman, L. F., Niedhammer, I., Chea, M., & Goldberg, M. (2003). Social relations and self-reported health: a prospective analysis of the French Gazel cohort. *Social Science and Medicine, 56,* 1817–1830.

Melchior, M., Niedhammer, I., Berkman, L. F., & Goldberg, M. (2003). Do psychosocial work factors and social relations exert independent effects on sickness absence? A six year prospective study of the GAZEL cohort. *Journal of Epidemiology and Community Health, 57,* 285–293.

Melzack, R. (1999). Pain and Stress: A New Perspective. In R.J. Gatchel & D. C. Turk (Eds.), *Psychological Factors in Pain. Critical Perspectives.* (pp. 89–106). New York: The Guilford Press.

Mondloch, M. V., Cole, D. C., & Frank, J. W. (2001). Working Paper # 72. Does how you do depend how you think you'll do? A structured review of the evidence for a relation between patients' recovery expectations and outcomes. *Canadian Medical Association Journal, 165,* 174–179.

Nachemson, A. L. (1991). *Back Pain. Causes, diagnosis, and treatment.* Stockhom.: The Swedish Council of Technology Assessment in Health Care.

Nachemson, A. L. & Andersson, G. B. J. (1982). Classification of low-back pain. *Scandinavian Journal of Work, Environment and Health, 8(2),* 134–136.

National Institute of Disability Management and Research (2000). *Code of practice for disability management. Describing effective benchmarks for the creation of workplace-based disability management programs.* National Institute of Disability Management and Research.

National Research Council, Panel on Musculoskeletal Disorders and the Workplace, Commission on Behavioral and Social Sciences and Education & Institute of Medicine (2001). *Musculoskeletal disorders and the workplace. Low back and upper extremities.* Washington, DC: National Academy Press.

Nordin, M., Hiebert, R., Pietrek, M., Alexander, M., Crane, M., & Lewis, S. (2002). Association of comorbidity and outcome in episodes of nonspecific low back pain in occupational populations. *Journal of Occupational and Environmental Medicine, 44,* 677–684.

Oleinick, A., Gluck, J. V., & Guire, K. (1996). Factors affecting first return to work following a compensable occupational back injury. *American Journal of Industrial Medicine, 30,* 540–555.

Ormel, J., Vonkorff, M., Oldehinkel, A. J., Simon, G., Tiemens, B. G., & Ustun, T. B. (1999). Onset of disability in depressed and non-depressed primary care patients. *Psychological Medicine, 29,* 847–853.

Pengel, L. H. M., Herbert, R. D., Maher, C. G., & Refshauge, K. M. (2003). Acute low back pain: systematic review of its prognosis. *British Medical Journal, 327,* 1–5.

Perez-Stable, E. J., Miranda, J., Munoz, R. F., & Ying, Y. W. (1990). Depression in medical outpatients. Underrecognition and misdiagnosis. *Archives Internal Medicine, 150,* 1083–1088.

Pransky, G., Benjamin, K., Hill-Fotouhi, C., Fletcher, K. E., Himmelstein, J., & Karz, J. (2002). Work-related outcomes in Occupational Low Back Pain: A Multidimensional Analysis, *Spine, 27*(3), 864–870.

Pransky, G., Benjamin, K., Hill-Fotouhi, C., Himmelstein, J., Fletcher, K. E., Katz, J. N. et al. (2000). Outcomes in work-related upper extremity and low back injuries: Results of a retrospective study. *American Journal of Industrial Medicine, 37,* 400–409.

Pransky, G., Benjamin, K., Himmelstein, J., Mundt, K., Morgan, W., Feuerstein, M. et al. (1999). Work-related upper-extremity disorders: prospective evaluation of clinical and functional outcomes. *Journal of Occupational and Environmental Medicine, 41,* 884–892.

Pransky, G., Katz, J. N., Benjamin, K., & Himmelstein, J. (2002). Improving the physican role in evaluation work ability and managing disability: a survey of primary care practitioners. *Disability & Rehabilitation, 24,* 867–874.

Prochaska, J. O. & Di Clemente, C. C. (1992). Stages of change in the modification of problem behaviors. *Progress in Behavior Modification, 28,* 183–218.

Prochaska, J. O., Velicer, W. F., Rossi, J. S., Goldstein, M. G., Marcus, B. H., Rakowski, W. et al. (1994). Stages of change and decisional balance for 12 problem behaviors. *Health Psychology, 13,* 39–46.

Reiso, H., Nygard, F., Jorgensen, S., Holanger, R., Soldal, D., & Bruusgaard, D. (2003). Back to Work: Predictors of Return to Work Among Patients With Back Disorders Certified As Sick: A Two-Year Follow-up Study. *Spine, 28,* 1468–1473.

Rossignol, M., Suissa, S., & Abenhaim, L. (1988). Working disability due to occupational back pain: three-year follow-up of 2,300 compensated workers in Quebec. *Journal of Occupational Medicine, 30,* 502–505.

Rossignol, M., Suissa, S., & Abenhaim, L. (1992). The evolution of compensated occupational spinal injuries: a three-year follow-up study. *Spine, 17(9),* 1043–1047.

Sandstrom, J. & Esbjornsson, E. (1986). Return to work after rehabilitation. The significance of the patient's own prediction. *Scandinavian Journal of Rehabilitation Medicine, 18,* 29–33.

Schade, B., Semmer, N., Main, C. J., Hora, J., & Boos, N. (1999). The impact of clinical, morphological, psychosocial and work-related factors on the outcome of lumbar discectomy. *Pain, 80,* 239–249.

Schultz, I. Z., Crook, J., Fraser, K., & Joy, P. W. (2000). Models of diagnosis and rehabilitation in musculoskeletal pain-related occupational disability. *Journal of Occupational Rehabilitation, 10,* 271–293.

Schultz, I. Z., Crook, J. M., Berkowitz, J., Meloche, G. R., Milner, R., & Zuberbier, O. A. et al. (2002). Biopsychosocial multivariate predictive model of occupational low back disability. *Spine, 27,* 2720–2725.

Selim, A. J., Ren, X., Gincke, G., Deyo, R., Rogers, W., Miller, D. et al. (1998). The importance of radiating leg pain in assessing health outcomes among patients with low back pain. Results from the Veterans Health Study. *Spine, 23,* 470–474.

Simon, G., Ormel, J., VonKorff, M., & Barlow, W. (1995). Health care costs associated with depressive and anxiety disorders in primary care. *American Journal of Psychiatry, 152,* 352–357.

Sinclair, S. J., Hogg-Johnson, S. A., Mondloch, M. V., & Shields, S. A. (1997). The effectiveness of an early active intervention program for workers with soft tissue injuries: the Early Claimant Cohort study. *Spine, 22,* 2919–2931.

Sinnott, P. (2003). *Administrative delay and secondary disability following acute occupational low back injury.* University of California in Berkeley.

Smith, J., Tarasuk, V., Ferrier, S., & Shannon, H. (1996). Relationship between workers' reports of problems and legitimacy and vulnerability in the workplace a duration of benefits for lost-time musculoskeletal injuries. American Journal of Epidemiology 143[11], S17.

Smith, J. M., Tarasuk, V., Shannon, H., Ferrier, S., & ECC Prognosis Modelling Group (1998). *Prognosis of musculoskeletal disorders: effects of legitimacy and job vulnerability.* (IWH Working Paper #67 ed.) Toronto: Institute for Work & Health.

Spitzer, W. O., LeBlanc, F. E., Dupuis, M., Abenhaim, L., Belanger, A. Y., Bloch, R. et al. (1987). Scientific approach to the assessment and management of activity-related spinal disorders: a monograph for clinicians. Report of the Quebec task force on spinal disorders. *Spine, 12(7S),* S4–S55.

Sullivan, M. J., Stanish, W., Waite, H., Sullivan, M., & Tripp, D. A. (1998). Catastrophizing, pain, and disability in patients with soft-tissue injuries. *Pain, 77,* 253–260.

Tarasuk, V. & Eakin, J. M. (1994). "Back problems are for life": perceived vulnerability and its implications for chronic disability. *Journal of Occupational Rehabilitation, 4(1),* 55–64.

Tarasuk, V. & Eakin, J. M. (1995). The problem of legitimacy in the experience of work-related back injury. *Qualitative Health Research, 5,* 204–221.

Theorell, T., Harms-Ringdahl, K., Ahlberg-Hulten, G., & Westin, B. (1991). Psychosocial job factors and symptoms from the locomotor system—a multicausal analysis. *Scandinavian Journal of Rehabilitation Medicine, 23,* 165–173.

Thomason, T. & Pozzebon, S. (1995). The effect of workers' compensation benefits on claims incidence in Canada. In Thomason T. & R. Chaykowski (Eds.), *Research in Canadian Workers' Compensation* (pp. 53–69). Kingston: IRC Press.

Troup, J. D. G., Martin, J. W., & Lloyd, D. C. E. F. (1981). Back pain in industry: a prospective study. *Spine, 6(1),* 61–69.

van der Giezen, A. M., Bouter, L. M., & Nijhuis, F. J. N. (2000). Prediction of return-to-work of low back pain patients sicklisted for 3-4 months. *Pain, 87,* 285–294.

van der Weide, W. E., Verbeek, J. H. A. M., Salle, H. J. A., & van Dijk, F. J. H. (1999). Prognostic factors for chronic disability from acute low-back pain in occupational health care. *Scandinavian Journal of Work, Environment and Health, 25,* 50–56.

Velicer, W. F., Norman, G. J., Fava, J. L., & Prochaska, J. O. (1999). Testing 40 predictions from the transtheoretical model. *Addictive Behaviors, 24,* 455–469.

Vlaeyen, J. W. & Linton, S. J. (2000). Fear-avoidance and its consequences in chronic musculoskeletal pain: a state of the art. *Pain, 85,* 317–332.

Von Korff, M. (1994). Studying the natural history of back pain. *Spine, 19,* 2041S–2046S.

Von Korff, M., Barlow, W., Cherkin, D., & Deyo, R. A. (1994). Effects of practice style in managing back pain. *Annals of Internal Medicine, 121,* 187–195.

Von Korff, M. & Simon, G. (1996). The relationship between pain and depression. *British Journal of Psychiatry - Supplement,* 101–108.

Waddell, G., Burton, A. K., & Main, C. J. (2003). *Screening to identify people at risk of long-term incapacity for work: A Conceptual and Scientific Review.* London.: The Royal Society of Medicine Press.

Waddell, G., Newton, M., Henderson, I., Somerville, D., & Main, C. J. (1993). A fear-avoidance beliefs questionnaire (FABQ) and the role of fear-avoidance beliefs in chronic low back pain and disability. *Pain, 52,* 157–168.

Waehrer, G. M., Miller, R., Ruser, J., & Leigh, J. P. (1998). Restricted work, workers' compensation, and days away from work.

Wang, H. (2000). *A follow-up study of workers with soft tissue injuries using the databases of the Ontario Workplace Safety & Insurance Board (WSIB).* Toronto: University of Toronto.

Wells, K. B., Hays, R. D., Burnam, M. A., Rogers, W., Greenfield, S., & Ware, J. E., Jr. (1989). Detection of depressive disorder for patients receiving prepaid of fee-for-service care - results from the medical outcomes study. *Journal of the American Medical Association, 262(23),* 3298–3302.

Yassi, A., Tate, R., Cooper, J. E., Snow, C., Vallentyne, S., & Khokhar, J. B. (1995a). Early intervention for back-injured nurses at a large Canadian tertiary care hospital: an evaluation of the effectiveness and cost benefits of a two-year pilot project. *Occupational Medicine, 45,* 209–214.

Yelin, E., Henke, C. J., & Epstein, W. V. (1986a). Work disability among persons with musculoskeletal conditions. *Arthritis and Rheumatism, 29(11),* 1322–1333.

Yelin, E. H. (1986). The Myth of Malingering: Why Individuals Withdraw from Work in the Presence of Illness. *Milbank Memorial Fund Quarterly/ Health and Society, 64 (40),* 622–647.

Yelin, E. H., Nevitt, M. C., & Epstein, W. (1980). Toward an epidemiology of work disability. *Milbank Memorial Fund Quarterly/ Health and Society, 58(3),* 386–415.

6

Musculoskeletal Injury

A Three-Stage Continuum from Cause to Disability to Decision

Anna Wright Stowell and Donald D. McGeary

BACKGROUND

The United States Department of Labor (DOL) (2000) defines a musculoskeletal disorder as an injury or disorder of the muscles, tendons, ligaments, joints, cartilage, and spinal discs. A report by the DOL in 2000 revealed 593,000 musculoskeletal disorders were reported in the U.S. in 1998, with an average of five work days lost per injury claim (U.S. Department of Labor, 2000). Andersson, Pope and Frymoyer (1984) found a lifetime incidence of spinal disorders ranging from 51.4% to 70%. A report by the National Research Council (National Research Council, 2001) revealed that approximately 1 million American workers took time of work due to the occurrence of at least one musculoskeletal disorder in 1999, resulting in over $50 billion worth of lost time from work. The prevalence of musculoskeletal disorders was predicted to increase to 18.4% in 2002 (Linton, 2002).

Musculoskeletal disorders are a major problem, not only in the United States, but also in other industrialized nations (Badley, Rasooly, & Webster, 1994; Bergman et al., 2001; Gatchel, Mayer, Capra, Diamond, & Barnett, 1986). Linton (2002) reviewed research from the Netherlands revealing a costly epidemic of musculoskeletal disorders similar to that of the United States. Furthermore, Bergman and colleagues (2001) examined the prevalence of chronic musculoskeletal pain (CMP) among the population of a subsection of southwest Sweden, and found a 34.5% rate of musculoskeletal pain. They note, however, that other studies have found a lower prevalence. The authors found that musculoskeletal pain prevalence was associated with age, gender, socioeconomic status and ethnicity.

The lifetime incidence of musculoskeletal pain has been found to range from 15% to 80%, and it is expected to increase (Anderson et al., 1984; Cats-Baril & Frymoyer, 1991; National Research Council, 2001). CMP disorders are among the most costly afflictions affecting workers the world over. Costs associated with

DOI: 10.1007/978-0-387-28919-9_6, © 2009 Springer Science+Business Media, LLC

musculoskeletal pain disorders have been estimated to be as high as $200 billion a year, with the majority of the costs accounted for by indirect sources (e.g., time away from work, National Research Council, 2001).

It is therefore well established that disabling medical conditions result in significant personal and financial costs to individuals and society as a whole. However, there is inconsistency as to what defines disability (Bickenbach, Chatterji, Badley, & Ustun, 1999; Susman, 1994; Usten, Saxena, Rehm, & Bickenbach, 1999). Many individuals refer to "disabled people" as those who are unable to perform specific tasks or skills (e.g., driving or showering unassisted), or those who are limited in some way (e.g., hearing or vision impaired). Yet, others, such as the Social Security Administration, refer to a disabled person as one who is unable to engage in active employment due to physical or psychological impairments for a minimum period of one year, or that the disability will result in death (Social Security Online, 2003). Obviously, there is disparity among groups as to how to classify someone as disabled (Matheson, 2001; Verbrugge & Jette, 1994). This is a problem that the World Health Organization (WHO) has attempted to remedy by devising a standard definition of disability. Hunter (2001) described the changes in the WHO's 1997 International Classification of Impairment, Activities, and Participation (ICIDH-2), which was a more inclusive improvement on the previous 1980 International Classification of Impairment, Disabilities, and Handicaps (ICIDH) definition (WHO 1998). The new definition reflects three main areas of function and disablement, which includes the following: physiologic and/or psychological impairment; activity limitations (e.g., activities of daily living); and, restricted societal participation (e.g., community activities or work, Hunter, 2001). This latest ICIDH-2 definition facilitates discussion when looking at how individuals become "disabled" across the course of pain or injury. Because of the three-fold interaction of biological, personal and societal factors, researchers may more easily evaluate people across the healthcare continuum (Bickenbach et al., 1999).

On the basis of a survey of the literature on musculoskeletal injury across multiple fields, there appears to be three primary stages that comprise an injury continuum, which can be termed the "CDD Injury Continuum." The stages are Cause, Disability, and Decision. Stage One (Cause) focuses on injury causation. The Cause Stage stems from musculoskeletal injury literature cited in the fields of physical therapy and industrial psychology. Stage Two (Disability) focuses on the progression from injury to disability. The Disability Stage stems from musculoskeletal injury literature cited in the fields of medicine and psychology. Stage Three (Decision) focuses on a person's decision to return to work (RTW) or adapt to long-term disability. The Decision Stage stems from musculoskeletal injury literature cited in the fields of epidemiology, sociology, psychology, and medical anthropology. For the remainder of this Chapter, we will cover theories or models associated with each of these three stages of the CDD Injury Continuum, and will explain each stage from different theoretical perspectives. We will then present additional information about the principle participants associated with the CDD Injury Continuum.

STAGE ONE: CAUSE

This first stage in the CDD Injury Continuum encompasses the origin of injury arising out of the physical therapy literature. Kumar (2001), a leader in the field of injury causation, provides an excellent overview of the risk factors and biomechanical basis of musculoskeletal injury. For the purpose of this discussion, injury is defined as the "mechanical disruption of tissues resulting in pain" (Kumar, 2001, p.19). Kumar proposes four major theories of injury causation: (1) *Multivariate Interaction Theory of Musculoskeletal Precipitation*; (2) *Differential Fatigue Theory*; (3) *Cumulative Load Theory*; and (4) *Overexertion Theory*. The following provides an overview of these four theories.

The Multivariate Interaction Theory of Musculoskeletal Precipitation

The *Multivariate Interaction Theory of Musculoskeletal Precipitation* asserts that injury is the result of a complex interaction between genetic, morphological, psychosocial, and biomechanical factors (Kumar, 2001). The number of potential variables is vast, as is the number of possible combinations of variables that might influence injury precipitation. Unfortunately, though relative weightings of variables are discussed in terms of impact on the individual, an actual algorithm for weighting such factors is not provided.

The Differential Fatigue Theory

The *Differential Fatigue Theory* posits that industries are economically motivated to employ workers in jobs that consist of repetitive functional tasks (Kumar, 2001). Such repetitive movements of workers serve to allow for greater quality control, increased productivity tracking and reduced training costs. The *Differential Fatigue Theory* asserts that the economic incentives for such repetitive tasks are at the cost of short-term fatigue and long-term increased likelihood for injury. This theory was built largely on the work of Kumar and Narayan (1998, as cited in Kumar, 2001) in which they studied the effect of maximal voluntary contraction of 14 trunk muscles during rotation. They found that, over time, as muscles fatigued, individuals were able to generate less force and were more likely to engage in abnormal or unnatural joint motion in response to the fatigue, as a means of compensating reduced function, thus leading to potential injury.

The Cumulative Load Theory

The *Cumulative Load Theory* asserts that although biological tissues are capable of self-repair, "mechanical degradation" occurs after repeated and prolonged use (Kumar, 2001). Prolonged loading on the muscles may result in permanent changes in the structure of the muscle that may lead, over time, to injury. Additionally, cumulative load, defined as the interaction of biomechanical load and exposure time to the load over the work life, may result in fatigue, which increases overall muscle stress (Kumar, 1990). This stress ultimately may impede the self-repair of an individual's muscles.

The Overexertion Theory

The *Overexertion Theory* posits that all physical activity consists of force generation/application, motion, and duration. Consequently, any physical activity that exceeds the limits of the individual will result in overexertion. If overexertion is sustained over time, or is due to extremes in either the force generated or the associated motion, injury is likely to result (see Kumar, 1994 for a detailed description of this model).

STAGE TWO: DISABILITY

The second stage in the CDD Injury Continuum (Disability) involves the multiple interactions among patients and providers, as well as other involved parties. Disability is a complex concept with great variance in how individuals seek to understand and treat the phenomenon. Understandably, models used to explain how disability is developed and maintained vary widely from dualistic models of either pure physical or psychosocial etiologies, to models indicative of a complex interaction between a variety of etiological phenomena. Harris (2000) indicates that the debate concerning the conception of disability has encompassed the consideration of physical and psychosocial factors, with no clear agreement as to which is most important in defining disability. Although some, according to Harris (2000), have been content to conclude that the dissolution of psychosocial factors associated with disability is sufficient to resolve serious disability. Further, the research literature is fraught with disagreement as to the etiological components of disability, as well as to the implications of etiology on treatment and compensation issues (Schultz, Crook, Fraser, & Joy, 2000).

Thus, it is important to examine the various models of disability that have been discussed in the literature as they relate to these concerns. As noted above, though a wide variety of models to explain disability have been proposed, discussed, and critiqued, only the most prominent of these will be discussed here. Schultz et al. (2000) distinguished the following first five models as most prominent, based on their extensive review of the literature, and the last has also been identified as useful. The models include: (1) *Biomedical Model*; (2) *Psychiatric Model*; (3) *Insurance Model*; (4) *Labor Relations Model*; (5) *Biopsychosocial Model*; and (6) *Sociomedical Model*. The following provides an overview of these six models.

The Biomedical Model

The *Biomedical Model* is one of the most widely recognized and utilized explanations of disability in the world today, even among the psychological and social work professions (Belar & Deardorff, 1999; Schultz et al., 2000). It has been noted that the primary tenet of the *Biomedical Model* is that disability is primarily attributable to some underlying biophysical abnormality due to organic pathology (Engel, 1977; Pledger, 2003). Schultz et al. (2000) explain that the *Biomedical Model* can be bisected into two articulations in which disability can be conceptualized as a disruption of an organism's machinery. The first is explainable through cellular biology, while the second is explained as a development from a linear progression of causal physical insults resulting in physical pathology, which manifests as disability symptoms. Pledger (2003) takes this conceptualization a step further by stating that the biomedical model fosters an understanding of disability as a functional deficit or disadvantage. Given the primary biomedical association between physical pathology and disability, it follows that successful treatment of the physical pathology should result in "curing" disability. It further follows that the intensity of symptoms associated with disability would be proportionate to the extent of the organic pathology.

Another central tenet of the *Biomedical Model* is the fundamental separation between the physical and the mental (Schultz et al., 2000; Turk & Okifuji, 2002). Obviously, there is a de-emphasis on the role of psychosocial factors in disability within the biomedical framework, in favor of a strong emphasis on physical, quantifiable factors. Schultz et al. (2000) point out that, expectedly, biomedical assessment has an emphasis on scientific measures yielding objective data such as lab or imaging tests. The authors also point out that evidence of psychosocial difficulty associated with disability is deemed less important than the data yielded by objective measures, and chalked up to "functional overlay." Treatment implications of the *Biomedical Model* generally include the physical treatment of disability by physicians, with an orientation toward curing, rather than managing disability (Belar & Deardorff, 1999; Olkin, 2002; Schultz et al., 2000). Schultz and colleagues (2000) further explain that biomedical disability treatment involves the diagnosis of organic pathology and attempts to cure the pathology often through physical treatments.

The *Biomedical Model* applies well to individuals suffering from acute or uncomplicated injuries, or individuals suffering from serious medical conditions (Schultz et al., 2000). However, this model has not been without its share of critics who seem primarily concerned with the de-emphasis of psychosocial factors in disability, as well as the inability of the *Biomedical Model* to consistently predict disability (Engel, 1977; Nielson & Weir, 2001; Schultz et al., 2000; Verbrugge & Jette, 1994). Nielson and Weir (2001) suggest that a comprehensive model of disability should be able to account for inconsistencies between reported pain and physical injury, such as: painful reactions to otherwise innocuous stimuli; the incongruence between the site of reported pain and the site of injury; the fact that the nature and location of pain can change over time; and the psychological processes which influence pain, all of which the *Biomedical Model* fails to do.

It has been widely noted that physical, objective biomedical assessment can fail to detect a specific organic origin to chronic pain, especially back pain (Schultz et al., 2000; Verbrugge & Jette, 1994). Concerns have been raised about the lack of consideration given within the *Biomedical Model* to psychosocial and environmental variables, which can impinge upon disability (Bickenbach et al., 1999; Harris, 2000; Verbrugge & Jette, 1994). Further, Belar and Deardorff (1999) share concerns that biomedical treatment of disability may leave individuals with disability complicated by psychosocial factors considered as "mental" cases to be treated psychiatrically rather than physically. Finally, the compensation implications of the *Biomedical Model* limit compensation to those individuals with objectively and scientifically identified organic pathology, to the exclusion of all others.

The Psychiatric Model

Just as the *Biomedical Model* seeks to explain disability in seemingly exclusive physical terms, the *Psychiatric Model*, seeks to explain disability and chronic pain as physical manifestations of psychological/psychiatric problems (Turk & Okifuji, 2002). Thus, the *Psychiatric Model* shares a commonality with the *Biomedical Model* in that disability is conceptualized in dualistic terms in which disability is either due to an organic problem or a psychiatric problem. Schultz et al. (2000) explain that the *Psychiatric Model* describes individuals experiencing chronic pain and disability, without a clear physical diagnosis, as homogeneous. The authors note that this model fosters reliance upon psychiatric diagnoses (with particular emphasis on Diagnostic and Statistical Manual—IV diagnoses (DSM-IV, American Psychiatric Association, 1994) including pain disorder, somatoform disorder, hypochondriasis, somatization disorder, factitious disorder, malingering, and conversion disorder. Unfortunately, as the authors point out, the reliance upon psychiatric diagnosis to explain disability precludes the consideration of comorbidity between physical and psychosocial factors. Also, given the relatively low base rates of many psychiatric disorders, this model runs the risk of overpathologizing psychiatrically "normal" individuals (Schultz et al., 2000). Thus, although the *Psychiatric Model* improves upon the *Biomedical Model* through the consideration of psychiatric influences on disability and the consequent consideration of such individuals for disability benefits, it also fosters a reliance upon diagnostic labels and continues to encourage a dualistic conceptualization of the complex disability phenomenon.

The Insurance Model

There are individuals who have sought to explain disability in terms of motivating factors contributing to disability symptomatology and have implicated secondary and tertiary gains in disability symptom manifestation (Ferrari & Kwan, 2001; Kwan, Ferrari, & Friel, 2001). Butler (2000) suggests that some disability models, like the *Biomedical* and *Psychiatric Models*, seek to inoculate as many people as possible from disability, regardless of motivation, while other models take motivation into account. Some have suggested that disability symptoms may be a manifestation of attempts to receive compensation for disability, which is the *Insurance Model* of disability, also referred to as the forensic or compensation model (Schultz et al., 2000). Whereas the two models above support an illness (physical or psychiatric) as the underlying mechanism driving disability, the *Insurance Model* attributes disability to a "dishonest" symptom magnification or manifestation, with a focus on the business of treating disability, rather than disability *per se*. Symptom exaggeration and malingering, for any reason, are, no doubt, present among the disabled population. A study by Mittenberg, Patton, Canyock, and Condit (2002) evaluated over 30,000 neuropsychology patients with personal injury, disability, criminal, or medical claims. They found a rate of 30% of disabled individuals identified as probable malingerers or symptom exaggerators, based on a variety of malingering measures. The authors, however, note that the research literature varies widely as to the extent of malingering as a function of litigation circumstances, type of injury/illness, malingering measures, and environment.

According to Schultz and colleagues (2000), under the *Insurance Model*, disabled individuals may be described as "sly" or "devious" individuals who are faking pain for financial compensation. Further, the intensity and duration of disability symptoms is hypothesized to vary relative to the amount of compensation received. Medelson stated that, "there are no malingerers in countries where there is no Workmens' Compensation Act" (as cited in Schultz et al., 2000, p.276). It is not being suggested that the *Insurance Model* assumes that all individuals experiencing long-term disability are "faking it." However, this model does seem to assume that these individuals are motivated by compensation until proven otherwise, in a "guilty-until-proven-innocent" fashion. Schultz et al. (2000) explain that the *Insurance Model* leaves the burden of proof of disability on the compensation claimant, who must be able to show that he or she is truly disabled. This model seems, then, to be akin to the *Biomedical Model* in its emphasis on compelling, objective data to prove that a disability really does exist, which may leave those who have a more complicated disability considered as malingerers, whether they are or not. Proponents of the model, in deference to this risk, have stated that the *Insurance Model*, while primarily trying to help those who truly need it without inflicting the extra costs associated with the treatment of those motivated by secondary gain, offers the secondary benefit of protecting society from abuse of the system (Schultz et al., 2000).

As one would expect, a large part of assessment in this model concerns "teasing apart" individuals who appear to be faking disability symptoms for monetary gain from those who are actually disabled. This has involved the use of various physical measures with the consideration of effort exerted, forensic techniques, and psychological measures, such as the Minnesota Multiphasic Personality Inventory—2 (MMPI-2, Butcher, Dahlstrom, Graham, Tellegen, & Kaemmer, 1989; Schultz et al., 2000). Schultz et al. (2000) point out, however, that the cost of exhaustive testing to identify malingerers may detract from savings associated with denying compensation to those who may not need it. The authors also suggest that costs associated with litigation for those who have been denied compensation, as well as system safeguards to prevent malingerers from obtaining compensation benefits, may also detract from the financial benefits of the *Insurance Model*. Most importantly, however, many wonder if the financial savings inherent to this model are worth the societal costs inherent to the risk run in this model of denying compensation to those who really need it (Butler, 2000; Schultz et al., 2000).

The Labor Relations Model

The *Labor Relations Model* of disability takes a unique approach in comparison to the other models discussed in this Chapter by placing at least some of the responsibility for the treatment and prevention of disability on the disabled individual's employer. Proponents of this model perceive the work environment to be a vital part of the individual's psychological, social, and physical life. Thus, returning an injured patient to work and helping him or her maintain employment is the highest priority (Schultz et al., 2000). Schultz and colleagues suggest that returning disabled individuals to work is considered mutually beneficial to the patient and employer (whose needs in the workplace are seen as complementary) under the *Labor Relations Model*.

Schultz and colleagues (2000) explain that assessment and treatment within the *Labor Relations Model* involve evaluations of a person's functional capacity (as alluded to above), as well as evaluations of the work place to help match one's work demands with his or her functional abilities. Further, because this model proposes that the workplace serve as a therapeutic medium for individuals with disabilities, assessment of psychosocial problems may be necessary to help develop appropriate work programs. Finally, the *Labor Relations Model* places a large emphasis on prevention of injury and disability through the workplace milieu, which may require work programs specifically tailored to this end (Schultz et al., 2000; Weir & Nielson, 2001).

Unfortunately, this model of disability proposes a complicated and possibly costly endeavor. First, if employers are to be made responsible for the *in vivo* treatment of disability at the workplace, a variety of expert consultants may be necessary to help plan job-site programs to meet these ends. These programs, after being planned, will require further expenditure of time and money in coordinating the cooperative efforts of individuals in the workplace to carry them out (Schultz et al., 2000; Williams & Westmorland, 2002). Furthermore, a disabled individual cannot simply return to his/her previous employment capacity. They must be matched to work that they can accomplish within the context of their physical limitations. Thus, this begs the question that job security may be vital to a person's well-being, but at what cost?

There are reports that work-based disability programs can be cost-effective. The cost benefits of implementing work-based disability prevention and management programs have been well-noted, with reported associated financial benefits in the millions of dollars (Mobley, Linz, Shukla, Breslin, & Deng, 2000; Silversides, 1998). One example of such savings is evident in a report concerning Chrysler Canada, who consulted an ergonomist regarding changes they could make in their Ontario plant employing over 6,000 individuals (Silversides, 1998). Silversides (1998) notes that the plant was reportedly spending almost 7% of their total payroll on Workers' Compensation benefits. After instituting recommended changes including longer training and introduction periods for jobs, breaks for exercise, redesigned tasks, and modified work for injured employees, the plant reported a 35% decrease in lost time from work and they decreased their payroll expenditure on Workers' Compensation benefits down to under 4% (Silversides, 1998).

In evaluating the cost effectiveness of an intervention, however, consideration of the program cost, and consideration of who will pay the cost, is important. First, the increased costs associated with the interventions outlined above are passed on to the employers, which may detract from the attractiveness of the *Labor Relations Model* to employers. Also, Schultz and colleagues (2000) suggest that small business owners may not be able to even implement this model due to these costs. Second, it is important to consider that the only disabled individuals who stand to benefit from this model are those who have a job to return to after their injury. Thus, although beneficial to the employed, the *Labor Relations Model* does not allow easy access to benefits for those not fortunate enough to be employed at the time of their injury. Finally, Butler (2000) notes that, even if an employer has the resources to coordinate, staff, and implement labor relations work programs, these programs can be difficult to sustain, as they are influenced by the constantly changing environment in which they are introduced (i.e., needs may wax and wane with flare-ups in employee illness).

The Biopsychosocial Model

Schultz et al. (2000) trace the etiology of the *Biopsychosocial Model* of disability 50 years ago to a meeting of the WHO in which health was defined as a multifaceted combination of biological/physical, emotional/psychological, and social well-being, as opposed to a mere absence of biological organic pathology. Thus, the WHO functionally recognized that health and, conversely, disability are defined by a complex interaction between a variety of factors. Further, Belar and Deardorff (1999) recount evidence dating back to the 1700's of individuals recognizing an interaction between the body and mind. The growing amount of evidence supporting a mind-body interaction eventually led to the conceptualization of a disability model which, instead of focusing on either psychosocial or physical etiologies in disability, focuses on conceptualizing disability as a consequence of the interaction between biological, psychological and social phenomena.

The *Biopsychosocial Model* is, as the name suggests, a multi-faceted model of pain and disability, which consideres biological, psychological, and social aspects (Crichton & Morley, 2002; Gatchel, 1996; Wright & Gatchel, 2002). Multiple dimensions of the *Biopsychosocial Model* contribute to disability through interaction, reciprocal determinism, and evolution (Crichton & Morley, 2002; Mayer, Gatchel, & Polatin, 1992; Turk & Monarch, 2002). As opposed to the biomedical and psychiatric approaches, that conceptualize disability dualistically as either due to the mind or the body, the *Biopsychosocial Model* considers disability as both a biological manifestation and a subjective experience of pathology based on the interaction between biological, psychological and social variables, which determine the severity and chronicity of pain. Not only do these multiple factors contribute to the etiology of disability, they have a reciprocal effect on one another to intensify and perpetuate each other and, consequently, the duration and intensity of disability symptomatology (Crichton & Morley, 2002). Schultz et al. (2000) also note that the *Biopsychosocial Model* distinguishes impairment from disability. According to the authors, impairment relates to the loss of physical function of a body system or body part, while disability relates specifically to one's inability to meet his or her personal, social, and occupational needs as a result of impairment. This consideration broadens the definition of the *Biopsychosocial Model* to include environmental factors, such that an individual with an impairment, who meets his or her needs within their environment, is not necessarily "disabled." However, it is questionable that this tenet suggests, as voiced by Harris (2000), that one who receives environmental accommodations to overcome a disability is no longer disabled.

Schultz and colleagues (2000) emphasize that one of the central tenets to the *Biopsychosocial Model* is the emphasis on the individual in treatment and conceptualization of disability. This emphasis is notable because many of the models described above do not have a strong patient focus. The *Insurance Model* seems to place a relatively greater focus on the treatment providers, while the *Labor Relations Model* shifts the focus to the disabled individual's employer. Schultz et al. (2000) note that the biomedical approach is structured in a way that fosters reliance by the patient on his or her physician, who is a "savior," of sorts. The *Biopsychosocial Model*, in contrast, emphasizes the role of the patient as, "... a collaborator [in treatment] and a comanager of his/her rehabilitation" (Schultz et al., 2000, p. 281–2). The authors explain that the "whole" person is the focal point of treatment, with the treatment goals aimed at improving the individual's quality of life and restoring his or her full functioning in physical, occupational, emotional, and social domains. Also, Kwan, Ferrari, and Friel (2001) stress that the *Biopsychosocial Model* of disability addresses all aspects of disability including consideration of possible patient motivators such as secondary and tertiary gains. To date, the *Biopsychosocial Model* remains one of the most comprehensive ways of conceptualizing and treating chronic pain (Mayer, Gatchel, & Evans, 2002).

As one would expect, assessment in the biopsychosocial context involves a comprehensive evaluation of a variety of domains including physical function, psychosocial variables, and occupational variables. Further, these data must then be integrated to provide a multidimensional understanding of disability in identifying treatment goals aimed at restoring the whole person back to full function. Congruent to the *Labor Relations Model*, there is also a strong goal that emphasizes helping the disabled individual return to work in as timely a manner as possible (Schultz et al., 2000). Schultz et al. (2000) note that the *Biopsychosocial Model* is applicable to a wide variety of disabilities, with compensation aimed at those who fail to experience symptom relief after rehabilitation and are unable to return to activity to a significant extent. In this model, the authors note that compensation can be used as an incentive to the patient's participation in his or her rehabilitation.

The Sociomedical Model: The Disablement Process

Verbrugge and Jette (1994) have improved upon previous models of disability inasmuch as they not only describe a comprehensive *Sociomedical Model*, focusing on medical and social aspects of disability, but also incorporate a variety of factors that impinge upon the progression of disability, either speeding it up or slowing it down. The authors note that their model is an adaptation of the International Classification of Impairments, Disabilities, and Handicaps (ICIDH) and the Nagi scheme. The ICIDH describes the development of disability as a progression from: (1) a pathological disease state; to (2) the impairment of physical or psychological functioning; to (3) disability defined, similarly to that of the *Biopsychosocial Model*, as an inability to perform normal activity; and finally to (4) handicap, described as an impairment- or disability-related inability to fulfill a "normal" role. The Nagi scheme defines the progression of disability from: (1) active pathology, interruption of normal processes; to (2) impairment of normal function; to (3) a limitation of the individual to perform as a normal whole; and finally, to (4) the development of role limitations due to impairment and limitations (i.e., disability).

Verbrugge and Jette's (1994) disablement process begins with the development of an organic pathology, which may become chronic and have effects that are not easily detected by objective testing. This pathology results in the development of structural/body system abnormalities (i.e., impairments) that may have significant psychological, physical, or social consequences. These impairments may not be congruent with the underlying pathology. In Verbrugge and Jette's main disablement pathway, impairments progress to functional limitations in which one's "fundamental" physical and social actions are restricted, and he or she is unable to perform "purposeful work." Finally, functional limitations progress to disability, which Verbrugge and Jette (1994) define as "difficulty doing activities in any domain of life (the domains typical for one's age-sex group) due to a health or physical problem," (p. 4). The authors outline appropriate assessment techniques throughout the progression of disability from appropriate medical measures of pathology and impairment, to tests of physical and mental functioning associated with functional limitations and measures of activity difficulties and performance of activities of daily living associated with disability.

As noted above, Verbrugge and Jette (1994) go beyond merely describing the progression of disability from pathology, to describing factors which may serve to intervene and exacerbate the progression. First, the authors note that there are certain long-standing characteristics that predispose an individual to experience a faster or slower progression from pathology to disability. These factors broadly include demographic, social, lifestyle, behavioral, psychological, environmental, and biological variables. Verbrugge and Jette (1994) further explain that either self- or other-imposed interventions may slow down the progression of the disablement process. For example, an individual's seeking of medical care or social support can help buffer against disablement progression at any of the four stages of the process described above. Exacerbators, on the other hand, may be intra- or extra-individual mediators that speed up disablement. The authors explain that there are three main types of exacerbators. First, iatrogenic effects of interventions, or interventions gone awry, may worsen an individuals' condition. Second, personal behavioral and emotional responses to injury and functional limitation (e.g., alcohol abuse and anger) can have deleterious effect on disablement. Finally, environmental variables (e.g., inflexible work hours, social prejudice, and architectural barriers) may contribute to one's handicap. Verbrugge and Jette (1994) explain that exacerbators may occur before, during, and in response to the disablement process.

STAGE THREE: DECISION

As has been reviewed in Stage Two, numerous physical, psychological, economic, social, and health care related factors influence the disability process. Though there is a great deal of research on the first two stages within the CDD Injury Continuum, little research exists to provide a theoretical understanding of the third stage in the continuum: Decision. Krause and colleagues (2001) recently reviewed the literature and found no comprehensive theories to explain the thoughts and behaviors that lead a work-disabled individual to return to work. Fortunately, since then, researchers have begun to explore this area, as return to work for a disabled worker not only can affect the individual worker in a positive economic and social manner, but also society as a whole in terms of reduced overall health care utilization and costs, increased workforce, and decreased need for training of new, replacement workers. Franche and Krause (2002) attempt to apply two existing theoretical models of motivation and behavior towards a better understanding of the decisions involved in return-to-work and, in turn, create a new theoretical model, unique to the return-to-work process. Their new model, the *Readiness for Return-to-Work*, stems from studying the *Readiness for Change Model* and the *Phase Model,* but it uniquely applies to the work environment. We will first provide a review of the two models upon which the Readiness for Return-to-Work Model is based; then, we will provide a brief overview of this work-application model.

The Readiness for Change Model

The *Readiness for Change Model* addresses motivational factors that influence behavioral change. This model, comprised of five motivational stages and a patient-based "decisional balance" self-analysis of the behavior in question, grew out of research aimed at health promotion and prevention (e.g., smoking cessation, condom use, sunscreen use, weight control, and exercise, Prochaska, 1994; Prochaska

& DiClemente, 1983; Prochaska, DiClemente, & Norcross, 1992; Prochaska, DiClemente, Velicer, Ginpil, & Norcross, 1985; Prochaska et al., 1994). Franche and Krause (2002) summarize the research supporting this model that demonstrates excellent predictive validity in the aforementioned areas and, in particular, in regards to smoking (Prochaska et al., 1985). The five stages are: (1) *precontemplation*—no thought of behavior change within the next six months; (2) *contemplation*—seriously thinking of initiating behavior change within the next six months; (3) *preparation*—serious thoughts of behavior change within the next month; (4) *action*—period lasting from zero to six months after overt behavioral change is initiated by patient; and lastly; (5) *maintenance*—begins six months after behavioral change has been initiated and continues until the behavior is no longer deemed a problem (Prochaska et al., 1994). Also, integral to the *Readiness for Change Model* is the concept of decisional balance (Prochaska et al., 1994). The decisional balance construct grew out of Janis and Mann's (1977) decision-making model, which posited four main categories of anticipated gains and losses that guide decision-making. Prochaska and colleagues (1994) found that utilizing their own five-stage model in combination with just one aspect of the aforementioned decision-making model allowed for prediction, with great accuracy, for the likelihood for behavioral change. The scanning of overall pros and cons involved in any potential behavioral change was the most beneficial element of the decision-making model, when considered along with the five-stage model of change (Janis & Mann, 1977; Prochaska et al., 1994).

The Phase Models

Another basis for the upcoming discussion of the *Readiness for Return-to-Work Model* is to consider disability in terms of phases. There are essentially two such models: the *Eight Phase Model of Disability* (Krause & Ragland, 1994) and the *Three Phase Model of Disability* (Frank, Sinclair, Hogg-Johnson, Beaton, & Cole, 1998). Within both of the models, the progression from one phase to the next is largely determined by duration of pain and/or disability and the related risks associated with each phase. Physical and injury-specific factors are generally deemed to carry more weight in terms of disability prediction, in the acute phases; whereas, psychosocial factors become paramount in the later subacute and chronic phases (Krause, Dasinger, Deegan, Rudolph, & Brand, 2001). As a patient's degree of risk increases within a phase, the more likely progression to the next stage will occur.

The Readiness for Return-to-Work Model

The *Readiness for Return-to-Work Model* encompasses the beliefs and behaviors of employees as the primary agents of change in the return to work process. It is built largely upon the Readiness for Change Model and is ultimately to be considered in conjunction with the *Phases Model of Disability* (Franche & Krause, 2002). Though the model is based on the same five stages of change as the Readiness for Change Model, the stages are now viewed within an occupational framework. Specifically, the *precontemplation* phase is associated with an exclusive focus on the recovery process, with no thought of immediate return to work. The *contemplation* phase begins when an injured worker views him or herself as potentially capable of returning to work within six months. This stage is characterized by ambivalence, when the patient vacillates while weighing the pros and cons of a return to work. The third stage, *preparation for action*, occurs when the worker begins to make active plans to return to work and solicit information regarding occupational modification options and also begins testing their own abilities. The fourth stage, the *action* stage, involves an actual return to work of some kind. Their perception of their own ability to succeed is of paramount importance in order to move to the next stage, maintenance. The last stage, *maintenance*, involves both physical and psychological prevention of relapse. Physically, employees must remain consistent with exercise regimens prescribed in earlier phases of disability. Additionally, psychologically, employees must prevent relapse via monitoring of mood, prevention of boredom, and other pre-determined, individual-specific psychological risk factors.

Within the *Readiness-for-Return-to-Work-Model*, two different sets of "dimension of change" principles help us to understand the interrelationships between the injured worker and the health care provider, the workplace and the insurer (Franche & Krause, 2002). The first has to do with time off of work and time since injury, and it grew out of the *Phases Model of Disability*. As each of these time frames lengthens, the likelihood of failing to return to work is increased. The second principle of dimension of change involves the concepts of decisional balance, self-efficacy, and change processes. These concepts evolved out of the *Readiness for Change Model* and help to further explain the beliefs and behaviors of an injured worker that lead to return to work. Franche and Krause (2002) describe the role of each of these concepts in detail, as they apply to the injured workers relationships with other involved parties, as discussed above.

Franche and Krause (2002), conclude that understanding an injury from the perpective of pain severity and functional ability alone is most easily done when based upon the *Phases Model of Disability*. Their own proposed *Readiness for Return-to-Work-Model* is likely to be most relevant when deciding upon an interventional approach for a specific injured employee, in order to maximize the likelihood of return to work. Ultimately, further research assessing the utility of a more integrated model based upon both the *Phases Model of Disability* and the *Readiness for Return-to-Work Model* is the next step in fully understanding both the prediction of return to work and the specific interventions needed to improve the odds for return to work.

PRINCIPLE PARTICIPANTS WITHIN THE THREE STAGES OF THE INJURY CONTINUUM

The agendas of many influences are at work throughout the CDD Injury Continuum. Providers, employers, patients, caretakers, and society as a whole all typically approach the injury, regardless of the stage, with a different point of view, different strategies, and different purposes. While the unique perspectives of these influencers have been previously explored, we will attempt to synthesize the literature and provide an overview that focuses on each influencer along the injury continuum.

Providers

Health care providers set the tone for how patients interpret and then respond to their injury. Many facets are involved in this intricate communication (e.g., the doctors' beliefs about injury, compensation, risk, and litigation). Ferrari and Kwan (2001) discuss the "sanctioning" of disability by providers. They suggest that patients will often seek out physicians who will diagnose in a "no-fault" manner that supports the sick role. Such diagnoses may include fibromyalgia, chronic fatigue syndrome, and multiple chemical sensitivities, all of which are associated with lack of definitive agreement among the medical community regarding etiologies and treatment planning. These diagnoses may also allow providers to avoid confrontation with a patient regarding the physician's impression of the patients' true physical abilities. Ferrari and Kwan (2001) elaborate further on the concept of diagnosing: "In eschewing the responsibility of adequately and honestly addressing the patient's true malady, a diagnostic label [is given] that leaves the patient contented and the physician self-satisfied" (Ferrari & Kwan, 2001, p 78–79). Such self-satisfaction may be derived from: (1) the physician's avoidance of potential litigation that may otherwise stem from such a patient-physician confrontation; and (2) from the financial incentives for a physician to maintain a long-term doctor-patient relationship (Ferrari & Kwan, 2001). Other researchers have also found that some providers operate from a "fear-avoidant" belief perspective, in which they communicate, contrary to available, current evidence, that a patient should stop an activity if they feel pain and not return to work until their pain is resolved (Linton, Vlaeyen, & Ostelo, 2002). In fact, Linton, et al. (2002) found that of 60 general practice physicians and 71 physical therapists who completed a questionnaire regarding their practice beliefs, fully 67% and 69%, respectively responded that they would advise avoidance of painful movements.

Moon and Liu (1998) studied the doctor-patient relationship from a cognitive-behavioral therapy perspective. In so doing, they acknowledge four tenets unique to the relationship. First, the physician is often not perceived by the patient as working in their best interest, but rather in the interest of the employer. Secondly, the primary goal of treatment is to return to work, not necessarily complete resolution of pain and a complete return to previous levels of functioning. This goal is frequently not in line with an injured workers expectation of treatment. Thirdly, physicians whose practices consist of many injured workers may harbor greater levels of cynicism and suspicion regarding their patients' complaints than do other physicians who see few work injured related patients, due to the role of potential secondary gain (e.g., financial incentives and time off of work). Kwan and Friel (2002) provide an overview of the primary issues involved in secondary gain. Lastly, the physician is only a limited patient advocate, as he or she has to balance the competing demands for increased time off for recovery from the patient and avoidance of creating a physician dependency that may further support the sick role. Moon and Lui (1998) summarize that a physician who uses a cognitive-behavioral approach from the outset may reduce disability days and reinforce return to work expectations and behaviors. Key components of such interactions would include: establishing goals for return to work at the outset of treatment; outlining a comprehensive treatment approach to the injury, rather than providing incremental education/information at each visit; actively involving the patient in treatment planning; and influencing the work environment (e.g., light duty and reasonable and obtainable work modifications).

Dasinger and colleagues (2001) further reviewed the literature regarding the unique doctor-patient relationship that is involved in the care of an injured worker.

They found that what little research exists on the subject all point to the same conclusion: communications of expectancy of return to work were paramount to aiding an injured worker to see such potential and make decisions accordingly. Specifically, they summarized previous research on the subject and found that providers who did not delay return to work nor communicate in an alarming manner to patients (e.g., use of words such as "injured" and "damaged," aided workers to return to work). Additionally, those who did not refer for numerous, unnecessary diagnostic procedures had patients who returned to work sooner. In order to more fully test two primary aspects of physician communication, that of proactive communication and the return to work recommendation, Dasinger and colleagues (2001) assessed the effect of such communication in a three-year retrospective study of 325 workers' compensation claims. They found that a positive return to work recommendation from the physician was associated with a 60% higher return to work rate during the subacute/chronic phase (>30 days of disability); whereas, physician proactive communication was a more important predictor of return to work during the acute phase (<30 days of disability). They suggest that the reason behind the lessening of impact of physician communication in the subacute and chronic phases may have more to do with overwhelming workplace factors and mounting psychological factors.

Employers

Factors associated with the work environment were partially addressed by the Americans with Disabilities Act (ADA) of 1990 (One Hundred First Congress of the United States of America, 1990). One of the intents of the ADA was to assist workers with reentry to the workplace following injury (Huang & Feuerstein, 1998). By evaluating all ADA-related litigation between 1990–1996, Huang and Feuerstein (1998) found that the top two areas of dispute surrounded the employer's termination of the worker and failure to provide reasonable return to work accommodation. The reasons for these alleged failures include an assumption on the employers' part that the employee is lacking in motivation to maintain productive work levels and possible expressions of frustration on the part of the employee stemming from difficulties with the workers' compensation system, pain, functional limitation, and perceived disinterest on the part of the employer. Within the workplace, social perceptions of the meaning of injury/disability may also lead to an air of stigmatization of the injured worker as a malingerer or other negative connotation (Huang & Feuerstein, 1998; Susman, 1994). Huang and Feuerstein (1998) conclude by underscoring the importance of identifying and implementing means of accommodating workers' upon return to work.

Teasell and Bombardier (2001) reviewed the literature and found that lack of available modified work and poor work autonomy were predictors of disability and poor return to work rates. Krause, Dasinger, and Neuhasuer (1998) provide an extensive review of modified return to work plans. They found that such programs, though seemingly costly and time-consuming at the onset, are actually associated with nearly twice the likelihood of an injured worker returning to work and half the number of lost days to injury. Further, they found the programs to be more cost-effective in the long run. Tate, Yassi, and Cooper (1999) also found modified return to work programs to be effective at reducing lost time to injury.

Patients

A study conducted in Sweden assessed layperson's viewpoint of the employer's response to an injured worker and the resulting impact on the injured worker (Nordqvist, Holmqvist, & Alexanderson, 2003). Based upon focus group data, consisting of workers' who had had work absence due to injury, several key employer factors were identified as part of an ideal "unambiguous return-to-work program": employers should contact the worker soon after sick leave begins; notify co-workers; make modifications to the work environment if need be and notify all as to who is in charge of such modifications, so they may be discussed if necessary; and lastly, encourage a positive work environment.

There is also research to suggest that there are some factors unique to the individual injured worker that may account for their return to work and maintenance of work. In assessing patients with chronic upper limb pain, Adams and Williams (2003) found that patients were more likely to return to work if they had been working just shortly before beginning pain management treatment. Additionally, patients who were psychologically robust, as measured by catastophizing less and asserting greater optimism about their capability of working, were also more likely to return to work. The propensity for catastrophizing among chronic pain patients is well documented (France, France, al'Absi, Ring, & McIntyre, 2002). In fact, catastrophizing has even been reported as the most common cognitive distortion associated with poor treatment response (Floreen, 2003). Patients' beliefs about the meaning of their injury are in fact a robust predictor of their disability progression.

Studies have shown that the following beliefs play a predictive role in the likelihood of recovery: initial perception of illness as "curable" (Petrie, Weinman, Sharpe, & Buckley, 1996); clinician driven exploration of patient's recovery expectations and assistance with revision to appropriate expectations of the recovery process (Mondloch, Cole, & Frank, 2001); viewing/experiencing the recovery process as better than expected and expectant return to work within three weeks (Cole, Mondloch, & Group, 2002); lack of anticipation of pain, as well as non-adherence to a fear-avoidance belief about physical activities (Al-Obaidi, Nelson, Al-Awadhi, & Al-Shuwaie, 2000); positive attitude about capacity for performance of activities of daily living (Sandstrom, 1986); and patients' self-perception of readiness for return to work (Marhold, Linton, & Melin, 2002; Sandstrom & Esbjornsson, 1986). Additionally, the role of spirituality has been implicated in patients who come to cope more effectively with disability. Treloar (2002) found that after interviewing nine adults with disabilities and 13 parents of children with disabilities, those who maintained a belief that their disability served a theological purpose experienced greater stability and more effective coping styles. Though the study did not focus on injured workers, it suggests that the role an injured workers' spiritual belief system serves, may need to be considered in future occupational research endeavors.

Despite all of this knowledge about injured workers, it appears we still do not have a representative sample of *all* occupational injury claimants. Those injured worker's who file workers' compensation claims may in fact be among the "worst of the worst" of the many injured patients. In Michigan, where report of a work-related injury is required by the physician, regardless of the workers' decision to file a workers' compensation claim, one study found that only 25% of the injured workers' actually filed a claim (Rosenman et al., 2000). Factors associated with claim filing included severity of the injury, increased length of employment, lower annual income, physician imposed activity restrictions, type of provider imposing restrictions, greater than one week of lost time from work and decreased overall current health status. Though this study focused largely on unionized autoworkers, it may reflect that the disability literature does not actually cover *all* work-related musculoskeletal injuries, but rather only the worst-case scenarios. Other researchers have found workplace disability to be underreported in another completely different but equally impactful way (Evanoff et al., 2002). Specifically, it has been found that much of the financial impact and lost productivity calculations are based on initial return-to work dates (Evanoff et al., 2002). This methodology leaves out the role of reinjury and/or reported persistent functional limitations that impact work productivity. Consequently, costs may continue to mount long after typical disability research stops the calculations. As a result, it is suggested that multiple measures to assess the costs incurred and productivity of workers after return to work is imperative in order to more fully understand the full array of impact of a work related injury.

Patient Caregivers

An additional area that is rarely discussed within the context of disability and return to work is the role of caregivers and social supports for the injured worker. One study followed 312 patients after lower extremity injury and found that return to work rates were positively correlated with the presence of strong social support (MacKenzie et al., 1998). Support from others has been further classified into two subgroups: perceived support, the perception that one is loved and valued and that help is available if needed; and received support, the actual direct aid to a disabled person, such as transportation, advice, and physical assistance (Kutner, 1987). Though support in general has been associated with more positive return to work outcomes (Mondloch et al., 2001), the Kutner work may provide stimulus for further research in this area. Such research may allow for pain management treatment to more fully address all factors that may lead to an increased return to work. Support is not only derived from individuals, but may also come in many forms from society as a whole.

Society

Much stigma surrounds the concept of disability in society today. Consider, a car parked in the parking lot, may draw thoughts of price, color, and style; while the same car, parked in a handicapped space with handicapped plates, may more frequently draw suspicious thoughts about the legitimacy of the drivers' disability. The disability stigma is constantly changing, given societies beliefs about disability at any given time. Susman (1994) summarizes the disability literature in terms of societal response to a disabled person. The associated stigma suggests that "...a person who has an impairment somehow gets lost to awareness and only the impairment itself remains seen" (Susman, 1994, p.19). Irving Zola takes this thought even further and writes, "No matter what label is used, it cannot help but equate the person totally with disability" (as cited in Susman, 1994, p.16). Many patients, regardless of type or origin or physical or emotional impairment, relate these feelings frequently.

Toward this end, there has been a recent movement to expand the understanding of disability beyond the psychology of the individual out to society as a whole;

the recent development of the field of "disability studies" exemplifies this movement. Olkin and Pledger (2003) describe disability studies as an "interdisciplinary field that seeks to legitimize the study of disability as a universal human condition" (p. 296). Individuals in this field seem to support a more "social" (or "socioecological") model of disability in which disability is described as a social, rather than psychological or physical, construct in which the limitations associated with disability are conceptualized as a function of an environment which fails to accommodate the needs of individuals with disabilities (Olkin, 2002; Tate & Pledger, 2003). It has been suggested that previous models of disability have perpetuated a dichotomous view of individuals as either "normal" or "disabled," (Olkin, 2002). Proponents of this "social" approach, however, advocate a sense of community among disabled individuals, as well as the depathologizing of disability per se. For a more detailed description of social disability and disability studies, see Olkin (2002), Tate and Pledger (2003), Pledger (2003), and Olkin and Pledger (2003).

In conclusion, the response to disability from a patient, physician, healthcare provider, insurance agent, or caregiver, whether personal or other-directed, plays a key role in the disabled person's self-perception of expected recovery and ultimate return to work. Consequently, additional discovery surrounding the role of the social environment is warranted to more fully understand all factors involved in disability and the decision to return to work.

CONCLUSION

Not only is there an increase in the incidence of musculoskeletal disorders and disabling medical conditions, there is a also a resulting significant rise in related personal and financial costs to individuals and society as a whole. With this in mind, we reviewed the literature and found little comprehensive attention had been given to *all* stages of musculoskeletal injury. Therefore, we analyzed the research and grouped the end-to-end process into a three-stage injury continuum: *Cause, Disability,* and *Decision*.

Some believe the *Cause* of disability is the result of complex interactions between genetic, morphological, psychosocial, and biomechanical factors. Others believe injury is caused by fatigue, mechanical degradation, or overexertion. The conception of *Disability* encompasses the consideration of physical and psychosocial factors with no clear agreement as to what is the most important factor in defining disability. While some look to biomedical treatment guidelines for musculoskeletal disorders, others explain disability in almost exclusive psychiatric terms. Proponents supporting primarily business and insurance interests suggest that disability symptoms may be a manifestation of attempts to receive compensation for disability. Contrary to this approach to disability is the labor relations viewpoint, which puts the responsibility for the treatment and prevention of liability on the disabled person's employer. There are also those professionals who take a broader, more inclusive view of disability, considering biological, psychological, and social aspects. Finally, there are many thoughts on what motivates an individual's *Decision* to return to work. Some believe it is personal motivation; still others think it is the amount and duration of pain; and more look to the person's employer as the primary agent of change.

TABLE 1. The Three-Stage CDD Injury Continuum and the Models on Which it is Based

Stage One—Cause →		Stage Two—Disability →		Stage Three—Decision	
Models	Key Tenets	Models	Key Tenets	Models	Key Tenets
Multivariate Interaction Fatigue Theory	Injury stems from complex interactions between genetics, morphological, psychological, and biomechanical factors.	*Biomedical Model*	Disability is due to underlying biophysical abnormality due to organic pathology. Physical and mental etiologies are separated.	*Readiness for Change Model*	Five motivational stages and a "decisional balance" explain the motivation behind behavioral change.
Differential Fatigue Theory	Injury stems from repetitive movements, resulting in fatigue and eventual inappropriate muscle use. The repetitive tasks assignments arise out of industries' own financial incentives for increased production with maximal efficiency.	*Psychiatric Model*	Disability is a physical manifestation of psychological/psychiatric problems.	*Phase Model*	Progression towards a decision to change behaviors revolves around timing: acute versus chronic.
		Insurance Model	The presence and strength of secondary and tertiary gains explain disability.	*Readiness for Return-to-Work Model*	The beliefs and behaviors of workers are the key components of change in the decision to return to work.
Cumulative Load Theory	Injury results from degradation of the muscles after prolonged use that is compounded by time on the job.	*Labor Relations Model*	Employers are partially responsible for treatment and prevention of disability, as the work environment is vital to an individual's psychological, social, and physical life.		
Overexertion Theory	Injury results from a combination of force generation, motion and duration.	*Biopsychosocial Model*	Disability is comprised of a complex interaction of biological, psychological, and social factors that influence an individual.		
		Sociomedical Model	Demographic characteristics and self- or other-imposed interventions may either exacerbate or buffer against the progression of disability.		

Regardless of the cause of the musculoskeletal injury, the disability, or the decisions to return to work, the progression of the disabled person through the CDD stages, is populated by an array of individuals, many with different points of view. Whether it is the provider, the employer, the caretaker, or even society as a whole, the patient is bombarded with intricate communications and varying belief systems, concerning injury, compensation, risk, and litigation.

Cause, Disability, and *Decision*: a continuum that spans the full range of a person's disability. Each individual stage in the musculoskeletal injury continuum must be thoroughly understood in part and in whole if we are to appreciate and apply the most effective and efficient treatment plans for disabled individuals.

REFERENCES

Adams, J. H., & de C. Williams, A. C. (2003). What affects return to work for graduates of a pain management program with chronic upper limb pain? *Journal of Occupational Rehabilitation, 13*(2), 91–106.

Al-Obaidi, S. M., Nelson, R. M., Al-Awadhi, S., & Al-Shuwaie, N. (2000). The role of anticipation and fear of pain in the persistence of avoidance behavior in the patients with chronic low back pain. *Spine, 25*(9), 1126–1131.

American Psychiatric Association (Ed.). (1994). *Diagnostic and Statistical Manual of Mental Disorders* (4 ed.). Washington, DC: American Psychiatric Association.

Anderson, G. B. J., Pope, M. H., & Frymoyer, J. W. (1984). Epidemiology. In M. H. Pope & J. W. Frymoyer (Eds.), *Occupational Low Back Pain*. New York: Praeger.

Badley, E. M., Rasooly, I., & Webster, G. K. (1994). Relative importance of musculoskeletal disorders as a cause of chronic health problems, disability, and health care utilization: findings from the 1990 Ontario Health Survery. *Journal of Rheumatology, 21*(505–514).

Belar, C. D., & Deardorff, W. W. (1999). *Clinical Health Psychology in Medical Settings, Revised*. Washington, D.C.: APA.

Bergman, S., Herrstrom, P., Hogstrom, K., Petersson, I. F., Svensson, B., & Jacobssen, L. T. H. (2001). Chronic musculoskeletal pain, prevalence rates, and sociodemographic associations in a Swedish population study. *Journal of Rheumatology, 28*, 1369–1377.

Bickenbach, J. E., Chatterji, S., Badley, E. M., & Ustun, T. B. (1999). Models of disablement, universalism and the international classification of impairments, disabilities and handicaps. *Social Science & Medicine, 48*, 1173–1187.

Butcher, J. N., Dahlstrom, W. G., Graham, J. R., Tellegen, A. M., & Kaemmer, B. (1989). *MMPI-2: Manual for the administration and scoring*. Minneapolis, MN: University of Minnesota Press.

Butler, R. J. (2000). Economic incentives in disability insurance and behavioral responses. *Journal of Occupational Rehabiliation, 10*(1), 7–19.

Cats-Baril, W. L., & Frymoyer, J. W. (1991). Identifying patients at risk of becoming disabled because of low-back pain. The Vermont rehabilitation engineering center predictive model. *Spine, 16*, 605–607.

Cole, D. C., Mondloch, M. V., & Group, E. P. M. (2002). Listening to workers: How recovery expectations predict outcomes. *Candian Medical Association Journal, 166*(749–754), 749–754.

Crichton, P., & Morley, S. (2002). Treating pain in cancer patients. In D. C. Turk & R. J. Gatchel (Eds.), *Psychological Approaches to Pain Management: A Practitioner's Handbook* (2nd ed.). New York: Guilford Press.

Dasinger, L. K., Krause, N., Thompson, P. J., Brand, R. J., & Rudolph, L. (2001). Doctor proactive communication, return to work recommendation, and duration of disability after a workers' compensation low back injury. *Journal of Occupational and Environmental Medicine, 43*(6), 515–525.

Engel, G. L. (1977). The need for a new medical model: A challenge for biomedicine. *Science, 196*(4286), 129–136.

Evanoff, B., Abedin, S., Grayson, D., Dale, A. M., Wolf, L., & Bohr, P. (2002). Is disability underreported following work injury? *Journal of Occupational Rehabilitation, 12*(3), 139–150.

Ferrari, R., & Kwan, O. (2001). The no-fault flavor of disability. *Medical Hypotheses, 56*(1), 77–84.

Floreen, H. (2003). A rehabilitation model of treatment, *Solving the puzzle of chronic pain: Understanding etiology, planning treatment* (Vol. Module 6, pp. 66). Dallas, TX: American Society of Professional Education.

France, C. R., France, J. L., al'Absi, M., Ring, C., & McIntyre, D. (2002). Catostrophizing is related to pain ratings, but not nociceptive flexion reflex threshold. *Pain, 99*, 459–463.

Franche, R. L., & Krause, N. (2002). Readiness for return to work following injury or illness: Conceptualizing the interpersonal impact of health care, workplace, and insurance factors. *Journal of Occupational Rehabilitation, 12*(4), 233–256.

Frank, J., Sinclair, S., Hogg-Johnson, S., Beaton, D., & Cole, D. (1998). Preventing disability from work-related low-back pain: New evidence gives new hope—if we can just get all the players on the same side. *Canadian Medical Association Journal, 158*(12), 1625–1631.

Gatchel, R. J. (1996). Psychological disorders and chronic pain: Cause and effect relationships. In R. J. Gatchel & D. C. Turk (Eds.), *Psychological Approaches to Pain Management: A Practitioner's Handbook* (pp. 33–52). New York: Guilford.

Gatchel, R. J., Mayer, T. G., Capra, P., Diamond, P., & Barnett, J. (1986). Millon behavioral health inventory: Its utility in predicting physical function in patients with low back pain. *Archives of Physical Medicine and Rehabilitation, 67*, 878–882.

Harris, J. (2000). Is there a coherent social conception of disability? *Journal of Medical Ethics, 26*, 95–100.

Huang, G. D., & Feuerstein, M. (1998). Americans with Disabilities Act litigation and musculoskeletal-related impairments: Implications for work re-entry. *Journal of Occupational Rehabilitation, 8*, 91–102.

Hunter, J. (2001). Chronic pain and the concept of disablement. *The Clinical Journal of Pain, 17*(S), 10–11.

Janis, I. L., & Mann, L. (1977). *Decision making: A psychological analysis of conflict, choice, and commitment*. New York: Free Press.

Krause, N., Dasinger, L. K., Deegan, L. J., Rudolph, L., & Brand, R. J. (2001). Psychosocial job factors and return-to-work after compensated low back injury: A disability phase-specific analysis. *American Journal of Industrial Medicine, 40*(4), 374–392.

Krause, N., Dasinger, L. K., & Neuhauser, F. (1998). Modified work and return to work: A review of the literature. *Journal of Occupational Rehabilitation, 8*, 113–140.

Krause, N., Frank, J. W., Dasinger, L. K., Sullivan, T., & Sinclair, S. J. (2001). Determinants of duration of disability and return to work after work-related injury and illness: Challenges for future research. *American Journal of Industrial Medicine, 40*, 464–484.

Krause, N., & Ragland, D. R. (1994). Occupational disability due to low back pain: A new interdisciplinary classification used in a phase model of disability. *Spine, 19*, 1011–1020.

Kumar, S. (1990). Cummulative load as a risk factor for low-back pain. *Spine, 15*, 1311–1316.

Kumar, S. (1994). A conceptual model of oxerexertion, safety, and risk of injury in occupational settings. *Human Factors, 36*(2), 197–209.

Kumar, S. (2001). Theories of musculoskeletal injury causation. *Ergonomics, 44*(1), 17–47.

Kutner, N. G. (1987). Social ties, social support, and perceived health status among chronically disabled people. *Social Science & Medicine, 25*(1), 29–34.

Kwan, O., Ferrari, R., & Friel, J. (2001). Tertiary gain and disability syndromes. *Medical Hypotheses, 57*(4), 459–464.

Kwan, O., & Friel, J. (2002). Clinical relevance of the sick role and secondary gain in the treatment of disability syndromes. *Medical Hypotheses, 59*(2), 129–134.

Linton, S. J. (2002). A cognitive-behavioral approach to the prevention of chronic back pain. In D. C. Turk & R. J. Gatchel (Eds.), *Psychological Approaches to Pain Management: A Practitioner's Handbook* (2nd ed.). New York: Guilford.

Linton, S. J., Vlaeyen, J., & Ostelo, R. (2002). The back pain beliefs of health care providers: Are we fear-avoidant? *Journal of Occupational Rehabilitation, 12*(4), 223–232.

MacKenzie, E. J., Morris, J. A., Jurkovich, G. J., Yasui, Y., Cushing, B. M., Burgess, A. R., et al. (1998). Return to work following injury: The role of economic, social and job-related factors. *American Journal of Public Health, 88*(11), 1630–1637.

Marhold, C., Linton, S. J., & Melin, L. (2002). Identification of obstacles for chronic pain patients to return to work: Evaluation of a questionnaire. *Journal of Occupational Rehabilitation, 12*, 65–76.

Matheson, L. N. (2001). Disability methodology redesign: Considerations for a new approach to disabilty determination. *Journal of Occupational Rehabilitation, 11*(3), 135–142.

Mayer, T. G., Gatchel, R. J., & Evans, T. H. (2002). Chronic low back pain. In R. H. Fitzgerald, H. Kauger & A. L. Malkani (Eds.), *Orthopadics* (pp. 1192–1197). St. Louis: Mosby.

Mayer, T. G., Gatchel, R. J., & Polatin, P. B. (1992). The functional restoration programme for the postoperative and chronic low back pain patient. In M. I. V. Jayson (Ed.), *The Lumbar Spine and Back Pain* (pp. 517–535). Great Britain: Butler & Tanner, Ltd.

Mittenberg, W., Patton, C., Canyock, E. M., & Condit, D. C. (2002). Base rates of malingering and symptom exaggeration. *Journal of Clinical and Experimental Neuropsychology, 24*, 1094–1102.

Mobley, E. M., Linz, D. H., Shukla, R., Breslin, R. E., & Deng, C. (2000). Disability case management: An impact assessment in an automotive manufacturing organization. *Journal of Occupational and Environmental Medicine, 42*(6), 597–602.

Mondloch, M. V., Cole, D. C., & Frank, J. W. (2001). Does how you do depend on how you think you'll do? A systematic review of the evidence for a relation between patients' recovery expectations and health outcomes. *Candian Medical Association Journal, 165*(10), 174–179.

Moon, S., & Liu, J. (1998). The physician/patient encounter from a cognitive behavioral therapy perspective. *Journal of Occupational Rehabilitation, 8*(2), 153–172.

National Research Council. (2001). *Musculoskeletal Disorders and the Workplace: Low Back and Upper Extremities*. Washington, D.C.: National Academy Press.

Nielson, W. R., & Weir, R. (2001). Biopsychosocial approaches to the treatment of chronic pain. *Clinical Journal of Pain, 17*(4 Suppl), S114–127.

Nordqvist, C., Holmqvist, C., & Alexanderson, K. (2003). Views of laypersons on the role employers play in return to work when sick-listed. *Journal of Occupational Rehabilitation, 13*(1), 11–20.

Olkin, R. (2002). Could you hold the door for me? Including disability in diversity. *Cultural Diversity & Ethnic Minority Psychology, 8*, 130–137.

Olkin, R., & Pledger, C. (2003). Can disability studies and psychology join hands? A new model of disability. *American Psychologist, 58*, 296–304.

One Hundred First Congress of the United States of America. (1990). *Americans with Disabilities Act of 1990*. Retrieved August 7, 2003, from *http://www.usdoj.gov/crt/ada/pubs/ada.txt*

Petrie, K. J., Weinman, J., Sharpe, N., & Buckley, J. (1996). Role of patients' view of their illness in predicting return to work and functioning after myocardial infarcation: Longitudinal study. *British Medical Journal, 312*(May), 1191–1194.

Pledger, C. (2003). Discourse on disability and rehabilitation issues: Opportunities for psychology. *American Psychologist, 58*, 279–284.

Prochaska, J. O. (1994). Strong and weak principles for progressing from precontemplation to action on the basis of twelve problem behaviors. *Health Psychology, 13*(1), 47–51.

Prochaska, J. O., & DiClemente, C. C. (1983). Stages and processes of self-change in smoking: Toward an integrative model. *Journal of Consulting & Clinical Psychology, 51*, 390–395.

Prochaska, J. O., DiClemente, C. C., & Norcross, J. C. (1992). In search of how people change: Applications to addictive behaviors. *American Psychologist, 47*(9), 1102–1114.

Prochaska, J. O., DiClemente, C. C., Velicer, W. F., Ginpil, S., & Norcross, J. C. (1985). Predicting change in smoking status for self-changers. *Addictive Behaviors, 10*(4), 395–406.

Prochaska, J. O., Velicer, W. F., Rossi, J. S., Goldstein, M. G., Marcus, B. H., Rakowski, W., et al. (1994). Stages of change and decisional balance for 12 problem behaviors. *Health Psychology, 13*(1), 39–46.

Rosenman, K. D., Gardiner, J. C., Wang, J., Biddle, J., Hogan, A., Reilly, M. J., et al. (2000). Why most workers' with occupational repetitive trauma do not file for workers' compensation. *Journal of Occupational and Environmental Medicine, 42*(1), 25–34.

Sandstrom, J. (1986). Clinical and social factors in rehabilitation of patients with chronic low back pain. *Scandinavian Journal of Rehabilitation Medicine, 18*, 35–43.

Sandstrom, J., & Esbjornsson, E. (1986). Return to work after rehabilitation. The significance of the patient's own prediction. *Scandinavian Journal of Rehabilitation Medicine, 18*, 29–33.

Schultz, I. Z., Crook, J., Fraser, K., & Joy, P. W. (2000). Models of diagnosis and rehabilitation in musculoskeletal pain-related occupational disability. *Journal of Occupational Rehabilitation, 10*(4), 271–293.

Silversides, A. (1998). Disability management efforts can reduce number of injuires, improve bottom line. *Canadian Medical Association Journal, 159*, 268–269.

Social Security Online. (2003). *Disability planner: What we mean by disability*. Retrieved July 23, 2003, from http://www.ssa.gov/dibplan/dqualify4.htm

Susman, J. (1994). Disability, stigma and deviance. *Social Science and Medicine, 38*(1), 15–22.

Tate, D., & Pledger, C. (2003). An integrative conceptual framework of disability. *American Psychologist, 58*, 289–295.

Tate, R. B., Yassi, A., Cooper, J., & Ryan, J. (1999). Predictors of time loss after back injury in nurses. *Spine, 24*(18), 1930–1936.

Teasell, R. W., & Bombardier, C. (2001). Employment-related factors in chronic pain and chronic pain disability. *Clinical Journal of Pain, December 2001 supplement*, S39–S45.

Treloar, L. L. (2002). Disability, spiritual beliefs and the church: The experiences of adults with disabilities and family members. *Journal of Advanced Nursing, 40*(5), 594–603.

Turk, D. C., & Monarch, E. S. (2002). Biopsychosocial perspective on chronic pain. In D. C. Turk & R. J. Gatchel (Eds.), *Psychological Approaches to Pain Management: A Practitioner's Handbook* (2nd ed.). New York: Guilford.

Turk, D. C., & Okifuji, A. (2002). Psychological factors in chronic pain. *Journal of Consulting & Clinical Psychology, 70*, 678–690.

U.S. Department of Labor. (2000). Lost-worktime injuries and illnesses: Characteristics and resulting time away from work, 1998, Publication USDL 00–115. Washington D.C.: U.S. Department of Labor.

Usten, T. B., Saxena, S., Rehm, J., & Bickenbach, J. (1999). Are disability weights universal? WHO/NIH Joint project CAR study group [comment]. *Lancet, 354*(9186), 1306.

Verbrugge, L. M., & Jette, A. M. (1994). The disablement process. *Social Science & Medicine, 38*(1), 1–14.

Weir, R., & Nielson, W. R. (2001). Interventions for disability management. *Clinical Journal of Pain, Etiology, Prevention, Treatment, and Disability Management of Chronic Pain, 17*(4 (Supplement)), S128–S132.

Williams, R. M., & Westmorland, M. (2002). Perspectives on workplace disability management: A review of the literature. *Work, 19*, 87–93.

World Health Organization. (1998). Bone and joint decade 2000–2010. *ACTA Orthopaedics Scandinavia, 69*, 219–220.

Wright, A. R., & Gatchel, R. J. (2002). Occupational rehabilitation: Interdisciplinary management of work-related musculoskeletal pain and disability. In D. C. Turk & R. J. Gatchel (Eds.), *Psychological Approaches to Pain Management: A Practitioner's Handbook* (2nd ed.). New York: Guilford.

7

Outcome Measures in Prediction of Occupational Disability

Peter Polatin, Richard C. Robinson, and J. P. Garofalo

INTRODUCTION

Chronic pain is a costly and debilitating medical condition. In the United States, approximately 80% of visits to physicians are related to pain (1). Pain affects more than 50 million Americans and consumes more than $70 billion in health care costs and lost productivity (2). The complex nature of pain demands assessment and treatment of both the biological and the psychosocial factors that exacerbate and maintain its symptoms and dysfunctions.

No single instrument can adequately assess pain, functional capacity, disability, emotional distress, and primary/secondary gain issues. A combination of subjective self report measures and objective physical and behavioral measures, along with historic/financial data allows the clinician to have the most in-depth assessment, in a "stepwise approach" (3) to the biopsychosocial assessment of chronic pain patients.

SELF-REPORT MEASURES

Pain and reactive emotional distress are subjective experiences. However, the assessment of subjective experience can still be undertaken when suitable instruments are used, which have demonstrated adequate reliability and validity. Reliability is equivalent to consistency and validity is equivalent to accuracy. For example, an archer who is able to hit the same area of a target repeatedly, would have aim that could be considered reliable. However, only if the archer is able to hit the bull's eye consistently, could her aim be considered reliable and valid. Below are several examples of self-report measures with adequate reliability and validity.

DOI: 10.1007/978-0-387-28919-9_7, © 2009 Springer Science+Business Media, LLC

Pain Affecting Function

Million Visual Analogue Scale (VAS; (4). This visual analogue scale is used to rate the patient's degree of pain on a scale from 0 (no pain) to 10 (worst possible pain). The scale consists of a 10-centimeter horizontal line hashed at two-point intervals. The patient is asked to mark an "X" on the line to represent current level of pain. Many studies support the use of the VAS with chronic pain patients, and the VAS has demonstrated good psychometric properties, especially when a ruler is used to determine the exact placement of the patient's mark. An additional benefit of the VAS is that is appears to have adequate responsiveness to change (4,5).

The Dallas Pain Questionnaire (DPQ). The DPQ is a 15-item analogue, self-report scale assessing perceived pain and disability. Million, Haavik-Nilson, Jayson and Baker (6) developed the scale, and validated it through correlation with clinicians' findings. Each response is scored on a scale of 0 to 10, and the total score is the sum of all responses. Scores of 0 to 39 indicate "mildly disabling pain"; 40 to 84 indicate "moderately disabling pain"; and 85 and above indicate "severely disabling pain". The Dallas Pain Questionnaire has particular utility when the self-report of pain exceeds what would be expected given physical findings, suggesting the potential existence of a psychosocial component to the patient's disability (7).

Oswestry Pain Disability Questionnaire (8). The Oswestry is a self-rating scale designed to assess the degree of subjective functional impairment the patient reports experiencing in a variety of activities of daily living as a result of pain. The Oswestry offers six choices under each activity of daily living, ranging from the least indicative of impaired functioning to the most indicative of impaired functioning. Test-retest reliability ranges from .94 to .99, and internal consistency was found to be .71. Validity was determined to be adequate through correlation between the Oswestry and scales on the Roland-Morris Questionnaire and other related scales (9).

Roland and Morris Disability Questionnaire (RMDQ; (10)). The RMDQ is a 24 item, "yes"/"no," self-report questionnaire that was derived from the longer Sickness Impact Profile. In recent years, the RMDQ has gained popularity, because of its ease of use. The SIP has adequate psychometric properties, and when the RMDQ has been studied, adequate reliability and sensitivity to clinical change has been noted (10).

Multidimensional Pain Inventory (MPI; (11)). The MPI is a 56-item, self-report questionnaire that assesses several dimensions of pain; including severity, social support and affective distress. Using statistical means, Turk and Rudy (12) derived a classification system for pain patients based on the patient's scores on the MPI scales. These classifications describe the way in which patients manage their pain as well as the impact of the pain on major life domains, and include a "Dysfunctional," "Interpersonally Distressed," and "Adaptive Coper" style. The psychometric properties of the MPI and the classification system are sound (13).

Depression

As pain becomes chronic, patients often will report problems with sleep, appetite, libido, and energy. There may be social withdrawal and progressive loss of enjoyment in recreational activities. They begin to appear depressed. In one carefully controlled study of chronic pain patients, Polatin and colleagues (14) found a point prevalence of 45% and a lifetime prevalence of 64% for major depressive disorder. Not only is depression a frequent consequence of pain, but the fatigue, difficulty with attention and pessimistic outlook associated with depression interfere with the patient's ability to participate in treatment.

Beck Depression Inventory (BDI-2). The Beck Depression Inventory (15) is a 21-item self-report measure designed to assess depressive symptomatology with numerically graded response which can be filled out by a patient without clinical supervision in approximately five minutes. A total score of 0–10 is considered normal; 11–14 indicates mild depression; 15–18 represents moderate depression; 19–30 reflects severe depression; and 30+ indicates very severe depression. Research using the BDI-2 has established good psychometric properties with test-retest reliabilities ranging from .48 to .86, and a mean internal consistency of .86 (16). A major strength of the BDI-2 is that is well-known by many practitioners and third party payors. In addition, the BDI-2 is commonly used to assess pre to post changes in depressive symptomatology (9).

Hamilton Psychiatric Rating Scale for Depression (HAM-D; (17)). The HAM-D assesses depressive symptomatology using a semi-structured interview format. It consists of 17 items rated on a 3- to 5-point scale. The following cut-off scores are used to assess severity of depression: <12 (none to minimal); 12–20 (mild to moderate); 21–29 (moderate to severe); 30+ (severe). The HAM-D has demonstrated an inter-rater reliability correlation coefficient of .9 (18), and has demonstrated acceptable concurrent validity of .73 with the BDI-2 (16). The HAM-D in combination with the BDI-2 captures both the patient's perception of their distress as well as the clinician's perception. However, the redundancy of the HAM-D in combination with BDI-2, along with the training required to ensure proper administration, argues for the use of the BDI-2 when time does not allow for a more thorough investigation of depressive symptoms.

Physical and Emotional Well-Being

In recent years, the importance and appreciation for the concept of "quality of life" has received increasing attention. Although quantifying this concept and capturing all the relevant domains that factor into quality of life can be challenging, several well-validated and relatively easy to administer instruments have been developed and implemented.

Medical Outcomes Short Form-36 Health-Status Survey (SF-36; (19)). The SF-36 is a 36-item, self-report questionnaire that assesses mental and physical health-related quality of life. It yields eight individual scales, as well as two standardized summary scales (the Mental Component Scale and the Physical Component Scale). Numerous studies reported in the SF-36 manual have shown high reliability coefficients for each of the eight scales. The psychometric properties of the SF-36 have been demonstrated to be excellent. SF-36 scales have also been found to correlate well with other health-related measures. In addition, there are good normative data for various medical populations published in the SF-36 manual, including a spinal population (19). However, caution must be exercised when using the individual scales to assess the impact of an intervention of a particular patient (20).

Global Psychological Status

These instruments are often used by psychologists as part of a comprehensive test battery to identify psychological "barriers to recovery" in a chronic pain patient. They may also be used to demonstrate improvement in pain, functioning and psychiatric symptoms during or after treatment.

Minnesota Multiphasic Personality Inventory-Second Edition (MMPI-2; (21)). The MMPI-2 is a 567-item, self-report measure of personality functioning and psychiatric symptoms. There are 10 empirically-derived clinical scales and numerous supplementary scales. The MMPI-2 normative sample closely approximated 1980 census data, and demonstrated adequate internal consistency and test-retest reliability (21). Several validity scales are provided to assess the test-taking attitudes of the patient. In the assessment of chronic pain patients, the MMPI-2 is useful in the identification of psychopathology as well as personality and behavioral characteristics, treatment planning, and prediction of treatment outcome (22).

Millon Behavioral Medicine Diagnostic (MBMD) (23). The MBMD is a 165-item, self-report inventory that is designed to assess psychological factors that can influence the treatment course of medical patients. The developers of the MBMD describe it as a substantial upgrading of their previous Millon Behavioral Health Inventory (MBHI). The MBMD yields 29 clinical scales, 3 response pattern scales, 1 validity indicator, and 6 negative health habits indicators. It is appropriate for use with adult clinical and rehabilitation patients (aged 18–85) who are undergoing medical care or surgical evaluation. The MBMD has demonstrated satisfactory reliability with an internal consistency estimate of .79, and test-retest estimates with a median value of .83 (23).

Structured Clinical Interview for DSM-IV (SCID) (24). The SCID is a structured interview that allows for the diagnosis of specific psychiatric disorders. The major advantage of the SCID over unstructured or semi-structured interviews is that it has high inter-rater reliability and has repeatedly been proven as a valid measure. In fact, the SCID is considered by most in the mental health field as the "gold standard" of psychiatric diagnosis. As with the other instruments in this section, the SCID must be administered by a trained clinician and is best suited for identifying psychopathology rather than monitoring treatment outcomes.

BEHAVIORAL MEASURES

In addition to self-report paper and pencil tests, more objective measures of behavior determined by physical and psychosocioeconomic factors lend additional depth to the assessment of the chronic pain patient.

Observed Behavior

Waddell Nonorganic Signs ("Behavioral Signs"). In 1980, Waddell (25) described behaviors by back pain patients on physical examination that he termed nonorganic or "behavioral signs." Since that time, these signs have been integrated into many clinicians' assessments. The eight original signs are the following: (1) Superficial Tenderness; (2) Nonanatomic Tenderness; (3) Axial Loading; (4) Simulated Rotation; (5) Distraction Straight Leg Raising; (6) Regional Weakness; (7) Regional Sensory Change; and (8) "Overreaction" to Examination (grimacing, sighing, guarding, bracing, and rubbing). Waddell hypothesized that the presence of several of these signs (i.e., three or more) suggested that the patient dos not have a simple, straightforward physical problem. When used with appropriate cut-off scores the *behavioral signs* have adequate inter-rater reliability and clinical validty (9).

Outcome Measures

Work Return. Whether or not a patient returns to work, either spontaneously or after a therapeutic intervention, is a critical measure of recovery. Typically, work return within six months to one year of last contact is the usual interval, although some studies will monitor subjects for up to two years (26).

Work Retention. A patient may return to work, but whether or not he actually continues working up to the time of the follow-up interview is a more robust measure of recovery. Retention may be affected by a number of psychosocioeconomic factors, such as rapport with the employer, state of the economy, and psychological status (26).

Health Care Utilization. A patient may return to work, but how much more medical treatment he seeks and receives is another measure of therapeutic success. There are several individual queries which, when grouped together, provide a composite index of health care utilization. *Additional* **surgery** *to the same area of injury* is potentially the most costly element. *Number of subsequent* **health care visits** *for the same problem*, even if derived as a rough estimate within certain specified ranges (0–5, 5–10, 10–20) adds to the index. *Number of* **prescribed medications** *being used* also provides information about future health care cost. The final dimension of socioeconomic outcomes considered in the evaluation systems for occupational musculoskeletal disorders is **case closure.** Not only is case closure a demonstrated major area of indemnity cost that generally represents 10% to 30% of workers' compensation claim costs, but in certain venues, the cost of case closure in some cases is well over 90% of total claims cost. Often certain related secondary costs must be considered related to the occupational injury claim (26).

Medication Misuse. The proper medicinal use of opioids, in light of their well-established history and current relationship to social ills, continues to be debated and remains unclear in several areas of medicine. Controversy over the prescription of opioids for chronic non-malignant pain continues despite the growing acceptance of this practice. Indeed, past research supports the beneficial use of opioids for non-cancer pain (27).

TABLE 1. Portenoy's Predictive Factors for Problematic Drug Use

Probably more predictive
- Selling prescription drugs
- Prescription forgery
- Stealing of "borrowing drugs from others
- Injecting oral formulations
- Obtaining prescription drugs from nonmedical sources
- Concurrent abuse of alcohol or illicit drugs
- Multiple dose escalations or other noncompliance with therapy despite warnings
- Multiple episodes of prescription "loss"
- Repeatedly seeking prescriptions from other clinicians or room emergency rooms without informing prescriber of after warning to desist
- Evidence of deterioration in the ability to function at work, in the family, or social that appear to be relate to drug use
- Repeated resistance to changes in therapy despite clear evidence of adverse physical or psychological effects form the drug

Probably less predictive
- Aggressive complaining about the need for more drug
- Drug hoarding during periods of reduce symptoms
- Requesting specific drugs
- Openly acquiring similar drugs form other medical sources
- Unsanctioned dose escalation or other noncompliance with therapy on one or two occasions
- Unapproved use of the drug to treat another symptoms
- Reporting psychic effects not intended by the clinician
- Resistance to a change in therapy associated with "tolerable" adverse effects with expressions of anxiety related to the return of severe symptoms

Currently, there is limited research on the risk factors for opioid misuse in chronic pain patients. Portenoy (27) describes several risk factors that he believes are important. He has operationalized behaviors that seem related to loss of control with regard to the drug use, compulsive drug use, and use despite harm. They are listed in Table 1.

In addition, Portenoy (1996) highlights the assumptions from clinical experience that patients with a history of substance abuse, a personality disorder, or chaotic familial relationships should be prescribed opioids cautiously. Clearly, more research is needed in this area and several different investigators are developing empirically sound screening instruments to detect opioid misuse. However, the close monitoring behaviors that are "warning signs" of opioid misuse (early refills) can determine if the patient is either misusing his medication or receiving ineffective pain relief.

FUNCTIONAL AND PHYSICAL MEASURES

While subjective and behavioral measures of disability status are important in measuring therapeutic success, more specific human performance parameters of *physical* and *functional* capacity are necessary to determine work capability and vocational status (28). These measures may, in turn, be compared to and matched with the known functional requirements of a job description to which the patient is being returned or for which he/she is being trained. For such a measure to be found useful, there should be a normative data base as well as a carefully described testing protocol that has accepted inter-test and inter-rater reliability (28).

Physical Measures

Physical measures include *range of motion* (ROM) determinations of a given joint or joints which were previously injured or medically impaired, and isolated *strength* measures for pararticular muscles moving these previously affected joints.

Range of Motion

For spinal motion (cervical, thoracic, and lumbar), the most accepted methodology is dual inclinometer measurement, described in the AMA Guides to the Evaluation of Permanent Impairment (29). Both saggital and axial motion may be determined by this technique, and these measurements have been correlated with impairment schedules which are in current use in most state juridictions in the United States.

For joint motion, use of a goniometer is recommended. Description of acceptable methodology may also be found in the AMA Guides (29), covering both the upper and lower extremities. This technique is also tied to impairment schedules as mentioned above.

Strength Measures

Manual motor testing, familiar to all physical therapists, is clinically useful in physical rehabilitation, but is not objective enough for documentation purposes. Isometric, isokinetic, or isodynamic protocols may be utilized to obtain strength measures. Isometric techniques involve measuring muscle force against a stationary load, such as a spring loaded or hydraulic device. Isometric techniques are used for assessment of grip strength, pinch strength, and isolated strength around any joint in the extremities in which motion is not permitted during the testing. Isometric devices (30) may be used for multiposition spinal strength testing as well. Isokinetic technology measures muscle strength at a fixed and constant rate of movement, which can be adjusted by the measurement device. Isokinetic devices may be applicable for isolated joints as well as spinal protocols (30). Isodynamic measurements do not fix either position or speed, and tend to be the least reliable and most subjective of these measures, although they lend themselves more easily to specific ergonomic situations. However, such measurements have less applicability for documentation purposes (30).

Functional Measures

Functional capacity tests are typically grouped into an ergonomic, work readiness evaluation referred to as a *functional capacity evaluation* (FCE), originally described by Isernhagen (31).

Activity Tests

The purpose of these tests is to evaluate a patient's capacity to perform activities of daily living (ADLs) relevant to a previously injured body part. Capacity is assessed according to defined normal values relative to speed of task, position tolerance, or repetitions per unit of time. Depending on the location of the injury, these whole body activity tests would include lifting, bending, sitting, squatting, kneeling, walking, running, reaching, carrying, peg board, keying, etc.

Cardiovascular and Upper Body Endurance

Assessment of overall *cardiovascular endurance* is performed on either a treadmill or stationary bicycle by use of a standardized protocol (30). Similarly, *upper body endurance* may be assessed by a protocol on either an Upper Body Ergometer (UBE) or rowing machine (30).

Effort

Physical and functional testing provides valuable information about a patient's status, but it may be influence by the test participant's willingness to perform at his or her maximal ability. Therefore, an integral component of such testing is an assessment of *effort*. The observing tester may express an opinion about effort expended on an ordinal scale, judging by visible exertion, substitution patterns, pulse and respiratory rate, or diaphoresis (32). A component of the test itself may allow for determination of maximal exertion, such as comparing the hip motion as measured by an inclinometer on the sacrum and straight leg raise as measured by inclinometer on the anterior thigh when measuring lumbar mobility. A difference of 15 degrees or more suggests suboptimal bending (33). The testing device may have a feature that determines effort on the measured task. Some of the isokinetic strength devices such as the Cybex TEF (trunk extensor/flexor) have a software computer program that measures the average points variance (APV) at all points along the curve of exertional effort. Extreme variations in that reading suggest poor effort on the testing (34). Finally, inconsistency in the testing, with variable performance, is suggestive of poor effort.

CONCLUSIONS

The assessment of occupational disability is complex, because it requires the careful evaluation of multiple dimensions of a disease process according to biopsychosocial and functional parameters. It is important to be aware of how the patient describes and visualizes himself within the context of perceived disability, but these measures may have inherent bias and are influenced by outside factors related to social relationships, economic and financial issues, and emotional determinants. Behavioral measures offer us a realistic view of how the individual "walks the walk", as opposed to how he/she "talks the talk". Ultimately, it is what the patient actually does that determines his disability status. Finally, human performance measures of physical and functional capacity provide relevant information about work readiness, adaptability to vocational tasks, and willingness to commit to a productive vocational role. The use of any one category of these measures does not give the full picture. The careful interpretation of results from all three types of tests can provide the clinician with an accurate multidimensional assessment of pre-treatment status and outcome after occupational rehabilitation.

REFERENCES

1. Woodwell, D.A. (2000). *National Ambulatory Medical Survey: 1998 Summary Advanced Data from Vital and Health Statistics No. 315* Hyattsville, MO: National Center for Health Statistics.
2. Mayer, T.G., Gatchel, R.J., & Polatin, P.B, (Eds.) (2000). *Occupational Musculoskeletal Disorders: Function, Outcomes and Evidence.* Philadelphia: Lippincott Williams & Wilkins.
3. Gatchel, R.J. (2001). A Biopsychosocial Overview of Pre-Treatment Screening of Patients with Pain. *The Clinical Journal of Pain, 17,* 92–199.
4. Million, S., Hall, W., Haavik, N.K., Baker, R.D., & Jayson, M.I.V. (1982). 1981 Volvo Award in Clinical Science: Assessment of the progress of the back-pain patient. *Spine, 7,* 204–212.
5. Gatchel, R.J., Mayer, T.G., Capra, P., Diamond. P., & Barnett, J. (1986). Quantification of lumbar function. Part VI: The use of psychological measure in guiding physical functional restoration. *Spine, 11,* 36–42.
6. Million, R., Haavik-Nilsen, J., Jayson, M.I.V., & Baker, R.D. (1981). Evaluation of low back pain and assessment of lumbar corsets with and without back supports. *Annals of the Rheumatic Diseases, 40,* 449–454.
7. Capra, P., Mayer, T.G., & Gatchel, R.J. (1985). Adding psychological scales to your back pain assessment. *The Journal of Musculoskeletal Medicine, 2,* 41–52.
8. Fairbanks, J.C., Couper, J., Davies, J.B., & O'Brien, J.P. (1980). The Oswestry low back pain disability questionnaire. *Physiotherapy, 66,* 271–273.
9. Gatchel, R.J. (2001). *A Compendium of Outcome Instruments for Assessment and Research of Spinal Disorders LaGrange,* IL: North American Spine Society.
10. Roland, M., & Morris, R. (1983). A study of the natural history of back pain. Part I: Development of a reliable and sensitive measure of disability and low back pain. *Spine, 8,* 141–144.
11. Kerns, R.D., Turk, D.C., & Rudy, T.E. (1985). The West Haven-Yale Multidimensional Pain Inventory. *Pain, 23,* 345–356.
12. Turk, D., & Rudy, T. (1988). Toward an empirically derived taxonomy of chronic pain patients: Integration of psychological assessment data. *Journal of Consulting & Clinical Psychology, 56,* 233–238.
13. Turk, D.C., & Rudy, T.E. (1990). Robustness of an empirically derived taxonomy of chronic pain patients. *Pain, 42,* 27–35.
14. Polatin, P.B., Kinney, R.K., Gatchel, R.J., Lillo, E., & Mayer, T.G. (1993). Psychiatric illness and chronic low-back pain. The mind and the spine–Which goes first? *Spine, 18(1),* 66–71.
15. Beck, A.T., Ward, C.H., Mendelson, M.M., Mock, J., & Erbaugh, J. (1961). An inventory for measuring depression. *Archives of General Psychiatry, 4,* 561–571.
16. Beck, A.T., Steer, R.A., & Garbin, M.G. (1988). Psychometric properties of the Beck Depression Inventory: Twenty-five years of evaluation. *Clinical Psychology Review, 8,* 77–100.
17. Hamilton, M. (1960). A rating scale for depression. *Journal of Neurology, Neurosurgery & Psychiatry, 23,* 56–62.
18. Rush, A.J., Beck, A.T., Kovacs, M., & Hollon, S. (1977). Comparative efficacy of cognitive therapy and pharmacotherapy in the treatment of depressed outpatients. *Cognitive Therapy and Research, 1,* 17–37.
19. Ware, J.E., & Sherbourne, C.D. (1992). The MOS 36-Item Short-Form Health Survey (SF-36). I. Conceptual framework and item selection. *Medical Care, 30,* 473–483.
20. Gatchel, R.J., Polatin, P.B., Mayer, T.G., Robinson, R., & Dersh, J. (1998). Use of the SF-36 health status survey with a chronically disabled back pain population: Strengths and limitations. *Journal of Occupational Rehabilitation, 8,* 237–246.
21. Butcher, J.N., Dahlstrom, W.G., Graham, J.R., Tellegen, A.M., & Kaemmer, B. (1989). MMPI-2: *Manual for the administration and scoring Minneapolis,* MN: University of Minnesota Press.
22. Gatchel, R.J., & Weisberg, J.N. (2000). *Personality Characteristics of Patients with Pain* Washington, DC: American Psychological Association Press.
23. Millon, T., Green, C., & Meagher, R. (1983). *Millon Behavioral Health Inventory.* 3rd. ed Minneapolis: National Computer Systems.
24. First, M.B., Spitzer, R.L., Gibbon, M., & Williams, B.W. (1994). *Structured Clinical Interview for Axis I DSM-IV Disorders* New York: Biometrics Research Department, New York State Psychiatric Institute.

25. Waddell, G., McCulloch, J., Kummel, E., & Venner, R. (1980). Non-organic physical signs in low back pain. *Spine, 5,* 117–125.
26. Mayer, T.G., Prescott, M., & Gatchel, R.J. (2000). Objective outcomes evaluation: Methods and evidence. In T.G. Mayer, P.B. Polatin & R.J. Gatchel (Eds.), *Occupational Musculoskeletal Disorders: Function, Outcomes and Evidence.* Philadelphia: Lippincott Williams & Wilkins.
27. Portenoy, R., & Foley, K. (1986). Chronic use of opioid analgesics in nonmalignant pain: Report of 38 cases. *Pain, 25,* 171–186.
28. Mayer, T. (2000). Chapter 30: Quantitave Physican and Functional Assessment. In T. Mayer, R. Gatchel, P. Polatin (Eds), *Occupational Musculoskeletal Disorders: Function, Outcomes and Evidence.*, pp. 547–560; Lippincot, Williams, & Wilkins, Philadelphia.
29. American Medical Association. (2000). *Guides to the Evaluation of Permanent Impairment,* 5th edition revised, Chicago, American Medical Association.
30. Flores, L., Gatchel, R., & Polatin, P. (1997). Objectification of functional improvement after nonoperative care. *Spine, 22,* 1622–1633.
31. Isernhagen, S. (1995). *The Comprehensive Guide to Work Injury Management.* Gaithersberg, Md., Aspen Publications.
32. Reneman, M., Jasgers, J., Westmaas, M., Goeken, L. (2002). The reliability of determining effort level of lifting and carrying in a functional capacity evaluation. *Work, 18,* 23–27.
33. Mayer, T., Pope, M., Tabor, J., Bovasso, E., Gatchel, R. (1994). Physical progress and residual impairment quantification after functional restoration. I. Lumbar mobility. *Spine, 19,* 389–394.
34. Hazard, R., Reid, S., Fenwick, J., Reeves, J. (1988). Isokinetic trunk and lifting strength measures: variability as an indicator of effort. *Spine, 13,* 54–57.

8

Tailoring Psychosocial Treatment for Patients with Occupational Disability

Richard C. Robinson, Robert J. Gatchel, and Travis Whitfill

INTRODUCTION

The cost of occupational musculoskeletal pain is staggering in terms of its impact on patients, family members, the economy and society. The annual cost of musculoskeletal disorders, when diagnosis, treatment, lost work days and compensation claims are calculated, amounts to tens of billions of dollars each year (Gatchel & Mayer, 2000). According to the US Department of Labor, 5.2 million injuries and illnesses were reported in private industry workplaces during 2001. This results in a rate of 5.7 cases per 100 equivalent full-time workers (Bureau of Labor Statistics, 2002). Of the 5.2 million total injuries and illnesses, 2.6 million (or 2.8 per 100 workers) were *lost workday cases*; that is, they required recuperation *away from work* or restricted duties at work, or both (Bureau of Labor Statistics, 2002). While the lost workday cases have continued to decrease in number each of the last several years, along with the total number of injury and illness cases, the cost of such cases requires that every effort be made to deal effectively with each.

Among lost workday cases, the most costly are those involving recuperation away from work. Away from work cases account for 60% of lost workday injuries/illnesses, and apply to 1.7 per 100 workers (Bureau of Labor Statistics, 2002). Common occupations, such as truck driving, nursing, janitorial services and cooking, compose 4 of the 10 careers with the highest number of cases resulting in time away from work. These 10 occupations account for one-third of the cases requiring recuperation away from work. (1995) Sprains and strains account for 40% of the total number of injuries, with the back being the most affected body region (U.S. Department of Labor, 2000). Of note, 5% of the work force accounts for 80% of the benefits, such as health care costs, short term disability and workers' compensation, paid as a result of workplace injuries and illnesses (Butler, 2000).

As the field of pain and disability management continues to evolve, the process of refining models is constantly occurring. As recently as 20 years ago, the biomedical model of pain and disability dominated the landscape. However, the biopsychosocial

DOI: 10.1007/978-0-387-28919-9_8, © 2009 Springer Science+Business Media, LLC

approach to pain management has become the new model from which the majority of pain and disability management specialists operate. In the traditional biomedical model, pain was thought to have a direct relationship with the amount and degree of tissue damage. In this traditional model, pain and disability were broken down into functional and organic categories. In organic categories, the pain and disability were seen as "real problems," compared to those illnesses which fell into the functional category. With the functional category, physical problems were perceived as situations in which the physical symptom was serving some sort of psychological function for the patient (Turk, 1996). For instance, a patient who is angry with his/her employer develops back pain as a way of punishing the employer, as well as punishing himself.

Although the traditional medical model is still applicable in many situations, with regard to chronic long-standing illnesses the biopsychosocial approach is more appropriate. In the biopsychosocial approach, a distinction is made between *disease* and *illness*. *Disease* is considered the objective biological problem, such as tissue damage. *Illness* is understood as all the subjective feelings, behaviors and thoughts related to the disease process. It is important to note that the biological aspect of the biopsychosocial approach is not de-emphasized. Rather, psychosocial variables are given a much more prominent role than in the biomedical approach, especially when discussing factors that maintain or exacerbate illness.

Despite the demonstrated effectiveness of many interdisciplinary pain treatment programs to address the complex nature of chronic pain and disability in patients with a variety of musculoskeletal disorders (Gatchel et al., 2003; Mayer, Gatchel, Polatin & Evans, 1999; Robbins et al., 2003), efforts to empirically examine tailored treatments is still in its infancy. However, relevant psychosocial factors that impact treatment have been rigorously investigated. These factors include the need to address psychopathology, the need to consider the impact of childhood abuse, and the need to understand a person's pattern of management and coping with life's difficulties.

PSYCHOSOCIAL FACTORS AND PAIN

Research over the past three decades has clearly demonstrated the central importance of psychosocial factors in the perception and reporting of chronic pain and disability (Flor & Turk, 1984; Fordyce, 1976; Fordyce, 1988; Fordyce, Fowler, Lehmann & Delateur, 1968). As early as 1959, Engel (1959) argued that the perception of pain is a psychological phenomenon. He also described personality characteristics that he hypothesized predisposed individuals to chronic pain. These characteristics included a history of defeat, significant guilt, unsatisfied aggressive impulses, and a propensity to develop pain in response to a real or imagined loss. Gatchel and Epker (1999) provided an updated review of many of the psychosocial risk factors.

Melzack and Wall's (1965) gate control theory of pain represented an important milestone by hypothesizing that central nervous system mechanisms provided the physiological basis for psychological involvement in pain perception. Specifically, these researchers theorized that a neurophysiological mechanism in the spinal cord (located in the dorsal horns) acted as a gate for pain signals, and allowed for modulation from various sources. Thus, the gate control theory integrated peripheral stimuli with cortical variables, explaining the impact that mood states may have on pain perception.

Psychopathology and Pain

The central importance of psychosocial factors in the pain perception process has come to be accepted by the scientific community. The majority of the research conducted in this area has focused on the relationship between pain and depression. Several studies have reported extremely high rates of major depressive disorder in chronic pain patients with current and lifetime rates of 45% and 65%, respectively, in the chronic low back population, and both current and lifetime rates of about 80% in the chronic upper extremity population (Kinney, Gatchel, Polatin, Fogarty & Mayer, 1993; Polatin, Kinney, Gatchel, Lillo & Mayer, 1993). It should be noted, however, that the reported prevalences of depression in chronic pain patients vary a great deal. In fact, rates between 31% and 100% have been reported (Romano & Turner, 1985). Most studies report prevalences that can be classified in the moderately high range. For instance, a study conducted by Banks and Kerns (1996) addressed this issue through a review of 14 studies that utilized the Diagnostic and Statistical Manual (DSM) criteria for diagnosing major depression in chronic pain patients. The authors reported that 9 of the 14 studies reviewed reported prevalences of major depression in chronic pain patients to be between 30% and 54%. These percentages can be compared with recent estimates of current and lifetime major depression for the entire United States population, which are 5% and 17%, respectively (Blazer, Kessler, Mcgonagle & Swartz, 1994).

Fishbain, Cutler, Rosomoff, and Rosomoff (1997) attempted to explore this relationship through a meta-analysis of studies that concerned both chronic pain and depression, and reported a number of interesting findings. Of the 23 studies that were reviewed, 21 related the severity of pain to the degree of depression. Each of the three studies reviewed that focused on the association between pain duration and the development of depression found a relationship between these two variables. In addition, a relationship was found between pain frequency and depression in all four of the studies reviewed. The authors reviewed two studies that looked at the association between depression and the number of pain sites. Both of these studies reported a relationship between the two variables, with multiple pain site patients being much more likely to be depressed than single site pain patients.

Demographic and work-related variables that impact the risk of disability due to the combination of depression and chronic pain have also been explored in the literature, but with mixed findings (Averill, Novy, Nelson & Berry, 1996). A study by Averill and colleagues (1996) provided some clarity to this issue with a group of 254 chronic pain patients. In addition to addressing pain-related variables, the authors of this study conducted a comprehensive examination of a number of demographic and work-related variables. Overall, the variable of work status (employment) was the most highly related to increased depression in chronic pain patients, followed by education level, and marital status. The strong relationship between work status and depression in chronic pain patients is consistent with an earlier study by Magni and colleagues (1994) in which unemployment was associated with increased levels of depression. With respect to education level, lower levels of education related to increased depressive symptoms in chronic pain patients. The authors postulate that this finding may be the result of the fewer alternative work options that are available to those with lower education levels. In addition, reasoning skills that are more concrete in nature, and less flexibility in coping options, are also proposed as possible explanations. As for marital status, single status was found to be highly related to increased levels of depression. This finding is in contrast to an earlier study by Haythronthwaite, Sieber, and Kerns (1991) that found no relation between depression and marital status in chronic pain patients.

In addition to the three variables that accounted for the majority of the variance (work status, education level, and marital status), an interaction was also found between depression and several other variables. With respect to demographic variables, age and gender interacted with depression, with younger women endorsing more depressive symptomatology than younger men, and older men scoring higher than older women. In addition, it should be noted that no relation was found between ethnicity and depression among the chronic pain patients. As for work-related variables, a significant interaction was found between planned litigation and work status, which is consistent with the results of Tait, Chibnall, and Richardson (1990). Chronic pain patients who were working and planning litigation had higher levels of depression than patients who were working and not planning litigation; patients who were both not working and not planning litigation were more depressed than those who were not working, but were planning litigation. In explaining these findings, the authors postulate that depression in individuals that are both working and litigating may be the result of an "internal conflict" about their two contradictory roles. As for those who are neither working nor litigating, the authors suggest that feelings of powerlessness and hopelessness may be responsible for their depressive symptomatology.

A number of studies have looked at the way in which co-occurrence of depression and chronic pain impacts treatment and subsequent disability. Weickgenant, Slater, Patterson, Atkinson, Grant, and Garfin (1993) found that chronic low back pain patients with depression avoid activities more than those who do not suffer from depression. The authors also reported that depressed patients engage in more self-blame and display a greater tendency to avoid social support and behaviors aimed at problem solving. Dworkin, Handlin, Richlin, Brand, and Vannucci (1985) looked at a group of chronic pain patients and determined that those suffering from depression were less likely to benefit from treatment. Haley, Turner, and Romano (1985) reported that chronic pain patients treated with antidepressant medications reported less pain-related symptoms, while Von Korff and Simon (1996) found that patients' depressive symptoms improve when their pain symptoms are alleviated. In addition to these findings, it has also been noted that depressed patients magnify the perception of pain and have a lower pain tolerance (Averill et al., 1996).

In summary, it is clear that a relationship exists between depression and chronic pain. The degree of depression is related to the presence, frequency, duration, and severity of pain. There is also a strong relationship between depression and the number of pain sites. Depressed chronic pain patients tend to magnify their symptoms, avoid more activities, benefit less from treatment, and engage in more self-blaming behaviors. Work status, level of education, and marital status appear to be the most important correlates of depression in chronic pain population. In addition to these three variables, a number of other demographic, pain-related, and work-related variables appear to be associated with depression in the chronic pain population. This information is of use because it can aid in predicting pain patients that are at risk for developing depression, and becoming increasingly disabled due to the combination of depression and chronic pain. With these patients, early preventative treatments may decrease the likelihood of long-term disability.

The Relationship between Pain and Psychopathology: Cause or Effect?

It is evident that chronic pain is a complex psychophysiological behavior pattern that is not amenable to simple component analyses of psychological, social, and physical factors. One of the more vexing questions about the relationship between pain and psychopathology involves the following, "which comes first, the pain or psychopathology?" This question does not have a simple answer, but researchers are beginning to develop a better understanding of the relationship between pain and psychopathology.

Several studies have provided evidence that chronic pain clearly contributes to the expression of psychological distress and psychopathology. Sternbach, Wolf, Murphy, and Akeson (1973) compared the Minnesota Multiphasic Personality Inventory (MMPI) profiles of acute and chronic pain patients and found that the chronic pain patients reported significantly more psychological distress as measured by the first three clinical scales of the MMPI (Scale 1-Hypochondriasis; Scale 2- Depression; and Scale 3-Hysteria; also known as the neurotic triad). Barnes, Gatchel, Mayer, and Barnett (Barnes, Gatchel, Mayer & Barnett, 1990) obtained similar results with the MMPI, finding that six months after successfully completing an intensive three-week rehabilitation program, when a majority of the patients had returned to work, previously elevated measures of distress had returned to normal levels.

Polatin, Kinney, Gatchel, Lillo, and Mayer (Polatin et al., 1993) also attempted to delineate the complex relationship between psychopathology and pain. Using the Structured Clinical Interview for the Diagnostic and Statistical Manual of Mental Disorders-III-Revised, Polatin and colleagues (1993) found that of 200 chronic low back pain (CLBP) patients, 77% met lifetime diagnostic criteria for psychiatric disturbances. The most common diagnoses were depression, substance abuse, and anxiety disorders. In addition, 51% of the patients met criteria for a personality disorder. Gatchel, Polatin, Mayer, and Garcy (1994b) examined 152 CLBP patients prior to undergoing an intensive three week functional restoration program, and found that 90% of the CLBP patients met criteria for a lifetime Axis I diagnosis; the most prevalent diagnoses being major depression and substance abuse.

Although more prospective studies need to be conducted to examine the extent to which psychopathology predisposes an individual to pain, research into personality disorders provides us with clues. Personality disorders are defined by the DSM-IV as life-long maladaptive patterns of perceiving, relating to, and thinking about the environment and oneself, that are exhibited in a wide range of social and personal contexts (American Psychiatric Association, 1994). According to this definition, personality disorders can not result from the stress associated with dealing with chronic pain. Fishbain and colleagues (Fishbain, Goldberg, Meagher, Steele & Rosomoff, 1986) found an incidence of 58.4% of Axis II disorders in CLBP patients. Other researchers have found similar incidence rates of Axis II pathology, which are at or above 50% for CLBP populations, far above the percentage found in the general population (Gatchel, Polatin, Mayer & Garcy, 1994a).

Research investigating childhood abuse and pain also provides us with information about the ways disruptive developmental experiences impact personality, psychopathology, and pain. As early as 1859, Briquet in his *Traite de l'hysterie* believed there to be a relationship between childhood abuse and somatoform disorders (Mai & Merskey, 1980). Since that time, several studies have demonstrated an association between pain and abuse (Benson, Hanson & Mararazzo, 1959; Hodgkins & Watson, 1994).

Schofferman, Anderson, Hines, Smith, and White (1992) investigated spinal surgery outcomes and psychosocial risk factors, including physical abuse, sexual abuse, substance abuse by caregivers, abandonment, and emotional neglect. As expected, most of the patients who denied all of these risk factors had positive outcomes, but significantly fewer patients who reported three or more of these risk factors had positive outcomes. Essentially the same group of investigators, also found a high correlation between childhood trauma and CLBP (Schofferman, Anderson, Hines, Smith & Keane, 1993). These findings are consistent with a study by McMahon, Gatchel, Polatin, and Mayer (1997). These investigators found that female CLBP patients had a higher rate of childhood abuse than a control group without a history of chronic pain. Further, CLBP patients with a history of childhood abuse had more lifetime Axis I diagnoses, more lifetime Axis II diagnoses, a lower return to work rate, and a higher number of post-discharge (McMahon et al., 1997).

DEVELOPMENTAL STAGES OF PAIN

Gatchel (1991) attempted to clarify the above complex relationship among pain, psychopathology and personality by theorizing about the progression from acute to chronic pain. He refers to the psychological changes that occur as a person progresses from acute to chronic pain as a "layering of behavioral/psychological problems over the original nociception of the pain experience itself" (p.34). His model is based on a three-stage progression from acute to sub-acute to chronic disability following the experience of pain as a result of an identifiable injury. Stage 1 encompasses the accompanying emotional reactions (e.g., fear, anxiety, and worry) that arise as a consequence of perceived pain. Stage 2 begins when the pain persists past a reasonable acute time period. It is at this stage that the development or exacerbation of psychological and behavioral problems occurs. Gatchel (1991) notes that the form these difficulties take depends primarily on the premorbid personality and psychological characteristics of the individual (i.e., a diathesis), as well as current socioeconomic and environmental stressors. For instance, an individual with a tendency to become depressed may develop a depressive disorder in response to the economic and social stress of being unable to work as a result of pain (Gatchel & Turk, 1996). Such a "diathesis-stress" model has also been recently amplified by Weisberg and colleagues (1996).

This complex interaction of physical and psychosocioeconomic factors leads to Stage 3 of the model. As the patient's life begins to totally and completely revolve around the pain as a result of the chronic nature of the problem, the patient begins to accept the sick role. By doing so, the patient is excused from normal responsibilities and social obligations, which may serve to reinforce the maintenance of the sick role.

Further adding to the "layers" of behavioral and psychosocial difficulties is the addition of physical deconditioning, which generally accompanies patients during their progression toward chronic disability. The physical deconditioning syndrome typically leads to the progressive lack of use of the body, as when an individual is physically and emotionally distressed. Research has shown that this physical deconditioning can produce a circular effect, leading to increased mental deconditioning. The combined interaction of the symptoms as they reinforce one another negatively impacts the emotional well being and self esteem of an individual (Gatchel & Turk, 1996). Conversely, the same negative emotional reactions can reinforce the physical deconditioning through decreased motivation to participate in work and recreational activities. Further complicating the process, when patients engage in an activity that produces acute pain, they are likely to associate the pain with the initial hurt. This causes patients to fear and avoid pain and possible pain-producing situations. Unfortunately, pain often accompanies physical reconditioning and the additional steps needed in order to resume normal responsibilities and social obligations. Therefore, patients must be taught that hurt and harm are not the same (Fordyce, 1988).

OTHER FACTORS ASSOCIATED WITH CHRONIC PAIN

The Influence of Job Satisfaction and Chronic Pain on Disability

Another factor that is associated with chronic pain, and subsequent disability, is job satisfaction. A number of retrospective studies have found an association between pain and job satisfaction (Bigos et al., 1986), as have several prospective studies (Bigos et al., 1991; Cats-Baril & Frymoyer, 1991; Croft et al., 1995). In each of these studies, decreased job satisfaction was related to increased pain-related symptoms and in many cases it was also related to increased chronicity.

A study by Williams and colleagues (1998) investigated the role of job satisfaction in the progression from acute to chronic pain. Specifically, the authors looked at the extent to which job satisfaction predicted disability, pain, and psychological distress six months following the onset of low back pain in 82 males. The results of this study indicated that job satisfaction may serve a protective role against the development of chronic pain and disability following an initial acute onset of back pain. These findings also revealed that dissatisfaction with one's job may increase the risk of long-term disability.

Vingard and colleagues (2000) addressed the association between job satisfaction and pain-related disability in a sample of 2118 males and females. In contrast to earlier studies (Bigos et al., 1991; Croft et al., 1995), the results of this investigation indicated that job dissatisfaction increased the risk of low back pain in males, but did not in females. In addition, an increased risk of low back pain was seen in men who reported "mostly routine work and no possibilities for learning;" (p. 498) however, this was also not the case in females. (Vingard et al., 2000) As a possible explanation of these findings, the authors proposed that females might be more satisfied with their work situations or have lower overall job expectations than men. Although previous studies have found an association between job satisfaction and pain in both males and females, this study raises the possibility that this association may differ by gender. However, additional research is necessary to more fully explore this possibility.

Coping

The ways an individual manages and copes with general stressors, and the multifaceted stress of chronic pain, have been implicated as important in relation to emotional distress, psychopathology, and predicting who will become chronic. The Multidimensional Pain Inventory (MPI), formerly the West-Haven Yale Multidimensional Pain Inventory, developed by Kerns, Turk, and Rudy (1985) is one of the most widely used measures in the pain area. The MPI is a brief self-report instrument that examines the person's perception of pain and coping ability.

The MPI helps to identify patients having difficulty coping with their pain and can guide the implementation of pain reduction interventions. Turk and Rudy (1988) identified three coping styles using a cluster analysis on the MPI scales with a heterogeneous group of chronic pain patients: dysfunctional (43%), interpersonally distressed (28%), and adaptive copers (29.5%). The dysfunctional group members reported that their pain, and the interference caused by their pain, was extreme. Patients in the interpersonally distressed group reported a lack of support, caring, and understanding from their family members and significant others. In contrast, individuals in the adaptive copers group reported high levels of activity and life control as well as lower levels of pain intensity, perceived interference, and affective distress.

Brown and Nicassio (1987) have described adaptive coping strategies that are similar to the activities of adaptive copers on the MPI. These investigators noted an association between reduction in pain perception and active coping strategies such as staying busy, distraction techniques, and ignoring the pain. In contrast, more passive strategies, such as limiting one's activities and wishful thinking, appear associated with more severe pain. These studies highlight the importance of coping, both in relation to pain and psychopathology.

Catastrophizing

The role of catastrophizing in the prediction of chronic pain and disability has gained increased attention in recent years. Catastrophizing involves thinking negatively, and in an exaggerated fashion, about events and stimuli. This can be applied to how persons perceive their pain or their ability to cope with their pain. (Sullivan, Stanish, Waite, Sullivan & Tripp, 1998) In one of the first studies to address this variable, Butler, Damarin, Beaulieu, Schwebel, and Thorn (1989) looked at cognitive strategies and postoperative pain in a sample of general surgical patients and found that increased catastrophizing was associated with higher levels of postoperative pain intensity. Main and Waddell (1991) also looked at this variable and found a strong relationship between catastrophizing and depressive symptoms in a sample of low back pain patients. Further, of the cognitive variables investigated by the authors, catastrophizing was determined to have the "greatest potential for understanding current low back symptoms" (Main & Waddell, 1991, p. 287). Jacobsen and Butler (1996) examined the role of catastrophizing in 59 females who had undergone surgery for breast cancer and found that increased catastrophizing was associated with more intense pain and greater use of analgesic medications. In addition, age was determined to be an important predictor of catastrophizing and postoperative pain, with younger aged patients being more likely to catastrophize and endorse greater levels of pain. A study by Sullivan and colleagues (1998) investigated the function of catastrophizing in the prediction of pain and disability in a sample of 86 patients with various types of soft-tissue injuries. In this study, catastrophizing was associated with perceived disability, reported pain intensity, and employment status. In addition, catastrophizing "contributed to the prediction of disability over and above the variance accounted for by pain intensity" (p. 253) and was related to disability independent of anxiety and depression levels.

Individuals who catastrophize experience increased pain intensity and, in one study, used larger amounts of analgesics. Younger patients appear to possess a greater tendency to catastrophize, which may result in the experience of higher levels of pain. Catastrophizing appears to be an important variable in the prediction of disability following an injury, with one study finding it to be a more powerful predictor than pain intensity. Fortunately, catastrophizing is amenable and especially suited for cognitive-behavioral interventions.

MATCHING THE RIGHT TREATMENT WITH THE RIGHT PATIENT

On the basis of the above discussion, there can be no question that psychosocial and behavioral factors play a significant role in the perception, experience, and response to pain. Research has revealed that groups of patients may differ in psychosocial and behavioral characteristics, even when the medical diagnosis is identical (e.g., Turk & Gatchel, 1999). Likewise, individuals with the same medical diagnosis may vary greatly in their response to their symptoms. Turk and colleagues, for example, have revealed that patients with diseases and syndromes as varied as back pain, headache, and metastatic cancer, may display comparable adaptation patterns, whereas patients with the same diagnosis may actually show great variability in their degree of disability (e.g., Turk & Gatchel, 1999; Turk, Okifuji, Sinclair & Starz, 1998).

As Turk and Gatchel (1999) have indicated, the traditional approach of "lumping" patients with the same medical diagnosis or set of symptoms together (e.g., back pain, fibromyalgia, temporomandibular disorder), and then to treat them all the same way, is not appropriate. That is because many of these common diagnoses are relatively gross categories, and there may be unique individual differences of patients who fall under these generic diagnoses. Thus, some patients may respond quite positively to a certain treatment, whereas others may actually show no improvement at all. Therefore, it is becoming more important to match a particular intervention to specific patient characteristics. As Turk (1990) originally emphasized, the "pain patient homogeneity" myth must be debunked, and patient differences need to be taken into account in order to tailor the appropriate treatment program. Turk and Okifuji (2001) have provided a comprehensive review of the importance of the treatment-matching process and literature to support greater clinical efficacy of such a matching approach strategy.

Psychosocial Profiles

A number of studies have already demonstrated that patients classified into different subgroups based on their behavioral and psychosocial characteristics responded differentially to identical treatments (Epker & Gatchel, 2000; Turk, 2002). This has been fairly consistently observed across different types of pain syndromes (e.g., cancer, fibromyalgia, headache, low back pain and temporomandibular joint [TMJ]). The differences in the psychosocial profiles displayed by patients has led to attempts to categorize different subgroups of patients and then to evaluate differential response to a treatment. Turk and Okifuji (1998) have demonstrated the effective use of the Multidimensional Pain Inventory (MPI) as one way to categorize subgroups of patients. As previously outlined in this chapter, a cluster analysis of the MPI yielded three distinct profiles: *Adaptive Copers*, *Dysfunctional Copers* and *Interpersonally Distressed*.

Turk and Okifuji (1998) have reviewed additional research demonstrating the utility of the MPI with various chronic pain conditions, including headache, TMJ pain and fibromyalgia. Assessment of such MPI profiles will help to "tailor" the needs for treatment strategies to account for the different personality characteristics of patients. For example, patients with an interpersonally distressed profile may need additional clinical attention addressing interpersonal skills to perform effectively in a group-oriented treatment program. Pain patients with dysfunctional and interpersonally distressed profiles display more indications of acute and chronic personality differences, relative to adaptive coper profile patients, and they would therefore require more clinical management (e.g., Etscheidt, Steiger & Braverman, 1995). Such additional attention, however, would not necessarily be essential for adaptive coper profile patients.

Studies such as those above support the notion that, because patients' responses to treatment differ as a function of their psychosocial coping profiles, then specific treatment modalities are more likely to be better suited than others for each profile. An important issue for future clinical research is whether there are other types of biopsychosocial profiles that are more or less responsive to different treatment modalities. For example, variables that have been found to be predictors of pain-related disability outcomes, such as catastrophizing, fear of movement/reinjury, pain beliefs, anxiety and depression, and their interactions with environmental factors such as workplace variables, health care and system variables, need to be more closely evaluated (Turk & Monarch, 2002).

Stages of Change Model

Currently, the biopsychosocial approach to treatment tailors the treatment to each individual patient. However, many, such as Kerns and colleagues (1997), have attempted to apply DiClemente and Prochaska's (1982) stages of change model to the tailoring of treatment.

Jensen (1996), as well as others, have attempted to use the "Stages of Change Model" to engage patients in attempting more adaptive coping behaviors. Jensen has recommended using a motivational interviewing approach that incorporates the model described by DiClemente and Prochaska (1982). This model has been shown to be applicable in many disorders, such as smoking cessation and exercise (Jensen, 1996). The model assumes that patients are at different levels of readiness for change. Each level recommends a different approach to engaging the patient. The first stage is known as *Precontemplation*. In this stage, people are not even thinking or contemplating about change and may exhibit active resistance. These are individuals who may have family members telling them to change, yet they feel no real internal pressure to begin thinking about the steps to make the change. This may be relevant for chronic pain patients in that some patients may have difficulty complying with the recommended exercises or relaxation techniques that could prove helpful in ameliorating their discomfort. The second stage is known as *Contemplation*. During this stage, the person is seriously considering making changes. Often times these people are going through the process of deciding whether the change would be valuable to them or not. From a pain perspective, these are individuals who now are thinking about asking for a referral from their primary care physician. The third stage is known as *Preparation*. The person in this stage is no longer thinking about whether to make a change or not, but has decided to make the change and is beginning to take steps to prepare for this change. For instance the person decides that they are going to follow-up on the recommendation to start aquatics therapy or to meet with a psychologist for biofeedback. The next stage is *Action*. This stage involves the person taking steps that lead to the desired change. Attending the biofeedback sessions, following through on exercise at the gym, meeting with a cognitive—behavioral therapist on a regular basis to look at both adaptive and non-adaptive thoughts are all examples of behaviors that chronic pain patients may engage. Finally, the last stage is known as *Maintenance*, although it is not necessarily appropriate to say this is the last stage. *Maintenance* involves those activities that help a person sustain change. For example, regular follow-ups with their physician or continued engagement in exercise despite no longer seeing a physical therapist are all examples of *Maintenance* level behavior. Of note in this model is the idea that patients often cycle back through stages (Jensen, 1996).

According to this model, the patient should be approached differently depending on their stage in the model. For instance, it is likely that many precontemplators are not going to make it into treatment because they have not even considered the option of making change. However, if a person is contemplating change, rather than recommending techniques to help them manage their pain, it is much more useful to help them weigh the pros and cons of change. Although most clinicians believe that they have help to offer a patient and feel compelled to offer treatment, it is noteworthy to remember in this model that patients have a right to choose to get help or not. Taking more of a neutral stance in which you are simply presenting the facts of changing versus not changing can often be helpful with these individuals. Further, if someone is in the maintenance stage they may only need help maintaining the goals they have achieved rather than going over the rationale for change once again. This can often be seen as "preaching to the choir."

Although taking a biopsychosocial approach has proven effective in treating many chronic pain conditions, not all patients appear to respond to therapy in the same way. From a biopsychosocial perspective, failures to respond to treatment could be related to biological, psychological, social factors or a combination thereof. Using the Stages of Change Model, and specifically using the Pain Stages of Change Questionnaire developed by Kerns and colleagues (1997), has been one attempt to understand the failures of pain patients to improve.

Based on the Pain Stages of Change Questionnaire, four scales were developed: precontemplation, contemplation, action and maintenance. The scale has been shown to have sound psychometric properties (Kerns et al., 1997). However, applying the stages of change to the treatment of chronic pain patients is still in the process of being investigated to determine how useful it is in predicting outcome to treatment. Preliminary evidence does exist regarding the model's usefulness. Kerns and colleagues (1997) found that the precontemplation scale was negatively related to measures of belief and control over pain, as well as to coping behaviors. However, the action and maintenance scales were positively associated with the same factors. In a later study, Kerns and Rosenberg (2000) found out that the Pain Stages of Change Questionnaire was able to successfully differentiate patients who engaged in pain self-management treatment versus those who either dropped out or did not complete. In addition, Jensen and colleagues (2000) evaluated the Pain Stages of Change Questionnaire by evaluating if the questionnaire classified persons with chronic pain into specific stages of readiness to self-manage pain. These researchers investigated 110 subjects with varying chronic pain conditions. And while internal consistency and concurrent validity of the Pain Stages of Change Questionnaire were strong, the ability of the tool to classify individuals into one of four of the stages did not seem to be as useful. The Stages of Change Model remains promising, but additional research is still required.

CONCLUSION

Although systematic tailoring of treatment is still under investigation, tailoring treatment to a patient has always occurred. Clinicians may attempt to use biofeedback with certain patients, while opting to use hypnosis for others. Examining the decisions that clinicians make and determining the most salient variable to consider when tailoring treatment will continue to occur. Currently, the evidence supports taking into account several psychosocial variables, including current psychopathology, coping style, workers' compensation status and readiness for change.

REFERENCES

American Psychiatric Association. (1994). *Diagnostic and Statistical Manual of Mental Disorders* (4th ed.). Washington: APA.

Averill, P. M., Novy, D. M., Nelson, D. V. & Berry, L. A. (1996). Correlates of depression in chronic pain patients: A comprehensive evaluation. *Pain, 65*, 93–100.

Banks, S. M. & Kerns, R. D. (1996). Explaining the high rates of depression in chronic pain: A diathesis-stress framework. *Psychological Bulletin, 119(1)*, 95–110.

Barnes, D., Gatchel, R. J., Mayer, T. G. & Barnett, J. (1990). Changes in MMPI profiles of chronic low back pain patients following successful treatment. *Journal of Spinal Disorders, 3*, 353–355.

Benson, R. C., Hanson, K. H. & Mararazzo, J. D. (1959). Atypical pelvic pain in women: Gynecologic-psychiatric considerations. *American Journal of Obstetrics and Gynecology, 77*, 806–825.

Bigos, S. J., Battie, M. C., Spengler, D. M., Fisher, L. D., Fordyce, W. E., Hansson, T. H., et al. (1991). A prospective study of work perceptions and psychosocial factors affecting the report of back injury. *Spine, 16(1)*, 1–6.

Bigos, S. J., Spengler, D. M., Martin, N. A., Zeh, J., Fisher, L., Nachemson, A., et al. (1986). Back injuries in industry: A retrospective study. *Spine, 11*, 241–256.

Blazer, D. G., Kessler, R. C., McGonagle, K. A. & Swartz, M. S. (1994). The prevalence and distribution of major depression in a national community sample: The national comorbidity survey. *American Journal of Psychiatry, 151*, 979–986.

Brown, G. K. & Nicassio, P. M. (1987). Development of questionnaire for the assessment of active and passive coping strategies in chronic pain patients. *Pain, 31*, 53–64.

Bureau of Labor Statistics. (1995). *Workplace Injuries and Illnesses in 1994* (No. 95–508). Washington, DC: U.S. Department of Labor.

Bureau of Labor Statistics. (2002). 2002, from http://data.bls.gov/surveymost

Butler, R. J. (2000). Economic incentives in disability insurance and behavioral responses. *Journal of Occupational Rehabiliation, 10(1),* 7–19.

Butler, R. W., Damarin, F. L., Beaulieu, C., Schwebel, A. L. & Thorn, B. E. (1989). Assessing cognitive coping strategies for acute postsurgical. *pain*, 139–153.

Cats-Baril, W. L. & Frymoyer, J. W. (1991). Identifying patients at risk of becoming disabled because of low-back pain. The Vermont rehabilitation engineering center predictive model. *Spine, 16*, 605–607.

Croft, P. R., Papageorgiou, A. C., Ferry, S., Thomas, E., Jayson, M. I. V. & Silman, A. J. (1995). Psychological distress and low back pain. Evidence from a prospective study in the general population. *Spine, 20*, 2731–2737.

DiClemente, C. C. & Prochaska, J. O. (1982). Self-change and therapy change of smoking behavior: A comparison of processes of change in cessation and maintenance. *Addictive Behaviors, 7(2),* 133–142.

Dworkin, R., Handlin, D., Richlin, D., Brand, L. & Vannucci, C. (1985). Unraveling the effects of compensation, litigation, and employment on treatment response in chronic pain. *Pain, 23*, 49–59.

Engel, G. L. (1959). "Psychogenic" pain and the pain-prone patient. *American Journal of Medicine*, 899–918.

Epker, J. & Gatchel, R. J. (2000). Coping profile differences in the biopsychosocial functioning of TMD patients. *Psychosomatic Medicine, 62*, 69–75.

Etscheidt, M. A., Steiger, H. G. & Braverman, B. (1995). Multidimensional pain inventory profile classifications and psychopathology. *Journal of Consulting & Clinical Psychology, 51*, 29–36.

Fishbain, D. A., Cutler, R., Rosomoff, H. L. & Rosomoff, R. S. (1997). Chronic pain-associated depression: Antecedent or consequence of chronic pain? A review. *Clinical Journal of Pain, 13*, 116–137.

Fishbain, D. A., Goldberg, M., Meagher, B. R., Steele, R. & Rosomoff, H. (1986). Male and female chronic pain patients categorized by DSM-III psychiatric diagnostic criteria. *Pain, 26*, 181–197.

Flor, H. & Turk, D. C. (1984). Etiological theories and treatments for chronic back pain: I. Somatic models and interventions. *Pain, 19*, 105–121.

Fordyce, W. (1976). *Behavioral Methods of Control of Chronic Pain and Illness*. St. Louis: Mosby.

Fordyce, W. E. (1988). Pain and suffering: A reappraisal. *American Psychologist, 43*, 276–283.

Fordyce, W. E., Fowler, R. S., Lehmann, J. F. & DeLateur, B. J. (1968). Some implications of learning in problems of chronic pain. *Journal of Chronic Diseases, 21*, 179–190.

Gatchel, R. J. (1991). Early development of physical and mental deconditioning in painful spinal disorders. In T. G. Mayer, V. Mooney & R. J. Gatchel (Eds.), *Contemporary Conservative Care for Painful Spinal Disorders* (pp. 278–289). Philadelphia: Lea & Febiger.

Gatchel, R. J. & Epker, J. T. (1999). Psychosocial predictors of chronic pain and response to treatment. In R. J. Gatchel & D. C. Turk (Eds.), *Psychosocial Factors in Pain: Critical Perspectives* (pp. 412–434). New York: Guilford Publications, Inc.

Gatchel, R. J. & Mayer, T. G. (2000). Occupational Musculoskeletal Disorders: Introduction and Overview of the Problem. In T. G. Mayer, R. J. Gatchel & P. B. Polatin (Eds.), *Occupational Musculoskeletal Disorders: Function, Outcomes, and Evidence* (pp. 3–8). Philadelphia: Lippincott Williams & Wilkins.

Gatchel, R. J., Polatin, P. B., Mayer, T. G. & Garcy, P. D. (1994a). Psychopathology and the rehabilitation of patients with chronic low back pain disability. *Archives of Physical Medicine and Rehabilitation, 75*, 666–670.

Gatchel, R. J., Polatin, P. B., Mayer, T. G. & Garcy, P. D. (1994b). Psychopathology and the rehabilitation of patients with chronic low back pain disability. *Archives of Physical Medicine & Rehabilitation, 75* (6), 666–670.

Gatchel, R. J., Polatin, P. B., Noe, C. E., Gardea, M. A., Pulliam, C. & Thompson, J. (2003). Treatment- and cost-effectiveness of early intervention for acute low back pain patients: A one-year prospective study. *Journal of Occupational Rehabilitation, 13*, 1–9.

Gatchel, R. J. & Turk, D. C. (1996). *Psychological Approaches to Pain Management: A Practitioner's Handbook*. New York: Guilford Publications, Inc.

Haley, W. E., Turner, J. A. & Romano, J. M. (1985). Depression in chronic pain patients: Relation to pain, activity, and sex differences. *Pain, 23*, 337–343.

Haythornwaite, J. A., Sieber, W. J. & Kerns, R. D. (1991). Depression and the chronic pain experience. *Pain, 46*, 177–184.

Hodgkins, A. D. & Watson, J. P. (1994). Psychiatric morbidity and illness in women with chronic pelvic pain. *Journal of Psychosomatic Research, 38*, 3–9.

Jacobsen, P. B. & Butler, R. W. (1996). Relation of cognitive coping and catastrophizing to acute pain and analgesic use follwoing breast cancer surgery. *Journal of Behavioral Medicine, 19*, 17–23.

Jensen, M. E., Nielson, W. R., Romano, J. M., Hill, M. L. & Turner, J. A. (2000). Further evaluation of the pain stages of change questionnaire: Is the trans theoretical model of change useful for patients with chronic pain? *Pain, 86*, 255–264.

Jensen, M. P. (1996). Enhancing motivation to change in pain treatment. In R. J. Gatchel & D. C. Turk (Eds.), *Psychological Approaches to Pain Management: A Practitioner's Handbook* (pp. 78–111). New York: Guilford Publications, Inc.

Kerns, R. D. & Rosenberg, R. (2000). Predicting responses to self-management treatments for chronic pain: Application of the pain stages of change model. *Pain, 84*, 49–55.

Kerns, R. D., Rosenberg, R., Jamison, R. N., Caudill, M. A. & Haythornthwaite, J. A. (1997). Readiness to adopt a self-management approach to chronic pain: The Pain Stages of Pain Questionnaire (PSOCQ). *Pain, 72*, 227–234.

Kerns, R. D., Turk, D. C. & Rudy, T. E. (1985). The West Haven-Yale Multidimensional Pain Inventory. *Pain, 23*, 345–356.

Kinney, R. K., Gatchel, R. J., Polatin, P. B., Fogarty, W. J. & Mayer, T. G. (1993). Prevalence of psychopathology in acute and chronic low back pain patients. *Journal of Occupational Rehabilitation, 1993*, 95–103.

Magni, G., Moreschi, C., Rigatti-Luchini, S. & Mersky, H. (1994). Prospective study on the relationship between depressive symptoms and chronic musculoskeletal pain. *Pain, 56*, 289–298.

Mai, F. M. & Merskey, H. (1980). Briquet's treatise on hysteria: Synopsis and commentary. *Archives of General Psychiatry, 37*, 1401–1405.

Main, C. J. & Waddell, G. (1991). A comparison of cognitive measures in low back pain: Statistical structure and clinical validity at initial assessment. *Pain, 56*, 287–298.

Mayer, T., Gatchel, R., Polatin, P. & Evans, T. (1999). Outcomes comparison of treatment for chronic disabling work-related upper extremity disorders. *Journal of Occupational and Environmental Medicine, 41*, 761–770.

McMahon, M. J., Gatchel, R. J., Polatin, P. B. & Mayer, T. G. (1997). Early childhood abuse in chronic spinal disorder patients. A major barrier to treatment success. *Spine, 22(20)*, 2408–2415.

Melzack, R. & Wall, P. D. (1965). Pain mechanisms: A new theory. *Science, 50*, 971–979.

Polatin, P. B., Kinney, R. K., Gatchel, R. J., Lillo, E. & Mayer, T. G. (1993). Psychiatric illness and chronic low-back pain. The mind and the spine–Which goes first? *Spine, 18(1)*, 66–71.

Robbins, H., Gatchel, R. J., Noe, C., Gajraj, N., Polatin, P., Deschner, M., et al. (2003). A prospective one-year outcome study of interdisciplinary chronic pain management: Compromising its efficacy by managed care policies. *Anesthesia & Analgesia, 97*, 156–162.

Romano, J. M. & Turner, J. A. (1985). Chronic pain and depression: Does the evidence support a relationship? *Psychological Bulletin, 97*, 18–34.

Schofferman, J., Anderson, D., Hines, F., Smith, G. & White, A. (1992). Childhood psychological trauma correlates with unsuccessful lumbar spine surgery. *Spine, 17(6S)*, S138–S144.

Schofferman, J., Anderson, D., Hines, R., Smith, G. & Keane, G. (1993). Childhood psychological trauma and chronic refractory low-back pain. *Clinical Journal of Pain, 9*, 260–265.

Sternbach, R. A., Wolf, S. R., Murphy, R. W. & Akeson, W. H. (1973). Traits of pain patients: The low-back "loser". *Psychosomatics, 14*, 226–229.

Sullivan, M. J., Stanish, W., Waite, H., Sullivan, M. & Tripp, D. A. (1998). Catastophizing, pain and disability in patients with soft-tissue injury. *Pain, 77*, 253–260.

Tait, R. C., Chibnall, J. T. & Richardson, W. D. (1990). Litigation and employment status: Effects on patients with chronic pain. *Pain, 43*, 37–48.

Turk, D. & Rudy, T. (1988). Toward an empirically derived taxonomy of chronic pain patients: Integration of psychological assessment data. *Journal of Consulting & Clinical Psychology, 56*, 233–238.

Turk, D. C. (1996). Biopsychosocial perspective on chronic pain. In R. J. Gatchel & D. C. Turk (Eds.), *Psychological Approaches to Pain Management* (pp. 3–32). New York: Guilford Press.

Turk, D. C. (2002). Clinical effectiveness and cost effectiveness of treatment for patients with chronic pain. *Clinical Journal of Pain, 18*, 355–365.

Turk, D. C. & Gatchel, R. J. (1999). Psychosocial factors and pain: Revolution and evolution. In R. J. Gatchel & D. C. Turk (Eds.), *Psychosocial Factors in Pain: Critical Perspectives*. New York: Guilford.

Turk, D. C. & Monarch, E. S. (2002). Biopsychosocial perspective on chronic pain. In D. C. Turk & R. J. Gatchel (Eds.), *Psychological Approaches to Pain Management: A Practitioner's Handbook* (2nd ed.). New York: Guilford.

Turk, D. C. & Okifuji, A. (1998). Treatment of chronic pain patients: Clinical outcomes, cost-effectiveness, and cost-benefits of multidisciplinary pain centers. *Critical Reviews in Physical and Rehabilitation Medicine, 10,* 181–208.

Turk, D. C. & Okifuji, A. (2001). Matching treatment to assessment of patients with chronic pain. In D. C. Turk & R. Melzack (Eds.), *Handbook of Pain Assessment* (2nd ed.). New York: Guilford.

Turk, D. C., Okifuji, A., Sinclair, J. D. & Starz, T. W. (1998). Interdisciplinary treatment for fibromyalgia syndrome: Clinical and statistical significance. *Arthritis Care & Research, 11,* 186–195.

Turk, D. C. & Rudy, T. E. (1990). Robustness of an empirically derived taxonomy of chronic pain patients. *Pain, 42,* 27–35.

U.S. Department of Labor. (2000). Lost-worktime injuries and illnesses: Characteristics and resulting time away from work, 1998, Publication USDL 00–115. Washington D.C.: U.S. Department of Labor.

Vingard, E., Alfredsson, L., Hagberg, M., Kilvom, A., Theorell, T., Waldenstrom, M., et al. (2000). To what extent do current and past physical and psychological occupational factors explain care-seeking for low back pain in a working population? *Spine, 25,* 493–500.

Von Korff, M. & Simon, G. (1996). The relationship between pain and derpssion. *british Hournal of Psychiatry, Supplement 30,* 101–108.

Weickgenant, A. L., Slater, M. A., Patterson, T. L., Atkinson, J. H., Grant, I. & Garfin, S. R. (1993). Coping activities in chronic low back pain: Relationship to pain and disability. *Pain, 53,* 95–103.

Weisberg, J. N., Gallagher, R. M. & Gorin, A. (1996, November 1996). *Personality disorder in chronic pain: A longitudinal approach to validation of diagnosis.* Paper presented at the 15th Annual Scientific Meeting of the American Pain Society, Washington, DC.

Williams, R. A., Pruitt, S. D., Doctor, J. N., Epping-Jordan, J. E., Wahlgren, D. R., Grant, I., et al. (1998). The contribution of job satisfaction to the transition from acute to chronic low back pain. *Archives of Physical Medicine and Rehabilitation, 79,* 366–374.

II

PREDICTION OF DISABILITY IN PAIN-RELATED AND PSYCHOLOGICAL CONDITIONS

A. PREDICTION OF CHRONIC PAIN DISABILITY

9

Determinants of Occupational Disability Following a Low Back Injury

A Critical Review of the Literature

Joan Crook, Ruth Milner, Izabela Z. Schultz, and Bernadette Stringer

INTRODUCTION

Low back musculoskeletal injuries pose a formidable health care problem for injured workers, industries and compensation systems. The lifetime prevalence of low back pain ranges from 60 to 90% and the annual incidence is 5% (1). While only a small proportion of acute back injuries progress on to disability and chronicity, it is these cases that contribute most to the economic and social burden of illness and the individual's physical, economic and psychological difficulties (1–5). It would be useful, therefore, to be able to predict, shortly after injury, those workers who are at high risk for continued disability.

The desire to predict injury or disability led to a profusion of studies, each claiming to have found a significant explanatory factor. The research task is exceedingly complex, however. Factors associated with an increased risk for injury are not necessarily the same as those associated with a worse prognosis (6). Some factors, for example heavy work/labor, may be both a risk factor for back injury (7–12) and a prognostic factor for continued work loss.

A number of studies also suggest that there is high variability in subacute and chronic pain conditions (13–15) and their trajectories (6;16), including the course of

This chapter originally appeared in the *Journal of Occupational Rehabilitation, 12*, 277–295, (2002) and is reprinted by permission.

DOI: 10.1007/978-0-387-28919-9_9, © 2009 Springer Science+Business Media, LLC

back pain (17;18). It is now clear that there is a wide range of outcomes in workers whose injuries initially appear similar.

Today little is known about those workers who are at high risk for developing a chronic problem and continued work disability. Although a number of studies have identified many potential factors associated with a poor prognosis in musculoskeletal pain, few of the studies meet accepted methodological standards for studies of prognosis.

Several narrative reviews have been undertaken (9;19–25), most identifying methodological difficulties in the studies reviewed. Unfortunately, the reviews themselves did not assess the studies systematically. Linton (24) and Turner et al., (26) completed systematic searches of the literature, and only included prospective studies. Krause et al. (27), in their review of the determinants of disability and return to work, chose to address key issues and challenges for future research. While not a systematic review, it is thoughtful and informative in identifying research needs.

Overall objectives of this paper include the comprehensive review of prognostic indicators of work disability in the occupational back pain literature, the assessment of the methodological quality of this literature and, finally, the synthesis of findings into a concise summary.

METHODS

The Literature Search

The literature review guidelines outlined by Oxman and Guyatt (28) were followed. These guidelines stress the importance of a rigorous process for locating studies for review and assessing the validity of these primary studies.

MEDLINE (1965 to 2000), PsycINFO (1967-2000), and EMBASE (1965 to 2001) were searched using dialogue. Review articles and bibliographies of relevant articles were also used and then their references were searched. The Institute for Work and Health, Toronto, Ontario provided bibliographies and working papers relevant to the topic. The Workers' Compensation Board of British Columbia (WCB-BC) bibliographic database for Multivariate Prediction of Occupational Disability was searched.

The first author and a medical librarian reviewed the most relevant articles and developed a search strategy based on all keywords associated with both the back and the study type. There was no specified time limit. Language choice was English. Literature searches were performed with respect to clinical disorder and publication type. The most relevant outcome for injured workers was return to work (RTW), because the social and economic consequences of musculoskeletal injury are of greatest importance to workers, families, insurers and society.

The references of retrieved articles were hand-searched for those missed by the computer searches. The 1999–2000 issues of Spine, Pain, the Scandinavian Journal of Rehabilitation Medicine and the Clinical Journal of Pain were also hand-searched because of their specific relevance to the subject matter and to ensure that the most recent articles would not be overlooked. Finally, experts and conference presenters were consulted for additional references.

The Screening Criteria

Each abstract was reviewed using the following methodological criteria. Original investigations of musculoskeletal soft tissue problems/pain/injury of the spine (thoracic or lumbar) were selected. Only prospective cohort studies of patients suffering from nonspecific spinal and low back pain (or musculoskeletal pain with a subgroup of back pain sufferers) were included. Nonspecific pain was defined as pain, with or without radiation, without specific underlying pathologies such as tumors, fractures, infection and inflammatory disorders. Participants must have entered the study within six months of injury or pain episode and have had at least one follow-up assessment. Randomized Control Trials (RCT) were included if they were analyzed as cohort studies with therapy as a prognostic factor.

Two trained research assistants reviewed each abstract independently and identified those that met the screening criteria. When abstracts were equivocal, the articles were retrieved and screened. If the research assistants did not agree on a decision regarding an abstract, discrepancies were noted, discussed and resolved. When disagreements could not be resolved, a conservative approach was used and the article was included for an in-depth review.

The Methodological Review Process

The authors, affiliations, and journal names of selected articles were masked. Each article was randomly assigned to and independently reviewed by one of two "blinded" reviewers who used structured assessment forms. The reviewers were qualified researchers trained in the use of the assessment form. A trial sample of five articles was independently reviewed by each of the reviewers. Discrepancies were noted, discussed, and resolved.

Methodological Standards Applied to Prognostic Studies

The methodological criteria used to judge quality were adapted from those developed by Laupacis et al., (29), Sackett and Whelan (30) and further modified by two of the authors (Crook and Milner).

Nineteen methodological criteria for prognostic studies were developed and scored (1 point = criteria met; 0.5 = criteria possibly met; 0 = criteria not met). Those studies that achieved 15 points out of a total of 19 possible points were selected for this review (Appendix 1). The rationale for each of the nineteen methodological criteria follows.

These guidelines are useful for the systematic review of the research literature and provide an efficient and effective method for evaluating studies of prognosis.

The better study design identifies participants at an early and uniform point in the course of their condition and follows them forward prospectively. As diagnosis is often problematic in musculoskeletal disorders, it is necessary to include specific criteria in relation to pain (e.g. body region) or type (musculoskeletal, headache), severity, and comorbidity. Prognosis is affected by the study population and the time sampled in the clinical course of the impairment and therefore both require precise definition. The pathways by which participants entered the study sample must be thoroughly delineated and properly selected to avoid bias. All persons entering the study must be accounted for and their clinical status reported. The follow up should be sufficiently long for the outcome of interest to have occurred. We considered one year from the onset of symptoms the necessary minimum length.

Objective, reproducible, and valid outcome criteria should be used and applied in a consistent manner. The examination for important prognostic events must be carried out by clinicians who are "blinded" to the outcome and to whether the participant had a potential prognostic factor. Study participants should be given the same tests at prescribed intervals and at the end of the study to avoid diagnostic suspicion bias. The appropriate analysis should have been adjusted for confounding factors. For example, pain disability data may be affected by age, gender, and time since injury. In addition, multivariate statistical analysis is needed to understand the interactions between variables.

LITERATURE SEARCH RESULTS

MEDLINE and EMBASE yielded 960 abstracts and PsycINFO 192. There were 1018 abstracts reviewed from the bibliographic database from WCB-BC and the "hand searched" journals. Of these 2170 abstracts, sixty-eight (4%) met the screening criteria. Hard copies of all these articles were independently reviewed by the "blinded" reviewers and 19 articles met the methodological standards. Two studies met the methodological criteria but the analyses were only descriptive and did not constitute a true prediction so were not included in this analysis (31;32).

Several articles reported on the same study, but either had a different focus or were reporting on a different follow-up time period. These articles included: Lloyd and Troup, (33) and Troup et al., (34), Rossignol et al., (35) and Abenhaim et al., (36), Macfarlane et al., (37) and Thomas et al., (38), Hazard et al., (39), Hazard et al., (40), and Reid et al., (41), Crook and Moldofsky, (16;42), and Crook et al., (6), Epping-Jordan et al., (43), Wahlgren et al., (44), and Williams et al., (5), Gatchel et al. (45;46), Indahl et al., (47), and Haldorsen et al., (48). The authors of this review chose the articles with a follow-up period of one year or more. Other papers based on the same study were reviewed for additional details of the study methodology.

Description of Samples Included in the Review

The 19 prognostic studies that met the methodological criteria are summarized in Table 1. Most researchers used a definition of a "case" to include body site (low back, spine), symptom (pain), and injury type (soft tissue, musculoskeletal, non-specific). Inclusion and exclusion criteria were used to further delineate a definition of a case.

The source of data for these studies ranged from general practice (38;49-51) through specialty back clinics, orthopedic services, occupational clinics (52;53), and administrative databases involving back injury claims (3;36;54-56). Studies designed to generate an inception cohort with follow up visits at specific times occasionally included extensive lists of variables, but at the other extreme the administrative databases were limited by the routine data available and their reliability.

TABLE 1. Prognostic Studies That Met Methodological Criteria

Author	Method score	Sample size	Sample	Follow-up time	Outcome measures	Analysis	Significant predictors	Odds ratio (95% CI)
Abenhaim et al. (1988)	16/19	2342	Back injury claim	3 years	Recurrence of back pain	Poison regression	Sex (males) Age (10 years) Thoracic (lower) Nurses and drivers most at risk	1.85 (1.50–2.27) 0.93 (0.88–0.98) 0.73 (0.60–0.88) 2.62 (1.80–3.82) 1.64 (1.13–2.36)
Burton & Tillotson (1991)	15/19	109	Low back trouble from orthopedic OP clinic and GP office	1, 3 months, 1 year	Improved/not improved	Discriminant function	Improvement: Frequency of pain Job Previous treatment SLR Leg traction Site Pain Extension	 Negative Negative Negative Positive Positive Negative Negative Positive
Carey et al. (2000)	15/19	1246	Low back pain <10 weeks	2, 4, 8, 12 and 24 weeks and 22 months	Remitting vs. unremitting pain	Logistic regression	Functional disability Sciatica	
Cheadle et al. (1994)	17.5/19	28,473	WCB claims involving at least 4 days of time lost from work All injury types	35.4 months 18 months minimum	Duration of time lost	Cox PH regression models Kaplan Maier estimates	Initial hospitalization Dx of carpal tunnel Sprain back/neck Age >45 30–44 Female sex	0.48 (0.46–0.51) 0.55 (0.50–0.60) 0.79 (0.72–0.82) 0.67 (0.64–0.69) 0.78 (0.76–0.81) 0.85 (0.82–0.88)
Cherkin et al. 1996	16/19	219	Back pain first visit to GP	1,3,7 weeks 1 year	Good vs. Poor outcome: Symptom satisfaction	Multivariate logistic regression	Depression Pain below knee	2.3 (1.4–3.6) 2.4 (1.1–5.0)

(*cont.*)

TABLE 1. *(Cont.)*

Author	Method score	Sample size	Sample	Follow-up time	Outcome measures	Analysis	Significant predictors	Odds ratio (95% CI)
Coste et al. (1994)	15/19	103	Nonspecific back pain <72 hrs in primary care	3 months	Time to Return To Work (RTW)	Kaplan-Meier PH models	Sex (Male)	0.62 (0.35–1.06)
							Previous chronic episode	0.30 (0.08–1.02)
							Pain worse on standing at onset	0.52 (0.30–1.03)
							Pain worse on lying at onset	0.56 (0.29–0.93)
							Disability status on entry	0.65 (0.36–1.14)
							Compensation status	0.53 (0.30–0.94)
							Poor job satisfaction	0.57 (0.24–1.13)
Crook et al. (1998)	17/19	148	Injured workers not RTW by 91–97 days	9, 15, 21 months	Number of days until first day of RTW	Cox Proportional Hazards	Age	0.98 (0.96–0.99)
							Sex (female)	0.59 (0.43–1.02)
							Positive psychological distress	0.45 (0.25–0.81)
			Soft tissue injuries			Regression Model	Functional disability	0.97 (0.93–1.00)
							Modified job	1.93 (1.54–2.42)
Engel et al. (1996)	16/19	1059	Primary care patients with back pain	1 year post index visit	Health care costs	Multivariate logistic regression	Chronic pain grade:	Adj. OR (95% CI)
							II	1.4 (0.8–2.4)
							III	2.8 (1.6–5.0)
							IV	7.2 (4.0–13.0)
							Days in pain:	
							31–89	2.4 (1.4–4.1)
							90–180	3.3 (2.1–5.3)
							SCL-90 depression:	
							1.01–1.6	1.1 (0.7–1.8)
							> 1.6	1.2 (0.7–1.9)
							Disability pay: In past ever	1.7 (1.0–2.7)

							Diagnosis:	
							Disc	3.7 (2.4–5.7)
							Arthritis	1.2 (0.7–2.1)
							Other	1.0 (reference)
Gatchel et al. (1995a)	16/19	421	New episode of Low Back Pain (LBP) (<6 weeks) reported to 3 clinics	12 months	Working vs. not working because of injury	Logistic regression	Pain and disability scale	1.55 (1.96–1.22)
							Gender (Female)	0.24 (0.59–0.10)
							Worker's Compensation Board case	0.13 (0.48–0.34)
Haldorsen et al. (1998)	15/19	260	Back pain On sick leave for 8–12 weeks	3, 6, 12 months	RTW/NRTW	Discriminant function	RTW:	
							Internal locus of control	Positive
							Lateral mobility to right	Negative
							Lateral mobility to left	Negative
							Work ability for ordinary work	Positive
							Number of x-rays taken	Negative
							Physical activity	Positive
							Number of children	Negative
							Number of years in occupation	Negative
Hemingway et al. (1997)	17/19	5620	Non-industrial civil servants workforce absences due to back pain	33–61 months = 48 months	Short (≤7d) vs. long (>7d) absences	Poison regression adjusted rate ratios	RR of long absences: Number of back pain self reports on entry:	
							1	1.90 (1.29–2.81)
							2	3.02 (2.09–4.36)
							3	4.63 (2.75–7.82)
							Control over work.	
							Low (vs. high)	1.64 (1.25–2.14)

(cont.)

TABLE 1. *(Cont.)*

Author	Method score	Sample size	Sample	Follow-up time	Outcome measures	Analysis	Significant predictors	Odds ratio (95% CI)
Indahl et al. (1995)	15.5/19	985	Acute back pain off work for 8 weeks	3 months 1 year	Days on sickness leave	Cox PH	Intervention: Light mobilization	 2.23 (1.75–2.84)
Infante-Rivard & Lortie (1996)	15.5/19	305	First compensated episode of back pain	Time until RTW (1228 days max.)	Time until RTW	Cox PH	Factors that favour RTW:	
							Younger age	1.43 (1.04–1.98)
							History of strain or sprain	2.20 (1.24–3.91)
							<30 days from injury to Rx	1.30 (0.96–1.77)
							Good flexion	1.52 (1.04–2.24)
							Absence of neurological signs	1.40 (0.98–2.00)
							>24 months duration of employment	1.49 (1.10–2.03)
							Public industry work	1.63 (1.21–2.19)
							Take unscheduled breaks	1.45 (1.06–1.97)
Klenerman et al. (1995)	15/19	300	Musculoskeletal LBP with 1 week before visit to GP	2, 12 months	Pain and disability	Multiple regression		R^2 P
							"Demographic" model	.122 .0002
							"Historical" model	.147 .0038
							"Fear-avoidance" model	.137 .0002
							All	.319 .0017
Sinclair et al. (1997)	17/19	885	Injured workers LBP off work at initial contact (within 21 days)	12 months	Cumulative time on wage replacement benefits	Kaplan Maier estimate	Filing claim likely to affect job (males)	0.59 (1.47–0.78)
						Cox PH	Reporting previous claim, surgery or hospitalization for another condition (females)	0.83 (0.67–1.03)

Tate et al. (1999)	16/19	320	Soft tissue back injuries in hospital nurses	6 months	Duration of time loss from work	Logistic regression	Previously injured	2.96 (0.98–8.96)
							Disability score (Oswestry)	1.14 (1.09–1.19)
							Pain score	0.70 (0.52–0.93)
Thomas et al. (1999)	16/19	180 consulted GP	Population based-participants recruited before onset of LBP consulation	12 months	Persistent disabling LB pain	Stepwise logistic regression	Women	2.26 (1.0 to 5.1)
							Not first episode of low back pain	2.76 (0.8 to 9.9)
							Not satisfied with employment situation	2.62 (1.2 to 5.8)
							Radiating leg pain	1.89 (0.8 to 4.4)
							Widespread pain	3.44 (1.3 to 9.3)
							Spinal restrictions 2–5	3.08 (1.3 to 7.3)
van der Weide et al. (1999)	16/19	120	Workers on sick leave with LBP for 10 days ® referred to occupational physicians with guidelines re: care	3, 12 months	Time to RTW	Kaplan-Meiler, Cox PH	Intervention	1.3 (0.88–1.9)
							Radiating pain	0.45 (0.30–0.70)
							Functional disability	0.82 (0.73–0.90)
							Work tempo/quantity	0.82 (0.73–1.00)
							Problematic relations with colleagues	0.92 (0.73–1.00)
Volinn et al. (1991)	15/19	18,372 Males 6,723 Females	Industrial insurance claim for back sprain	4 years	>90 days off work = chronicity of disability	Logistic regression	Males	Females
							Age > 40 2.14 (1.77–2.58)	1.88 (1.46–2.41)
							Wage >2000 0.57 (0.47–0.68)	0.51 (0.33–0.79)
							W/D/0 children 2.11 (1.20–3.44)	2.54 (1.55–4.16)
							Nan-Powers Index: >50 0.46 (1.05–1.48)	NS
							Occupation: Laborer/trans. 1.25 (1.05–1.48)	NS

The definition of inception cohort is a group assembled at some common point in the course of their injury/episode (preferably at the earliest possible point), but varies according to the purpose of the study. In low back injuries, the inception cohort could be identified from date of injury, date of first visit, date of first claim or a point following first treatment for the injury. This variability causes difficulties in interpreting the prognostic variables because they must be viewed in the context of the timing of assessment.

In specific studies of post-injury low back pain prognosis, follow-up times are specific and most participants are seen within a short range of time. When administrative databases are used the times can be quite variable. For the purposes of this review, the outcomes of interest must have been measured as close to 12 months as possible, with the exception of two papers that reported a shorter follow-up. These will be reported separately.

Table 2 organizes the variables observed in these studies. Within each domain, however, the variables range from one to many, depending on the availability and interest. For example, the domain Medical/Physical can include detailed complete physical examinations or one or two measures, only.

Sample sizes of each paper are shown in Table 1 and vary from small numbers (100-300) in the dedicated studies to large database studies with up to 28,473 cases. The smaller the sample size, the fewer variables that can be studied, limiting the number of predictors.

Statistical analyses deemed adequate to measure the strength of association were Cox's regression modelling (for continuous data) or logistic regression (for dichotomous data). Descriptive data were not considered to be robust enough to merit inclusion. The authors estimated or reported Odds Ratios or Relative Risks for categorical and continuous data, respectively. The strength of the association between each variable (prognostic factor) and the five outcomes selected (see below) are reported. Any results for which the confidence limits do not include the value one (no difference) are considered to be strong associations.

Outcomes

The outcomes have been sorted into five categories (*i.e. Time to RTW (Time Lost), Recurrence/Improvement, Working/Not Working, Health Care Costs and Persistent Disability/Pain*) and each study was assigned to one of the categories (Table III). Time to RTW (Time Lost) is a category for specific time losses due to low back injury or time from injury to return to work. The *Recurrence/Improvement* category encompasses papers which report recurrence or improvement as the main outcomes of interest. In these papers, non-recurrence is assumed to equal improvement although non-improvement does not equate to recurrence. Non-improvement may indicate the chronicity of the injury only. The category *Working/Not Working* includes papers which distinguish between participants who have returned to work by a specified time (usually 12 months) and those who have not. *Health Care Costs* is a very specific outcome and includes only one paper. *Persistent Disability/Pain* is a composite of papers having pain, disability, or both as the main outcome.

TABLE 2. Prognostic Factors Measured in the Studies Reviewed

	Authors	Socio demographics	Medical/physical	History of back pain	Pain	Psychological	Social/Family	Functional disability	Health status	Workplace	Lifestyle	Compensation	Intervention
1	Abenhaim, 1988	√	√		√								
2	Burton, 1991	√	√	√	√				√	√	√		
3	Carey, 2000	√	√		√	√	√	√	√				
4	Cheadle, 1994	√	√										
5	Cherkin, 1996	√		√		√		√	√	√	√		
6	Coste, 1994	√	√	√	√	√		√		√			
7	Crook, 1998	√	√	√	√	√	√	√		√			
8	Engel, 1996	√	√		√		√	√				√	
9	Gatchel, 1995a	√			√	√		√	√			√	
10	Haldorsen, 1998	√	√			√	√		√	√	√		
11	Hemingway, 1997	√		√	√					√			
12	Indahl, 1995	√											√
13	Infante-Rivard, 1996	√	√	√				√		√			
14	Klenerman, 1995	√		√	√	√		√					
15	Sinclair, 1997	√	√	√	√			√	√	√		√	
16	Tate, 1999	√			√			√		√			
17	Thomas, 1999	√		√	√			√	√	√	√		
18	van der Weide, 1999	√			√	√		√	√	√			
19	Volinn, 1991	√					√			√		√	

TABLE 3. Summary of Prognostic Factors within Outcomes

	Outcomes				
Prognostic factor	Time to RTW (Time Lost)	Recurrence/ Improvement	Working/ Not Working	Health Care Costs	Persistent Disability/ Pain
Demographic	Older – *Crook* Older – *Cheadle* Younger®* *Infant-Rivard* Females – *Crook* Males – *Coste* Females – *Cheadle*	Older – *Abenhaim* Males – *Abenhaim*	Older – *Volinn* Number of children Haldorsen Females – *Gatchel*		Demographic model – *Klenerman* Females – *Thomas*
Psychological distress	Psychological distress - *Crook*		Internal locus of control – *Haldorsen*	Depression – *Engel*	Depression – *Cherkin* Fear Avoidance model – *Klenerman*
Functional disability	Functional disability – *Crook* Disability score – *Tate* Disability status – *Coste* Functional disability – *van der Weide*		Pain and disability – *Gatchel* Physical activity – *Haldorsen*		Functional disability – *Carey*
Modified job	Availability favors RTW – *Crook*				
Light mobilization	Intervention favors RTW – *Indahl*				
Referral to occupational physicians with guidelines re:care	Intervention favors RTW – *van der Wiede*				
WCB claims	Males – Previous claim – *Sinclair* Compensation status – *Coste*		WCB case – *Gatchel*		
Hospitalization	Hospitalization – *Cheadle*				

Time since injury	<30 days to Rx®* – *Infante-Rivard*			Number days in pain – *Engel*	
Duration of employment	>2 years employment®* – *Infante-Rivard*				
Physical indicators	Good flexion/absence of neurological sings®* – *Infante-Rivard* Sprain back/neck/ carpal tunnel – *Cheadle* Pain worse on standing and lying – *Coste*	Thoracic – *Abenhaim* SLR < 50° – *Burton* Traction relieves pain – *Burton* Lower extremity – *Burton* Lumbar extension – *Burton*	Lateral mobility to right and left – *Haldorsen* Number of x-rays – *Haldorsen*	Disc/Arthritis – *Engel*	Sciatica – *Carey* Radiating leg pain – *Thomas*
Work environment	Public industry Unscheduled breaks – *Infante-Rivard* Work tempo/quantity – *van der Weide* Poor job satisfaction – *Coste* Problematic relations with colleagues – *van de Wiede*	Nurses and drivers – *Abenhaim* Job exertion – *Burton*	Low control over work – *Hemingway*** Work ability for ordinary work – *Haldorsen* Number of years in ordinary occupation – *Haldorsen*	Disability pay – *Engel*	No job satisfaction – *Thomas*
Pain	Radiating pain – *van der Weide*	Pain below knee – *Cherkin*		Pain grade – *Engel*	Widespread pain – *Thomas*
Previous episode	Previous chronic episode – *Coste* Previous injury – *Tate*	Previous Rx – *Burton* Frequency of persis- tent trouble – *Burton*			Historical model – *Klenerman*

*® Reverse.
** short (≤7 days) vs. long (>7 days)

RESULTS

Time to RTW (Time Lost)

There were eight papers which specified time to return to work as a continuous variable (6;47;50;53-57). In these papers, 14 different domains encompassing 22 variables provided prognostic evidence affecting return to work. In the demographic domain, four papers identified older age and/or female sex as deterrents for return to work (6;50;54;55). One paper (6) found evidence of psychological distress and four papers identified functional disabilities (6;50) (53;57) as important predictors of non-return to work. Looking at workplace factors, the availability of modified jobs (6) and light mobilization (47) predicted faster return to work. Referral to clinics geared to occupational injuries, less than 30 days from injury to treatment, and more than two years on the job were good predictors of faster return (53). Workplace factors like job problems or problems with colleagues (50;53;55) were deterrents to recovery. Radiating pain (53) and pain that was worse on standing and lying (50) also negatively affected a return to work.

Clinical indicators such as no pain (50), no sprains (54), good flexion (55), plus the absence of neurological signs (55) were good predictors. Previous hospitalization was a negative factor (54) as was a previous episode of back pain (50;57). Finally, workers' compensation status was noted by two authors to be either positive or negative, depending on the claim (50;56).

Recurrence/Improvement

Three papers (36;49;52) identified one or both of these outcomes. Variables identified as prognostic of these outcomes can be characterized into five domains—demographic, physical, pain, history, and work environment. In the demographic domain, young workers were less, and male workers were more, vulnerable to recurrence. Physical indicators which predicted recurrences were a Straight Leg Raise of less than 50°, pain in the lower extremity/below knee, and poor lumbar extension. One paper identified nurses and drivers as being the most likely occupational groups to have a recurrence.

Working/Not Working

Return to work at a specified time was expressed as a categorical outcome and named "Working/Not Working". Four papers used this outcome (3;45;48;58) and predictive variables can be classified into six domains (i.e. demographic, psychological, functional disability, physical indicators, work environment and WCB claims).

Older age (3) and female sex (45) are negative factors. In addition, the more children and the more of them living at home, the less likely the participant is to return to work (48). One author identified locus of control (48) and two authors functional disability (45;48) as strongly predictive. The physical indicators predicting return to work were a low number of X-rays and greater mobility (48). The work environment domain showed that low control over work was a negative factor (58). Proportionately more workers had a workers' compensation claim in the group which did not return to work (45).

Health Care Costs

Only one paper addressed the health care costs of a low back injury. Engel et al., (51) identified five domains (i.e. psychological factors, time since injury, physical factors, work environment and pain) which reflected increased costs. The variables which increased the demand for health care were depression, number of days in pain, pain grade, arthritis in addition to injury, and disability pay.

Persistent Disability/Pain

These were sufficiently different from Recurrence indicators to merit a further classification. Seven domains in three papers were identified (38;59;60). In the demographic domain, a summary variable developed to include several demographic variables was predictive (60). Female sex (38), depression (49), fear avoidance (60), and functional disability (59) were predictive of persistent disability. The physical variables, radiating leg pain and widespread pain (38), were both negative factors, as were previous episodes (60). Finally, job dissatisfaction predicted persistent disability (38).

DISCUSSION

The reader can have more confidence in recent research results because the methodological quality of prognostic studies has substantially improved over the past ten years. Nevertheless, there still remain methodological challenges that require discussion. The heterogeneity of low back pain poses challenges for case definition (61). Although most researchers have adopted the body zone and symptom type classification (62), an adequate method of classifying low back musculoskeletal disorders has not yet been developed.

Further, a number of studies suggest that there is a wide range of outcomes in workers whose injuries initially appear similar (16;63). As Feinstein (64) suggested, members of a cohort may be heterogenous on prognostic factors that determine susceptibility to the outcome event. Consequently, prognostic stratifications are necessary to discern baseline prognostic factors. For example, Crook and Moldofsky (16) developed cluster groupings of baseline variables (i.e. pain sites, functional limitations, and pain behaviors) of workers who had not returned to work three months after the injury. Their purpose was to divide the original cohort into subgroups of injured workers who were similar in their prognostic expectations and to follow them over time. If prognostic stratification is used, as the Crook and Moldofsky (16) analysis suggests, the results of therapeutic maneuvers or specific focussed interventions can be compared within, or targeted toward, specific prognostic strata.

If stratified results are reported and multiple follow up assessments (over years) performed, then it would be possible to understand how prognostic factors might operate at different times following the onset of symptoms. To understand changes in prognostic status over time requires the use of multiple measurement periods and survival analysis techniques using Cox regression and time-dependent covariates (6;27;65). Ultimately, these results would enable the development of interventions that are differentially focussed on prognostically stratified groups and introduced at the most appropriate time during the course of the injury and at the most optimum cost.

Further, estimates of prognosis may be systematically different depending on the outcome measure used, that is, how success or failure is defined. In addition, important prognostic information may be lost in studies that have only one assessment period after injury or treatment or use only dichotomous outcome variables (e.g., return to work or not, successful or not). The varied definitions of outcome in the literature reflect the relative values of the different parties and purposes of the evaluation. Some concern the return of the injured worker to full employment, some the time it takes to reach that stage, and others, permanent disability, chronic pain, or health care costs (27). In our opinion, the most clinically relevant, socially relevant, and adequately variable outcomes for worker populations are number of days of work absenteeism or length of work absenteeism during a specified time period.

Because of the diverse outcomes and the complexity of the injury, it is not surprising that prognostic factors are extremely variable and that multiple domains are included in the search for any factor that will assist in the prediction of a satisfactory or unsatisfactory outcome. A variety of prognostic factors and outcomes are likely to be important as this review suggests.

Prognostic for all of the outcomes, except in the assessment of health care costs, are the demographic variables. Regardless of the outcome studied, it appears that the older worker is negatively affected by the low back injury. The results for gender are mixed, but most studies report that females are more likely to be negatively affected. In addition, the number of children at home negatively affects the outcomes, perhaps by creating a physically and psychologically demanding environment counterproductive to recovery. It may also be highly correlated with socioeconomic variables that affect the outcome independent of the injury. Depression or other psychological distress indicators did not appear to play a part in the development of recurrences, but were a major factor in persistence, time lost and increased health care costs. Surprisingly, the workplace factors—modified job, light mobilization and referral to appropriate occupational physicians were only recorded by the authors who looked at Time to RTW as an outcome. Presumably, these would potentially represent major variables for other outcomes (including health care costs) since these factors or variations of them might be expected to appear in administrative databases as well as be of interest to investigators.

Based on the results of this systematic review, the process of compiling of lists of risk factors for disability, including the so-called "yellow flag" approach (25;66), by health care and compensation systems will be problematic. Such an approach does indicate, however, the complexity and magnitude of the problem of deciding upon the best approach for rehabilitation. Despite the best intentions to the contrary, however, such lists of variables may not possess the requisite degree of methodologically rigorous empirical validation. Their authors may not have been in a position to consider the methodological rigor of studies reporting lists of predictors. Further, the "yellow flag" approaches (25;66;67), do not indicate which of the variables are modifiable and which are not. Is it possible to modify the residual impairment affecting functional status and work capacity with improved clinical intervention? To what degree is it possible to alter the injured person's perception of injury/illness? Further research is required to answer these questions. In the meantime, the prognostic variables outlined in the tables and the frequency with which they are reported provide the most succinct summary of the evidence at present.

More recently, researchers are combining primary data from the injured worker and the workplace with administrative databases in an attempt to understand a full range of factors for delayed return to work (27;68). By placing the study within a larger context of a workers' compensation system, the social and economic consequences of back injury can be more readily understood.

What is needed for the future is a comprehensive multivariate biopsychosocial job-related model of work disability. The results presented here would provide a good baseline for such a model. The key groups of variables to be included should be those reflected in the tables of this review. Only a comprehensive model developed on the basis of sound methodological criteria could or should become a foundation for the practical applications in health care and compensation systems to identify workers at highest risk of disability and provide appropriate rehabilitation programming. Until such a model is developed and validated, caution should be exercised on implementation and proliferation of various non-evidence-based lists of predictive factors. Clearly, to date, the findings of many studies on predictors of disability, conducted largely independently from each other, have not reached the level of integration required to provide unequivocal recommendations to various health care and compensation systems.

ACKNOWLEDGMENTS: Funding for this project was provided by the Workers' Compensation Boards of British Columbia and Alberta as a part of a major study on Multivariate Prediction of Occupational Disability: Low Back. The authors would like to thank Wendy Hunt, M.L.S., Assistant Librarian; Wendy Meloche, B.A., Research Coordinator; Oonagh Zuberbier, B.G.S., B.A., Research Assistant—Workers' Compensation Board of British Columbia.

REFERENCES

1. Spitzer WO, LeBlanc FE, Dupuis M. Scientific approach to the assessment and management of activity-related spinal disorders: A monograph for clinicians. Report of the Quebec Task Force on spinal disorders. *Spine* 1987; 12; S1–S59.
2. Webster BS, Snook SH. The cost of compensable low back pain. *J Occup Med* 1990; 32: 13–15.
3. Volinn E, Van Koevering D, Loeser JD. Back sprain in industry: The role of socioeconomic factors in chronicity. *Spine* 1991; 16: 542–48.
4. Hashemi L, Webster BS, Clancy EA, Volinn E. Length of disability and cost of workers' compensation low back pain claims. *J Occup Environ Med* 1997; 39: 937–45.
5. Williams RA, Pruitt SD, Doctor JN, Epping-Jordan JE, Wahlgren DR, Grant I, Patterson TL, Webster JS, Slater MA, Atkinson JH. The contribution of job satisfaction to the transition from acute to chronic low back pain. *Arch Phys Med Rehabil* 1998; 79: 366–74.
6. Crook J, Moldofsky H, Shannon H. Determinants of disability after a work related musculoskeletal injury. J Rheumatology 1998; 25: 1570–1577.
7. Battiè MC, Bigos SJ. Industrial back pain complaints: A broader perspective. *Orthop Clin North Am* 1991; 22: 273–82.
8. Borenstein D. Low back pain: Current opinion. *Rheumatism* 1990; 2: 233–41.
9. Frank JW, Kerr MS, Brooker A, DeMaio SE, Maetzel A, Shannon HS, Sullivan TJ, Norman RW, Wells RP. Disability resulting from occupational low back pain: Part I: What do we know about primary prevention? A review of the scientific evidence on prevention before disability begins. *Spine* 1996; 21: 2908–17.
10. Frank JW, Brooker A, DeMaio SE, Kerr MS, Maetzel A, Shannon HS, Sullivan TJ, Norman RW, Wells RP. Disability resulting from occupational low back pain: Part II: What do we know about secondary

prevention? A review of the scientific evidence on prevention after disability begins. *Spine* 1996; 21: 2918–29.

11. Frymoyer JW, Cats-Baril WL. An overview of the incidences and costs of low back pain. *Orthop Clin North Am* 1991; 22: 263–71.
12. Heliövaara M. Risk factors for low back pain and sciatica. *Ann Med* 1989; 21: 257–64.
13. Von Korff M, Ormel J, Keefe FJ, Dworkin SF. Grading the severity of chronic pain. *Pain* 1992; 50: 133–49.
14. Klapow JC, Slater MA, Patterson TL, Doctor JN, Atkinson JH, Garfin SR. An empirical evaluation of multidimensional clinical outcome in chronic low back pain patients. *Pain* 1993; 55: 107–18.
15. Tunks E. Is there a chronic pain syndrome? In: Lipton S, Tunks E, Zoppi M, eds. *Advances in pain research and therapy*. New York: Raven Press, 1990. pp. 247–66.
16. Crook J, Moldofsky H. The clinical course of musculoskeletal pain in empirically derived groupings of injured workers. *Pain* 1996; 67: 427–33.
17. Von Korff M, Saunders K. The course of back pain in primary care. *Spine* 1996; 21: 2833–39.
18. Linton SJ, Hallden K. Risk factors and the natural course of acute and recurrent musculoskeletal pain: developing a screening instrument. In: Jensen TS, Turner JA, Wiesenfeld-Hallin Z, eds. *Proceedings of the 8th World Congress on Pain, Progress in Pain Research and Management. Volume 8*. Seattle, Washington: IASP Press, 1997, pp. 527–36.
19. Valat J, Goupille P, Vèdere V. Low back pain: Risk factors for chronicity. *Rev. Rhum.* (English Edition). 1997; 64: 189–94.
20. Turk DC. The role of demographic and psychosocial factors in transition from acute to chronic pain. In: T. S. Jensen, J. A. Turner, Z. Wiesenfeld-Hallin, eds. *Proceedings of the 8th World Congress on Pain, Progress in Pain Research and Management.* Volume 8. Seattle, Washington: IASP Press, 1997, pp. 185–213.
21. Weiser S, Cedraschi C. Psychosocial issues in the prevention of chronic low back pain - a literature review. *Bailliére's Clinical Rheumatology* 1992; 6: 657–684.
22. Bongers PM, de Winter CR, Kompier MAJ, Hildebrandt VH. Psychosocial factors at work and musculoskeletal disease. *Scand J Work Environ Health* 1993; 19: 297–312.
23. Hudak PL, Cole DC, Frank JW. Perspectives on prognosis of soft tissue musculoskeletal disorders. *Int J Rehabil Res* 1998; 21: 29–40.
24. Linton SJ. A review of psychological risk factors in back and neck pain. *Spine* 2000; 25: 1148–56.
25. Main CJ, Spanswick CC, eds. *Pain Management: An interdisciplinary approach*. Edinburgh: Churchill Livingstone, 2000.
26. Turner JA, Franklin G, Turk DC. Predictors of chronic disability in injured workers: A systematic literature synthesis. *Am J Ind Med* 2000; 38: 707–22.
27. Krause N, Frank JW, Sullivan TJ, Dasinger LK, Sinclair SJ. Determinants of duration of disability and return to work after work-related injury and illness: Challenges for future research. Invited paper for special issue of *Am J Ind Med* 2001; 40: 464–84.
28. Oxman AD, Guyatt GH. Validation of an index of the quality of review articles. *J Clin Epidemiol* 1991; 44: 1271–78.
29. Laupacis A, Wells G, Richardson S, Tugwell P, for the Evidence-Based Medicine Working Group. Users' Guides to the Medical Literature V. How to use an article about prognosis. *JAMA* 1994; 272: 234–37.
30. Sackett DL, Whelan G. Cancer risk in ulcerative colitis: Scientific requirement for the study of prognosis. *Gastroenterology* 1980; 78: 1632–35.
31. Hellsing A, Linton SJ, Kälvemark M. A prospective study of patients with acute back and neck pain in Sweden. *Phys Ther* 1994; 74: 116–28.
32. Nordin M, Skovron ML, Hiebert R, Weiser S, Brisson PM, Campello M, Harwood K, Crane M, Lewis, S. Early predictors of delayed return to work in patients with low back pain. *J Musculo Pain* 1997; 5: 5–27.
33. Lloyd DCEF, Troup JDG. Recurrent back pain and its prediction. *J Soc Occup Med* 1983; 33: 66–74.
34. Troup JDG, Martin JW, Lloyd DCEF. Back pain in industry: A prospective survey. *Spine* 1981; 6: 61–69.
35. Rossignol M, Suissa S, Abenhaim L. Working disability due to occupational back pain: Three-year follow-up of 2,300 compensated workers in Quebec. *J Occup Med* 1988; 30: 502–5.

36. Abenhaim L, Suissa S, Rossignol M. Risk of recurrence of occupational back pain over three year follow up. *B J Ind Med* 1988; 45: 829–33.
37. Macfarlane GJ, Thomas E, Croft PR, Papageorgiou AC, Jayson MIV, Silman AJ. Predictors of early improvement in low back pain amongst consulters to general practice: The influence of pre-morbid and episode-related factors. *Pain* 1999; 80: 113–119.
38. Thomas E, Silman AJ, Croft PR, Papageorgiou AC, Jayson MIV, Macfarlane GJ. Predicting who develops chronic low back pain in primary care: A prospective study. *BMJ* 1999; 381: 1662–67.
39. Hazard RG, Haugh LD, Reid S, Preble JB, MacDonald L. Early prediction of chronic disability after occupational low back injury. *Spine* 1996; 21: 945–51.
40. Hazard RG, Haugh LD, Reid S, McFarlane G, MacDonald L. Early physician notification of patient disability risk and clinical guidelines after low back injury A randomized, controlled trial. *Spine* 1997; 22: 2951–58.
41. Reid S, Haugh LD, Hazard RG, Tripathi M. Occupational low back pain: Recovery curves and factors associated with disability. *J Occup Rehab* 1997; 7: 1–14.
42. Crook J, Moldofsky H. The probability of recovery and return to work from work disability as a function of time. *Qual Life Res* 1994; 3: S97–S109.
43. Epping-Jordan JE, Williams RA, Pruitt SD, Patterson TL, Grant I, Wahlgren DR, Slater, MA, Webster, JS, Atkinson, JH. Transition to chronic pain in men with low back pain: Predictive relationships among pain intensity, disability, and depressive symptoms. *Health Psychol* 1998; 17: 421–27.
44. Wahlgren DR, Atkinson JH, Epping-Jordan JE, Williams RA, Pruitt SD, Klapow JC, Patterson, TL, Grant I, Webster JS, Slater, MA. One-year follow-up of first onset low back pain. *Pain* 1997; 73: 213–21.
45. Gatchel RJ, Polatin PB, Mayer TG. The dominant role of psychosocial risk factors in the development of chronic low back pain disability. *Spine* 1995; 20: 2702–9.
46. Gatchel RJ, Polatin PB, Kinney RK. Predicting outcome of chronic back pain using clinical predictors of psychopathology: A prospective analysis. *Health Psychol* 1995; 14: 415–20.
47. Indahl A, Velund L, Reikeraas O. Good prognosis for low back pain when left untampered: A randomized clinical trial. *Spine* 1995; 20: 473–77.
48. Haldorsen EMH, Indahl A, Ursin H. Patients with low back pain not returning to work: A 12-month follow up study. *Spine* 1998; 23: 1202–8.
49. Cherkin DC, Deyo RA, Street JH, Barlow W. Predicting poor outcomes for back pain seen in primary care using patients' own criteria. *Spine* 1996; 21: 2900–2907.
50. Coste J, Delecoeuillerie G, Cohen de Lara A, Le Parc JM, Paolaggi JB. Clinical course and prognostic factors in acute low back pain: An inception cohort study in primary care practice. *BMJ* 1994; 308: 577–80.
51. Engel CC, Von Korff M, Katon WJ. Back pain in primary care: Predictors of high health-care costs. *Pain* 1996; 65: 197–204.
52. Burton AK, Tillotson KM. Prediction of the clinical course of low-back trouble using multivariable models. *Spine* 1991; 16: 7–14.
53. van der Weide WE, Verbeek JHAM, Salle HJA, van Dijk FJH. Prognostic factors for chronic disability from acute low-back pain in occupational health care. *Scand J Work Environ Health* 1999; 25: 50–56.
54. Cheadle A, Franklin G, Wolfhagen C, Savarino J, Liu PY, Salley C, Weaver, M. Factors influencing the duration of work-related disability: A population based study of Washington state workers' compensation. *Am J Public Health* 1994; 84: 190–196.
55. Infante-Rivard C, Lortie M. Prognostic factors for return to work after a first compensated episode of back pain. *Occup Environ Med* 1996; 53: 488–94.
56. Sinclair SJ, Hogg-Johnson S, Mondloh MV, Shields SA. The effectiveness of an early active intervention program for workers with soft-tissue injuries. *Spine* 1997; 22: 2919–31.
57. Tate RB, Yassi A, Cooper J. Predictors of time loss after back injury in nurses. *Spine* 1999; 24: 1930–1935.
58. Hemingway H, Shipley MJ, Stansfeld S, Marmot M. Sickness absence from back pain, psychosocial work characteristics and employment grade among office workers. *Scand J Work Environ Health* 1997; 23: 121–29.
59. Carey TS, Garrett JM, Jackman AM. Beyond the good prognosis. *Spine* 2000; 25: 115–20.

60. Klenerman L, Slade PD, Stanley IM, Pennie B, Reilly JP, Atchison LE, Troup JDG, Rose MJ. The prediction of chronicity in patients with an acute attack of low back pain in a general practice setting. *Spine* 1995; 20: 478–84.
61. Cole DC, Hudak PL. Prognosis of nonspecific work-related musculoskeletal disorders of the neck and upper extremity. *Am J Ind Med* 1996; 29: 657–68.
62. Croft PR. Soft tissue rheumatism. In: Selman AR, Hochberg MC, eds. *Epidemiology of the rheumatic diseases*. New York: Oxford University Press, 1993, pp. 375–421.
63. Von Korff M. Studying the natural history of back pain. *Spine* 1994; 19: 2041S–6S.
64. Feinstein AR. *Clinical biostatistics*. St. Louis, MO: CV Mosby, 1977.
65. Hogg-Johnson S, Frank JW, Rael E. Prognostic risk factor models for low back pain: Why they failed and a new hypothesis. Institute for Work and Health, Working Paper #19. 1994.
66. Kendall NAS, Linton SJ, Main CJ. Guide to assessing psychosocial yellow flags in acute low back pain: risk factors for long-term disability and work loss. Wellington, New Zealand, Enigma Publishing Ltd., 1997.
67. Black C, Cheung L, Cooper J, Curson-Prue S, Doupe L, Guirguis S, Haines T, Hawkins L, Helmka S, Holness L, Levitsky M, Liss G, Malcolm B, Painvin C, Wills M. Injury/Illness and Return to Work/Function: A practical guide for physicians. 2000. http/://www.wsib.on.ca/wsib/wsibsite.nsf/LookupFiles/DownloadableFilePhysiciansRTWGuide/$File/RTWGP.pdf.
68. Schultz IZ, Crook JM, Berkowitz J, Meloche GR, Milner R, Zuberbier OA, Meloche, W. Biopsychosocial multivariate predictive model of occupational low back disability. Accepted by *Spine* for publication December 2002.

APPENDIX

Methodological Assessment Criteria

Sampling

- Inception cohort defined in relation to symptom onset/injury?
- Early and uniform point in time?
- Referral pattern described?
- Did the referral pattern avoid bias?

Case Definition

- Operational definition of cases (i.e., inclusion criteria?)
- Exclusion criteria identified?

Follow-up

- Follow-up of >80% of total sample?
- Were all patients entered into the study accounted for in the results?
- Was follow-up sufficiently long (at least 1 year from onset of symptoms)?
- Was the clinical status of the patient known?

Outcome

- Were the outcome criteria appropriate to the research question?
- Was the outcome assessment "blind"?
- Was at least one outcome criteria objective, reproducible and accurate?

Prognostic Factors

- Were potential prognostic factors identified and measured?
- Were the measurement instruments valid and reliable?

Analysis

- Was adjustment for important prognostic factors carried out (or appropriate multivariate techniques)?
- Are the estimates (e.g., relative risk, relative odds) of the outcome complete?
- Did they give confidence intervals?
- Did they allow for analysis of subgroups?

Scoring: Yes = 1, Unclear = 0.5, No = 0

10

Biopsychosocial Multivariate Predictive Model of Occupational Low Back Disability

Izabela Z. Schultz, Joan M. Crook, Jonathan Berkowitz, Gregory R. Meloche, Ruth Milner, and Oonagh A. Zuberbier

INTRODUCTION

Low back injury rates have stabilized (Murphy & Volinn, 1999), but the growing economic burden of low back occupational disability (Volinn, Van Koevering & Loeser, 1991) has fuelled an extensive international research effort to identify risk factors for this condition. Over 1000 research and review papers were published in the last decade (Crook et al., 2002). Several empirically-based prediction models have been constructed (Feuerstein & Thebarge, 1991; Frymoyer, 1992; Gatchel, Polatin & Kinney, 1995; Halpern et al., 2001; Hazard et al., 1996; Linton & Hallden, 1997) to parallel theoretical models of occupational musculoskeletal disability (Schultz et al., 2000). At present, however, a limited convergence remains among different empirically-derived models and between empirical and theoretical models.

Fragmentation of studies on predictors of disability, varying degrees of empirical validation of predictive models, and poor differentiation and overlapping boundaries among diverse (i.e. clinical, actuarial, community health, compensation, disability-management, stage-of-disability, pain-site specific, and occupational) models of disability markedly hamper progress in this area. Concurrently, a proliferation of lengthy lists of risk factors for disability, including the so-called yellow, blue and black flags for disability (Linton & Hallden, 1998; Main & Spanswick, 2000) sought after by compensation systems, often lack requisite empirical validation for back-injury claim and disability management applications. Moreover, the mere length and breadth of such lists in the absence of empirically-based actuarial decision making rules implies that "anything that goes wrong" (medically, psychologically or occupationally) in

This chapter originally appeared in *Spine, 27*, 2220–2725 (2002) and is reprinted by permission of Lippincott Williams and Wilkins.

DOI: 10.1007/978-0-387-28919-9_10, © 2009 Springer Science+Business Media, LLC

the workers' life constitutes a potential risk for disability. Indiscriminate use of such systems likely poses a significant legal, economic and human suffering threat.

A recent systematic review of the literature (Crook et al., 2002) identified numerous methodological problems limiting the validity and generalizability of empirically-derived predictors and predictive models. Of 2170 studies screened in MEDLINE (1965 to 2000), PsycINFO (1967–2000), and EMBASE (1965 to 2000) for prediction of low back disability, only 19 met methodological standards. Problems related to lack of an overarching conceptual framework, differing levels of empirical validation of predictive factors, diversity of methodological designs, cohorts, sampling procedures, and outcome procedures, and differences in health care and compensation systems (Krause et al., 2001; Schultz et al, 2000). Moreover, heavy reliance on self-report rather than adherence to a multi-trait, multi-method approach (Campbell & Fiske, 1959) further restricted the generalizability of findings.

Studies that withstood methodological scrutiny (Crook et al., 2002) yielded the following groups of prognostic factors: sociodemographic, medical/physical, pain behavior, work-related, compensation-related, and psychological. There continues to be a need, however, for an empirically-validated, integrated, biopsychosocial model of return to work specific to the workers' compensation environment. Such a model would use empirically-based formulas derived from multivariate analysis, provide an empirical index of probability of return to work, and apply the most clinically and legally defensible multivariate, multi-method data collection approach. Ultimately, such actuarially-based, rather than judgment-based, predictions (Dawes, Faust & Meehl, 1989) will identify injured workers at the highest risk for chronicity and match disability management and rehabilitative approaches to workers' individual profiles of modifiable and non-modifiable risk factors.

METHODS

A multivariate biopsychosocial model of occupational disability formed the conceptual and practical framework for this study. An extensive literature search was undertaken to augment the systematic review described above. Important prognostic determinants of occupational disability following low back injury were divided into four major domains: Physical Examination and Medical History, Pain Behavior, Workplace and Psychosocial. As many potential relevant risk factors as possible were found for each domain. Experts in each of the four areas were consulted. Once predictors were identified, existing standardized, psychometrically-tested instruments were chosen to measure the constructs. When reliable and valid instruments did not exist, new scales were developed and tested.

A *Standardized Comprehensive Physical Examination* and pertinent medical history were developed for assessment and diagnosis (Hunt et al., 2001; Zuberbier, Kozlowski, et al., 2001; Zuberbier, Hunt, et al., 2001).

The *Pain Behavior Taxonomy (PBT)* was developed to measure "behavior associated with pain" (Keefe & Block, 1982; Keefe, Wilkins & Cooke, 1984; Prkachin, 1992). Pain behaviors such as guarding, touching, words, sounds, and facial expressions were observed and assessed during the standardized physical exam (Prkachin, Hughes, et al., 2002; Prkachin, Schultz, et al., 2002).

TABLE 1. Standardized Psychosocial Measuring Instruments Selected for the Study

Instrument	Variables
Short Form-36 Health Survey (SF-36)	Physical functioning Role-physical Bodily pain General health Vitality Social functioning Emotional functioning Mental health
State—Trait Anxiety Inventory (STAI) State Scale	Anxiety
Center for Epidemiological Studies-Depression (CES-D)	Depression
Visual Analogue Scale	Pain right now
Short Form McGill Pain Questionnaire (SF-MPQ)	Affective pain Sensory pain
Pain Drawing	Pain right now
Western Ontario and McMaster Universities (WOMAC) Scale	Physical functioning
Chronic Pain Grade (Von Korff)	Pain intensity Disability
Pain Disability Index (PDI)	Pain disability
Duke—UNC Functional Social Support Questionnaire	Functional social support
Job Content Questionnaire (Karasek)	Skill discretion at work Decision authority Job security Co-worker support Supervisory support Psychological demand Physical demand
Sickness Impact Profile (Roland)	Disability

The *Workplace Protocol* assessed variables including management involvement in health and safety, safety and accountability, disability claims management, work accommodation, company environment and organizational culture, and labor involvement in health and safety. Job characteristics included physical demands, employee tenure, company size and union status (Habeck et al., 1991; Schultz et al., 2002 (submitted for publication)).

The *Psychosocial Protocol* (Table 1) consisted of a number of standardized and newly developed measures designed to assess depression, anxiety, pain, general health status, social support at home and work, work satisfaction, perceptions of disability, expectations of recovery, and both workers' compensation and employer's response to the claim.

Study Design

A cohort longitudinal study design with two randomly selected cohorts of compensated low-back-injured workers was used. If participants remained off work 4–6 weeks after their original injury, they were classified "subacute". If they remained off work for 6–12 months after their original injury, they were classified "chronic."

The study received Ethics Approval from the University of British Columbia. When informed consent was obtained participants were assured that their study responses would not be available to any workers' compensation staff.

To qualify for the study, participants had to be off work due to "subacute" or "chronic" low back injury, have a low back injury claim with the Workers' Compensation Board of British Columbia (WCB-BC), be on active wage loss, be receiving WCB benefits, be at least 18 years old, be able to read English, have no history of back surgery, and not be pregnant.

Each week appropriate workers were identified from the WCB-BC computerized claim registry. Workers residing one hour (by car) from the WCB-BC were contacted by phone and those who met the inclusion criteria were invited to join the study.

Consenting participants underwent medical, pain behavior, workplace, and psychosocial assessments at the initial visit. A subset of workers returned for a repeat assessment three days later to test reliability of newly developed study instruments and physical exam items. Participants returned for a full reassessment three months later, with additional inquiry into their current work status.

Companies employing study participants were contacted and management representatives responsible for health and safety provided Workplace Protocol information.

The outcome variable used in the study was return-to-work status, i.e., return-to-work (RTW) or non-return-to-work (NRTW) at three month follow-up. The overall correct classification rate of participants was assessed for all prognostic variables. Stepwise logistic regression models were developed with variables entered in blocks (i.e. demographic, medical, pain behavior, workplace, and psychosocial factors). Variables were retained if they had a significance level of $p<0.10$. A final integrated model was constructed using the significant predictors from each block and selected significant predictors from bivariate analysis.

RESULTS

Sampling Frame and Demographic Factors

Nine hundred and eighty seven workers with subacute back injuries were identified, 864 could be contacted, 579 were deemed eligible and 247 (43%) consented to participate. One hundred and ninety two (78%) of these presented for the first examination. Eighty-three percent (160) of the subacute participants attended the three month follow-up visit. Thirty-two participants (17%) did not return for any follow-up*. There were no statistically significant differences between those participants whom returned for follow-up and those whom did not.

*Of these, sixteen did not respond to scheduling attempts, seven were away on vacation or had moved for work, five declined to participate, two were disgruntled with the WCB-BC for claim reasons, two had too much back pain, and one worked prohibitively long hours.

TABLE 2. Demographic Characteristics of the Low Back Pain Sample

Age (yr)	41.0 ± 10.3
Sex (% male/female)	73/27
Education (%)	
Grade School	5
High School	56
College/University/Technical School	40
Marital Status (%)	
Married/Common law	68
Single (never married)	18
Widowed/Separated/Divorced	15
Number of Dependents in Family (median)	2
Percent of Family Income Provided by Worker	
More than 75%	54
50%–75%	30
25%–50%	11
0%–25%	5
Union Membership (%)	
Union	63
Non-Union	7
Current Employment (mean)	
Years in job	8.1 ± 7.6
Years with employer	8.3 ± 7.4

Of the 422 chronically disabled workers contacted, 372 were reached and 202 were eligible to participate. Of these, 129 declined or were unable to participate. Sixty-one chronically disabled workers attended their first visit and fifty-six workers (92%) returned for their three month follow-up visit. The five participants lost to follow-up did not respond to scheduling attempts. Once more, there were no statistically significant differences between those participants whom returned for follow-up and those whom did not.

Demographics

Table 2 presents the demographic profile of the participants. The candidate demographic variables were subgroup (subacute/chronic), marital status, number of adults dependent on family income, percent of total income worker provided to the family, highest educational level, employment status, union membership, age, total time (years) held current job, and total (years) employed by present employer. The variables retained in the model were subgroup, union membership, years holding current job, and years employed by present employer. Odds ratios showed subacute study participants were 7.0 times more likely to return to work than chronic participants. Union members were 2.6 times more likely to return to work than non-members.

A flat prediction (no model) that 100% of participants would return to work would have correctly classified 51.3% of participants. Using demographic variables only, the correct classification (CC) rate rose to 68.3%. The model was equally accurate in predicting RTW (CC = 68.3%) and NRTW (CC = 67.7%).

Medical History

Candidate variables included medical red flags, injury intensity, perception of severity of disability, active treatment, Waddell symptoms, psychological distress in the last month, pre-injury psychological distress, passive treatments, and medication use. The final model retained perception of severity of disability, injury intensity, and Waddell symptoms. Only perception of severity of disability was highly significant. The overall correct classification rate for this model was 65.4% (CC = 70.5% for RTW and CC = 59.8% for NRTW).

Range of Motion

Eight variables were calculated: T12 and S1-2 extension and flexion, and T12 and S1-2 left and right lateral flexion. The model retained only T12 extension and S1-2 left lateral flexion, and produced an overall correct classification rate of 62.0% (CC = 68.8% for RTW and CC = 54.5% for NRTW).

Physical Exam

The candidate predictive variables included nerve root tension, lumbar nerve root function, functional tests, Waddell signs, left and right leg typical sciatica, current pain, worst pain during exam, time to complete walk, gait, physical signs of exaggerated pain behaviors, and clinical impressions of radiculopathy and mechanical non-specific low back pain. Worst pain during exam, time to complete walk, and right leg typical sciatica remained in the model. This model correctly classified 68.8% of RTW and 54.5% of NRTW for an overall classification rate of 62.0%.

Pain Behavior

Five pain behaviors were coded during the physical exam: guarding, touching, words, sounds, and facial expression. Only guarding (defined as behavior that prevents or alleviates pain, including stiffness, hesitation, limping, bracing, and flinching) (Prkachin, Schultz et al., 2002) was a significant predictor, achieving a modest correct classification rate of 57.8%. It was a much better predictor of NRTW (70.7%) than RTW (40.9%).

Psychosocial

The next model used standardized psychosocial instruments and the final model retained percent body pain right now (Pain Drawing), Physical Functioning, Vitality, and Health Transition (SF-36 Health Survey), Skill Discretion (Job Content Questionnaire) and State Anxiety (State-Trait Anxiety Inventory). The model gave a correct classification rate of 68.6% (CC = 70.6% for RTW and CC = 66.3% for NRTW).

Workplace

The candidate predictive variables included safety environment, disability management, senior management involvement in health and safety, company environment, work accommodation and availability of work capacity evaluation, as reported by

TABLE 3. Final Integrated Logistic Regression Model of RTW/NRTW

	B	SE	Sig	Odds Ratio
VARIABLE				
Subgroup	−1.396	0.546	0.011	0.248
SF-36 Vitality	−0.031	0.011	0.006	0.969
SF-36 Health Transition*	−0.832	0.367	0.023	0.435
Feel job threatened due to injury	0.617	0.331	0.062	1.854
Problem better or worse than expected	−0.610	0.199	0.002	0.544
Guarding	−0.098	0.033	0.003	0.907
Perception of severity of disability	−0.540	0.264	0.041	0.583
Time to complete walk	−0.012	0.005	0.022	0.988
Right leg typical sciatica	−1.534	0.762	0.044	0.216
Constant	11.788	2.316	0.000	

**Health transition* is defined as change in health status, for better or worse.

company management. The model retained work accommodation. It produced an overall classification rate of 58.2% and was significantly better at classifying RTW (73.7%) than NRTW (40%).

Final Integrated Model

A final model was developed using the significant predictors from the previous blocks. The candidate variables were: group (subacute or chronic), union membership, total time in current job, total time employed by employer, percent body pain right now, physical functioning, vitality and health transition, state anxiety, skill discretion, guarding (pain behavior), injury intensity, perception of severity of disability, Waddell symptoms, T12 extension, worst pain during the exam, time to complete walk, and right leg typical sciatica.

In addition, the pool of predictors was expanded to include individual items that were significant predictors of RTW/NRTW in bivariate analysis. These items assessed the WCB and employer's response (treated fairly by WCB regarding his/her claim, and feeling threatened regarding job due to injury) and expectations of recovery (problem better or worse than expected). The final model retained a selection of variables from among the medical, pain behavior, and psychosocial factors, and achieved an overall correct prediction rate of 77.6%. The model correctly classified 80.5% of RTW and 74.4% of NRTW (Table 3).

DISCUSSION

The study allowed for a systematic comparison of the return-to-work predictive power of multivariate occupational disability determinants. It clearly demonstrated that the predictive power of individual groups of variables, although statistically significant, was not particularly strong and ranged from 57.8% for pain behavior to 68.6% for psychosocial variables. Since the Integrated Model of Disability constructed in this study was developed within the workers' compensation environment, the adherence to the medico-legal principle of cross-validation through the use of multiple sources and methods of data collection was followed. The "winning" predictors were derived from three methods (Amick III et al., 2000) self-report on a paper-and-pencil questionnaire, (Burton et al., 1995) physical examination, and (Campbell & Fiske, 1959) behavioral pain observation. This resulted in a significantly improved rate of prediction accuracy: 80.5% for return to work and 74.4% for failure to return to work. Such accurate, validated, multi-method, empirically-derived formulas offer an empirical link to enhanced secondary disability prevention strategies, rehabilitative interventions and legal defensibility of disability claim decisions.

The results confirmed superiority of the biopsychosocial model over the biomedical model (Feuerstein & Thebarge, 1991; Turk, 1996; Waddell, 1987; Waddell, 1992). The predictive factors identified by the Integrated Model actually covered a biopsychosocial spectrum. They included physical/medical factors, psychosocial factors, pain behavior-guarding, and a workplace-related factor, namely, the belief that the worker's job was threatened due to injury.

Analysis of the Integrated Model revealed the significance of workers' cognitions (i.e. perceptions of current health and physical status, and expectations of recovery). Conspicuously missing from the model were measures of psychopathology, particularly depression and anxiety. This finding was consistent with recent systematic reviews of the literature (Linton, 2000; Main & Spanswick, 2000; Turk, 1997), which have emphasized the role of cognitive factors in the development of pain and disability. It appeared that psychopathological variables were less important for disability prediction models with a workers' compensation population. Cognitively-based measures of perceptions, beliefs and expectations may have more effectively captured and subsumed emotional distress common to chronic pain disability. Furthermore, an adaptation-oriented, cognitive-behavioral model of psychosocial determinants of disability lends itself better to multi-modal interventions, particularly in the subacute stage, where the focus is upon education, management of expectations, and gradual activation.

Fear of job loss, embedded in workers' expectations of recovery, constitutse an important but often forgotten predictor of disability (Cole et al., 2002). Job insecurity factors require particular attention in designing early intervention studies and must include early employer involvement for work-attached individuals. Clinically, fear of job loss likely blend in with other aspects of emotional distress related to back pain. The present study did not confirm the postulated significance of macro-level workplace organizational factors (Amick III et al., 2000; Habeck et al., 1991). This can likely be explained by insufficient heterogeneity among employers involved in the study and low correlation between employer and worker perceptions of the workplace organization. However, the results of our study, which underscored the role of work accommodation as a predictor of disability, are promising for future research and consistent with the literature (Krause, Dasinger & Neuhauser, 1998; Pransky et al., 2002).

Medical/physical variables contributed to the Integrated Model. In this study, sciatica was among the best predictors, consistent with a study by Carey et al. (Carey, Garrett & Jackman, 2000). Time to complete walk, a behavioral measure of functional status, was also considered among the best predictors, concordant with studies using other functional status measures (Carey, Garrett & Jackman, 2000; Coste et al., 1994; Cooke, Moldofsky & Shannon, 1998; Gatchel, Polatin & Kinney, 1995; Haldorsen, Indahl & Ursin, 1998; van der Weide et al., 1999).

Pain behavior-guarding (Prkachin, Schultz et al., 2002) was also identified among the best predictors of disability. This was consistent with the results of the study by Öhlund (Öhlund et al., 1994) which showed positive correlations between the total score on the Pain Behavior Rating Scale (Richards et al, 1992) and failure to return to work. There were no studies to date, however, that reported a specific relationship between guarding and return to work. There was no consensus on what the theoretical and clinical construct was underlying guarding behavior. In medical conceptualization it was a reflection of tenderness and pain. In psychological conceptualization, it was reflective of fear of movement and fear avoidance (Burton et al., 1995; Klenerman et al., 1995). Components of pain-related distress from a biopsychosocial perspective reflected both conceptualizations. (Waddell & Main, 1998). Anticipatory guarding may lead to increase in muscular activation and pain (Skouen et al., 2002), which, in turn, may lead to even more distress, more guarding and more disability.

Several researchers (Gatchel, Polatin & Kinney, 1995; Hazard et al., 1996; Linton & Hallden, 1998; Nordin et al., 1997) have reported on the development of short standardized indices to screen for early identification of those at risk for chronic disability. This study built on those efforts and offered several advantages. As noted, this work was based on a comprehensive biopsychosocial model, theoretically-derived and empirically-validated. The psychometric properties of all newly developed measures were tested. The clinical and work status of the injured workers were known at outcome.

The multivariate prediction model developed in this study was specifically applicable to the workers' compensation context and its generalizability to other contexts was unknown. It was validated on combined groups of subacute and chronic low back-injured workers, which reduced its dependence on a specific stage of disability. However, it is still likely to perform better on subacute rather than chronically disabled workers, given smaller total number and participation rate of chronically disabled workers. The model also performed better in predictions of who would likely return to work as compared to who would not, and its validated time frame was three months after the initial evaluation. It is too labor intensive for mass applications in case-and disability-management by lay users. However, the paper-and-pencil-measured predictors identified in this study may form a starting point for the development and validity of a risk-for-disability questionnaire, which could be used for such purposes (Cats-Baril & Frymoyer, 1991; Frymoyer & Cats-Baril, 1987; Linton & Hallden, 1998).

Finally, the review of the best performing return-to-work variables suggested that most of the predictive factors were potentially amenable to change. A clear link to secondary prevention and early intervention with workers at high risk for low back disability emerged in this study. Secondary prevention interventions should be designed to address modifiable, cognition-based factors implicated in occupational disability. A well-coordinated, educational, and early activation approach involving primary care physicians, employers, and workers' compensation systems, and targeting workers' beliefs, perceptions, and expectations, would likely be most effective. Such intervention should be supported by a randomized controlled trial with a follow-up longer than three months, ranging from one to two years, depending on the purpose of the study.

Ability to identify those workers in chronic stage of work disability who are or are not likely to return to work is also important. Recent studies (Haldorsen et al., 2002; Skouen et al., 2002), demonstrated that for workers with poor prognosis, involving psychosocial problems and generalized pain, extensive multidisciplinary program with significant cognitive-behavioural component had been more effective than usual treatment. For the remaining chronically disabled workers, however, light multidisciplinary program, with exercise, lifestyle and fear-avoidance advice, was more cost-beneficial.

ACKNOWLEDGMENTS: The authors wish to gratefully acknowledge the contributions of Dr. Gordon Waddell, Dr. Ken Prkachin, Dr. David Hunt, Dr. Alec Ostry, Dr. Peter Joy and the financial support of the British Columbia and Alberta Workers' Compensation Boards, Canada.

REFERENCES

Amick III, B.C., Habeck, R.V., Hunt, A., et al. (2000). Measuring the impact of organizational behaviors on work disability prevention and management. *Journal of Occupational Rehabilitation, 10*, 21–38.

Burton, A.K., Tillotson, K.M., Main, C.J., et al. (1995). Psychosocial predictors of outcome in acute and subchronic low back trouble. *Spine, 20*, 722–28.

Campbell, D.T., & Fiske, D.W. (1959). Convergent and discriminant validation by the multitrait-multimethod matrix. *Psychological Bulletin, 56*, 81–105.

Carey, T.S., Garrett, J.M., Jackman, A.M. (2000). Beyond the good prognosis. *Spine, 25*, 115–20.

Cats-Baril, W.L., Frymoyer, J.W. (1991). Identifying patients at risk of becoming disabled due to low back pain: The Vermont Rehabilitation Engineering Center predictive model. *Spine, 16*, 605–7.

Cole, D.C., Mondlock, M.V., Hogg-Johnson, S., et al. (2002). Listening to injured workers: How recovery expectations predict outcomes—a prospective study. *Canadian Medical Association Journal, 166*, 749–54.

Coste, J., Delecoeuillerie, G., Cohen de Lara, A., et al. Clinical course and prognostic factors in acute low back pain: An inception cohort study in primary care practice. *British Medical Journal, 308*, 577–80.

Crook, J., Milner, R., Schultz, I., et al. (2002). Determinants of occupational disability following a low back injury: A critical review of the literature. Accepted for publication in *Journal of Occupational Rehabilitation* December 2002.

Crook, J., Moldofsky, H., & Shannon, H. (1998). Determinants of disability after a work related musculoskeletal injury. *Journal of Rheumatology, 25*, 1570–1577.

Dawes, R.M., Faust, D., & Meehl, P.E. (1989). Clinical versus actuarial judgment. *Science, 243*, 1668–74.

Feuerstein, M., & Thebarge, R.W. (1992). Perceptions of disability and occupational stress as discriminatory of work disability in patients with chronic pain. *Journal of Occupational Rehabiliation, 1*, 185–95.

Frymoyer, J.W. (1992). Predicting disability from low back pain. *Clinical Orthopedics, 279*, 101–9.

Frymoyer, J.W., & Cats-Baril, W. (1987). Predictors of low back pain disability. *Clinical Orthopedics, 221*, 90–98.

Gatchel. R,J., Polatin, P.B., & Kinney, R.K. 91995). Predicting outcome of chronic back pain using clinical predictors of psychopathology: A prospective analysis. *Health Psychology, 14*, 415–20.

Habeck, R.V., Leahy, M.J., Hunt, H.A., et al. (1991). Employer factors related to workers' compensation claims and disability management. *Rehabilitation Counseling Bulletin, 34*, 210–226.

Haldorsen, E.M.H., Grasdal, A.L., Skouen, J.S., et al. (2002). Is there a right treatment for a particular patient group? Compaison of ordinary treatment, light multidisciplinary treatment, and extensive multidisciplinary treatment for long-term sick-listed employees with musculoskeletal pain. *Pain, 95*, 49–63.

Haldorsen, E.M.H., Indahl, A., & Ursin, H. (1998). Patients with low back pain not returning to work: A 12-month follow up study. *Spine, 23*, 1202–8.

Halpern, M., Hiebert, R., Nordin, M., et al. (2001). The test-retest reliability of a new occupational risk factor questionnaire for outcome studies of low back pain. *Applied Ergonomics, 32*, 39–46.

Hazard, R.G., Haugh, L.D., Reid, S., et al. (1996). Early prediction of chronic disability after occupational low back injury. *Spine, 21*, 945–51.

Hunt, D.G., Zuberbier, O.A., Kozlowski, A.J., et al. (2001). Reliability of the lumbar flexion, lumbar extension and passive straight leg raise test in normal populations embedded within a complete physical examination. *Spine, 26*, 2714–18.

Keefe, F.J., & Block, A.R. (1982). Development of an observation method for assessing pain behavior in chronic low back pain patients. *Behavior Therapy, 13*, 363–365.

Keefe, F.J., Wilkins, R.H., & Cook, W.A. (1984). Direct observation of pain behavior in low back pain patients during physical examination. *Pain, 20*, 59–68.

Klenerman, L., Slade, P.D., Stanley, I.M., et al. (1995). The prediction of chronicity in patients with an acute attack of low back pain in a general practice setting. *Spine, 20*, 478–84.

Krause, N., Dasinger, L.K., Neuhasuer, F. (1998). Modified work and return to work: A review of the literature. *Journal of OccupationalRehabilitation, 8*, 113–39.

Krause, N., Frank, J.W., Sullivan, T.J., et al. (2001). Determinants of duration of disability and return to work after work-related injury and illness: Challenges for future research. Invited paper for special issue of *American Journal of Industrial Medicine. 40*, 464–84.

Linton, S.J. (2000). A review of psychological risk factors in back and neck pain. *Spine, 25*, 1148–56.

Linton, S.J., & Halldén, K. (1997). Risk factors and the natural course of acute and recurrent musculoskeletal pain: Developing a screening instrument. In: Jensen TS, Turner JA, Wiesenfeld-Hallin Z, eds. *Proceedings of the 8th World Congress on Pain, Progress in Pain Research and Management.* Volume 8, 527–36. Seattle, Washington: IASP Press.

Linton, S.J., & Halldén, K. (1998). Can we screen for problematic back pain? A screening questionnaire for predicting outcome in acute and subacute back pain. *Clinical Journal of Pain, 14*, 209–15.

Main, C.J., & Spanswick, C.C. (Eds.) (2000). *Pain Management: An Interdisciplinary Approach*. Edinburgh: Churchill Livingstone.

Murphy, P.L., & Volinn, E. (1999). Is occupational low back pain on the rise? *Spine, 24*, 691–697.

Nordin, M., Skovron, M.L., Hiebert, R., et al. (1997). Early predictors of delayed return to work in patients with low back pain. *Journal of Musculoskeletal Pain, 5*, 5–27.

Öhlund, C., Lindström, J., Areskoug, B., et al. (1994). Pain behavior in industrial subacute low back pain. Part I. Reliability: concurrent and predictive validity of pain behavior assessments. *Pain, 58*, 201–9.

Pransky, G., Benjamin, K., Hill-Fotouhi, C. et al. (2002). Work-related outcomes in occupational low back pain: A multidimensional analysis. *Spine, 27*, 684–870.

Prkachin, K.M. (1992). The consistency of facial expressions of pain: A comparison across modalities. *Pain, 51*, 297–306.

Prkachin, K.M., Hughes, E., Schultz, I., et al. (2002). Real-time pain assessment of pain behavior during clinical assessment of low-back pain patients. *Pain, 95*, 23–30.

Prkachin, K.M., Schultz, I., Berkowitz, J., et al. (2002). Assessing pain behavior in real time: Concurrent validity and examiner sensitivity. *Behavior Research and Therapy, 40*, 595–607.

Richards, J.S., Nepomuceno, C., Riles, M., et al. (1982). Assessing pain behavior: The UAB pain behavior scale. *Pain, 14*, 393–98.

Schultz, I.Z., Crook, J., Fraser, K, et al. (2000). Models of diagnosis and rehabilitation in musculoskeletal pain-related occupational disability. *Journal of Occupational Rehabilitation, 10*, 271–93.

Schultz, I.Z., Ostry, A., Milner, R.A., et al. (2002). In search of workplace predictors of disability: The relationship between workplace organization and workers' compensation disability claim rates. Submitted for publication 2002.

Skouen, J.S., Grasdal, A.L., Haldorsen, E.M.H., et al. (2002). Relative cost-effectiveness of extensive and light multidisciplinary treatment programs *versus* treatment as usual for patient with chronic low back pain on long-term sick leave. *Spine, 27*, 901–10.

Turk, D.C. (1996). Biopsychosocial perspective on chronic pain. In: R.J. Gatchel & D.C. Turk (Eds.), *Psychological Approaches to Pain Management: A Practitioner's Handbook*, 3–32. New York: Guilford Press.

Turk, D.C. (1997). The role of demographic and psychosocial factors in transition from acute to chronic pain. In: Jensen, TS, Turner, JA, Wiesenfeld-Hallin, Z., eds. *Proceedings of the 8th World Congress on Pain, Progress in Pain Research and Management*. Volume 8. Seattle, 185–213. Washington: IASP Press.

van der Weide, W.E., Verbeek, J.H.A.M., Salle, H.J.A. et al. (1999). Prognostic factors for chronic disability from acute low-back pain in occupational health care. *Scandinavian Journal of Work and Environmental Health, 25*, 50–56.

Volinn, E., Van Koevering, D., Loeser, J.D. (1991). Back sprain in industry: The role of socioeconomic factors in chronicity. *Spine, 16*, 542–48.

Waddell, G. (1987). A new clinical model for the treatment of low-back pain. *Spine, 12*, 632–44.

Waddell, G. (1992). Biopsychosocial analysis of low back pain. *Baillière's Clinical Rheumatology, 6*, 523–57.

Waddell, G., & Main, C.J. (1998). A new clinical model of low back pain and disability. In: G. Waddell (Ed.), *The Back Pain Revolution*, 223–40. Edinburgh: Churchill Livingstone.

Zuberbier, O., Kozlowski, A.J., Hunt, D.G., et al. (2001). An analysis of the convergent and discriminant validity of published lumbar flexion, extension, and lateral flexion scores. *Spine, 26*, E472–E478.

Zuberbier, O.A., Hunt, D.G., Kozlowski, A.J., Berkowitz, J., Schultz, I.Z., Crook, J.M. et al. (2001). Commentary on the AMA Guides' lumbar impairment validity checks. *Spine, 26*, 2735–37.

11

Whiplash and Neck Pain-Related Disability

Jerome A. Schofferman and Mary E. Koestler

INTRODUCTION

Chronic neck pain results in significant costs to individuals because of pain, suffering, and personal losses; and to society due to increased health care costs, disability payments, and loss of work productivity. Many people have an episode of acute neck pain, but only in a few does the pain become chronic. This chapter will examine chronic neck pain, particularly whiplash, with an emphasis on the potential predictors of chronic pain and long-term disability. In order to accomplish this, we will briefly discuss the structural causes for chronic neck pain after trauma and the results of the most important evidence-based treatments.

Whiplash is one important cause of neck pain. The term "whiplash" is potentially confusing because it describes both a mechanism of injury and the symptoms caused by an injury. According to the Quebec Task Force on Whiplash-Associated Disorders, the mechanism of injury is any incident that causes the head and neck to move suddenly and forcefully in one direction and then recoil in the opposite direction (Spitzer, Skovron, Salmi, Cassidy, Duranceau, Suissa, & Zeiss, 1995). In whiplash due to motor vehicle accident (MVA), the actual biomechanical injury is due to the thorax moving forward and upward while the neck and head remain stationary. These forces can produce shear injury to the discs, facet joints, and soft tissues. The magnitude of injury, pain, and impairment varies greatly from person to person. Some patients are not injured at all in a MVA, but others develop chronic problems. Although it may seem counterintuitive, the correlation between the vehicular damage, relative speeds of the vehicles, and the degree of pain and impairment is poor.

Whiplash has a very negative public image. The mere mention of the term brings up a picture of a person with a neck brace who is exaggerating his or her symptoms in the hope of obtaining a large financial settlement. Although some individuals may try to take advantage of any situation, even a car accident, whiplash is very real, and is responsible for a significant amount of pain, suffering, and disability.

DOI: 10.1007/978-0-387-28919-9_11, © 2009 Springer Science+Business Media, LLC

We have chosen to state our conclusions here, and then review the evidence to support them.

- Chronic or frequently recurring neck pain occurs in about 14% of the general population (Berglund, Alfredsson, Cassidy, Jensen, & Nygren, 2000).
- Most patients with acute neck pain after MVA recover within three to six months, but 18% to 40% develop chronic pain of variable intensity (Berglund et al, 2000; Radanov, Sturzenegger, & Stefano, 1995).
- About 4% to 8% of whiplash patients become partially or totally disabled (Gozzard, Bannister, Langkamer, Khan, Gargan, & Foy, 2001; Radanov et al, 1995).

Based on the preponderance of published studies, and giving more weight to the prospective clinical cohorts than the population-based studies, a rather clear picture emerges. It is not possible to predict the clinical outcome of a particular individual with neck pain after MVA. However, among large cohorts of patients with acute whiplash, by far the strongest predictor of high risk for poor outcome is severe neck pain at the initial evaluation. Other strong predictors that correlate with poor outcome are headache, especially if it is severe, multiple areas of pain, marked restriction of cervical range of motion, and the presence of radicular symptoms and signs (Cote, Cassidy, Carroll, Frank, & Bombardier, 2001; Scholten-Peeters, Verhagen Bekkering, van der Windt, Barnsley, Oostendorp, & Hendriks 2003). Psychologically, patients who cope well tend to do better than those who are very concerned with their long-term prognosis. Although patients with prior psychological illness tend to fare worse, there are no other psychological factors that correlate with outcome. Although litigation itself does not appear to alter outcome, there appears to be less chronic whiplash in cultures with no compensation for pain and suffering.

Many patients with chronic neck pain will improve after their primary structural injuries (disc, facet joints), secondary problems (posture, deconditioning), and secondary psychological problems (depression, fear-avoidance) are evaluated and appropriately treated (Garvey, Transfeldt, Malcolm, & Kos, 2002; Lord, Barnsley, Wallis, McDonald, & Bogduk, 1996; Palit, Schofferman, Goldthwaite, Reynolds, Kerner, Keaney, & Lawrence-Miyasaki, 1999; Vendrig, van Akkerveeken, & McWhorter, 2000).

In population-based epidemiological studies, the prognosis for whiplash varies according to the population studied and the insurance or compensation system in which the MVA occurred. These statistical correlations cannot be and should not be used to evaluate, treat, or render a legal opinion for an individual patient, nor to attribute poor outcome to social, cultural, or compensation systems. There is a strong correlation between retention of a lawyer and worse outcome, but it is not clear if the most severely injured are just more likely to seek counsel (Cote et al, 2001). Some, but not all studies found patients who were at fault for the MVA tend to recover faster. Using insurance company records, in a no-fault, no tort system, there is a shorter mean time to case closure, although the correlation of time to case closure with pain and disability is significant it is not totally accepted (Cassidy, Carroll, Cote, Lemstra, Berglund, & Nygren, 2000; Scholten-Peters et al, 2003). Even using this population-based outcome parameter, the intensity of neck pain, the level of physical functioning, and the presence or absence of depression correlate strongly with outcome (Cassidy et al., 2000). Cultural factors may play a role. In societies without compensation for pain or suffering and where people do not readily seek redress through the legal system, there appears to be less chronic whiplash (Obelieniene, Schrader, Bovim, Miseviciene, & Sand, 1999). There is a lack of data regarding the results of any form of clinical social, or cultural interventions that can be inferred from these and similar data.

The relationship between injury and outcome is more like a Moebius strip than a straight line. There are complex and reciprocal relationships between pain, disability, psychosocial, and cultural factors in whiplash and other forms of chronic spine pain (Linton, 2000). In chronic neck pain, for most patients, the biological factors (primary structural pathology and secondary deconditioning) are probably the most important to account for the pain, but these have been virtually ignored in most outcome studies. Using a modern, thorough, and evidence-based evaluation, the structural problems can usually be identified and treated. There is no evidence that psychosocial factors *cause* the pain. However, they may account for much of the disability. Although psychological factors cannot predict which patients will develop chronic problems, coping styles and beliefs, not psychopathology may play an important role. Depression and anxiety are usually secondary to pain and impairment. Psychosocial factors probably exert their greatest influence in determining the level of impairment and the transition from acute to chronic pain and disability, rather than the level of pain.

NATURAL HISTORY OF WHIPLASH

Fortunately, most persons involved in an MVA do not develop neck pain. Of those who do have pain, most improve within a few weeks or months (Radanov et al, 1995). Pain, if it occurs, usually begins almost immediately, but about 22% of whiplash patients do not appear to be injured at the scene (Spitzer et al, 1995). Early interventions may decrease the incidence of chronic neck pain and disability due to whiplash (Pettersson & Toolanen, 1998; Rosenfeld, Seferiadis, Carlsson, & Gunnarsson, 2003). The use of intravenous corticosteroids within the first six hours of MVA has been shown to decrease the incidence of chronic pain (Pettersson et al, 1998). Patients who are able to maintain normal or nearly normal function or who are in an active physical rehabilitation program soon after MVA also have a lower incidence chronic pain (Borchgrevink, Kaasa, McDonagh, Stiles, Haraldseth, & Lereim, 1998; Rosenfeld et al., 2000) Obviously, it is not possible to say if these patients who are able to function normally were less seriously injured, if early activity prevents excess joint and soft tissue problems, or if the lowered incidence is psychologically related.

The natural history of whiplash has been well studied and systematically reviewed, and is generally favorable (Cote et al., 2001; Scholten-Peeters et al., 2003; Spitzer et al., 1995). However, 18–40% of patients with acute neck pain after MVA develop chronic neck pain, and 5 to 7% develop partial or total long-term disability (Berglund et al., 2000; Gozzard et al., 2001; Radanov et al., 1995). However, some have opined that chronic whiplash rarely occurs in certain cultures that do not have a compensation system, and infer that chronic pain and disability are driven predominantly by cultural and financial factors (Schrader, Obelieniene, Bovim, Surkiene, Mickeviciene, Miseviciene, & Sand, 1996; Partheni, Constantoyannis, Ferrari, Nikiforidis, Voulgaris, & Papadakis, 2000; Obelieniene et al., 1999).

Radanov (1995) performed a two-year prospective longitudinal cohort study of 117 patients seen within one week of a MVA. They collected comprehensive demographic, physical, and psychological data at the initial evaluations. After two-years, 21 patients (18%) still had symptoms related to the MVA, and 82% had recovered. Only 5 patients were disabled, three of whom were able to work part-time.

Berglund and associates (2000) retrospectively evaluated the prevalence of chronic neck pain in four groups of patients identified through insurance records: persons previously involved in MVA with *no* acute neck pain, persons previously involved in MVA *with* acute neck pain, and two separate control groups of patients with no prior MVA. The study was performed 7 years after the MVA, and all liability claims and litigation had been settled. They found the prevalence of chronic neck pain in the two control groups was 14.5%, and the prevalence of chronic neck pain in patients with no acute neck pain despite MVA was about 14%. However, the prevalence of chronic neck pain in those patients who had acute neck pain after MVA was 39.6%, nearly three times greater than the other groups. The authors did not measure function or return to work.

There are three papers that report on the same cohort of 61 patients followed prospectively at the Bristol Royal Infirmary for 2, 10.8, and 15 years (Gargan & Bannister, 1990; Norris & Watt, 1983; Squires, Gargan, & Bannister, 1996). Unfortunately, many patients were lost to follow-up, which makes the results somewhat difficult to interpret. The authors evaluated pain directly and disability indirectly by describing severe pain as that which "disrupted work and other activities." At 10 and 15 years about 7% and 8% had disabling symptoms, but because of the small remaining sample size, the confidence intervals reflect a great deal of potential overlap. Nonetheless, this disability prevalence is similar to that described by Radanov et al. (1995).

In summary, the prognosis for neck pain due to whiplash is generally good. About 60% to 70% of patients will recover by three to six months. After six months, the incidence of recovery slows significantly and almost becomes asymptotic with about 82% of patients fully recovered by two years. Although an additional number of patients do recover, some others may get worse. The prevalence of patients who are partly or completely disabled after two years is about 4 to 8% based on several prospective studies (Radanov et al., 1995; Squires et al., 1996).

SYMPTOMS OF WHIPLASH

Pain

Neck Pain

Neck pain is the predominant symptom of whiplash. Pain is usually located in the mid to low cervical region. It may be midline or on either side of the midline. It is very common for pain to be referred to the trapezius muscles, shoulders, interscapular region, or arms in a nondermatomal distribution. Some patients experience pain in the anterior neck. Less commonly pain may be felt in the face. If there is a lateral disc herniation, there may be arm pain in the dermatome of the involved nerve root. These patients are generally more straight-forward in terms of diagnosis and treatment.

Headache

Headache is the second most common symptom, and is best referred to as cervicogenic headache (CHA). The headache may vary in severity and frequency. It is often confused with migraine or tension-type headache. It virtually always involves the base of the skull, but frequently radiates to the crown of the head and frontal regions. It is often unilateral, but the side can vary even in the same patient. It is often precipitated by cervical range of motion, especially prolonged or repeated end-range flexion, extension, or axial rotation.

Whiplash Associated Disorders

There are many other symptoms associated with whiplash injury that are referred to as whiplash associated disorders (WAD). Some of the symptoms and the range of WAD symptoms reported include visual disturbances (2–54%), dizziness (53%), ringing in the ears (7–14%), weakness (68%), fatigue, poor concentration or memory, difficulty sleeping, and even low back pain (39–50%) (Barnsley, Lord, & Bogduk, 2002; Rosenfeld et al., 2003). Some or all of these symptoms are noted in virtually all prospective studies on whiplash, although the prevalence may vary. The combination of symptoms may suggest to physicians unfamiliar with WAD that the problems including the neck pain may all be psychological rather than structural. However, the pattern is so common among patients, so well described in the literature, and often improved with effective treatment of the neck disorder, that it appears far more likely the symptoms are organically based, even if poorly understood.

Psychological Disorders and Whiplash

Psychological factors are involved in virtually all patients with acute and chronic pain. In some persons psychological factors can help a person function despite pain. In others, psychological factors may worsen pain, and certainly impact the degree of impairment, and disability.

The relationship between chronic pain, chronic neck pain due to whiplash and psychological factors is complex and multi-layered, and there are many questions.

- What are the psychological consequences of chronic neck pain and impairment?
- Is chronic neck pain due to whiplash different from other chronic musculoskeletal pain problems?
- Is there evidence that pre-existing psychological factors or illnesses predispose patients to chronic pain and disability after whiplash?
- Does litigation and the potential for financial gain perpetuate pain and disability?

Fortunately there is an abundance of published literature on each aspect.

Psychological Abnormalities in Chronic Neck Pain Due to Whiplash

In acute neck pain, particularly after trauma such as MVA, there may be anxiety and fear (Mayou, Bryant, & Duthie, 1993). In any chronic pain state there may be depression, anxiety, substance abuse disorder, cognitive impairment, and post-traumatic stress disorder. Patients may be overly focused on physical sensations and seemingly overly concerned about their health. There may be anger and hostility, feelings of self-doubt, and loss of control (Peebles, McWilliams, & MacLennan, 2001). There may be cognitive and behavioral disorders as well.

Mayou et al. (1993) followed a group of MVA patients for one year to evaluate the early and late psychological consequences. Patients were initially evaluated at a mean of 25 days after MVA and then again at 3 and 12 months. Almost 20% suffered acute stress syndrome characterized by mood disorder and horrific memories of the accident. At one-year, 5% of patients met criteria for post-traumatic stress disorder (PTSD), 18% had travel anxiety, and 12% had a mood disorder.

In the evaluation and treatment of a particular patient with chronic pain due to whiplash and psychological changes, it is not possible to know which came first. If the psychological problems are secondary to the pain, and the pain is effectively treated, then psychological factors may be expected to improve. Wallis, Lord, and Bogduk (1997) treated 17 patients with cervical facet syndrome and psychological changes using the Symptom Checklist 90-Revised (SCL-90-R) as an outcome measure. In all patients in whom pain was improved by radiofrequency neurotomy (RFN), improvement in the SCL-90-R followed. In all but one of the patients who did not improve after RFN, the SCL-90-R did not change. The authors concluded that the psychological abnormalities in these patients were secondary to the chronic structural pain, and psychological abnormalities improved after pain improved.

We have reported that psychological and cognitive abnormalities may be overlooked by treating physicians (Schofferman & Young, 2003) We evaluated 34 patients with chronic neck pain seen at a mean of 29 months after injury who had symptoms of personality change, memory loss, emotional lability, or difficulty with simple calculations. Two-thirds had been injured in MVA. We referred these patients for neuropsychological testing (NPT). No patient had normal NPT, 4 (12%) had cognitive impairment only, 11 (32%) had psychological disorder only [depression (8), PTSD (2), and adjustment disorder (1)], and 19 (56%) had both. Perhaps most remarkably, the patients had previously seen an average of 4 (range 2 to 7) physicians without either a psychological or cognitive disorder being mentioned.

Linton (2000) reviewed the potential psychosocial risk factors in back and neck pain. Most of the data concerned injured workers and most studies emphasized low back pain patients. Some of his conclusions are directly applicable to whiplash. Linton opined that the evidence was strong that psychosocial variables are linked to the transition from acute to chronic pain; cognitive factors are related to the development of pan and disability; depression, anxiety, and distress are related to pain and disability, and psychosocial factors may be used as predictors of the risk for developing long-term pain and disability (although the evidence specific for whiplash reaches an opposite conclusion on this last point). He added that passive coping style, disability, fear-avoidance beliefs, and beliefs about the meaning of the pain are all related to pain and disability.

Chronic Whiplash versus Other Chronic Musculoskeletal Disorders

Wallis and associates (1997) described what they believed was a characteristic profile for chronic whiplash patients by using the SCL-90-R. However, Peebles and associates (2001) compared the SCL-90-R results in 61 patients with chronic neck pain due to whiplash to patients with 91 patients with chronic pain due to other musculoskeletal injuries. They found no differences between the two groups. Both had the same abnormalities. There were similar elevations in the somatization, depression, obsessive-compulsive, and psychoticism scales in each. They did not think there was a characteristic chronic whiplash psychological profile.

Are There Psychological Predictors of Chronic Pain and Impairment?

Radanov and associates (1996) compared a group of 21 patients with chronic pain after whiplash to 21 patients matched for age, gender, and education who had recovered completely from acute whiplash. They concluded that psychological problems were a consequence rather than a cause of pain and other symptoms in whiplash. The same author (Radanov et al., 1991) had also shown that neither psychosocial factors nor personality traits were significant factors predicting illness behavior.

Gargan et al. (1997) recorded symptoms and psychological test scores of 50 patients seen within one week of acute whiplash injury, and then again three months and two years later. Two years after MVA, one-third of patients still had intrusive or disabling symptoms. At the initial visit, psychological testing was normal in 82% of patients, but at the three months re-evaluation, psychological testing had become *abnormal* in 81%, and at two years, psychological test scores were still abnormal in 69%. There was no correlation between the severity of the symptoms at two years and the initial psychological testing. Those patients who has developed psychological abnormalities by three months had a worse prognosis than those whose scores remained normal. They concluded that the psychological changes were the result of the pain, not the cause.

Other authors feel psychological factors might play a role. Buiternhuis and associates (2003) evaluated the role of coping styles with respect to recovery from whiplash in a Dutch prospective cohort. After one year, 40% of men and 50% of women still had neck pain. Patients, especially men, "who seek distraction, avoid thinking about the problem, and try to feel better by smoking, drinking or relaxing have a longer duration of neck pain" (Buiternhuis et al., 2003). Those who experience fear, annoyance, anger or feel inadequate also have worse prognosis. Conversely, those who seek social support, and share their concerns with others have a shorter duration of pain. Patients with severe pain intensity also had a worse prognosis.

Olsson and associates (2002) evaluated 123 whiplash patients four weeks after their MVA with the West Haven-Yale Multidimensional Pain Inventory (MPI). The MPI separates patients into three groups: adaptive copers, interpersonally distressed, and dysfunctional. In their study, it is remarkable that after one year, 79% of patients had some degree of pain due to the MVA. In the adaptive coper group (48 patients), one-third were pain free, one-third had infrequent pain, and one-third had frequent pain. In both the dysfunctional and interpersonally distressed groups, 93% had residual pain and none were pain free. However, the only cluster that discriminated among groups was the interference variable. In general, patients whose pain interfered greatly with their daily activities had greater pain frequency at one year.

Gozzard et al. (2001) looked at factors that might affect employment and disability after whiplash. They found that of the 586 patients in their retrospective review, 40 (7%) had not returned to work. The strongest predictor of prolonged disability was the intensity of symptoms. There was a prior psychological illness in 10 (25%) of patients who did not return to work and 59 (11%) of those who did return, a difference that is significant. Other significant factors that predicted greater disability included heavy labor and the presence of neurological symptoms or signs. Interestingly the self-employed returned to work sooner, but recovered significantly more slowly than employees.

The Role of Litigation and Compensation

Secondary gain is defined as any gain due to illness or injury. Gain comes in many forms, only one of which is financial. Intuitively, it might seem that the presence of potential financial recovery after MVA would exacerbate and/or prolong pain and impairment. It is very important to distinguish between workers' compensation claims and personal injury claims, something that not all studies have done and a distinction that many clinicians do not make. Virtually every study has shown that injured workers with LBP have more pain and take longer to recover than patients with similar injuries who are not involved in workers compensation litigation. This is very different from personal injury litigation. It is useful to examine the data, although it is not possible in this context to review all pertinent studies, others have attempted to do so.

Scholten-Peeters et al. (2003) performed a systematic review of prospective cohort studies to evaluate prognostic factors associated with recovery or chronicity. They concluded that compensation was not associated with prolonged recovery, nor was a high acute psychological response. With regard to the influence of legal and compensation factors on outcome, Cote et al. (2001) stated, "...it is not possible to comment on the consistency of evidence." They did reiterate the results of the single Cassidy study discussed above (2000). Barnsley et al. (1998) reviewed the published evidence to 1994 regarding the role of litigation. They concluded that the well-performed studies of whiplash patients showed that the likelihood of developing chronic symptoms was independent of litigation. Boon and Smith (2002) reached a similar conclusion after their review of the literature.

Swartzman and associates (1996) retrospectively compared the outcomes of whiplash patients currently in litigation with those who had completed litigation in a Canadian population. Active litigants reported more pain than postlitigants, even when results were adjusted for the time interval since the accident, but there were no differences in function or employment status.

Norris and Watt (1983) attempted to evaluate the role of filing claims on recovery. They found that patients who had more pain and more objective findings were more likely to file claims. They found no statistical improvement after litigation was settled. In fact, 39% improved, 55% did not change, and 5% got worse after settlement.

Sapir and Gorup (2001) compared the results of radiofrequency neurotomy (RFN) for cervical facet syndrome due to whiplash in litigants with nonlitigants. There was no difference in the pain levels between groups before RFN or in response to treatment. We performed a prospective longitudinal cohort study of patients with low back and/or neck pain after MVA (Schofferman & Wasserman, 1994) All patients were involved in personal injury litigation. We observed significant improvements in pain and function and 97% of patients had returned to work. Although there was no control group, these patients appeared to respond to treatment no differently from patients who were not involved in litigation.

However there is an opposite point of view. Some investigators feel that chronic whiplash does not occur outside the medical-legal context and in cultures that do not offer redress for pain and suffering via a tort system. The studies of twenty years ago and more that have supported a "litigation neurosis" were methodologically flawed and are now generally disregarded. Schrader et al. (1996) performed a retrospective review of whiplash in Lithuania using an unvalidated questionnaire. They located 202 persons involved in MVA. Thirty-two reported pain initially, but only 9 had pain at one week. The prevalence of long-term neck pain was no different to controls. However, this study did not have near the sufficient statistical power to draw any conclusions and was totally dependent on recall. Obelieniene et al. (1999) studied the results of whiplash in Lithuania prospectively. They found that neck pain did not persist for longer than 3 weeks and at two and twelve months, accident victims had no greater prevalence of neck pain than controls. The authors concluded the absence of an increased prevalence of chronic neck pain was due to the absence of a litigation system for financial recovery and/or cultural factors (Schrader et al., 1996; Obelieniene et al., 1999). Studies in Germany (Bonk, Ferrari, & Giebel, 2000) and Greece (Partheni et al., 2000) also reached the conclusion that chronic whiplash is very rare in societies with a low rate of litigation.

STRUCTURAL CAUSES OF NECK PAIN AFTER WHIPLASH

The most common structural causes of chronic neck pain in general and of whiplash in particular have been well studied (Bogduk and Aprill, 1993 ; Chabot & Montgomery, 1995) and recently reviewed briefly (Feng & Schofferman, 2003). It is noteworthy that the long-term studies of the outcome of neck pain due to whiplash do not consider the structural basis for pain or the results of treatment. If whiplash were a purely psychological or secondary gain problem, one might anticipate great difficulty in isolating the cause or causes of the pain, and even more difficulty demonstrating a response to treatment. However, using modern diagnostic testing, the structural cause of chronic neck pain after trauma can usually be isolated (Bogduk and Aprill, 1993).

In a rear-impact MVA, the upper body is thrust forward, leaving the head and neck behind, which in essence forces the head and neck backward. Perhaps most important, the upper body moves forward, which causes the neck to form an unnatural S-shape and places great forces on the facet joints and discs. The head and neck then recoil and accelerate forward, but most likely, the structural damage has already occurred Even in low speed collisions, the forces can be high enough to injure joints, discs, muscles, and ligaments.

Facet Joint Pain

Facet joints *alone* are the cause of neck pain in at least 23% of patients with chronic axial neck pain due to trauma (Bogduk & Aprill, 1993). Neck pain from both facet joints and discs are the cause in an additional 41%. Facet joints facilitate smooth motion, but limit excess motion. Facet joints can be injured acutely by traumas such as whiplash and from chronic overuse. There are no specific symptoms for facet joint pain, but their referral patterns are well known (Aprill, Dwyer, & Bogduk, 1990). There are no specific findings on examination, but anecdotally, painful facets are tender upon direct pressure while normal joints are not. We believe that many patients diagnosed with myofascial pain actually have facet joint pain, because it is not possible to isolate tender muscles from tender facet joints while palpating the neck. The only way to reliably diagnose facet joint pain is by injection, specifically local anesthetic blockade of the nerve supply to the putative painful joint.

Disc Pain

It is established that intrinsic disc pathology can be a source of pain, yet many physicians cling to the belief that discs cause pain only when they compress or irritate a nerve root or the spinal cord. Using strict criteria and studying the facet joints and discs at only C4/5, C5/6, and C6/7, it was estimated that cervical discs *alone* are the cause of pain in at least 20% of patients with chronic neck pain due to trauma (Bogduk & Aprill, 1993). The facet joints plus discs are the cause in at least an additional 41%.

The symptoms of discogenic pain are not specific, but the referral topography during discography has been elucidated (Slipman, Plastaras, Patel, Chow, & Issac, 2002). Physical examination is also not specific for discogenic pain but can help exclude true radiculopathy, myelopathy, and systemic or neurological illnesses. Radiographs may disclose disc space narrowing and osteophyte formation at levels of degenerated discs. MRI may disclose disc desiccation or herniation. However, MRI alone cannot determine whether a disc is painful, and therefore must always be interpreted in conjunction with the history, examination, and other tests.

Cervicogenic headache (CHA) may arise from the upper facet joints, C2/3 or C3/4 discs, atlanto-axial joint, or atlanto-occipital joint disruption. Although pain may be felt in the distribution of the greater occipital nerve (GON), GON entrapment is rarely the primary cause. Muscle spasm may aggravate the underlying pain.

Soft Tissue and Other Myofascial Pain

We are not aware of reasonable peer reviewed data that that demonstrate soft tissues alone can be a primary cause of moderate to severe chronic neck pain or CHA. Muscles certainly may become painful "guarding" a deeper structural abnormality and thereby worsen pain, however. Despite the phrase "chronic strain or strain" being used often, especially in the medical-legal context, again we are not aware of any peer-reviewed publications that demonstrate such a primary entity.

PREDICTORS OF PROLONGED RECOVERY: CHRONIC WHIPLASH AND WHIPLASH ASSOCIATED DISORDERS

Potential Predictors of Outcome

Potential predictors of chronic neck pain and disability can be categorized into demographics, crash-related mechanics, initial level of pain, presence of other symptoms, physical examination findings, radiographic abnormalities, initial treatment rendered, and psychological abnormalities including the effects of litigation. Several prospective longitudinal cohort studies have looked at the issue of potential predictors of chronic pain and disability after whiplash and there are several systematic reviews.

Scholten-Peeters et al. (2003) reviewed 50 papers consisting of 29 cohorts and 12 were considered to be high quality by their predetermined standards. They did not include pure population-based studies that employed time to case closure or treatment duration as major outcome measures because they felt their correlation with symptoms and disability were not clear. They opined that the prognosis factor for any individual item was not strong with respect to each individual patient. However, when groups of patients were evaluated, there was strong evidence that high initial pain intensity at the initial evaluation was the best predictor of poor outcome. Other somewhat useful predictors were the presence of a high number of complaints, prior psychological problems, and nervousness. They found no correlation with outcome for older age, female gender, initial psychological response, x-ray findings, and litigation.

Cote et al. (2001) performed a systematic review that included 13 cohorts, but they did include population-based studies. They found there was evidence that greater intensity of neck pain, greater intensity of headache, and the presence of radicular signs or symptoms at initial evaluation correlated with worse outcome, as did older age, and female gender. Based on the population-based studies they reviewed and the cohort they reported, they concluded that prognosis varied greatly according to the population sampled and the type of insurance or compensation system in effect. However, even in the population-based studies, a higher level of pain, lower level of physical functioning, and the presence of depression were strongly associated with a longer time to case closure, a primary outcome measure (Cassidy et al., 2000).

The Quebec Task Force presented its monograph in 1995, and could only include papers published before 1993. A great deal has been published since then (Spitzer et al., 1995). In addition to literature review, they reported on a large population-based cohort. About half the patients had only whiplash versus half with whiplash plus other injuries (not defined). Their outcomes of interest were absence from usual activities, recurrence or relapse, and financial costs. About 47% had returned to usual activities by one month, 64% by two months, 87% by six months and 97% by twelve months. Factors associated with a longer absence were female gender, older age, multiple injuries, greater collision severity, among others. There was a recurrence rate of 6.8%. The 11% who were disabled for more than six months accounted for 32% of the costs and the 2% who were disabled at twelve months accounted for 14% of the costs.

In the Radanov et al. (1995) study discussed previously, in addition to charting the natural history of whiplash, the authors compared those who recovered with those who did not, searching for predictors of chronic pain and disability. Significant correlates with poor outcome included older age, higher intensity of initial neck pain or headache, more rotated or inclined head position at impact, higher number of other symptoms, greater prevalence of headache prior to the MVA, a higher degree of injury-related cognitive impairment, and more concern or worry about the long-term effects of the accident. There was no significant differences between groups for other psychological variables, gender, or vocation.

Kasch et al. (2001) prospectively followed 141 Danish patients with acute whiplash to determine the prevalence of long-term "handicap." They excluded patients with prior neck or low back pain. At one year after injury, 11 (8%) had not returned to their usual level of work or activity and an additional 4% had returned only to modified work. They found reduced range of motion of the neck at the initial evaluation to be the single best predictor of long-term disability. Specificity for predicting disability was increased by adding pain intensity and the presence of numerous other body complaints, but at the expense of some loss of sensitivity. There was no predictive value for age, gender, speed differences between collision vehicles, type of early treatment, psychometric testing (Millon Behavioral Health Inventory), or litigation initiated within the first month of MVA.

Kyhlback et al. (2002) attempted to identify predictors of perceived disability and subjective pain in whiplash patients. They found that at their initial visits, patients with greater pain and disability had worse perceived self-efficacy for their ability to perform activities of daily living. These same patients did worse at one year compared to those with less pain, less disability, and greater self-efficacy. Although the authors concluded that it was self-efficacy that determined outcome, it is not at all clear that it was not just that those with increased pain had worst prognosis.

SUMMARY AND CONCLUSIONS

It may be useful to summarize our findings. Chronic or frequently recurring neck pain occurs in about 14% of the general population. Most patients with acute neck pain after MVA recover within three to six months, but 18% to 40% develop chronic pain. In some people it is mild, but in a few it is severe. About 4% to 8% of whiplash patients become partially or totally disabled.

It is not possible to predict the clinical outcome of a particular individual with neck pain after MVA. The strongest predictor of high risk for poor outcome is severe neck pain at the initial evaluation. Other strong predictors that correlate with poor outcome are headache, especially if it is severe, multiple areas of pain, marked restriction of cervical range of motion, and the presence of radicular symptoms and signs. Although there are no good psychological predictors of outcome, patients who cope well tend to do better than those who are very concerned with their long-term prognosis. Depression is usually secondary to pain and impairment. Psychosocial factors probably exert their greatest influence in determining level of impairment and the transition from acute to chronic pain and disability, rather than the presence or intensity of pain. Although the presence of litigation does not appear to alter outcome, there is less chronic whiplash in cultures with no compensation for pain and suffering, but even then, the intensity of neck pain, the level of physical functioning, and the presence or absence of depression correlate strongly with outcome.

REFERENCES

Aprill, C., Dwyer A., & Bogduk, N. (1990). Cervical zygapophyseal joint pain patterns. II: A clinical evaluation. *Spine, 15(6),* 458–461.

Barnsley, L., Lord, S.M., & Bogduk, N. (2002). The pathophysiology of whiplash. In: Malanga, G.A. & Nadler, S.F. (Ed.), *Whiplash*. Philadelphia: Hanley & Belfus.

Berglund, A., Alfredsson, L., Cassidy, J.D., Jensen, I., & Nygren, A. (2000). The association between exposure to a rear-end collision and future neck or shoulder pain: A cohort study. *Journal of Clinical Epidemiology, 53*, 1089–1094.

Bogduk, N. & Aprill, C. (1993). On the nature of neck pain, discography and cervical zygapophysial joint blocks. *Pain, 54*, 213–217.

Bonk, A.D., Ferrari, R., & Giebel, G.D. (2000). Prospective randomized controlled study of activity versus collar, and the natural history for whiplash injury in Germany. *Journal Muscle Pain, 8*, 123–132.

Boon, A.J. & Smith, J. (2002). Whiplash-associated disorders: Prognosis after injury. In: Malanga, G.A. & Nadler, S.F. *Whiplash*. (pp. 79–96). Philadelphia: Hanley & Belfus.

Borchgrevink, G.E., Kaasa, A., McDonagh, D., Stiles, T.C., Haraldseth, O., & Lereim, I. (1998). Acute treatment of whiplash neck sprain injuries. *Spine, 23(1)*, 25–31.

Buitenhuis, J., Spanjer, J., & Fidler, V. (2003). Recovery from acute whiplash: The role of coping styles, *Spine, 28(9)*, 896–901.

Cassidy, J.D., Carroll, I.J., Cote, P., Lemstra, M., Berglund, A., & Nygren, A. (2000). Effect of eliminating compensation for pain and suffering on the outcome of insurance claims for whiplash injury. *New England Journal of Medicine, 342*, 1179–1186.

Chabot, M.C. & Montgomery, D.M. (1995). The pathophysiology of axial and radicular neck pain. *Seminar Spine Surgery, 7*, 2–8.

Cote, P., Cassidy, J.D., Carroll, L., Frank, J.W., & Bombardier, C. (2001). A systematic review of the prognosis of acute whiplash and a new conceptual framework to synthesize the literature, *Spine, 26(19)*, E445–E458.

Feng, F. & Schofferman, J. (2003). Chronic neck pain and cervicogenic headaches. *Current Treatment Options in Neurology, 5*, 493–498.

Gargan, M.F., & Bannister, G.C. (1990). Long-term prognosis of soft-tissue injuries of the neck, *The Journal of Bone & Joint Surgery, 72-B(5)*, 901–903.

Gargan, M., Bannister, G., Main, C., & Hollis, S. (1997). The behavioural response to whiplash injury, *The Journal of Bone & Joint Surgery, 79-B(4)*, 523–526.

Garvey, T.A., Transfeldt, E.E., Malcolm, J.R., & Kos, P. (2002). Outcome of anterior cervical discectomy and fusion as perceived by patients treated for dominant axial-mechanical cervical spine pain. *Spine, 27(17)*, 1887–1895.

Gozzard, C., Bannister, G., Langkamer, G., Khan, S., Gargan, M., & Foy, C. (2001). Factors affecting employment after whiplash injury, *The Journal of Bone & Joint Surgery, 83-B(4)*, 506–509.

Kasch, H., Bach, F.W., & Jensen, T.S. (2001). Handicap after acute whiplash injury: A 1-year prospective study of risk factors, *Neurology, 56*, 1637–1643.

Kyhlback, M., Thierfelder, T., & Soderlund, A. (2002). Prognostic factors in whiplash-associated disorders, *International Journal of Rehabilitation Research, 25*, 181–187.

Linton, S.J. (2000). A review of psychological risk factors in back and neck pain, *Spine, 25(9)*, 1148–1156.

Lord, S.M., Barnsley, L., Wallis, B.J., & Bogduk, N. (1996). Percutaneous radio-frequency neurotomy for chronic cervical zygapophyseal joint pain. *New England Journal of Medicine, 335*, 1721–1726.

Mayou, R., Bryant, B., & Duthie, R. (1993). Psychiatric consequences of road traffic accidents, *British Medical Journal*, 307, 647–651.

Norris, S.H., & Watt, I. (1983). The prognosis of neck injuries resulting from rear-end vehicle collisions, *The Journal of Bone & Joint Surgery, 65-B(5)*, 608–611.

Obelieniene, D., Schrader, H., Bovim, G., Miseviciene, I., & Sand, T. (1999). Pain after whiplash: A prospective controlled inception cohort study, *Journal of Neurol Neurosurg Psychiatry, 66*, 279–283.

Olsson, I., Bunketorp, O., Carlsson, S.G., & Styf, J. (2002). Prediction of outcome in whiplash-associated disorders using West haven-Yale Multidimensional Pain Inventory. *Clinl J Pain, 18*, 238–244.

Palit, M., Schofferman, J., Goldthwaite, N., Reynolds, J., Kerner, M., Keaney, D., & Lawrence-Miyasaki, L. (1999). Anterior discectomy and fusion for the management of neck pain. *Spine, 24*, 2224–2228.

Partheni, M., Constgantoyannis, C., Ferrari, R., Nikiforidis, G., Voulgaris, S., & Papadakis, N. (2000). A prospective cohort study of the outcome of acute whiplash in greece. *Clinical Experimental Rheumatology, 18*, 67–71.

Peebles, J.E., McWilliams, L.A., & MacLennan, R. (2001). A comparison of Symptom Checklist 90-revised profiles from patients with chronic pain from whiplash and patients with other musculoskeletal injuries, *Spine, 26(7)*, 766–770.

Pettersson, K. & Toolanen, G. (1998). High-dose methylprednisolone prevents extensive sick leave after whiplash injury. *Spine, 23(9)*, 984–989.

Radanov, B.P., Begre, S., Sturzenegger, M., & Augustiny, K.F. (1996). Course of psychological variables in whiplash injury—A 2-year follow-up with age, gender, and education pair-matched patients. *Pain, 64*, 429–434.

Radanov, B.P., Stefano, G., Schnidrig, A., & Ballinari, P. (1991). Role of psychosocial in recovery from common whiplash. *The Lancet, 338*, 712–715.

Radanov, B.P., Sturzenegger, M., & Stefano, G.D. (1995). Long-term outcome after whiplash injury: A 2-year follow-up considering features of injury mechanism and somatic, radiologic, and psychosocial findings, *Medicine, 74(5)*, 281–297.

Rosenfeld, M., Seferiadis A., Carlsson J, & Gunnarsson R. (2003) Active intervention in patients with whiplash-associated disorders improves long-term prognosis. Spine, *28(22)*, 2491–2498.

Sapir, D.A. & Gorup, J.M. (2001). Radiofrequency medial branch neurotomy in litigant and nonlitigant patients with cervical whiplash. *Spine, 26(12)*, E268–E273.

Schofferman, J. & Wasserman, S. (1994). Successful treatment of low back and neck pain after motor vehicle accident despite litigation. *Spine, 19(9)*, 1007–1010.

Schofferman, J. & Young, M. (2003). Previously unrecognized cognitive and psychological disorders in patients with chronic neck pain due to whiplash and other forms of cervical trauma. Presentation North American Spine Society, San Diego, CA, October, 2003.

Scholten-Peeters, G.G., Verhagen, A.P., Bekkering, G.E., van der Windt, D.A., Barnsley, L., Oostendorp, R.A., & Hendriks, E.J. (2003). Prognostic factors of whiplash-associated disorders: A systematic review of prospective cohort studies. *Pain, 104(1–2)*, 303–322.

Schrader, H., Obelieniene, D., Bovim, G., Surkiene, D., Mickeviciene, D., Miseviciene, I., & Sand, T. (1996). Natural evolution of late whiplash syndrome outside the medicolegal context. *Lancet, 347*, 1201–1211.

Slipman, C.W., Plastaras, C., Patel, R., Chow, D., & Issac, Z. (2002). Provocative cervical discographic symptom mapping. Presented at the 21st Annual Meeting, Cervical Spine Research Society, December.

Spitzer, W.O., Skovron , M.L., Salmi, L.R., Cassidy , J.D., Duranceau, J., Suissa, S., & Zeiss, E. (1995). Scientific monograph of the Quebec task force on whiplash associated disorders. *Spine*, 20(8S), 8S–58S.

Squires, B., Gargan, M.F., & Bannister, G.C. (1996). Soft-tissue injuries of the cervical spine: 15-year follow-up, *The Journal of Bone & Joint Surgery, 78-B(6), 955–957.*

Swartzman, L.C., Teasell, R.W., Shapiro, A.P., & McDermid, A.J. (1996). The effect of litigation status on adjustment to whiplash injury. *Spine, 21(1)*, 53–58.

Vendrig, A.A., van Akkerveeken, P.F., & McWhorter, K.R. (2000). Results of a multimodal treatment program for patients with chronic symptoms after a whiplash injury of the neck. *Spine, 25(2)*, 238–244.

Wallis, B.J., Lord, S.M., & Bogduk, N. (1997). Resolution of psychological distress of whiplash patients following treatment by radiofrequency neurotomy: A randomised, double-blind, placebo-controlled trial, *Pain, 73*, 15–22.

12

Disability in Fibromyalgia

Akiko Okifuji

CLINICAL FEATURES

Fibromyalgia syndrome (FMS) is a chronic, musculoskeletal pain disorder, characterized by diffuse pain and a lowered pain threshold at certain anatomical points ("tender points"). FMS may be accompanied by other pain, and functional comobidity factors, and mood disturbance. Most commonly, patients complain of chronic fatigue, diffuse tenderness and aches, and sleep disturbance. Anxiety and depression are also common mood problems. The list of the prevalent symptoms, based upon 434 treatment seeking patients is listed in Table 1.

FMS is a commonly occurring pain disorder, with an estimated prevalence ranging from 0.6% to 11% in Western countries with prevalence in the average population approximately 2% (Wolfe, Ross, Anderson, Russell, & Hebert, 1995). The variability of the prevalence rates seems to be the result of methodological differences across studies. FMS is one of the disorders commonly seen by rheumatologists in North America (White, Speechley, Harth, & Ostbye, 1995). There seems to be a consistent gender differences in the prevalence. A large scale, community-based study in Ontario, Canada by White et al. (1999c) estimated that the prevalence of FMS is 1.6% in men and 5% in women. However, a population survey study in Norway shows a much lower rate of 0.6% in women aged 26 to 55 (Forseth, Gran, & Husby, 1997).

CURRENT CLASSIFICATION CRITERIA

The research efforts to better understand FMS proliferated in the 70's and 80's. However, the criteria used to define FMS varied across studies; this lack of consented classification criteria resulted in large variability in patient selections, and thus equivocality of research results became more the rule than the exception. In a concerted effort to achieve a uniformed classification criteria, a multicenter study was conducted (Wolfe et al., 1990). Clinicians at each site tested a number of FMS-relevant parameters in FMS patients (as diagnosed by the "usual" ways of their practice) as well as patients with other chronic musculoskeletal pain disorders. The two groups

DOI: 10.1007/978-0-387-28919-9_12, © 2009 Springer Science+Business Media, LLC

TABLE 1. Clinical Presentation of Fibromyalgia Syndrome ($n = 434$ in Ongoing Interdisciplinary Treatment Trial)

Fatigue	98%
Muscle tenderness	95%
Sleep disturbance	90%
"Pain all over"	88%
Joint pain/tenderness	85%
Morning stiffness	80%
Paresthesia	76%
Anxiety	74%
Depression	72%
Headaches	66%
Feeling cold	63%
Night sweats	54%
Dry/itchy eyes	54%
Change in bowel habits	53%
Jaw pain	51%

of patients were compared on various parameters including combinations of several criteria. In short, the parameters most discriminating FMS from other chronic musculoskeletal pain disorders were identified.

Two parameters distinguished FMS patients from others. The American College of Rheumatology (ACR) criteria, it is called, consists of 1) history of widespread pain (3 months or longer) and 2) presence of hyperalgesic responses to at least 11 of 18 designated tender points (TPs, see Table 2 and Figure 1). The validity of the ACR criteria, like the validity of any other criteria for classifying FMS, is difficult to evaluate due to the absence of a "gold standard" for diagnosing FMS. The lack of concurrent diagnostic procedures leads to a circular argument between the classification of FMS and delineation of the characteristics associated with FMS. However, the primary purpose of the ACR criteria is to implement a consistent measure to

TABLE 2. The 1990 ACR Criteria for the Classification of FMS

1. Presence of widespread pain for at least 3 months. Pain must be present in all of the body quadrants and axial skeletal area.
2. Presence of pain in at least 11 of 18 tender points on digital palpation with approximately 4kg force. Tender points are located in 9 bilateral sites as described below:

   Occiput: at the suboccipital muscle insertions.
   Low cervical: at the anterior aspects of the intertransverse spaces at C5–C7.
   Trapezius: at the midpoint of the upper boarder.
   Supraspinatus: at origins, above the scapula spine near the medial boarder.
   Second rib: at the second costochondral junctions, just lateral to the junctions on upper surfaces.
   Lateral epicondyle: at 2 cm distal to the epicondyles.
   Gulteal: in upper outer quadrants of buttocks in anterior fold of muscle.
   Greater trochanter: posterior to the trochanteric prominence.
   Knee: at the medial fat proximal to the joint line.

Source: Adapted from Wolfe et al., 1990.

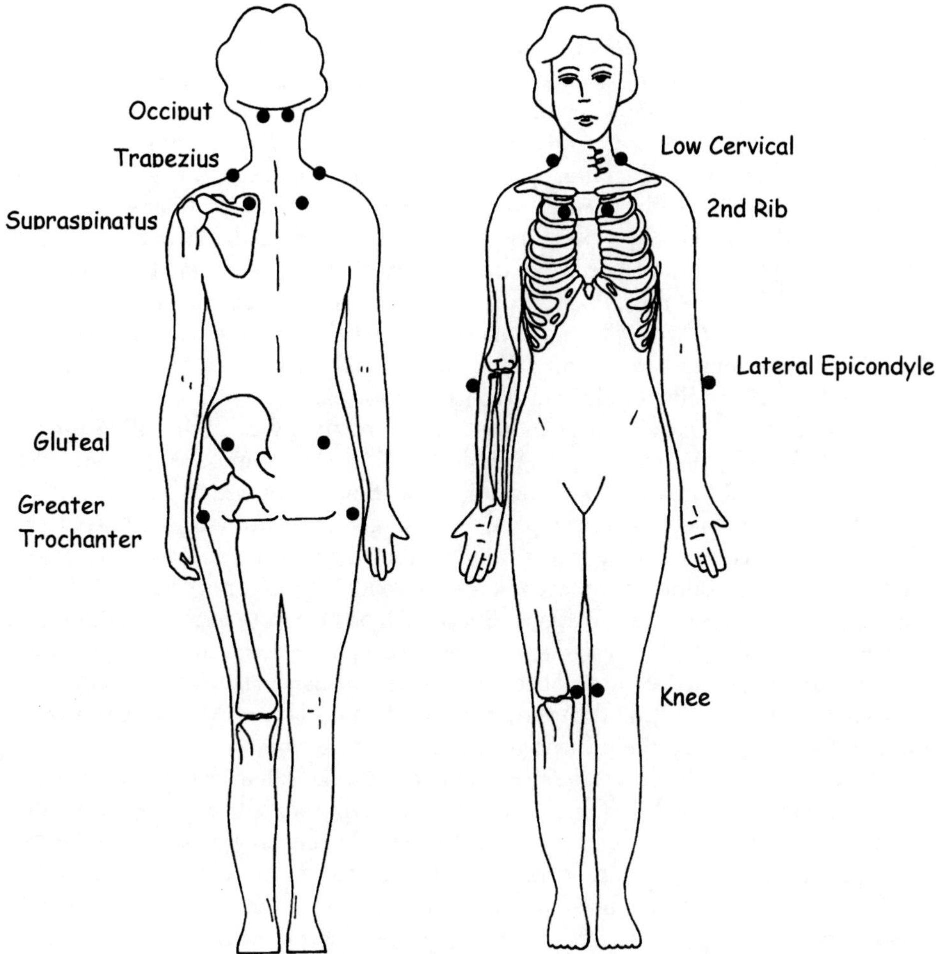

Figure 1. Locations of Tender Points.

identify cases of FMS thereby making integration of knowledge across published reports possible. The contribution of the ACR criteria to research has been apparent. Since its publication, the majority of published reports on FMS specify their subjects using the ACR criteria. Although clinical diagnosis of FMS still relies largely upon clinical presentations of the symptoms, patients can now be identified as ACR criteria positive or negative.

POSSIBLE MECHANISMS

Despite extensive research, the etiology and pathophysiology of FMS are still not well understood. Subtle abnormalities in local muscles, such as hypoxia (Bengtsson & Henriksson, 1989), decreased levels of ATP and phosphocreatine (Park, Phothimat, Oates, Hernanz-Schulman, & Olsen, 1998), and metabolic abnormalities (Sprott et al., 1998) are indicated. However, the diffuse and multifactorial nature of the disorder suggests that the role of peripheral mechanisms is likely limited.

Prevalent complaints of sleep disturbance has led some to consider the possibility that FMS is a variant of a sleep disorder. An early experimental study showed the development of FMS-like symptoms following repeated deprivation of stage IV sleep (Moldofsky, Scarisbrick, England, & Smythe, 1975). This result was recently replicated (Lentz, Landis, Rothermel, & Shaver, 1999). Electroencephalographic (EEG) studies have shown that FMS patients commonly experience the intrusion of alpha wave during the delta-wave sleep period (Branco, Atalaia, & Paiva, 1994; Drewes et al., 1995). However, this is not a definitive characteristic; Carette and colleagues (1995) found only 36% of FMS patients they tested showed abnormal alpha intrusion. Thus, the common complaint of unrestorative sleep may not be accounted for solely by the EEG finding of alpha-delta sleep abnormality.

The accumulation of research evidence consistently indicates that FMS is associated with diffusely diminished pain thresholds (Kosek, Ekholm, & Hansson, 1996; Lautenbacher & Rollman, 1997; Okifuji, Turk, Sinclair, Starz, & Marcus, 1997) most likely due to abnormal central pain processing at the central level. FMS patients exhibit slower recovery from experimentally inflicted pain than do healthy individuals, suggesting the notion of ineffective diffuse noxious inhibitory control (DNIC) in FMS patients in response to provoked pain (Kosek & Hansson, 1997). Furthermore, FMS is associated with hyperalgesia following repeated electric muscle stimulation and infusion of hypertonic saline (Sorensen, Graven-Nielsen, Henriksson, Bengtsson, & Arendt-Nielsen, 1998), and capsaicin-induced vasodilation (Morris, Cruwys, & Kidd, 1998), supporting the presence of central sensitization.

Taken together, it seems to be reasonable to postulate that FMS is a disorder of malfunctioning pain modulation. Support for this hypothesis is seen in research that has shown various neurobiological and neurochemical abnormalities in FMS. For example, FMS may involve an abnormality in the activation of *N*-methyl-D-aspartate (NMDA) receptors that has been linked to hyperalgesia (Meller & Gebhart, 1993). Plasma levels of nitric oxide (NO), which plays a role intracellularly in the activation of NMDA, were significantly elevated following a vein distension test (Nicolodi, Volpe, & Sicuteri, 1998). In addition, the effectiveness of ketamine in reducing pain in FMS patients (Graven-Nielsen et al., 2000) is consistent with excessive NO production as a cause of hyperalgesia in FMS.

Additionally, empirical support exists that demonstrates reduced serotonin (5-HT) levels in FMS patients as compared to others. 5-HT influences pain, mood, and sleep, all of which are affected in FMS. Plasma (Wolfe, Russell, Vipraio, Ross, & Anderson, 1997b) and cerebrospinal fluid levels of 5-HT (Russell, Vaeroy, Javors, & Nyberg, 1992b), the transfer ratio of tryptophan (Yunus, Dailey, Aldag, Masi, & Jobe, 1992), and the reuptake site density of 5-HT (Russell et al., 1992a) are all lower in FMS patients.

Neuroendocrine responses to stress are also abnormal in FMS. A subnormal adrenocorticotropic hormone (ACTH) response to exogenous corticotropin-releasing hormone (CRH) and insulin-induced hypoglycemia, along with a blunted cortisol response (Adler, Kinsley, Hurwitz, Mossey, & Goldenberg, 1999) and impaired sympathetic reactivity in response to stressors such as cold, physical exertion, and noise (Okifuji & Turk, 2002) have all been reported in FMS. Patients with FMS are also more likely to develop hypotension during an orthostatic stressor

(Bou-Holaigah et al., 1997). An intriguing link between aberrant stress responses and symptoms of FMS and other disorders is possible dysregulation of proinflammatory cytokines (Watkins, Maier, & Goehler, 1995; Zachrisson et al., 2002).

The difficulty in identifying a definitive pathology has led some to speculate that FMS may be psychological in origin (Ford, 1997). Concurrent depression is diagnosed in 14–71% of FMS patients (Alfici, Sigal, & Landau, 1989; Walker et al., 1997). These rates are higher than the prevalence of depression in healthy community populations (Myers et al., 1984). However, similar prevalence rates for depression occur in many chronic medical illnesses. Further, in contrast to FMS patients seen in the clinic, the prevalence of psychiatric disorders in persons who meet criteria for FMS but who are not actively seeking treatment is comparable to that found in healthy community samples (Aaron et al., 1996). Research seeking a common biological marker for depression and FMS has not been productive. In sum, the research findings to date do not indicate that depression causes or maintains FMS.

CURRENT TRENDS IN TREATMENT

No therapeutic modality is universally effective for all FMS patients. Most treatments provide some relief for a subset of their symptoms. Pharmacologically, a low-dose tricyclic antidepressant (TCA), non-opioid as well as opioid analgesics, sedatives, and muscle relaxants are commonly used. Other common modalities include exercise, education, stress-management skill training, and cognitive-behavioral approaches. The manifestation of FMS is generally multifactorial, with symptoms encompassing physical, psychophysiological, functional, cognitive, behavioral, and affective domains. Thus it is not surprising that no single modality effectively manages all aspects of FMS. Indeed, Okifuji and Ashburn (2001) have reported that each modality seems to target different areas. For example, the low dose amitriptyline seems to improve pain, sleep, and fatigue whereas activating physical exercise seems to reduce hyperalgesia. Many have conceptualized FMS as a multifactorial complex pain disorder and thus a multidisciplinary approach has been recommended (Patkar, Bilal, & Masand, 2003). The current evidence suggests that a multidisciplinary approach appears to benefit patients in both pain and functional domains (Okifuji & Ashburn, 2001).

PHENOMENOLOGY OF FMS

FMS is not lethal or progressive; however, the condition is quite debilitating and patients with FMS report a severely compromised quality of life (QOL). QOL is a multi-factorial, multi-level concept. In FMS, various disease-related factors as well as factors that are independent of the FMS contribute to the overall QOL. However, one of the factors that is significant to changes in QOL for patients with FMS is how FMS affects their ability to function in their lives.

There is little question that FMS imposes adverse impacts on patients' lives. FMS patients tend to report a lowered sense of physical well-being, greater long-term health concerns (Ejlertsson, Eden, & Leden, 2002; Wolfe, 1997) and elevated health care utilization (Bombardier & Buchwald, 1996; White, Speechley, Harth, & Ostbye, 1999b; Wolfe, 1994). FMS seems to be a compounding factor in disability associated with other disease conditions such as systemic lupus (Middleton, McFarlin, & Lipsky, 1994). Furthermore, FMS patients tend to rate their quality of life as significantly more compromised, compared to other chronically ill patients (Burckhardt, Clark, & Bennett, 1993).

HEALTH CARE UTILIZATION

FMS is a costly illness. Wolfe et al. (1997a) conducted the first multicenter study on the healthcare utilization of FMS patients in seven healthcare centers. On average, FMS patients had one hospitalization every three years and approximately 10 outpatient visits per year. The mean annual cost for outpatient care, medications, and hospitalization in 1996 dollars was $2,274. Regression analysis revealed that the annual cost was related to the number of comorbidities, perceived disability, and perceived severity of FMS. In Canada investigators reported FMS patients had 7 physician visits in the 6 months prior to the study (Dobkin, De Civita, Bernatsky, Kang, & Baron, 2003). The regression analysis revealed that the number of physician visits was mostly related to younger age and greater number of co-morbid symptoms.

The results from a recent study suggest that health care cost associated with FMS may be rapidly climbing. Based upon the claim data of a Fortune 100 manufacturer, Robinson et al. (2003) compared the annual medical, pharmaceutical, and work-loss cost between FMS claimants and randomly selected claimants. The comparison revealed that the cost for the FMS claimants were substantially greater ($5,945) than that of the others ($2,486). When the figure was recalculated only for the employee claimants, FMS employees incurred a cost of $7,776 per year.

WORK DISABILITY

Given the multiple symptoms, including chronic fatigue, pain, and sleep disturbance, it should perhaps not be surprising that many FMS patients find it difficult to maintain their productivity in the workforce. Work disability is prevalent in FMS. Bombardier and Buchwald (1996) reported that 35% of FMS patients and over 50% of FMS patients with concurrent chronic fatigue syndrome were unable to be gainfully employed due to their illness.

In a small sample of FMS patients with a mean age of 43, Martinez et al. (1995) reported that 30% had reduced their work hours and 65% had a fall in their family income. A recent report by Assefi et al. (2003) estimates that approximately half of the patients with FMS lost jobs due to the hardship associated with FMS. Even for those currently employed, many patients reduced their working hours (mean hours: 41–45 hours per week prior to the FMS onset vs. 31–32 hours per week currently).

This is not to say that FMS patients willingly terminate their employment. The results from narrative interviews (Liedberg & Henriksson, 2002) indicate that FMS patients consider a work role to be an important part of their self image. However, it appears patients carefully review the work environment for such factors as the physical demands of work, the requirement for physical movement and the opportunity to move around, when they evaluate their ability to stay at work. In addition to their physical ability to perform tasks, comobid conditions, such as fatigue and compromised ability to concentrate, may significantly interfere with certain occupational requirements. Moreover, the availability of psychosocial support at work seems essential. Many FMS patients feel that others do not understand their pain and suffering for their "invisible" illness. Acceptance of their frequent leaves for visiting health care providers may also influence their sense of well-being at work.

It is important to note that although FMS is considered a pain disorder, other symptoms are also important to consider in understanding how occupationally disabled patients perceive themselves. The comparison between working and non-working FMS patients (Henriksson & Liedberg, 2000) demonstrates that fatigue, irritability, and gastrointestinal discomfort were significant discriminating variables whereas the two groups did not differ in age, duration of symptoms, number of pain locations or pain-free time periods.

COMPENSATION ISSUES

The difficulty in maintaining gainful employment may lead FMS patients to apply for financial compensation for their disability. The prevalence of receiving financial compensation for their condition varies greatly from study to study. In one study, 55% of patients reported receiving either temporary or permanent disability compensation (Martinez, Ferraz, Sato, & Atra, 1995). In the multicenter study, Wolfe et al (1997) found that approximately 15% of FMS patients receive compensation from Social Security Disability and an additional 10% receive other types of financial compensation for disability. Needless to say, the decision to award compensation for FMS is based not only upon clinical factors but also political and economical factors. For example, only a small fraction of the disability compensation is provided for FMS in the US, whereas in Canada, McCain et al. (1989) reported that 9% of all disability compensation was paid for FMS.

Some FMS seems to be triggered by accidental injuries. There is some evidence that FMS patients with injurious onset may experience greater severity in their symptoms when compared with FMS patients whose symptoms begin insidiously (Turk, Okifuji, Starz, & Sinclair, 1996b). As in the case of other chronic pain syndromes, the issue of secondary gain impacting the severity of FMS has been of considerable interest. However, the greater level of perceived disability in FMS with the injurious onset still held even when the status of receiving financial compensation was controlled (Turk et al., 1996b). Similarly, Moldofsky, Wong, and Lue (1993) reported that the resolution of litigation for post-accident FMS patients does not seem to improve their FMS symptoms.

FUNCTIONAL DISABILITY

One of the prominent features of FMS is functional disability. Functional disability associated with FMS may be comparative in degree to other chronic illnesses such as rheumatoid arthritis (Martinez et al., 1995) and spondyloarthropathy (Heikkila, Ronni, Kautiainen, & Kauppi, 2002). Others have shown that FMS patients claim a greater degree of perceived disability compared to people with chronic non-FMS conditions such as diffuse (but not FMS) musculoskeletal pain (White, Speechley, Harth, & Ostbye, 1999a) and spinal cord injury (Cardol et al., 2002).

Relatively little is known about the factors contributing to the significant decline in functional ability in FMS patients. Mood disturbance, such as depression and anxiety, is significantly related to self-reported disability (Kurtze, Gundersen, & Svebak, 1999; Sherman, Turk, & Okifuji, 2000; White, Nielson, Harth, Ostbye, & Speechley, 2002). Lifestyle of patients may also impact their self-evaluation of disability. FMS patients who smoke tend to report a higher degree of functional disability than those who don't smoke (Yunus, Arslan, & Aldag, 2002b). There also seems to be a positive relationship between body mass index and self-reported disability (Yunus, Arslan, & Aldag, 2002a). There is suggestive support that pain sensitivity for TPs may be associated with disability, however, as will be discussed later, subjective disability may not necessarily correspond with objective findings. Interestingly, although it is reasonable to point to the severity of illness as a primary determinant of disability, self-reported disability seems fairly independent of disease severity (Hawley, Wolfe, & Cathey, 1988).

Exercise intolerance is also frequently noted for FMS patients. At times this creates a clinical challenge when the treatment plan includes activating physical therapy. Research investigating the baseline level of physical conditioning for FMS patients, however, has yielded conflicting results. Some studies showed a below average level of aerobic conditioning in the majority of FMS patients (Bennett et al., 1989; Mannerkorpi, Burckhardt, & Bjelle, 1994) whereas others report that FMS patients' aerobic capacity does not differ significantly from age-matched healthy individuals although FMS patients consistently rate the exercise as more demanding (Mengshoel, Forre, & Komnaes, 1990; Nielens, Boisset, & Masquelier, 2000; Norregaard, Bulow, & Danneskiold-Samsoe, 1994). However, research is more consistent with respect to the ability to performmuscle strengthening tasks; FMS patients exhibit a significantly lower degree of strength and endurance than do healthy people (Norregaard et al., 1994) and chronic myofascial pain patients (Jacobsen & Holm, 1992). Surface electromyographic activity during isokinetic tasks reveals no specific abnormality in the fatigue mechanisms in the local muscles of FMS patients (Elert, Rantapaa-Dahlqvist, Henriksson-Larsen, Lorentzon, & Gerdle, 1992).

OBSERVED VERSUS PERCEIVED DISABILITY: INDIVIDUAL DIFFERENCES

As noted earlier, subjective reports and objective findings do not always correlate in FMS. Turk and his associates (1996a) found that the relationships between pain and perceived disability and between pain and observed physical functioning were significant, whereas there was no association found between observed physical functioning and self-reported disability. These results suggest that FMS is associated with an inability to perceive accurately one's physical ability. Similar results have recently been reported by others (Hidding et al., 1994).

Although the discrepancy seems to be fairly common, FMS patients are a heterogeneous group and large variability in the degree to which actual and perceived functional ability differ may vary across patients. Turk et al. (1998) further analyzed the data on the basis of the psychosocial subgroups of FMS and found that indeed, those patients whose coping was fairly adaptive did not show that discrepancy. The results suggest that perceived functional disability may not depend solely upon actual ability, but the relationship between them is moderated by how patients interpret their plight. Beliefs, expectations, and mood state have been shown to influence the relationship between the actual and perceived physical ability in individuals with chronic pain (Blalock et al., 1992).

One potential cognitive-behavioral mediatior for the discrepancy is fear of physical activity and related avoidance. Vlaeyen et al. (1995) state that fear that physical activity may aggravate pain may lead to excessive guarding and avoidance of functional activity, leading to further deconditioning and disability in chronic pain patients. The vicious cycle of fear, deactivation, and disability may provide a feedback toa patient's belief about their physical ability, and thus, these patients may underestimate their ability to perform physical tasks. However, the recent study by de Gier et al (2003) has shown that although FMS patients with a high level of fear of physical activity exhibited lower tolerance and endurance for the physical task, the effect disappeared when pain intensity was taken into consideration. This result is at variance with the multiple studies testing low back patients (eg, Al-Obaidi, Nelson, Al-Awadhi, & Al-Shuwaie, 2000). The authors speculate that the level of the physical task may not have beenthreatening enough to create the appropriate level of fear-avoidance in their patients. Further research may clarify this point.

SUMMARY: RISK FACTORS FOR DISABILITY IN FMS

The literature provides an abundant volume of evidence that FMS, although not lethal, is a disabling pain disorder that disrupts patients' daily lives and work capacities. Surprisingly little has been done empirically to delineate risk factors for chronic disability in FMS. However, a review of the literature provides us some hypotheses. First, mood disturbance, particularly symptoms of depression and anxiety disorders, seem to be consistently related to disability. Of course, the expressed relationship is correlational and does not indicate directionality. However, the presence of mood disturbance is clearly an indication of further deterioration of patients' functional ability and thus management of mood disturbance may be an important factor in improving patients' function.

A few studies also indicate that smoking and obesity may significantly contribute to functional disability. These two factors are generally related to a sedentary life style, which may mediate the relationship. The results clearly suggest that researchers and clinicians may need to pay close attention to patients' life style issues to evaluate their disability status.

Factors associated with work disability appear to include multiple components including physical and cognitive demands of the job and social relationships at the workplace. Gainful employment may also be impacted by socioeconomic factors such as availability of income source, trends of the job market, and value of the skills of the person. A systematic approach to further delineate specifics is needed. However, for now, clinicians may wish to consider referring FMS patients for counseling, as assistance with problem solving may help them maintain their employment status.

Finally, it is important to rememberthe heterogeneity of FMS patients. How patients adapt and cope with their FMS varies greatly across individuals. Cognitive appraisals of their plight, how patients' pain complaints are handled at home and at work, expectation of how physical activities affect their pain, and the availability of environmental resource to accommodate any changes that their FMS requires, all seem to have an impact on patients' adaptation. Further research investigating these factors in relation to disability will help us better understand and manage this complex, debilitating pain disorder.

REFERENCES

Aaron, L. A., Bradley, L. A., Alarcon, G. S., Alexander, R. W., Triana-Alexander, M., Martin, M. Y., & Alberts, K. R. (1996). Psychiatric diagnoses in patients with fibromyalgia are related to health care-seeking behavior rather than to illness. *Arthritis Rheum, 39*(3), 436–45.

Adler, G. K., Kinsley, B. T., Hurwitz, S., Mossey, C. J., & Goldenberg, D. L. (1999). Reduced hypothalamic-pituitary and sympathoadrenal responses to hypoglycemia in women with fibromyalgia syndrome. *Am J Med, 106*(5), 534–43.

Alfici, S., Sigal, M., & Landau, M. (1989). Primary fibromyalgia syndrome—a variant of depressive disorder? *Psychother Psychosom, 51*(3), 156–61.

Al-Obaidi, S. M., Nelson, R. M., Al-Awadhi, S., & Al-Shuwaie, N. (2000). The role of anticipation and fear of pain in the persistence of avoidance behavior in patients with chronic low back pain. *Spine, 25*(9), 1126–31.

Assefi, N. P., Coy, T. V., Uslan, D., Smith, W. R., & Buchwald, D. (2003). Financial, occupational, and personal consequences of disability in patients with chronic fatigue syndrome and fibromyalgia compared to other fatiguing conditions. *J Rheumatol, 30*(4), 804–8.

Bengtsson, A., & Henriksson, K. G. (1989). The muscle in fibromyalgia—a review of Swedish studies. *J Rheumatol Suppl, 19*, 144–9.

Bennett, R. M., Clark, S. R., Goldberg, L., Nelson, D., Bonafede, R. P., Porter, J., & Specht, D. (1989). Aerobic fitness in patients with fibrositis. A controlled study of respiratory gas exchange and 133 xenon clearance from exercising muscle. *Arthritis Rheum, 32*(4), 454–60.

Blalock, S., DeVellis, B., DeVellis, R., Giorgino, K., Sauter, S., Jordan, J., Keefe, F., & Mutran, E. (1992). Psychological well-being among people with recently diagnosed rheumatoid arthritis. Do self-perceptions of abilities make a difference? *Arthritis Rheum, 35*(11), 1267–72.

Bombardier, C. H., & Buchwald, D. (1996). Chronic fatigue, chronic fatigue syndrome, and fibromyalgia. Disability and health-care use. *Med Care, 34*(9), 924–30.

Bou-Holaigah, I., Calkins, H., Flynn, J. A., Tunin, C., Chang, H. C., Kan, J. S., & Rowe, P. C. (1997). Provocation of hypotension and pain during upright tilt table testing in adults with fibromyalgia. *Clin Exp Rheumatol, 15*(3), 239–46.

Branco, J., Atalaia, A., & Paiva, T. (1994). Sleep cycles and alpha-delta sleep in fibromyalgia syndrome. *J Rheumatol, 21*(6), 1113–7.

Burckhardt, C. S., Clark, S. R., & Bennett, R. M. (1993). Fibromyalgia and quality of life: a comparative analysis. *J Rheumatol, 20*(3), 475–9.

Cardol, M., de Jong, B. A., van den Bos, G. A., Beelem, A., de Groot, I. J., & de Haan, R. J. (2002). Beyond disability: perceived participation in people with a chronic disabling condition. *Clin Rehabil, 16*(1), 27–35.

de Gier, M., Peters, M. L., & Vlaeyen, J. W. (2003). Fear of pain, physical performance, and attentional processes in patients with fibromyalgia. *Pain, 104*(1–2), 121–30.

Dobkin, P. L., De Civita, M., Bernatsky, S., Kang, H., & Baron, M. (2003). Does psychological vulnerability determine health-care utilization in fibromyalgia? *Rheumatology (Oxford), 42*(11), 1324–31.

Drewes, A. M., Nielsen, K. D., Taagholt, S. J., Bjerregard, K., Svendsen, L., & Gade, J. (1995). Sleep intensity in fibromyalgia: focus on the microstructure of the sleep process. *Br J Rheumatol, 34*(7), 629–35.

Ejlertsson, G., Eden, L., & Leden, I. (2002). Predictors of positive health in disability pensioners: a population-based questionnaire study using Positive Odds Ratio. *BMC Public Health, 2*(1), 20.

Elert, J. E., Rantapaa-Dahlqvist, S. B., Henriksson-Larsen, K., Lorentzon, R., & Gerdle, B. U. (1992). Muscle performance, electromyography and fibre type composition in fibromyalgia and work-related myalgia. *Scand J Rheumatol, 21*(1), 28–34.

Ford, C. V. (1997). Somatization and fashionable diagnoses: illness as a way of life. *Scand J Work Environ Health, 23*(Suppl 3), 7–16.

Forseth, K.O., Gran, J.T., & Husby, G. (1997). A population study of the incidence of fibromyalgia among women aged 26–55 years. *Br J Rheumatol, 36*, 1318–1323.

Graven-Nielsen, T., Aspegren Kendall, S., Henriksson, K. G., Bengtsson, M., Sorensen, J., Johnson, A., Gerdle, B., & Arendt-Nielsen, L. (2000). Ketamine reduces muscle pain, temporal summation, and referred pain in fibromyalgia patients. *Pain, 85*(3), 483–91.

Hawley, D. J., Wolfe, F., & Cathey, M. A. (1988). Pain, functional disability, and psychological status: a 12-month study of severity in fibromyalgia. *J Rheumatol, 15*(10), 1551–6.

Heikkila, S., Ronni, S., Kautiainen, H. J., & Kauppi, M. J. (2002). Functional impairment in spondyloarthropathy and fibromyalgia. *J Rheumatol, 29*(7), 1415–9.

Henriksson, C., & Liedberg, G. (2000). Factors of importance for work disability in women with fibromyalgia. *J Rheumatol, 27*(5), 1271–6.

Hidding, A., van Santen, M., De Klerk, E., Gielen, X., Boers, M., Geenen, R., Vlaeyen, J., Kester, A., & van der Linden, S. (1994). Comparison between self-report measures and clinical observations of functional disability in ankylosing spondylitis, rheumatoid arthritis and fibromyalgia. *J Rheumatol, 21*(5), 818–23.

Jacobsen, S., & Holm, B. (1992). Muscle strength and endurance compared to aerobic capacity in primary fibromyalgia syndrome. *Clin Exp Rheumatol, 10*(4), 419–20.

Kosek, E., Ekholm, J., & Hansson, P. (1996). Modulation of pressure pain thresholds during and following isometric contraction in patients with fibromyalgia and in healthy controls. *Pain, 64*(3), 415–23.

Kosek, E., & Hansson, P. (1997). Modulatory influence on somatosensory perception from vibration and heterotopic noxious conditioning stimulation (HNCS) in fibromyalgia patients and healthy subjects. *Pain, 70*(1), 41–51.

Kurtze, N., Gundersen, K. T., & Svebak, S. (1999). Quality of life, functional disability and lifestyle among subgroups of fibromyalgia patients: the significance of anxiety and depression. *Br J Med Psychol, 72 (Pt 4)*, 471–84.

Lautenbacher, S., & Rollman, G. B. (1997). Possible deficiencies of pain modulation in fibromyalgia. *Clin J Pain, 13*(3), 189–96.

Lentz, M. J., Landis, C. A., Rothermel, J., & Shaver, J. L. (1999). Effects of selective slow wave sleep disruption on musculoskeletal pain and fatigue in middle aged women. *J Rheumatol, 26*(7), 1586–92.

Liedberg, G. M., & Henriksson, C. M. (2002). Factors of importance for work disability in women with fibromyalgia: an interview study. *Arthritis Rheum, 47*(3), 266–74.

Mannerkorpi, K., Burckhardt, C. S., & Bjelle, A. (1994). Physical performance characteristics of women with fibromyalgia. *Arthritis Care Res, 7*(3), 123–9.

Martinez, J. E., Ferraz, M. B., Sato, E. I., & Atra, E. (1995). Fibromyalgia versus rheumatoid arthritis: a longitudinal comparison of the quality of life. *J Rheumatol, 22*(2), 270–4.

McCain, G. A., Cameron, R., & Kennedy, J. C. (1989). The problem of longterm disability payments and litigation in primary fibromyalgia: the Canadian perspective. *J Rheumatol Suppl, 19*, 174–6.

Meller, S. T., & Gebhart, G. F. (1993). Nitric oxide (NO) and nociceptive processing in the spinal cord. *Pain, 52*(2), 127–36.

Mengshoel, A. M., Forre, O., & Komnaes, H. B. (1990). Muscle strength and aerobic capacity in primary fibromyalgia [see comments]. *Clin Exp Rheumatol, 8*(5), 475–9.

Middleton, G. D., McFarlin, J. E., & Lipsky, P. E. (1994). The prevalence and clinical impact of fibromyalgia in systemic lupus erythematosus [see comments]. *Arthritis Rheum, 37*(8), 1181–8.

Moldofsky, H., Scarisbrick, P., England, R., & Smythe, H. (1975). Musculosketal symptoms and non-REM sleep disturbance in patients with "fibrositis syndrome" and healthy subjects. *Psychosom Med, 37*(4), 341–51.

Moldofsky, H., Wong, M. T., & Lue, F. A. (1993). Litigation, sleep, symptoms and disabilities in postaccident pain (fibromyalgia). *J Rheumatol, 20*(11), 1935–40.

Morris, V., Cruwys, S., & Kidd, B. (1998). Increased capsaicin-induced secondary hyperalgesia as a marker of abnormal sensory activity in patients with fibromyalgia. *Neurosci Lett, 250*(3), 205–7.

Myers, J. K., Weissman, M. M., Tischler, G. L., Holzer, C. E. d., Leaf, P. J., Orvaschel, H., Anthony, J. C., Boyd, J. H., Burke, J. D., Jr., Kramer, M., & et al. (1984). Six-month prevalence of psychiatric disorders in three communities 1980 to 1982. *Arch Gen Psychiatry, 41*(10), 959–67.

Nicolodi, M., Volpe, A. R., & Sicuteri, F. (1998). Fibromyalgia and headache. Failure of serotonergic analgesia and N- methyl-D-aspartate-mediated neuronal plasticity: their common clues. *Cephalalgia, 18 Suppl 21*, 41–4.

Nielens, H., Boisset, V., & Masquelier, E. (2000). Fitness and perceived exertion in patients with fibromyalgia syndrome. *Clin J Pain, 16*(3), 209–13.

Norregaard, J., Bulow, P. M., & Danneskiold-Samsoe, B. (1994). Muscle strength, voluntary activation, twitch properties, and endurance in patients with fibromyalgia. *J Neurol Neurosurg Psychiatry, 57*(9), 1106–11.

Okifuji, A., & Ashburn, M. (2001). Fibromyalgia: Comprehensive evaluation. *Crit Rev Phys Rehab Med, 13*(1), 24–54.

Okifuji, A., & Turk, D. C. (2002). Stress and psychophysiological dysregulation in patients with fibromyalgia syndrome. *Appl Psychophysiol Biofeedback, 27*(2), 129–41.

Okifuji, A., Turk, D. C., Sinclair, J. D., Starz, T. W., & Marcus, D. A. (1997). A standardized manual tender point survey. I. Development and determination of a threshold point for the identification of positive tender points in fibromyalgia syndrome. *J Rheumatol, 24*(2), 377–83.

Park, J. H., Phothimat, P., Oates, C. T., Hernanz-Schulman, M., & Olsen, N. J. (1998). Use of P-31 magnetic resonance spectroscopy to detect metabolic abnormalities in muscles of patients with fibromyalgia. *Arthritis Rheum, 41*(3), 406–13.

Patkar, A. A., Bilal, L., & Masand, P. S. (2003). Management of fibromyalgia. *Curr Psychiatry Rep, 5*(3), 218–24.

Robinson, R. L., Birnbaum, H. G., Morley, M. A., Sisitsky, T., Greenberg, P. E., & Claxton, A. J. (2003). Economic cost and epidemiological characteristics of patients with fibromyalgia claims. *J Rheumatol, 30*(6), 1318–25.

Russell, I. J., Michalek, J. E., Vipraio, G. A., Fletcher, E. M., Javors, M. A., & Bowden, C. A. (1992a). Platelet 3H-imipramine uptake receptor density and serum serotonin levels in patients with fibromyalgia/fibrositis syndrome [see comments]. *J Rheumatol, 19*(1), 104–9.

Russell, I. J., Vaeroy, H., Javors, M., & Nyberg, F. (1992b). Cerebrospinal fluid biogenic amine metabolites in fibromyalgia/fibrositis syndrome and rheumatoid arthritis. *Arthritis Rheum, 35*(5), 550–6.

Sherman, J. J., Turk, D. C., & Okifuji, A. (2000). Prevalence and impact of posttraumatic stress disorder-like symptoms on patients with fibromyalgia syndrome. *Clin J Pain, 16*(2), 127–34.

Sorensen, J., Graven-Nielsen, T., Henriksson, K. G., Bengtsson, M., & Arendt-Nielsen, L. (1998). Hyperexcitability in fibromyalgia. *J Rheumatol, 25*(1), 152–5.

Sprott, H., Bradley, L. A., Oh, S. J., Wintersberger, W., Alarcon, G. S., Mussell, H. G., Tseng, A., Gay, R. E., & Gay, S. (1998). Immunohistochemical and molecular studies of serotonin, substance P, galanin, pituitary adenylyl cyclase-activating polypeptide, and secretoneurin in fibromyalgic muscle tissue. *Arthritis Rheum, 41*(9), 1689–94.

Turk, D. C., Okifuji, A., Sinclair, J. D., & Starz, T. W. (1996a). Pain, disability, and physical functioning in subgroups of patients with fibromyalgia. *J Rheumatol, 23*(7), 1255–62.

Turk, D. C., Okifuji, A., Starz, T. W., & Sinclair, J. D. (1996b). Effects of type of symptom onset on psychological distress and disability in fibromyalgia syndrome patients. *Pain, 68*(2–3), 423–30.

Vlaeyen, J. W., Kole-Snijders, A. M., Boeren, R. G., & van Eek, H. (1995). Fear of movement/(re)injury in chronic low back pain and its relation to behavioral performance. *Pain, 62*(3), 363–72.

Walker, E. A., Keegan, D., Gardner, G., Sullivan, M., Katon, W. J., & Bernstein, D. (1997). Psychosocial factors in fibromyalgia compared with rheumatoid arthritis: I. Psychiatric diagnoses and functional disability. *Psychosom Med, 59*(6), 565–71.

Watkins, L. R., Maier, S. F., & Goehler, L. E. (1995). Immune activation: the role of pro-inflammatory cytokines in inflammation, illness responses and pathological pain states. *Pain, 63*(3), 289–302.

White, K. P., Nielson, W. R., Harth, M., Ostbye, T., & Speechley, M. (2002). Chronic widespread musculoskeletal pain with or without fibromyalgia: psychological distress in a representative community adult sample. *J Rheumatol, 29*(3), 588–94.

White, K. P., Speechley, M., Harth, M., & Ostbye, T. (1995). Fibromyalgia in rheumatology practice: a survey of Canadian rheumatologists. *J Rheumatol, 22*(4), 722–6.

White, K. P., Speechley, M., Harth, M., & Ostbye, T. (1999a). Comparing self-reported function and work disability in 100 community cases of fibromyalgia syndrome versus controls in London, Ontario: the London Fibromyalgia Epidemiology Study. *Arthritis Rheum, 42*(1), 76–83.

White, K. P., Speechley, M., Harth, M., & Ostbye, T. (1999b). The London Fibromyalgia Epidemiology Study: direct health care costs of fibromyalgia syndrome in London, Canada. *J Rheumatol, 26*(4), 885–9.

White, K. P., Speechley, M., Harth, M., & Ostbye, T. (1999c). The London Fibromyalgia Epidemiology Study: the prevalence of fibromyalgia syndrome in London, Ontario. *J Rheumatol, 26*(7), 1570–6.

Wolfe, F. (1994). When to diagnose fibromyalgia. *Rheum Dis Clin North Am, 20*(2), 485–501.

Wolfe, F. (1997). The fibromyalgia problem [editorial; comment]. *J Rheumatol, 24*(7), 1247–9.

Wolfe, F., Anderson, J., Harkness, D., Bennett, R. M., Caro, X. J., Goldenberg, D. L., Russell, I. J., & Yunus, M. B. (1997a). A prospective, longitudinal, multicenter study of service utilization and costs in fibromyalgia. *Arthritis Rheum, 40*(9), 1560–70.

Wolfe, F., Ross, K., Anderson, J., Russell, I. J., & Hebert, L. (1995). The prevalence and characteristics of fibromyalgia in the general population. *Arthritis Rheum, 38*(1), 19–28.

Wolfe, F., Russell, I. J., Vipraio, G., Ross, K., & Anderson, J. (1997b). Serotonin levels, pain threshold, and fibromyalgia symptoms in the general population. *J Rheumatol, 24*(3), 555–9.

Wolfe, F., Smythe, H. A., Yunus, M. B., Bennett, R. M., Bombardier, C., Goldenberg, D. L., Tugwell, P., Campbell, S. M., Abeles, M., Clark, P., & et al. (1990). The American College of Rheumatology 1990 Criteria for the Classification of Fibromyalgia. Report of the Multicenter Criteria Committee [see comments]. *Arthritis Rheum, 33*(2), 160–72.

Yunus, M. B., Arslan, S., & Aldag, J. C. (2002a). Relationship between body mass index and fibromyalgia features. *Scand J Rheumatol, 31*(1), 27–31.

Yunus, M. B., Arslan, S., & Aldag, J. C. (2002b). Relationship between fibromyalgia features and smoking. *Scand J Rheumatol, 31*(5), 301–5.

Yunus, M. B., Dailey, J. W., Aldag, J. C., Masi, A. T., & Jobe, P. C. (1992). Plasma tryptophan and other amino acids in primary fibromyalgia: a controlled study. *J Rheumatol, 19*(1), 90–4.

Zachrisson, O., Regland, B., Jahreskog, M., Jonsson, M., Kron, M., & Gottfries, C. G. (2002). Treatment with staphylococcus toxoid in fibromyalgia/chronic fatigue syndrome–a randomised controlled trial. *Eur J Pain, 6*(6), 455–66.

13

Musculoskeletal Disorders, Disability, and Return-to-Work (Repetitive Strain)

The Quest for Objectivity

J. Mark Melhorn and Eric M. Kennedy

INTRODUCTION

The huge costs of work-related musculoskeletal pain and its associated disability are not new or unique to the population of the United States. Many historical manifestations of workplace pain have been related to innovation and changing technology. Incidence rates and symptom severity have had an interesting relationship to public concern and governmental decisions.

Musculoskeletal pain is often separated into two categories: occupational and non-occupational. This distinction is often considered when reviewing the outcome of treatment but is commonly overlooked during treatment. This legal distinction is not required by the physician for treatment of the condition but has importance for the patient. Injuries or illnesses can cause musculoskeletal pain in the workplace. An occupational injury by definition is one that results from a work-related event or from a single instantaneous exposure in the work environment. Injuries are reportable by the employer on the Occupational Safety and Health Administration (OSHA) 300 log if they result in lost work time; require medical treatment (other than first aid); or if the worker experiences loss of consciousness, restriction of work activities or motion, or is transferred to another job (United States Bureau of Labor Statistics, 1997). An occupational illness is any abnormal condition or disorder (other than one resulting from an occupational injury) caused by exposure to a factor(s) associated with employment. Included are acute and chronic illnesses or diseases which may be caused by inhalation, absorption, ingestion, or direct contact (United States Bureau of Labor Statistics, 1997). Musculoskeletal injuries are often defined as traditional traumatic injuries such as fractures, sprains, strains, dislocations, or

DOI: 10.1007/978-0-387-28919-9_13, © 2009 Springer Science+Business Media, LLC

lacerations, while musculoskeletal illnesses are commonly called cumulative trauma disorders (CTD), repetitive motion injuries (RMI) or musculoskeletal disorders (MSD).

Work-related musculoskeletal disorders are very costly to the economy. In 1997, direct health costs for both injuries and illnesses for the nation's work force were over $418 billion with estimated indirect costs of $837 billion (Brady et al., 1997). Private industry reported 6.1 million injuries and illnesses with a case rate of 7.1 cases per 100 equivalent full-time workers (United States Department of Labor, 1999). Reducing the costs associated with workplace disability has clearly become a priority for the American public and the American business community. A complicating factor is the variation in workers' compensation from state to state. Although described as a system, it isn't; each state, US territory, and all US federal employees have different and separate workers' compensation laws and regulations. The workers' compensation system is designed to be a no-fault and exclusive remedy. The workers and their dependents are not required to prove fault for personal injuries, diseases, or deaths arising out of and in the course of employment. The employer agrees to provide rapid payment to the injured worker for lost wages and medical care costs in exchange for limiting or eliminating the employer's potential liability for said occupational illness, injuries and death and, thereby, the possibility of large tort verdicts.

Occupational medicine presents a number of challenges to the physician. Management of work-related musculoskeletal pain is often frustrating. Patients may have more complaints and longer recovery times, require longer and more frequent office visits, and may be accompanied by the employer or nurse case manager during the office visit. They frequently have more questions about work status, require more phone calls, and have more paper work requirements. Many have attorneys and they commonly require a permanent physical impairment rating with subsequent depositions or mandatory court appearances. Treatment outcomes often shift from good to poor (Kasdan, Vender, Lewis, Stallings, & Melhorn, 1996). The negative shift in outcome indicates that workers' compensation involvement introduces additional factors that influence patients and complicate treatment efforts. Traditional Western medical education is heavily weighted in the scientific study of the biologic systems of health and disease, often to the exclusion of such factors (Zeppieri, 1999). Physicians who provide care to those with work-related injuries are often inadequately prepared to deal with the biosocial (also labeled as psychosocial or biopsychosocial) issues—including motivation, social factors, psychological overlays, economic incentives, and legal complications—that influence the outcomes of treatment (Melhorn, 1998e). Those physicians who are adequately prepared are often faced with the difficult task of separating fact from fiction. Occasionally, the patient's symptoms can be disproportional to the clinic examination. Since an occupationally related OSHA event requires only a complaint of pain, multiple subjective issues must be reviewed. This can make the clinical picture confusing and require more tests and studies to be used to arrive at the appropriate medical diagnosis than a similar non-occupational patient. Other factors impacting treatment costs might include: somatization behavior among patients and medicalization among physicians (Barsky & Borus, 1995); cost shifting from commercial insurance to workers' compensation insurance (Butler, 1996); and removing disincentives for early return to work (Filan, 1996). The occupational physician must recognize, understand and address these factors to achieve the more favorable outcomes that are seen in non-workers' compensation injuries and illnesses.

WHO PAYS FOR DISABILITY

Surprisingly little work has been done to address this question. Workers' compensation and Social Security Disability Insurance (SSDI) are economic mainstays of disabled workers and their families. These programs were designed to help replace the lost earnings of covered workers who meet certain eligibility criteria. Yet neither program seeks to replace the full earnings loss due to disability; as a consequence, the disabled individual inevitably shoulders some of the financial burden of disability. Most workers' compensation programs aim to replace two-thirds of lost gross earnings. Commonly, the workers' compensation benefits payment is not taxed. This can result in a significant increase in the total take home amount, which on occasions could be equal to their usual after tax paycheck. All programs have initial waiting periods that are uncompensated and all have statutory caps on weekly compensation benefits. Many individuals also have private disability insurance, either provided by the employer or personally purchased. When this payment is added to the non-taxed workers' compensation benefits, the total amount may be more than when the individual is working. Permanent disability benefits are very rarely provided for a lifetime and only a few states provide any cost of living adjustments for long-term benefits. Not infrequently, workers must also pay for the costs of litigating for the benefits they receive. It seems clear that, for some injured workers, a sizeable gap can exist between losses incurred by the disabled individual and the transfer payments typically provided. The gap is especially large in the case of persons who lose time from work while disabled and particularly where a full job loss results from the condition.

Although the injured worker sometimes bears the cost of disability there is also cost to employers and society at large. The employers' costs are increased when insurance premiums are increased or in the case of self-insured employers the cost falls directly to the bottom line. Additionally, employers' costs are increased by such items as replacement workers, lost productivity, reduced quality, internal personnel and administrative costs to process the claim and benefits. A common "rule of thumb" is that the indirect costs of disability are a multiple of between four and ten times the direct costs of medical and indemnity. Obviously, the precise multiple can only be determined through careful economic analysis and will vary by state, industry, employer, and many other factors. Society as a whole pays the cost from loss or reduction in productive citizenry, social programs to assist the disabled, loss of function to the individual, their family, and many other direct and indirect costs. Perhaps the most tangible cost that society pays is that of increased product pricing to cover the manufacturers cost of disability. Obviously, in most cases, the disability costs discussed above are ultimately passed through to the consumer.

OPPORTUNITIES FOR REDUCING DISABILITY

Everyone loses when patients are disabled for long periods of time. The insurer, employer, and society suffer the economic losses while the employee suffers the individual losses. The opportunity to change the current lose-lose situation to win-win lies in prompt treatment and early return-to-work. The best interest of the injured worker, the financial interests of the employer and the insurer, and the intended fairness of the system would be served best by a joint effort of all parties to reduce the period of disability and promote return to work.

Physicians

Physicians must be the patient advocate and help end the antagonism between employers and employees. The treating physician can improve the quality of life for the injured worker by using the science of medicine to treat the anatomical injury, thereby decreasing the physical impairment and the physician can use the art of medicine to treat the biopsychosocial issues, thereby decreasing the disability from the injury resulting in less handicap for the individual and improved treatment outcomes at a lower financial cost.

This approach provides treating physicians with a unique opportunity and obligation to provide reasonable work-guides in an effort to reduce work disability, improve the outcome for work related injuries, and advance the quality of life for their patients. Returning the individual to work requires a balance between the demands of the job and the capability of the patient. Many studies have demonstrated the advantages of early return to work for the injured workers (Melhorn, 1996b; Cook, Birkholz, King, & Szabo, 1995; Melhorn & Wilkinson, 1996; Melhorn, 1997a; Melhorn, 1997b; Melhorn, 1997c; Ballard, Baxter, Bruening, & Fried, 1986; Bruce & Bruce, 1996; Burke, Harms-Constas, & Aden, 1994; Centineo, 1986; Day, McCabe, & Alexander, 1993; Devlin, O'Neill, & MacBride, 1994; Gice & Tompkins, 1988; Goodman, 1989; Groves & Gallagher, 1993; Grunet et al., 1992; Kasdan & June, 1993; Nathan, Meadows, & Keniston, 1993). Examples of these benefits include: better self image (Bernacki & Tsai, 1996), improved ability to cope (Bigos et al., 1986), improved work survivability (Melhorn, 1996b), improved ability to be self sufficient and, therefore, in the best interest of the patient (employee) (Burke et al., 1994; Devlin et al., 1994; Bruce et al., 1996; Dworkin, Handlin, Richlin, Rrand, & Vannucci, 1985; Hall, McIntosh, Melles, Holowachuk, & Wai, 1994). Conversely, prolonged time away from work makes recovery and return to work progressively less likely (Strang, 1985).

Return to work guides are not an exact science. Often, physicians find this requirement frustrating and time consuming. Commonly, little or no formal training occurs during residency training. Occasionally, the patient wants to negotiate the workplace guides or simply refuses to go back to work, often resulting in a no-win situation. It is important for the physician to provide guidance. Workplace guides are simply guides and not written in stone. However, it should be understood that the employer must interpret the work guides and thus should be related in terms that can be easily applied to the workplace. Workplace guides need to be flexible and should be adjusted with the individual patient's response to treatment. An understanding of the symptoms, signs, job description, essential functions of the job, accommodation options, employer willingness, employee willingness, previous workplace guides (family physician, company physician, or other), response to previous modified work activities, and current work status are required to provide reasonable workplace guides. As the healing continues, both job demands and ability to meet those demands tend to increase. This allows for a natural transition from accommodated work to regular work. These reports should be understandable in lay terms with restrictions expressed in terms of functional impairment (lifting and motion limits) rather than job category (carpenter, truck driver), unless the physician is sure of the exact physical requirements of the job.

In 1990, when it enacted the Americans with Disabilities Act (ADA), Congress adopted a definition of the term "disability" that had been used under Title V of the Rehabilitation Act since the 1970s. The definition included individuals with a physical or mental impairment that substantially limits at least one major life activity, individuals with a history of such impairment, and people who are regarded by others or perceived as having such impairment.

The importance of preventing disability and medically unnecessary time off from work can be placed in perspective by considering the origin of the Americans with Disabilities Act (United States Congress, 1991). People with amputations, on crutches, in wheelchairs, spastic, blind, deaf, in constant pain and crippled with rheumatoid arthritis, weakened and slowly dying from diabetes, cancer, or AIDS, or otherwise substantially limited in performing life activities insisted so strongly on their right to work that Congress passed the ADA.

Employers, Employees, and Case Managers

Employers, employees, case managers, human resources personnel, and others play a vital role in reducing medically unnecessary time off from work as well. Too often the worst disability cases have much less to do with the biology of the case and hinge to a greater extent on the psychology of the case. This can perhaps be best illustrated by examining the answer to the following questions.

- Who is more likely to get injured, a person who likes his job or a person who hates his job?
- Two workers are injured. One likes his job and the other hates his job. Who is coming back to work sooner?

In general terms employers have a great deal of control over employees. Employers can dictate when to come to work, when to leave, what to wear, the precise method of accomplishing tasks, when to have lunch, and when to have breaks. Often employees work in situations where they share their supervisor with fifty or more other employees. The lack of control, communication and individual attention can lead to dissatisfaction that manifests itself in a variety of destructive ways. When an employee presents with a disability claim the dynamics of the situation is often abruptly changed. Suddenly, a supervisor that may not have even known their name before contacts the employee. Case managers, human resources personnel, and others begin asking how they feel and if they think that they can come back to work. The shift in control may be attractive to the employee and they may elect to drag out the new situation. Employers should take every opportunity to empower and communicate with employees before an injury occurs so that the shift is less attractive. Employer, human resources, case managers, and others that manage the case need to understand that "the issue" is often "not the issue". The underlying problem may be a disgruntled employee (often justifiably so) that is using the disability system to bring attention to unresolved issues.

REVIEWING DISABILITY TERMS

Depending upon one's definition of disability, between 35 and 46 million Americans can be labeled as disabled. Unlike other human conditions such as poverty, gender, childhood, old age, and race, the definition of disability and the determination of who is disabled continue to challenge governments and adjudicating bodies. Thus, the definitions of disability expand and contract more along political and ideological lines than according to any clear physical determinations. Since no standardized or generally accepted definition exists, calculating the cost of disability is even more difficult. If the cost of exclusion from the workplace, medical care, legal services, and earning replacements are summed, the 1980 estimate was $177 billion or approximately 6.5% of the gross domestic product (Demeter, Andersson, & Smith, 2001).

Precise definitions, communication, and role awareness are essential parts of disability management. Disability arises out of an individual's inability to perform a task successfully because of an insufficiency in one or more areas of functional capability: physical function or mental function. Disability is not necessarily related to any health impairment or medical condition; although a medical condition or impairment may cause or contribute to disability. Disability requires a conceptual definition. Disability is the gap between what a person can do and what the person needs or wants to do and may be temporary or permanent. It is defined by the American Medical Association Guides to the Evaluation of Permanent Impairment (AMA Guides) (2000) as an alteration of an individual's capacity to meet personal, social, or occupational demands or statutory or regulatory requirements, because of an impairment. In addition, there are degrees of disability, usually termed partial or complete. Many factors affect these determinations because disability refers to the fit between ability and functional requirement. Disability includes the medical impairment, the demands of the task, and the individual. Factors such as age, regional job opportunities, IQ, educational level, and biopsychosocial issues are important to how the disability affects an individual's life (Melhorn, 2001). Therefore, disability is usually not determined by a physician.

Impairment is defined as the loss of a physiologic function or of an anatomic structure. Evaluation of impairment is addressed by the AMA Guides (2000) and is defined as a deviation from normal in a body part or organ system and its functioning. Impairment assessment is deemed a medical evaluation, while disability is determined in an operational setting, such as the workplace or in a structured, functional capacity evaluation where observations are made of the individual's capacity to carry out particular tasks or perform specified functions. Therefore, an impaired person (i.e. reduced grip strength) is not necessarily disabled (i.e. inability to work).

The law is a term lawyers often use to refer to the controlling rules of litigation and is made up of statutes, regulations, and common law. Statutes and regulations are written documents that explicitly define certain rules and duties, although they are often subject to differing interpretations. The common law is simply prior judicial decisions (precedents) that impose obligations and liability on certain persons. For example, if a shop owner is negligent in not shoveling the sidewalk and a person slips on it and falls, the shop owner is liable for the damages to that person. While certain legal principles are fairly uniform, the law does vary from state to state and from state courts to federal courts.

Determination of causation, apportionment, and aggravation is a vital requirement to allow for the speedy resolution of the workers' compensation legal requirements. These three words can often delay or limit treatment, reduce or eliminate financial restitution, and adversely impact the outcome of care for the work-injured patient. Causation is defined as a physical, chemical, or biologic factor that contributed to the occurrence of a medical condition (AMA, 2000). To decide that a factor alleged to have caused or contributed to the occurrence or worsening of a medical condition has actually done so is necessary to verify both of the following: the alleged factor could have caused or contributed to worsening of the impairment which is a medical determination, and the alleged factor did cause or contribute to worsening of the impairment, which is a non-medical determination. Apportionment is an estimate of the degree to which each of various occupational and nonoccupational factors may have caused or contributed to a particular impairment. Aggravation means that a physical, chemical, or biologic factor, which may or may not be work related, contributed to the worsening of a preexisting medical condition. However, if the information is insufficient to accurately assign causation, determine apportionment, or assess change resulting in aggravation, then the physician needs to explain that decision.

Possibility and probability are terms that refer to the likelihood or change that an injury or illness was caused by or aggravated by a particular factor. Possibility sometimes is used to imply a likelihood of less than 50 percent while probability is used to imply greater than 50 percent.

Work related injuries do not occur in a vacuum. The impact of the injury and the outcome of treatment are influenced by the biopsychosocial issues that make each individual unique and each patient's injury different. Taking the standard approach that a privately insured patient's biopsychosocial issues are the same as those of a patient with carpal tunnel seeking workers' compensation, may result in a poor outcome for the patient and a discouraged treating physician. If physicians elect to treat workers' compensation patients, they need to do it right. Physicians should address all the critical issues: age, gender, genetics, workplace, nonwork environment, biopsychosocial issues, work status, impairment, disability, and handicaps. Learning this art of medicine will improve the physician's skills for all patients and make each physician a better all-around physician.

STEPS FOR THE PHYSICIAN

Obviously, disability management represents an area of medicine that has a large financial impact upon society. It is only in recent times that disability and impairment have been accorded legal status. Despite the large expenditures of money, time, personnel, and resources there exists no single comprehensive compendium of information on disability, the role of physicians in diagnosing and quantifying impairment, the role of lay professionals (most notably lawyers, vocational experts and forensic economists) in translating medically derived impairment into legally allowable disability for financial reimbursements, and an analysis of the social and legal constructs upon which disability determination is to be based. Impairment and disability evaluations encompass medical and non-medical aspects of injuries and illnesses and are effectively accomplished only when both components are properly managed. A physician not involved in the patient's care through a process called an independent medical evaluation often completes these evaluations.

Physicians can be a major force in serving the public good and in reducing costs of work-related disability for a number of reasons. Physicians are usually patient advocates. As that advocate and in the best interest of society, physicians should encourage rehabilitation, not disability. Many studies have shown that early return to work results in a better outcome for work-related injuries and improves the quality of life for the patient (Melhorn, 1997d; Melhorn, 1998b; Melhorn, 1996b; Melhorn, 1998d; Derebery & Tullis, 1983; Dworkin et al., 1985; Feuerstein et al., 1993; Christian, 2000). Early intervention by the physician and rehabilitation counselor at the time of injury can facilitate a positive attitude and empower the worker to resist the negative effect of a system which discourages early return to work (Mundy, Moore, Corey, & Mundy, 1994). For instance, the current Social Security disability system discourages potentially disabled workers from even attempting rehabilitation. To be eligible for disability benefits, a claimant must prove that he or she is unable to engage in any substantial gainful employment because of a medical impairment that is anticipated to continue for at least 12 months (Yelin, 1989). On the other hand, to be eligible for rehabilitation, the claimant must demonstrate both the potential for work and that rehabilitation would be beneficial. Physicians should discourage patients from prolonging disability beyond medical necessity, as this has been shown to have negative impact on the patient's total health. Patients with extended disability often become depressed, show decreased motivation, and their medical outcomes are usually worse than patients who are placed into early return to work programs (Zeppieri, 1999). Additionally, the individual who has chronic pain suffers less when his or her life has purpose and meaning. Gainful employment frequently serves as a distraction from pain (Dent, 1985). Individuals with legitimate painful injuries should be appropriately compensated for pain and suffering, but an alternative to the current reimbursement system is needed. The compensation and disability system must be changed so that it encourages early intervention, prevention of chronicity with incentives towards rehabilitation, and early return to work.

Specific steps for the physician to help patients avoid work-related disability include the following (Florence, 1979):

1. Do not commit to a diagnosis that the injury is work-related without reasonable certainty.
2. Do evaluate the physical and emotional components of each patient individually.
3. Do inform the patient of the diagnosis with care.
4. Do put reasonable limits on rest and physical therapy.
5. Do avoid addictive medications.
6. Do treat physical problems with reasonable and structured activities, giving plenty of reassurance and encouragement.
7. Do encourage early return to safe work when reasonable.
8. Do take a positive role in getting the patient back to work and use rehabilitation specialists and/or case managers.
9. Do intercept the patient on the way to permanent compensation—do not exploit the system.

10. Do remember that emotional illness cannot be cured by surgery and often can be made worse.
11. Do support legislative changes to reward the injured worker for getting well and back on the job—rather than the current system which encourages disability.
12. Continue to be the patient's advocate.

STEPS FOR THE EMPLOYER

With the total cost of disability running as high as 10 to 15 percent of payroll in some organizations employers should be very interested in controlling these costs. However, employers often view these costs as part of doing business. It is surprising how many employers have little or no real process for dealing with disability management. Even those that do, often place most of the responsibility in the hands of one or two people on the corporate staff. In order for return-to-work processes to be effective the responsibility must permeate the organization. Some specific steps for employers to help employees avoid work-related disability include:

1. Do maintain active and effective safety processes that keep injuries and illnesses from occurring.
2. Do not wait until an injury or illness occurs to discuss your return-to-work policies and procedures with employees, supervisors, and managers.
3. Do empower employees before an injury or illness occurs to deal with issues important to them. Empowering them before disability reduces the attractiveness of using the disability system to work out issues that have nothing to do with disability.
4. Do communicate job demands clearly and concisely to the medical providers involved in managing disability claims. This can be accomplished in a variety of ways including job descriptions, videotape, oral statements, and physician tours of your facility.
5. Do report claims promptly and completely to required parties that could include the safety department, human resources department, medical department and others.
6. Do thorough investigations of reported claims and make changes to keep additional disability from occurring.
7. Do accept an employee at the work site who is less than fully recovered from injury.
8. Do be creative and flexible when matching job tasks to the identified capabilities of your employee.
9. Do use ergonomists, case managers, and other professionals to develop modified work that meets employee capability.
10. Do communicate with all involved at least once per week.

UNDERSTANDING THE INJURED WORKER

Return to work is only one part of injury and restoration of function. The injured worker must move through five steps from injury to resolution. These steps are:

1. Injury and its relationship to the workplace
2. Diagnosis and treatment
3. Off work and return to work
4. Impairment and disability
5. Settlement and resolution

1. *Injury and its relationship to the workplace.* The injury or illness is the event that triggers the workers compensation claim. Injuries are easy to understand. The individual usually has a cut, break, or strain. The relationship to the workplace is easy to understand with a specific event, a specific injury, and a specific diagnosis. Illnesses for this article are limited to musculoskeletal disorders. Examples include tendonitis, nerve entrapments, and musculoskeletal pain or musculoskeletal disorders sometimes called cumulative trauma disorders. With the longer onset of symptoms and lack of a specific event, it is sometimes difficult to demonstrate the work-relatedness. Physicians are often asked to determine work-relatedness. This requires an understanding of the symptoms (what hurts), the signs (the clinical examination), support tests (like nerve conduction studies or x-rays), the diagnosis, and the natural disease process based on the diagnosis. This opinion is often given to a reasonable degree of medical probability (likely to occur 51 percent of the time), which is a legal rather than medical definition of probability.

2. *Diagnosis and treatment.* The diagnosis is based on collecting the information for symptoms, signs, and tests, which are analyzed for a conclusion. The diagnosis may be easy or difficult depending on the information available and the physician's experience and skills. Treatment is traditionally based on the diagnosis. For example, a simple fractured wrist is treated with a cast because medical outcome studies have demonstrated a reasonable outcome with casting. Treatment protocol or guides have been developed for many diagnoses. When a specific diagnosis is not available, the treatment becomes less specific and less effective.

3. *Off work and return to work.* The ability to return to work is dependent on the injury, the individual, the physician, the employer, and the support services. Each may have a different agenda with different goals. The benefits and predictive factors will be discussed.

4. *Impairment and disability.* Impairment and disability have been previously defined. Determining the percentage of impairment and understanding how this converts into disability for the individual are required before settlement and resolution can occur.

5. *Settlement and resolution.* After injury, diagnosis, treatment, and return to work, the physician is often asked to provide the impairment, which is converted to a disability by the legal system to offer a settlement and provide for resolution of the process. This step often is the most frustrating for the individual worker who often is unfamiliar with the medical terms, legal processes, and the concept of a cash settlement for their injury rather than a return to their pre-injury state.

THE BENEFITS OF RETURN TO WORK

Within the current workers' compensation system, the physician can improve the quality of life for the injured worker through medical care, return to work, and prevention. Early return to work can result in a win-win situation for everyone. Employers, patients, lawyers, and the courts often assume that time away from work after an illness or injury is necessary. They typically remain unquestioning as long as a doctor makes a medical diagnosis or verifies that there is ongoing treatment. But they neglect to inquire whether the patient is actually unable to do any productive work safely. Lost workdays can be medically necessary or medically unnecessary. Certain injuries/illnesses will require that the employee/patient be off work. Other injuries/illnesses may allow the employee/patient back to work with restrictions, accommodations, or modifications. These lost workdays would be considered medically necessary days. Lost workdays because of poor or slow communication between the physician and the employer, inadequate information, litigation over benefits, disputes over other matters, lack of cooperation by any party, administrative delays, or lack of desire on the part of the individual/employee are medically unnecessary.

Unnecessary lost workdays mean lost dollars in workers' compensation and benefits. The national average lost time claim costs more than \$19,000 in medical and indemnity payments, compared with the average medical-only claim that costs less than \$400 (Macher, 1998). Christian (2000) surveyed occupational health physicians on their clinical experience regarding medically necessary days off work after injury. The majority said that less than 10% of the employees/patients would require a few days off work. Almost half the doctors surveyed place the percentage at 5 percent. The actual national average is 24 percent. Using this range of 5 to 10% would suggest that 60 to 80 percent of the lost workdays involve medically unnecessary time off from work. More than two-thirds of the physicians surveyed gave the following reasons for the medically unnecessary time off work: the treating physician is unwilling to force a reluctant patient back to work (the most common reason cited), the treating physician is not equipped to determine the right restriction and limitations on work activity, the employer has a policy against light-duty work, the employer can't find a way to temporarily modify a job, the treating physician feels caught between the employer's and the employee's version of events, the treating physician has been given too little information about the physical demands of the job to issue a work release for the patient, and a conflict exists between the opinions of two physicians.

RETURN TO WORK

Who is able to return to work depends as much on the injury as it does on the individual employee and the employer. Job satisfaction is the foremost factor correlating with an early return to work (Bigos et al., 1992; Fordyce, Bigos, Battie, & Fisher, 1992). Persons with high levels of discretion are more than two times as likely to be working as those with less autonomy. Those with high demands and little autonomy to deal with them are far less likely to return to work after a disabling injury. An unpleasant and stressful work environment will greatly reduce the probability for return to work. The individual employer has the greatest opportunity to reduce losses in the workers' compensation system and to return the injured employee to work. A single supportive phone call from the employer to the injured worker would be a strong force in motivating the patient to return to work especially if the patient is experiencing depression or has a need for emotional support. Unfortunately, some employers respond angrily to the injured worker and refuse to file an initial report of injury. Thus, not even the insurer has the opportunity to deal with the injured worker. Occasionally, the employer is simply happy to be rid of the injured worker and does as little as possible to promote his or her return to work. Considering the prevalence of psychiatric co-morbidity, it is possible to understand that attitude. Depressed, anxious, or substance abusing people do not make the most desirable and productive employees. Unions with rigid seniority policies may assign the easier jobs to workers with more seniority instead of to those with limited abilities. This practice also hampers return to work efforts. Unions with strict rules prohibiting a worker from crossing trades can also hinder return to work. The physician must be actively involved in addressing these issues to facilitate the transitional work, which requires a partnership between the patient, the family, the healthcare provider, the employer, and the insurer. The overriding objective is a safe, speedy return to work with the interests of the patient being the primary responsibility.

Early identification and early intervention is most successful and helpful in returning the injured worker to the workplace. A treating physician can look for and respond to the Five D's as described by Brena and Chapman (as cited in Black & Martin, 1988):

1. Dramatization (vague, diffused non-anatomical pain complaints)
2. Drugs (misuse of habit-forming pain medications)
3. Dysfunction (bodily impairment related to various physical and emotional factors)
4. Dependency (passivity, depression, and helplessness)
5. Disability (pain contingent on financial compensation and pending litigation claims)

Appropriate work guidelines require an understanding of the injury, the patient, and the job. Fortunately, physicians can make a fair estimate of the time required for healing based on empiric knowledge of specific injuries. The patient needs to be an active participant in the return to work guides, but they should not decide them. Patients possess unique knowledge of their job and their ability to perform their job. However, they sometimes overstate them and thus all employee statements of occupational requirement should be checked against other sources such as employer statements, first hand knowledge and job descriptions.

The physician must blend the patient's information with the employer's information. The National Institute for Occupational Safety and Health (NIOSH) and the Equal Employment Opportunities Commission (EEOC with regard to the ADA) has been encouraging employers to develop job descriptions that outline the essential functions of a job. Essential functions are that part of the job that must be performed and cannot be easily modified (American College of Occupational and Environment Medicine, 1997; Colledge, Johns, & Thomas, 1999; Equal Employment Opportunity Commission, 1989; Equal Employment Opportunity Commission, 1995). The U.S. Department of Labor has provided guides for work by weight. By combining these elements, safe and reasonable work guidelines can be provided that will allow the injured employee to return to the appropriate work while using the workplace as an integral part of the therapy program, thus providing for cost-effective rehabilitation. Physicians who treat work-related injuries realize that there is no easy table for developing work guidelines. The process is slow, time consuming, and often frustrating for both the patient and physician. The benefits to the employee/patient, employer and society are significant and worthy of the effort (Melhorn, 1996b).

EXAMPLES OF BENEFITS

In a study by Melhorn (1996b) of 109 employees, a new term, "work survivability," is suggested for measuring treatment outcomes for work-related injuries. The effects of continuation of employment (no lost workdays) and early return-to-work (no more than 15 lost workdays) on work survivability and treatment outcomes were reviewed. Work survivability did not increase the risk of recurrence of cumulative trauma disorders problems. This article provides strong evidence that continued employment or early return-to-work is the most important element of work survivability.

Taylor (cited in Mayer et al., 1986) reviewed the benefits of return to work, emphasized that many companies sponsor early return to work programs, and that the employees are better off financially than workers who choose other options, such as alternative vocational rehabilitation or job retraining.

Roehl (1998) reported that early return to work results in the happiest employees after a work injury. When work injuries occur, the employee's quality of life may quickly deteriorate. Their steady income may be interrupted resulting in financial and social changes. Family dynamics may become strained adding stress to the worker. Trying to maintain a modified work environment decreases the impact of these non-workplace issues for the injured employee.

Oleinick, Gluck, and Guire (1996) found, in a study of 8,628 Michigan workers with compensable back injuries, that after 8 weeks off work, the chances of returning the employee to gainful employment were very low and once financial support ended, significant quality of life issues developed for the injured worker. Gilbert, Kerley, Lowdermilk, and Panus (2000) found that individuals who returned to work earlier were usually more compliant with their medical treatment and usually had a better outcome with less impairment.

Shin and colleagues (2000) reviewed patients with occupational carpal tunnel syndrome, nerve conduction velocity studies, and a closed workers' compensation status. Early return to work and surgical release of the carpal tunnel was performed in 57% of patients while the other 43% were treated conservatively with continuation of work. Overall, 82% of patients returned to full work status, whereas 18% had duty modifications. Surgical treatment decreased the rate of duty modifications and disability ratings compared with non-surgical treatment and reduced the odds of incurring disability. Despite the generally held belief that the outcome of treatment of occupational carpal tunnel syndrome is poor, the present study shows that both surgical and non-surgical treatment is effective. However, patients treated with surgery had decreased disability when compared with those who were treated conservatively. Pransky et al. (as cited in Khan & Birch, 2000) found that individuals who remained employed had a greater reduction in symptom severity over time and were significantly more likely to report improvement in their problem than those who were unemployed.

Welch, Hunting, and Nessel-Stephens (1999) reported that acute musculoskeletal injuries in construction workers frequently resulted in chronic symptoms which have substantial effects on the worker's quality of life. Job accommodations were helpful, but difficult to do for construction work. They concluded that these findings point to the need for heightened efforts for injury prevention in this industry.

Guirguis (1999) examined the relationships between unemployment and the worker's mental, physical and social well being. When unemployment or being out of work is due to injury or sickness, the effects are compounded by mental and social factors. In an effort to prevent prolonged unemployment due to injury or sickness, changes were made to existing disability income supplement plans to redirect their focus from basic income support to active employment measures. This was intended to reduce individual dependency on financial assistance and encourage individuals to take personal responsibility for getting back to work. The various disability insurance plans require primary care physicians to provide opinions and participate in the recovery and safe return to work of injured or sick persons. The physician approach to medical care of the injured/sick person with employment problems should focus on return to work as a goal of treatment. The patient should be seen as part of a social or environmental system and not as an isolated individual. The physician has a significant role to play in the diagnosis, determining functional abilities and participation in the return to work plan. The physician positive participation, not only provides an intrinsic cost saving value in insurance costs, but more important, helps patients maintain gainful employment. Work often helps in regaining health.

Tan et al (1997) demonstrated that goal setting improved the individual's motivation and provided a more favorable opportunity for early return to work. Garcy, Mayer, and Gatchel (1996) found that work injured patients with chronic disabling spinal disorders who complete a tertiary functional restoration program are at relatively low risk for either a recurrent spinal disorder or new musculoskeletal injury claim (with or without disability) after returning to work. No major physical or psychological risk factors for recurrent injury could be identified in this large cohort. These findings argue powerfully against employer bias in not rehiring employees with previous chronic disabling spinal disorders or discriminating in pre- or re-employment on the basis of possible re-injury risk factors after an appropriate rehabilitation program.

PREDICTIVE FACTORS FOR RETURN TO WORK

Individual risk factors include: age, gender, and biopsychosocial variables (Melhorn, 1998f). The biopsychosocial components include: personality traits, psychological dysfunction (depression), coping ability, attitude toward life, attitude toward one's own health, overall poor health, lower socioeconomic status, lower intelligence, marital problems, living alone, financial problems, child rearing problems, interpersonal conflicts, job dissatisfaction, perceived administrative workplace stress, anatomical loss of function, attorney involvement, delayed intervention and return to work programs, depression, drinking, experiencing occupational mental stress, family members with disabilities, interpersonal conflict at home or work, legislative rules or requirements, less education, less motivated individuals, lower annual family incomes, marital status (widowed, separated, or divorced), multiple parts of the body involved, multiple workers' compensation status, not currently working, persistent pain, poor history of onset, psychological factors—"work caused my problem", receiving compensation, smoking, stress in daily activities, and unreasonable workplace guides (Hales & Bernard, 1996).

Hurrell and Murphy (1992) developed a model to help describe the complexity by which these factors interact. This model includes individual factors, job stressors, non-work factors, buffers, acute reactions and illness. Three mechanisms have been suggested to account for associations between psychosocial factors and musculoskeletal disorders (Bernard, Sauter, & Fine, 1993; Bongers, de Winter, Kompier, & Hildebrandt, 1993; Sauter & Swanson, 1995; Ursin, Edresen, & Ursin, 1988):

1. Psychosocial demands may overwhelm the individual's coping mechanism and produce a stress response. This stress response may increase muscle tension or static loading of muscles (Waersted, Bjorklund, & Westgaard, 1986; Waersted et al., 1986).
2. Biopsychosocial demands may affect musculoskeletal disorders awareness and reporting or increase its attribution to the work environment (Melhorn, 1998b).
3. In some work situations, biopsychosocial demands may be highly correlated with increased physical demands. Therefore, any association between biopsychosocial factors and musculoskeletal disorders may actually reflect an association but not a cause between physical factors and musculoskeletal disorders (Hales et al., 1996).

Carmona et al. (1998) reported that among patients receiving workers' compensation, those exposed to higher levels of bending and twisting of their hands and wrists, women were slower to return to work after carpal tunnel release surgery. Likewise, Ahlgren and Hammarstrom (1999) found that men showed a higher level of return to work than women, although women were better educated.

Crook, Moldofsky, and Shannon (1998) concluded that the negative effect of psychological distress and functional disability on return to work rates must be considered in the design and delivery of rehabilitation programming for workers with musculoskeletal soft tissue injuries. The employers' provision of a modified job was particularly important in the prevention of continued disability. The rate of return to work for men was 1.5 times that for women, and 20% less for every 10-year increase in age. Controlling for sex and age, psychological distress and functional disability were associated with a slower rate of return to work. The rate of return to work for workers who were provided with modified jobs was 2 times higher than for those with no such accommodation in employment.

Gard and Sandberg (1998) reviewed motivation and return to work. The primary predictor of return to work was the injured workers' opinion whether they could do as much work as their colleagues, quantitatively and qualitatively. The relationship with their coworkers was central to the injured worker's self-confidence; of particular importance was feeling that their work was done in a manner satisfactory to themselves and acceptable to others. Everyday responsibility, feedback and support in daily work tasks were also important.

Murphy (1994) showed that the job-satisfaction scores of 107 work-injured employees were correlated with return to work status at 20 weeks post-injury. There was a slight tendency for the more satisfied employees to be back at work.

Filan (1996) found that compensation encouraged a slower return to work after surgery. The current compensation system could save millions of dollars each year by incorporating incentives to return to work without sacrificing good surgical results.

Muller (Muller, 1992) reported that injured workers who were young and had a high level of education were more likely to attempt return to work while those with a high Social Security benefit were less likely to make a return to work attempt.

Lawrence, Doll, and McWhinnie (1996) found that time back to normal activity postoperatively is influenced by a number of factors unrelated to health status and is an unreliable proxy for it. Time to normal is therefore, not a good outcome measure for quantifying the benefits of surgical interventions.

Burdorf, Naaktgeboren, and Post (1998) reported that workers with complaints of the neck or shoulder and upper extremities in the previous 12 months before an injury are more likely to be off work or more difficult to return to work after a work related injury.

JOB RISK FACTORS

Workplace or employer risk factors can be placed into three broad categories:

1. Job or task demands,
2. Organizational structure,
3. Physical work environment, as seen in Table 3.

As discussed above, the individual risk factors become contributors, moderators, and buffers as to how the workplace may affect the individual's likelihood for early return to work.

1. Job or Task Demands

The job or task demands may have physical stressors. Physical stressors are described as:

- Repetitive movements,
- Forceful exertions,
- Awkward postures,
- Static muscle loads,
- Cold temperatures,
- Local or segmental vibration,
- Occupational stress, and
- Combinations of above.

For each of these factors one must consider both the amplitude and duration of the exposure. This list has been developed from epidemiological associations (Hales et al., 1996). Most epidemiological studies sample working populations with the focus often restricted to repetitive and high physical loads, certain wrist and hand postures, and vibration associated with work tasks. Non-occupational (non-work environment) physical factors (those associated with sports, hobbies, activities of daily living, and previous traumas) are potential confounders that have not been thoroughly investigated. The effects of inactivity have not been addressed. Some older studies suggest unaccustomed work to be a major etiologic factor for tendon disorders but the magnitude of this risk has not been evaluated in recent studies. The recognition of physical load factors has remained mostly at a qualitative level with little information on the exposure-effect relationship. One notable exception to this is the NIOSH lifting guide that was originally published in 1981 and then updated in 1991. This guide requires the user to collect workplace measurements (i.e. vertical distance to load, horizontal distance to load and frequency of lift) that are then placed into calculations to quantifiably determine the acceptable load to lift, given the measurements that formed the input. These epidemiological studies that have put an emphasis on the assessment of physical workloads often have not included psychosocial factors or vice versa. As a result of these experimental designs, not much has been determined about the role of physical versus psychosocial factors for different outcomes. Pending prospective medical evidence, there appears to be a relationship between certain jobs and certain job characteristics that include frequent repetitions, high forces, awkward postures, vibration, and cold. Although control measures may be costly, they can be cost-effective if they reduce disability and increase productivity (Webster & Snook, 1994). The non-work environment could include similar activities and, therefore, should also be modified for each individual.

The choices that employees make in how they use their body (body mechanics) can be directly related to job demands, but are determined by the individual. For example, it is possible for an employer to supply chairs that have many ergonomic features that have the potential to reduce the job demands. However, the individual operator's use of those features ultimately determines whether the demands are in fact reduced. Changing employee behavior as a group can be a daunting task. There is a much higher likelihood of success in changing the individual behavior of an injured worker since pain can serve as a great motivator and the behavior that needs to be modified is usually very specific.

2. Organizational Structure

The process of manufacturing is a blending of the input (raw materials) by the processing system into the output (finished product) using the people, materials, methods, machines, and environment. The people factor has been the most difficult to evaluate and quantify. In recent years the people factor has received increasing focus. The Accredited Standards Committee (ASC) Z365 and NIOSH have included work organization (biosocial) factors in their lists of work-related risk factors. In particular work organization factors that are thought to contribute include machine paced work, incentive pay, electronic monitoring of employees, lack of control, and monotonous work. The subject of biosocial issues is further clouded by discussions that focus on non-work issues such as the demands arising from roles outside of work (i.e. parent, spouse, or children) and individual worker factors such as genetic factors (i.e. gender and intelligence), acquired aspects (i.e. social class, culture, educational status), and disposition factors (i.e. personality traits, and characteristics and attitudes such as life and job satisfaction).

This lack of specific information regarding the functional limits of the human body, dose relationships to development of musculoskeletal pain, or individual tolerance thresholds has hampered the employer's ability to design and implement safety programs. Industry is directed by OSHA Guides and the Americans with Disabilities Act (ADA) to establish occupational programs that should include prevention, identification of risk, education, monitoring, medical management, and modification of the workplace (Anfield, 1992). Prevention is now possible by identifying individuals at increased risk by using a risk assessment instrument. Risk assessment instruments currently being used include questionnaires, limited physical measurements, and supporting nerve function studies (Melhorn, 1996c). For example, the CtdMAP™ meets the requirements of a disease-specific instrument for MSD and has been previously validated (Melhorn, 1996c; Melhorn, 1996a; Melhorn et al., 1996; Melhorn, 2002; Melhorn, 1997a; Melhorn, 1997b; Melhorn, 1997c; Melhorn, 1998a; Melhorn, 1998c; Melhorn, 1998g; Melhorn, Wilkinson, Gardner, Horst, & Silkey, 1999). This instrument contains 89 questions and 38 physical measurements and takes approximately 30 minutes to complete. The individual risk range is 1 to 7, where 4 is the average, 1, 2, 3 are below average and 5, 6, 7 indicate above average risk. Through awareness of individual and job risk potential, both the employer and the individual can then institute proven programs to change the individuals' risk level which could include education about cumulative trauma disorders and musculoskeletal disorders (CTD/MSD), education about the workplace, education about ergonomic use of the extremities, and exercise programs.

A 2001 National Academy of Sciences report on musculoskeletal disorders and the workplace concluded that scientific evidence showed musculoskeletal disorders can be reduced with well-designed intervention programs. This conclusion was made with the understanding that the connection between the workplace and these disorders is complex, partly because of the individual characteristics of workers, such as age, gender, and lifestyle (Barondess et al., 2001). To be most effective, the procedures thought to be the most reliable preventives should be implemented earlier rather than later in the continuum for musculoskeletal pain (Melhorn & Barr, Jr., 2001). Examples of successful programs include: a 1991 study for a major American bakery (Rystrom & Eversman, Jr., 1991), a 1992 Johns Hopkins Hospital program (Bernacki, Guidera, Schaefer, Lavin, & Tsai, 1999), a 1995 meatpacking plant project (Genaidy, Delgado, & Bustos, 1995), a 1996 prospective study with aircraft employees (Melhorn, 1996a), a 1996 prospective study with manufacturer of plastic products (Melhorn et al., 1996), a 1997 prospective study with aircraft employees (Melhorn, 1997a), a 1998 prospective study for new employees post-hire and preplacement (Pransky & Long, 1998), a 1998 California county government study on ergonomic improvements (Anderson, 1998), a 1999 prospective study with aircraft employees by integrating a traditional occupational medicine clinic (physician on site) and a risk assessment instrument (Melhorn et al., 1999), a 1999 medical center early return-to-work policy (Nassau, 1999), a 1999 employee pre-placement assessments study (Nachreiner et al., 1999), a 2000 study on case-by-case costs associated with cumulative trauma disorders (Vaughn-Miller, 2000), a 2001 study on aircraft employees for medical intervention (Melhorn, Wilkinson, & Riggs, 2001), a 2001 study using a self-rating assessment of physical capacities compared with matched physical performance (Klipstein, Huwiler, & Widmer, 2001), a 2001 study on workplace organizational factors and job risk (Shannon, Robson, & Sale, 2001), a 2001 study which reviewed medical treatment of current employees and found that traditional medical treatment of musculoskeletal disorders could be enhanced by using a risk assessment instrument (Melhorn, Wilkinson, & O'Malley, 2001), and a 2002 study evaluating the effectiveness of a consultative workplace risk assessment team in reducing the rate and severity of injury among cleaners, (Carrivick, Lee, & Yau, 2002).

3. Physical Work Environment

The physical work environment results from capital investment in equipment and buildings. From a retrofit standpoint this can be difficult to improve due to financial and technological constraints. However, professional ergonomists routinely assist employers in developing options for improving the fit between workers and their work. These options for improvement are usually geared towards groups of employees that perform a similar task. However, in ADA and return-to-work cases the ergonomist will usually focus modifications on the individual limitations of the person involved. This is often called an accommodations assessment. An understanding of the impact of methods, materials, and people can allow for the changes to be made at the time of retooling or building a new facility. This is usually the most cost efficient way to make changes to the environment.

SUMMARY

Preventing disability and musculoskeletal pain is challenging. Physicians cannot prove or disprove the existence of pain clinically. A person complaining of work-related musculoskeletal pain may or may not have nociception, suffering, pain behavior, impairment, or disability. When diagnostic evaluations have ruled out treatable nociception and when impairment has been addressed, targets for intervention include the suffering component (emotional distress), pain behaviors, and disability issues. With traumatic injuries occurring at a rate of 7.1 per 100 equivalent full-time employees in the private business sector at an estimated cost of over $1.25 trillion, there is a need for better disability management. Since work related injuries require complex decision making and require the physicians to draw upon their understanding of basic medical and surgical principles, their experiences, and their familiarity with the literature to formulate a reasonable diagnosis and an appropriate treatment plan, reasonable return to work guides can be challenging. Secondary gains and biopsychosocial issues can intentionally or unintentionally impact the outcome of treatment and the length or severity of the disability.

However, for early return to work to be successful and to reduce unnecessary work disability, a partnership between the patient, family, healthcare provider, employer, and insurer is required (Melhorn, 2000). Communication and education are key issues. The workplace guides must be safe and allow for a speedy return to work with the interests of the patient being the primary responsibility. Early return to work has been demonstrated to be in the patient's best interest (Melhorn, 1996b; Cook et al., 1995; Melhorn et al., 1996; Melhorn, 1997a; Melhorn, 1997b; Melhorn, 1997c; Ballard et al., 1986; Bruce et al., 1996; Burke et al., 1994; Centineo, 1986; Day et al., 1993; Devlin et al., 1994; Gice et al., 1988; Goodman, 1989; Groves et al., 1993; Grunet et al., 1992; Kasdan et al., 1993; Nathan et al., 1993). Examples of these benefits include: better self image (Bernacki et al., 1996), improved ability to cope (Bigos et al., 1986), improved work survivability (Melhorn, 1996b), and improved ability to be self sufficient (Burke et al., 1994). These benefits result in a win-win for employee and employer (Devlin et al., 1994; Bruce et al., 1996; Dworkin et al., 1985; Hall et al., 1994).

Conversely, prolonged time away from work makes recovery and return to work progressively less likely (Strang, 1985). In today's environment where outcomes are important and economics matter greatly, the physician is in a unique position to provide better management of work-related injuries. However, this management does not occur in a vacuum. The employer, case manager, human resources department, and other specialists play important roles. Improved outcomes are possible when the physician treats the whole patient. This whole patient approach requires an understanding of the factors that contribute to the poorer outcomes, medical treatment plans that include options to address the biopsychosocial issues, and early return to work guides. These inclusive medical treatment plans aid in the patient's recovery and rehabilitation while avoiding many of the pitfalls of the workers' compensation system. This approach requires a team effort on the part of the patient, physician, employer, insurer, and government, but the benefits are significant and well worth the additional effort.

REFERENCES

Ahlgren, C. & Hammarstrom, A. (1999). Has increased focus on vocational rehabilitation led to an increase in young employees' return to work after work-related disorders? *Scand J Public Health, 27,* 220–227.

American Medical Association (2000). Philosophy, Purpose, and Appropriate Use of the *Guides.* In L.Cocchiarella & G. B. J. Andersson (Eds.), *Guides to the Evaluation of Permanent Impairment* (5th ed., pp. 1–16). Chicago, IL: American Medical Press.

American College of Occupational and Environmental Medicine (1997). ACOEM's eight best ideas for workers' compensation reform. *American College of Occupational and Environment Medicine Conference, 4,* 4.

Anderson, D. (1998). RSI can strain the bottom line. *Business Health, 16,* 44–45.

Anfield, R. N. (1992). Americans with Disabilities Act of 1990 a primer of title I provisions for occupational health care professionals. *J Occup Environ Med, 34,* 503–517.

Ballard, M., Baxter, P., Bruening, L., & Fried, S. (1986). Work therapy and return to work. *Hand Clin, 2,* 247–258.

Barondess, J. A., Cullen, M. R., de Lateur, B. J., Deyo, R. A., Donaldson, K. S., & Drury, C. G. (2001). *Musculoskeletal disorders and the workplace: Low back and upper extremities.* Washington, DC: National Academy of Sciences.

Barsky, A. J. & Borus, J. F. (1995). Somatization and medicalization in the era of managed care. *JAMA, 274,* 1931–1934.

Bernacki, E. J., Guidera, J. A., Schaefer, J. A., Lavin, R. A., & Tsai, S. P. (1999). An ergonomics program designed to reduce the incidence of upper extremity work related musculoskeletal disorders. *J Occup Environ Med, 41,* 1032–1041.

Bernacki, E. J. & Tsai, S. P. (1996). Managed care for workers' compensation: Three years of experience in an "employee choice" state. *J Occup Environ Med, 38,* 1091–1097.

Bernard, B. P., Sauter, S. I., & Fine, L. J. (1993). Hazard evaluation and technical assistance report: Los Angeles Times, Los Angeles, CA. *NIOSH, Report No. HHE 90-013-2277.*

Bigos, S. J., Battie, M. C., Spengler, D. M., Fisher, L. D., Fordyce, W. E., Hansson, T. et al. (1992). A longitudinal, prospective study of industrial back injury reporting. *Clin Orthop, 279,* 21–34.

Bigos, S. J., Spengler, D. M., Martin, N. A., Zeh, J., Fisher, L. D., & Nachemson, A. L. (1986). Back injuries in industry: A retrospective study. III. Employee related factors. *Spine, 11,* 252–256.

Black, J. L. & Martin, M. J. (1988). Musculoskeletal symptoms and anxiety disorders. When do aches signal a treatable psychiatric problem? *J Musculoskeletal Med, 9,* 97–84.

Bongers, P. M., de Winter, C. R., Kompier, M. A. J., & Hildebrandt, V. H. (1993). Psychosocial factors at work and musculoskeletal disease. *Scand J Work Environ Health, 19*, 297–312.
Brady, W., Bass, J., Royce, M., Anstadt, G., Loeppke, R., & Leopold, R. (1997). Defining total corporate health and safety costs: Significance and impact. *J Occup Environ Med, 39*, 224–231.
Bruce, W. C. & Bruce, R. S. (1996). Return-to-work programs in the unionized company. *J Workers Compensation, 38*, 9–17.
Burdorf, A., Naaktgeboren, B., & Post, W. (1998). Prognostic factors for musculoskeletal sickness absence and return to work among welders and metal workers. *J Occup Environ Med, 55*, 490–495.
Burke, S. A., Harms-Constas, C. K., & Aden, P. S. (1994). Return to work/work retention outcomes of a functional restoration program: A multi-center, prospective study with a comparison group. *Spine, 19*, 1880–1885.
Butler, R. J. (1996). Increasing claims for soft tissue injuries in workers' compensation, cost shifting and moral hazard. *J Risk Uncertainty, 12*, 379–393.
Carmona, L., Faucett, J., Blanc, P. D., & Yelin, E. (1998). Predictors of rate of return to work after surgery for carpal tunnel syndrome. *Arthritis Care Res, 11*, 298–305.
Carrivick, P. J. W., Lee, A. H., & Yau, K. K. W. (2002). Effectiveness of a workplace risk assessment team in reducing the rate, cost, and duration of occupational injury. *J Occup Environ Med, 44*, 155–159.
Centineo, J. (1986). Return-to-work programs: cut costs and employee turnover. *Risk Management, 33*, 44–48.
Christian, J. (2000). Reducing disability days: healing more than the injury. *J Workers Compensation, 9*, 30–55.
Colledge, A. L., Johns, Jr. R. E., & Thomas, M. H. (1999). Functional ability assessment: Guidelines for the workplace. *J Occup Environ Med, 41*, 172–180.
Cook, A. C., Birkholz, S., King, E. F., & Szabo, R. M. (1995). Early mobilization following carpal tunnel release. A prospective randomized study. *J Hand Surg, 20B*, 228–230.
Crook, J., Moldofsky, H., & Shannon, H. (1998). Determinants of disability after a work related musculoskeletal injury. *J Rheumatol, 25*, 1570–1577.
Day, C. S., McCabe, S. J., & Alexander, G. (1993). Return to Work as an Outcome Measure in Hand Surgery. In *Presented at the Annual Meeting* (pp. 28–29). American Society for Surgery of the Hand, Baltimore.
Demeter, S. L., Andersson, G. B. J., & Smith, G. M. (2001). *Disability Evaluation*. St. Louis, MO: Mosby.
Dent, G. L. (1985). Curing the disabling effects of employee injury. *Risk Management, 1*, 30–31.
Derebery, V. J. & Tullis, W. H. (1983). Delayed recovery in the patient with a work compensable injury. *J Occup Environ Med, 25*, 829–835.
Devlin, M., O'Neill, P., & MacBride, R. (1994). Position paper in support of timely return to work programs and the role of the primary care physician. *Ont Med Assoc, 61*, 1–45.
Dworkin, R. H., Handlin, D. S., Richlin, D. M., Rrand, L., & Vannucci, C. (1985). Unraveling the effects of compensation, litigation, and employment on treatment response in chronic pain. *Pain, 23*, 49–59.
Equal Employment Opportunity Commission (1989). *Job advertising and pre-employment inquiries under the age discrimination in employment act.* (vols. N-915.043) Washington, DC: United States Government Printing Office.
Equal Employment Opportunity Commission (1995). Equal Employment Opportunity Commission issues final enforcement guidance on preemployment disability-related questions and medical examinations under the Americans with Disabilities Act. *Equal Employement Opportunity Commission News, 95*, 1–5.
Feuerstein, M., Callan-Harris, S., Hickey, P., Dyer, D., Armbruster, W., & Carosella, A. M. (1993). Multidisciplinary rehabilitation of chronic work-related upper extremity disorders: long-term effects. *J Occup Environ Med, 35*, 396–403.
Filan, S. L. (1996). The effect of workers' or third-party compensation on return to work after hand surgery. *Med J Aust, 165*, 80–82.
Florence, D. W. (1979). Diary of a work-related disability. *Legal Aspects of Medical Practice, 8*, 5–10.
Fordyce, W. E., Bigos, S. J., Battie, M. C., & Fisher, L. D. (1992). MMPI Scale 3 as a predictor of back injury report: what does it tell us? *Clin J Pain, 8*, 222–226.
Garcy, P., Mayer, T. G., & Gatchel, R. J. (1996). Recurrent or new injury outcomes after return to work in chronic disabling spinal disorders. Tertiary prevention efficacy of functional restoration treatment. *Spine, 21*, 952–959.

Gard, G. & Sandberg, A. C. (1998). Motivating factors for return to work. *Physiother Res Int, 3,* 100–108.

Genaidy, A. M., Delgado, E., & Bustos, T. (1995). Active microbreak effects on musculoskeletal comfort ratings in meatpacking plants. *Ergonomics, 38,* 326–336.

Gice, J. H. & Tompkins, K. (1988). Cutting costs with return-to-work programs. *Risk Management, 35,* 62–65.

Gilbert, S., Kerley, A., Lowdermilk, A., & Panus, P. C. (2000). Nontreatment variables affecting return-to-work in Tennessee-based employees with complaints of low back pain. *Tenn Med, 93,* 167–171.

Goodman, R. C. (1989). An aggressive return-to-work program in surgical treatment of carpal tunnel syndrome: A comparison of costs. *Plast Reconstr Surg, 89,* 715–717.

Groves, F. B. & Gallagher, L. A. (1993). What the hand surgeon should know about workers' compensation. *Hand Clin, 9,* 369–372.

Grunet, B. K., Devine, C. A., Smith, C. J., Matloub, H. S., Sanger, J. R., & Yousif, N. J. (1992). Graded work exposure to promote work return after severe hand trauma: A replicated study. *Ann Plast Surg, 29,* 532–536.

Guirguis, S. S. (1999). Unemployment and health: physicians' role. *Int Arch Occup Environ Health, 72 Suppl,* S10–S13.

Hales, T. R. & Bernard, B. P. (1996). Epidemiology of work-related musculoskeletal disorders. *Ortho Clinic N Am, 27,* 679–709.

Hall, H., McIntosh, G., Melles, T., Holowachuk, B., & Wai, E. (1994). Effect of discharge recommendations on outcome. *Spine, 19,* 2033–2037.

Hurrell, J. J. & Murphy, L. R. (1992). Psychological job stress. In W.N.Rom (Ed.), *Environmental and occupational medicine* (pp. 675–684). New York: Little, Brown and Company.

Kasdan, M. L. & June, L. A. (1993). Returning to work after a unilateral hand fracture. *J Occup Environ Med, 35,* 132–135.

Kasdan, M. L., Vender, M. I., Lewis, K., Stallings, S. P., & Melhorn, J. M. (1996). Carpal tunnel syndrome. Effects of litigation on utilization of health care and physician workload. *J Ky Med Assoc, 94,* 287–290.

Khan, R. & Birch, R. (2001). Iatropathic injuries of peripheral nerves. *J Hand Surg, 83B,* 1145–1148.

Klipstein, A., Huwiler, H. J., & Widmer, M. (2001). [Management of non-specific musculoskeletal disorders: Role of ergonomics]. *Ther Umsch, 58,* 515–520.

Lawrence, K., Doll, H., & McWhinnie, D. (1996). Relationship between health status and postoperative return to work. *J Public Health Med, 18,* 49–53.

Macher, A. (1998). *Annual Statistical Bulletin.* Noca Raton, FL: National Council on Compensation Insurance, Inc.

Mayer, T. G., Gatchel, R. J., Kishino, N. D., Keeley, J., Mayer, H., Capra, P. et al. (1986). A prospective short-term study of chronic low back pain patients utilizing novel objective functional measurement. *Pain, 25,* 53–68.

Melhorn, J. M. (1996a). A prospective study for upper-extremity cumulative trauma disorders of workers in aircraft manufacturing. *J Occup Environ Med, 38,* 1264–1271.

Melhorn, J. M. (1996b). CTD injuries: An outcome study for work survivability. *J Workers Compensation, 5,* 18–30.

Melhorn, J. M. (1996c). Cumulative trauma disorders: How to assess the risks. *J Workers Compensation, 5,* 19–33.

Melhorn, J. M. (1997a). CTD Solutions for the 90's: Prevention. In *Seventeenth Annual Workers' Compensation and Occupational Medicine Seminar* (17 ed., pp. 234–245). Boston, MA: Seak, Inc.

Melhorn, J. M. (1997b). Identification of Individuals at Risk for Developing CTD. In D.M.Spengler & J. P. Zeppieri (Eds.), *Workers' Compensation Case Management: A Multidisciplinary Perspective* (pp. 41–51). Rosemont, IL: American Academy of Orthopaedic Surgeons.

Melhorn, J. M. (1997c). Physician Support and Employer Options for Reducing Risk of CTD. In D.M.Spengler & J. P. Zeppieri (Eds.), *Workers' Compensation Case Management: A Multidisciplinary Perspective* (pp. 26–34). Rosemont, IL: American Academy of Orthopaedic Surgeons.

Melhorn, J. M. (1997d). Work Restrictions for Return to Work. In J. P. Zeppieri & D. M. Spengler (Eds.), *Workers' Compensation Case Management: A Multidisciplinary Perspective* (pp. 249–266). Rosemont, IL: American Academy of Orthopaedic Surgeons.

Melhorn, J. M. (1998a). Cumulative trauma disorders and repetitive strain injuries. The future. *Clin Orthop, 351,* 107–126.

Melhorn, J. M. (1998b). Pain responses in patients with upper-extremity disorders. [Letter]. *J Hand Surg, 23A,* 954–955.

Melhorn, J. M. (1998c). Prevention of CTD in the Workplace. In *Workers' Comp Update 1998* (pp. 101–124). Walnut Creek, CA: Council on Education in Management.

Melhorn, J. M. (1998d). Rediscovering occupational orthopaedics for the next millennium. *J Bone Joint Surg, 81A,* 587–591.

Melhorn, J. M. (1998e). The Future of Musculoskeletal Disorders (Cumulative Trauma Disorders and Repetitive Strain Injuries) in the Workplace - Application of an Intervention Model. In T.G.Mayer, R. J. Gatchel, & P. B. Polatin (Eds.), *Occupational Musculoskeletal Disorders Function, Outcomes, and Evidence* (pp. 353–367). Philadelphia, PA: Lippincott, Williams & Wilkins.

Melhorn, J. M. (1998f). Understanding the types of carpal tunnel syndrome. *J Workers Compensation, 7,* 52–73.

Melhorn, J. M. (1998g). Upper-extremity cumulative trauma disorders in workers in aircraft manufacturing [Letter, Response] Upper extremities cumulative trauma disorders. *J Occup Environ Med, 40,* 12–15.

Melhorn, J. M. (2000). Workers' compensation: Avoiding the work-related disability. *J Bone Joint Surg, 82A,* 1490–1493.

Melhorn, J. M. (2001). Workers' Compensation for Fractures and Dislocations. In J.D.Heckman & R. W. Bucholz (Eds.), *Rockwood and Green's Fractures In Adults* (5th ed., pp. 2247–2263). Philadelphia, PA: J B Lippincott Company.

Melhorn, J. M. (2002). CTD's: Assessment of Risk (Risk Assessment Applications in the Workplace). In J.Williams (Ed.), *Proceedings of McPherson College Science Symposium April 26–27, 1996* (pp. 161–166). McPherson, KS: McPherson College.

Melhorn, J. M. & Barr, J. S., Jr. (2001). *Occupational Orthopaedics and Workers' Compensation: A Multidisciplinary Perspective 2001.* (2001 ed.) Rosemont, IL: American Academy of Orthopaedic Surgeons.

Melhorn, J. M. & Wilkinson, L. K. (1996). *CTD Solutions for the 90's: A Comprehensive Guide to Managing CTD in the Workplace.* Wichita, KS: Via Christi Health Systems.

Melhorn, J. M., Wilkinson, L. K., Gardner, P., Horst, W. D., & Silkey, B. (1999). An outcomes study of an occupational medicine intervention program for the reduction of musculoskeletal disorders and cumulative trauma disorders in the workplace. *J Occup Environ Med, 41,* 833–846.

Melhorn, J. M., Wilkinson, L. K., & O'Malley, M. D. (2001). Successful management of musculoskeletal disorders. *J Hum Ecolog Risk Assessment, 7,* 1801–1810.

Melhorn, J. M., Wilkinson, L. K., & Riggs, J. D. (2001). Management of musculoskeletal pain in the workplace. *J Occup Environ Med, 43,* 83–93.

Muller, L. S. (1992). Disability beneficiaries who work and their experience under program work incentives. *Soc Secur Bull, 55,* 2–19.

Mundy, R. R., Moore, S. C., Corey, J. B., & Mundy, G. D. (1994). Disability syndrome: The effects of early vs delayed rehabilitation intervention. *American Association Occupational Health Nursing Journal, 42,* 379–383.

Murphy, G. C. (1994). Job satisfaction of and return to work by occupationally injured employees. *Psychol Rep, 75,* 1441–1442.

Nachreiner, N., McGovern, P., Kochevar, L. K., Lohman, W. H., Cato, C., & Ayers, E. (1999). Preplacement assessments: Impact on injury outcomes. *American Association Occupational Health Nursing Journal, 47,* 245–253.

Nassau, D. W. (1999). The effects of prework functional screening on lowering an employer's injury rate, medical costs, and lost work days. *Spine, 24,* 269–274.

Nathan, P. A., Meadows, K. D., & Keniston, R. C. (1993). Rehabilitation of carpal tunnel surgery patients using a short surgical incision and an early program of physical therapy. *J Hand Surg, 18A,* 1044–1050.

Oleinick, A., Gluck, J. V., & Guire, K. (1996). Factors affecting first return to work following a compensable occupational back injury. *Am J Ind Med, 30,* 540–555.

Pransky, G. S. & Long, R. (1998). Screening for carpal tunnel syndrome in the workplace. *J Occup Environ Med, 40,* 421–422.

Roehl, W. K. (1998). Return to work - clearing the liability and productivity hurdles that trip up even the most savvy employers. In *Workers' Comp Update 1998* (pp. 13–30). Walnut Creek, CA: Council on Education in Management.

Rystrom, C. M. & Eversman, W. W., Jr. (1991). Cumulative Trauma Intervention in Industry: A Model Program for the Upper Extremity. In M.L.Kasdan (Ed.), *Occupational Hand & Upper Extremity Injuries & Diseases* (pp. 489–506). Philadelphia: Hanley & Belfus, Inc.

Sauter, S. L. & Swanson, N. G. (1995). The relationship between workplace psychosocial factors and musculoskeletal disorders in office work: suggested mechanisms and evidence. In *Repetitive motion disorders of the upper extremity* (pp. 65–76). Rosemont, IL: American Academy of Orthopaedic Surgeons.

Shannon, H. S., Robson, L. S., & Sale, J. E. (2001). Creating safer and healthier workplaces: Role of organizational factors and job characteristics. *Am J Ind Med, 40,* 319–334.

Shin, A. Y., Perlman, M., Shin, P. A., & Garay, A. A. (2000). Disability outcomes in a worker's compensation population: surgical versus nonsurgical treatment of carpal tunnel syndrome. *Am J Orthop, 29,* 179–184.

Strang, J. P. (1985). The chronic disability syndrome. In G.M.Aronoff (Ed.), *Evaluation and Treatment of Chronic Pain* (pp. 247–258). Baltimore, MD: Urban & Schwarzenberg.

Tan, V., Cheatle, M. D., Mackin, S., Moberg, P. J., & Esterhai, J. L., Jr. (1997). Goal setting as a predictor of return to work in a population of chronic musculoskeletal pain patients. *Int J Neurosci, 92,* 161–170.

United States Bureau of Labor Statistics (1997). *Occupational Injuries and Illnesses: Counts, Rates, and Characteristics, 1994.* (April 1997 ed.) (vols. Bulletin 2485) Washington, DC: United States Government Printing Office.

United States Congress (1991). *Americans with Disabilities Act 42 USC 12101.* Washington, DC: United States Government Printing Office.

United States Department of Labor (1999). *Workplace injuries and illnesses in 1997.* (vols. USDL 98–494) Washington, DC: United States Government Printing Office.

Ursin, H., Edresen, I. M., & Ursin, G. (1988). Psychological factors and self-reports of muscle pain. *Eur J Appl Physiol, 57,* 282–290.

Vaughn-Miller, C. (2000). Put your money where your injuries are like your CTDs. *J Workers Compensation, 10,* 100–106.

Waersted, M., Bjorklund, R., & Westgaard, R. H. (1986). Generation of muscle tension related to a demand of continuing attention. In B.G.Knave & P. G. Wideback (Eds.), *Work With Display Units* (pp. 288–293). New York: Elsevier Science North-Holland.

Webster, B. S. & Snook, S. H. (1994). The cost of compensable upper extremity cumulative trauma disorders. *J Occup Environ Med, 7,* 713–718.

Welch, L. S., Hunting, K. L., & Nessel-Stephens, L. (1999). Chronic symptoms in construction workers treated for musculoskeletal injuries. *Am J Ind Med, 36,* 532–540.

Yelin, E. (1989). Displaced concern: the social context of the work disability problem. *Milbank Mem Fund Q, 67 (suppl 2, pt 1),* 114–166.

Zeppieri, J. P. (1999). The Physician, the Illness, and the Workers' Compensation System. In J.H.Beaty (Ed.), *Orthopaèdic Knowledge Update 6* (pp. 131–137). Rosemont, IL: American Academy of Orthopaedic Surgeons.

14

Predicting Disability from Headache

Jonathan Borkum

SCOPE OF THE PROBLEM

In over two dozen studies, disability from the main forms of headache has been quantified (see Table 1). Absenteeism from tension-type headache alone is the equivalent of 0.4 to 1.2 days per year for every person in the workforce (Pryse-Phillips, Findlay, Tugwell, Edmeads, Murray, & Nelson, 1992; Schwartz, Stewart, Simon, & Lipton, 1998). Migraines cause the average sufferer to lose approximately 4.6 workdays annually (e.g., Steiner, Scher, Stewart, Kolodner, Liberman, & Lipton, 2003; Von Korff, Stewart, Simon, & Lipton, 1998). With a 1-year migraine prevalence of about 10% in the United States and Europe (Rasmussen, 2001), this translates to 0.5 days per year of migraine-related absenteeism in the general population. Thus, we would expect all forms of headache together to produce at least the equivalent of 1 lost workday per year for every employed person. (The few studies so far of "headache" as a general category give a lower figure, about 0.6 lost workdays, but their results have been variable and preliminary.) If we include partial loss of productivity due to ineffectiveness while working with a headache, the number of lost workday equivalents would be approximately tripled.

The aggregate economic impact is significant, estimated at \$10–\$13 billion annually for migraine alone, primarily from indirect costs due to lost workplace productivity (Ferrari, 1998; Hu, Markson, Lipton, Stewart, & Berger, 1999). For all headaches, the estimate is twice as high, \$20–\$26 billion (Stewart, Ricci, Chee, Morganstein, & Lipton, 2003). And this assumes that we restrict our analysis to people who are, in fact, working. In severe headache, the unemployment rate may be four times higher than the regional average (20% vs. 5%, Von Korff, Ormel, Keefe, & Dworkin, 1992).

How do we account for such profound impact? We will take up this question below, when we consider the specific types of primary headache disorders. First, however, we will try to identify those at greatest risk for disability and reduced quality of life.

DOI: 10.1007/978-0-387-28919-9_14, © 2009 Springer Science+Business Media, LLC

TABLE 1. Disability Due to Headaches

Source (1st Authors, Date)	HA Type	Sample	N (% female)	Country	Retrospective vs. Prospective	Time Period[a]	Denominator[b]	Absent[c] (days/yr)	Red. Eff.[d]
Stewart, Ricci, 2003	Any	Popul.	28902 (56%)	United States	Retrospective	2 weeks	Gen. Popul.	0.226	1.013
Boardman, 2002	Any	Popul.	2662 (56%)	United Kingdom	Retrospective	3 months	Gen. Popul.	1.327	—
Schwartz, 1997	Any	Popul.	13343	United States	Retrospective	1 year	Gen. Popul.	0.777	1.732
Nikiforow, 1979	Any	Popul.	2018 (59%)	Finland	Retrospective	1 year	Gen. Popul.	0.086	—
Benassi, 1986	Any	Popul.	514 (37%)	San Marino	Retrospective	1 year	Gen. Popul.	0.658	—
Pop, 2002	Any	1 Employer	1082 (11%)	Netherlands	Retrospective	4 weeks	Employees	1.235	0.780
Von Korff, 1992	Any	Prim. Care	779	United States	Retrospective	6 months	HA Popul.	20.2[e]	—
Micieli, 1995	Any	HA Clinic	400 (67%)	Italy	Retrospective	8 weeks	HA Popul.	26.4	—
Lavados, 1998	TTH	Popul.	1385 (53%)	Chile	Retrospective	1 year	Gen. Popul.	0.106 m, 0.565 f	—
Schwartz, 1998	ETTH	Popul.	13,345	United States	Retrospective	1 year	Gen. Popul.	0.284	0.849
Schwartz, 1998	CTTH	Popul.	13,345	United States	Retrospective	1 year	Gen. Popul.	0.072	0.211
Rasmussen, 1992	TTH	Popul.	740 (48%)	Denmark	Retrospective	1 year	Gen. Popul.	0.820	—
Pryse-Phillips, 1992	TTH	Popul.	1573	Canada	Retrospective	Last HA	TTH Popul.	c. 1.21	—
Micieli, 1995	CTTH	HA Clinic	83 (70%)	Italy	Retrospective	8 weeks	CTTH Popul.	44.4	—
Steiner, 2003	Migraine	Popul.	4007 (63%)	England	Retrospective	1 year + global	Mig. Popul.	5.7	—
Stewart, Lipton, Whyte, 1999	Migraine	Popul.	97 (84%)	United States	Retrospective	3 months	Mig. Popul.	6.4	—

Stewart, Lipton, Whyte, 1999	Migraine	Popul.	100 (80%)	United Kingdom	Retrospective	3 months	Mig. Popul.	3.2	—
Stewart, Lipton, Simon, 1999	Migraine	Popul.	82	United States	Prospective	3 months	Mig. Popul.	3.6	6.4
Von Korff, 1998	Migraine	Popul.	212	United States	Prospective	3 month diary	Mig. Popul.	4.36	7.80
Schwartz, , 1997	Migraine	Popul.	13343	United States	Retrospective	4 weeks	Gen. Popul.	0.443	0.641
Lavados, 1997	Migraine	Popul.	1385 (53%)	Chile	Retrospective	1 year	Mig. Popul.	9.4 m, 9.7 f	—
Stewart, 1996	Migraine	Popul.	1663	United States	Retrospective	Selected by subj.	Mig. Popul.	7.441[f]	—
Stang, 1993	Migraine	Popul.	4800 migraineurs	United States	Retrospective	2 weeks	Mig. Popul.	4.075 bed rest	—
Pryse-Phillips, 1992	Migraine	Popul.	1573	Canada	Retrospective	Last HA	Mig. Popul.	c. 2.66	—
Rasmussen, 1992	Migraine	Popul.	740 (48%)	Denmark	Retrospective	1 year	Gen. Popul.	0.270	—
Green, 1977	Migraine	Popul.	14893 (67%)	England	Retrospective	?	Mig. Popul.	c. 4	—
Mushet, 1996	Migraine	1 Employer	59 migr. (98% f)	United States	Prospective	8–18 wks	Mig. Popul.	2.820	—
Osterhaus, 1992	Migraine	Prim. Care	501 (89%)	United States	Retrospective	1 month	Mig. Popul.	26.4	28.9
Lambert, 2002	Migraine	HA Clinics	134 (87%)	Canada	Retrospective	4 weeks	Mig. Popul.	6.5	10.4
Gerth, 2001	Migraine	HA Clinics	2670 (82%)	25 Countries	Retrospective	4 weeks	Mig. Popul.	8.32	11.23
Laloux, 1998	Migraine	HA Clinics	89 (87%)	Belgium	Prospective	3 months	Mig. Popul.	3.91	3.68
Cortelli, 1997	Migraine	HA Clinics	298 (75%)	5 Countries	Retrospective	3 months	Mig. Popul.	10.0	—

Note. CTTH = Chronic tension-type headache; ETTH = Episodic tension-type headache; Gen. Popul. = General population; HA = Headache; Mig. Popul. = Migraine population; TTH = Tension-type headache.

[a] For retrospective studies, the recall interval; for prospective studies, the period of diary data collection

[b] Whether lost workdays are reported per person in the general population, per worker at a given company, or per person with a particular headache disorder

[c] Days of work absenteeism, per person per year

[d] In lost workday equivalents, per person per year (e.g., 1/2 day worked at 50% effectiveness counts as 1/4 lost workday equivalent)

[e] Includes absenteeism from school or housework

[f] Includes unpaid work

General Predictors

Disability, once acquired, tends to persist. Thus, among primary care patients with at least a moderate level of headache-related disability at baseline, 80% were still disabled at one-year follow-up. In contrast, only 16% of headache patients with initially low disability proceeded to moderate or high levels over the year (Von Korff, et al., 1992). These results were corroborated in a prospective 3-year population study: 92% of patients who initially had moderate or high disability from headache remained disabled after 3 years. Only 12% of initially non-disabled subjects became disabled over the same interval (Von Korff, et al., 1992). Thus, there seems to be little movement between disability categories. Disability status has prognostic as well as descriptive value.

The relationship of headache frequency to *perceived* disability is uncertain. Some authors have found an association (e.g., Marcus, 2000), while others, using such global psychometrics as the Headache Disability Inventory (HDI), Migraine-Specific Quality of Life Questionnaire (MSQ), and the Life Interference scale of West Haven-Yale Multidimensional Pain Inventory, have found none (e.g., Jacobson, Ramadan, Aggarwal, & Newman, 1994; Magnusson & Becker, 2002, 2003; Martin, Pathak, Sharfman, Adelman, Taylor, Kwong, & Jhingran, 2000). When the measure is lost workdays, however, the association is clear: Chronic headaches (> 180 days/year) involve considerably more disruption than their less frequent analogues (e.g., Bigal, Rapoport, Lipton, Tepper, & Sheftell, 2003; Lantéri-Minet, Auray, El Hasnaoui, Dartigues, Duru, Henry, Lucas, Pradalier, Chazot, & Gaudin, 2003). This effect can be seen economically: Among members of a health maintenance organization, people reporting at least 90 headache days over the preceding 6 months had an unemployment rate of 18.7%, vs. 7.5% for those with 30 or fewer headache days (Stang, Von Korff, & Galer, 1998).

High pain intensity seems to be necessary but not sufficient for disability. It is exceptionally rare for people to miss work due to mild headaches. As pain increases beyond a rating of "5" on a 0–10 scale, the probability of absenteeism rises steadily (Stewart, Shechter, & Lipton, 1994). This suggests that even a partial reduction in pain could bring a marked improvement in functional capacity.

Nonetheless, among people with moderate or severe pain, functioning varies widely (Stewart, et al., 1994). We might expect such variability to correlate with other behavioral factors, and a study by Von Korff et al. suggests that it does. Specifically, among people with intense headaches, those who reported marked functional impairment were also more likely to have seen a doctor at least monthly for pain, to regard their health as poor, and to report pain-related interference in a number of daily activities. A slightly higher proportion of disabled than non-disabled persons had elevated scores on a depression scale as well (36% vs. 31%), but it was the illness perception and behavior that seemed most distinguishing (Von Korff, et al., 1992).

We might suspect that beneath these characteristics lies an external locus of control, a limited self-efficacy for coping with pain, or an illness focus, but these hypotheses have yet to be examined. It does appear that disability is better predicted by negative affect, whether as a psychological symptom (Trask, Iezzi, & Kreeft, 2001) or as a response to pain (Passchier, de Boo, Quaak, & Brienen, 1996) than by headache characteristics. The literature on headaches in general, however, will take us no further. To dig deeper, we must examine the specific, common forms of headache disorders.

Migraine

The one-year prevalence of migraine is about 6% in men and c. 15–18% in women (Rasmussen, 2001). African-Americans and Asian-Americans appear to be at lower risk than Caucasians (Stewart, Lipton, & Liberman, 1996). Prevalence peaks at ages 35–40, key years in the workforce (Stewart, Lipton, Celentano, & Reed, 1992).

By current diagnostic criteria, migraine pain has at least 2 of the following characteristics: moderate or severe intensity, pulsating quality, unilateral location, and aggravation by or causing avoidance of routine physical activities such as walking or climbing stairs. Attacks last for 4–72 hours untreated, and are accompanied by nausea, vomiting, and/or a painful aversion to both light and sound (Headache Classification Subcommittee, 2004). Indeed, so intense are migraines that during episodes, sufferers often score in the impaired range on a mental status exam (Meyer, Thornby, Crawford, & Rauch, 2000). Clearly, a person with migraines could have trouble functioning at work.

This realization is captured in methodology used by the World Health Organization to measure the disability burden imposed by various illnesses (Murray & Lopez, 1996). Focus groups comprised of health professionals drawn from 25 countries placed severe migraine episodes (during an attack) in the highest disability class, along with quadriplegia, active psychosis, and dementia (Murray & Lopez, 1997).

In the United States (although not in Canada or Europe), migraineurs have, on average, a lower socioeconomic status than people without the disorder (Breslau & Rasmussen, 2001). Although the direction of causality has not been established, the high unemployment rate seen for intense headaches supports the "downward drift" hypothesis, in which migraines disrupt one's career path (Stang, et al., 1998).

We have seen that migraineurs incur, on average, about 4.6 lost workdays per year. However, individuals vary considerably (Edmeads & Mackell, 2002), with 25% of migraine sufferers accounting for approximately 90% of the total lost work time (Stewart, Lipton, & Simon, 1996). The source of these differences is only now being subjected to examination.

Predictors

Cultural factors and/or differences in health care system may be relevant. For example, migraineurs in France seem to have lower levels of disability than those in the United States, both by self-report (Henry, Auray, Gaudin, Dartigues, Duru, Lantéri-Minet, Lucas, Pradalier, Chazot, & El Hasnaoui, 2002) and by work attendance records (Michel, Dartigues, Lindoulsi, & Henry, 1997).

Women with migraine generally report a higher rate of disability than men, which presumably reflects the greater duration, intensity, and number of associated symptoms (e.g., nausea) among female as compared with male migraineurs (Stewart, et al., 1994). Age has a weak, curvilinear relationship, with disability being slightly higher in middle adulthood, after correcting for headache characteristics (Stewart, Lipton, & Kolodner, 2003).

Of note, migraine need not be an isolated disorder. People with migraine have 3–6 times the risk of major depression (Breslau, Lipton, Stewart, Schultz, & Welch, 2003), up to 13 times the risk of panic disorder (Breslau & Davis, 1993), and higher levels of trait negative affect (Breslau, Chilcoat, & Andreski, 1996). So far, studies have not teased apart the effects of migraine itself vs. comorbidities on work functioning (Edmeads & Mackell, 2002). However, depression and migraine have independent effects on quality of life (Lipton, Hamelsky, Kolodner, Steiner, & Stewart, 2000) and hence, we may presume, on disability. Thus, to improve functioning, both the migraines and any accompanying psychological disorder would need to be addressed.

Similarly, the use of passive coping strategies ("retreating," "resting" and "worrying" on the Pain Coping Inventory) is associated with greater disability. Possibly, this could reflect a tendency to use passive coping specifically for the most severe pain. However, the effects of pain-related "worrying" on quality of life are partially independent of migraine intensity (Passchier, Mourik, McKenna, van den Berg, & Erdman, 2001). Presumably, "worrying" has similar direct effects on disability.

Lost productivity due to migraines correlates with headache intensity, frequency, and exacerbation by routine activity (Stewart, Lipton, & Kolodner, 2003). This implies that reducing migraine symptoms will improve functioning, and indeed data have been supportive (e.g., Cortelli, Dahlöf, Bouchard, Heywood, Jansen, Pham, Hirsch, Adams, & Miller, 1997; Wells & Steiner, 2000). Conversely, factors that predict a long-term increase in migraine frequency would augur increased disability as well. Thus, the risk factors for chronic daily headache are of considerable interest.

Chronic Daily Headache

For some migraineurs, the disorder seems to follow a "malignant" course, culminating in a continuous, treatment-refractory, highly disabling headache (Granella, Cavallini, Sandrini, Manzoni, & Nappi, 1998; Loder & Biondi, 2003). Such "transformed migraine" is a subtype of chronic daily headache, defined as headache at least 4 hours per day, for at least 15 days per month, over 2 months or more (Silberstein, Lipton, Solomon, & Mathew, 1994). Between 3% and 6% of the general population has chronic daily headache (Castillo, Munoz, Guitera, & Pascual, 1999; Pascual, Colás, & Castillo, 2001; Prencipe, Casini, Ferretti, et al., 2001; Scher, Stewart, Liberman, & Lipton, 1998).

In a population-based study in France, 18.5% of people with chronic daily headache, vs. 4.3% of people with episodic migraine, scored in the "severe disability" range on a measure of lost productivity time (Lantéri-Minet, et al., 2003). The excess disability was due specifically to people whose chronic daily headaches had migrainous features, suggesting that transformed migraine may have a particularly deleterious effect on functioning. Similar findings have been reported in large clinical samples (Bigal, et al., 2003; Meletiche, Lofland, & Young, 2001).

Predictors

Fortunately for prevention, the transformation from episodic to chronic headache usually takes place gradually, after over at least a year. Moreover, the risk of developing chronic daily headache over the course of a year is a positively accelerating function of baseline headache frequency. Thus, people who report more than one headache per week, or a pattern of increasing headache frequency, appear to be at greater risk (Scher, Stewart, Ricci, & Lipton, 2003).

In people with episodic migraines, overuse of symptomatic medications is a strong predictor of long-term transformation into chronic daily headache. For example, in a large, population-based study (N = 32,067), daily or weekly analgesic use was associated with a 13-fold increased risk of chronic migraine 11 years later, and a 6-fold increased risk of nonmigrainous (mostly tension-type) headaches (Zwart, Dyb, Hagen, Svebak, & Holmen, 2003). Because presence of headache was not assessed at baseline, it is possible that the medication use was a result rather than a cause of frequent headaches. However, other prospective studies have associated symptomatic medications with persistence vs. remission of chronic daily headache (Lu, Fuh, Chen, Juang, & Wang, 2001; Wang, Fuh, Liu, Hsu, Wang, & Liu, 2000).

Still, although the relative risk is high, the absolute risk is low. Of 2,490 participants who had been taking analgesics at least weekly in the 1984–1986 period, only 76 (3.1%) had chronic migraine in 1995–1997 (Zwart, et al., 2003). The risk may be specific to people with a history of episodic migraines (Bahra, Walsh, Menon, & Goadsby, 2003; Lance, Parkes, & Wilkinson, 1988).

Because high medication use may be a marker for disease severity or comorbid conditions, a causal association has not been proven (Scher, Lipton, & Stewart, 2002). However, there are plausible mechanisms, including a decline in receptor sensitivity (Nicolodi, Del Bianco, & Sicuteri, 1997), up-regulation of pain excitatory systems by opiates ("opioid-induced hyperalgesia;" Mao, 2002), and depletion of serotonin in pain inhibitory pathways (Srikiatkhachorn, Maneesri, Govitrapong, & Kasantikul, 1998). Moreover, tapering from overused medications has been associated with clinical improvement (Mathew, 1997) and decreased sensitivity to experimental pain (Fusco, Colantoni, & Giacovazzo, 1997).

Now, if high medication use is causal then so, likely, are psychological factors. In clinical settings, patients cite being unable to cope with the pain as the primary impetus to take medications (Gerber, Miltner, & Niederberger, 1988), and training in coping skills may improve later abstinence (Grazzi, Andrasik, D'Amico, Leone, Usai, Kass, & Bussone, 2002). Psychometrically, difficulty concentrating during a headache, and reacting to pain with physical signs of anxiety, are also slightly correlated with a tendency to use medications (Asmundson, Wright, Norton, & Veloso, 2001). Unfortunately, catastrophization has not yet been studied as a factor in headache medication use.

Other risk factors have been identified as well. In a Norwegian population selected for initial absence of analgesic use, a low socioeconomic status at baseline was associated with chronic daily headache at 11-year follow-up (Hagen, Vatten, Stovner, Zwart, Krokstad, & Bovim, 2002). Similarly, in a large American study, educational attainment at baseline predicted remission from chronic daily headache one year later. People who had attended graduate school were 5 times more likely than those who had not finished high school to have spontaneous remission of chronic daily headache (Scher, et al., 2003).

Also, people who are divorced, widowed, or separated seem to be more likely to have chronic daily headache than those who are single or currently married (Scher, et al., 2003). And being divorced, widowed or separated seems to reduce the probability that chronic daily headache will remit over 1 year of follow-up (Scher, et al., 2003).

Now, it is tempting to speculate that low socioeconomic status and divorce, separation, or death of a spouse, are demographic indices of a high level of life stress. And although there have been no prospective studies examining life stress directly, there is supportive data from a population-based case-control approach (Stewart, Scher, & Lipton, 2001). Compared with people having episodic headache, those with chronic daily headache were more likely to report having moved, having had a change (generally, loss) in an important relationship, having had significant problems with children, or having experienced some other extremely stressful ongoing situation in the year before or the year that chronic daily headache began. People with episodic and chronic headache did not report different numbers of life stresses in the years following onset, implying that the association was indeed causal (Stewart, Scher, & Lipton, 2001). Similar results have been reported in retrospective studies of clinical samples in chronic daily (Giglio, Bruera, & Leston, 1995; Mathew, Stubits, & Nigam, 1982; Sandrini, Manzoni, Zanferrari, & Nappi, 1993) and other headaches (De Benedittis, Lorenzetti, & Pieri, 1990).

Of course life stress raises the question of coping. Unfortunately, there is little data on this point. In a 6.5-year longitudinal study, depression predicted lack of long-term improvement in a clinical sample of migraineurs (Mongini, Keller, Deregibus, Raviola, Mongini, & Sancarlo, 2003). However, in a large community sample, only a weak trend in the same direction was found on 2-year follow-up (OR = 1.4, 95% CI = 1.0, 2.0; Breslau, et al., 2003). More clearly, depression seems related to *current* disability. Tschannen, et al. report a correlation of 0.46 between the Pain Disability Index and the Beck Depression Inventory in a mixed clinical sample, 74% of whom had near-daily headache (Tschannen, Duckro, Margolis, & Tomazic, 1992). Other psychological variables have not been examined.

Physical variables predicting chronic daily headache have also been identified. In a prospective study, obesity was a strong risk factor for onset of chronic daily headache (Scher, et al., 2003). In a population-based case-control study, frequent snoring and report of sleep problems was similarly a risk factor, independent of obesity and hypertension (Scher, Stewart, & Lipton, 2002; Scher, Lipton, & Stewart, 2002).

Chronic Tension-Type Headache

A common form of chronic daily headache, chronic tension-type headache, has received separate research scrutiny. By current diagnostic criteria, the pain has at least 2 of: bilateral location, non-pulsating (pressing or tightening) quality, mild or moderate intensity, and no aggravation by routine physical activity such as walking or climbing stairs. Painful avoidance of light and sound cannot both be present, nor can moderate or severe nausea. Duration of individual attacks can vary, but is greater than 30 minutes. As in all forms of chronic daily headache, the total number of headache days per year exceeds 180. Episodic tension-type headache is similar, but with no accompanying nausea (anorexia can occur during attacks) and fewer than 180 headache days per year (Headache Classification Subcommittee, 2004).

The prevalence of chronic tension-type headache is 3%, and is remarkably constant in studies from Europe, Asia, South America, and the United States (Jensen, 2003; Rasmussen, 2001). In the United States, it appears to be twice as prevalent among women (Schwartz, et al., 1998). There is no clear trend with age, but education level (and thus, presumably socioeconomic status) shows a mild inverse relationship. There is a weak trend for African-Americans to be at lower risk than whites, after correction for potential confounds (Schwartz, et al., 1998).

Now, in a large population-based study in the United States, only 2.2% of respondents met the diagnostic criteria for chronic tension-type headache, and of them, only 11.8% (about one-quarter of one percent of the total sample) reported missed workdays. However, these subjects had very high absenteeism, an average of 27.4 annual workdays each. Thus, the impact on individuals was quite high (Schwartz, et al., 1998).

Moreover, if we add to this the disability caused by the more-prevalent episodic form (see Table 1), the combined economic loss from tension-type headache is similar to that for migraines. Indeed, in Denmark, episodic and chronic tension-type headache together accounted for 0.82 missed workdays annually for each employed person in the country, or 14% of total sick days (Rasmussen, Jensen, & Olesen, 1992).

Similar impact is suggested by unemployment figures. Among enrollees in a health maintenance organization, those consulting a physician for tension-type headache had the same high rate of unemployment (14.2%) as those consulting for migraine with aura (14.0%) or migraine in general (11.2%). The high unemployment rate persisted after controlling for age, gender, education, depression, and even frequency of headache. The primary difference from migraines was that people with tension-type headache tended not to attribute their being out of work to the headaches (Stang, et al., 1998).

Predictors

So who is at risk for such profound personal impact? So far, the little data we have points to psychological variables. Thus, Hursey and Jacks (1992) report that fear of pain played a significant role in the capacity of tension-type headaches to disrupt enjoyable activities. Moreover, French, Holroyd and coworkers found that among patients presenting clinically with chronic tension-type headache, the belief that the headaches were potentially under one's control (internal locus of control) accounted (inversely) for variance in disability scores not accounted for by pain severity. Further, the belief that one actually possesses the skills for preventing and managing headaches (self-efficacy) accounted for additional variance (French, Holroyd, Pinell, Malinoski, O'Donnell, & Hill, 2000). As fear of pain appears to be uncorrelated with locus of control, self-efficacy, and catastrophizing (Hursey & Jacks, 1992), a number of psychological variables may contribute independently to disability.

Post-Traumatic Headache

In clinical samples, traumatic onset seems to be associated with greater disability (Marcus, 2003; Scharff, Turk, & Marcus, 1995). The reason is not yet known, but we may venture a guess. Post-traumatic headaches are generally one part of a constellation of symptoms, including fatigue, dizziness, tinnitus, depression, irritability, and reports of impaired concentration and memory (Duckro & Chibnall, 1999). Between 30% and 70% of patients referred for treatment of post-traumatic headaches also meet the diagnostic criteria for Posttraumatic Stress Disorder (PTSD; Chibnall & Duckro, 1994; Hickling, & Blanchard, 1992; Hickling, Blanchard, Silverman & Schwartz, 1992), which can itself be a significant source of disability (Brunello, Davidson, Deahl, Kessler, Mendlewicz, Racagni, Shalev, & Zohar, 2001). Indeed, even survivors of motor vehicle accidents who do *not* have headaches report elevated levels of physical symptoms, affective distress, short-term memory impairment, and signs of PTSD (Tatrow, Blanchard, Hickling, & Silverman, 2003). Thus, depending on the case, disability in posttraumatic headache could be due to headache, postconcussion syndrome, Posttraumatic Stress Disorder, and/or depression.

Predictors

Of these, only depression has been examined directly. Specifically, Duckro and colleagues report a correlation of 0.50 between self-rated disability (on the Pain Disability Index) and score on the Beck Depression Inventory in a clinical series (Duckro, Chibnall, & Tomazic, 1995). We may note, too, that an acute stress reaction immediately after injury helps identify those at risk for later chronic neck and head pain (Drottning, Staff, Levin, & Malt, 1995; Sterling, Kenardy, Jull, & Vicenzino, 2003). Thus, we might speculate that pain, affective distress, and disability are closely entwined in post-traumatic headaches.

Alternatively, Schrader and coworkers have noted that post-traumatic headache does not seem to occur in Lithuania where, at least at the time of the research, accident insurance and a belief that whiplash could be disabling were both rare (Schrader, Obelieniene, Bovim, Surkiene, Mickeviciene, Miseviciene, & Sand, 1996). This raises the possibility that headache and disability arise together from compensation practices and/or cultural beliefs (Obelieniene, Schrader, Bovim, Miseviciene, & Sand, 1999). However, the role of these variables in post-traumatic headache specifically (vs. the broader category of minor head injury) does not seem to have been examined further.

Cervicogenic Headache

Cervicogenic headaches are those in which the pain is traceable to definite neck pathology. Diagnostic criteria include unilateral head pain that is always on the same side, unilateral neck pain on the same side as the headache, objectively and subjectively restricted neck range of motion, reproduction of the pain with palpation of the neck or occipital area of the head, and relief of pain after greater occipital nerve or C2 nerve block (Sjaastad, Fredriksen, & Pfaffenrath, 1998). When it follows an injury, cervicogenic headache is a restrictively and precisely defined subset of post-traumatic headache.

Of note, cervicogenic headache is associated with high rates of disability, with 25% of patients out of work at 4 weeks, and 15% at 1-year post-injury. Moreover, at 1 year, 67% report ongoing compromise (albeit usually minor) in work or social functioning (Drottning, 2003; Drottning, Staff, & Sjaastad, 2002). Thus, factors that predict the persistence of cervicogenic headache are relevant to identifying high risk patients for occupational disability.

The primary data so far available are from a one-year, prospective study of 587 consecutive patients (49% female) presenting to the emergency room after a whiplash (Drottning, 2003; Drottning, et al., 2002). Of them, 20 went on to develop lasting cervicogenic headache by the strict research criteria. From the data given, relative risks can readily be computed (Greenberg, Daniels, Flanders, Eley, & Boring, 2001). In particular, a pre-injury history of significant headache and persistence of neck pain and dizziness four weeks after injury, are each associated with a statistically significant 6-fold increase in risk for chronic cervicogenic headache.

Still, the low incidence of strictly defined chronic cervicogenic headache means that any one predictor has very low specificity. For example, only 10% of people with dizziness at 4 weeks post-injury go on to long-term headache. Drottning (2003) suggests that the co-occurrence of multiple predictors should alert us to cases in need of more intensive treatment. And here, too, we may note the persistence of disability, for it appears that 60% of those who were out of work at one month were still out of work at one year. Thus, early assessment of disability appears crucial for identifying high risk patients.

MEASURING HEADACHE-RELATED DISABILITY

Although a number of psychometrically sound disability measures are available (Holroyd, 2002), only two headache-specific instruments seem to have found common use: the *Migraine Disability Assessment Scale* (MIDAS; Stewart, Lipton, Dowson, & Sawyer, 2001), and the *Headache Disability Inventory* (HDI; Jacobson, et al., 1994; Jacobson, Ramadan, Norris, & Newman, 1995). Of these, the MIDAS seems to have the strongest validation and the closest relationship to lost workdays. Despite its name, items on the MIDAS refer to "headache" in general, and hence may turn out to be useful for other types of headache disorders.

The HDI, in contrast, seems to be a slightly stronger measure of emotional impact than disability (Holroyd, Malinoski, Davis, & Lipchik, 1999). The items that deal with functioning are somewhat global (e.g., "Because of my headaches I feel restricted in performing my routine daily activities"), and are sensitive to the intensity but not frequency of headache (Jacobson, et al., 1994). Two other measures, the *Headache Impact Test* (HIT and HIT-6; Ware, Bjorner, & Kosinski, 2000) and the *Migraine-Specific Quality of Life Questionnaire* (MSQ; Martin, et al., 2000) have promising psychometric properties but have seen little application so far.

CONCLUSIONS

Thus, we have seen a number of candidate risk factors for headache-related disability, given in Table 2.

FUTURE DIRECTIONS

In studies so far, the emphasis has been on demonstrating the magnitude of disability caused by recurrent headaches. This project has been worthwhile, for historically

TABLE 2. Risk Factors for Disability from Headache

Strong	Probable	Possible
Predictors of Later Disability		
Current disability	Depression	High life events stress
High use of acute HA meds (migraine)	Onset with physical trauma	Sleep difficulty
	Increasing HA frequency	Depression (migraine)
	Low SES	High use of acute HA meds (TTH)
	Obesity	Stress reaction to injury (PTH)
		Pre-injury history of HA (CEH)
		Neck pain and dizziness at 4 wks post-injury (CEH)
Correlates of Current Disability		
Pain intensity (> 5/10)		Distress at pain
HA frequency		Worrying about pain
Depression		Low internal locus of control (TTH)
		Low self-efficacy (TTH)
		Fear of pain (TTH)

Note: CEH = Cervicogenic headache; HA = Headache; PTH = Post-traumatic headache; SES = Socioeconomic status; TTH = Tension-type headache.

the impact of headaches has been under-appreciated. Clearly, however, it is time to expand the scope of research. Because disability is, in a sense, a behavioral response to pain, psychologists have much to contribute (Holroyd, 2002). Useful questions include:

1. To what extent does psychological treatment reduce disability, and how can this effect be optimized? Early results have been encouraging (e.g., Holroyd, O'Donnell, Stensland, Lipchik, Cordingley, & Carlson, 2001), but a great deal of work remains. At the least, it makes sense to include disability and/or quality of life measures in treatment outcome studies (Holroyd, 2002).

2. What are the main contributors to headache-related disability? There is clearly a need for longitudinal studies of headache incorporating psychological variables. The role of depression, both as a source of disability (including in tension-type headache), and as an indicator of long-term clinical course (in migraine), needs to be clarified. Patients sometimes relate fear that mental or physical exertion will be exacerbating. From the chronic pain literature, other candidates include fear of the pain itself, catastrophic thinking about pain, avoidance of potentially exacerbating activities, anger that an injury has occurred, and cuing and reinforcement of a pain focus by one's family or compensation systems. Of course, equally disabled individuals could differ markedly in the key underlying variables. Moreover, given preliminary data that people can desensitize to certain headache triggers through exposure (Philips & Jahanshahi, 1985; Martin, 2001), it may be useful to examine whether disability (avoidance) predicts a later increase in headache frequency or intensity.

3. Stratified care, in which treatment intensity is matched to the severity of symptoms, has received support for choosing among acute migraine medications (Lipton, Stewart, Stone, Láinez, & Sawyer, 2000). In stratified care, what are the appropriate high intensity behavioral treatments for frequent migraines or chronic

daily headache? Simply increasing the number of sessions of, e.g., biofeedback or relaxation training may not be effective (Barton & Blanchard, 2001). By analogy to other forms of chronic pain syndrome, directly addressing the variables thought to mediate disability may have more promise.

4. Is life events stress in fact an important contributor to the conversion of episodic to chronic headaches? Can daily hassles, pain catastrophizing, or a comorbid anxiety disorder cause the same deterioration in clinical course? Of course the mechanisms of such an effect deserve considerable scrutiny, on a behavioral (e.g., medication overuse), cognitive/affective, and psychophysiological level.

5. If the course of migraine is indeed affected by the amount of life stress, can the impact be mitigated by appropriate skills training, for example in stress hardiness, problem solving therapy, or headache management? Of course, the ability to prevent chronic daily headache would be a tremendous contribution of psychological treatments, and does not seem unlikely from the risk factors so far identified.

In the clinical context, of course, the questions are much the same, except that treatment cannot be postponed until all the research is complete. Current disability, risk of future disability, and such possible contributors as depression, fear of pain, pain-related catastrophizing, and preemptive avoidance of activities should be included in the assessment. The presence of conditions likely to be mediating disability should, of course, be treated on the reasonable presumption that they are contributing.

In essence, then, an assessment of disability should be included routinely in research and clinical work. As level of disability may be independent of the exact type of headache (Scharff, et al., 1995), it requires separate evaluation. All of this commends a multiaxial description of headaches, analogous to the system used for psychiatric disorders in DSM-IV, such as that proposed by Lake and colleagues (Lake, Saper, Hamel, & Kreeger, 1995):

I: Diagnosis, frequency, and severity of headaches
II: Analgesic or migraine abortive use, overuse, and abuse
III: Triggers and aggravators, behavioral and stress-related risk factors
IV: Comorbid psychiatric disorders
V: Functional impact and disability

REFERENCES

Asmundson, G. J. G., Wright, K. D., Norton, P. J., & Veloso, F. (2001). Anxiety sensitivity and other emotionality traits in predicting headache medication use in patients with recurring headaches: Implications for abuse and dependency. *Addictive Behaviors*, *26*, 827–840.

Bahra, A., Walsh, M., Menon, S., & Goadsby, P. J. (2003). Does chronic daily headache arise de novo in association with regular use of analgesics? *Headache*, *43*, 179–190.

Barton, K. A., & Blanchard, E. B. (2001). The failure of intensive self-regulatory treatment with chronic daily headache: a prospective study. *Applied Psychophysiology and Biofeedback*, *26*, 311–318.

Benassi, G., D'Alessandro, R., Lenzi, P. L., Manzaroli, D., Baldrati, A., & Lugaresi, E. (1986). The economic burden of headache: An epidemiological study in the Republic of San Marino. *Headache*, *26*, 457–459.

Bigal, M. E., Rapoport, A. M., Lipton, R. B., Tepper, S. J., & Sheftell, F. D. (2003). Assessment of migraine disability using the Migraine Disability Assessment (MIDAS) questionnaire: a comparison of chronic migraine with episodic migraine. *Headache*, *43*, 336–342.

Boardman, H. F., Thomas, E., Croft, P. R., & Millson, D. S. (2003). Epidemiology of headache in an English district. *Cephalalgia, 23*, 129–137.

Breslau, N., & Davis, G. C. (1993). Migraine, physical health and psychiatric disorder: a prospective epidemiologic study in young adults. *Journal of Psychiatric Research, 27*, 211–221.

Breslau, N., & Rasmussen, B. K. (2001). The impact of migraine: Epidemiology, risk factors, and co-morbidities. *Neurology, 56*(Suppl. 1), s4–s12.

Breslau, N., Chilcoat, H. D., & Andreski, P. (1996). Further evidence on the link between migraine and neuroticism. *Neurology, 47*, 663–667.

Breslau, N., Lipton, R. B., Stewart, W. F., Schultz, L. R., & Welch, K. M. A. (2003). Comorbidity of migraine and depression: investigating potential etiology and prognosis. *Neurology, 60*, 1308–1312.

Brunello, N., Davidson, J. R. T., Deahl, M., Kessler, R. C., Mendlewicz, J., Racagni, G., Shalev, A. Y., & Zohar, J. (2001). Posttraumatic Stress Disorder: Diagnosis and epidemiology, comorbidity and social consequences, biology and treatment. *Neuropsychobiology, 43*, 150–162.

Castillo, J., Munoz, P., Guitera, V., & Pascual, J. (1999). Epidemiology of chronic daily headache in the general population. *Headache, 39*, 190–196.

Chibnall, J. T., & Duckro, P. N. (1994). Post-traumatic stress disorder in chronic post-traumatic headache patients. *Headache, 34*, 357–361.

Cortelli, P., Dahlöf, C., Bouchard, J., Heywood, J., Jansen, J.-P., Pham, S., Hirsch, J., Adams, J., & Miller, D. W. (1997). A multinational investigation of the impact of subcutaneous sumatriptan. III. Workplace productivity and non-workplace activity. *Pharmacoeconomics, 11*(Suppl. 1), 35–42.

De Benedittis, G., Lorenzetti, A., & Pieri, A. (1990). The role of stressful life events in the onset of chronic primary headache. *Pain, 40*, 65–75.

Drottning, M. (2003). Cervicogenic headache after whiplash injury. *Current Pain and Headache Reports, 7*, 384–386.

Drottning, M., Staff, P. H., Levin, L., & Malt, U. F. (1995). Acute emotional response to common whiplash predicts subsequent pain complaints. *Nordic Journal of Psychiatry, 49*, 293–299.

Drottning, M., Staff, P. H., & Sjaastad, O. (2002). Cervicogenic headache (CEH) after whiplash injury. *Cephalalgia, 22*, 165–171.

Duckro, P. N., & Chibnall, J. T. (1999). Chronic posttraumatic headache. In: A. R. Block, E. F. Kremer, & E. Fernandez (Eds.), *Handbook of pain syndromes: biopsychosocial perspectives* (pp. 303–320). Mahwah, NJ: Lawrence Erlbaum Associates.

Duckro, P. N., Chibnall, J. T., & Tomazic, T. J. (1995). Anger, depression, and disability: A path analysis of relationships in a sample of chronic posttraumatic headache patients. *Headache, 35*, 7–9.

Edmeads, J., & Mackell, J. A. (2002). The economic impact of migraine: An analysis of direct and indirect costs. *Headache, 42*, 501–509.

Ferrari, M. D. (1998). The economic burden of migraine to society. *Pharmacoeconomics, 13*, 667–676.

French, D. J., Holroyd, K. A., Pinell, C., Malinoski, P. T., O'Donnell, F., & Hill, K. R. (2000). Perceived self-efficacy and headache-related disability. *Headache, 40*, 647–656.

Fusco, B. M., Colantoni, O., & Giacovazzo, M. (1997). Alteration of central excitation circuits in chronic headache and analgesic misuse. *Headache, 37*, 486–491.

Gerber, W. D., Miltner, W., & Niederberger, U. (1988). The role of behavioral and social factors in the development of drug-induced headache. In: H.-C. Diener & M. Wilkinson (Eds.), *Drug-induced headache* (pp. 65–74). NY: Springer-Verlag.

Gerth, W. C., Carides, G. W., Dasbach, E. J., Visser, W. H., & Santanello, N. C. (2001). The multinational impact of migraine symptoms on healthcare utilization and work loss. *Pharmacoeconomics, 19*, 197–206.

Giglio, J. A., Bruera, O. C., & Leston, J. A. (1995). Influence of transformation factors on chronic daily headache. *Headache, 35*(Suppl. 14), 165.

Granella, F., Cavallini, A., Sandrini, G., Manzoni, G. C., & Nappi, G. (1998). Long-term outcome of migraine. *Cephalalgia, 18*(Suppl. 2), 30–33.

Grazzi, L., Andrasik, F., D'Amico, D., Leone, M., Usai, S., Kass, S. J., & Bussone, G. (2002). Behavioral and pharmacologic treatment of transformed migraine with analgesic overuse: Outcome at 3 years. *Headache, 42*, 483–490.

Green, J. E. (1977). A survey of migraine in England 1975–1976. *Headache, 17*, 67–68.

Greenberg, R. S., Daniels, S. R., Flanders, W. D., Eley, J. W., & Boring, J. R. III. (2001). *Medical epidemiology* (3rd ed.). NY: McGraw-Hill.

Hagen, K., Vatten, L., Stovner, L J., Zwart, J. A., Krokstad, S., & Bovim, G. (2002). Low socio-economic status is associated with increased risk of frequent headache: a prospective study of 22,718 adults in Norway. *Cephalalgia*, *22*, 672–679.

Headache Classification Subcommittee of the International Headache Society. (2004). International classification of headache disorders (2nd ed.). *Cephalalgia*, *24*(Suppl. 1).

Henry, P., Auray, J. P., Gaudin, A. F., Dartigues, J. F., Duru, G., Lantéri-Minet, M., Lucas, C., Pradalier, A., Chazot, G., & El Hasnaoui, A. (2002). Prevalence and clinical characteristics of migraine in France. *Neurology*, *59*, 232–237.

Hickling, E. J., & Blanchard, E. B. (1992). Post-traumatic stress disorder and motor vehicle accidents. *Journal of Anxiety Disorders*, *6*, 285–291.

Hickling, E. J., Blanchard, E. B., Silverman, D. J., & Schwartz, S. P. (1992). Motor vehicle accidents, headaches and post-traumatic stress disorder: assessment findings in a consecutive series. *Headache*, *32*, 147–151.

Holroyd, K. A. (2002). Assessment and psychological management of recurrent headache disorders. *Journal of Consulting and Clinical Psychology*, *70*, 656–677.

Holroyd, K. A., Malinoski, P., Davis, M. K., & Lipchik, G. L. (1999). The three dimensions of headache impact: pain, disability and affective distress. *Pain*, *83*, 571–578.

Holroyd, K. A., O'Donnell, F. J., Stensland, M., Lipchik, G. L., Cordingley, G. E., & Carlson, B. W. (2001). Management of chronic tension-type headache with tricyclic antidepressant medication, stress management therapy, and their combination: a randomized controlled trial. *JAMA*, *285*, 2208–2215.

Hu, X. H., Markson, L. E., Lipton, R. B., Stewart, W. F., & Berger, M. L. (1999). Burden of migraine in the United States: disability and economic costs. *Archives of Internal Medicine*, *159*, 813–818.

Hursey, K. G., & Jacks, S. D. (1992). Fear of pain in recurrent headache sufferers. *Headache*, *32*, 283–286.

Jacobson, G. P., Ramadan, N. M., Aggarwal, S. K., & Newman, C. W. (1994). The Henry Ford Hospital Headache Disability Inventory (HDI). *Neurology*, *44*, 837–842.

Jacobson, G. P., Ramadan, N. M., Norris, L., & Newman, C. W. (1995). Headache Disability Inventory (HDI): short-term test-retest reliability and spouse perceptions. *Headache*, *35*, 534–539.

Jensen, R. (2003). Diagnosis, epidemiology, and impact of tension-type headache. *Current Pain and Headache Reports*, *7*, 455–459.

Lake, A. E. III, Saper, J. R., Hamel, R. L., & Kreeger, C. (1995). Proposal for a multiaxial diagnostic system for headache. *Headache*, *35*, 285–286.

Laloux, P., Vakaet, A., Monseu, G., Jacquy, J., Bourgeois, P., & van der Linden, C. (1998). Subcutaneous sumatriptan compared with usual acute treatments for migraine: clinical and pharmacoeconomic evaluation. *Acta Neurologica Belgica*, *98*, 332–341.

Lambert, J., Carides, G. W., Meloche, J. P., Gerth, W. C., & Marentette, M. A. (2002). Impact of migraine symptoms on health care use and work loss in Canada in patients randomly assigned in a phase III clinical trial. *Canadian Journal of Clinical Pharmacology*, *9*, 158–164.

Lance, F., Parkes, C., & Wilkinson, M. (1988). Does analgesic abuse cause headaches de novo? *Headache*, *28*, 61–62.

Lantéri-Minet, M., Auray, J.-P., El Hasnaoui, A., Dartigues, J.-F., Duru, G., Henry, P., Lucas, C., Pradalier, A., Chazot, G., & Gaudin, A.-F. (2003). Prevalence and description of chronic daily headache in the general population in France. *Pain*, *102*, 143–149.

Lavados, P. M., & Tenhamm, E. (1997). Epidemiology of migraine headache in Santiago, Chile: a prevalence study. *Cephalalgia*, *17*, 770–777.

Lavados, P. M., & Tenhamm, E. (1998). Epidemiology of tension-type headache in Santiago, Chile: a prevalence study. *Cephalalgia*, *18*, 552–558.

Lipton, R. B., Hamelsky, S. W., Kolodner, K. B., Steiner, T. J., & Stewart, W. F. (2000). Migraine, quality of life, and depression: a population-based case-control study. *Neurology*, *55*, 629–635.

Lipton, R. B., Stewart, W. F., Stone, A. M., Láinez, M. J. A., & Sawyer, J. P. C. (2000). Stratified care vs. step care strategies for migraine: The Disability in Strategies of Care (DISC) Study: A randomized trial. *JAMA*, *284*, 2599–2605.

Loder, E., & Biondi, D. (2003). Disease modification in migraine: A concept that has come of age? *Headache*, *43*, 135–143.

Lu, S. R., Fuh, J. L., Chen, W. T., Juang, K. D., & Wang, S. J. (2001). Chronic daily headache in Taipei, Taiwan: Prevalence, follow-up and outcome predictors. *Cephalalgia*, *21*, 980–986.

Magnusson, J. E., & Becker, W. J. (2002). A comparison of disability and psychological factors in migraine and transformed migraine. *Cephalalgia*, *22*, 172–178.

Magnusson, J. E., & Becker, W. J. (2003). Migraine frequency and intensity: relationship with disability and psychological factors. *Headache*, *43*, 1049–1059.

Mao, J. (2002). Opioid-induced abnormal pain sensitivity: Implications in clinical opioid therapy. *Pain*, *100*, 213–217.

Marcus, D. A. (2000). Identification of headache subjects at risk for psychological distress. *Headache*, *40*, 373–376.

Marcus, D. A. (2003). Disability and chronic posttraumatic headache. *Headache*, *43*, 117–121.

Martin, B. C., Pathak, D. S., Sharfman, M. I., Adelman, J. U., Taylor, F., Kwong, J., & Jhingran, P. (2000). Validity and reliability of the Migraine-Specific Quality of Life Questionnaire (MSQ Version 2.1). *Headache*, *40*, 204–215.

Martin, P. R. (2001). How do trigger factors acquire the capacity to precipitate headaches? *Behaviour Research and Therapy*, *39*, 545–554.

Mathew, N. T. (1997). Transformed migraine, analgesic rebound, and other chronic daily headaches. *Neurologic Clinics*, *15*(1), 167–186.

Mathew, N. T., Stubits, E., & Nigam, M. P. (1982). Transformation of episodic migraine into daily headache: analysis of factors. *Headache*, *22*, 66–68.

Meletiche, D. M., Lofland, J. H., & Young, W. B. (2001). Quality-of-life differences between patients with episodic and transformed migraine. *Headache*, *41*, 573–578.

Meyer, J. S., Thornby, J., Crawford, K., & Rauch, G. M. (2000). Reversible cognitive decline accompanies migraine and cluster headaches. *Headache*, *40*, 638–646.

Michel, P., Dartigues, J. F., Lindoulsi, A., & Henry, P. (1997). Loss of productivity and quality of life in migraine sufferers among French workers: Results from the GAZEL cohort. *Headache*, *37*, 71–78.

Micieli, G., Frediani, F., Cavallini, A., Rossi, F., Bussone, G., Merli, S., & Nappi, G. (1995). Quantification of headache disability: A diagnostic-based approach. *Headache*, *35*, 131–137.

Mongini, F., Keller, R., Deregibus, A., Raviola, F., Mongini, T., & Sancarlo, M. (2003). Personality traits, depression and migraine in women: a longitudinal study. *Cephalalgia*, *23*, 186–192.

Murray, C. J. L., & Lopez, A. D. (Eds.) (1996). *The global burden of disease*. Cambridge, MA: Harvard University Press.

Murray, C. J. L., & Lopez, A. D. (1997). Regional patterns of disability-free life expectancy and disability-adjusted life expectancy: Global Burden of Disease study. *Lancet*, *349*, 1347–1352.

Mushet, G. R., Miller, D. W., Clements, B., Pait, G., & Gutterman, D. L. (1996). Impact of sumatriptan on workplace productivity, nonwork activities, and health-related quality of life among hospital employees with migraine. *Headache*, *36*, 137–143.

Nicolodi, M., Del Bianco, P. L., & Sicuteri, F. (1997). The way to serotonergic use and abuse in migraine. *International Journal of Clinicial Pharmacology Research*, *17*(2/3), 79–84.

Nikiforow, R., & Hokkanen, E. (1979). Effects of headache on working ability: A survey of an urban and a rural population in Northern Finland. *Headache*, *19*, 214–218.

Obelieniene, D., Schrader, H., Bovim, G., Miseviciene, I., & Sand, T. (1999). Pain after whiplash: A prospective controlled inception cohort study. *Journal of Neurology, Neurosurgery and Psychiatry*, *66*, 390–392.

Osterhaus, J. T., Gutterman, D. L., & Plachetka, J. R. (1992). Healthcare resource and lost labour costs of migraine headache in the U.S. *Pharmacoeconomics*, *2*, 67–76.

Pascual, J., Colás, R., & Castillo, J. (2001). Epidemiology of chronic daily headache. *Current Pain and Headache Reports*, *5*, 529–536.

Passchier, J., de Boo, M., Quaak, H. Z. A., & Brienen, J. A. (1996). Health-related quality of life in chronic headache patients is predicted by the emotional component of their pain. *Headache*, *36*, 556–560.

Passchier, J., Mourik, J.C., McKenna, S. P., van den Berg, M., & Erdman, R. A. M. (2001). Evaluation of the Dutch version of the migraine quality of life instrument (MSQOL) and its application in headache coping. *Cephalalgia*, *21*, 823–829.

Philips, H. C., & Jahanshahi, M. (1985). Chronic pain: an experimental analysis of the effects of exposure. *Behaviour Research and Therapy*, *23*, 281–290.

Pop, P. H. M., Gierveld, C. M., Karis, H. A. M., & Tiedink, H. G. M. (2002). Epidemiological aspects of headache in a workplace setting and the impact on the economic loss. *European Journal of Neurology*, *9*, 171–174.

Prencipe, M., Casini, A. R., Ferretti, C., Santini, M., Pezzella, F., Scaldaferri, N., & Culasso, F. (2001). Prevalence of headache in an elderly population: Attack frequency, disability, and use of medication. *Journal of Neurology, Neurosurgery, and Psychiatry*, *70*, 377–381.

Pryse-Phillips, W., Findlay, H., Tugwell, P., Edmeads, J., Murray, T. J., & Nelson, R. F. (1992). A Canadian population survey on the clinical, epidemiologic and societal impact of migraine and tension-type headache. *Canadian Journal of Neurological Sciences*, *19*, 333–339.

Rasmussen, B. K. (2001). Epidemiology of headache. *Cephalalgia*, *21*, 774–777.

Rasmussen, B. K., Jensen, R., & Olesen, J. (1992). Impact of headache on sickness absence and utilisation of medical services: a Danish population study. *Journal of Epidemiology and Community Health*, *46*, 443–446.

Sandrini, G., Manzoni, G. C., Zanferrari, C., & Nappi, G. (1993). An epidemiological approach to the nosography of chronic daily headache. *Cephalalgia*, *13*(Suppl. 12), 72–77.

Scharff, L., Turk, D. C., & Marcus, D. A. (1995). Psychosocial and behavioral characteristics in chronic headache patients: support for a continuum and dual-diagnostic approach. *Cephalalgia*, *15*, 216–223.

Scher, A. I., Stewart, W. F., Liberman, J., & Lipton, R. B. (1998). Prevalence of frequent headache in a population sample. *Headache*, *38*, 497–506.

Scher, A. I., Lipton, R. B., & Stewart, W. (2002). Risk factors for chronic daily headache. *Current Pain and Headache Reports*, *6*, 486–491.

Scher, A. I., Stewart, W. F., & Lipton, R. B. (2002). Snoring and chronic daily headache: Results from the Frequent Headache Epidemiology Study. *Neurology*, *58*(Suppl. 3), A332.

Scher, A. I., Stewart, W. F., Ricci, J. A., & Lipton, R. B. (2003). Factors associated with the onset and remission of chronic daily headache in a population-based study. *Pain*, *106*, 81–89.

Schrader, H., Obelieniene, D., Bovim, G., Surkiene, D., Mickeviciene, D., Miseviciene, I., & Sand, T. (1996). Natural evolution of late whiplash syndrome outside the medicolegal context. *Lancet*, *347*, 1207–1211.

Schwartz, B. S., Stewart, W. F., & Lipton, R. B. (1997). Lost workdays and decreased work effectiveness associated with headache in the workplace. *Journal of Occupational and Environmental Medicine*, *39*, 320–327.

Schwartz, B. S., Stewart, W. F., Simon, D., & Lipton, R. B. (1998). Epidemiology of tension-type headache. *JAMA*, *279*, 381–383.

Silberstein, S. D., Lipton, R. B., Solomon, S., & Mathew, N. (1994). Classification of daily and near-daily headaches: Proposed revisions to the IHS criteria. *Headache*, *34*, 1–7.

Sjaastad, O., Fredriksen, T. A., & Pfaffenrath, V. (1998). Cervicogenic headache: diagnostic criteria. *Headache*, *38*, 442–445.

Srikiatkhachorn, A., Maneesri, S., Govitrapong, P., & Kasantikul, V. (1998). Derangement of serotonin system in migrainous patients with analgesic abuse headache: Clues from platelets. *Headache*, *38*, 43–49.

Stang, P. E., & Osterhaus, J. T. (1993). Impact of migraine in the United States: Data from the National Health Interview Survey. *Headache*, *33*, 29–35.

Stang, P., Von Korff, M., & Galer, B. S. (1998). Reduced labor force participation among primary care patients with headache. *Journal of General Internal Medicine*, *13*, 296–302.

Steiner, T. J., Scher, A. I., Stewart, W. F., Kolodner, K., Liberman, J., & Lipton, R. B. (2003). The prevalence and disability burden of adult migraine in England and their relationships to age, gender and ethnicity. *Cephalalgia*, *23*, 519–527.

Sterling, M., Kenardy, J., Jull, G., & Vicenzino, B. (2003). The development of psychological changes following whiplash injury. *Pain*, *106*, 481–489.

Stewart, W. F., Lipton, R. B., Celentano, D. D., & Reed, M. L. (1992). Prevalence of migraine headache in the United States: Relation to age, income, race, and other sociodemographic factors. *JAMA*, *267*, 64–69.

Stewart, W. F., Shechter, A., & Lipton, R. B. (1994). Migraine heterogeneity: Disability, pain intensity, and attack frequency and duration. *Neurology*, *44*(Suppl. 4), s24–s39.

Stewart, W. F., Lipton, R. B., & Liberman, J. (1996). Variation in migraine prevalence by race. *Neurology*, *47*, 52–59.

Stewart, W. F., Lipton, R. B., & Simon, D. (1996). Work-related disability: Results from the American Migraine Study. *Cephalalgia*, *16*, 231–238.

Stewart, W. F., Lipton, R. B., Simon, D., Liberman, J., & Von Korff, M. (1999). Validity of an illness severity measure for headache in a population sample of migraine sufferers. *Pain*, *79*, 291–301.

Stewart, W. F., Lipton, R. B., Whyte, J., Dowson, A., Kolodner, K., Liberman, J. N., & Sawyer, J. (1999). An international study to assess reliability of the Migraine Disability Assessment (MIDAS) score. *Neurology, 53*, 988–994.

Stewart, W. F., Lipton, R. B., Dowson, A. J., & Sawyer, J. (2001). Development and testing of the Migraine Disability Assessment (MIDAS) Questionnaire to assess headache-related disability. *Neurology, 56*(Suppl. 1), s20–s28.

Stewart, W. F., Scher, A. I., & Lipton, R. B. (2001). The Frequent Headache Epidemiology Study (FrHE): Stressful life events and risk of chronic daily headache. *Neurology, 56*, A138–A139.

Stewart, W. F., Lipton, R. B., & Kolodner, K. (2003). Migraine Disability Assessment (MIDAS) Score: Relation to headache frequency, pain intensity, and headache symptoms. *Headache, 43*, 258–265.

Stewart, W. F., Ricci, J. A., Chee, E., Morganstein, D., & Lipton, R. (2003). Lost productive time and cost due to common pain conditions in the U.S. workforce. *JAMA, 290*, 2443–2454.

Tatrow, K., Blanchard, E. B., Hickling, E. J., & Silverman, D. J. (2003). Posttraumatic headache: Biopsychosocial comparisons with multiple control groups. *Headache, 43*, 755–766.

Trask, P. C., Iezzi, T., & Kreeft, J. (2001). Comparison of headache parameters using headache type and emotional status. *Journal of Psychosomatic Research, 51*, 529–536.

Tschannen, T. A., Duckro, P. N., Margolis, R. B., & Tomazic, T. J. (1992). The relationship of anger, depression, and perceived disability among headache patients. *Headache, 32*, 501–503.

Von Korff, M., Ormel, J., Keefe, F. J., & Dworkin, S. F. (1992). Grading the severity of chronic pain. *Pain, 50*, 133–149.

Von Korff, M., Stewart, W. F., Simon, D. J., & Lipton, R. B. (1998). Migraine and reduced work performance. A population-based diary study. *Neurology, 50*, 1741–1745.

Wang, S. J., Fuh, J. L., Liu, C. Y., Hsu, L. C., Wang, P. N., & Liu, H. C. (2000). Chronic daily headache in Chinese elderly. Prevalence, risk factors, and biannual follow-up. *Neurology, 54*, 314–319.

Ware, J. E., Jr., Bjorner, J. B., & Kosinski, M. (2000). Practical implications of item response theory and computerized adaptive testing. *Medical Care, 38*(Suppl. II), II-73–II-82.

Wells, N. E. J., & Steiner, T. J. (2000). Effectiveness of eletriptan in reducing time loss caused by migraine attacks. *Pharmacoeconomics, 18*, 557–566.

Zwart, J.-A., Dyb, G., Hagen, K., Svebak, S., & Holmen, J. (2003). Analgesic use: A predictor of chronic pain and medication overuse headache. The Head-HUNT study. *Neurology, 61*, 160–164.

B. PREDICTION OF DISABILITY AFTER HEAD INJURY

15

Prediction of Disability after Mild Traumatic Brain Injury

Nancy Canning and Ronald M. Ruff

INTRODUCTION

The goal of this chapter is to present the topic of Mild Traumatic Brain Injury (MTBI) within a transdisciplinary, biopsychosocial context. After defining MTBI, citing its incidence in the United States and reviewing diagnostic criteria, we will focus on the question: *What are the outcome predictors for individuals who have incurred a MTBI?* In other words, are there risk factors for certain sets of symptoms associated with how an individual will respond to a MTBI, or "early markers" for predicting the likelihood of developing a persistent postconcussional disorder?

To date, there have been few studies that have examined outcome predictors for MTBI. The impetus for having these determinants is two-fold: to serve current patients most effectively and to analyze trends that would enable us to create public policies that will serve this population. Ultimately, the goal is also to institute preventative measures that would reduce the size of the population that currently requires service. Given the current status, we first explored how clinicians' prognostications might help identify a clinical model for predicting outcome. Second, we examined the complexities involved in designing research paradigms whose goal is to develop a model for prediction.

DEFINITION

Traumatic Brain Injury (TBI) refers to a physiological disruption of brain functioning caused by an external force resulting in an acceleration/deceleration or a direct blow to the head. TBI does not include hereditary, congenital or degenerative processes,

DOI: 10.1007/978-0-387-28919-9_15, © 2009 Springer Science+Business Media, LLC

stroke, post surgical complications or disease processes, (e.g., tumors, aneurysms, encephalitis, anoxia). TBI should also not be confused with whiplash, where damage is to extra-cranial structures and not directly related to cerebral injury. However, whiplash may occur concurrently with brain trauma. Whiplash is a forceful cervical flexion-extension, with or without a torsional (twisting) component. It results in pathological lesions to peripheral nerves, muscles and vascular structures in the head and neck, but not to the central nervous system (Snyder and Nussbaum, 1998), as would be the case with diffuse axonal injury. TBI is classified by its level of severity into "severe," "moderate" or "mild." After reviewing incidence and prevalence of TBI in general, we will focus on MTBI.

INCIDENCE AND PREVALENCE

Statistics on the etiology of TBI from the Center for Disease Control (2002) indicate that transportation-related injuries are the leading cause of TBI (44%). The breakdown within this category is as follows: 62% are occupants in enclosed motor vehicles, 13% are pedestrians, 7% involved bicycles, 6% involved motorcycles and 12% are classified as "other." Falls account for 26% of TBI, most of which involve children less than five years old and adults older than 75. Firearm and non-firearm assaults account for 8% and 9% of the injuries, respectively.

The 1999 CDC *Report to Congress* on TBI in the United States reported the following statistics (Center for Disease Control, 2001):

- Every 21 seconds, one person in the United States sustains TBI.
- More than 1.5 million people will sustain TBI annually (incidence rate of 100 per 100,000)
- 50,000–52,000 people die of TBI annually.
- TBI is more than twice as likely in males than as in females.
- 91% of firearm-related TBI results in death.
- There are currently 5.3 million Americans living with a disability as a result of TBI.

These statistics estimate that the incidence of TBI has not only reached epidemic proportions, but that compared to 1992 data, the number of individuals has increased from 1.3 million in 1992 to 1.5 million in 1999. In the preceding decades, the mortality rate was considerably higher, approximately 200,000, 50% of whom died within the first 2 hours post-trauma. The introduction of seatbelts and other safety precautions (which reduced mortality by 57%) combined with better emergency medical care at the trauma scene appear to be the primary factors for this great decline. However, more people surviving TBI has also meant an increase in the amount of treatment and aftercare required. 1995 data estimated the lifetime costs for direct and indirect services for TBI in the United States at $56.3 billion (Thurman, 2001).

The 1998 NIH *Consensus Statement* on rehabilitation of persons with traumatic brain injury concluded that "since TBI may result in lifelong impairment of an individual's physical, cognitive, and psychosocial functioning and prevalence is estimated to be 2.5 million to 6.5 million individuals, TBI is a disorder of major public health significance" (National Institute of Health, 1998). The Brian Injury

Association (2001a) estimated that each year, 80,000 Americans experience the onset of long-term disability secondary to TBI. The CDC's current estimate is that approximately 2% of the American population is living with a disability as a result of traumatic brain injury (Center for Disease Control, 2002).

Of the annual incidence of 1.5 million TBIs, it is estimated that approximately 80% are of mild severity, with the remaining 20% more or less evenly split between moderate and severe TBIs (Krauss, McArthur, Silverman and Jayaraman, 1996). It also has been estimated that the majority of TBI patients whose injury is of mild severity either see their primary care physician days after their injury or seek no care at all (Kay, Newman, Cavallo, Erzrachi and Resnick, 1992; Langlois et al., 2003; Mellick, Gerhart and Whiteneck, 2003; Sosin, Sniezek and Thurman, 1996). Hence, the CDC's most recent *Report to Congress* (which utilizes different algorithms to predict disability) cautioned that their earlier estimate of 5.3 million Americans living with disability as a result of TBI may have under-represented true incidence, in part because their data only reflects individuals who were admitted to hospitals (Langlois et al., 2003). That is, it and the majority of research reflects about 20% of the total TBI population who seek hospital treatment. It does not account for MTBI patients who were discharged from emergency rooms without being admitted, for individuals who visited outpatient clinics or for whatever reason, received no treatment at all. As we will discuss later in this chapter, the fact that we cannot identify the majority of the MTBI population has major implication for being able to predict outcome.

The majority of TBI cases are classified as "mild" and are thought to be largely unrecognized and untreated. Hence, MTBI is often referred to as the "silent epidemic" (Brain Injury Society, 2001). The 1998 NIH Consensus statement indicated that "*mild TBI is significantly under diagnosed and the likely societal burden therefore even greater*" [italics added]. The Traumatic Brain Injury Act of 1999—which allocates Federal funding for additional research, protection and advocacy for individuals with TBI was the first Federal recognition of TBI and MTBI as epidemics (Berube, 2001; Brain Injury Association, 2001). The first step in addressing the MTBI epidemic was to identify this hidden population.

The first multi-center study that evaluated successively admitted MTBI patients to the ER documented that most patients experienced cognitive, physical and emotional symptoms within 72 hours following the accident (Levin et al., 1987c). As a group, MTBI patients made a full recovery within 1 to 3 months post injury. Subsequent studies continued to find that the majority of MTBI patients made a full recovery, but they also identified a minority of 10 to 20% whose complaints persisted after 3 months (Alexander, 1995; Binder, Rohling and Larrabee, 1997; Wong, Regennitter and Barrios, 1994). In fact, these patients often presented with chronic symptoms over 12 months post-injury.

This 10 to 20% of the MTBI patients were the first subgroup to be identified and referred to as the "Miserable Minority" (Ruff, Camenzuli and Mueller, 1996a). What distinguishes this subgroup is both their clinical presentation of unresolved symptoms and the fact that they seek treatment. Neuropsychologists must determine if the sequelae of these patients reflects: (1) neurogenic etiology, (2) post-morbid psychogenic etiology, (3) pre-morbid psychological problems, (4) non-neurological physical residuals associated with the accident, (5) malingering, or (6) any combination of the above. Given the annual incidence rate of approximately 1.5 million TBI survivors in the United States alone, combined with the fact that 80% are MTBIs, the Miserable Minority of 10 to 20% comprises 150,000 to 300,000 individuals each year. For medical practitioners to diagnose a Post-concussion Syndrome (PCS) or for psychologists to diagnose a Postconcussional Disorder (PCD), the patient's acquired physical, emotional or cognitive symptoms must be the direct consequence of a concussion. Thus, it is essential for practitioners across disciplines to agree on a clear definition of cerebral concussion (Ruff, 1999).

DIAGNOSIS OF MTBI

Practically speaking, different phases of recovery focus on different aspects of injury at different times. Immediately after injury, the severity of the insult must be determined to guide treatment in the acute phase. Teasdale and Jennet's (Teasdale and Jennett, 1974) Glasgow Coma Scale (GCS) is internationally recognized for assigning a common grading system for assessment of initial insult based on eye opening, verbal and motor response (see Table 1).

The GCS was designed by neurosurgeons for triaging patients. It is extremely time-sensitive and should not be utilized without careful consideration of the time parameters (Ruff and Jurica, 1999). Although when placed in the appropriate time context, a GCS of 13 or 14 can support a TBI diagnosis of a mild severity, the GCS is not to be considered as a reliable tool for diagnosing MTBI per se. For example, a MTBI patient who was rendered unconscious for 20 minutes and is examined during this time will have a GCS of 3. Conversely, a patient with a severe TBI can have a GCS of 15 two days following the accident. Although the GCS has been shown to be a reasonable predictor of short-term outcome for moderate to severe TBI, it also has been shown to be less robust for predicting post-triage outcome, especially as the level of severity decreases (Burnett et al., 2003; Stambrook, Moore, Lubusko, Peters and Blumenschein, 1993). For this reason, several grading systems emerged that classified the severity of head injuries based on either the duration or the severity of symptoms (Whyte, Cifu, Dikmen and Temkin, 2001).

In 1993, the American Congress of Rehabilitation Medicine (ACRM) established a set of diagnostic criteria that could be applied retrospectively based on the lengths of loss of consciousness and/or posttraumatic amnesia and the presence of neurological signs (see Table 2) (American Congress of Rehabilitation Medicine, 1993).

In 1997, the American Academy of Neurology (AAN) published a practice parameter for the management of concussion in sports (American Academy of Neurology, 1997). The ANN criteria break down concussions into three grades (see Table 3).

As a comparison of Tables 2 and 3 shows, the ACRM and AAN criteria for concussion are not incompatible, but grade symptoms over time differently. In 1994, the fourth edition of the Diagnostic and Statistical Manual of Mental Disorders

TABLE 1. Glasgow Coma Scale Scores and Associated TBI Levels

Score	Level
3 to 8	Severe
9 to 12	Moderate
13 to 15	Mild

TABLE 2. ACRM MTBI Criteria

Inclusion Criteria—one or more must be manifested:

- Any period of loss of consciousness for up to 30 minutes
- Any loss of memory for events immediately before and after the accident for as much as 24 hours
- Any alteration of mental state at the time of accident (dazed, disoriented, or confused)
- Focal neurological deficit(s) that may or may not be transient.

Exclusion Criteria—one or more must be manifested:

- Loss of consciousness exceeding 30 minutes
- Posttraumatic amnesia (PTA) persisting longer than 24 hours
- After 30 minutes, the GCS falling below 13

(American Psychiatric Association, 1994) indirectly defined concussion when it included an experimental definition for a Postconcussional Disorder (PCD). Criteria for diagnosis include a loss of consciousness of 5 minutes and persistent physical, cognitive and emotional residual 3 months following the concussion.

In the interest of arriving at a unified definition of MTBI, an integration of two of these classifications has been proposed. Table 4 illustrates the incorporation of the ACRM and DSM-IV criteria. Type I is modeled on ACRM, Type III matches the DSM-IV criteria, and Type II bridges the gap between all three definitions (Ruff and Grant, 1999; Ruff and Jurica, 1999).

Various studies have tried to break-down MTBI into sub-types that would help identify segments of the population by correlating symptoms with different levels. Alexander suggested that MTBI be broken into two groups: patients with a GCS of 15 and those with a GCS of 13 or 14. He identified the first group as the "true Milds" and the second group as those who are more likely to have longer periods of LOC or confusion and amnesia (Alexander, 1995). Another approach has been to measure attentional deficits with various neuropsychological instruments to see if patterns of specific deficits (selective, sustained or divided attention, error commission) characterize distinct clusters of symptoms (Chan, Hoosain, Lee, Fan and Fong, 2003; Cicerone, 1996). The Crash Injury Engineering Network (CIREN) has focused on examining the crash circumstances of TBIs with a GCS of 13 to 15 (Dischiner et al., 2003).

Levin and colleagues have proposed a classification that is combined with neuroimaging. Patients with positive CT or MRI findings are classified as moderate or "complicated" whereas those without positive neuroimaging are referred to as

TABLE 3. AAN Criteria for Concussion

Criteria	Grade 1	Grade 2	Grade 3
Loss of consciousness (LOC)	None	None	Any loss, whether brief (seconds) or prolonged (minutes)
Confusion	Momentary	Transient	Present
Mental status	Abnormalities resolve in less than 15 minutes	Abnormalities last more than 15 minutes, but less than 1 hour	Abnormalities last more than 15 minutes and may persist after 1 hour

TABLE 4. Proposed Classifications for MTBI

Criteria	Type I	Type II	Type III
Loss of consciousness (LOC)	Altered state or transient loss	Definite loss with time unknown or less than 5 minutes	Loss of 5 to 30 minutes
Posttraumatic amnesia (PTA)	1–60 seconds	60 seconds to 12 hours	> 12 hours to 24 hours
Neurological symptoms	One or more	One or more	One or more

"uncomplicated" (Levin et al., 1987a). Similarly, Prigitano and colleagues have suggested that "Mild" also be sub-divided into "complicated" and "uncomplicated" MTBI. The former is distinguished by the presence of a space-occupying lesion, LOC and the preponderance of cognitive over affective symptoms, whereas the latter have an absence of space-occupying lesions, brief, if any LOC and primarily affective symptoms (Borgaro, Prigatano, Kwasnica and Rexer, 2003).

A review of all of the above proposed sub-classifications raised the following questions: if neuroimaging is a critical element of the diagnosis, how are those patients diagnosed without CT or MRI scans? And similarly, how do we diagnose MTBI in the ER by incorporating cognitive and affective symptoms, when these are not yet manifested or documented? These classifications seem to obfuscate the distinctions between MTBI and PCD. Thus, we suggest that the diagnosis of MTBI rely on LOC, PTA and neurological symptoms, and classifications for PCD include all available data including neuroimaging, documentation of cognitive, emotional and physical symptoms.

Given that the diagnosis of MTBI is dependent on LOC, PTA and neurological symptoms, we proposed a scale analogous and complementary to the GCS; see Appendix A (Ruff, 2003). For patients with GCS scores of 13, 14 or 15, the California Concussion Scale (CCS) provides a quick and easy classification for rating LOC, PTA and neurological symptoms. This tool should be utilized in conjunction with the Galveston Orientation Amnesia Test (Levin, O'Donnell and Grossman, 1979) and has two benefits. (1) The CCS can be administered retrospectively and (2) it provides for a gradation of 3–15 scores just for MTBI patients.

In conclusion, it is paramount that a unified classification system be developed that provides diagnostic classifications that sub-classifies the severity of MTBI. A separate diagnostic classification system should be developed for Postconcussional Disorders.

CLINICAL PREDICTION OF OUTCOME

Once a patient is diagnosed with MTBI, part of their treatment plan is a prognosis that we render based on clinical experience. Prognosticating, or predicting outcome is based on estimation of who the individual was prior to injury, expectations of how an individual will respond to his or her injury, and the progress he or she will make in response to treatment. If all individuals were characteristically identical and received the same quality of care, predicting outcome would be relatively straight forward. However, individual differences that include variable personality patterns and skills that affect the ability to adjust to change, as well as the fact that people have different resources available to them and receive a variety of treatments, confounds any such linear model.

"Outcome" can be defined as expected consequences or how we think things will turn out. Ideally, there would be a formula from which expected outcome could be derived. How we predict outcome is largely based on a set of variables that include demographic information, estimates of pre-morbid functioning, measurements that assess the effect of the injury and co-morbid issues on post-morbid functioning.

The first hurdle in predicting outcome is defining what "good outcome" means and recognizing that expectations tend to be very different for each individual. For the treating neurosurgeon, a positive outcome is that damage was averted or reduced, with minimal gross residua. For the patient, the best outcome is to achieve pre-morbid functioning, i.e., to return to who they were before their injury and to resume life as if their injury never happened. The goal of family members tends to be similar to the patient's, coupled with a desire that the patient receives appropriate treatments. For the rehabilitation staff, good outcome is the patient achieving as high a level of independent functioning as is reasonable for the injuries the patient has incurred. For insurance providers, good outcome is viewed in terms of functional recoveries tied to specific treatment goals. Once the goals are reached or the patient's recovery plateaus, then treatments are stopped. A vocational therapist views good outcome as returning to work. All these examples demonstrate the lack of a unified definition of outcome.

To help overcome this hurdle, the following figure (Figure 1) presents a conceptual model that integrates the multiple perspectives of the patient, caregivers,

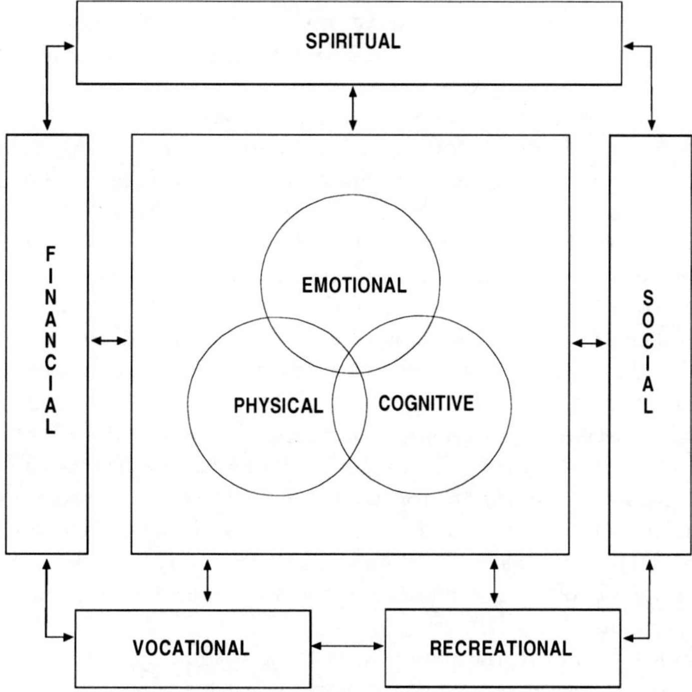

Figure 1. Ruff Conceptual Model.

treatment providers and policy makers within a dynamic context that recognizes and respects individual differences (Ruff, 1999; Ruff and Hibbard, 2003). The overlapping circles are based on how we organize the domains of functioning subserved by the brain and represent the integration of physical, emotional and cognitive dimensions. These intrapersonal dimensions must be placed within a socio-historical context that includes how we feel about ourselves, how we interact with others, and how others interact with us. The bi-directional arrows among the squares account for how the interpersonal dimensions of work, finances, social life, recreation and spirituality interact with these core domains.

Within the rehabilitation context, these dimensions are isolated as domains of functioning that can be assessed by different specialists to describe strengths, weaknesses and deficits. This multidisciplinary approach—which has been used as far back as post-WWI (Gutman, 1997)—recognizes that simply being medically cleared does not mean that individuals should be discharged without follow up as if their injury never happened. Instead, many patients will need additional services to achieve optimal outcomes. Based on 1997 data from 14 states, the CDC currently estimates that of the one quarter million people hospitalized for TBI annually, about a third of adults will require help with daily activities one year post discharge (Langlois et al., 2003). Ultimately, the multidisciplinary approach attempts to capture how the unique interaction of these dimensions accounts for individual differences and creates separate, but composite identities for the patients we treat.

The second hurdle for predicting outcome is recognizing and controlling for the fact that these domains of individual functioning are assessed over *time*. Although there is as yet not set of standards for defining this continuum of time (Bullinger et al., 2002), there is general agreement that for assessment and outcome studies, it should be broken down into three periods: pre-morbid (pre-injury), co-morbid (at the time of injury) and post-morbid (post-injury). As with all research, the greatest challenge is how to make generalizations about populations and the individuals they represent.

Individuals have a variety of physical, cognitive and emotional capacities, characteristics and vulnerabilities before being injured, that with the location and severity of injury in large part determines their initial response. Estimates of *premorbid* functioning are necessary to establish a baseline against which response to treatment and post-morbid strengths and weaknesses can be compared (Hall, Wallbom and Englander, 1998; Ruff, Mueller and Jurica, 1996b). Population-based outcome studies analyze trends that help us make generalizations about people who share sets of characteristics and create predictor variables, i.e., the premorbid demographic variables and medical and psychiatric risk factors that contribute to making some individuals more likely to incur TBI. These studies provide guidelines for how individuals who share a number of characteristics might be expected to function, or how they might respond to different treatments. Case studies attempt to test these rules.

Evaluating how *co-morbid* factors contribute to the patient's presentation is also key. In addition to the location and severity of insult, the degree to which the most common physical symptoms that accompany TBI are present—including orthopedic injuries, vestibular problems, headaches, pain and fatigue—in large part determines their initial response.

After injury (*morbid*), the patient's outcome is impacted by both pre-morbid and co-morbid factors, the pattern of recovery, the effects of financial and behavioral

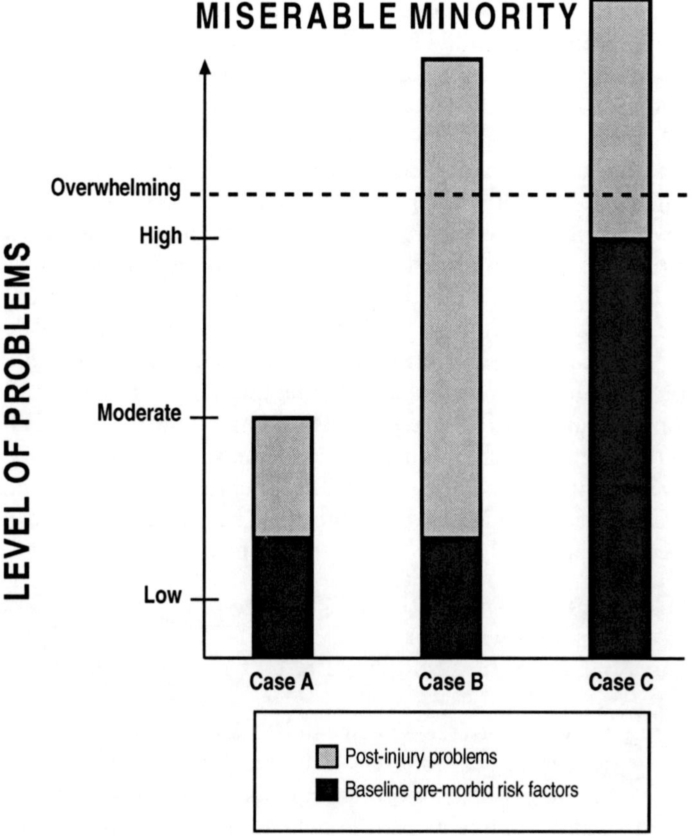

Figure 2. Cumulative Stress Model.

problems on families, and whether or not litigation is pursued. Above all, it is the interaction of these factors over time that determines the patient's outcome.

The second step in addressing how outcome measures assess patients is to recognize that despite the linear progression of time, those intrapersonal and interpersonal concepts continue to interact dynamically. Figure 2 above, which is based on cumulative stress paradigms, builds on the model presented in Figure 1. This model illustrates how many of the problems related to conducting outcome studies and making predictions about individual behavior are based on the fact that people respond differently to sequelae and that over time, an individual's response to their injury and residua changes.

This clinical model illustrates how many variables must be considered when rendering a clinical diagnosis, including demographics, pre-morbid risk factors, co-morbid conditions and post-morbid response to injury can result in very different outcomes. This model is based on the assumption that increased risk factors are associated with an increase of poor outcome. The black bars represents the baseline levels of pre-morbid risk factors that vary between individuals, such as age, previous concussion or emotional problems. The gray bars represent the impact of co-morbid and post-morbid variables resulting in MTBI, such as pain or orthopedic injuries, cognitive and emotional residua or inadequate financial or social support. These two factors vary greatly between individuals.

Figure 2 presents three sample cases of MTBI that illustrate this variability. In Case A, the individual has a low level of premorbid vulnerabilities that combine with the post-injury residua to result in a moderate level of problems, but enough reserve capacity or "head room" to manage additional problems of daily functioning. In Case B, the individual also has a low level of premorbid risk factors, but the post-accident residua are significantly more pronounced (orthopedic injury, headaches, vestibular problems, chronic pain, sleep disturbance, fatigue, anxiety). This individual's "head room" of resources is overwhelmed by the immediate impact and sequelae of injury. In Case C, the individual has a high level of pre-morbid risk factors, such as learning disability or ADHD, a history of substance abuse, poor psychosocial adjustment or increased age. Even before injury, this individual had considerably fewer resources to draw upon to manage life's stressors. Thus, their response to MTBI reflects a combination of increased vulnerability and inadequate resources.

Case A represents the majority of MTBI patients who make a quick recovery. Cases B and C represent the Miserable Minority. These three cases illustrate several points that pertain specifically to predicting outcome.

- The fact that people begin with different levels of premorbid risk factors alone suggests that some people are more vulnerable to incurring TBI. Post-injury, they already have fewer resources in reserve or "head room" to dedicate to recovery.
- Levels of pre-morbid stress—which can be based on any of the dimensions in Figure 1—further reduce resources available for recovery.
- An increased number of co-morbid stressors, such as headache, dizziness and orthopedic pain, will likely result in increased post-morbid levels of stress.
- Each additional pre-, co- and post-morbid factor subtracts from an individual's overall resources that are available for rehabilitation.
- Untreated, some stressors may resolve, but persistent stress tends to have a cumulative effect over time (Ruff, 2003).

Thus, there is an inverse relationship between the number of pre-morbid risk factors and the availability of resources individuals have to devote to recovery.

Together, these two clinical models help organize the symptomatic complexity of MTBI. With these in mind, let us now turn first to issues specific to predicting outcome for this population and then review problems related to conducting outcome studies.

ISSUES RELATED TO OUTCOME STUDIES

Inclusion of Key Variables

When investigating predictors of outcome, both the severity of the initial insult, premorbid vulnerabilities and psychosocial behavior must be considered. Prior to diagnostic criteria for MTBI being more clearly established and distinguished from Postconcussional Disorder (PCD), as well as from more severe levels of TBI, more weight was given to demographic factors. In the past decade, equal weight has been given to emotional (e.g., anxiety and depression), behavioral (e.g., substance abuse), cognitive (e.g., learning disabilities) and physical (e.g., neurological insults and other medical conditions) issues (Hall, Bushnik, Lakisic-Kazazic, Wright and Cantagallo, 2001; MacMillan, Hart, Martelli and Zasler, 2002). However, it is the dynamic relationship among all these variables that makes describing individuals and the aggregate MTBI population such a moving target.

Diagnostic muddle resulted in either an overlap or poor discrimination between different diagnostic entities, especially the comorbidity of MTBI, PCD and psychiatric conditions (anxiety, depression, PTSD). The diagnostic criteria established by AAN and ACRM were efforts not only to define the severity of injury, but also intended to serve as guidelines for treatment planning and expectations for outcome. At this time, there are three primary factors that must be incorporated into outcome studies.

Demographic Factors

The chief variables used in predicting outcome are age at the time of injury, gender, level of education, employment status, marital status, ethnicity and socio-economic status. Studies to date have been able to associate different etiologies with specific demographic variables. For example, children and older adults are at the highest risk for TBI secondary to falls. While an earlier study thought it was premature to conclude that the elderly had a uniformly poor outcome post-TBI, it is generally believed that older adults fare worse than younger patients with similar injuries, if for no other reason than the concept of cognitive reserve (Ferrel and Tanev, 2002; Kesler, Adams, Blasey and Bigler, 2003). In fact, it appears that MTBI in the geriatric population due to falls is on the rise (Adekoya, Thurman, White and Webb, 2002).

Because of a rise in risk-seeking behaviors, males between the ages of 18–25 are at the highest risk for TBI (as well as for spinal cord injury). Women may be at greater risk for more severe injuries secondary to domestic violence (Farace and Alves, 2001), but gender, minority status, age, substance abuse and low SES may also play a role (Wagner, Sasser, Hammond, Wierciesiewski and Alexander, 2000). While the role of socioeconomic status alone is not clear (that is, whether the conditions of poverty increase risk of TBI), it is hypothesized that if individuals who receive treatment from publicly supported programs uniformly receive substandard care, public policy related to resource allocation would have a more direct impact on the outcome of lower SES individuals (Reynolds, Page and Johnston, 2001).

Premorbid Medical Conditions

Although it is unknown whether certain physical illnesses make some individuals more vulnerable to TBI, in one study, 84% with TBI had co-occurring disabilities (Moscato, Trevisan and Willer, 1994). It is also not known whether TBI is a risk factor for Alzheimer's Disease (Rapoport and Feinstein, 2000; Smith, Uryu, Saatman, Trojanowski and McIntosh, 2003), or conversely, whether dementia places individuals at higher risk for TBI. As with many other conditions, such as stroke, the primary risk factor for TBI is a history of previous TBI or other neurological insults.

Premorbid Psychiatric Conditions

The conditions that contribute most to prediction of outcome are mood disorders, personality disorders, learning disorders, substance abuse and PTSD. In the absence of clear, documented history, however, it is difficult to distinguish between the cognitive and affective components of behavior and to determine how much was premorbid, how much is due (organically) to the injury itself, and how much is an emotional response with no obvious physiological basis. For example, the question of whether diminished cognitive functioning leads to depression or whether idiopathic depression causes difficulties in cognitive function (for example, working memory, recall/retrieval problems) is not limited to MTBI. However, the inability to clearly delineate deficits has implications for treatment. There also are no clear roadmaps that guide the practitioner through the coincidence of DSM-IV-TR psychopathology and MTBI. Although certain personality types appear to be more vulnerable to catastrophic responses or difficulties adjusting to sequelae (Ruff and Richardson, 1999), without corroboration from a third party, premorbid psychological functioning can confound post-injury evaluation, especially when trying to assess personality functioning issues.

Methodological Considerations

Variability

Overall, it is difficult to capture the variability of the combination of level of injury, the pace of recovery and measurable outcomes over time. First and foremost, the rules that apply to the readily identifiable population of moderate to severe brain injury that receives treatment do not apply to MTBI. Specifically, the relationship between level of severity and outcome at different points of time (1, 5 or 10 years) is still equivocal, especially with MTBI (Hammond et al., 2001; Novack, Bush, Meythaler and Canupp, 2001; van Baalen et al., 2003). That is, the variability in levels of function over up to 10 years post injury—whether the individual has improved, declined, or is unchanged across neuropsychological domains—may not necessarily be associated with the initial level of injury severity (Millis et al., 2001), but instead with the kind and quality of care received. Most studies have found no association between the subjective impact of MTBI that results in a diagnosis of PCS and the demographic, pre-morbid risk factors, type of injury, length of LOC or PTA or post-morbid factors that often correlate with more severe brain injury (Karzmack, Hall and Englander, 1995).

Second, comparing data in follow-up studies is complicated by the variable number of years post-injury, as well as the fact that they use different measures to gather data across time—from the initial insult to more than 10 years post. The data from each point in time that can be gathered to serve different purposes—initial triage, treatment planning, estimating length of hospital stay, and estimating the type and amount of services needed—does not necessarily apply equally in predicting acute outcome for patients with severe TBI outcome.

Study Samples

There are at least three levels of population sampling. At the most global level, there is a population of all individuals who sustain TBI, approximately 80% of whom are considered MTBI. As discussed earlier in this chapter [see Incidence and

Prevalence, above], studies have been limited because they only are able to identify the TBI patients who seek hospital treatment. Of the approximately 20% who do seek medical services, a very small percentage actually receive any form of treatment other than medications for acute pain. Indeed, data is typically confined to ER admissions, yet many individuals may seek assistance from their primary care physician, or from an osteopath, chiropractor or acupuncturist. Although this percentage has remained relatively stable over the past decade, changes in reimbursement rates ultimately may reduce the number of admissions, which in turn only may allow researchers to capture an even smaller random sample from this pool (Hoffman et al., 2003).

The second population sampling is comprised of those 20% that seek medical services. This sample was captured in the three center study mentioned earlier in this chapter (Levin et al., 1987c). The advantage of this sample, as well as archival and large centralized databases, is that these individuals are not self-selected. It is among this group that we believe that 80–90% make a favorable recovery. Thus to capture the Miserable Minority of 10 to 20% represents multiple challenges. If the investigators are interested in identifying a group of 30 patients that fall in the Miserable Minority, then the required sample size for this study should be between 150 to 300 MTBI patients.

This leads us to the third population sampling, which is comprised of much smaller clinical sample sizes. For example, if 50 MTBI are compared to 50 control participants, then the results are difficult to interpret unless the percentage of those individuals that fall in the Miserable Minority are identified. If 2 out of the 50 fall in the Miserable Minority, then one would not expect significant group differences. However, if 45 of the patients fall in the Miserable Minority, then group comparisons are more likely yield significant differences. *The fact that 10–20% of the MTBI patients fall in the Miserable Minority has not been sufficiently recognized in research designs and therefore has likely led to multiple false positives and false negatives.* As an analogy, assume that 10–20% of HIV+ patients develop AIDS. Does it make sense to study 50 HIV+ patients and then offer conclusions about AIDS or HIV without knowing if any of the HIV+ patients also have AIDS?

Sample size impacts the power of all studies. In addition to small study samples and only a small percentage of the MTBI population being studied due to difficulties identifying the population (Gollaher et al., 1998), these studies suffer from the self-selection and recruitment biases that are inherent in clinical samples (Karzmack et al., 1995). Most longitudinal studies of MTBI, which are volunteer-based, suffer from very high drop out rates. It has not been determined whether patient's symptoms resolve and patients thereby disqualify themselves from studies and that the remaining individuals who actually participate completely in studies have enough motivation to do so, or whether other factors are at play. The end result is a very limited picture of a very small part of the actual MTBI population, which makes it questionable how reliable these predictors could be.

Assuming that the MTBI population can be identified, the most problematic variable for predicting outcome, formulating diagnostic criteria and applying them as guidelines for treatment planning, is the construct of time. We have discussed how different measurements of severity and duration of symptoms has made diagnosis of MTBI difficult [see Diagnosis of MTBI, above]. The following six points summarize how the same problems that plague diagnosis equally impact outcome studies.

Symptoms May Not Be Pronounced Enough for an Individual to Seek Treatment

Why do only a small percentage of individuals who incur MTBI seek medical services and receive a diagnosis? The NIH consensus team found that the most critical problem related to treating the 'silent epidemic' was that MTBI was under-diagnosed. Are the symptoms of the majority of MTBI subclinical? Does MTBI affect a population that may be under-insured compared to other segments of our population? Are they fully recovered and not in need of services? To date, our studies cannot answer these questions. It is unfortunate that in the absence of data, personal biases about patients' motivation, levels of pain and functionality have filled this research void. It is ironic that patients who do seek treatment are often labeled negatively.

Because the majority of studies are conducted on the clinical sample of MTBI patients who sought treatment and agreed to participate in programs, most studies cite recruitment and self-selection biases as major weaknesses. Several recent studies have attempted to address different dimensions of this problem. A study by McCullagh and Feinstein (2003) used Canadian population-based administrative data to compare pre- and post-injury healthcare utilization. Another study, which appears to be the first to examine a non-referred population, used demographic data from the U.S. Army database on Vietnam-era veterans and a follow-up questionnaire to explore factors associated with long-term outcome (Vanderploeg, Curtiss, Duchnick and Luis, 2003). The CDC's response to the NIH consensus statement was to organize state-based surveillance systems to collect data which are now just beginning to bear fruit (Langlois et al., 2003).

Symptoms May Not Be Pronounced Enough to Be Defined as Deficits on Either Medical or Neuropsychological Tests

The general lack of objective evidence from neuroimaging to independently and objectively identify physiological deficits to support neuropsychological tests, behavioral evidence or subjective complaints, is perhaps the biggest strike against individuals with MTBI (Bigler, 2001; Friedman, Brooks, Jung, Hart and Yeo, 1998; Lewine, Davis, Sloan, Kodituwakku and Orrison, 1999; Ruff, Cullum and Luerssen, 1989; Sarno et al., 2000). People, including medical professionals, believe, treat and study what they can see. For this reason, adopting Levin or Prigatano's division of MTBI into "complicated" and "uncomplicated"—essentially patients with positive CT scans and those with negative scans—would at least identify a subset of the MTBI population with measurable outcome variables that could be studied.

It is unfortunate that the invisible nature of MTBI just as often results in the individual being accused of malingering (Hilsabeck & Irby, 1999; Langeluddecke & Lucas, 2003; Sbordone, Seyranian & Ruff, 2000) as of "just" having premorbid psychological problems that are unrelated to traumatic injury. Undoubtedly, some people who have incurred MTBI are malingering in order to make financial or emotional secondary gains. While there are some measures to assist practitioners in the detection of malingering, there are no standard tools to assess secondary gain (Hilsabeck & Irby, 1999; Iverson & Binder, 2000) or to distinguish between unconscious motivation and conscious misrepresentation.

There May Be an Obvious Lack of Agreement Between Medical and Neuropsychological Tests and Behavioral Observations

Since the deficits in MTBI tend to be relatively subtle, a person with MTBI may be aware that "something is not right," but to the casual observations of family, friends or co-workers, he or she appears to be back to normal. Symptoms that may be readily identifiable in daily living skills may not be apparent on a CT scan or fall easily into the domains of behavior evaluated by formal neuropsychological measures. Indeed, many of the symptoms that follow MTBI such as anger, pain, irritability and disinhibition are subjective phenomena and cannot be objectively quantified. Given the lack of standardized definitions coupled with the different viewpoints inherent in the various disciplines, a lack of agreement should be expected.

The Pathophysiology of MTBI May Follow a Different Time Course Than Moderate to Severe TBI

Since TBI is graded by degree of deficit over a specific time course, if objective evidence that may have existed during the acute stage of injury was not gathered, it may be no longer available in the chronic stage, despite the fact that the patient may continue to report problems. For example, biochemical markers such as the serum marker astroglial protein S-100B, the presence of the apolipoprotein E-epsilon4 (APOE-epsilon4) allele and neuron specific enolase are being explored to improve the sensitivity of ER assessment (Chin, 2003; Jancin, 2002; Nathoo, Chetry, van Dellen, Connolly & Naidoo, 2003). Wallesch (2001) has recently argued that in order to improve prognostic predictions, all MTBI patients should receive the same exam as patients with more obvious, severe damage, including the use of CT to detect diffuse axonal injury (DAI) or MR technologies to look for biochemical markers. Others have suggested that a combination of symptoms and biochemical markers may help predict which MTBI patients are at risk for developing PCD (deKruijk et al., 2002; Herrmann et al., 2001; Savola & Hillbom, 2003).

There is some indication that the time course of diffuse axonal injury and inflammatory responses may be significantly longer than once believed and that biological markers only become evident in the chronic stage of injury (Lenzinger, Morganti-Kossmann, Laurer & McIntosh, 2001; Vink, 1989). As researchers and practitioners, we need to take patients with MTBI seriously and continue to look for physiological bases for symptoms as long as they persist (Bigler, 2001).

Symptoms May Be Present Only Under Certain Conditions or Wax and Wane Independent of Any Obvious Physiological Etiology, Psychosocial Stressors, or Environmental Factors

The symptoms associated with MTBI cut across neuropsychological domains. Deficits are associated with cognitive and emotional functioning. Individuals with more moderate to severe TBI have just as wide a range of symptoms, but their deficits are often more focal and associated with specific brain regions. In the case of frontal damage, however, there is considerably more diversity of symptomatology and inconsistency in its presentation. Damage in this region of the brain is most often associated with overall cognitive slowing, attentional difficulties, executive and affect regulation problems (Kay, 1986; Levin, Benton, Muizelaar & Eisenberg, 1996; Levin, Grafman & Eisenberg, 1987b; Vogenthaler, 1987).

Symptoms Vary Based on Physiological and Psychosocial Issues

While it may seem obvious that medication can impact physical, cognitive and emotional functioning, it should be no less obvious that an individual's level of pain or fatigue will take its toll on performance, regardless of how much effort is exerted. In fact, maximal effort or "overdoing it" often results in symptom exacerbation and a downward spiraling effect. That is, increased stress often disrupts sleep, which increases fatigue and results in lower levels of performance, which creates more stress, etc. Financial stress due to lost work time almost invariably leads to familial stress and less time to relax, socialize with friends and generally "recharge." As illustrated in Figure 1, we must be able to account for the interrelationships of these variables and how they fluctuate over time.

Outcome Measures

Assessing functional status and predicting outcome are now essential to TBI rehabilitation programs, both for treatment planning and for securing funding for treatment and aftercare. Much of this assessment is primarily for diagnostic purposes, rather than for treatment considerations. When evaluating outcome measures it is important to consider 1) whether the measures provide indicators for short-term and/or long-term outcome, 2) to which segment of the population they apply, and 3) what functional dimensions the measure purports to predict.

To date, no measure has emerged that is universally-administered and comprehensively evaluated outcome. To achieve a comprehensive assessment, a long list of predictors should be included. However, the focus of predicting outcome has been based on the severity of the brain trauma, that is, length of LOC, duration of PTA or level of function at discharge. Age has emerged as a powerful predictor. In recent years, premorbid factors have been shown to impact outcome, including: multiple trauma, education level, employment status pre-injury, type and length of employment pre-injury, gender and ethnicity. Moreover, a history of substance abuse or psychiatric issues are thought to correlate premorbid coping skills with post-morbid disability (MacMillan 2002).

Unfortunately, there has been little consensus on which variables, individually or in combination, are the most significant predictors. Few, if any variables are independent. As a concession to the number of variables that influence outcome, many studies apply multivariate techniques. Although the huge variability in instruments, definitions and methodologies make it difficult to compare studies, one key problem is that studies examine patients at different points in time, generally either 3-, 6-, 12- or 24-months post-injury. However, for MTBI populations, the most glaring problem is the lack of outcome studies conducted with large sample sizes that are representative and distinguish between the recovered majority and the Miserable Minority.

Each of the scales used for short- and long-term evaluation of predominantly the moderate to severe TBI population has been shown to have strengths and weaknesses, with varying levels of sensitivity and specificity. Regardless of what they were designed to measure, they have been used independently or in combination with one another to assess functional status, evaluate treatment, predict employment and community integration and identify at-risk individuals. Predicting service utilization, or what services should be used for how long, has remained problematic, especially in relation to estimates of long-term disability and workmen's compensation insurance claim costs.

Short-term outcome measures collect demographic data and evaluate two major areas: injury severity and functional status (for a review of measures, see Hall et al., 2001). The GCS score and neuroimaging assess injury severity in the acute stage. The Galveston Orientation and Amnesia Test (GOAT) was designed to determine when patients emerge out of PTA and are able to reliably undergo neuropsychological testing. The Orientation Log (O-LOG) was designed to document the length of LOC and PTA.

Other measures were developed to assess specific functional areas during the course of hospitalization or treatment. The Functional Independence Measure (FIM), which assesses the level of independence in self-care over the course of rehabilitation hospitalization has been adopted by Medicare for making length of stay decisions. The Glasgow Outcome Scale (GOS) was originally conceived as a companion to the GCS for capturing the degree of disability and predicting outcome. It is still used internationally, but its poor sensitivity (van der Naalt, van Zommeren, Stuiter & Minderhoud, 1999) has resulted in it largely being replaced by the Disability Rating Scale (DRS). The DRS was designed in the rehabilitation setting to assess moderate-to-severe TBI by tracking from initial coma to post-discharge status. Since its items are more dependent on longer-term recovery (Hammond et al., 2001), the FIM has been shown to be more effective in predicting longer-term outcomes. The DRS appears to be more sensitive to changes over a shorter term. The FIM's motor score also has been shown to be a good predictor of length of stay and overall FIM discharge score (Hall et al., 2001). FIM and DRS scores were reliably predicted by comparing GOAT scores and age at the time of injury (Zafonte et al., 1997).

Long-term outcome measures have been used to gather descriptive statistics about the incidence of TBI and to measure treatment effectiveness. These measures assess and attempt to predict community integration, employment-related issues, and to a lesser degree, quality of life issues. The current standard for measuring these outcomes is the International Classification of Disability (ICF), which is an updated classification of functioning, disability and health from the WHO International Classification of Impairments, Disabilities and Handicaps (ICIDH) (1980). It's key definitions include description of body structure and function (impairment), activity (disability) and participation (handicap) (World-Health-Organization, 2001).

A major goal of these long-term outcome measures has been to estimate the type and cost of services each individual will need and for how long to determine immediate and future public financial burden, as well as to prospectively determine the types of services that need to be developed for patients and caregivers. Longitudinal studies have been used to reveal the nature and severity of longer-term deficits. For example, such studies were the basis of determining that longer-term cognitive remediation and rehabilitation aftercare programs were needed (Alaoui et al., 1998). The Functional Integration Log (FIL) and DRS together have been shown to be effective for retrospective and prospective assessment of rehabilitation outcome (Schatz, Hillary, Moelter & Chute, 2002). An early retrospective 10-year follow-up of severe TBI determined that these individuals continued to make improvement throughout those

10 years, i.e., that recovery continued beyond the usually quoted 24-month period (Sbordone, Liter & Pettler-Jennings, 1995). Although the CDC continues to revise its formulas, psychosocial disability, rather than physical and cognitive disability, may be a better predictor of service use (Hodgkinson, Veerabangsa, Drane & McCluskey, 2000).

Rather than attempt to single out any one measure or demographic statistic, many more recent study designs attempt to reflect a biopsychosocial model in which a complex of predictor variables are dynamically inter-dependent. For example, while an individual's perspective of their quality of life is affected by their level of independence, level of income, where they live and the quality of their support network, their employment status and level of income is a primary determinant in measuring their quality of life (Corrigan, Bogner, Mysiw, Clinchot & Fugate, 2001).

The Ruff Neurobehavioral Inventory (Ruff & Hibbard, 2003) was developed to capture outcome based on the patient's perspective modeled after Figure 1 shown in this chapter. Various scales were developed for each of the three intrapersonal dimensions; the *physical* domain is comprised of a Neurological, Pain and Somatic Scales, the *emotional* domain of an Anger, Anxiety, Depression, Paranoia, PTSD and Substance Abuse Scales and the *cognitive* domain is evaluated according to an Attention, Memory, Language and Executive Functioning Scales. The interpersonal dimensions assess *quality of life* according to scales that capture Physical or Sexual Abuse, Activities of Daily Living, Psychosocial Integration, Vocation and Finance, and Spirituality. Since outcome is judged according to premorbid functioning, all of these scales are examined from two different points in time: currently and premorbidly. This provides a comparison of the patient's baseline or premorbid level of functioning and the post-morbid status. Finally, the RNBI includes four validity scales to rule out overly positive or negative response styles.

Issues Related to Predicting Employment Status

Over the past two decades, assessment of outcome has shifted from rate of survival to long-term functional status of the working population of individuals between the ages of 16 and 64 who incur TBI. Disability has an immense financial impact on individuals, their families and society as a whole in the form of lost wages, workforce productivity and the burden of providing services.

The ability to live independently and return to work are thought to be major factors in individuals' perceived overall quality of life. Not returning to work is associated with poorer psychosocial adjustment and increased somatic complaints (Kreutzer et al., 2003). TBI patients were at higher risk for developing depressive symptoms, especially if they were unemployed or impoverished pre-injury (Seel et al., 2003). Hence, biopsychosocial predictive models need to be developed to identify high-risk patients.

As with the evolution of the TBI literature into finer definitions and more robust studies, the literature on outcome specifically related to employment has gone from simply counting how many people returned to work after discharge to developing more of an operational definition for "successful employment." Since higher levels of education could predict return to work, but could not predict the level of work responsibility, full- or part-time capacity, or how well the individual will function (Gollaher et al., 1988), more questions are being asked about pre-morbid employment status. For example, was the individual employed pre-injury and if so, how long were they engaged in what type of employment?

Post-morbid variables, such as the availability of family emotional and financial support, of post-acute rehabilitation and vocational rehabilitation services, as well as the patients' awareness of their difficulties, also can play an important role (Novack et al., 2001). There also are attempts to better describe post-morbid employment, starting with how long a period of time there was between injury and return to work, whether the individual returned to the same position with the same employer and how long they remained at work. Were their job responsibilities modified and were they working the same number of hours and receiving the same level of compensation? And finally, what impact did job changes have on job satisfaction?

Regardless of how much an individual wishes to return to work, a high level of employer support is needed for developing alternate duties and accommodation. Several studies have examined employer's inclinations and incentives to hold or modify a position for a TBI patient. In general, employers were found to be less tolerant of and less likely to accommodate cognitive and behavioral deficits than physical disabilities (Blair & Spellacy, 1989).

Return to work rates were moderated by types of employment, primarily whether there was latitude in job descriptions to allow for adjustments and accommodations (Crisp, 1992). MTBI patients who pre-morbidly had greater job independence and decision making latitude had higher rates of return to work. Thus, higher level white collar managers were more likely to return to work than clerical, sales, service, manual labor and trade workers (Friedland and Dawson, 2001). In addition, individuals who retained the ability to drive and non-minority group members were more likely to be stably employed (Kreutzer et al., 2003).

Studies that attempt to predict return to work or employment status use a combination of measures and indicators that include of length of PTA, assessment of cognition, disability levels, GCS scores, functional status, length of acute hospital stay and prior occupation. Although an earlier study found that the GCS alone was not predictive of employment or community integration (Neuman & Bowen, 1996), a more recent study by Wagner (2000) found that the most significant single outcome predictor of long-term disability and community integration for individuals hospitalized with TBI was injury severity (as represented by the GCS score), especially when it was combined with premorbid demographic variables.

The Functional Assessment Measure (FAM) is an adjunct to the FIM (known as the FIM-FAM). The fact that it did not prove to be a good predictor of employment status and community integration after 24 months post-discharge may reflect ceiling effects (Gurka et al., 1999). The DRS Employability and FAM employment questions correlated well, but since information from the FAM did not really add to the DRS (Hall et al., 2001), the DRS is the measure most consistently used. It alone has most consistently shown its usefulness in predicting employment outcome (Hall et al., 2001; Ponsford, Oliver, Curran & Ng, 1995).

One study found length of PTA and the number of complaints 3-months post, but not gender, age or education to be significant (Van Der Naalt, et al, 1999). Another study found that the deficits exhibited 6-months post and pre-morbid variables of age, education, employment status and history of alcohol abuse to be more predictive of outcome (Novak, et al, 2001). Still, yet another study found that 12-months post-injury, a combination of education level, psychiatric history, violent mechanism of injury, discharge status, pre-morbid substance abuse and injury severity were predictive of employment status for individuals with moderate to severe TBI (Wagner, Hammond, Sasser & Wiercisiewski, 2002). For more severe TBI, demographic characteristics, especially age, were found to be the best predictors of employment 4-years post and patients who had been employed pre-injury were 3 to 5 times more likely to be employed post (Keyser-Marcus et al., 2002). The variability of the patient population and the fact that these studies evaluate patients at different points in time make valid comparisons difficult.

Outcomes and Employment for MTBI

As discussed above, describing outcome for a population that has not been adequately identified is problematic at best. Nearly all of the literature on predicting outcome is based on the identifiable population of patients who seek and receive treatment, the vast majority of whom are classified as having moderate to severe brain injuries.

Virtually all the measures that have been developed to predict outcome, including employment, are designed to assess levels of function in rehabilitation settings within the first several months post-injury. Since all these measures were developed to assess more severe levels of brain injury, ceiling effects preclude their applicability or usefulness with MTBI. For example, for predicting who would benefit from early intervention, the predictors of age, injury severity score, CT scan or length of stay cannot be used to identify cognitive deficits in MTBI as they can with more severe injuries (Orest, 1999).

Most studies have found no association between the subjective impact of MTBI that results in a diagnosis of PCS and the demographic, pre-morbid risk factors, type of injury, length of LOC or PTA or post-morbid factors that often correlate with more severe brain injury (Karmack, 1995). Some measures (the FIM or DRS), combined with GCS scores, length of LOC, PTA and demographic variables can yield better predictors of longer-term outcome in moderate to severe TBI. Yet few similar combinations have been proven to be good predictors of employment and community integration (Gurka et al., 1999). For example, the GCS score alone was not found to be predictive of employment status in moderate to severe MTBI (van der Naalt et al., 1999). The FIM's motor score has been shown to have poor sensitivity for evaluation of MTBI. With the exception of the GOAT, none of the inpatient rehabilitation measures (FIM, FAM, DRS) have proven sensitive for evaluation of MTBI, let alone predictability of employment (Hall et al., 2001).

There is very limited literature on MTBI population and employment. Much of it is related to what is now euphemistically termed "effort" measures (see, e.g., Binder & Rohling 1996). In other words, the focus is on determining whether or not the patient is malingering or faking bad, with the goal of denying to the malingerer disability and compensation claims. There is considerably less effort invested in examining the methodological issues related to describing this population (see discussion above), to determining why an individual's performance would be sub-optimal or to convincingly differentiate between fatigue, medication side-effects, attentional fluctuation, diminished self-confidence, anxiety, posttraumatic stress, depression, treatment received or socioeconomic status. An emerging number of neuropsychologists believe that the MTBI cause no neurological residua and therefore, these patients should be able to return to work.

One recent longitudinal study (intake, 3- and 12-months post-injury) is the only study we found that actually looked at compensation seeking practices and return to work rates for MTBI patients (Reynolds, et al 2003). Its findings examined compensation-seeking behavior among MTBI patients. This study confirmed that compensation seeking of any type was associated with a delayed return to work. The mean delay for patients in litigation to return to work was 7 months, as compared to 6 weeks for patients receiving employer-based compensation (sick pay, workers' compensation) and 4 days for individuals not seeking any compensation at all. They noted that insurance and worker's compensation systems might play a role in how long the patient is involved in seeking compensation. They suggested that "the need to repeatedly convince skeptical insurers that one is ill sometimes leads to adoption of a disability mentality and an associated delay in return to work" (p. 146).

No demographic variables (age, gender, years of education, ethnicity, SES) were found to be predictive of litigation-seeking behavior in this study. However, higher age and SES were associated with initial administrative compensation. Both types of compensation seeking were associated with increased use of prescription medication, although it was unclear whether it was related to subjective complaints or the nature of injury. The authors concluded that we need to consider and better understand precipitating factors (events associated with initial symptom presentation) and perpetuating factors (conditions that maintain symptoms after the trigger disappears) of this population.

Identifying the Miserable Minority

As discussed earlier in this chapter, the vast majority of MTBI patients are thought to go undetected because their symptoms are minor and resolve within several days. They do not seek medical treatment, and hence elude datasets that attempt to describe this population. A small subset of the larger MTBI population that does seek medical care and treatment are the basis of what we know about MTBI. Most of these individuals recover within one to three months and then disappear from the radar screen. The even smaller subset of patients that do not fully recover by three months post-injury is the Miserable Minority.

The only agreed upon criterion for diagnosis of the Miserable Minority is prolonged disability by the persistence of a complex of interactive symptoms that DSM-IV has crystallized into the diagnosis of Post-concussional Disorder (PCD). Some initial symptoms, such as vomiting and nausea tend to resolve quickly, whereas headache and dizziness tend to endure. Somatic symptoms that develop hours to weeks after initial insult also tend to be more enduring: sleep disturbance, fatigue, hypersensitivity to light and sound, blurred or double vision or tinnitus. Cognitive complaints generally include: reduced attention, concentration and short-term memory, slowed thinking and difficulty multi-tasking. Symptoms of depression, such as increased irritability and frustration, and anxiety also commonly develop (Mittenberg, Tremont, Zielinski, Fichera & Rayls, 1996; Ruff et al., 1996a). More recently, it has been suggested that this cluster of symptoms are presented by chronic pain (CP) as well as MTBI patients. However, the MTBI population tended to report greater cognitive symptoms and the CP patients reported higher rates of emotional symptoms (Smith-Seemiller, Fow, Kant & Franzen, 2003). As with the Reynolds study (above), the impact of medication on symptom endorsement remains an important unanswered question.

Since it is thought that one of the reasons the Miserable Minority's symptoms persist is because untreated initial symptoms become self-perpetuating and self-reinforcing, the limited research on this population has focused on early identification. One early study suggested that level of psychological distress, rather than demographic, pre-morbid risk, injury-related or post-morbid factors was strongly related to the development of persistent PCD (Karzmack et al., 1995). That is, this population self-selected based on subjective evaluation of the impact of the injury and symptoms playing a larger role in PCD symptomatology than any pre- or post-morbid factors.

The question of whether our samples of MTBI is based on biased a population with complaints of pre-existing problems was explored in recent study (McCullagh & Feinstein, 2003). This study compared MTBI patients who agreed with patients who did not agree to participate in a study. The authors found that the individuals who had fewer post-injury symptoms were less likely to participate. However, this study found no differences between the groups in their premorbid utilization of medical services. For those patients who agreed to participate in the study, the post-accident residuals were worse and they sought more treatments.

In a more recent study, key predictors of six-month outcome were the presence of headache, dizziness and nausea at the time of initial presentation (Jancin, 2002). Patients with all three symptoms had only a 50% recovery rate at six months, as compared to a 78% recovery rate for patients who presented with none of these symptoms. The other major predictor of long-term outcome is a range of symptoms of perceived vulnerability that take the form of acute anxiety and posttraumatic stress (Harvey & Bryant, 1998). Especially when these symptoms remain untreated or were resistant to treatment, there appeared to be an overlap of postconcussional disorder and posttraumatic stress (Friedland & Dawson, 2001).

The results of several studies strongly suggest that identification of individuals at risk for persistent PCD and implementation of focused treatment reduces symptom duration. Brief, cognitive-behavioral therapy has been shown to assist in increased realistic assessment of the effects of concussion, ward off misattribution of responsive symptoms to organic brain injury, and self-reinforcing behaviors that perpetuate difficulties (Mittenberg et al., 1996). In a randomized controlled trial, it was found that for MTBI patients who were not admitted to the hospital, but presented with PCD symptoms, increased anxiety, depression or posttraumatic stress to emergency services and general practitioners, routine follow-ups with specialists reduced the severity of PCD symptoms (Friedland & Dawson, 2001). Both studies strongly suggest that the role of post-morbid support (Novack et al., 2001) should not be underestimated when charting a patient's course of recovery. At this point in time, we have the following recommendations to offer:

- Take all patients seriously, regardless of GCS score, length of LOC or PTA. Ruling out a concussion should be done with respect and dignity towards patients, especially if there is emotional overlay.
- Look for risk factors and early indicators of the potential to develop PCD.
- Treat all pain (headache, orthopedic) and vestibular symptoms aggressively.
- Provide education, realistic expectations for symptom relief as well as close to the time of injury as possible.

- If symptoms persist following three months post-accident, provide counseling and make referrals that target symptoms (neurologists, orthopedists, ophthalmologists, physical therapy, speech therapy, brief psychotherapy).

SUMMARY AND CONCLUSIONS

The importance of early studies of patients with brain injury is that they were the first efforts to collect descriptive data on the population. From these studies, descriptive statistics on incidence helped document which populations have been most vulnerable and begin to define risk factors for TBI. Data from these early studies was instrumental in making policy the changes on automobile, motorcycle and bicycle safety guidelines and establish preventive strategies to reduce incidence and lower mortality rates, as well as in the areas of domestic violence and gun control legislation. The time has come to move beyond descriptive studies and tackle the immense challenges of defining and capturing the complexities of outcome subsequent to MTBI.

Although the amount of progress that has been made to further our understanding of MTBI is impressive, we are just starting to study how to reliably predict outcome for these individuals. The accumulation of longitudinal data for the moderate and severe TBI population is better established in databases that were designed for long-term outcome studies (e.g., the Coma Databank, the Model Systems database). These outcome studies and public healthcare data show great promise in our ability to analyze trends and identify risk factors, even though the unique parameters of MTBI make it difficult to generalize these datasets to that population. Nonetheless, these studies can in part guide us in designing future studies by showing how different factors require different weighting across time.

Although progress has been made in the development of diagnostic criteria, we still lack a unified and standardized definition for MTBI and PCD. MTBI can be clearly differentiated from moderate to severe TBI, but we still need to explore the utility of more refined gradation with the spectrum of MTBI (Ruff & Jurica, 1999). Improved technology may reveal neurological or biochemical markers for both prospective and retrospective diagnosis (Bigler, 2001).

The largest problem that remains for us to address relative to predicting outcome is the identification of the elusive MTBI population that goes untreated. Public health policies that have focused on education and prevention strategies are one way to reach this group. The flip side is that increased awareness of MTBI may in part be responsible for escalation of claims made, and the iatrogenic effect of "disability industry" treatment providers may in fact be making the Miserable Minority more miserable. For the MTBI patients that we can identify, the disability industry would serve them better if we shifted our focus away from diagnosis and put our energy into increasing the availability and quality of services and into developing treatments that can improve their sense of well-being. Thus, a balance between careful diagnoses and efficacious treatments must lead the way towards improving the outcome of the Miserable Minority.

REFERENCES

Adekoya, N., Thurman, D. J., White, D. D., and Webb, K. W. (2002). Surveillance for Traumatic Brain Injury Deaths–United States, 1989–1998. *MMWR Surveillance Summary 51*, SS10: 1–16.

Alaoui, P., Mazaux, J., Masson, F., Vecsey, J., Destaillats, J., Maurette, P., Vanier, M., Levin, H., Joseph, P., and Barat, M. (1998). Long term neuropsychological outcome after traumatic brain injury. *Annales de Readaptation et de Medecine Physique 41,* 4: 171–81.

Alexander, M. P. (1995). Mild traumatic brain injury: pathophysiology, natural history and clinical management. *Neurology 45,* 1253–60.

American Academy of Neurology (1997). Practice Parameter: the management of concussion in sports. *Neurology 48,* 581–85.

American Congress of Rehabilitation Medicine (1993). Definition of mild traumatic brain injury. *Journal of Head Trauma Rehabilitation 8,* 86–87.

American Psychiatric Association (1994). *Diagnostic and statistical manual of mental disorders (4th ed.).* Washington, D.C.: Author.

Berube, J. (2001). The Traumatic Brain Injury Act amendments of 2000. *Journal of Head Trauma Rehabilitation 16,* 2: 210–13.

Bigler, E. D. (2001). The lesion(s) in traumatic brain injury: implications for clinical neuropsychology. *Archives of Clinical Neuropsychology 16,* 2: 95–131.

Binder, L. M., and Rohling, M. L. (1996). Money matters: A meta-analytic review of the effects of financial incentives on recovey after closed-head injury. *American Journal of Psychiatry 153:* 7–10.

Binder, L. M., Rohling, M. L., and Larrabee, J. (1997). A review of mild head trauma. Part I: Meta-analytic review of neuropsychological studies. *Journal of Clinical Experimental Neuropsychology 19,* 3: 421–31.

Blair, J. R., and Spellacy, F. J. (1989). Employer acceptability of behavioral changes with traumatic brain injury. *The Journal of Rehabilitation 55,* 3: 46–49.

Borgaro, S. R., Prigatano, G. P., Kwasnica, C., and Rexer, J. L. (2003). Cognitive and affective sequelae in complicated and uncomplicated mild traumatic brain injury. *Brain Injury 17,* 3: 189–98.

Brain Injury Association, U. S. A. The costs and causes of traumatic brain injury. Retrieved October 20, 2003 from: www.biausa.org.

Brain Injury Society, U.S.A. About traumatic brain injury. Retrieved October 10, 2003 from: http://www.virtualtrials.com.

Bullinger, M., Azouvi, P., Brooks, N., Basso, A., Christensen, A. L., Gobiet, W., Greenwood, R., Hutter, B., Jennet, B., Maas, A. I., Truelle, J. L., and von Wild, K. R. (2002). Quality of life in patients with traumatic brain injury-based issues, assessment and recommendations. *Restoration, Neurology and Neuroscience 20,* 3–4: 111–24.

Burnett, D. M., Kolakowsky-Hayner, S. A., Slater, D., Stringer, A., Bushnik, T., Zafonte, R., and Cifu, D. X. (2003). Ethnographic analysis of traumatic brain injury patients in the national Model Systems database. *Archives of Physical Medicine and Rehabilitation 84,* 2: 263–67.

Center for Disease Control, U. S. A. National center for injury prevention and control. Retrieved October 25, 2003 from: http://www.cdc.gov.

Center for Disease Control, U. S. A. Traumatic Brain Injury in the United States: A Report to Congress. Retrieved November 25, 2003 from: http://www.cdc.gov.

Chan, R. C. K., Hoosain, R., Lee, T. M. C., Fan, Y. W., and Fong, D. (2003). Are there sub-types of attentional deficits in patients with persisting post-concussive symptoms? A cluster analytical study. *Brain Injury 17,* 2: 131–48.

Chin, J. (2003). Significance of serum neuron-specific enolase in patients with acute traumatic brain injury. *Traumatology 6,* 1: 218–21.

Cicerone, K. (1996). Attention deficits and dual task demands after mild traumatic brain injury. *Brain Injury 10,* 2: 79–89.

Corrigan, J. D., Bogner, J. A., Mysiw, W. J., Clinchot, D., and Fugate, L. (2001). Life satisfaction after traumatic brain injury. *Journal of Head Trauma Rehabilitation 16,* 6: 543–55.

Crisp, R. (1992). Return to work after traumatic brain injury. *The Journal of Rehabilitation 58,* 4: 27–34.

deKruijk, J. R., Leffers, P., Menheere, P. P. C. A., Meerhoff, S., Rutten, J., and Twijnstra, A. (2002). Prediction of post-traumatic complaints after mild traumatic brain injury: early symptoms and biochemical markers. *Journal of Neurology Neurosurgery and Psychiatry 73,* 6: 727–33.

Dischiner, P., Read, K., Kerns, T., Ho, S., Kufera, J., Burch, C., Jawed, N., Burgess, A., and Bents, F. (2003). Causes and outcomes of mild traumatic brain injury: An analysis of CIREN data. *Annual Proceedings of the Association for the Advancement of Automotor Medicine 47:* 577–89.

Farace, E., and Alves, W. M. (2001). Review: Women have worse outcomes than men after traumatic brain injury. *Evidence-based Mental Health 4,* 12: 58.

Ferrel, R. B., and Tanev, K. S. (2002). Traumatic brain injury in older adults. *Current Psychiatry Reports 4*, 5: 354–62.

Friedland, J. F., and Dawson, D. R. (2001). Function after motor vehicle accidents: a prospective study of mild head injury and posttraumatic stress. *The Journal of Nervous and Mental Disease 189*, 7: 426–34.

Friedman, S., Brooks, W., Jung, R., Hart, B., and Yeo, R. (1998). Proton MR spectroscopic findings correspond to neuropsychological function in traumatic brain injury. *American Journal of Neuroradiology 19*, 10: 1879–77.

Gollaher, K., High, W. M., Sherer, M., Bergloss, P., Boake, C., Young, M. E., and Ivanhoe, C. (1988). Prediction of employment outcome one to three years following traumatic brain injury (TBI). *Brain Injury 12*, 4: 255–63.

Gollaher, W. H., Sherer, M., Bergloff, P., Boake, C., Young, M. E., and Ivanhoe, C. (1998). Prediction of employment outcome one to three years following traumatic brain injury (TBI). *Brain Injury 12*, 4: 255–63.

Gurka, J. A., Felmingham, K. L., Baguley, I. J., Schotte, D. E., Crooks, J., and Marosszeky, J. E. (1999). Utility of the functional assessment measure after discharge from inpatient rehabilitation. *Journal of Head Trauma Rehabilitation 14*, 3: 247–56.

Gutman, S. A. (1997). Occupational Therapy's Link to Vocational Reeducation 1910–1925. *The American Journal of Occupational Therapy 51*, 10: 907–15.

Hall, K. M., Bushnik, T., Lakisic-Kazazic, B., Wright, J., and Cantagallo, A. (2001). Assessing traumatic brain injury outcome measures for long-term follow-up of community-based individuals. *Archives of Physical Medicine and Rehabilitation 82*, 3: 367–74.

Hall, K. M., Wallbom, A. S., and Englander, J. (1998). Premorbid history and traumatic brain injury. *Neurorehabilitation 10:* 3–12.

Hammond, F. M., Grattan, K. D., Sasser, H. C., Corrigan, J. D., Bushnik, T., and Zafonte, R. D. (2001). Long-term recovery course after traumatic brain injury: A comparison of the functional independence measure and disability rating scale. *Journal of Head Trauma Rehabilitation 16*, 4: 318–29.

Harvey, A. G., and Bryant, R. A. (1998). Predictors of acute stress following mild traumatic brain injury. *Brain Injury 12*, 2: 147–54.

Herrmann, M., Curio, N., Jost, S., Grubich, Ebert, A. D., Fork, M. L., and Synowitz, H. (2001). Release of biochemical markers of damage to neuronal and glial brain tissue is associated with short and long-term neuropsychological outcome after traumatic brain injury. *Journal of Neurology Neurosurgery and Psychiatry 70:* 95–100.

Hilsabeck R. C., and Irby J. W. (1999). Effects of litigation and malingering on MMPI-2 performance in mild TBI. *Archives of Clinical Neuropsychology 14*, 8: 741.

Hodgkinson, A., Veerabangsa, A., Drane, D., and McCluskey, A. (2000). Service utilization following traumatic brain injury. *Journal of Head Trauma Rehabilitation 15*, 6: 1208–26.

Hoffman, J. M., Doctor, J. N., Chan, L., Whyte, J., Jha, A., and Dikmen, S. (2003). Potential impact of the new medicare prospective payment system on reimbursement for traumatic brain injury inpatient rehabilitation. *Archives of Physical Medicine and Rehabilitation 84*, 8: 1165–72.

Iverson, G. L., and Binder, L. M. (2000). Detecting exaggeration and malingering in neuropsychological assessment. *Journal of Head Trauma Rehabilitation 15*, 2: 829–58.

Jancin, B. (2002). Predicting long-term outcomes after mild traumatic brain injury. *Family Practice News 32*, 14: 18.

Karzmack, P., Hall, K., and Englander, J. (1995). Late-onset post-concussion symptoms after mild brain injury: The role of premorbid, injury-related, environmental and personality factors. *Brain Injury 9*, 1: 21–26.

Kay, T. (1986). *Minor head injury: An introduction for professionals*. Southboro, MA: National Head Injury Foundation.

Kay, T., Newman, B., Cavallo, M., Erzrachi, O., and Resnick, M. (1992). Toward a neuropsychological model of functional disability after mild traumatic brain injury. *Neuropsychology 6:* 371–84.

Kesler, S. R., Adams, H. F., Blasey, C. M., and Bigler, E. D. (2003). Premorbid intellectual functioning, education and brain size in traumatic brain injury: An investigation of the cognitive reserve hypothesis. *Applied Neuropsychology 10*, 3: 153–62.

Keyser-Marcus, L. A., Bricout, J. C., Wehman, P., Campbell, L. R., Cifu, D. X., Englander, J., High, W., and Zafonte, R. D. (2002). Acute predictors of return to employment after traumatic brain injury: A longitudinal follow-up. *Archives of Physical Medicine and Rehabilitation 83*, 5: 635–41.

Krauss, J. F., McArthur, D. L., Silverman, T. A., and Jayaraman, M. (1996). Epidemiology of brain injury. In R.K. Narayan, J.E. Wilberger and J. T. Povlishock, Eds.), *Neurotrauma*. New York: McGraw-Hill.

Kreutzer, J. S., Marwitz, J. H., Walker, W., Sander, A., Sherer, M., Bogner, J. A., Fraser, R., and Bushnik, T. (2003). Moderating factors in return to work and job stability after traumatic brain injury. *Journal of Head Trauma Rehabilitation 18,* 2: 128–38.

Langeluddecke, P. M., and Lucas, S. K. (2003). Quantitative measures of memory malingering on the Wechsler Memory Scale—Third edition in mild head injury litigants. *Archives of Clinical Neuropsychology 18,* 2: 181–97.

Langlois, J. A., Kegler, S. R., Butler, J. A., Johnson, R. L., Reichard, A. A., Coronadao, V. G., Anbesaw, W. S., and Thurman, D. J. (2003). Traumatic brain injury-related hospital discharges: Results for a 14-state surveillance system, 1997. *MMWR Surveillance Summary 52,* SS04: 1–39.

Lenzinger, P. M., Morganti-Kossmann, M. C., Laurer, H. L., and McIntosh, T. K. (2001). The duality of the inflammatory response to traumatic brain injury. *Molecular Neurobiology 24,* 1–3: 169–81.

Levin, H. S., Amparo, E., Eisenberg, H. M., Williams, D. H., High, W. M. J., McArdle, C. B., and Winer, R. L. (1987a). Magnetic resonance imaging and computerized tomography in relation to the neurobehavioral sequelae of mild and moderate head injuries. *Journal of Neurosurgery 66:* 706–13.

Levin, H. S., Benton, A. L., Muizelaar, J. P., and Eisenberg, H. M., Eds. (1996). *Catastrophic Brain Injury*. New York: Oxford University Press.

Levin, H. S., Grafman, J., and Eisenberg, H. M., Eds. (1987b). *Neurobehavioral Recovery from Head Injury*. New York: Oxford University Press.

Levin, H. S., Mattis, S., Ruff, R. M., Eisenberg, H. M., Marshall, L. F., Tabaddor, K., High, W. M., and Frankowski, R. F. (1987c). Neurobehavioral outcome following minor head injury: A three-center study. *Journal of Neurosurgery 66,* 234–243.

Levin, H. S., O'Donnell, V. M., and Grossman, R. G. (1979). The Galveston Orientation and Amnesia Test: A practical scale to assess cognition after head injury. *Journal of Nervous and Mental Disorders 167:* 675–84.

Lewine, J. D., Davis, J. T., Sloan, J. H., Kodituwakku, P. W., and Orrison, W. W., Jr. (1999). Neuromagnetic assessment of pathophysiologic brain activity induced by minor head trauma. *American Journal of Neuroradiology 20,* 5: 857–66.

MacMillan, P. J., Hart, B. L., Martelli, M. F., and Zasler, N. D. (2002). Pre-injury status and adaptation following traumatic brain injury. *Brain Injury 16,* 1: 41–49.

McCullagh, S., and Feinstein, A. (2003). Outcome after mild traumatic brain injury: an examination of recruitment bias. *Journal of Neurology, Neurosurgery and Psychiatry 74,* 1: 39–45.

Mellick, D., Gerhart, K. A., and Whiteneck, G. G. (2003). Understanding outcomes based on the post-acute hospitalization pathways followed by persons with traumatic brain injury. *Brain Injury 17,* 1: 55–71.

Millis, S. R., Rosenthal, M., Novack, T. A., Sherer, M., Nick, T. G., Kreutzer, J. S., High, W. M., and Ricker, J. H. (2001). Long-term neuropsychological outcome after traumatic brain injury. *Journal of Head Trauma Rehabilitation 16,* 4: 343–55.

Mittenberg, W., Tremont, G., Zielinski, R. E., Fichera, S., and Rayls, K. R. (1996). Cognitive-behavioral prevention of postconcussion syndrome. *Archives of Clinical Neuropsychology 11,* 2: 139–45.

Moscato, B. S., Trevisan, M., and Willer, B. S. (1994). The prevalence of traumatic brain injury and co-occurring disabilities in a national household survey of adults. *Journal of Neuropsychiatry and Clinical Neuroscience 6,* 2: 134–42.

Nathoo, N., Chetry, R., van Dellen, J. R., Connolly, C., and Naidoo, R. (2003). Apolipoprotein E polymorphism and outcome after closed traumatic brain injury: Influence of ethnic and regional differences. *Journal of Neurosurgery 98,* 2: 302–06.

National Institute of Health, U. S. A. (1998). Rehabilitation of persons with traumatic brain injury. *NIH Consensus Statement Online 16,* 1: 1–41.

Neuman, V., and Bowen, A. (1996). Lack of occupation after traumatic brain injury: who is affected? *Injury 27,* 5: 369.

Novack, T. A., Bush, B. A., Meythaler, J. M., and Canupp, K. (2001). Outcome after traumatic brain injury: Pathway analysis of contributions from premorbid, injury severity, and recovery variables. *Archives of Physical Medicine and Rehabilitation 82,* 3: 300–05.

Orest, M. (1999). Cognitive screening in mild traumatic brain injuries: Analysis of the neurobehavioral cognitive status exam when utilized during initial trauma hospitalization. *Physical Therapy 79*, 5: 518.

Ponsford, J. L., Oliver, J. H., Curran, C., and Ng, K. (1995). Prediction of employment status 2 years after traumatic brain injury. *Brain Injury 9*, 1: 11–20.

Rapoport, M. J., and Feinstein, A. (2000). Outcome following traumatic brain injury in the elderly: A critical review. *Brain Injury 14*, 8: 749–61.

Reynolds, W. E., Page, S. J., and Johnston, M. V. (2001). Coordinated and adequately funded state stress for rehabilitation of newly injured persons with tbi. *Journal of Head Trauma Rehabilitation 16*, 1: 34–46.

Ruff, R. M. (1999). Discipline specific approach versus individual care. In N. R. Varney and R. J. Roberts, Eds.), *Mild Head Injury: Causes, Evaluation and Treatment*. Mahwah, NJ: Erlbaum Associates.

Ruff, R. M. (2003). Sequelae of traumatic brain injury. In H. R. Winn, (Ed.), *Youman's Neurological Surgery* (Ch. 329, pp. 5181–5201). New York: W. B. Saunders Company.

Ruff, R. M., Camenzuli, L., and Mueller, J. (1996a). Miserable minority: emotional risk factors that influence the outcome of a mild traumatic brain injury. *Brain Injury 10*, 8: 551–65.

Ruff, R. M., Cullum, C. M., and Luerssen, T. G. (1989). Brain imaging and neuropsychological outcome in traumatic brain injury. In E. D. Bigler, R. A. Yeo and E. Turkheimer, (Eds.), *Neuropsychological Function and Brain Imaging*. New York: Plenum Publishing Corporation.

Ruff, R. M., and Grant, I. (1999). Postconcussional disorder: background to DSM-IV and future considerations. In N. R. Varney and R. J. Roberts, (Eds.), *Mild Head Injury: Causes, Evaluation and Treatment*. Mahwah, New Jersey: L. Erlbaum Associates.

Ruff, R. M., and Hibbard, K. M. (2003). *Ruff Neurobehavioral Inventory*. Lutz, FL: Psychological Assessment Resources, Inc.

Ruff, R. M., and Jurica, P. (1999). In search of a unified definition for mild traumatic brain injury. *Brain Injury 13*, 12: 943–52.

Ruff, R. M., Mueller, J., and Jurica, P. (1996b). Estimation of premorbid functioning after traumatic brain injury. *Neurorehabilitation 7*: 39–53.

Ruff, R. M., and Richardson, A. M. (1999). Mild traumatic brain injury. In J. Sweet, (Ed.), *Forensic Neuropsychology: Fundamentals and Practice*. Amsterdam: Swets and Zeitlinger.

Sarno, S., Erasmus, L. P., Lippert, G., Frey, M., Lipp, B., and Schlaegel, W. (2000). Electrophysiological correlates of visual impairments after traumatic brain injury. *Vision Research 40*, 21: 3029–38.

Savola, O., and Hillbom, M. (2003). Early predictors of post-concussion symptoms in patients with mild head injury. *European Journal of Neurology 10*, 2: 175–81.

Sbordone, R. J., Liter, J. C., and Pettler-Jennings, P. (1995). Recovery of function following severe traumatic brain injury: a retrospective 10-year follow-up. *Brain Injury 9*, 3: 285–99.

Sbordone, R. J., Seyranian, G. D., and Ruff, R. M. (2000). The use of significant others to enhance the detection of malingerers from traumatically brain-injured patients. *Archives of Clinical Neuropsychology 15*, 6: 465–77.

Schatz, P., Hillary, F. G., Moelter, S. T., and Chute, D. L. (2002). Retrospective assessment of rehabilitation outcome after traumatic brain injury: development and utility of the functional independence level. *Journal of Head Trauma Rehabilitation 17*, 6: 510–25.

Seel, R. T., Kreutzer, J. S., Rosenthal, M., Hammond, F. M., Corrigan, J. D., and Black, K. (2003). Depression after traumatic brain injury: A National Institute on Disability and Rehabilitation Research Model Systems multicenter investigation. *Archives of Physical Medicine and Rehabilitation 84*, 2: 177–84.

Smith, D. H., Uryu, K., Saatman, K. E., Trojanowski, J. Q., and McIntosh, T. K. (2003). Protein accumulation in traumatic brain injury. *Neuromolecular Medicine 4*, 1–2: 59–72.

Smith-Seemiller, L., Fow, N. R., Kant, R., and Franzen, M. D. (2003). Presence of post-concussion syndrome symptoms in patients with chronic pain vs mild traumatic brain injury. *Brain Injury 17*, 3: 199–206.

Snyder, P., and Nussbaum, P., Eds. (1998). *Clinical Neuropsychology: A Pocket Handbook for Assessment*. First ed. Washington, DC: American Psychological Association.

Sosin, D. M., Sniezek, J. E., and Thurman, D. J. (1996). Incidence of mild and moderate brain injury in the United States, 1991. *Brain Injury 10*, 1: 47–54.

Stambrook, M., Moore, A. D., Lubusko, A. A., Peters, L. C., and Blumenschein, S. (1993). Alternatives to the Glasgow Coma Scale as a quality of life predictor following traumatic brain injury. *Archives of Clinical Neuropsychology 8,* 2: 95–103.

Teasdale, G. M., and Jennett, B. (1974). Assessment of coma and impaired consciousness: a practical scale. *Lancet 2:* 81–84.

Thurman, D. J. (2001). The epidemiology and economics of head trauma. In L. Miller and R. Hayes, Eds.), *Head Trauma: Basic, Preclinical and Clinical Directions.* New York: Wiley & Sons.

van Baalen, B., Odding, E., Maas, A. I., Ribbers, G. M., Bergen, M. P., and Stam, H. J. (2003). Traumatic brain injury: classification of initial severity and determination of functional outcome. *Disability Rehabilitation 25,* 1: 9–18.

van der Naalt, J., van Zommeren, A. H., Stuiter, W. J., and Minderhoud, J. M. (1999). One year outcome in mild to moderate head injury: The predictive value of acute injury characteristics related to complaints and return to work. *Journal of Neurology Neurosurgery and Psychiatry 66:* 207–13.

Vanderploeg, R. D., Curtiss, G., Duchnick, J. J., and Luis, C. A. (2003). Demographic, medical, and psychiatric factors in work and marital status after mild head injury. *Journal of Head Trauma Rehabilitation 18,* 2: 148–63.

Vink, R. (1989). The role of excitatory amino acids and NMDA receptors in traumatic brain injury. *Science 244,* 4906: 793–801.

Vogenthaler, D. R. (1987). An overview of head injury: Its consequences and rehabilitation. *Brain Injury 1,* 1: 113–27.

Wagner, A. K., Hammond, F. M., Sasser, H. C., and Wiercisiewski, D. (2002). Return to productive activity after traumatic brain injury: Relationship with measures of disability, handicap, and community integration. *Archives of Physical Medicine and Rehabilitation 83,* 1: 107–14.

Wagner, A. K., Sasser, H. C., Hammond, F. M., Wierciesiewski, D., and Alexander, J. (2000). Intentional traumatic brain injury: Epidemiology, risk factors and associations with injury severity and mortality. *Journal of Trauma 49,* 3: 404–10.

Wallesch, C.-W., Curio, N., Galazky, I., Jost, S., and Synowitz, H. (2001). The neuropsychology of blunt head injury in the early postacute stage: Effects of focal lesions and diffuse axonal injury. *Journal of Neurotrauma 18,* 1: 11–20.

Whyte, J., Cifu, D., Dikmen, S., and Temkin, N. (2001). Prediction of functional outcomes after traumatic brain injury: A comparison of 2 measures of duration of unconsciousness. *Archives of Physical Medicine and Rehabilitation 82,* 10: 1355–59.

Wong, J., Regennitter, R., and Barrios, F. (1994). Base rate and simulated symptoms of mild head injury among normals. *Archives of Clinical Neuropsychology 9:* 441–26.

World-Health-Organization (2001). International classification of functioning, disability and health (ICF). Vol. WHA54.21.

Zafonte, R. D., Mann, N. R., Millis, S. R., Black, K. L., Wood, D. L., and Hammond, F. M. (1997). Posttraumatic amnesia: Its relation to functional outcome. *Archives of Physical Medicine and Rehabilitation 78,* 10: 1103–06.

Appendix A. *California Concussion Scale*

CALIFORNIA CONCUSSION SCALE (CCS)

The California Concussion Scale (CCS) is a practical rating for the severity of mild traumatic brain injury where the posttraumatic amnesia does not exceed 24 hours and the loss of consciousness is less than 30 minutes. For more several traumatic brain injury, the utilization of the Glasgow Coma Scale is recommended.

Posttraumatic Amnesia (PTA) **Estimated Duration ____**	**Reliability Code*** **1, 2, 3**
Greater than 24 hours**	0
Greater than 12 hours, but less than 24 hours	1
Greater than 1 hour, but less than 12 hours	2
Greater than 15 minutes, but less than 1 hour	3
Greater than 1 minute, but less than 15 minutes	4
Transient amnesia with a loss of memory for events immediately before or after the accident lasting less than 1 minute	5
No posttraumatic amnesia (continuous recall of events)	6

Loss of Consciousness (LOC) **Estimated Duration ____**	**Reliability Code*** **1, 2, 3**
Greater than 30 minutes	0
Greater than 5 minutes, but less than 30 minutes	1
Less than 5 minutes or definite loss of consciousness with duration unknown	2
Altered mental state (e.g., transient loss of consciousness, disoriented, confused)	3
No loss of consciousness	4

Focal Neurological Signs (permanent or temporary)	**Reliability Code*** **1, 2, 3**
4 or more signs	1
3 signs	2
2 signs	3
1 sign	4
No neurological signs	5

TOTAL CCS SCORE: ________

(From 3 to 15)

*Reliability: 1 = Reliable documentation by health care provider; 2 = Questionable and inconsistent documentation; 3 = Unreliable

**Greater impairment indicates a moderate to severe brain injury. Thus, do not use the CCS alone.

16

Prediction of Vocational Functioning from Neuropsychological Data

Thomas J. Guilmette

Approximately 1.5 million to 2 million traumatic brain injuries (TBI) occur each year in the United States with an estimated incidence rate of 100 per 100,000 persons (NIH Consensus Development Panel on Rehabilitation of Persons With Traumatic Brain Injury, 1999). Of those, males are injured at approximately twice the rate of females and 70,000 to 90,000 individuals are left each year with long-term disabling deficits. The majority of these injuries occur to persons who are of working age. Thus, deficits associated with TBI can persist for decades and result in a significant loss of income or earning potential, costly lifetime expenses, inability to function in the community, and devastating changes in marital, family, and social relationships.

The most common deficits associated with TBI are characterized by changes in physical, cognitive, and behavioral/emotional functioning. Each brain injury is unique, which makes it difficult to predict long term outcome. In addition, the resulting impairments are a function of several factors including severity of injury, premorbid functioning and demographic factors, secondary injuries, availability of treatment and social/family support, and the extent of localized damage to specific brain areas. However, there are some deficits in each domain that tend to be more frequent than others The most common long term physical deficits can include decreased muscle strength and control, poor balance, problems walking, headaches, seizures, vision changes, incontinence, and slurred speech (dysarthria). Unlike many other types of traumatic injuries that result in long term disability, the residual physical problems tend not to interfere with employment as much as the cognitive and behavioral/emotional problems do.

Within the cognitive domain, TBI survivors may exhibit a host of problems including, but not limited to, decreased attention/concentration, memory (particularly with recent memory and new learning), ability to think quickly (mental processing speed), and problem solving and organizational skills. There may also be problems with impulsivity and distractibility. Depending on the type and severity of impairment, cognitive deficits can interfere significantly with a range of everyday behaviors

DOI: 10.1007/978-0-387-28919-9_16, © 2009 Springer Science+Business Media, LLC

such as living independently, handling finances, making healthcare and legal decisions, and returning to work or school.

In many cases, the most disabling effects of TBI are due to the emotional and behavioral changes that can occur post-injury. These can include a range of behaviors such as behavioral disinhibition, apathy, emotional dyscontrol, childishness, social inappropriateness, depression, and excessive irritability. The hallmark of problems in this domain has largely to do with the inability to control emotions/behavior or regulating responses to circumstances. For example, some TBI survivors can become excessively irritable from even minor annoyances and exhibit little frustration tolerance. They can overreact and respond impulsively to situations and people, which can have adverse effects on safety and effective problem solving. Conversely, they may also exhibit little to no initiative or motivation to accomplish important tasks such as paying bills, looking for employment, or in some cases even taking care of personal hygiene. In addition, there is frequently a loss of insight and awareness into one's impairments and change in functioning. Thus, TBI survivors frequently underestimate or deny the effects of their brain injury on their functioning and may consequently refuse assistance or therapy. By overestimating abilities, TBI survivors may insist on returning to their previous jobs or of assuming the same responsibilities that they had pre-injury, without any modifications or assistance. The ramifications for post-injury re-employment in these types of cases can be significant.

Head injury severity is an important, although not the sole, component in attempting to predict long term outcome. Generally, more severe injuries result in greater disability, although this is not always the case. Most injuries (approximately 75%) are considered mild and the remaining constitute the moderate to severe range. In addition, injuries can be open or closed. In an open head injury the brain is penetrated by an object (knife, nail, gunshot, etc.), which tends to result in more localized brain damage. In a closed head injury, the head usually strikes an object or is shaken violently but there is no penetration of the brain by an external object. This usually causes more widespread or diffuse damage to brain cells (neurons) as neurons throughout the brain are stretched and torn; a process known as diffuse axonal injury or DAI. Further trauma can also occur if the brain strikes the inside of the skull, which can result in focal bruising or contusions.

DETERMINING INJURY SEVERITY

Classification of TBI is based on injury severity. The main criteria for establishing severity of TBI include duration of loss of consciousness (LOC), admitting or initial Glasgow Coma Scale (GCS) score, length of posttraumatic amnesia (PTA), and neuroimaging results, usually based on patient's brain CT scan.

It is possible to sustain a brain injury without losing consciousness although at least some alteration in a person's mental status (i.e., evidence of confusion, lack of memory for the trauma or events surrounding it, feeling dazed, etc.) is necessary in order to establish that the brain, and not just the head, was injured. Loss of consciousness can last seconds or be permanent as in the case of a person who does not evolve from a coma after years or decades. Generally, the longer LOC extends, then the more the severe the injury and greater disability frequently results. Loss of consciousness less than 20 or 30 minutes is indicative of a mild brain injury. There is some disagreement about length of unconsciousness necessary for a moderate brain injury. Some have suggested 30 minutes to six hours whereas others support 30 minutes to 24 hours. However, loss of consciousness greater than 24 hours is generally indicative of severe brain injury.

When head trauma patients first arrive at the emergency room, determining their best motor response, their best verbal response, and how easily they can be made to open their eyes assesses their responsiveness. A patient's responsiveness in each of these three domains is assigned a number from one to four or six, which results in a total score of 3-15. The higher the score the more responsive the patient is. A GCS of 13-15 is reflective of a mild head injury, 9-12 is considered a moderate injury, and less than 9 is consistent with a severe TBI.

After TBI survivors regain consciousness there is a period when the patient is in a state of posttraumatic amnesia (PTA). During this time, survivors are confused and disoriented (i.e., unable to state the date, where they are, and in some cases unable to state their own name). In addition, the person is unable to learn new information or remember events that happened since the injury. Their recall lasts just seconds or minutes and so they will usually forget what happened moments before. Gradually this period of PTA recedes and there is a return to more normal memory functioning although memory may never reach its premorbid levels. Posttraumatic amnesia that persists for less than 24 hours reflects a mild brain injury, PTA that extends from 24 hours to about seven days is reflective of a moderate injury, and greater than seven days is diagnostic of a severe TBI. In more severe injuries, there may also be a loss of memory for events that happened before the injury that may extend from seconds to years. This loss of memory for events that happened pre-injury is known as retrograde amnesia and generally remits as the person improves. It is generally not diagnostic of injury severity.

The results of a patient's brain imaging (CT or Magnetic Resonance Imaging [MRI]) can also provide evidence of injury severity and the potential effects of their brain damage on future functioning. That is, even though TBI is most associated with diffuse and nonspecific brain damage, particular parts of the brain may sustain bruises (contusions), bleeding (hemorrhages), and swelling (edema). It is important to also appreciate that evidence of trauma on CT or MRI does not necessarily reflect how those specific brain areas may function. Brain imaging techniques provide a "view" inside the skull that allows the radiologist to determine if there is something in the brain that does not belong there, such as a tumor or bleeding, or if brain structures are damaged (bruised). However, these images do not provide information about how well the brain *functions*.

PREDICTING RETURN TO WORK

The Complexities of Work Prediction

Predicting who will and will not return to work following a moderate to severe brain injury is a complicated endeavor. Multiple factors determine the employability and employment options of TBI survivors including the state of the economy and the availability of jobs in the survivor's community, which are obviously well beyond the influence of rehabilitative treatment. Furthermore, employment is not a homogeneous entity and TBI survivors do not exhibit homogeneous strengths and weaknesses. Jobs differ greatly in terms of their physical and intellectual requirements in the same way that persons recovering from TBI differ greatly with regard to their physical and cognitive functioning. For example, severe visual spatial deficits or impaired balance may preclude someone from returning to his/her job as a carpenter but perhaps would not interfere with the job of a receptionist or a journalist. Impaired memory may make it impossible for someone to resume a law practice although a repetitive assembly job may not be beyond this same patient's capability. Thus, global probability statements about returning to work need to be interpreted with caution.

The return-to-work (RTW) literature on TBI survivors reveals a wide range of employment outcomes post-injury. Interpreting prior research is complicated by the use of heterogeneous samples (i.e., including mild, moderate, and severe TBI survivors within the same sample under study), evaluating survivors at different follow-up periods post-injury, a lack of consistent rehabilitative treatments and interventions across studies, inconsistent definitions of work or productivity, considering full and part-time employment as equivalent outcomes, and analyzing or omitting different variables that may contribute to successfully returning to work. Also, most studies examine TBI survivors at a specific point in time post-injury, such as one year, two years, and so on. However, what is frequently missing is how long the survivor was able to stay in the job he/she acquired. The stability of employment following TBI is as important as becoming employed initially.

Return to work rates vary considerably. Recent studies that were solely or primarily conducted with moderate to severe TBI samples revealed RTW rates that varied from 10.2 % for a group of severely brain injured patients evaluated at 12 months post-injury (Novack, Alderson, Bush, Meythaler, & Canupp, 2000) to 71% of patients employed or in educational/vocational training nearly two years post-injury (Sherer, Bergloff, High, & Nick, 1999). In the former study only 2% of the severe TBI sample was employed at six months post-injury and in the latter study all 76 TBI patients had participated in a post-acute brain injury program, which reflects a relatively select sample of survivors who had received specialized rehabilitative treatment. Time post-injury influences employment rates as the Novack et al. (2000) article reflects although even at an average of 14 years post-injury, only 60.5% of a severe TBI sample in Israel was employed and of those 39% were in non-competitive positions (Hoofien, Gilboa, Vakil, & Donovick, 2001).

When assessing RTW capability, several factors need to be considered including demographic and pre-injury characteristics, injury severity, age, and physical, behavioral, and cognitive functioning. Ponsford and colleagues also described that employer support, the availability of job modifications and alternative duties, and patient determination were important RTW variables whereas pre-existing personality and social problems, multiple trauma, lack of employer support, and the availability of financial support from spouses or others tended to decrease the likelihood of returning to employment (Ponsford, Olver, Curran, & Ng, 1995).

Injury Severity and Demographic Variables

Injury severity as measured by GCS and other factors has been inconsistently shown to be predictive of RTW rates in moderate to severe TBI. For example, higher GCS scores at admission to the acute hospital were among the three best predictors of employment in a group of 74 moderate to severe TBI patients (Ponsford, Olver, Curran, & Ng, 1995). GCS scores greater than 9 as well as discharge from acute care to home (and not to rehabilitation or other facilities, which reflects less severe injuries), were associated with a significantly higher likelihood of returning to productive employment in a sample of 105 mild to severe TBI patients (Wagner, Hammond, Sasser, Wiercisiewski, & Norton, 2000; Wagner, Hammond, Sasser, Wiercisiewski, & Norton, 2002). Flemming, Tooth, Hassell, and Chan (1999) also found initial GCS scores predictive of those who were able to resume work from those who could not (GCS = 7.7 vs. 6.4, respectively) as well as length of PTA (35 vs. 53 days, respectively). Average coma length combined with length of PTA were found to be longer with unemployed vs. employed severe TBI survivors (108 vs. 28 days, respectively) at 16 months post injury although GCS scores were not different between the two groups (Cattelani, Tanzi, Lombardi, Mazzuchi, 2002). Other researchers have also not found GCS scores or other injury severity variables to be related to employment (Ip, Dornan, & Schentag, 1995; Keyser-Marcus, Bricout, Wehman et al., 2002; Novack Bush, Meythaler, & Canupp, 2001; Sherer, Bergloff, High, & Nick, 1999).

Premorbid and demographic factors have also been shown to be related to employment. A number of studies have demonstrated that younger age at the time of injury is associated with increased probability of employment (Felmingham, Baguley, & Crooks, 2001; Ip, Dornan, & Schentag, 1995; Novack, Bush, Meythaler, & Canupp, 2001), particularly with TBI survivors less than age 40 (Keyser-Marcus et al., 2002; Ponsford, Olver, Curran, & Ng, 1995). Others, however, have not found this association (Cattelani, Tanzi, Lombardi, & Massuchi, 2002; Flemming, Tooth, Hassell, & Chan, 1999).

TBI survivors who were employed before their injury are more likely to return to work (Flemming, Tooth, Hassell, & Chan, 1999) and perhaps 3 to 5 times more likely to return to work than those who were unemployed at the time of their trauma (Keyser-Marcus et al., 2002). In addition, higher levels of education (generally high school level or higher), the absence of alcohol and drug abuse premorbidly, higher socio-economic status, and a lack of social and behavioral problems pre-dating the injury are all associated with increased probability of employment post-injury (Hoofien, Vakil, Gilboa, Donovik, & Barak, 2002; Ip, Dornan, & Schentag, 1995; Novack, Bush, Meythaler, & Canupp, 2001; Sherer, Bergloff, High, & Nick, 1999; Wagner, Hammond, Sasser, & Wiercisiewski, 2002). In addition, some evidence suggests that those employed in higher status occupations and those with jobs that allow greater independent decision making have higher RTW rates than those in lower status occupations (Flemming, Tooth, Hassell, & Chan, 1999; Ruffolo, Friedland, Dawson, Colantonio, & Lindsay, 1999).

The Association between Neuropsychological Testing and Employability

Neuropsychological assessment can serve many purposes in the treatment of head injury survivors. For example, although neuroimaging procedures, such as CT and MRI, provide evidence of structural brain damage and are sometimes related to return to work (Groswasser, Reider-Groswasser, Schwab et al., 2002), these diagnostic methods do not give information about how a person functions or what types of cognitive impairments may have resulted from the injury. Thus, the only methodology that can determine the degree to which a person has sustained a loss of specific cognitive skills is through neuropsychological testing. Evaluations can also assist in determining the severity and type of cognitive impairments at different time periods post-injury, monitor extent of recovery, establish a plan for cognitive rehabilitation, evaluate psychological, emotional, and behavioral sequelae, and assess cognitive capacity to perform everyday activities such as handling finances, driving, living alone, and working.

Although neuropsychological assessment can provide extensive and detailed information about a patient's cognitive functioning, integrating that data into valid predictions about employability is difficult. For example, in a review of 23 studies concerning the relationship between neuropsychological test results and employment after TBI, the authors opined that early neuropsychological assessment (i.e, testing at resolution of PTA or ≤ one month post-injury) was strongly associated with predicting late employment outcome (Sherer, Novack, Sander et al., 2002). However, the relationship between late (i.e., ≥ six months post-injury) or concurrent neuropsychological assessment and employment prediction was inconclusive based on the available studies. The authors concluded, however, that their review "provides strong support for the relationship of neuropsychological test results to employment outcome after TBI" (Sherer, Novack, Sander et al., 2002, p. 176). Boake et al. (2001) found that just being able to complete at least one neuropsychological test during inpatient rehabilitation increased the probability by a factor of six of returning to competitive employment or attending school from one to four years post-injury. Even among those who could complete at least one neuropsychological test, only 38% returned to productivity (compared to 6% of their sample who became productive but could not complete a neuropsychological test during rehabilitation).

A number of specific measures have been associated with return to work functioning. For example, better perceptual-motor functions, particularly Performance IQ, have predicted RTW (Bowman, 1996; Fraser, Dikmen, McLean, Miller, & Temkin, 1988; Ip, Dornan, & Schentag, 1995). Verbal and Full Scale IQ scores have also been associated with return to work as well as performance on specific WAIS-R subtests such as Picture Arrangement, Block Design, Similarities, and Digit Symbol (Fabiano & Crewe, 1995). Other researchers have reported that speed of mental processing as assessed by Wechsler IQ subtests, Trails A and B, and other measures is an important determiner of return to work capability (Bowman, 1996; Girard et al., 1996; Ip, Dornan, & Schentag, 1995; Ruff et al., 1993).

In addition to mental speed and perceptual deficits, impaired memory functioning for both verbal and nonverbal information has also been associated with higher rates of unemployment following TBI (Boake et al., 2001; Bowman, 1996; Schwab, Grafman, Salazar, & Kraft, 1993). Communication skills have also been associated with employment capabilities. For example, Isaki and Turkstra (2000) reported that a combination of three language tests separated a group of employed from unemployed moderate TBI survivors 1-4 years post-injury. Specifically, the most powerful discriminator between the two groups was a daily schedule test (from the Functional Assessment of Verbal Reasoning) that required reading, writing, problem solving, organization, working memory, and sustained attention.

Damage to the frontal lobes of the brain frequently results in significant alterations in behavioral regulation that can have important ramifications for RTW. These behavioral alterations, typically referred to as executive function deficits, can range from behavioral excesses characterized by impulsivity, disinhibition, distractibility, emotional lability, aggression, and social inappropriateness to behavioral deficiencies such as lack of drive and initiation, an inability to organize and carry out a plan of behavior, and impaired working memory and sustained attention. There is some evidence that neuropsychological measures of frontal and executive functioning can be useful in return to work prediction (Butler, Anderson, Furst, Namerow, & Satz,1989; Kibby, Schmitter-Edgecombe, & Long, 1998; Leahy & Lam, 1998) although due to the structure and predictability of testing, patients can perform well in the neuropsychological laboratory but exhibit severe impairments in the "real world." Thus, performance on standardized test instruments does not always reflect the behavioral abnormalities that frontal lobe patients can exhibit under more varied and less structured circumstances.

Butler and colleagues (Butler et al., 1989), for example, used standard neuropsychological measures as well as behavioral observations (Behavioral Assessment of Vocational Skills: BAVS) of 20 brain-injured patients who were instructed to assemble a wheelbarrow using written instructions. During the assembly the subjects were interrupted at several points, asked to perform other tasks, and offered criticism when an error was made. The trained observers rated the patients on their ability to follow directions, maintain their attention, tolerate frustration, and on several other variables. Although a number of the neuropsychological tests were related to job performance during a three-month volunteer work trial in a rehabilitation program, the BAVS was the only significant predictor of vocational functioning in a multiple regression analysis. Simpson and Schmitter-Edgecombe (2002) used a self-report behavioral questionnaire of frontal lobe functioning (Brock Adaptive Functioning Questionnaire: BAFQ) completed by TBI survivors and combined that data with patient demographics, injury characteristics, and social and physical variables to predict occupational status with 77.4% accuracy. Their prediction rate, without using any cognitive status variables or neuropsychological test results, was slightly higher than the prediction rate of 68.3% described by Fleming et al. (1999) who used a combination of injury variables, demographic characteristics, disability/functional levels, and cognitive screen results.

Regardless of the methods used for assessment, it is clear that behavioral problems post-injury, even for those TBI survivors without any history of substance abuse or psychological disorders premorbidly, adversely affect employment post-trauma (Cattelani et al., 2002). Employers do not want workers who cannot get along with others or who are difficult to manage or supervise due to behavioral dyscontrol. Even without overt behavioral problems, TBI survivors who report significant psychological or emotional distress are less likely to be employed two years post-injury than those survivors who do not report such psychological problems (Felmingham, Baguley, & Crooks, 2001). However, sometimes a lack of psychological distress can be due to a lack of awareness of one's injury and its effects on a person's functioning. In these cases, a lack of awareness is actually detrimental to vocational functioning. Sherer and colleagues found a positive relationship between insight and employment outcome in 66 TBI patients (Sherer et al., 1998). They reported that TBI survivors with accurate self awareness about the effects of their injury on their functioning were almost 2.5 times more likely to have a favorable vocational outcome than patients with inaccurate self awareness.

Greenspan and colleagues (Greenspan et al., 1996) found that functional limitations alone (i.e., dependence for some aspects of self care such as dressing, grooming, toileting, mobility, etc.) greatly influenced RTW. For example, in their sample of 343 previously employed TBI hospitalized patients interviewed by phone at one year post-injury, 76% of patients who were dependent on others with one or more aspects of their self care were unemployed whereas only 6% of the TBI survivors were unemployed when they were completely independent in all self care domains. However, Novack et al. (2001) did not find functional status at six months post-injury to be related to outcome, including employment, at 12 months post-injury although cognitive status at six months was related to outcome at one year.

Limitations of Neuropsychological Testing in Predicting Employment

The issue of predicting everyday functioning, including work, from neuropsychological test data is known as ecological validity. Historically, neuropsychological tests were developed to assess specific cognitive or brain functions, and not everyday abilities. In addition, testing is typically conducted in an environment that is designed to maximize the patient's performance (i.e., quiet, distraction-free, supportive, responsive to patient fatigue or need for additional time or help, etc.), which is not the context in which most of us work (i.e., chaotic, unstructured, demanding, etc.). Thus, both the neuropsychological tests and the conditions under which they are administered tend to reduce the ecological validity of neuropsychological measures predicting work behavior (Sbordone, 2001; Sbordone & Long, 1996).

After reviewing the literature on the use of neuropsychological tests to predict vocational functioning, Guilmette and Kastner (1996) and Sbordone and Guilmette (1999) concluded that no one specific test or procedure could accurately predict one's employability in general. Leblanc and colleagues further confirmed this finding when they compared work simulation results with a neuropsychological battery for 127 moderate to severe TBI survivors (Leblanc, Hayden, & Paulman, 2000). Possl et al. (2001) also described the difficulties of predicting employment by examining 43 brain damaged patients (most were severe TBI survivors) who had participated in a post-acute, comprehensive rehabilitation day clinic. Based on a retrospective analysis of their estimated degree of neuropsychological and psychological deficits, patients were classified into four groups of potential employability. Their study highlighted the difficulty of predicting long term employment outcome given that 4 of 11 patients with the best vocational prognosis experienced vocational problems or retired and 3 of 10 patients with the worst employment prognosis successfully returned to their previous jobs.

In summarizing their review of the literature on predicting employment from neuropsychological test results, Guilmette and Kasner (1996) concluded the following: in general, the greater the level of cognitive dysfunction, the less the likely the patient will be employable; assessing work capabilities is generally more valid for specific jobs than for the world of work in general; predicting employability is increased by assessing those skills that a person will need to demonstrate in order to be successful in a particular job (i.e., verbal skills for jobs with significant verbal component or perceptual functions for jobs requiring spatial skills,.); psychosocial functioning and psychological adjustment are important to consider in evaluating work potential; and, obtaining collateral information about the patient's everyday functioning and self care activities from family or behavioral ratings will augment neuropsychological test results.

Leblanc, Hayden, and Paulman (2000) also asserted that identifying specific cognitive deficits that may correspond to specific vocational abilities increases prediction of work success more than global neuropsychological performance predicts general work capabilities. They indicated that, "neuropsychological assessment can serve a valuable purpose in identifying neurocognitive deficits... and can serve a very important function in generating hypotheses about how deficits identified on standard testing might influence behaviors in more natural environments" (pp. 1038). Knowledge about a person's cognitive deficits could potentially lead to modifications in the work environment and/or teaching the patient strategies to compensate for his/her impairments, which can maximize performance on the job.

Johnstone, Schopp, Harper, and Koscuilek (1999) found that relative cognitive decline from estimated premorbid level of functioning was a better predictor of vocational outcome than the absolute level of impairment among a group of TBI survivors enrolled in a vocational rehabilitation program. Contrary to most studies, they reported that the greater the decline from one's premorbid level of functioning, the greater the likelihood of successfully returning to work. They concluded that neuropsychological testing can be beneficial in rehabilitation planning and in providing information to clients about their relative loss of functioning, which can be helpful for them to understand the degree to which they must adjust to their deficits or the likelihood of being able to return to their previous job. Johnstone et al. (2003) also found that the odds of having a successful vocational outcome was 14 times higher if vocational counseling was provided, which seems to further support that improving adjustment to injury and altering expectations for vocational success can be helpful in returning TBI survivors to work.

SUMMARY

Based on the available literature, the use of neuropsychological data to predict vocational functioning can be summarized by the following:

- Neuropsychological testing is helpful to identify the cognitive strengths and weaknesses of the patient in order best match the patient's cognitive profile with appropriate occupations.
- Global performance on neuropsychological tests is only marginally related to employability although generally the more severe the cognitive impairments, the less likely the TBI survivor will be able to return to work.
- The cognitive areas that seem most related to employability are perceptual functions, mental processing and motor speed, memory, executive functions, and language abilities.
- Neuropsychological test results are most valid in predicting employability when they address the specific abilities necessary for specific jobs or occupations.
- Behavioral and social problems as well as emotional maladjustment—as gleaned from patient and collateral report—decrease the employability of the

TBI survivor and thus need to be incorporated into conclusions about the likelihood of RTW.

- Functional and everyday problems with self care are associated with a decreased likelihood of returning to work.
- Premorbid characteristics, particularly age, education, employment status, substance and drug abuse, and psychosocial functioning should be combined with the post-injury cognitive status when making RTW predictions.
- Injury severity as assessed by GCS and length of PTA also seem to contribute to the chances of employment post-injury.
- Assessing (and increasing) insight and awareness appear to play an important role in a person's ability to return to work.
- Encouraging employers to adopt job and environmental modifications will generally increase the probability of successful re-employment for many TBI patients.
- There are multiple factors associated with RTW that cannot be accounted for by neuropsychological data, injury severity, or premorbid characteristics that affect RTW and which cannot always be measured or anticipated.

REFERENCES

Boake, C., Millis, S.R., High, W.M. Jr., Delmonico, R.L., Kreutzer, J.S., Rosenthal, M., Sherer, M., & Ivanhoe, C.B. (2001). Using early neuropsychologic testing to predict long-term productivity outcome from traumatic brain injury. *Archives of Physical Medicine and Rehabilitation, 82*, 761–768.

Bowman, M.L. (1996). Ecological validity of neuropsychological and other predictors following head injury. *The Clinical Neuropsychologist, 10*, 10, 382–396.

Butler, R.W., Anderson, L., Furst, C.J., Namerow, N.S., & Satz, P. (1989). Behavioral assessment in neuropsychological rehabilitation: A method for measuring vocational-related skills. *The Clinical Neuropsychologist, 3*, 235–243.

Cattelani, R., Tanzi, F., Lombardi, F., & Mazzucchi, A. (2002). Competitive re-employment after severe traumatic brain injury : Clinical, cognitive and behavioural predictive variables. *Brain Injury, 16*, 51–64.

Drake, A.I., Gray, N., Yoder, S., Pramuka, M., & Llewellyn, M. (2000). Factors predicting return to work following mild traumatic brain injury: A discriminant analysis. *Journal of Head Trauma Rehabilitation, 15*, 1103–1112.

Fabiano, R.J., & Crewe, N. (1995). Variables associated with employment following severe traumatic brain injury. *Rehabilitation Psychology, 40*, 223–231.

Felmingham, K.L., Baguley, I.J., & Crooks, J. (2001). A comparison of acute and postdischarge predictors of employment 2 years after traumatic brain injury. *Archives of Physical Medicine and Rehabilitation, 82*, 435–439.

Fleming, J., Tooth, L., Hassell, M., & Chan, W. (1999). Prediction of community integration and vocational outcome 2–5 years after traumatic brain injury rehabilitation in Australia. *Brain Injury, 13*, 417–431.

Fraser, R., Dikmen, S., McLean, A., Miller, B., & Temkin, N. (1988). Employability of head injury survivors: First year post-injury. *Rehabilitation Counseling Bulletin, 31*, 276–288.

Girard, D., Brown, J., Burnett-Stolnack, M., Hashimoto, H., Hier-Wellmer, S., Perlman, O.Z., & Seigerman, C. (1996). The relationship of neuropsychological status and productive outcomes following traumatic brain injury. *Brain Injury, 10*, 663–676.

Greenspan, A.I., Wrigley, J.M., Kresnow, M., Branche-Dorsey, C.M., & Fine, P.R. (1996). Factors influencing failure to return to work due to traumatic brain injury. *Brain Injury, 10*, 207–218.

Groswasser, Z., Reider-Groswasser, I.I., Schwab, K., Ommaya, A.K., Pridgent, A., Brown, H.R., Cole, R., & Salazar, A.M. (2002). Quantitative imaging in late TBI. Part II: Cognition and work after closed and penetrating head injury: A report of the Vietnam head injury study. *Brain Injury, 16*, 681–690.

Guilmette, T.J., & Kastner, M.P. (1996). The prediction of vocational functioning from neuropsychological data. In R.J. Sbordone & C.J. Long (Eds.), *Ecological validity of neuropsychological testing* (pp. 387–412). Delray Beach, FL: GR Press/St. Lucie Press.

Hoofien, D., Gilboa, A., Vakil, E., & Donovick, P.J. (2001). Traumatic brain injury (TBI) 10–20 years later: A comprehensive outcome study of psychiatric symptomatology, cognitive abilities and psychosocial functioning. *Brain Injury, 15*, 189–209.

Hoofien, D., Vakil, E., Golboa, A., Donovick, P.J., & Barak, O. (2002). Comparison of the predictive power of socioeconomic variables, severity of injury and age on long-term outcome of traumatic brain injury: Sample-specific variables versus factors as predictors. *Brain Injury, 16*, 9–27.

Ip, R.Y., Dornan, J., & Schentag, C. (1995). Traumatic brain injury: Factors predicting return to work or school. *Brain Injury, 9*, 517–532.

Isaki, E., & Turkstra, L. (2000). Communication abilities and work re-entry following traumatic brain injury. *Brain Injury, 14*, 441–453.

Johnstone, B., Schopp, L.H., Harper, J., & Koscuilek, J. (1999). Neuropsychological impairments, vocational outcomes, and financial costs for individuals with traumatic brain injury receiving state vocational rehabilitation services. *Journal of Head Trauma Rehabilitation, 14*, 220–232.

Johnstone, B., Vessell, R., Bounds, T., Hoskins, S., & Sherman, A. (2003). Predictors of success for state vocational rehabilitation clients with traumatic brain injury. *Archives of Physical Medicine and Rehabilitation, 84*, 161–167.

Keyser-Marcus, L.A., Bricout, J.C., Wehman, P., Campbell, L.R., Cifu, D.X., Englander, J., High, W., & Zafonte, R.D. (2002). Acute predictors of return to employment after traumatic brain injury: A longitudinal follow-up. *Archives of Physical Medicine and Rehabilitation, 83*, 635–641.

Kirby, M., Schmitter-Edgecombe, M., & Long, C. (1998). Ecological validity of neuropsychological tests: Focus on the California Verbal Learning Test and the Wisconsin Card Sorting Test. *Archives of Clinical Neuropsychology, 13*, 523–534.

LeBlanc, J.M., Hayden, M.E., & Paulman, R.G. (2000). A comparison of neuropsychological and situational assessment for predicting employability after closed head injury. *Journal of Head Trauma Rehabilitation, 15*, 1022–1040.

Leahy, B., & Lam, C. (1998). Neuropsychological testing and functional outcome for individuals with traumatic brain injury. *Brain Injury, 12*, 1025–1035.

NIH Consensus Development Panel on Rehabilitation of Persons With Traumatic Brain Injury. (1999). Rehabilitation of persons with traumatic brain injury. *Journal of the American Medical Association, 282*, 974–983.

Novack, T.A., Alderson, A.L., Bush, B.A., Meythaler, J.M., & Canupp, K. (2000). Cognitive and functional recovery at 6 and 12 months post-TBI. *Brain Injury, 14*, 987–996.

Novack, T.A., Bush, B., Meythaler, J.M., & Canupp, K. (2001). Outcome after traumatic brain injury: Pathway analysis of contributions from premorbid, injury severity, and recovery variables. *Archives of Physical Medicine and Rehabilitation, 82*, 300–305.

Ponsford, J.L., Olver, J.H., Curran, C., & Ng, K. (1995). Prediction of employment status 2 years after traumatic brain injury. *Brain Injury, 9*, 11–20.

Possl, J., Jurgensmeyer, S., Karlbauer, F., Wenz, C., & Goldenberg, G. (2001). Stability of employment after brain injury: A 7-year follow-up study. *Brain Injury, 15*, 15–27.

Ruff, R.M., Marshall, L.F., Crouch, J., et al. (1993). Predictors of outcome following severe head trauma: Follow-up data from the traumatic coma data bank. *Brain Injury, 7*, 101–111.

Ruffolo, C.F., Friedland, J.F., Dawson, D.R., Colantonio, A., & Lindsay, P.H. (1999). Mild traumatic brain injury from motor vehicle accidents: Factors associated with return to work. *Archives of Physical Medicine and Rehabilitation, 80*, 392–398.

Sbordone, R.J. (2001). Limitations of neuropsychological testing to predict the cognitive and behavioral functioning of persons with brain injury in real-world settings. *NeuroRehabilitation, 16*, 199–201.

Sbordone, R.J., & Guilmette, T.J. (1999). Ecological validity: Prediction of everyday and vocational functioning from neuropsychological test data. In J. Sweet (Ed.), *Forensic neuropsychology: Fundamentals and practice* (pp. 227–254). Lisse, The Netherlands: Swets & Zeitlinger.

Sbordone, R.J., & Long, C.J. (Eds.) (1996). *Ecological validity of neuropsychological testing.* Delray Beach, FL: GR Press/St. Lucie Press.

Schwab, K., Grafman, J., Salazar, A.M., & Kraft, J. (1993). Residual impairments and work status 15 years after penetrating head injury: Report from the Vietnam Head Injury Study. *Neurology, 43*, 95–103.

Sherer, M., Bergloff, P., High, W. Jr., & Nick, T.G. (1999). Contribution of functional ratings to prediction of longterm employment outcome after traumatic brain injury. *Brain Injury, 13*, 973–981.

Sherer, M., Bergloff, P., Levin, E., High, W.M., Jr., Oden, K.E., & Nick, T.G. (1998). Impaired awareness and employment outcome after traumatic brain injury. *Journal of Head Trauma Rehabilitation, 13*, 52–61.

Sherer, M., Novack, T.A., Sander, A.M., Struchen, M.A., Alderson, A., & Thompson, R.N. (2002). Neuropsychological assessment and employment outcome after traumatic brain injury: A review. *The Clinical Neuropsychologist, 16*, 157–178.

Simpson, A., & Schmitter-Edgecombe, M. (2002). Prediction of employment status following traumatic brain injury using a behavioural measure of frontal lobe functioning. *Brain Injury, 16*, 1075–1091.

Wagner, A.K., Hammond, F.M., Sasser, H.C., Wiercisiewski, D., & Norton, H.J. (2000). Use of injury severity variables in determining disability and community integration after traumatic brain injury. *Journal of Trauma Injury, Infection, and Critical Care, 49*, 411–419.

Wagner, A.K., Hammond, F.M., Sasser, H.C., Wiercisiewski, D., & Norton, H.J. (2002). Return to productive activity after traumatic brain injury: Relationship with measures of disability, handicap, and community integration. *Archives of Physical Medicine and Rehabilitation, 83*, 107–114.

C. PREDICTION OF DISABILITY AFTER PSYCHOLOGICAL TRAUMA

17

The Role of Individual Factors in Predicting Posttraumatic Stress Disorder

Marilyn L. Bowman

INTRODUCTION

This chapter will review the factors that contribute to the risk of PTSD in individuals who have faced a severely threatening experience such as an assault, an accident, or participation in war. It will review the epidemiological evidence, which shows that although most adults in even peacetime democracies have encountered such challenging experiences, most do not develop PTSD. The gap in rates between exposure to threatening events and the incidence of event-focused mental disorder is accounted for by individual differences in long-standing traits, beliefs, and aspects of personal history. The chapter will examine the role of important traits that include the ability to regulate emotions, as well as the presence of certain longstanding dysfunctional thoughts and beliefs. Additional individual differences arising from prior experiences, behavior, and mental disorder will be reviewed. The chapter will not examine the role of demographic variables other than sex, as the other factors appear to have only minor effects. Finally, the chapter will consider the implications of the data for diagnosis, case management, and rehabilitation.

The chapter will mainly review evidence relating to peacetime civilian life, with only brief references to the literature on war veterans. That literature is extensive, especially in the United States, and it suffers from some research problems. In most of the studies there was no effort made to validate the veterans' self-reported military experience against the official combat records to ensure that threatening exposure(s) had been experienced. This has allowed ambiguity including fraud concerning

DOI: 10.1007/978-0-387-28919-9_17, © 2009 Springer Science+Business Media, LLC

stressor events, undermining the validity of research based on this population (Burkett & Whitley, 1998). Data from such veteran samples will be used sparingly, if it directly addresses conceptual issues broader than simple incidence rates.

"TRAUMATIC" EVENTS (TEs)

In general people who are faced with an event that threatens death or serious injury are at increased risk of suffering short-term emotional disarray that in some individuals turns into a long-term disorder. Posttraumatic stress disorder (PTSD) is the diagnostic term for this, defined as an anxiety disorder in the Diagnostic and Statistical Manual of Mental Disorders (American Psychiatric Association, 1994). The current 4th edition (DSM-IV) is the third edition to include the disorder, which first entered the manual in the 1980 edition arising from disorders identified in returning Vietnam war veterans in the United States. The manual requires seven criteria to be met. The stressor must be threatening to life or health and must elicit intense feelings of fear, horror or helplessness. Three symptom-cluster criteria are set, essentially including re-experiencing, avoidance, and persistent symptoms of increased arousal. The symptom pattern must be in place at least one month, and finally, "the disturbance must cause clinically significant distress or impairment in social, occupational or other important areas of functioning" (p. 429). The DSM-IV asserts that the event (specifically its "severity, duration, and proximity") is the most important factor causing the disorder, although it acknowledges that other factors may influence the disorder.

The disorder is named "posttraumatic," which is unfortunate, in that this term implies backward reasoning to declare an event as "traumatic," yet this term is only logically applied to the subjective responses of an individual. An event that actively threatens death or injury should be more objectively labeled so as to separate out the qualities of an event from the subjective response of an individual to the event. I will use the term TE to refer to the idea of a threatening or toxic event, to ensure that the concept of exposure to an objectively threatening event is separated from the subjective response of an individual to it.

Models in Popular Culture and Mental Health Practice

In popular culture, however, events are typically described as "traumatic," and are believed to cause the mental disorder of PTSD. These popular beliefs are consistent with two competing 20th century mental health models that are often considered to be contradictory. The first half-century was influenced by Freudian ideas in which adult emotional disorder ("neurosis") was attributed to unresolved emotional conflicts that were experienced early in childhood. The latter half of the century was influenced by behavioral models that emphasized the role of conditioned learning of fear responses to more recent events. Both models are strongly environmentalist, differing essentially in attributing emotional regulation disorders either to very early experience or to more current experience. Most psychological treatment and counseling is based on these models either explicitly or implicitly, seeking evidence of early conflicts with parents, or evidence of more recent emotionally-challenging experiences as important elements in understanding the current emotional disorder.

THE VARIETY OF RESPONSES TO TE EXPOSURES

Individuals differ significantly in the ways they respond to TE exposures. In cases known to me, three men were seriously injured in a mine explosion. After physically recovering, one returned to work in the mine and the second man returned to work on lighter duties above ground because of residual physical disabilities. The third man fully recovered physically but was permanently disabled from returning to work because of chronic PTSD elicited by even remote sounds of the working mine. In another event, bears attacked two woodsmen. The man who was directly mauled developed PTSD, while the man who succeeded in chasing the bear away did not. In contrast, when two women tree-planters were attacked by bears, it was the one who chased the bear away who developed PTSD, while the woman who was mauled did not suffer any mental disorder. These cases illustrate the variations of response to threatening events, and indicate that additional individual factors determine whether some individuals develop a mental disorder after a TE exposure. The question thus arises as to the quantity of variation: Is PTSD to be mostly expected after a TE, or is it a more rare and atypical response? Epidemiological data allow us to answer this question.

A. Epidemiology: The Prevalence of TE Exposure and PTSD Response

If PTSD is mostly determined by exposure to a TE, then the prevalence rates of TE exposures and the prevalence rates of PTSD responses should be very similar. Huge epidemiological studies of the lifetime prevalence of threatening events in the lives of adults in the United States have found high levels of these events. In the National Comorbidity Study (NCS) of nearly 6,000 adults representative of the general population, 61% of the men and 51% of the women had experienced events that met the "threatening" criterion required by the diagnostic criteria (Kessler, Sonnega, Bromet, Hughes & Nelson, 1995). A large representative study of adults done in the Detroit area found even higher rates, with 92% of the men and 87% of the women reporting such experiences (Breslau et al., 1998). Similar lifetime rates for experiencing such events were reported from Canada, with 81% of men and 74% of women (Stein, Walker, Hazen & Forde, 1997). Overall then, the significant majority of adults in these affluent, peacetime democracies have been confronted with threatening events that met the stressor criterion in the DSM. To the extent that this exposure determines PTSD, then PTSD rates should be similar.

Studies of the lifetime prevalence of PTSD report rates that are significantly lower than the exposure rates to threatening events. The NCS data, probably the best in the world to date, show lifetime PTSD rates of 5% in men and 10% in women (Kessler et al., 1995). The Detroit study found a lifetime rate of 6.2% in men, and 13% in women (Breslau, Davis, Andreski & Peterson, 1991). The Canadian study reported on "past- month" prevalence rates, finding 1.2% in men, and 2.7% in women (Stein et al., 1997). A superbly inclusive study in Iceland was able to study half of the entire cohort of individuals born in 1931, reporting lifetime prevalence in these Icelandic men of Zero %, and of 1.3% of women, using international criteria for the disorder (Lindal & Stefansson, 1993). In young adults in Munich, although 26% of the men had TE exposures only 1% ever met PTSD criteria, and although 18% of the young women reported TE exposures, only 2.2% met criteria for PTSD (Perkonigg, Kessler,

Storz & Wittchen, 2000). A recent study to re-examine epidemiological data to determine actual impairment suffered by individuals with various mental disorders, found that about 30% of those who met diagnostic criteria were not clinically significantly impaired (Narrow, Rae, Robins & Regier, 2002). Unfortunately the data about PTSD were not in a form that could be re-examined in that study, so we can only speculate that it too would be associated with lower rates of actual clinical impairment than the official diagnosis rate might imply.

Overall the pattern of the data is clear. Exposure to threatening events is quite high in the general population, yet occurrence of the event-attributed disorder of PTSD is quite low. In addition, data are consistent that females respond with the disorder about twice as frequently as men do. This sex difference is one of the very few reliable demographic factors that have been found to affect the incidence of the disorder.

Studies have gone beyond general community surveys examining general exposures and the disorder, to look at the conditional risk of developing PTSD in individuals specifically exposed to different kinds of threatening events. The main finding is that conditional risk varies tremendously across samples. Even the high and prolonged life-threatening experience of combat for example, yields significant differences in PTSD rates in different combat groups. These rates vary from a low of less than one % in one sample (Lee, Vaillant, Torrey & Elder, 1995), to rates that go as high as 48% in a group of 'body-handlers" in the first Gulf war (Sutker, Uddo, Brailey, Vasterling & Errera, 1994). The largest general survey of Vietnam veterans reported rates of around 15% (Kulka et al., 1990).

Civilian Life Events

In civilian life conditional risk also varies greatly in different groups. Across thirty years of terrorist bombings and attacks in Northern Ireland, there was no significant increase in hospital admission rates for mental disorder, although this is a modern state with good services and data, in contrast to many other settings of communal violence (Summerfield, Loughrey, Nikapota & Parry-Jones, 1997). In the more extreme levels of violence of civil wars in Algeria, Cambodia, Ethiopia and Gaza, the average rate of PTSD was 23%, but varied from 16% in Ethiopia to more than double that in Algeria (de Jong, Komproe & Van Ommeren, 2001). PTSD rates for the shared experience of handling dead bodies similarly ranged from 48% in the US veterans in the first Gulf war (see above), to zero in the staff who handled the dead bodies after a terrible fire on an oil platform in the North Sea near Scotland (Alexander, 1993).

Intentionality of the Event

It is widely assumed in the PTSD literature that experiencing an intentional assault has greater emotional impact than experiencing an impersonal accident or natural disaster. Even in the realm of intentional attacks however, there are significant variations in how individuals respond, with results that at times are counter-intuitive in not matching the severity of harms. Among those closely involved in a mass shooting in Texas, PTSD rates in the rescue workers were higher (35%) in those who were not injured than in those who were injured (13%) (North, Smith & Spitznagel, 1994).

In the large Detroit study, the greater rate of PTSD in women was discovered to arise from their greater risk of developing the disorder after violent assault, in that 36% of women responded to violent assault with the disorder, while only 6% of the men did (Breslau, Chilcoat, Kessler, Peterson & Lucia, 1999b).

Effects of Time Since Event

Because lives change with time, and the PTSD model in the DSM asserts that proximity to the event is a determining factor, individuals exposed to a TE should show a reduction in the disorder across the passage of time. General psychological research shows that events that contribute to either feelings of happiness or of distress seem to have only temporary effects on overall basic well-being levels, which instead represent deeper, more long-standing individual differences (Suh, Diener & Fujita, 1996). Emotional disorder after the sudden death of a loved one, for example, shows naturally-occurring recovery over time (Bonanno & Kaltman, 2001). The literature specific to PTSD shows this general pattern as well, with naturally occurring recovery independently of any treatment (Feinstein & Dolan, 1991), and with even loss of memory for the experience of the disorder by one year post-event (North, Smith & Spritznagel, 1997). Despite these general findings, there is evidence that a small subset of individuals develops a prolonged disorder, and a smaller subset even develops a delayed traumatic response after initially resilient responding. This has been found both in children (Greenberg & Keane, 2001) and in adults (McFarlane, 1988a), casting a question on the DSM proximity model.

Research methods affect findings, and this can be significant because most studies of PTSD are done retrospectively studying individuals after they have experienced a TE, have developed PTSD, and have sought treatment. A meta-analysis across multiple studies found that trauma severity variables had weaker effects on distress when samples were followed prospectively, which is the more superior, but rare, research method (Brewin, Andrew & Valentine, 2000). This general research method problem means that not only are many research samples highly biased and thus less likely to provide insights about general or typical human responses to TE exposures, but it also means that the strength of the findings risks being altered by the choice of method.

Summary of Epidemiological Data

1. The rate of exposure to significantly threatening life events is high, affecting the majority of adults in affluent, peacetime democracies.
2. The lifetime rate of PTSD is quite low, ranging roughly around 8% in peacetime, with women showing a rate twice that of men.
3. Even without treatment, recovery of emotional disturbance arising from a threatening life event is seen in most cases; a small minority does not recover emotional self-regulation, and a smaller proportion even becomes more disturbed over time.
4. These data suggest that additional individual factors are more powerful in the development of the disorder, than is the TE exposure.

B. Individual Traits of Personality and Abilities Affect Response

Individual factors that increase the probability of the development of a disorder are called risk factors. While some social advocates argue against identifying risk factors in PTSD as "blaming the victim", in fact any logical scientific understanding of the factors that contribute to a disorder is part of the necessary work to properly diagnose and treat it. Similar risk factor research in schizophrenia for example, was able to identify genetic factors that increase the probability of the disorder more effectively than any other factor.

In the case of PTSD, the personality trait that refers to a general tendency to experience negative affect (emotions including anxiety and depression) upon experiencing life events, has been found a powerful risk factor for PTSD. The trait has been called "temperament" in the studies of infants and children, where it is found to be a longitudinally stable individual factor across early childhood (Kagan, 1989), (Schwartz, Snidman & Kagan, 1999), late childhood (Block & Robins, 1993), and across adulthood (Costa & McCrae, 1994), (McCrae & Costa, 1994). It has been studied as the personality trait of negative affectivity (Tellegen et al., 1988) or neuroticism in adults, with a stability coefficient of 0.53 over 30 years of adulthood (Finn, 1986). A different disposition or personality trait of responding with greater adaptiveness to life events also shows longitudinal stability relatively independent of the nature of events. It has been studied under different terms such as resilience (Garmezy, 1991), hardiness (Kobasa, Hilker & Maddi, 1979), and happiness (Myers & Diener, 1995; Diener, Oishi & Lucas, 2003).

The relative stability of the traits of neuroticism (N) and of resilience in different individuals arises in part from a genetic component which appears to be associated with a transporter gene for serotonin (Lesch, 2003). Large twin studies consistently find high rates of MZ concordance for neuroticism (Loehlin, 1989), and for additional risk traits such as impulsivity and risk-taking (Loehlin, 1992) associated with increased risk for later TE exposures, (Stein, Jang, Taylor, Vernon & Livesley, 2002). In combination such traits as these show a significant genetic role in the development of PTSD (True et al., 1993), with varying genetic contributions to different symptoms in the disorder (True & Lyons, 1999).

Neuroticism is strongly associated with PTSD as both a correlate and as a predictive risk factor for the disorder. In studies of combat veterans, high trait N has been found as a correlate of the diagnosis independent of combat exposure (Talbert, Braswell, Albrecht, Hyer & Boudewyns, 1993) that contributes more to PTSD than does combat (Casella & Motta, 1990). It was a pre-war predictor of later PTSD both in U.S. (Sutker, Bugg & Allain, 1991; Schnurr, Friedman & Rosenberg, 1993) and Australian veterans (O'Toole, Marshall, Schureck & Dobson, 1998). Personality traits accounted for more of the variations in distress-disorder than did the experience of combat (Sutker, Davis, Uddo & Ditta, 1995). Emotional competence during college predicted later combat disorder in WWII, in a longitudinal study that eventually followed men across 50 years (Lee et al., 1995). In the studies that directly examined the relative power of combat events vs. personality traits in predicting PTSD, traits were more powerful.

Within civilian life, similar findings of the power of trait N (or its close correlate, trait anxiety) on the prediction of PTSD and other event-attributed emotional disorder, have been reported. Across a seven year span trait N accounted for more distress symptoms than intrusive life events did in individuals in a community sample (Ormel & Wohlfarth, 1991). In another large community sample studied over a 10-year period, trait emotionality accounted for 47% of emotional distress symptoms, while stressful life events contributed 38% (Aldwin, Sutton & Lachman, 1996). Across other civilian events trait emotionality accounts for more of the distress disorder than actual exposure severity, including in children experiencing natural disasters (Lonigan, Shannon, Taylor, Finch & Sallee, 1994) and in parents' responding to their children's' cancers (Kazak et al., 1998). Trait N differentiated individuals seeking treatment from their siblings (Mook et al., 1997), and high trait N differentiated between severely burned patients with and without PTSD (Fauerbach, Lawrence, Schmidt, A.M. & Costa, 2000), and within patients after a heart attack (Pedersen, Middel & Larsen, 2002).

A long series of studies of firemen fighting periodic giant bush fires in Australia has had the benefit of obtaining information about individuals prior to their exposure to the fires and the injuries and property losses that often occur. Psychiatrist Alexander McFarlane has reported that stressor severity had no reliable relationship with subsequent psychiatric disorder (McFarlane, 1988b) and that cases often developed after a delay rather than immediately (McFarlane, 1988a). In addition, pre-fire neuroticism was the best predictor of PTSD after the fire (McFarlane, 1989), while actual harms and losses played a relatively minor role in the disorder (McFarlane, 1990). A similar pattern in which subjective trait qualities of the individual were more predictive of responses than objective features of the event, was found in a large review of studies of the effects of violence on individuals (Weaver & Clum, 1995).

While trait N is a precursor predicting PTSD after TE exposure, other personality traits themselves predict exposure to threatening events, which are not random but differentially clustered in certain individuals' lives. Sensation-seeking, impulsivity, and openness to experience appear to represent a different route to PTSD, through increasing exposure to threatening events. They are traits shown early in life, with significant genetic loading (Loehlin, 1992) accounting for their longitudinal stability, and they represent risk factors for exposure to TEs, typically through individuals initiating acts that result in untoward events. For example 47% of the variance in combat exposure was associated with such genetic factors (True & Lyons, 1999).

General reasoning ability serves as a mild moderator of the relationship between threatening events and PTSD. Longitudinal studies of children growing up in environments with high rates of threatening events show that intelligence is part of resiliency in the children who manage these experiences without suffering disorder (Fergusson & Lynskey, 1996). Among military veterans, pre-combat intelligence and education levels have been consistently associated with PTSD, always in the direction that lower intelligence/education is a risk factor for the disorder (Pitman, Orr, Lowenhagen & Macklin, 1991; Kaplan et al., 2002; McNally & Shin, 1995; Macklin et al., 1998). Low education was a risk factor for PTSD in women who were diagnosed with the disorder four months after a pregnancy loss (Englehard, van den Hout, Kindt, Arntz & Schouten, 2003), and low education pre-military was a risk factor for combat-related PTSD in a large twin study (Koenen et al., 2002).

Summary: Longstanding trait N is a significant risk factor for PTSD to develop after TE exposure, and long-standing traits of impulsivity and sensation-seeking are risk factors for more TE exposures and thus risk of PTSD. The enduring trait of general intelligence serves to promote resiliency when facing threatening events.

C. Individual Beliefs about Self, Emotions, and the World Affect Response

Beliefs, attitudes, thoughts, appraisals, and expectations about the self and about the world help individuals to assign meaning to events, and function as risk factors for the prediction of PTSD. Beliefs tend to be rather stable across time. The stable personality trait of N is correlated with a tendency to selectively perceive and remember fearful and negative stimuli (Derryberry & Reed, 1994; Reed & Derryberry, 1995). The negative emotionality trait is also associated with the general tendency to focus on feeling states rather than thoughts or actions, along with a general tendency to attribute blame to self as a stable, internal appraisal (Berenbaum, Fujita & Pfennig, 1995).

Beliefs about the self and the meaning of emotion affect the emotional responses of individuals after a TE exposure, and different thoughts can determine the meaning of events and thus affect emotional experience. Basic laboratory studies done in the 1960's showed how different meanings can determine emotional responses to a challenging stimulus. Participants were all shown a documentary film about circumcision rites in an Australian aboriginal group, with different voice-overs given to different groups of participants in the study. Among the different participant groups one group received a calm, intellectual narration emphasizing the importance of the ritual in the community, contrasting with another narration that emphasized the pain, the bloodiness and the risks of infection and death; other 'intermediate" narration conditions were given to other groups. Participants who heard the calm narrative responded with little arousal, while those with the dramatically different narration were highly emotionally aroused, both on self-report and by objective psychophysiological recordings (Speisman, Lazarus, Mordkoff & Davison, 1964). Since this early study similar findings have been widely replicated, and there is a general consensus that the meanings that individuals place on events can be a more powerful determinant of their responses than implicit and objective features of the events. In the case of PTSD a number of beliefs and thoughts are salient in those who develop the disorder (Ehlers & Clark, 2000) and in treating it (Parrot & Howes, 1991). In particular, negative beliefs about the self and the world are risk factors for developing and maintaining PTSD after a TE (Dunmore, Clark & Ehlers, 2001; Ehlers, Maercker & Boos, 2000). The belief that the self is vulnerable and has low self-efficacy differentiates those who develop PTSD after a TE exposure in many studies (Benight & Harper, 2002; Carlier, Lambers & Gersons, 2000; Dutton, Burghardt, Perrin, Chrestman & al., 1994), though not all (Ferren, 1999).

Beliefs that emotional arousal is itself a sign of danger or harm done, also increase the risk of PTSD (Smith & Bryant, 2000; Mayou, Ehlers & Bryant, 2002). It has been studied under the construct of anxiety sensitivity (Reiss, Peterson, Gursky & McNally, 1986) in laboratory and clinical samples, where it represents a combination of trait anxiety with the belief that emotional arousal symptoms represent harm (Taylor & Cox, 1998; Taylor, 1999). Anxiety sensitivity is a significant correlate of N (Cox, Borger, Taylor, Fuentes & Ross, 1999) and is a risk factor for PTSD (Asmundson, Bonin & Frombach, 2000; Schmidt & Lerew, 1998). It is also a correlate of treatment efficacy: among those whose treatment for PTSD was successful, reduction in anxiety sensitivity was a key factor in recovery (Fedoroff, Taylor, Asmundson & Koch, 2000). The belief that other PTSD symptoms (such as intrusion) are dangerous also serves as a risk factor for the disorder and for its persistence across time (Ehlers,

Mayou & Bryant, 1998; Mayou et al., 2002). PTSD patients with these symptoms appraise them as more unacceptable than do control patients who also experience them at the same rates (Reynolds & Brewin, 1998).

Beliefs about the general benevolence or danger of the world (Janoff-Bulman, 1989) and its fairness (Lerner, 1980) contribute to well-being (e.g. after bereavement, (Bonanno et al., 2002)) or to the development of disorder. These beliefs appraising the risks of the world may be anchored in realistic evaluations of events, or can arise from highly specific and inaccurate belief systems, such as in the case of koro. Koro is an intense fear, horror and sense of helplessness that at times becomes an epidemic afflicting hundreds of Chinese men. In this disorder an individual suffers from a culturally-defined delusion that his penis is retracting into his abdomen (Mo, Chen, Li & Tseng, 1995). The men and their terrified families attempt occasionally horrific measures to grab the organ to safely secure it, but end up with hospital admissions as the terror of the trauma affects them all. In fact there is no phenomenon affecting the organ, it is entirely a traumatic response to a delusional belief that has its roots in prohibitions about the dangers of masturbation. Under more ordinary conditions, beliefs about the availability for example of social support, were more important in mitigating distress in a community sample in the U.S. than was the actual provided social support (Krause, 1997). Appraisals of events were correlated with PTSD symptoms while actual injury severity was not, in soldiers injured in the war in Croatia (Sivik, Delimar, Korenjak & Delimar, 1997).

D. Personal History Factors: Events, Behavior, and Mental Disorder

Several aspects of pre-event personal history serve as individual risk factors for PTSD, including histories of previous TE exposures, of conduct problems, and of psychiatric disorder.

Prior exposures to challenging experiences should yield habituation to the stimuli, adaptation of responses, and skill learning relating to emotional regulation in humans, rather than simple conditioned fears as could be expected in simple organisms. Humans show complex individual differences in these processes, in that while most people do show the ability to navigate their way through threatening events and to recover adequate functioning, the small minority who develop PTSD show a different pattern of response. Those with PTSD show a failure to habituate, and an inability to develop emotional control or to return regulation of thoughts to a pre-event level. This represents a sensitization process rather than an immunization or learning process, and such sensitization to threatening stimuli has been reported as a feature of those who develop PTSD. Previous TE exposures were a risk factor for PTSD after violence in civilian life (Breslau, Chilcoat, Kessler & Davis, 1999a; Yehuda, Resnick, Schmeidler, Yang & Pitman, 1998), after September 11, 2001 in New York (Galea, Ahern & Resnick, 2002), and in veterans who had suffered child abuse (Bremner, Southwick, Johnson, Yehuda & Charney, 1993). The literature is not entirely consistent, however, and other studies report contrary findings for the effects of previous TE exposures, with no differences in PTSD rates (Falsetti & Resick, 1995; Corneil, Beaton, Murphy, Johnson & Pike, 1999). An exceptionally interesting finding hinting at the power of individual differences in capacity to learn from prior TE exposures, was reported in a study of psychiatric nurses assaulted by patients.

Among those with histories of past assaults, the nurses broke into two clusters of very different response patterns (Wykes & Whittington, 1998). One group had significantly low distress, while the other had significantly high. This suggests that one group consisted of individuals who had been able to adapt and learn how to manage their responses to this challenging feature of their job, while the other group had become sensitized to it as an enduring source of trauma.

High proportions of individuals who develop PTSD have a history of previous mental disorder, and such a history represents a risk factor for PTSD. In most cases where an individual has PTSD and another lifetime mental disorder, the other disorder preceded PTSD in the large NCS American sample (Kessler et al., 1995), and in an Australian veteran sample (O'Toole et al., 1998). After the September 11, 2001 attacks in New York, PTSD rates nearly tripled (to 33%) in individuals with psychiatric outpatient status, compared to rates of 13% in those with medical outpatient status (Franklin, Young & Zimmerman, 2002). The role of prior psychiatric history has also been found in smaller studies such as the study of the Texas mass shooting (North et al., 1994). After that event, it was learned that 92% of the men who developed PTSD had a history of alcohol abuse as did 83% of the women who developed PTSD. Further, while 13% of those directly injured developed PTSD, those not injured had a rate of 35% PTSD, and those who were only witnesses to the aftermath of the killings showed a PTSD rate of 27%. In general, a history of depression was a strong risk factor for PTSD in the group, and similar findings of the role of pre-event depression as a risk factor for PTSD have been reported in other major samples (Breslau, Davis, Peterson & Schultz, 1997). In general, having another pre-event psychiatric disorder appears to double the risk of developing PTSD after a threatening event (North et al., 1999)

Histories of conduct disorder and personality disorders such as antisocial and borderline personality disorder are also associated with PTSD, typically as pre-event risk factors. These are "Axis II" disorders in the Diagnostic Manual, which means they develop early in life and represent long-standing patterns of behavior, rather than reactive syndromes that come and go. Childhood behavior disorders were identified as a risk for adult PTSD in the first big US epidemiological study (Helzer, Robins & McEvoy, 1987) and in the later NCS (Kessler et al., 1995). Within children, those who are hyperactive and impulsive tend to initiate high risk acts more frequently than other children (Farmer & Peterson, 1995), and antisocial behavior by age 10 results in a doubling of exposures to threatening events over the next 20 years (Champion, Goodall & Rutter, 1995). Within adults, a childhood history of conduct disorder was a risk factor for PTSD in veterans (King, King, Foy & Gudanowski, 1996), and more particularly in a twin study with veterans, where it both predicted more TE exposure and also PTSD (Koenen et al., 2002). Other behavior that does not meet full criteria for personality disorder but represents untrustworthy acts and antisocial attitudes specifically reported in PTSD but not in other psychiatric disorders, may confound clinical management. Reports have noted that veterans with PTSD differ from those with other mental disorders, showing increasing exaggeration over time of the severity of the TE exposure (Southwick, Morgan, Nicolaou & Charney, 1997), exaggeration of pre-event competencies (Johnson-Greene et al., 1997), and symptom exaggeration (Frueh, Gold & de Arellano, 1997).

Brain function and PTSD: There is considerable interest in the possibility that PTSD is associated with unique features of brain-adrenal stress hormone production, and that even the anatomy of certain brain areas might be different among those with PTSD. As this issue is complex and the details exhaustive, this chapter will not go into the details. The most accurate summary at this point is that there is no specific pattern of brain chemistry response after a threatening event, rather, it appears to vary depending on numbers of prior TE exposures (Yehuda et al., 1998). Similarly, it is not yet clear that there is any change in the size of the hippocampus among those with PTSD despite early reports suggesting this was a finding and a change arising from the TE exposure (Bremner et al., 1995). The best evidence to date, from a twin study to allow identification of pre-event genetic factors, suggests that small hippocampal volume may be a pre-existing risk factor for the development of PTSD if a TE exposure occurs (Gilbertson, Shenton & Ciszewski, 2002).

E. Implications for Diagnosis of PTSD, for Case Management, and for Rehabilitation

While research can tell us in general what factors are important when findings are averaged across a group, in clinical practice professionals are faced with an individual who will vary from the group means in many unpredictable ways associated with the factors reviewed in earlier sections of this chapter. It is this unique pattern of factors that must be considered in diagnosis, case management, and rehabilitation in order to avoid the "ecological fallacy" of assuming that a general population finding can be applied to an abnormal individual. In addition to this general problem, PTSD has further unique definitional features in the DSM that compel scrupulous attention to the validity of the diagnosis. First, it is relatively unique among mental disorders in being attributed to a specific external event for which some other party might be held responsible. Secondly, unfortunately the defining features of the disorder in the Diagnostic Manual include a contradictory mixture of elements. The current edition of the Manual allows the stressor event to be something that threatens others, with the clinical individual only "confronted" with awareness of this. This language opens the door for claims of fear and horror that would not be considered typical emotions arising from an event that was only heard about. In addition, the Manual uses backward reasoning in which reported emotions of fear and horror are used to define an event as a "traumatic" stressor; this is especially problematical if the event was not directly experienced.

With those problems confounding the current definition, diagnosis must be very carefully done in order to ensure it is valid for the individual, because the diagnosis may be used for purposes beyond clinical care. It may be intended for use as the basis of medico-legal claims for personal injury awards, for diminished responsibility in criminal actions, or for disability-related compensation claims. From the outset it may be important to have the occurrence of the putative threatening event validated through independent, objective investigation, as up to 13% of claims of military experience were fraudulent in one sample (Baggaley, 1998). Symptom exaggeration affecting self-reports has also been found in veteran samples (Frueh, Smith & Barker, 1996), thus it is important to use multiple methods to assess functioning including measures with validity indicators, as well as independent information about impairments in everyday functioning. If the diagnosis is justified, the clinician must pay attention to additional individual risk factors contributing to the expression of the disorder in this individual in light of the evidence that most people exposed to threatening events do not develop the disorder. Additional individual risk factors that must be considered include those outlined in this chapter. The clinician must understand these individual pre-event factors in order to assess what portion of the disorder arises from the event, and what portion represents the operation of other individual risk factors; the Diagnostic Manual notes that such other factors may contribute to the disorder. This chapter has reviewed evidence that PTSD may represent an exacerbation of long-standing acute Axis I psychiatric disorders or a continuation of long-standing Axis II personality disorders, as well as reflecting long-standing temperament, competencies, and beliefs. The clinician must examine all of these in order to develop an accurate understanding of the roots of the disorder in a particular individual.

The mix of individual factors contributing to the expression of PTSD may affect case management and rehabilitation. Some individuals may have to be treated to come to terms with a temperament inclined to generate negative emotions of fear and anxiety. This might require methods including cognitive and medical approaches rather than intensely emotional imaginal exposure treatments which evidence suggests they might be unable to tolerate (Foa, Keane & Friedman, 2000) or with which they are unwilling to comply (Scott & Stradling, 1997). Other individuals may respond well to imaginal exposures (Tarrier & Humphreys, 2000), yet need to have cognitive biases and dysfunctional beliefs addressed in cognitive-behavioral treatment. Those with long-standing depression or alcohol abuse may need treatment directed to those problems. Those with long-standing personality disorders may prove quite difficult to help (Simon, 2002). They are less likely to recover from PTSD over time (Malta, Blanchard, Taylor, Hickling & Freidenberg, 2002), consistent with the nature of those disorders; this may present a significant problem if the diagnosis of PTSD provides an opening to desired resources such as long-term compensation.

SUMMARY

1. Most individuals who encounter even severely threatening events do not develop PTSD or any other event-focused mental disorder; a small minority does.
2. Most individuals respond with a mixture of emotions at the time of a TE exposure, and gradually recover their abilities to regulate their thoughts and emotions with the passage of time.
3. Individual factors that contribute to a failure to regulate thoughts and emotions include two main factors and several life history factors. The personality trait of "negative emotionality" (the tendency to respond to life events with negative emotions, or "neuroticism"), and a cluster of typical beliefs, are the two main factors contributing to a failure to recover emotional well-being.
4. Life history factors that may also contribute to failures to recover include past histories of substance abuse, conduct or antisocial personality disorder, previous TE exposures with poor recovery, and pre-event psychiatric disorder.
5. Because PTSD is unique among mental disorders in being attributed to an external event that may form the basis for special claims to disability compensation or diminished criminal responsibility, diagnosis must be done with

exceptional care. To ensure validity, case examination must include information about prior history of experiences, actions, and psychiatric diagnoses and independent and objective validation of the threatening event exposure, and about actual functioning effectiveness to ensure the case meets the diagnostic criterion of clinical significance.

6. Treatment may have to vary to accommodate individual differences in negative affectivity and individual differences in beliefs and thoughts about self, emotions and the world, and to ensure attention to pre-event behavioral and psychiatric histories that may be associated with co-morbid disorders that also require treatment.

REFERENCES

Aldwin, C. M., Sutton, K. J., & Lachman, M. (1996). The development of coping resources in adulthood. *Journal of Personality, 64*(4), 837–871.

Alexander, D. A. (1993). Stress among police body handlers: a long-term follow-up. *British Journal of Psychiatry, 163*, 806–808.

American Psychiatric Association. (1994). *Diagnostic and statistical manual of mental disorders.* (4th ed.). Washington DC: Author.

Asmundson, G. J. G., Bonin, M. F., & Frombach, I. K. (2000). Evidence of a disposition toward fearfulness and vulnerability to posttraumatic stress in dysfunctional pain patients. *Behaviour Research & Therapy, 38*(8), 801–812.

Baggaley, M. (1998). "Military Munchausen's": Assessment of factitious claims of military service in psychiatric patients. *Psychiatric Bulletin, 22*(3), 153–154.

Benight, C. C., & Harper, M. L. (2002). Coping self-efficacy perceptions as a mediator between acute stress response and long-term distress following natural disasters. *Journal of Traumatic Stress, 15*(3), 177–186.

Berenbaum, H., Fujita, F., & Pfennig, J. (1995). Consistency, specificity, and correlates of negative emotions. *Journal of Personality & Social Psychology, 68*(2), 342–352.

Block, J., & Robins, R. W. (1993). A longitudinal study of consistency and change in self-esteem from early adolescence to early adulthood. *Child Development, 64*(3), 909–923.

Bonanno, G., & Kaltman, S. (2001). The varieties of grief experience. *Clinical Psychology Review, 21*(5), 705–734.

Bonanno, G., Wortman, C. B., Lehman, d. R., Tweed, R. G., Haring, M., Sonnega, J., Carr, D., & Nesse, R. M. (2002). Resilience to loss and chronic grief; A prospective study from preloss to 18-months postloss. *Journal of Personality and Social Psychology, 83*(5), 1150–1164.

Bremner, J. D., Randall, P., Scott, T. M., Bronen, R. A., Seibyl, J. P., Southwick, S. M., Delaney, R. C., McCarthy, G., Charney, D. S., & Innis, R. B. (1995). MRI-based measurement of hippocampal volume in patients with combat-related posttraumatic stress disorder. *American Journal of Psychiatry, 152*(7), 973–981.

Bremner, J. D., Southwick, S. M., Johnson, D. R., Yehuda, R., & Charney, D. S. (1993). Childhood physical abuse and combat-related posttraumatic stress disorder in Vietnam veterans. *American Journal of Psychiatry, 150*(2), 235–239.

Breslau, N., Chilcoat, H. D., Kessler, R. C., & Davis, G. C. (1999a). Previous exposure to trauma and PTSD effects of subsequent trauma: Results from the Detroit Area Survey of Trauma. *American Journal of Psychiatry, 156*(6), 902–907.

Breslau, N., Chilcoat, H. D., Kessler, R. C., Peterson, E. L., & Lucia, V. C. (1999b). Vulnerability to assaultive violence: further specification of the sex difference in post-traumatic stress disorder. *Psychological Medicine, 29*(4), 813–821.

Breslau, N., Davis, G. C., Andreski, P., & Peterson, E. (1991). Traumatic events and posttraumatic stress disorder in an urban population of young adults. *Archives of General Psychiatry, 48*, 216–222.

Breslau, N., Davis, G. C., Peterson, E. L., & Schultz, L. (1997). Psychiatric sequelae of posttraumatic stress disorder in women. *Archives of General Psychiatry, 54*(1), 81–87.

Breslau, N., Kessler, R. C., Chilcoat, H. D., Schultz, L. R., Davis, G. C., & Andreski, P. (1998). Trauma and posttraumatic stress disorder in the community: The 1996 Detroit area survey of trauma. *Archives of General Psychiatry, 55*(7), 626–632.

Brewin, C. R., Andrew, B., & Valentine, J. D. (2000). Meta-analysis of risk factors for posttraumatic stress disorder in trauma-exposed adults. *Journal of Consulting and Clinical Psychology, 68*(5), 748–766.

Burkett, B. G., & Whitley, G. (1998). *Stolen valor: How the Vietnam generation was robbed of its heroes and its history.* Dallas TX: Verity Press.

Carlier, I. V. E., Lambers, R. D., & Gersons, B. P. R. (2000). The dimensionality of trauma: a multidimensional scaling comparison of police officers with and without posttraumatic stress disorder. *Psychiatry Research, 97*(1), 29–39.

Casella, L., & Motta, R. W. (1990). Comparison of characteristics of Vietnam veterans with and without Posttraumatic Stress Disorder. *Psychological Reports, 67*(2), 595–605.

Champion, L. A., Goodall, G., & Rutter, M. (1995). Behaviour problems in childhood and stressors in early adult life: I. A 20 year follow-up of London school children. *Psychological Medicine, 25*(2), 231–246.

Corneil, W., Beaton, R., Murphy, S., Johnson, C., & Pike, K. (1999). Exposure to traumatic incidents and prevalence of posttraumatic stress symptomatology in urban firefighters in two countries. *Journal of Occupational Health Psychology, 4*(2), 131–141.

Costa, P. T., & McCrae, R. R. (1994). Stability and change in personality from adolescence through adulthood. In C. F. Halverson, G. A. Kohnstamm, & R. P. Martin (Eds.), *The developing structure of termperament and personality from infancy to adulthood*, (pp. 139–150). Hillsdale NJ: Lawrence Erlbaum Associates.

Cox, B. J., Borger, S. C., Taylor, S., Fuentes, K., & Ross, L. M. (1999). Anxiety sensitivity and the five-factor model of personality. *Behaviour Research & Therapy, 37*(7), 633–641.

de Jong, J. T., Komproe, I. H., & Van Ommeren, M. (2001). Lifetime events and posttraumatic stress disorder in 4 postconflict settings. *Journal of the American Medical Association, 286*(5), 555–562.

Derryberry, D., & Reed, M. A. (1994). Temperament and attention: Orienting toward and away from positive and negative signals. *Journal of Personality & Social Psychology, 66*(6), 1128–1139.

Diener, E., Oishi, S., & Lucas, R. e. (2003). Personality, culture, and subjective well-being: Emotional and cognitive evaluations of life. *Annual Review of Psychology, 54*, 403–425.

Dunmore, E., Clark, D., & Ehlers, A. (2001). A prospective investigation of the role of cognitive factors in persistent posttraumatic stress disorder (PTSD) after physical or sexual assault. *Behaviour Research & Therapy, 39*(9), 1063–1084.

Dutton, M. A., Burghardt, K. J., Perrin, S. G., & Chrestman, K. R. (1994). Battered women's cognitive schemata. *Journal of Traumatic Stress, 7*(2), 237–255.

Ehlers, A., & Clark, D. M. (2000). A cognitive model of posttraumatic stress disorder. *Behaviour Research and Therapy, 38*(4), 319–345.

Ehlers, A., Maercker, A., & Boos, A. (2000). Posttraumatic stress disorder following political imprisonment: The role of mental defeat, alienation, and perceived permanent change. *Journal of Abnormal Psychology, 109*(1), 45–55.

Ehlers, A., Mayou, R. A., & Bryant, B. (1998). Psychological predictors of chronic posttraumatic stress disorder after motor vehicle accidents. *Journal of Abnormal Psychology, 107*(3), 508–519.

Englehard, I. M., van den Hout, M. A., Kindt, M., Arntz, A., & Schouten, E. (2003). Peritraumatic dissociation and posttraumatic stress after pregnancy loss: A prospective study. *Behaviour Research & Therapy, 41*(1), 67–78.

Falsetti, S. A., & Resick, P. A. (1995). Causal attributions, depression, and posttraumatic stress disorder in victims of crime. *Journal of Applied Social Psychology, 25*(12), 1027–1042.

Farmer, J. E., & Peterson, L. (1995). Injury risk factors in children with attention deficit hyperactivity disorder. *Health Psychology, 14*, 325–332.

Fauerbach, J. A., Lawrence, J. W., Schmidt, C. W., A.M., M., & Costa, P. T. (2000). Personality predictors of injury-related posttraumatic stress disorder. *Journal of Nervous & Mental Disease, 188*(8), 510–517.

Fedoroff, I. C., Taylor, S., Asmundson, G. J. G., & Koch, W. J. (2000). Cognitive factors in traumatic stress reactions: Predicting PTSD symptoms from anxiety sensitivity and beliefs about harmful events. *Behavioural & Cognitive Psychotherapy, 28*(1), 5–15.

Feinstein, A., & Dolan, R. (1991). Predictors of post-traumatic stress disorder following physical trauma: An examination of the stressor criterion. *Psychological Medicine, 21*, 85–91.

Fergusson, D. M., & Lynskey, M. T. (1996). Adolescent resiliency to family adversity. *Journal of Child Psychology & Psychiatry, 37*(3), 281–292.

Ferren, P. M. (1999). Comparing perceived self-efficacy among adolescent Bosnian and Croatian refugees with and without posttraumatic stress disorder. *Journal of Traumatic Stress, 12*(3), 405–420.

Finn, S. E. (1986). Stability of personality self-ratings over 30 years: Evidence for an age/cohort interaction. *Journal of Personality and Social Psychology, 50*, 813–818.

Foa, E. B., Keane, T. M., & Friedman, M. J. (Eds.). (2000). *Effective treatments for PTSD*. New York: The Guilford Press.

Franklin, C. L., Young, D., & Zimmerman, M. (2002). Psychiatric patients' vulnerability in the wake of the September 11th terrorist attacks. *Journal of Nervous & Mental Disease, 190*(12), 833–838.

Frueh, B. C., Gold, p. B., & de Arellano, M. A. (1997). Symptom overreporting in combat veterans evaluated for PTSD: Differentiation on the basis of compensation seeking status. *Journal of Personality Assessment, 68*(2), 369–384.

Frueh, B. C., Smith, D. W., & Barker, S. E. (1996). Compensation seeking status and psychometric assessment of combat veterans seeking treatment for PTSD. *Journal of Traumatic Stress, 9*(3), 427–440.

Galea, S., Ahern, J., & Resnick, H. (2002). Psychological sequelae of the September 11 terrorist attacks in New York City. *New England Journal of Medicine, 346*(13), 982–987.

Garmezy, N. (1991). Resilience and vulnerability to adverse developmental outcomes associated with poverty. *American Behavioral Scientist, 34*(4), 416–430.

Gilbertson, M. W., Shenton, M. E., & Ciszewski, A. (2002). Smaller hippocampal volume predicts pathologic vulnerability to psychological trauma. *Nature Neuroscience, 5*(11), 1242–1247.

Greenberg, H. S., & Keane, A. (2001). Risk factors for chronic posttraumatic stress symptoms and behavior problems in children and adolescents following a home fire. *Child & Adolescent Social Work Journal, 18*(3), 205–221.

Helzer, J. E., Robins, L. N., & McEvoy, L. (1987). Post-traumatic stress disorder in the general population: findings of the Epidemiologic Catchment Area Survey. *New England Journal of Medicine, 317*(26), 1630–34.

Janoff-Bulman, R. (1989). Assumptive worlds and the stress of traumatic events: Applications of the schema construct. *Social Cognition, 7*(2), 113–136.

Johnson-Greene, D., Dehring, M., Adams, K. M., Miller, T., Arora, S., Beylin, A., & Brandon, R. (1997). Accuracy of self-reported educational attainment among diverse patient populations: A preliminary investigation. *Archives of Clinical Neuropsychology, 12*(7), 635–643.

Kagan, J. (1989). Temperamental contributions to social behavior. *American Psychologist, 44(4), 668–674.*

Kaplan, Z., Weiser, M., Reichenberg, A., Rabinowitz, J., Caspi, A., Bodner, E., & Zohar, J. (2002). Motivation to serve in the military influences vulnerability to future posttraumatic stress disorder. *Psychiatry Research, 109*(1), 45–49.

Kazak, A. E., Stuber, M. L., Barakat, L. P., Meeske, K., Guthrie, D., & Meadows, A. T. (1998). Predicting posttraumatic stress symptoms in mothers and fathers of survivors of childhood cancers. *Journal of the American Academy of Child & Adolescent Psychiatry, 37*(8), 823–831.

Kessler, R., Sonnega, A., Bromet, E., Hughes, M., & Nelson, C. B. (1995). Posttraumatic stress disorder in the National Comorbidity Survey. *Archives of General Psychiatry, 52*, 1048–1060.

King, D. W., King, L. A., Foy, D. W., & Gudanowski, D. M. (1996). Prewar factors in combat-related posttraumatic stress disorder: Structural equation modeling with a national sample of female and male Vietnam veterans. *Journal of Consulting and Clinical Psychology, 64*(3), 520–531.

Kobasa, S., Hilker, R., & Maddi, S. (1979). Who stays healthy under stress?, *Journal of Occupational Medicine, 21, 595–598.*

Koenen, K. C., Harley, R., Lyons, M., Wolfe, J., Simpson, J. C., Goldberg, J., Eisen, S. A., & Tsuang, M. (2002). A twin registry study of familial and individual risk factors for trauma exposure and posttraumatic stress disorder. *Journal of Nervous & Mental Disease, 190*(4), 209–218.

Krause, N. (1997). Anticipated support, received support, and economic stress among older adults. *Journal of Gerontology, 52B*, 284–293.

Kulka, R. A., Schlenger, W. E., Fairbank, J. A., Hough, R. L., Jordan, B. K., Marmar, C. R., & Weiss, D. S. (1990). *Trauma and the Vietnam war generation: Report of findings from the national Vietnam veterans readjustment study.* New York: Brunner/Mazel.

Lee, K. A., Vaillant, G. E., Torrey, W. C., & Elder, G. H. (1995). A 50-year prospective study of the psychological sequelae of World War II combat. *American Journal of Psychiatry, 152*(4), 516–522.

Lerner, M. J. (1980). *The belief in a just world.* New York: Plenum.

Lesch, K. P. (2003). Neuroticism and serotonin: A developmental genetic perspective. In R. Plomin, J. C. Defries, I. W. Craig, & P. McGuffin (Eds.), *Behavioral genetics in the postgenomic era*, (pp. 389–423). Washington DC: American Psychological Association.

Lindal, E., & Stefansson, J. G. (1993). The lifetime prevalence of anxiety disorders in Iceland as estimated by the National Institute of Mental Health Diagnostic Interview Schedule. *Acta Psychiatrica Scandinavica, 88*(1), 29–34.

Loehlin, J. C. (1989). Partitioning environmental and genetic contributions to behavioral development. *American Psychologist, 443*, 1285–1292.

Loehlin, J. C. (1992). *Genes and environment in personality development.* Newbury Park, CA: sage.

Lonigan, C. J., Shannon, M. P., Taylor, C. M., Finch, A. J., & Sallee, F. R. (1994). Children exposed to disaster: II. Risk factors for the development of post-traumatic symptomatology. *Journal of the American Academy of Child and Adolescent Psychiatry, 33*(1), 94–105.

Macklin, M. L., Metzger, L. J., McNally, R. J., Litz, B. T., Lasko, N. B., Orr, S. P., & Pitman, R. K. (1998). Lower precombat intelligence is a risk factor for posttraumatic stress disorder. *Journal of Consulting and Clinical Psychology, 66*(2), 323–326.

Malta, L. S., Blanchard, E. B., Taylor, A. E., Hickling, E. J., & Freidenberg, B. M. (2002). Personality disorders and posttraumatic stress disorder in motor vehicle accident survivors. *Journal of Nervous and Mental Disease, 190*(11), 767–774.

Mayou, R. A., Ehlers, A., & Bryant, B. (2002). Posttraumatic stress disorder after motor vehicle accidents: 3-year follow-up of a prospective longitudinal study. *Behaviour Research & Therapy, 40*(6), 665–675.

McCrae, R. R., & Costa, P. T. (1994). The stability of personality: observations and evaluations. *Current Directions in Psychological Science, 3*(6), 173–175.

McFarlane, A. (1989). The aetiology of post-traumatic morbidity: predisposing, precipitating, and perpetuating factors. *British Journal of Psychiatry, 154*, 221–228.

McFarlane, A. C. (1988a). The longitudinal course of posttraumatic morbidity: The range of outcomes and their predictors. *Journal of Nervous and Mental Disease, 176*(1), 30–39.

McFarlane, A. C. (1988b). Relationship between psychiatric impairment and a natural disaster: The role of distress. *Psychological Medicine, 18*, 129–139.

McFarlane, A. C. (1990). An Australian disaster: The 1983 bushfires. *International Journal of Mental Health, 19*(2), 36–47.

McNally, R. J., & Shin, L. M. (1995). Association of intelligence with severity of posttraumatic stress disorder symptoms in Vietnam combat veterans. *American Journal of Psychiatry, 152*(6), 936–938.

Mo, G. M., Chen, G. Q., Li, L. Z., & Tseng, W. S. (1995). Koro epidemics in Southern China. In T. Y. Lin, W. S. Tseng, & E. K. Yeh (Eds.), *Chinese societies and mental health*, (pp. 231–246). Hong Kong: Oxford University Press.

Mook, J., Schreuder, B. J. N., van der Ploeg, H., Bramsen, I., van Tiel-Kadiks, G. W., & Feenstra, W. (1997). Psychological complaints and characteristics in postwar children of Dutch World War II victims: Those seeking treatment as compared with their siblings. *Psychotherapy & Psychosomatics, 66*(5), 268–275.

Myers, D. G., & Diener, E. (1995). Who is happy? *Psychological Science, 6*(1), 10–19.

Narrow, W. E., Rae, D. S., Robins, L. N., & Regier, D. A. (2002). Revised prevalence estimates of mental disorders in the United States, using a clinical significance criterion to reconcile 2 surveys' estimates. *Archives of General Psychiatry, 59*(2), 115–123.

North, C. S., Nixon, S. J., Shariat, S., Mallonee, S., McMillen, J. C., Spitznagel, E. L., & Smith, E. M. (1999). Psychiatric disorders among survivors of the Oklahoma City bombing. *Journal of the American Medical Association, 282*(8), 755–762.

North, C. S., Smith, E. M., & Spitznagel, E. L. (1994). Posttraumatic stress disorder in survivors of a mass shooting. *American Journal of Psychiatry, 151*(1), 82–88.

North, C. S., Smith, E. M., & Spritznagel, E. L. (1997). One-year follow-up of survivors of a mass shooting. *American Journal of Psychiatry, 154*(12), 1696–1702.

O'Toole, B. I., Marshall, R. P., Schureck, R. J., & Dobson, M. (1998). Posttraumatic stress disorder and comorbidity in Australian Vietnam veterans: risk factors, chronicity and combat. *Australian & New Zealand Journal of Psychiatry, 32*(1), 32–42.

Ormel, J., & Wohlfarth, T. (1991). How neuroticism, long-term difficulties, and life situation change influence psychological distress: A longitudinal model. *Journal of Personality and Social Psychology, 60*(5), 744–755.

Parrot, C., & Howes, J. L. (1991). The application of cognitive therapy to posttraumatic stress disorder. In T. M. Vallis, J. L. Howes, & P. C. Miller (Eds.), *The challenge of cognitive therapy: Applications to nontraditional populations*, (pp. 85–109). New York: Plenum.

Pedersen, S. S., Middel, B., & Larsen, M. L. (2002). The role of personality variables and social support in distress and perceived health in patients following myocardial infarction. *Journal of Psychosomatic Research, 53*(6), 1171–1175.

Perkonigg, A., Kessler, R. D., Storz, S., & Wittchen, H. U. (2000). Traumatic events and post-traumatic stress disorder in the community: prevalence, risk factors and comorbidity. *Acta Psychiatrica Scandinavica, 101*(1), 46–59.

Pitman, R. K., Orr, S. P., Lowenhagen, M. J., & Macklin, M. L. (1991). Pre-Vietnam contents of post-traumatic stress disorder veterans' service medical and personnel records. *Comprehensive Psychiatry, 32*(5), 416–422.

Reed, M. A., & Derryberry, D. (1995). Temperament and attention to positive and negative trait information. *Personality & Individual Differences, 18*(1), 135–147.

Reiss, S., Peterson, R., Gursky, D., & McNally, R. (1986). Anxiety sensitivity, anxiety frequency and the prediction of fearfulness. *Behaviour Research and Therapy, 24*, 1–8.

Reynolds, M., & Brewin, C. R. (1998). Intrusive cognitions, coping strategies and emotional responses in depression, post-traumatic stress disorder and a non-clinical population. *Behaviour Research & Therapy, 36*(2), 135–147.

Schmidt, N. B., & Lerew, D. R. (1998). Prospective evaluation of psychological risk factors as predictors of functional impairment during acute stress. *Journal of Occupational Rehabilitation, 8*(3), 199–212.

Schnurr, P. P., Friedman, M. J., & Rosenberg, S. D. (1993). Premilitary MMPI scores as predictors of combat-related PTSD symptoms. *American Journal of Psychiatry, 150*, 479–483.

Schwartz, C., Snidman, N., & Kagan, J. (1999). Adolescent social anxiety as an outcome of inhibited temperament in childhood. *Journal of the American Academy of Child & Adolescent Psychiatry, 38*(8), 1008–1015.

Scott, M. J., & Stradling, S. G. (1997). Client compliance with exposure treatments for posttraumatic stress disorder. *Journal of Traumatic Stress, 10*(3), 523–526.

Simon, R. I. (2002). Distinguishing trauma-associated narcissistic symptoms from posttraumatic stress disorder: A diagnostic challenge. *Harvard Review of Psychiatry, 10*(1), 28–36.

Sivik, T., Delimar, D., Korenjak, P., & Delimar, N. (1997). The role of blood pressure, cortisol, and prolactine among soldiers injured in the 1991–93 war in Croatia. *Integrative Physiological & Behavioral Science, 32*(4), 364–372.

Smith, K., & Bryant, R. A. (2000). The generality of cognitive bias in acute stress disorder. *Behaviour Research & Therapy, 3*(7), 709–715.

Southwick, S. M., Morgan, C. A., Nicolaou, A. L., & Charney, D. S. (1997). Consistency of memory for combat-related traumatic events in veterans of operation Desert Storm. *American Journal of Psychiatry, 154*(2), 173–177.

Speisman, J. C., Lazarus, R. S., Mordkoff, A. M., & Davison, L. (1964). Experiential reduction of stress based on ego-defense theory. *Journal of Abnormal and Social Psychology, 68*, 367–380.

Stein, M. B., Jang, K. L., Taylor, S., Vernon, P. A., & Livesley, W. J. (2002). Genetic and environmental influences on trauma exposure and posttraumatic stress disorder symptoms: a twin study. *American Journal of Psychiatry, 159*(10), 1675–1681.

Stein, M. B., Walker, J. R., Hazen, A. L., & Forde, D. R. (1997). Full and partial posttraumatic stress disorder: Findings from a community survey. *American Journal of Psychiatry, 154*(8), 1114–1119.

Suh, E., Diener, E., & Fujita, F. (1996). Events and subjective well-being: Only recent events matter. *Journal of Personality & Social Psychology, 70*(5), 1091–1102.

Summerfield, D. A., Loughrey, G., Nikapota, A., & Parry-Jones, W. (1997). Civil violence. In D. Black, M. Newman, J. Harris-Hendriks, & G. Mezey (Eds.), *Psychological trauma: a developmental approach*, (pp. 156–160 148–175). London: Gaskell.

Sutker, P. B., Bugg, F., & Allain, A. N. (1991). Psychometric prediction of PTSD among POW survivors. *Psychological Assessment, 3*(1), 105–110.

Sutker, P. B., Davis, J. M., Uddo, M., & Ditta, S. R. (1995). War zone stress, personal resources, and PTSD in Persian Gulf War returnees. *Journal of Abnormal Psychology, 104*(3), 444–452.

Sutker, P. B., Uddo, M., Brailey, K., Vasterling, J. J., & Errera, P. (1994). Psychopathology in war-zone deployed and nondeployed Operation Desert Storm troops assigned graves registration duties. *Journal of Abnormal Psychology, 103*, 383–390.

Talbert, F. S., Braswell, L. C., Albrecht, J. W., Hyer, L. A., & Boudewyns, P. A. (1993). NEO-PI profiles in PTSD as a function of trauma level. *Journal of Clinical Psychology, 49*(5), 663–669.

Tarrier, N., & Humphreys, L. (2000). Subjective improvement in PTSD patients with treatment by imaginal exposure or cognitive therapy: Session by session changes. *British Journal of Clinical Psychology, 39*(1), 27–34.

Taylor, S. (Ed.). (1999). *Anxiety sensitivity: Theory, research, and treatment of the fear of anxiety.* Mahweh NJ: Lawrence Erlbaum Associates.

Taylor, S., & Cox, B. J. (1998). Anxiety sensitivity: Multiple dimensions and hierarchic structure. *Behaviour Research & Therapy, 36*(1), 37–51.

Tellegen, A., Lykken, D. T., Bouchard, T. J., Wilcox, K. J., Segal, N. C., & Rich, S. (1988). Personality similarity in twins reared apart and together. *Journal of Personality and Social Psychology, 54*(6), 1031–1039.

True, W. R., & Lyons, M. J. (1999). Genetic risk factors for PTSD: A twin study. In R. Yehuda (Ed.), *Risk factors for posttraumatic stress disorder,* (pp. 61–78). Washington DC: American Psychiatric Press.

True, W. R., Rice, J., Eisen, S. A., Heath, A. C., Goldberg, J., Lyons, M. J., & Nowak, J. (1993). A twin study of genetic and environmental contributions to liability for posttraumatic stress symptoms. *Archives of General Psychiatry,* 50(April), 257–264.

Weaver, T. L., & Clum, G. A. (1995). Psychological distress associated with interpersonal violence: A meta-analysis. *Clinical Psychology Review, 15*(2), 115–140.

Wykes, T., & Whittington, R. (1998). Prevalence and predictors of early traumatic stress reactions in assaulted psychiatric nurses. *Journal of Forensic Psychiatry, 9*(3), 643–658.

Yehuda, R., Resnick, H. S., Schmeidler, J., Yang, R.-K., & Pitman, R. K. (1998). Predictors of cortisol and 3-Methoxy-4-hydroxy-phenylglycol responses in the acute aftermath of rape. *Biological Psychiatry, 43*(11), 855–859.

18

Posttraumatic Stress Disability after Motor Vehicle Accidents

Impact on Productivity and Employment

William J. Koch and Joti Samra

IMPACT ON PRODUCTIVITY AND EMPLOYMENT

Motor vehicle accidents (MVAs) are a leading cause of Posttraumatic Stress Disorder (PTSD, Norris, 1992). A recent meta-analysis of conditional prevalence suggests that approximately 15 percent of MVA survivors will suffer from PTSD as long as 1 year post-MVA (Shercliffe, 2001). Because MVA-related losses may be compensated through either personal injury litigation or Workers' Compensation claims, it behooves us to better understand the relationship of PTSD to functional disability in employment settings. This chapter will discuss what we know of the general effects of PTSD on income and employment, followed by a discussion of likely connections between the emotional, cognitive and behavioral domains of PTSD and functional disability. Recommended assessment methods for detecting symptom-disability pathways for the individual will be described as well as relevant case examples. By pathways, we mean the route through which particular mental health problems affect individuals' abilities to work.

EFFECTS OF PTSD ON INCOME AND EMPLOYMENT

Posttraumatic stress has been associated with impairment in social, financial, physical, and psychological functioning (Amaya-Jackson et al., 1999). Individuals who report posttraumatic stress symptoms (PTSS) are more likely to report impaired social support, to report that their income poorly meets their needs, to have spent more than 7 days in bed in the preceding 3 months, to report suicidal thoughts, to report increased general medical and mental health outpatient visits, and to use psychotropic drugs (Amaya-Jackson et al., 1999). Individuals who meet diagnostic criteria for

DOI: 10.1007/978-0-387-28919-9_18, © 2009 Springer Science+Business Media, LLC

PTSD are more functionally impaired than are individuals who meet sub-threshold levels of PTSS (Amaya-Jackson et al., 1999). Additionally, individuals with PTSD are more likely than those without PTSD to have other co-morbid psychiatric disorders (Sautter et al., 1999; Solomon & Davidson, 1997). For example, it has been reported that 40–50%, or more, of PTSD patients have comorbid depression (Blanchard & Hickling, 1997; Kessler, Sonnega, Bromet, Hughes, & Nelson, 1995). This, of course, places individuals with PTSD and comorbid depression at greater risk for the economic losses associated with depression, a double whammy if one believes that these different disorders have independent negative effects on economic functioning.

The negative impact of PTSD upon employment has been relatively well established. In their review of the labor force participation research for individuals who have suffered traumatic exposure (i.e., to combat, childhood abuse, concentration camp experiences, and refugee status), Fairbank, Ebert, and Zarkin (1999) found a consistent pattern whereby exposure to traumatic stress is associated with reduced labor market outcomes. Among male monozygotic twin pairs of American Vietnam veterans, a diagnosis of PTSD was associated with a higher likelihood of unemployment at follow-up, even when controlling for genetic factors (McCarren, James, Goldberg, Eisen, True, & Henderson, 1995). Male Vietnam veterans with PTSD have been found to be five times as likely to be unemployed, in comparison to veterans without PTSD (Kulka et al., 1990). Even after statistically adjusting for the economic effects of variables such as demographic factors, depression, alcohol abuse/dependence, chronic medical conditions, and panic disorder, women veterans with PTSD have been found to be ten times more likely than women veterans without PTSD to be unemployed, and male veterans with PTSD are three times more likely to be unemployed, in comparison to their veteran counterparts without PTSD (Zatzick et al., 1997). Middle-aged Cambodian refugees who live in the US and have PTSD have lower annual incomes and are more likely to be receiving public financial assistance than similar refugee adults without a mental health diagnosis (Sack, Clarke, Kinney, Belestos, Chanrithy, & Seeley, 1995). Finally, symptomatic status has been directly related to economic variables. Vietnam veterans with higher PTSD symptom scores have been found to have significantly lower incomes, lower educational attainment, and greater unemployment than those with lower symptom scores, independent of degree of combat exposure and service unit (Vincent, Chamberlain, & Long, 1994). In conclusion, PTSD appears to be associated with markedly reduced employment and thus persons with this diagnosis are at risk for lost wages. However, this conclusion about PTSD's economic implications is taken from samples (war veterans, refugees) that may be different on other dimensions from MVA survivors with resulting work disability. There are no published studies to our knowledge that indicate the economic impact of PTSD following MVAs specifically. In addition, the association of PTSD with underemployment merely indicates that the individual who earns a PTSD diagnosis is at some increased risk for reduced employment. The reader should remind him/herself that risk factors for lesser employment are not synonymous with under-employment. Applying actuarial data to individual cases requires a functional assessment of the individual that relates his/her symptoms to reduced attendance or productivity in the work setting. Group differences (e.g., between PTSD and non-PTSD samples) in economic performance obscure important differences between those PTSD individuals who suffer significant functional disadvantage secondary to their psychological disorder and those who, despite having the same diagnosis, suffer no such functional disadvantage by dint of personal or environmental advantages. Thus, it is important in any given case to investigate the pathways through which specific psychological disorders, or their symptoms, produce work disability in the individual case.

RESEARCH ON PREDICTORS OF DISABILITY

Little research has been conducted that is directly relevant to the prediction of work disability among PTSD sufferers. There are scattered studies within the general disability literature that may be relevant. Kouzis and Eaton (1994) in a large study with 1,463 adults found that depression, in particular, was associated with work disability. Regehr, Goldberg, Clancy, and Knott (2003) utilized a small sample of 86 paramedics to investigate the predictors of mental health stress leave. High levels of PTSD symptoms were associated with previous stress leave, however, the strongest factor in predicting stress leave were personality characteristics of suspiciousness, hostility and isolation. Emsley, Seedat, and Stein (2003) studied 124 South African Security Force members who had taken early retirement secondary to PTSD. Of note among this clinical sample, 90 percent had negative feelings about their previous work and over half believed that changes in the work environment played a substantial role in their emotional discomfort. A large study of 1038 middle-aged Finnish men (Krause et al., 1997) examined the predictors of disability. While they did not study PTSD, per se, they found that psychosocial constructs such as mental strain on the job, job dissatisfaction, limited communication with fellow workers, and less social support from supervisors all contributed to disability. Another large study from Finland followed up 15,348 workers over six years. Life dissatisfaction predicted disability for both genders, while interpersonal conflict at work predicted disability in women, and monotonous work, neuroticism, and daily stressors predicted disability in men (Appelberg, Romanov, Heikkilae, & Honkasalo, 1996). Another Scandinavian study (Olstad, Sexton, & Sogaard, 2001) found that social support appeared to buffer work-related stress.

The findings above are relevant to the prediction of work disability for the following reasons. First, it is likely that high levels of PTSD and depressive symptoms place an individual at risk for work disability. Second, social/interpersonal factors such as the individual's own hostility and social isolation, neuroticism (perhaps best conceptualized here as a predisposition to emotional distress), social support both within and outside the work setting, perceived or actual low support from employers, and work/life dissatisfaction are all variables that may influence the person's ability to work productively. At the end of this chapter, we discuss possible avenues for research to shed more light on this area.

PATHWAYS BETWEEN PTSD AND FUNCTIONAL DISABILITY

To meet symptomatic criteria for PTSD, one must have a combination of symptoms sampled from each of three theoretically distinct clusters: (a) re-experiencing symptoms (e.g., distressing nightmares of the MVA, distress following reminders of the

MVA); (b) avoidant or numbing symptoms (e.g., behavioral or cognitive avoidance of reminders, emotional numbing, loss of recreational/social interests); and (c) hyperarousal symptoms (e.g., irritability, sleep disturbance). To meet full diagnostic criteria for PTSD under DSM-IV rules, the individual must also meet certain duration requirements, and more importantly, the symptoms must be associated with severe distress or disability in his/her social or occupational roles. The importance of taking into account functional disability is illustrated by the findings of Peters, Slade, and Andrews (1999) and Andrews Slade, and Peters (1999), who found that using ICD-10 criteria for PTSD (without a functional impairment or clinically significant distress criterion) resulted in twice the rate of PTSD as found with DSM-IV criteria. Therefore, meeting symptomatic criteria alone is insufficient to demonstrate functional disability.

Disability may be defined as a behavioral deficit that is an inability to perform some task or an inability to control some maladaptive behavior that interferes with task performance. To use a personal example, the first author would be functionally disabled as a Sherpa on Mt. Everest for a number of reasons. First, his current aerobic fitness (as observed by his track star daughter) would not meet the job requirements. Second, his spatial disability (as observed by his wife) might result in his walking off a cliff. Third, his height phobia (a psychological disorder) might result in emotional discomfort and possibly outright avoidance of 8,000 meter mountains. Thus, the first writer is functionally disabled as a Sherpa because of physical, cognitive, and emotional impairments. Luckily, no one has asked him to make a living by climbing mountains.

Domains of Work Disability

What is a PTSD sufferer's equivalent of the first author's disability as a Sherpa? This is a question too seldom asked by forensic assessors. If a MVA survivor meets symptomatic criteria for PTSD, the first question a claims adjudicator or forensic assessor must ask him/herself is *how* the individual's PTSD symptoms lead to deficits in important occupational skills. To address this problem, one must take a common sense approach to conceptualizing employability. What does it take to be an adequate worker in modern society?

Mobility

First, the person must be able to attend work. That is, he/she must not have any obstacles to mobility with respect to getting to the office, factory, or retail outlet. There may be some workers who do not need to commute to work (e.g., homemakers, telecommuters), but they are likely still in the minority, and they may have their own motor vehicle travel requirements. Fear and avoidance of motor vehicle travel, whether as drivers or passengers, are high prevalence problems with MVA survivors and can lead directly to work impairment. We will give an example below.

> "Jane Doe," a 30-year-old married woman, survived two separate MVAs within a space of five years. She developed PTSD with associated driving phobia subsequent to the first MVA, but recovered substantial driving mobility following a course of cognitive-behavioral therapy (CBT), and remained fully employed albeit somewhat apprehensive about automobile travel leading up to the second MVA.

> Subsequent to the second MVA, she relapsed with a severe depression and a more severe fear and avoidance of motor vehicle travel. She did not respond positively to a second course of CBT for her driving fears and thus remained both fearful and avoidant of automobile travel. At the time of this writing, this person was on long term disability because the large retail chain in which she held a middle management position had no job opportunities within easy pedestrian or mass transit access and also required her to drive among different stores to conduct her middle management duties. Adding to her stress, this woman impulsively sold her home and purchased another within walking distance of one of her employer's stores, only to learn that the employer could not offer her a position in that particular store. Thus, because of her apprehension and avoidance of driving, she could neither drive to her place of work, nor could she engage in the necessary driving required during her work hours.

Ms. Doe illustrates the negative impact PTSD-related fear and avoidance can have on an individual's ability to attend work, independent of her ability to perform necessary job tasks once she arrives at the work site.

Emotional Control and Interpersonal Skills

Problematic anger is often part of the presentation of PTSD. The reader acquainted with PTSD will recall that "irritability or outbursts of anger" (APA, 1994, p. 428) is part of the diagnostic criteria for this condition. It is also notable that anger problems frequently complicate PTSD (Chemtob, Novaco, Hamada, Gross, & Smith, 1997), and interfere in successful treatment of PTSD (e.g., Taylor, Fedoroff, Koch, Thordarson, Fecteau, & Niki, 2001). The following example illustrates how problematic anger can complicate occupational functioning.

> "John Smith," a 35-year-old single automobile sales manager, sustained a PTSD following injuries sustained in a MVA. Mr. Smith was able to sustain employment as a sales manager in a large retail auto dealer but was vulnerable to job loss/disability through (a) fear and avoidance of driving, and (b) angry verbal outbursts. He was fortunate enough to live within walking distance of the car dealership, and was allowed to avoid test drives with customers given his managerial status. He also had an understanding employer who accommodated his anger outbursts because of Mr. Smith's previous positive work history. The employer showed great tolerance for this particular employee who "blew up" on multiple occasions with sales and clerical staff, and walked off the job site impulsively on two occasions following anger outbursts. With a less understanding employer, Mr. Smith may have been terminated from his managerial position and then, as he feared, would have to find work as a car salesman, which would require him to accompany customers on test drives.

Mr. Smith's case is a good example of how anger control problems play an important role in employability and work performance, and how PTSD may negatively affect employment performance in an individual case.

Stress Resilience

Because part of the symptomatic presentation of PTSD involves high levels of autonomic arousal and vigilance for threat, PTSD sufferers may experience those corollaries of hypervigilance such as fatigue, demoralization, and malaise. The following case illustrates the impact of these PTSD side effects on employability.

> "Bill Jones" was a 38-year-old married corrections worker. He suffered a PTSD and co-morbid Panic Disorder in a MVA during which he also suffered a severe orthopedic injury. Following recovery from his orthopedic injury, he returned to work. By his report, following his return, he found the every day stressors of his work in the corrections environment more stressful than he had before his injury. He frequently suffered full or limited symptom panic attacks on the job site secondary to interpersonal conflict or otherwise feeling threatened. He would frequently retreat to the staff room where he felt less vulnerable. If around work-related stressors for too long, he would suffer panic attacks that were very distressing to him. Despite sympathetic co-workers and supervisors, he had to take more sick days than he did previous to the MVA, most often following work shifts that involved some type of stressful interpersonal conflict with inmates. One year after his return to full time work, he had used his full allotment of sick time (calculated at 1.25 days per month), and an additional 10 days taken as unpaid leave. His supervisor also reported that Bill spent too much time in the staff room during work shifts, resulting in less positive work evaluations than he had previously received.

This case illustrates how the hypervigilance symptoms associated with PTSD and associated panic attacks can negatively affect both work attendance and work performance.

RECOMMENDED ASSESSMENT METHODS

Mobility Deficits Secondary to Fear

Clinicians should start with the simplest of questions. "How do you get to work?" and "Do you find yourself having problems getting to work because you are afraid?" These questions follow naturally from either parts of standard symptomatic inquiries about either PTSD or Specific Phobias of driving and so are not difficult to include in a forensic, clinical or vocational inquiry. It is wise to probe more deeply than some clinicians might to determine just what the person is fearful of happening on the way to work. Some MVA survivors with driving fears may think that you are inquiring about the obvious. They will respond "Well, I will be in another accident." However, it is important for rehabilitation purposes to know whether they are fearful that their driving competence is somehow impaired so that they are more likely to find themselves in a collision, if they feel that their physical injuries are such that they will be more severely or permanently impaired if they aggravate the injury through another collision, if other drivers on the roads are particularly untrustworthy, or if they think that they will become so stressed while driving that they will have a panic attack and lose control in some dangerous or embarrassing fashion. As the reader can appreciate, these different responses have different rehabilitation implications. The first author has, in fact, assessed and treated driving phobics who reported having been warned by medical specialists that if they were to be in another MVA, they might aggravate their previous injury with catastrophic consequences. Psychometric measures that can be helpful in assessing such mobility problems include the

Accident Fear Questionnaire (AFQ; Kuch, Cox, & Direnfeld, 1995), Anxiety Sensitivity Index (ASI; Reiss, Peterson, Gursky, & McNally,1986), and the Mobility Inventory (Chambless, 1985). The AFQ measures avoidance of motor vehicle travel and related concepts, the ASI measures fear of bodily sensations and is strongly associated with panic disorder, PTSD, and the frequency of panic attacks (e.g., Taylor, Koch, & McNally, 1992). The Mobility Inventory measures avoidance of public, closed and open spaces common among agoraphobic patients.

Collateral interviews are also helpful in this regard. Spouses, co-workers, and supervisors may possess valuable insights on the individual's difficulties getting to work on time (e.g., "always late," "arrives at work every morning looking really stressed," "takes him a long time to work up his nerve to drive"). Spouses may have actually observed the person's fear during car travel (e.g., overly cautious driving, back seat driving as a passenger). Finally, behavioral observations of the person while either driving or riding in a vehicle can also be very enlightening with respect to the amount of vigilance, responses to different traffic densities and patterns, and maladaptive safety behaviors.

Interpersonal Difficulties Secondary to Irritability

While one might wish to use psychometric measures such as the State Trait Anger Expression Inventory (STAXI, Spielberger, 1996) to measure the severity of such difficulties, this is not a substitute for a behavioral analysis of how problematic expression of anger impairs the individual's employability and productivity. Again, the assessor should be asking the individual about the quality of his work relationships, how often he has lost his temper at work, and whether his anger or irritability have affected his work productivity. Collateral sources (e.g., work supervisors, co-workers, spouses) may give the clinician the best vantage point to understand how such mental health problems affect the individual's performance on the job. Specific inquiries might include questions about (a) changes in the persons's relationships with co-workers, (b) frequency of verbal or physical outbursts of anger, or (c) disciplinary steps taken at work in response to anger outbursts. Work records may include notes with respect to problematic anger outbursts, but they are likely to underestimate the occurrence of such events. It is likely important in determining the impact of such anger problems on an individual's work productivity to determine how many interpersonal interactions he/she must have on the job, with whom, and the economic risks associated with problematic interpersonal relationships. The economic consequences of an irritable employee are likely quite different for a shipping clerk who packages parts for delivery in a back room by himself, and an executive secretary who sets up appointments for the CEO with important customers.

Lowered Stress Tolerance

Again, much of the assessment of reduced stress tolerance requires interviews of both the person and collateral sources. It is important to ascertain whether the individual's demeanor, appearance, and subjective experience on the job site has changed subsequent to the index trauma. Does he/she require more frequent breaks (for other than physical reasons), take more sick days, or appear to avoid more stressful work activities? Does he/she complain of more physical symptoms of a potentially psychosomatic nature (e.g., headaches, fatigue, malaise, tension) while at work? Does he avoid or retreat from specific work activities because he/she finds such participation stressful?

SUMMARY

Epidemiological research suggests that PTSD is a general risk factor for underemployment and reduced economic functioning. However, further research is needed to extend this conclusion to MVA-PTSD sufferers specifically. This is especially important given the growing rate of personal injury claims implicating PTSD following MVAs.

On an idiographic level, one must determine how a PTSD sufferer's emotional symptoms lead to occupational dysfunction. We have outlined three potential pathways for such disability. Mobility problems secondary to fear of automobile travel may limit the person's ability to commute to work. Symptoms of anger and irritability may decrease the quality of a individual's interpersonal relations in the work place, making him/her an unwelcome and ineffective employee. Such inadequate interpersonal behavior may even lead to termination. Hypervigilance and lowered stress tolerance may lead a worker to avoid some work situations and use more sick days secondary to such correlates of PTSD as fatigue and malaise.

Further research is needed to better understand the employment implications of MVA-PTSD. There are a number of different avenues through which such research can be conducted. First, at the general population level, it seems that it is important to learn from members of the working public what personal mobility, emotional resiliency, social and environmental support, and interpersonal skills and relationships they require to comfortably tolerate a full time work position. Contrasted groups of workers differentiated by amount of sick days taken would also help us to understand the impact of these different variables on work attendance. Further research could then be conducted at both the group level for clinical cases (e.g., MVA-PTSD sufferers, or more generally MVA survivors with any injury) to determine the number of sick days associated with MVA-PTSD, as well as personality, work environment, and social support predictors of work attendance within these clinical groups. Beyond such large sample studies, we require some work on an idiographic level. As one example, we need case series research that studies how individual mental health symptoms (e.g., driving-related fear, PTSD symptoms) interfere with work attendance, productivity, and interpersonal functioning in the work setting.

REFERENCES

Amaya-Jackson, L., Davidson, J. R., Hughes, D. C., Swartz, M., Reynolds, V., George, L. K., & Blazer, D. G. (1999). Functional impairment and utilization of services associated with posttraumatic stress in the community. *Journal of Traumatic Stress, 12*, 709–724.

Appelberg, K., Romanov, K., Heikkilae, K., & Honkasalo, M.L. (1996). Interpersonal conflict s a predictor of work disability: A follow-up study of 15,348 Finnish employees. *Journal of Psychosomatic Research, 40*, 157–167.

Andrews, G., Slade, T., & Peters, L. (1999). Classification in psychiatry: ICD-10 versus DSM-IV. *British Journal of Psychiatry, 174*, 3–5.

Blanchard, E.B. & Hickling, E.J. (1997). *After the Crash: Assessment and Treatment of Motor Vehicle Accident Survivors.* Washington, D.C.: American Psychological Association.

Chambless, D.L. (1985). The Mobility Inventory for Agoraphobia. *Behaviour Research & Therapy, 23*, 35–44.

Chemtob, C.M., Novaco, R.W., Hamada, R.S., Gross, D.M. & Smith, G. (1997). Anger regulation deficits in combat-related posttraumatic stress disorder. *Journal of Traumatic Stress, 10*, 17–35.

Emsley, R.A., Seedat, S., & Stein, D.J. (2003). Posttraumatic stress disorder and occupational disability in South African Security Force members. *Journal of Nervous and Mental Disease, 191*, 237–241.

Fairbank, J. A., Ebert, L., & Zarkin, G. A. (1999). Socioeconomic consequences of traumatic stress. In P. A. Saigh & J. D. Bremner (Eds.), *Posttraumatic stress disorder: A comprehensive text* (pp. 180–198). Allyn & Bacon: Needham Heights, Massachusetts.

Kessler, R. C., Sonnega, A., Bromet, E., Hughes, M., & Nelson, C. B. (1995). Posttraumatic stress disorder in the national comorbidity survey. *Archives of General Psychiatry, 52*, 1048–1060.

Kulka, R.A., Schlenger, W.E., Fairbank, J.A., Hough, R.L., Jordan, B.K., Marmar, C.R., & Weiss, D.S. (1990). *Trauma and the Vietnam war generation: Report of findings from the National Vietnam Veterans Readjustment Study.* New York: Brunner/Mazel.

Kouzis, A.C. & Eaton, W.W. (1994). Emotional disability days: Prevalence and predictors. *American Journal of Public Health, 84*, 1304–1307.

Krause, N., Lynch, J., Kaplan, G.A., Cohen, R.D., Goldberg, D.E., & Salonen, J.T. (1997). Predictors of disability retirement. *Scandinavian Journal of Work, Environment and Health, 23*, 403–413.

Kuch, K., Cox, B.J., & Direnfeld, D.M. (1995). A brief self-rating scale for PTSD after road vehicle accident. *Journal of Anxiety Disorders, 9*, 503–514.

McCarren, M., Janes, G.R., Goldberg, J., Eisen, S.A., True, W.R., & Henderson, W.G. (1995). A twin study of the association of post-traumatic stress disorder and combat exposure with long-term socioeconomic status in Vietnam Veterans. *Journal of Traumatic Stress, 8*, 111–124.

Norris, F.H. (1992). Epidemiology of trauma: Frequency and impact of different potentially traumatic events on different demographic groups. *Journal of Consulting and Clinical Psychology, 60*, 409–418.

Olstad, R., Sexton, H.,& Sogaard, A.J. (2001). The Finnmark Study. A prospective population study of the social support buffer hypothesis, specific stressors and mental distress. *Social Psychiatry and Psychiatric Epidemiology, 36*, 582–589.

Peters, L., Slade, T., & Andrews, G. (1999). A comparison of ICD-10 and DSM-IV criteria for posttraumatic stress disorder. *Journal of Traumatic Stress, 12*, 33–343.

Regehr, C., Goldberg, G., Glancy, G.D., & Knott, T. (2002). Posttraumatic symptoms and disability in paramedics. *Canadian Journal of Psychiatry, 47*, 953–958.

Reiss, S., Peterson, R.A., Gursky, D.M., & McNally, R.J. (1986). Anxiety sensitivity, anxiety frequency and the prediction of fearfulness. *Behavior Research and Therapy, 24*, 1–8.

Sack, W. H., Clarke, G. N., Kinney, R., Belestos, G., Him, C., & Seeley, J. (1995). The Khmer Adolescent Project. II: Functional capacities in two generations of Cambodian refugees. *The Journal of Nervous and Mental Disease, 183*, 177–181.

Sautter, F. J., Brailey, K., Uddo, M. M., Hamilton, M. F., Beard, M. G., & Borges, A. H. (1999). PTSD and comorbid psychotic disorder: Comparison with veterans diagnosed with PTSD or psychotic disorder. *Journal of Traumatic Stress, 12*, 73–88.

Shercliffe, R. (2001). *Post-traumatic Stress Disorder in a Civilian Context: A Quantitative Review.* Unpublished Doctoral Dissertation. Simon Fraser University.

Solomon, S.D., & Davidson, J.R.T. (1997). Trauma: Prevalence, impairment, service use, and cost. *Journal of Clinical Psychiatry, 58*, 5–11.

Spielberger, C.D. (1996). *State-Trait Anger Expression Inventory: Professional Manual.* Odessa, FL: Psychological Assessment Resources.

Taylor, S., Fedoroff, I. C., Koch, W. J., Thordarson, D., Fecteau, G., & Niki, R. (2001). Posttraumatic stress disorder arising after road traffic collisions: Patterns of response to cognitive behavior therapy. *Journal of Consulting and Clinical Psychology, 69*, 541–551.

Taylor, S., Koch, W.J., & McNally, R.J. (1992). How does anxiety sensitivity vary across the anxiety disorders? *Journal of Anxiety Disorders, 6*, 249–259.

Vincent, C., Chamberlain, K., & Long, N. (1994). Relation of military service variables to posttraumatic stress disorder in New Zealand Vietnam war veterans. *Military Medicine, 159*, 322–326.

Zatzick, D. F., Weiss, D. S., Marmar, C. R., Metzler, T. J., Wells, K., Golding, J. M, Stewart, A., Schlenger, W. E., & Browner, W. S. (1997). Post- traumatic stress disorder and functioning and quality of life outcomes in female Vietnam veterans. *Military Medicine, 162*, 661–665.

19

Disability Following Posttraumatic Stress Disorder

Robert J. Sbordone

INTRODUCTION

This chapter will examine acute, chronic and complex Posttraumatic Stress Disorder, particularly its neuroendocrinological, neurophysiological and neuropsychological effects; the various risk factors for the development of Posttraumatic Stress Disorder, and its relationship to traumatic injury and comorbid psychiatric disorders. It will also examine the effect of PTSD on psychiatric and vocational disability, which may last a lifetime in some individuals.

POSTTRAUMATIC STRESS DISORDER

Posttraumatic Stress Disorder (PTSD) refers to the development of a set of specific symptoms following exposure to traumatic and physical events such as combat, fire, flood, molestation, natural disasters, rape or witnessing someone badly injured or killed, etc. According to the 4th edition of the *Diagnostic and Statistical Manual of Mental Disorders* (DSM-IV), (American Psychiatric Association 1994), an individual who develops PTSD must be confronted with an event or events that involve actual or threatened death or serious injury or threat to the physical integrity of self or others which produces intense feelings of fear, helplessness or terror. The diagnostic criteria for PTSD requires that the traumatic event be persistently re-experienced by either recurrent or intrusive recollections, distressing dreams, flashbacks, or by stimuli which symbolize or resembles some aspect of the traumatic event; conscious efforts to avoid specific thoughts, feelings, people, places or activities which could trigger recollections of the event; symptoms of emotional arousal (e.g., hypervigilance) and heightened reactivity (e.g., exaggerated startle responses).

DOI: 10.1007/978-0-387-28919-9_19, © 2009 Springer Science+Business Media, LLC

ACUTE STRESS DISORDER

The diagnosis of Acute Stress Disorder (ASD) was introduced in the *Diagnostic and Statistical Manual of Mental Disorders* (DSM-IV) by the American Psychiatric Association in 1994 and was conceptualized as an acute form of PTSD, which occurs within one month following exposure to a traumatic event. While ASD has been regarded as a predictor of a Posttraumatic Stress Disorder (Bryant and Harvey, 1997), Harvey and Bryant (1998) found that 40% of the individuals who met the diagnostic criteria for ASD did not develop chronic PTSD. The major difference between PTSD and ASD is that the latter requires the presence of significant dissociative symptoms where the patient reports a subjective sense of numbing, emotional detachment, or absence of emotional responsiveness; a reduction in awareness of his or her surroundings, derealization; depersonalization, or dissociative amnesia. The DSM-IV diagnostic criteria for ASD also place more stringent requirements on intrusive, avoidance and arousal symptoms than PTSD. While numerous structured interviews and self-report inventories currently exist to assess PTSD, only a few inventories have been developed to assess ASD (Briere, 2001, Bryant et al., 1998; Bryant & Harvey, 2000).

Role of Dissociation

One explanation of ASD argues that since dissociation is a primary coping mechanism for managing traumatic experiences, individuals who are exposed to traumatic events are likely to minimize the adverse emotional consequences of the trauma by restricting their awareness of the experience (van der Kolk & van der Hart, 1989). Foa and Hearst-Ikeda (1996), however, have argued that following a traumatic event, fear structures develop which contain the mental representations of the traumatic experience which produce an attentional bias to threat related material. These investigators have proposed that the initial dissociative responses following exposure to a traumatic event may impede deactivation of fear structures which results in impaired emotional functioning that may lead to chronic PTSD. Their theoretical explanation is corroborated by research studies which demonstrate that traumatic individuals frequently display disorganized and fragmented memories (Foa, Molnar, & Casman, 1995) and often develop overgeneral memories of the traumatic event (McNally, Lasko, Macklin and Pitman, 1995). Other investigators (e.g., Horowitz, 1986) have argued that dissociative responses are common and serve as adaptive short-term reactions to a traumatic event which may subsequently produce a resolution of the traumatic experience. Conversely, other research has shown that dissociative reactions at the time of traumatic event are highly predictive of chronic PTSD (McFarlane, 1986; Shalev, Orr, & Pitman, 1993; Shalev, Pei, Caneti & Schreiber, 1996; Solomon, & Mikulincer, 1992).

Bryant & Harvey (1997) have stressed that the role of dissociation in ASD is complicated by the ambiguity concerning when the dissociative response occurs. They point out that according to the DSM-IV criteria, the dissociative symptoms may occur either, during or after experiencing the traumatic event. This time frame, however, contrasts markedly to the requirement that the intrusive avoidance and arousal symptoms need to be experienced as ongoing problems. This also contrasts with the DSM-IV criteria that the symptoms of ASD persist for a minimum of two days following the traumatic experience.

COMPLEX PTSD

Although the DSM-IV presents criteria to allow clinicians to differentiate between an acute stress disorder and chronic Posttraumatic Stress Ddisorder (i.e., the duration of the patient's symptoms in the former is more than one month but less than three months, while the duration of symptoms of the latter is greater than three months), it fails to mention complex PTSD which is a broader and more severe form of Posttraumatic Stress Disorder that stems from early and repetitive psychological trauma (Herman, 1992; Smythe, 1999). Individuals with complex PTSD are likely to have had a history of sexual or physical abuse throughout their childhood or exposure to chronic trauma as adults (e.g., repeated physical and/or sexual abuse, frequent torture, or exposure to repeated combat trauma).

A number of investigators (e.g., Herman, 1993; Ide & Paez, 2000) have stressed that that the definition of PTSD contained in the DSM-IV implicitly refers to the development of symptoms following exposure to a single or discreet stressor rather than frequent or numerous exposure to stressors throughout one's life. Smyth (2000) has stressed the prognosis for complex PTSD is substantially worse than for simple PTSD. For example, he points out that individuals with complex PTSD exhibit symptoms such as severe affect regulation dysfunction approaching what is typically seen in individuals with bipolar and/or borderline personality disorders, and frequently exhibit somatic difficulties and dissociative symptoms. Thus, the symptom picture of individuals with complex PTSD, as a result of prolonged victimization, is far more complex than the simple PTSD patient (Ide & Paez, 2000).

Complex PTSD has also been defined as a syndrome with varied and divergent symptoms such as alteration in attention and consciousness which includes symptoms such as amnesia, transient dissociative episodes and depersonalization. These dissociative symptoms, however, may cause health professionals to misdiagnose many of these individuals with a closed head injury if they become involved in motor vehicle accidents. For example, when these individuals are seen by a physician in the emergency room or later by a neurologist, they frequently claim that they are unable to recall the accident or some of the events surrounding the accident even though they did not strike their head, lose consciousness, or display symptoms such as confusion or disorientation at the time of the accident. Unfortunately, as a result of their complex Posttraumatic Stress Disorder, their symptoms can be shaped over time by others, particularly those who are in a position of authority and control (e.g., attorneys, physicians, etc.) (Smyth, 1999).

CASE EXAMPLE

A 49-year-old female slipped and fell in the parking lot of a hardware store that was covered with snow and ice and landed on her buttocks. She immediately got up and finished loading her supplies into a car and drove approximately 12 miles home. The next day, she went to see her family physician and complained of stiffness and soreness in her lower back. She remained out of work for a week and returned to work without incident. Several months later, she became very depressed as a result of several tragic personal losses, which triggered a delayed Posttraumatic Stress Disorder as a result of a repeated childhood history of sexual molestation, physical abuse, and torture, which she had managed to repress. She consulted with an attorney, who suggested to her that she may have sustained a brain injury during her slip and fall accident. The attorney then referred her to a neurologist. When she saw the neurologist, she complained of symptoms that were similar to the information she had received from her attorney about closed head injuries. For example, she informed the neurologist that she had no recollection of the accident, and complained of severe problems with her recent memory, attention, and problem solving skills, even though she did not report any alteration of consciousness or head trauma when she was examined the day following her accident by her family physician. She was then referred for neuropsychological testing and was found to have moderate to severe neuropsychological impairments (most likely as a result of her extremely high levels of internal anxiety and/or the neurotoxic effects of her complex PTSD).

Based on her test scores, the neuropsychologist diagnosed a severe closed head injury. She was then encouraged by her attorney to quit her job since it would result in a larger financial award. Unfortunately, quitting her job created serious financial difficulties which resulted in frequent arguments with her husband, conflicts with her children, and feelings of worthlessness as a result of her perceived inability to contribute to her family's welfare. These problems exacerbated her delayed Posttraumatic Stress Disorder and resulted in her being placed in a psychiatric unit for several weeks. All of her symptoms and problems were attributed by her "treating doctors" to the "brain injury" she had sustained as a result of her slip and fall accident.

Individuals with complex PTSD symptoms can exhibit a wide spectrum of psychological impairment. While some of these individuals may exhibit high levels of interpersonal, social and vocational functioning, many are unable to function in society. Not uncommonly, the explanation given for their disability is "brain damage," rather than their complex Posttraumatic Stress Disorder, particularly if the healthcare professionals are unaware of the patient's history of repeated psychological trauma. In other cases, the symptoms of such individuals may be attributed to a borderline personality disorder (Briere, 1997; Herman, 1993; and Ide & Paez, 2000).

Historical Background

Psychological distress following exposure to a traumatic event has been described in many early literary works. For example, Samuel Pepy described PTSD symptoms after witnessing the great London fire during the 17th century (Boudewns, 1996). Descriptions of PTSD were also made by Abercrombie in 1928 and Brodie in 1837 (Millen, 1996). When PTSD symptoms were observed by military physicians during the first and second world wars, they were often given diagnoses such as "shell shock", "war neurosis", and "combat exhaustion". When such symptoms were reported by individuals who had filed personally injury lawsuits or workers compensation claims after they had been involved in a motor vehicle or railway accidents, their symptoms were often given pejorative labels such as "posttraumatic neurosis", "accident neurosis", or "railway spine" particularly when there was no evidence of physical injury (Sparr, 1995).

Although Grinker & Spiegel (1945) and Kardiner (1941) had described the short and long term psychological sequelae of PTSD in combat veterans, PTSD did not start gaining acceptance until a number of studies appeared in prominent medical and psychiatric journals describing the psychiatric symptoms of soldiers who had fought in Vietnam (Fox, 1972; Goldsmith & Cretekos, 1969). Other studies also appeared which described the psychological and emotional reaction of survivors to extreme trauma such as fires, explosions, floods, military combat, concentration camps and rape (eg., Horowitz, 1976). The empirical information and conceptual refinements generated by this research significantly advanced our understanding of posttraumatic stress responses and led to the inclusion of the diagnostic criteria for PTSD in the DSM-III-R; in 1980 which defined PTSD as a syndrome in response to a "stressor that would evoke significant symptoms of distress in almost everyone." (APA 1980, p. 238). The DSM-III criteria required that the individual who developed PTSD had to have been exposed to a traumatic event. The DSM-IV criteria (APA, 1994), however, significantly broadened the definition of a traumatic stressor to include stressors which were not directly experienced by the victim (e.g., being horrified by what had happened to others) (McNally, 2003). As a consequence, the DMS-IV has been criticized for its failure to discriminate between the symptoms of PTSD and normal distress reactions (e.g., learning about the 911 disaster). (Wakefield & Spitzer, 2002).

EPIDEMIOLOGY

Incidence of PTSD

Helzer, Robins & McEvoy (1987) investigated the incidence of PTSD in 2,493 Vietnam combat veterans. They found that the incidence of PTSD was 6.3% for veterans who were not wounded and 20% for veterans who were wounded in combat. Later, in a carefully designed study, Kulka et al., (1991) found that the incidence of PTSD was 15.2% in male and 8.5% in female Vietnam veterans, while the lifetime prevalence of PTSD in these groups was 30.9% and 26.9%, respectively with even higher ratios reported for veterans who had sustained physical injuries or who had served in high stress war zones. These investigators, however, pointed out that one of the limitations of this type of research is that many Vietnam veterans with PTSD are homeless or have dropped out of society. Thus, the prevalence rates in Vietnam veterans may be considerably higher since these veterans were most likely not included in these studies. For example, 70% of World War II combat veterans serving in the Pacific who had been captured and tortured by the Japanese were found to have PTSD in comparison to 18% of veterans who had never been captured and tortured (Sutker et al., 1993).

Kessler, Sonnega & Bromet (1995) estimated 7.9% of the general population (5% men and 10.4% women) has a lifetime history of PTSD. These findings are similar to previous estimates (6% males and 11.3% women) that were reported earlier by Breslau et al., (1991). The traumatic stressors most commonly associated with PTSD in women were rape and sexual molestation and were reported by 49% of the women with PTSD.

Is Exposure to a Traumatic Event Sufficient to Produce PTSD?

Although epidemiological studies have shown that while nearly seven out of ten people are exposed to at least one traumatic event during their lifetime (e.g., Norris, 1992), the lifetime prevalence of PTSD is only one out of twelve. This suggests that multiple risk factors determine whether a person develops PTSD after being exposed to a traumatic event, or severe and prolonged trauma. Thus, PTSD can best be considered a possible but not inevitable outcome to a traumatic event (Yehuda, McFarlane, & Shalev, 1998).

Risk Factors

One of the most salient predictors of chronic PTSD, is the nature of the traumatic stressor. Stressors such as torture or prolonged victimization are typically associated with the highest estimates of PTSD. For example, the prevalence of chronic PTSD among torture survivors such as prisoners of war and concentration camp survivors has been reported to be approximately 50% (Kluznick et al., 1986; Yehuda et al., 1995); while the prevalence rate of chronic PTSD of survivors of natural disasters was reported to be 4% (Shore et al., 1989).

McFarlane (2000) has argued that while the symptoms of PTSD typically resolve in the majority of individuals, some individuals are more likely to develop chronic and unremitting PTSD, which is often disabling. For example, a number of research studies (e.g., Paris, 2000) have shown that some individuals may be predisposed to chronic and disabling PTSD by personality traits that shape their cognitive processing of stressful events, prior life experiences, and their social support system. For example, Brewin, Andrews & Valentine (2000) performed meta-analyses on 14 separate risk factors for PTSD and the moderating effects of various sample and study characteristics including civilian/military status. They found that risk factors such as gender, age of trauma and race predicted PTSD in some populations, but not others. Other factors such as education, previous trauma and general childhood adversity predicted PTSD more consistently, but to a varying extent according to the population studied and the methods utilized. Although, factors such as psychiatric history and reported childhood abuse and family psychiatric history had more uniform predictive effects, factors operating during or after the trauma such as trauma severity, lack of social support, and additional life stress had somewhat stronger effects than pretraumatic factors.

Breslau, Davis & Andreski (1995) found that high scores in neuroticism (eg., a tendency to react with strong emotion to adverse events), one of the personality dimensions originally described by Eysenck (1989,1990), influenced the intensity of an individual's response to psychological stressors. Other studies have shown that neuroticism is often accompanied by variations in both psychophysiological and neurocognitive functions that have been associated with individuals who are at higher risk for PTSD (Orr & Pitman, 1999; Shalev, 1999). While impulsivity is not necessarily a risk factor for PTSD, the combination of impulsivity and neuroticism increased the risk for developing PTSD following trauma exposure (Paris, 2000).

Other research (e.g., Rahe, 1995) has shown that the risk for developing any type of psychological symptom following traumatic exposure does not revolve around single events but tends to increase with the cumulative number of adverse events or stressors the individual experiences throughout his or her lifetime. For example, the developmental psychopathology literature has shown that single adverse events rarely cause psychiatric disorders in children, whereas multiple events tend to place children at increased risk in an exponential manner (e.g., Rutter, 1989).

A number of investigators who have studied PTSD have noted that both innate and environmental factors play a major role in determining the resilience of an individual to develop PTSD. The most important risk factors appear to be a combination of genetic and environmental influences such as a previous psychiatric history, a family history of psychiatric illness, and a personality profile associated with an increased risk for psychopathology (eg., Breslau, et al., 1991; Breslau, et al., 1998).

Social factors may explain the discrepancy between exposure to adverse life events and PTSD. For example, studies have shown that the impact of traumatic events can be minimized by social support and amplified by the absence of such support (e.g., Schlenger, et al., 1992; Neria, Solomon & Bekel, 1998). These studies demonstrate that the social support system can be a crucial protective factor against the development of PTSD. Conversely, a weak social support system may actually predispose individuals to develop chronic PTSD.

Bromet, Sonnega and Kessler (1998) examined the association of childhood risk factors with exposure to trauma and PTSD in 5,877 respondents between the ages of 15 and 54. They examined risk factors such as pre-exposure affective, anxiety and substance use disorders; parental, mental and substance abuse disorders; parental aggression toward the respondent or toward the other parent; and a non-confiding relationship with mother during childhood. They found that a preexisting history of affective disorder predicted PTSD in women, while a history of anxiety disorder and parental mental disorder predicted PTSD in men.

Sedat & Stein (2000) examined men and women who presented with physical trauma after interpersonal violence. They found that women were more likely than men to have been previously assaulted or to have sustained injury by a relative or someone known to them. Other research has shown that women with PTSD from assaultive violence have more severe PTSD symptoms than men with assaultive violence, and that their symptoms persisted longer (eg., Breslau et al., 1999).

Sexual abuse during childhood has been found to significantly increase the risk of PTSD (Koss & Harvey, 1991). Women who were traumatized as children and were retraumatized as adults are more likely to have dissociative symptoms and attempt suicide than women who were only sexually assaulted as adults and women who had never been assaulted (Cloitre et al., 1997). Roberts et al., (1998) found that women who had been abused as a child and as an adult were at significantly greater risk for developing alcoholism and drug dependence than women who had been abused as adults only. Other studies have shown that women who were exposed to recurrent or chronic sexual and physical abuse were at greater risk of developing physical, psychiatric and PTSD symptoms (e.g., Yellowless & Kaushik, 1994).

Blanchard et al., (1996) assessed 158 motor vehicle victims who sought medical attention following a motor vehicle accident. They found that 62 (39%) of these individuals met the diagnostic criteria for PTSD as set forth in the DSM-III-R. Risk factors such as degree of injury, prior mood disorder (which included major depression, bipolar disorder and dysthymia), fear of death, and whether or not litigation had been initiated accounted for 70% of those diagnosed with PTSD.

Vietnam combat veterans who developed PTSD were found to have higher levels of pre-existing positive soft neurological signs than combat veterans who did not develop PTSD (Gurvits et al., 1996). For example, they were more likely to have had pre-existing histories of developmental delay, attention-deficit disorder, hyperactivity, learning problems, enuresis or head trauma.

Chronicity of PTSD Symptoms

Although the DSM-IV claims that approximately 50% of PTSD cases resolve within three months, Davidson et al., (1991) found that 47.9% of the adults with PTSD were still experiencing symptoms more than one year post-trauma. Similarly, Helzer et al., (1987) found that a third of the adult patients who had developed PTSD, were reporting symptoms three years following the traumatic event. Bryant et al., (2000) found that factors such as an avoidant coping style following a traumatic event, low intelligence, and unemployment at the time of the trauma were reliable predictors of the chronicity of PTSD.

Comorbidity of PTSD with Other Psychiatric Disorders

Comorbidity refers to the effects of one disorder on the presentation, course, biological parameters, and treatment outcome of another disorder (Bogenschutz & Nurnberg, 2000). PTSD has been shown to have a high rate of comorbidity with psychiatric, substance abuse, and somatization disorders. For example, Kessler et al., (1995) found that 88% of males and 75% of females with PTSD had at least one other psychiatric disorder. They found that patients with PTSD were almost eight times as likely to have three or more psychiatric disorders than individuals without PTSD. They also found that the incidence of somatization disorders in individuals with PTSD was 90 times more frequent than in individuals without PTSD.

Brady et al., (2000) found that the comorbidity of PTSD with substance abuse disorders was complex since a substance abuse disorder often develops as an attempt to self-medicate the painful symptoms of PTSD. However, they noted that comorbidity in PTSD was the rule rather than the exception. They stressed that PTSD with or without major depression appeared to be an important risk factor for suicidality. They also reported a study by Wunderlich et al., (1997) which found that 91% of individuals who had attempted suicide had at least one psychiatric diagnosis and that the highest risk for suicide attempts was among those individuals with PTSD. Ferrada-Noli et al., (1998) found that the presence of suicidal behavior was more frequent in individuals with the primary diagnosis of PTSD compared to all other diagnoses. They also found that PTSD patients were comorbidly depressed and reported more suicidal ideation than nondepressed patients with PTSD.

Research has demonstrated that while other psychiatric disorders may not be comorbid with PTSD, they are more frequently reported in individuals with PTSD. For example, Deering et al., (1996) found that panic disorders were more common in individuals with PTSD. Orsillo et al., (1996) found that the majority of Vietnam veterans who met the criteria for PTSD also met the criteria for social phobia when compared to a group of veterans without PTSD. Other research (Wunderlich, 1990) found that a history of childhood sexual abuse placed children at risk for the development of bulimia nervosa, but not anorexia nervosa. These investigators also found that childhood sexual abuse predicted significantly greater comorbidity of other psychiatric disorders including major depression, anxiety disorder, substance abuse or dependence, and personality disorders.

Individuals with PTSD have been found to have high rates of psychogenic or dissociative amnesia (Scheflin & Brown, 1996). Other studies (e.g., Brewerton et al., 1999) found that psychogenic amnesia was reported in 41% of women with PTSD in comparison to only 7% of women without PTSD. They also found that women with psychogenic amnesia had significantly higher rates of rape, childhood rape, molestation, aggravated assault, major depression, and an eating disorder than those without psychogenic amnesia. Harvey and Bryant (1998) found that peritraumatic dissociation or the presence of dissociative symptoms at the time of the traumatic event is a robust prognostic predictor of subsequent PTSD development and its severity.

Brady et al., (2000) has stressed that the relationship between PTSD and other comorbid psychiatric disorders is complex since PTSD may play a causal role in development in comorbid disorders, while the existence of prior psychiatric disorders appears to increase the vulnerability of individuals to develop PTSD following exposure to a traumatic event.

BIOLOGICAL CORRELATES OF PTSD

While many healthcare professionals have naively assumed that Posttraumatic Stress Disorder is a "psychological" or "mental" condition, their views are at variance with extensive body of research which demonstrates that PTSD is a physiological, endocrinological, and neurologically mediated disorder.

Physiological/Endocrinological Studies

Research has shown that profound and persistent alterations in physiological reactivity and stress hormone (cortisol) secretion occurs in patients with PTSD. For example, PTSD patients experience heightened physiological arousal in response to stimuli which are related to the traumatic event, characterized by significant increases in heart rate, skin conductance and blood pressure (Blanchard, Kolb and Gerardi, 1986; Malloy, Fairbanks and Kean, 1983; Pitman, Orr and Forgue, 1987; and van der Kolk, 1994). Drugs such as lactate (Riney, Aleem and Ortiz, 1987) or Yohimbine (Southwick, Krystal and Morgan, 1993) have been found to trigger panic attacks and flashbacks in PTSD patients by increasing their autonomic arousal levels. Ornitz and Pynoos (1989) found that PTSD patients have abnormalities in their habituation to the acoustic startle response which suggests that these patients have difficulty evaluating the significance of sensory stimuli while modulating their levels of physiological arousal. These studies suggest that chronic physiological arousal, combined with an inability to regulate their autonomic reaction to internal or external stimuli, can severely hinder patients with PTSD from effectively utilizing their emotions as warning signals and attend to incoming information in order to take necessary adaptive actions. Thus, patients with PTSD tend to immediately begin responding with fight or flight reactions without initially trying to cognitively determine the significance of the stimuli being received (van der Kolk, 1997).

PTSD patients have been found to have chronically high levels of sympathetic nervous system activity (Kosten, Mason and Giller, 1987) and increased levels of lymphocyte glucocorticoid receptors (McEwen & Sapolsky, 1995; Sapolsky, 2000). Yehuda, Southwick, & Mason (1990) and Yehuda & Southwick (1991) have proposed that the glucocorticoid system shuts down the body's biological reactions that are activated by acute stress through the release of cortisol which serves as an anti-stress hormone. Thus, low levels of glucocorticoids or cortisol would be expected to result in the development of high levels of catecholamine activity that is likely to produce fight or flight reactions, since the glucocorticoids and catecholamines modulate each other's effects.

Low levels of cortisol have been associated with increased vulnerability to PTSD. For example, McFarlane (1996) found that low cortisol levels in MVA victims, when they were seen in the emergency room, were highly correlated with the development of PTSD symptoms three months later. Urinary cortisol levels were also found to be lower in inpatient and outpatient combat veterans (Yehuda, Southwick and Mason, 1990) and in holocaust survivors (Yehuda, Kahana and Binder-Byrnes, 1995) with PTSD than comparison groups without PTSD.

Neurological/Brain Imaging Studies

Bremner et al., (1995) utilized magnetic resonance imaging (MRI) to determine the hippocampal volume of Vietnam combat veterans with PTSD. They found that combat veterans with PTSD had statistically smaller right hippocampal volume than combat veterans without PTSD who were matched for age, sex, race, years of education, socioeconomic status, body size, and years of alcohol use. Since the hippocampus mediates declarative memory, a decrease in hippocampal volume would be expected to produce deficits in short-term memory. In a subsequent study (Bremmer, 1999) found that hippocampal volume in combat veterans was correlated with deficits in verbal memory on neuropsychological testing. He stressed that PTSD patients demonstrate a variety of memory problems, including deficits in declarative memory (i.e. remembering facts or lists), fragmentation of autobiographic and trauma-related memories, and non-declarative memory (i.e. types of memory that cannot be willfully brought up into the conscious mind including motor memory such as how to ride a bicycle). He also stressed that since the hippocampus has a rich concentration of receptors for glucocorticoids and modulates glucocorticoid release through inhibitory effects on the hypothalamic-pituitary-adrenal axis, it plays a crucial role in the integration of cognitive, neurohormonal, and neurochemical responses to stress. He also points out that studies with normal human participants have shown that glucocorticoids have direct effects on memory functioning. For example, therapeutic doses of glucocorticoids (dexamethasone or cortisol) have been found to produce impairments in verbal declarative memory functioning in healthy humans. He points out that high stress-induced cortisol levels can lead to an exacerbation of memory deficits while an improvement in memory function occurs when stress-induced cortisol levels are reduced. Similarly, adults with PTSD who had histories of childhood physical or sexual abuse were found to have smaller (12%) left hippocampi than non-abused controls (Bremner et al., 1997). Gilbertson et al., (cited in McNally, 2003), has suggested that hippocampal atrophy may reflect preexisting PTSD risk factors.

Sapolsky and his associates (1995) have shown that the chronically high levels of corticoid activity as a resulted of prolonged stress can either produce reversible dendritic alterations in a neuronal loss, particularly in the hippocampus. They reported that animal studies have shown that exposure to glucocorticoids or to stress over the course of 21 days led to atrophy of dendritic branches in the pyramidal neurons in the CA region of the rat hippocampus which was accompanied by impairment of the initial learning of a spatial memory task on an eight arm radial maze. These investigators stressed that certain levels of glucocorticoids can cause reversible changes in the morphology of hippocampal neurons, and that longer periods of exposure to glucocorticoids produces irreversible hippocampal dysfunction resembling a pattern seen in aging animals at an accelerated rate. They also found that the older the animal, the more vulnerable it is to damage.

Recent studies utilizing magnetic resonance imaging to investigate myelination in vivo has shown that myelination in the frontal and temporal lobes continues into the mid to late 40's (Bartzokis et al., 2001) to compensate for a reduction in gray matter volume in these areas (Bartzokis et al., 2003). The process of myelination is believed to be crucial for normal adult brain function since it increases neuronal transmission speed and the integration of information across brain regions (e.g., Bartzokis, 2002). He has suggested that exposure to stress could interfere with this process and increase the likelihood of excretory amino acid toxicity of the oligodendrocytes which play a crucial role in the myelination process; resulting in a decrease of the speed of information processing and disruptions in the brain's ability to process information.

Research studies have shown that the limbic region of the brain plays a critical role in learning, memory and emotional regulation. Hamner, Lorberbaum and George (1999) have explored the impact of stress on the limbic system. Their findings suggested that the anterior cingulate gyrus may serve as a critical gating function in modulating condition/fear responses and is a key component to neural circuits involved in the pathophysiology of PTSD. For example, they have proposed that the amygdala-locus coeruleus-anterior cingulate circuit may play an important role in chronic noradrenergic activation which has been documented in PTSD patients. According to their model, efferent noradrenergic projections in the locus coeruleus may dampen anterior cingulate function, which in turn would allow the myriad of externally or internally driven stimuli to produce the exaggerated emotional and behavioral responses characteristic of PTSD.

Freedman et al., (1998) using proton magnetic resonance spectroscopy (a noninvasive technique for the in vivo measurement of the concentration of various compounds in the human brain to identify neuronal loss or damage) studied 21 veterans with PTSD and eight age-matched control veterans. They found that the N-acetyl-L-aspartic acid/creatine ratio was significantly lower for PTSD patients in the right medial temporal lobe in comparison to the left in patients with PTSD and those in the control group. Their findings suggest that the neuronal density of right-sided medial temporal structures in patients with combat related PTSD may have decreased.

Fernandez et al., (2001) studied positron emission tomographic measurements of regional cerebral blood flow in a male patient with war and torture related PTSD. They exposed this patient to war-related sounds which resulted in decreased cerebral blood flow in the insula, and the prefrontal and inferior frontal lobes, while increased blood flow was found in the cerebellum, precuneus and supplementary motor cortex. They noted that the pre-frontal and cingulate cerebral blood flow levels correlated with the patient's heart rate. Mirzaei et al., (2001) examined cerebral regional blood flow using single positron emission computer tomography. They found that cerebral blood flow was markedly more heterogeneous in patients suffering from PTSD than healthy controls. They concluded that severe psychological trauma induced by torture can cause neurobiological alterations which may contribute even after years following the original trauma to a number of complaints commonly expressed by patients suffering from PTSD.

Positron emission tomography (PET) was used to measure normalized regional cerebral blood flow in 16 women with histories of childhood sexual abuse: eight with current PTSD symptoms and eight without current PTSD symptoms (Shin et al., 1999). In separate script-driven imagery conditions, particpants recalled and imagined traumatic and neutral autobiographical events. Physiological responses and subjective ratings of their emotional state were measured for each condition. They found that in the traumatic condition vs. the neutral control conditions, both groups exhibited increased regional blood flow in the orbitofrontal cortex and anterior temporal poles, however, these increases were greater in the PTSD group than in the comparison group. The comparison group, on the other hand, exhibited regional blood flow increases in the insular cortex and anterior cingulate gyrus in comparison to the PTSD group. Regional cerebral blood flow decreases in the bilateral anterior frontal regions were greater in the PTSD group than in the comparison group. Only the PTSD group exhibited regional blood flow decreases in the left inferior frontal gyrus. These investigators concluded that the recollection and imagery of traumatic events vs. neutral events was accompanied by regional cerebral blood flow increases in the anterior paralimbic regions of the brain in trauma-exposed individuals with and without PTSD. However, the PTSD group had greater increases in the orbitofrontal cortex and the anterior temporal pole, while the comparison group had greater increases in the anterior cingulate gyrus.

Zubieta et al., (1999) examined the regional blood flow responses to a combat stress-related auditory stimulus in Vietnam veterans diagnosed with PTSD and age-matched combat exposed individuals without PTSD in a control group of twelve healthy people. The participants were studied twice while listening to combat sounds or white noise. They found significant increases in the blood flow to the medial prefrontal cortex in the PTSD patients, but not in the controls which correlated with physiological measures of the stress response. Their data support the involvement of the medial prefrontal cortex in the pathophysiology of PTSD which, they argue, may mediate some of the symptoms of PTSD.

PTSD patients have also been found to have significantly lower P300 amplitudes in comparison to a matched control group without PTSD (Charles et al., 1995). This finding suggests that patients with PTSD have defective information processing capabilities and are impaired with respect to their ability to discriminate between relevant and irrelevant information.

Neuropsychological Investigations of PTSD Patients

Detailed studies of other patient populations have shown that the frontal lobes play a crucial role in a patient's ability to sustain attention, concentration, executive functions, judgment, and encode and retrieve information from memory (Keane and Wolfe, 1990; Oscar-Berman and Bardenhagen, 1998). The frontal lobes also play a major role in the regulation of impulses, affect, mood stability and disinhibition (Fuster, 1997; Stuss and Benson, 1986). Since these functions are often problematic for patients with PTSD, Wolfe (1994) suggested that patients with PTSD may have abnormalities in their frontal brain systems. To test this hypothesis, Konen et al., (2001) administered neuropsychological tests and measures, that had been shown by prior research (e.g., Oscar-Berman and Bardenhagen, 1998) to be sensitive to frontal lobe dysfunction as well as standard neuropsychological tests, to identify abnormalities in pre-frontal brain systems in PTSD patients. They found that while PTSD subjects were unimpaired on standard neuropsychological tests and measures, they exhibited deficits on tests of frontal lobe functioning and on measures which were sensitive to different aspects of pre-frontal damage. Their findings demonstrate that PTSD patients have overlapping dysfunction in both the dorsolateral and ventral pre-frontal brain systems which implicated frontal system involvement. They also noted that their findings would explain the memory difficulties that PTSD patients exhibit that are mediated by the pre-frontal cortex such as deficits in working memory (eg., the ability to hold information in a temporary short-term store).

Sachinvala et al., (2000) examined the range and degree of compromised cognitive and functional capacities and the mood state of Vietnam veterans with PTSD in comparison to control subjects for age, sex and level of education. They found that PTSD subjects performed significantly less well on the cognitive evaluation protocol (CEP), a touch screen computer assessment instrument that was self-administered by the subjects twice, one month apart, for the cognitive domains of attention, memory and functional capability.

In a review of the efficacy of neuropsychological tests to assess memory in PTSD patients, Wolfe and Schlesinger (1997) indicated that there was a growing body of evidence which suggests that cognitive alterations occur in PTSD patients. Specifically, they noted that PTSD patients may demonstrate enhanced learning and retention of some trauma stimuli as well as decreased memory functioning on stimuli or information which is non-trauma related. They concluded that the research literature suggests that the memory functioning of PTSD patients range from intact to mildly impaired on general tests of visual or verbal memory. However, at the same time, memory tests involving trauma-specific stimuli point to alterations in cognitive information processing, specifically an attentional bias manifested by changes in speed, accuracy and depth of processing.

CONTROVERSIAL ISSUES

Can PTSD Develop if the Patient Is Amnestic for the Traumatic Event?

Within the past decade, there has been considerable controversy as to whether an individual who has suffered an accident related brain injury can develop PTSD. One school of thought (e.g., Sbordone and Liter, 1995) has argued that if the brain injury results in a loss of consciousness, the individual is unable to develop vivid memories of the traumatic event necessary to generate intrusive recollections of the trauma which are essential in the development of PTSD. This argument receives support from several investigators. For example, Mayou, Bryant, and Duthio (1993) reported that none of the 51 patients who had been sustained mild traumatic brain injury as a result of a motor vehicle accident and reported loss of consciousness for more than five minutes, developed PTSD. Similarly, Warden et al., (1997) found that none of the 47 patients they examined who sustained a closed head injury developed PTSD if they were unable to recall the traumatic event. Although Malhi and Bartlett (1998) reported that only five individuals out of a total of 196 adults they examined who sustained closed head injuries as defined by either a Glasgow Coma Scale Score of 14 or less; documented loss of consciousness; or posttraumatic amnesia, developed

PTSD; all five of these individuals had either no or minimal loss of consciousness and were able to clearly recall the traumatic event. Middelboe et al., (1992) reported that only one out of a total of 51 patients who had been admitted to the hospital after a "minor head injury" was diagnosed with PTSD. Max et al., (1998) examined 50 children ranging in age from 6 to 14 utilizing psychiatric assessments that were repeated 3, 6, 12 and 24 months following the TBI. They found that only two (4%) of the subjects were found to have PTSD on at least one of the follow up assessments. These investigators, however, did not preclude children with preexisting PTSD in their study even though it is generally well known that "minor head injuries" may reactivate symptoms related to previous traumatic experiences. Thus, the diagnosis of PTSD that was given to these children may have reflected reactivation of preexisting childhood trauma (Berthier et al., 1998).

Sbordone and Liter (1995) examined 70 patients who had been previously diagnosed with either mild traumatic brain injury (MTBI) or PTSD. Each patient was interviewed by a board certified neuropsychologist and was asked to provide a detailed recollection of the events which preceded, occurred during, or followed the traumatic event to determine the extent of their recall, particularly whether they had amnesia for the traumatic event. They found that while all 42 PTSD patients were able to provide a detailed and emotionally charged recollection of these events, none of the 28 MTBI patients were able to recall the event or were observed to become emotionally upset when they were asked to discuss it. Virtually, none of the MTBI patients in this study reported PTSD symptoms such as nightmares, flashbacks, intrusive recollections, hypervigilance, phobic or startle reactions, or became emotionally upset whenever they were exposed to stimuli associated with the traumatic event. Both MTBI and PTSD patients, however, complained of similar cognitive and behavioral problems such as memory, word finding, problem solving difficulties, distractibility, photophobia, fatigue, diminished libido, and interpersonal difficulties.

These investigators stressed that if the traumatic event occurred prior to the onset of retrograde amnesia (e.g., becoming terrified while riding as a passenger in an automobile that was being driven in a reckless manner for several minutes prior to colliding with another vehicle) or after the cessation of anterograde amnesia (e.g., witnessing the death of a family member who sustained massive injuries several minutes after regaining consciousness following a motor vehicle accident), an MTBI patient could develop PTSD in response to these events rather than to their brain injury.

Since individuals with acute stress disorders frequently develop dissociative amnesia for some or all of the events surrounding a traumatic event, they are often diagnosed with a cerebral concussion rather than PTSD since they are unable to provide a detailed recollection of the traumatic event (e.g., motor vehicle accident). Similarly, Sbordone and Liter (1995) found that many patients who develop PTSD initially claimed that they had no recollection of the traumatic event, showed evidence of physiological arousal, and anxiety when they were asked to provide a chronological history of events leading up to the accident. For example, when these individuals were asked during the interview "what was going on in your head during the accident itself?" they typically replied, "I thought I was going to die."

Since the clinical interviews of these patients lasted between two and three hours, it is doubtful that these individuals would have had sufficient time to adequately recall the events leading up to the traumatic event if they were interviewed in a busy emergency room by a physician or later by a neurologist. These investigators have argued the initial claim of amnesia in the PTSD group most likely represented their conscious attempt to avoid discussing the emotionally charged traumatic event. In other words, their initial claim of having no memory of the traumatic event typically meant "I don't want to recall it."

The opposing viewpoint argues that PTSD can be developed following a closed head injury even if the trauma itself cannot be recalled (e.g., McMillan, 1991; 1996). For example, Bryant and Harvey (1998) studied the occurrence of acute stress disorder following mild traumatic brain injury to determine its utility in predicting PTSD. Utilizing a questionnaire (e.g., Acute Stress Disorder Inventory) and a structured clinical interview based on DSM IV criteria, they found that Acute Stress Disorder was diagnosed in 14% of adult patients who had sustained mild traumatic brain injury following a motor vehicle accident. In a followup study (Bryant and Harvey, 1999), 24% of these patients satisfied the criteria for PTSD. They also reported that 82% who had been initially diagnosed with an acute stress disorder went on to develop chronic PTSD. These investigators utilized the diagnostic criteria for mild traumatic brain injury which was defined as posttraumatic amnesia of less than 24 hours. They reported that the average duration of estimated posttraumatic amnesia in their subjects (222 patients between the ages of 16 and 65 years of age) was 9.4 hours with a range of five minutes to 24 hours. However, they appeared to have relied on the diagnosis of mild traumatic brain injury that had been initially given to these patients by physicians in a major trauma center, and did not exclude patients who may have had a preexisting exposure to a traumatic event or PTSD symptoms.

Case studies of patients who developed PTSD after they sustained a closed head injury have also been utilized to corroborate the development of PTSD in motor vehicle accidents. For example, King (1997) described a 21-year-old unemployed man who had been struck from behind by an automobile while hitchhiking. He reported that this patient developed PTSD after his accident, even though he had been given the diagnosis of a "mild head injury" at the time he was admitted to the hospital. This patient, however, was able to recall lying in the road shortly after the accident after being thrown out of his vehicle and seeing the car that him his vehicle turn around and head directly at him as he lay on the ground. As a result of this patient's orthopedic injuries, he was unable to transport himself to the side of the road and believed that the driver was intentionally trying to kill him in order to "finish him off." McMillan (1996) reported on ten cases who had developed PTSD symptoms from a total of 312 patients who had sustained closed head injuries ranging in severity from mild to severe. These patients, however, were able to either recall feeling shocked shortly after the accident, being trapped in their vehicle, being in pain or physically injured, and the distress of others involved in the accident. Four of these patients complained of survivor guilt as a result of two deaths which occurred (a child and a passenger), as well as injuries sustained by their passengers. Thus, it would appear that in these case studies, these patients recalled the traumatic event which produced their PTSD symptoms after their anterograde amnesia ended.

Bryant and Harvey, (1999) investigated the relationship between PTSD and post-concussion syndromes following a mild traumatic brain injury in survivors of motor vehicle accidents who had either sustained a mild traumatic brain injury or no traumatic brain injury at six months post-trauma for PTSD and postconcussive symptoms. They found that postconcussive symptoms were more evident in MTBI patients with PTSD than those without PTSD and in mild traumatic brain injury patients than non-mild traumatic brain injury patients. Utilizing an administered PTSD module from the Composite International Diagnostic Interview (CIDI) and a post-concussive symptom checklist, they concluded that their findings suggested that postconcussive symptoms may be mediated by an interaction of neurological and psychological factors following MTBI. Although their findings suggest that the presence of a mild traumatic brain injury may facilitate the development of PTSD symptoms, Warden et al., (1997) studied the frequency of PTSD in 47 active duty service members who had sustained moderate traumatic brain injury and had neurogenic amnesia for the events surrounding the traumatic event. They found that when they evaluated these patients with a modified mental state examination and other questions at various points during a 24-month followup, none of these patients met the full criteria for PTSD. They concluded that posttraumatic amnesia following moderate head injury may protect against recurrent memories of the traumatic event and development of PTSD.

Bryant (2001) examined the relationship between Posttraumatic Stress Disorder and mild brain injury through a review of the research literature. He noted that while a number of studies had investigated the initial Posttraumatic Sstress Disorder in patients who had sustained mild traumatic brain injury, he pointed out that one of the difficulties in evaluating the findings of different studies is that these studies utilized variable definitions of mild traumatic brain injury and different methods of patient recruitment (e.g., many of these studies included individuals who were currently involved in litigation). For example, his research studies relied on the definition of mild traumatic brain injury as put forth by the American Congress of Rehabilitation Medicine (1993). While this definition utilizes as one of its criteria: any loss of consciousness or posttraumatic amnesia of less than 24 hours, Sbordone and Saul (2000) have pointed out that these criteria could include individuals who had posttraumatic amnesia of less than one second, or many individuals with acute stress disorder (without brain injury) since these individuals frequently report dissociative amnesia for the accident. While Bryant (2001) cites a number of studies which demonstrate that patients can develop PTSD following a mild traumatic brain injury, a review of these studies reveals that these investigators in the studies relied heavily on PTSD questionnaires and structured PTSD interviews to arrive at the diagnosis of PTSD in patients who had sustained traumatic brain injuries.

McMillan (2001) has pointed out that the use of structured PTSD interviews and PTSD questionnaires may result in the misdiagnosis of PTSD in individuals with traumatic brain injuries. He cited the example of a 21-year-old male who had sustained a severe closed head injury which had disrupted his cognitive functioning, ability to return to work, and his life. He noted that when this patient was assessed five months postinjury on the Impact of Events Scale (Horowitz, Wilner, and Alvarez, 1979), the patient's score on this test was consistent with individuals who have been diagnosed with PTSD and satisfied the DSM-IV criteria for PTSD. He also noted that on the Posttraumatic Diagnostic Scale (PDS) (Foa et al., 1993), this patient's severity score also qualified him for a diagnosis of PTSD. Despite these findings, he noted that a clinical interview did not support the diagnosis of PTSD. For example, he pointed out that the patient's responses to the questionnaires were significantly colored by the general disruption to his life that the brain injury had caused, his cognitive deficits, and the fact that many of the symptoms he endorsed were common symptoms of traumatic brain injury. He stressed that this case study demonstrates that PTSD can be easily misdiagnosed in TBI cases since the cognitively impaired patient may not follow the questionnaire instructions consistently, was likely to have physical disabilities, and other injuries that were likely to interfere with their day-to-day life functioning. He stressed that this case study suggests that even sophisticated questionnaire measures can be misleading when evaluating TBI cases for the presence of PTSD.

McMillan's (2002) findings suggest that the different findings in the literature on the relationship between traumatic brain injury and PTSD may be, at least in part, due to the different methodologies utilized in these studies. For example, the studies which reported the relative absence of PTSD following a traumatic brain injury appear to have relied heavily on psychiatric interviews with these patients. The studies which reported that patients who sustained traumatic brain injuries also developed PTSD appear to have heavily relied on PTSD questionnaires and structured PTSD interviews.

Another explanation of the endorsement of PTSD symptoms in TBI patients could be due to pending litigation or secondary gain since it may increase the value of their case (Bryant et al., 2001). For example, Lees-Haley and Dunn (1994) have shown that 85% of the individuals with no history of PTSD were able to accurately endorse PTSD symptoms and experiences to satisfy the DSM-IV diagnostic criteria of PTSD. These authors have argued that lay persons may have some basic knowledge of PTSD through books, magazines, newspapers, television news programs, televisions talk shows and radio call-in programs hosted by psychologists and psychiatrists. Thus, an individual's scores on a PTSD questionnaire or structured interview could simply reflect their motivation to appear more disabled, particularly if litigation is pending.

DISABILITY FOLLOWING POSTTRAUMATIC STRESS DISORDER

There is evidence that PTSD is associated with long-term functional disability in some individuals. For example, Gruenert et al., (1992) reported relatively high levels of moderate to severe psychiatric symptoms which included flashbacks, avoidance, marital distress, irritability, fear of reinjury, and preoccupation with the appearance of the effected limb of burn survivors during an 18-month follow up evaluation of patients who had suffered traumatic work-related burn injuries. Michaels et al., (1998) evaluated 35 adults prospectively, who were returned to functional employment after injury, using demographic data, validated psychological and health measures, and the Michigan Critical Events Perception Scale. They found that approximately 10% of the variance of these individuals returning to work was accounted for by poor psychological outcome, which was largely attributed to PTSD symptoms. Similarly, Green et al., (1993) examined the influence on PTSD on subsequent levels of disability in motor vehicle accident victims. They found that individuals with PTSD had higher levels of disability utilizing the Sickness Impact Profile Scale, particularly in the domain of social functioning. They concluded that PTSD was associated with work-related dysfunction equal to that of individuals who had severe physical handicaps. Zatzick et al., (1997) examined female Vietnam veterans to determine whether their current PTSD symptoms were associated with impaired functioning. They found that

PTSD was associated with a significantly higher risk of poor functioning in five of the six outcome domains. They also found that PTSD was associated with significantly higher levels of bed days, poor physical health and unemployment.

Amir et al., (1997) studied the prevalence of fibromyalgia syndrome-related symptoms, quality of life, and functional impairment among PTSD patients in comparison to controls. They found 21% of the PTSD patients showed evidence of a fibromyalgia syndrome in comparison to none of the control subjects. They also noted that the subjects in the PTSD group were more physically tender than controls and reported more pain and a lower quality of life, higher functional impairment, and suffered more from psychological distress than PTSD patients who were not experiencing fibromyalgia syndrome.

Davis and Kutter (1998) examined the independent living skills, traumatic experiences, and symptoms of PTSD in women residing in a supportive housing program for women and in families who were homeless. These subjects' independent living skills were evaluated by the Kohlman Evaluation of Living Skills Scale and a structured interview format to determine whether they had met the diagnostic criteria for PTSD. They found that traumatic experiences and PTSD were more prevalent among women who were homeless than among women in the general population. Michaels et al., (2000) evaluated 247 patients without severe neurotrauma at the time of admission and at 6 and 12 months post-trauma. They found that at 12 months the work status, general health, and overall satisfaction of recovery was heavily dependent on these patient's mental health functioning. More specifically, they found that individuals who had developed symptoms of PTSD were at higher risk to be unemployed, have poor general health and be unsatisfied with their recovery. Similarly, Kimerling and Calhoun, (1994) found that individuals with PTSD were at elevated risk for health problems and were disproportionate users of the healthcare system. Finally, Leserman, et al., (1996) found that women with PTSD attending a clinic specializing in gastrointestinal problems tended to be sicker, have had more surgery, and more disabling symptoms than women without a history of PTSD.

The healthcare costs associated with a diagnosis of PTSD appears to be extremely high (Soloman and Davidson, 1997). For example, Miller et al., (1996) estimated that the true cost of trauma to PTSD victims was 450 billion dollars a year which included medical costs, lost earnings, public program costs related to victim assistance, pain and suffering, loss of quality of life, and jury awarded compensation. They also noted that very little of the mental health costs were spent on professional mental health treatment since many people who seek mental health professionals fail to realize that their symptoms could result from a traumatic experience, therefore, they fail to mention the trauma. They also noted that individuals with PTSD were more reluctant than others with emotional problems to seek professional help even if they know they need it.

Prigerson, Miciejewski and Rosenheck (2001) examined 587 persons ranging in age from 15 to 44 to determine the risk and course of PTSD associated with combat trauma relative to other traumas. They found that men who reported combat as their worst trauma were more likely to have lifetime PTSD, delayed PTSD symptom onset, be unemployed, divorced, and physically abusive to their spouses. Gregurek et al., (2001) examined 42 disabled Croatian war veterans ranging in age from 19 to 44 who were receiving long-term physical rehabilitation in a hospital setting. They found that patients with PTSD symptoms had significantly higher anxiety levels than patients without PTSD symptoms. However, they noted that the percentage of patients manifesting PTSD symptoms increased from 19% to 41% five years later, while the anxiety levels decreased in patients with PTSD who were not receiving long-term physical rehabilitation. They concluded that staying in the same homogeneous group for a substantial period of time, in combination with inadequate social support and deficient psychological care, contributed to the development of PTSD-related disability.

PSYCHOLOGICAL TREATMENT OF PTSD

While an exhaustive review of the efficacy of the various psychological treatments that have been utilized to treat patients with PTSD is beyond the scope of this chapter, treatments such as crisis intervention, hypnosis, psychodynamic treatment, cognitive treatment, behavioral treatment, and eye movement desensitization have been frequently utilized to treat patients with PTSD. While crisis intervention has been used to treat female assault and rape victims with some success (Burgess and Holmstrom, 1974), there is little empirical evidence that crisis intervention is effective in preventing the development of chronic PTSD (FOA and Meadows, 1997). Furthermore, if such interventions are made by inexperienced clinicians, their interventions may be harmful (McFarlane, 1989). Although hypnotic techniques have been widely used to treat PTSD patients, one of the major problems with using hypnosis is that some patients with PTSD appear to be resistant to hypnosis since they fear losing control, while others may respond by developing severe dissociative states (Shalev, Bonne and Eth, 1996). Psychodynamic treatment utilizing concepts such as denial, abreaction, and catharsis in dealing with PTSD patients has been reported to be helpful, however, many of the studies which have demonstrated improvement are confounded by methodological problems such as lack of inappropriate controls, inadequate assessment of outcome, etc. (Foa and Meadows, 1997).

Cognitive treatment approaches have also been utilized relying on the basic assumptions about the belief systems of individuals regarding personal safety, control, and survival. This form of treatment views the patient's PTSD symptoms as a set of self-protective strategies which are utilized to survive in a seemingly dangerous world (Horowitz, 1976). Cognitive treatment approaches have been found to be effective in reducing symptoms of stress, depression, avoidance, intrusion of traumatic memories, and also appear to improve the patient's self-concept (Shalev, Bonne and Eth, 1996).

Behavioral treatments using classic operant conditioning have been utilized to understand and treat patients with PTSD by focusing on extinguishing the conditioned responses of these patient to the conditioned stimuli through the use of techniques such as gradual desensitization or massive flooding which involves re-exposure to the conditioned stimuli, either using a live object or a situation related to trauma (in vivo), or mental imagery of the trauma (in vivo). Research (e.g., Shalev, Bonne and Eth, 1996) has shown that behavioral treatments such as flooding can not only reduce the patient's PTSD symptoms, but can also exacerbate them.

Eye movement desensitization consists of eliciting saccadic eye movements while the patient mentally focuses on the traumatic event and describes his or her feelings about the event (Shapiro, 1989). Despite reports of excellent treatment results, more control studies are needed to determine its effectiveness since there is no convincing theoretical basis to explain its rapid effect in reducing PTSD symptoms (McCulloch & Feldman, 1996).

SUMMARY

While exposure to a traumatic event appears necessary for the development of PTSD, it is not sufficient to cause PTSD since the vast majority of individuals who are exposed to a traumatic event do not develop PTSD. Multiple risk factors include, but are not limited to, female gender, social disadvantage, education, childhood adversity, genetic predisposition, childhood physical or sexual abuse, prior head trauma, psychiatric illness, and substance abuse appear to significantly increase the likelihood of whether an individual will develop PTSD. Patients with PTSD are almost eight times more likely to have three or more comorbid psychiatric disorders and ninety times as likely to have a comorbid somatization disorder than individuals without PTSD.

PTSD produces profound and long lasting alterations in physiological reactivity characterized by significant increases in heart rate, skin conductance and blood pressure. This chronic state of physiological arousal, combined with an inability to regulate the autonomic nervous system, severely handicaps PTSD patients from effectively utilizing their emotions as warning signals and results in the development of fight or flight reactions without attempting to cognitively determine the significance of the information received. PTSD also produces chronically high levels of sympathetic nervous system activity and lower glucocorticoid levels in response to acute stress which leads to high levels of catecholamine release that can be neurotoxic. This has been linked to the reduction of the volume of the hippocampus and to deficits in short-term memory. Neurodiagnostic testing, using positron emission tomography, cerebral blood flow, and other measures, has shown that alterations in functioning of cortical structures are commonly seen in patients with chronic PTSD. Neuropsychological testing has demonstrated that patients with PTSD frequently demonstrate cognitive impairments on neuropsychological tests of attention, concentration, recent memory, and executive functions.

Although considerable controversy exists at the present time as to whether patients can develop PTSD if they have sustained a closed head injury, the differing results obtained by investigators may reflect the different methodologies that were utilized in these studies. For example, studies which have reported little or no PTSD following closed head injuries have relied heavily on psychiatric interviews, while studies which reported the development of PTSD following closed head injuries have relied heavily on PTSD questionnaires and structured PTSD interviews. This later technique may produce a high false positive rate in the diagnosis of PTSD in patients with closed head injuries.

PTSD has been found to produce significant psychiatric disability which, in some individuals, can last their entire lifetime. Patients with chronic or complex PTSD are at higher risk of being unemployed, having disabling medical symptoms such as pain and discomfort and abuse alcohol, drugs and their spouses. While a variety of psychological treatment modalities have been utilized on PTSD patients, some of these treatments may actually exacerbate the patient's negative symptoms, while others may only be of limited value.

REFERENCES

Amaya—Jackson, L, & March, J. (1995). Posttraumatic stress disorder. In J. S. March (Ed.), Anxiety disorders in children and adolescents (pp. 276–300). New York: Guilford.

American Psychiatric Association. (1980). *Diagnostic and Statistical Manual of Mental Disorders, 3rd Ed.* Washington, D.C.: APA.

American Psychiatric Association. (1994). *Diagnostic and Statistical Mental Disorders*, 4th Ed. Washington, D.C.: APA.

Amir, M., Kaplan, Z., Neuman, L., Sharabani, R., Shani, N., & Buskila, D. (1997). Posttraumatic stress disorder, tenderness, and fibromyalgia. *Journal of Psychosomatic Research, 42 (6)*, 607–613.

Bartzokis, G., Beckson, M., Lu, P.H., Nuechterlein, K., Edwards, N., & Mintz, J. (2001). Age related changes in frontal and temporal lobe volumes in men: a magnetic resonance imaging study. *Archives of General Psychiatry, 58*, 461–465. *Neuropsychopharmacology, 27*, 672–683.

Bartzokis, G., Nuechterlein, K. H., Lu, P. H., Gitlin, M., Rodgers, S. & Mintz, J. (2003). Dysregulated brain development in adult men with schizophrenia: A magnetic resonance imaging study. *Society of Biological Psychiatry, 53*, 412–421.

Bartzokis, G. (2002). Schizophrenia: Breakdown in the well regulated lifelong process of brain development and maturation.

Begic, D., Hotujac, L., & Jokic-Bergic, N. (2001). Electroencephalogic comparison of veterans with combat-related posttraumatic stress disorder and healthy subjects. *International Journal of Psychophysiology, 40*, 167–172.

Berthier, M. L., Kulisevsky, J., Fernandez-Benitz, J. A., & Gironell, A. (1998). Reactivation of posttraumatic stress disorder after minor head injury. *Depression and Anxiety, 8*, 43–47.

Blake, D. D., Weathers, F. W., & Nagy, F. N. (1990). A clinical rating scale for assessing current and lifetime PTSD: The CAPS-1. *Behavior Therapist, 18*, 187–188.

Blanchard, E. B., Kolb, L. C., & Gerardi, R. J. (1986). Cardiac Response to relevant stimuli as an adjunctive tool for diagnosing posttraumatic stress disorder in Vietnam veterans. *Behavior Therapy, 17*, 592–606.

Blanchard, E. B., Hickling, E. J., Taylor, A. E., Loos, W. R., & Gerardi, R. J. (1996). Psychological morbidity associated with motor accidents. *Behavior Research and Therapy, 32*, 283–290.

Blanchard, E. B., Hickling, E. J., Forneris, C. A., Taylor, A. E., Buckley, T. C., Loos, W. R., & Jaccard, J. (1997). Prediction of remission of accurate posttraumatic stress disorder in motor vehicle accident victims. *Journal of Traumatic Stress, 10*, 215–234.

Bogenschultz, M. P. & Nurnberg, G. H. (2000). Theoretical and methodological issues in psychiatric comorbidity. *Harvard Review of Psychiatry, 8*, 18–24.

Boudewyns, P.A. (1996). Posttraumatic stress disorder: Conceptualization and treatment. In M. Hersen, KM. Eisler, & P. Miller, (Eds.). *Progress in behavior modification*, Vol. 3C, New York: Brooks Cole, 165–189.

Brady, K. T., Killen, T. K., Brewerton, T., & Lucerini, S. (2000). Corborbidity of psychiatric disorders and posttraumatic stress disorder. *Journal of Clinical Psychiatry*, 61 (suppl 7), 22–32.

Bremner, J. D., Southwick, S. M., & Johnson, D. R. (1993). Childhood physical abuse and combat-related post-traumatic stress disorder. *American Journal of Psychiatry, 150*, 234–239.

Bremner, J. D., Randall, P., Scott, T. M., Bronen, R. A., Shelby, J. P., Southwick, S. M., Delany, R. C., McCarthy, G., Charney, D. S, & Innis, R. B. (1995). MRI-based measurement of hippocampal volume in patients with combat-related posttraumatic stress disorder. *American Journal of Psychiatry, 152*, 973–981.

Bremner, J. D. (1999). Does stress damage the brain? *Society of Biological Psychiatry, 45*, 797–805.

Breslau, N., Davis, G. C., Andreski, P., & Peterson, E. (1991). Traumatic events and posttraumatic stress disorder in an urban population of young adults. *Archives of General Psychiatry, 48*, 216–316.

Breslau, N., Chilcoat, H. D., Kessler, R. C. & Davis, G. C. (1999) Previous exposure to trauma and PTSD effects of subsequent trauma. *American Journal of Psychiatry, 156*, 902–907.

Breslau, N., Davis, G. C., Peterson, E. L. & Schultz, L. R. (1998). A second look at comorbidity in victims of trauma: The posttraumatic stress disorder-major depression connection. *Biological Psychiatry, 48*, 902–909.

Brewerton, T., Dansky, B., & Kilpatrick, D. (1999). Bulimia nervosa, PTSD and "forgetting." Results from the national women's study, In L. M. Williams & V. L. Banyard (Eds.) *Trauma and Memory.* Thousand Oaks, CA: Sage Press, 127–138.

Brewin, C. R., Andrews, B., & Valentine, J. D. (2000). Meta-analysis of risk factors for posttraumatic stress disorders in trauma-exposed adults. *Journal of Consulting and Clinical psychology, 68(5)*, 748–766.

Briere. J. (1997). Psychological assessment of child abuse effects in adults. In J. P. Wilson & T. M. Keane (Eds.), *Assessing Psychological Trauma and PTSD* (pp. 43–68). New York: Guilford Press.

Briere, J. (2001) *Detailed Assessment of Posttraumatic Stress,* Odessa, FL: PAR.

Bromet, E., Sonnega, A., & Kesler, R. C. (1998). Risk factors for DSM-III-R posttraumatic stress disorders: Findings from the National Comorbidity Survey. *American Journal of Epidemiology, 147,* 353–361.

Bryant, R.A. & Harvey, A.G. (1997). Acute stress disorder: A critical review of diagnostic issues. *Clinical Psychology Review, 17, 753–757.*

Bryant, R.A. & Harvey, A.G. (1998). Relationship between acute stress disorder and posttraumatic stress disorder following mild traumatic brain injury. *American Journal of Psychiatry, 155, 625–629.*

Bryant, R.A., Harvey, A.G., Dang, S.T., & Sakerville, T. (1998). Assessing acute stress disorder: Psychometric prospective of a structured clinical interview. *Psychological Assessment, 10,* 215–220.

Bryant, R.A., & Harvey, A.G. (2000). Acute Stress Disorder: A handbook of Theory, Assessment, and Treatment. Washington, D.C.: American Psychological Association.

Bryant, R.A., Marosskeky, J. E. Crooks, J., Baguley, J., & Gurka, J. (2000). Coping style and posttraumatic stress disorder following severe traumatic brain injury. *Brain Injury, 14(2),* 175–180.

Buckley, T. C., Blanchard, E. B., & Hickling, E. J. (196). A prospective examination of delayed onset PTSD secondary to motor vehicle accidents. *Journal of Abnormal Psychology, 105, 617–625.*

Charles, G., Hansenne, M., Ansseau, M., Pichot, W., Machowski, R., Schittercatte, M., & Wilmotte, J. (1995) P300 in Posttraumatic stress disorder. *Biological Psychiatry, 32, 72–74.*

Cloitre, M., Scarvalone, P., Difede, J. F. (1997). Posttraumatic stress disorder, self and interpersonal dysfunction among sexually re-traumatized women. *Journal of Traumatic Stress, 10,* 437–452.

Davidson, J., Swartz, M., & Storck, M. (1985). A diagnostic and family study of posttraumatic stress disorder. *American Journal of Psychiatry, 142,* 90–93.

Davidson, J. R. T., Smith, R. D., & Kuder, H. S. (1989). Validity and reliability of the DSM-III criteria for posttraumatic stress disorder: Experience with a structured interview. *Journal of Nervous and Mental Diseases, 177,* 336–341.

Davidson, J. R. T., Huges, D., Blazer, D., & George, L. K. (1991). Posttraumatic stress disorder in the community: An epidemiological study. *Psychological Medicine, 21,* 1–19.

Davis, J. & Kutter, C. J. (1998). Independent living skills an posttraumatic stress disorder in women who are homeless: Implications for future practice. *The American Journal of Occupational Therapy, 52(1),* 39–44.

Deering, C. G., Glover, S. G. & Ready, D. (1996). Unique patterns of comorbidity in posttraumatic stress disorder from different sources of trauma. *Comprehensive Psychiatry, 37,* 336–346.

Delahanty, D. L., Herberman, H. B., Craig, K. J., Hayward, M. C., Fullerton, C. S., Ursano, R. J., & Baum, A. (1997). Acute and chronic distress and posttraumatic stress disorder as a function of responsibility for serious motor vehicle accidents. *Journal of Consulting and Clinical Psychology, 65,* 560–567.

Dirkzwager, A., Bramson, I., & Van der Ploeg. (2001) The longitudinal course of posttraumatic stress disorder symptoms among aging military veterans. *Journal of Nervous and Mental Disorders, 189,* 846–853.

Eysenck, M. W. (1989). Trait anxiety and stress. In S. Fisher & J. Reason (eds.), *Handbook of Life Stress Cognition and Health.* New York: Wiley.

Feehan, M., Nada-Raja, S., & Langley, J. D. (2001). The prevalence and correlates of psychological distress following physical and sexual assault in a young adult cohort. *Violence and Victims, 16(1),* 49–63.

Fernandez, M., Pissiota, A., Frans, O., Von Knorring, Fischer, H., & Fredrikson, M. (2001). Brain function in a patient with torture related post-traumatic stress disorder before and after fluoxetine treatment: A positron emission tomography provocation emission tomography study. *Neuroscience Letters, 297,* 101–104

Ferrada-Noli, M., Asberg, M. & Ormstad, K. (1998). Suicidal behavior after severe trauma, Part 1: PTSD Diagnoses, psychiatric. *Journal of Traumatic Stress, 11,* 103–112.

Foa, E.B. & Hearst-Ikeda, D. (1996). Emotional dissociation in response to trauma: An information-processing approach. In L. K. Michelson & W. J. Ray (Eds), *Handbook of dissociation:* Theoretical and clinical perspectives (pp 207–222). New York: Phenum.

Foa, E.B., Molnar, C., & Cushman, L. (1995). Changes in rape narratives during exposure therapy for post-traumatic stress disorder. *Journal of Tramatic Stress, 8,* 675–690.

Foa, E.B., & Meadows, E.A., (1997). Psychosocial treatments for post-traumatic stress disorder: a critical review. *Annual Review of Psychology 48*, 449–480.

Foa, E.B., Cashman, L., Jaycox, L., & Perry, K. (1997). The validation of a self-report measure of post-traumatic stress disorder: the post-traumatic diagnostic scale. *Psychological Assessment, 9*, 445–451.

Fox, R.P. (1972). Postcombat adaptation problems. *Comprehensive Psychiatry, 13*, 435–443.

Freedman, T. W., Cardwell, D., Karson, C. N., & Komoroski, R. A. (1998). In vivo proton magnetic resonance spectroscopy of the medial temporal lobes of subjects with combat-related post-traumatic stress disorder. *Magnetic Resonance in Medicine, 40(1)*, 66–71.

Fuster, J. M. (1997). *The Prefrontal Cortex* (3rd ed). New York: Lippincott-Raven.

Gerard, G., Hansenne, M., Ansseau, M., Pitchot, W., Machowski, R., Shittecatte, M., & Wilmotte, J. (1995). P300 in post-traumatic stress disorder. *Neuropsychology, 32*, 72–74.

Giaconia, R. M., Reinherz, H. Z., Silverman, A. B., Pakiz, B., Frost, A. K., & Cohen, E. (1995). Traumas and post-traumatic stress disorder in a community population of older adolescents. *Journal of The American Academy of Child and Adolescent Psychiatry, 34*, 1369–1380.

Gilbertson, M.W., Shenton, M.E., Ciszewski, A., Kasai, K., & Kasko, N.B. (2003). Hippocampal volume as a vulnerability factor for chronic post-traumatic stress disorder: MRI evidence from monozygotic twins discordant for combat exposure. Cited in McNally, R.J. Progress and controversy in the study of post-traumatic stress disorder. *Annual Review of Psychology. 54*, 229–252.

Charles, G., Hunsenne, M., Ansseau, M., Pitchot, W., Machowski, R., Schittecatte, M., & Wilmotte, J. (1995). P300 in post-traumatic stress disorder. *Neuropsychobiology 32*, 72–74.

Goldsmith, W. & Cretekos, C. (1969). Unhappy odysseys: Psychiatric hospitalizations among Vietnam returnees. *Archives of General Psychiatry, 20*, 78–83.

Green, M. M., McFarlane, A. C., Hunter, C. E., & Griggs, W. M. (1993). Undiagnosed post-traumatic stress disorder following motor vehicle accidents. *Medical Journal of Australia, 159*, 529–534.

Gregurek, R., Pavic, L., Vuger-Kovacic, Vukusic, H., Potrebica, S., Bitar, Z., Kovacic, D., Danic, S., & Klain, E. (2001). Increase of frequency of post-traumatic stress disorder in disabled war veterans during prolonged stay in a rehabilitation hospital. *Croatian Medical Journal, 42(2)*, 161–164.

Grinker, R. R. & Spiegel, R.R. (1945). *Men under Stress*. Philadelphia: Blackston.

Grunert, B. K., Devine, C. A., Matloub, H. S., Sanger, J. H., Yousif, N. J., Anderson, R. C., & Roell, S. M. (1992). Psychological adjustment following work-related hand injury: 18-month follow-up. *Annals of Plastic Surgery, 29(6)*, 537–542.

Gurvits, T. V., Gilbertson, M. W., Lasko, N. B., Orr, S P., & Pitman, R. K. (1996). Neurological status of combat veterans and adult survivors of sexual abuse PTSD. In Yehuda, R. & McFarlane, A. C. (Eds.). *Psychobiology of Posttraumatic stress disorder* Annals of the New York Academy of Sciences, Vol. 821. New York: New York Academy of Sciences, 468–471.

Hammarberg, M. (1992). PENN inventory for posttraumatic stress disorder: Psychometric properties. *Psychological Assessment, 4*, 67–76.

Hamner, M. B. (1994). Exacerbation of posttraumatic stress disorder symptoms with medical illness. *General Hospital Psychiatry, 16*, 135–137.

Hamner, M. B., Lorberbaum, J. P., & George, M. S. (1999). Potential role of the anterior cingulate cortex in PTSD: Review and hypothesis. *Depression and Anxiety, 9, 1*—14.

Harvey, A. G. & Bryant, R. A. (1998). The relationship between acute stress disorder and posttraumatic stress disorder: A prospective evaluation of motor vehicle accident survivors. *Journal of Consulting and Clinical Psychology, 66*, 507–512.

Helzer, J.E., Robins, L.N., & McEvoy, L. (1987). Posttraumatic stress disorder in the general population. *New England Journal of Medicine, 317*, 1630–1634.

Herman, J. (1993). Sequelae of prolonged and repeated trauma: Evidence for a complex posttraumatic syndrome, In J. Davidson & E. Foa (Eds.), *PTSD: DSM-IV and beyond*. Washington, D.C.: American Psychiatric Association Press.

Holbrook, T.L., Anderson, J. P., Sieber, W.J., Browner, D., & Hoyt, D. B. (1999). *The Journal of Trauma: Injury, Infection, and Critical Care, 46* (9), 765–773.

Horowitz, M. J. (1976). *Stress Response Syndrome*, New York: Aronson.

Horowitz, M. J. (1986). *Stress Response Syndromes* (2nd ed.) New York: Jason Aronson.

Horowitz, M. J., Wilner, W.R., & Alvarez, W. (1979). Impact of event scales: A measure of subjective stress. *Psychosomatic Medicine, 41*, 209–218.

Ide, M.S. & Paez, A. (2000). Complex PTSD: A review of current issues. *International Journal of Emergency Mental Health, 2(1)*, 43–51.

Kardiner, A, (1941). *The Traumatic Neuroses of War.* New York: Hoeber.
Keane, T. M., Wolfe, J., & Taylor, K. L. (1987). Posttraumatic stress disorder: Evidence for diagnostic validity and methods of psychological assessment. *Journal of Clinical Psychology, 43,* 32–43.
Kessler, R., Sonnega, A., & Bromet, E. (1995). Posttraumatic stress disorder in the National Comorbidity Survey. *Archives of General Psychiatry, 52,* 1048–1060.
Kimerling, R., & Calhoun, K. S. (1994). Somatic symptoms, social support, and treatment seeking among sexual assault victims. *Journal of Consulting and Clinical Psychology, 62,* 333–340.
King, N. (1997). Posttraumatic stress disorder and head injury as a dual diagnosis: "Islands" of memory as a mechanism. *Journal of Neurology, Neurosurgery, and Psychiatry, 62,* 82–84.
Kluznick, J. C.,Speed, N., & Van Valkenberg, C. (1986). Forty year follow up of United States prisoners of war. *American Journal of Psychiatry, 43,* 1443–1446.
Koenen, K. C., Driver, K. L., Oscar-Berman, M., Wolfe, J. Folsom, S., Huang, M. T., & Schlesinger, L. (2001). Measures of prefrontal system dysfunction in posttraumatic stress disorder. *Brain and Cognition, 45,* 64–78.
Koss, M. P., & Harvey, M. R. (1991). *The Rape Victim: Clinical an Community Interventions, 2nd ed.* Newbury Park, CA: Sage Publications.
Kosten, T. R., Mason, J. W., & Giller, E. L. (1987). Sustained urinary norepinephrine and epinephrine elevation in PTSD. *Psychoneuroendocrinology, 12,* 13–20.
Kulka, R. A, Schlenger, W. E., & Fairbank, J. A. (1991). Assessment of posttraumatic stress disorder in the community: Prospects and pitfalls from recent studies of Vietnam veterans: Psychological assessment. *Journal of Consulting and Clinical Psychology, 3,* 547–560.
Lees-Haley, P. & Dunn, J. T. (1994). The ability of naïve subjects to report symptoms of mild brain injury, post-traumatic stress disorder, major depression, and generalized anxiety disorder. *Journal of Clinical Psychology, 50(2),* 252–256.
Leserman, J., Drossman, D. A., Li, Z. (1996). Sexual and physical abuse history in gastroenterology practice: how types of abuse impact health status. *Psychosomatic Medicine, 58,* 538–547.
MacKenzie, E. J., Siegel, J. H. Shapiro, S., Moody, M., & Smith, R. T. (1988). Functional recovery and medical costs of trauma: An analysis by type and severity of injury. *Journal of Trauma, 28,* 281–297.
Malhi, G. S. & Bartlett, J. R. (1998). Loss of consciousness and posttraumatic stress disorder. *British Journal of Psychiatry, 173,* 537.
Malloy, P. F., Fairbanks, J. A., & Keane, T. M. (1983). Validation of a multi method assessment of posttraumatic stress disorders in Vietnam veterans. *Journal of Clinical and Consulting Psychology, 51,* 488–494.
March, J. S. (1993). The stress criterion in *DSM-IV* posttraumatic stress disorder. In Davidson, J. R. & Foa, E. B. (Eds.). *Posttraumatic Stress Disorder: DSM-IV and Beyond,* Washington, D.C.: American Psychiatric Press, 37–54.
Mayou, R., Bryant, B., & Duthie, R. (1993). Psychiatric consequences of road traffic accidents. *British Medical Journal, 307,* 647–651.
Max, J. E., Castillo, C. S., Robin, D. A., Lindgren, S. D., Smith, W. L., Sato, Y., & Arndt, S. (1998). Posttraumatic stress symptomology after childhood traumatic brain injury. *Journal of Nervous and Mental Disease, 186(10),* 589–596.
McCranie, E. W., Hyer, L. A., Boudewyns, P. A., & Woods, M. G. (1992). Negative parenting behavior, combat exposure and PTSD symptom severity: Test of a person-event interaction model. *Journal of Nervous and Mental Diseases, 180,* 431–438.
McCulloch, M. J., & Feldman, P., (1996). Eye movement desensitization utilizes positive visceral element of the investigatory reflex to inhibit the memories of posttraumatic stress disorder: a theoretical analysis. *British Journal of Psychiatry 169,* 571–579.
McFall, M. E., Smith, D. E., & Roszell, D. K. (1990). Convergent validity of measures of PTSD in Vietnam combat veterans. *American Journal of Psychiatry, 147,* 645–648.
McFarlane, A. C. (1986). Posttraumatic morbidity of a disaster. *Journal of Nervous and Mental Disease, 174,* 4–14.
McFarlane, A. C. (1989). The treatment of posttraumatic stress disorder. *British Journal of Psychiatry, 62,* 81–90.
McFarlane, A. C. (1996). Control response as a predictor of the development of PTSD following motor vehicle accidents. Paper presented at the New York Academy of Sciences, September, New York.
McFarlane, A. C. (2000) Posttraumatic stress disorder: A model of the longitudinal course and the role of risk factors. *Journal of Clinical Psychiatry, 61(5),* 15–23.

McMillan, T. M. (1991). Posttraumatic stress disorder and severe head injury. *Psychiatry, 159,* 431–433.

McMillan, T. M. (1996). Post-traumatic stress disorder following minor and severe closed head injury: 10 single cases. *Brain Injury, 40,* 749–758.

McMillan, T. M. (2001). Errors in diagnosing posttraumatic stress disorders after traumatic brain injury. *Brain Injury, 15,* 39–46.

McNally, R. J. (2003). Progress and controversy in the study of posttraumatic stress disorder. *Annual Review of Psychology, 54,* 229–252.

McNally, R. J., Lasko, N. B., Machlin, M. L., & Pitman, R. K. (1995). Autobiographical memory disturbances in combat-related posttraumatic stress disorder. *Behavioral Research Therapy, 33,* 619–630.

Michaels, A. J., Michaels, C. E., Smith, J. S., Moon, C. H., Peterson, C., & Long, W. B. (2000). Outcome from injury: General health, work status, and satisfaction 12 months after trauma. *Journal of Traumatic Injury, Infection, and Critical Care, 48(5),* 841–850.

Mild Traumatic Brain Injury Committee of the Head Injury Interdisciplinary Special Interest Group of the American Congress of Rehabilitation Medicine (1993). Definition of mild traumatic brain injury. *Journal of Head Trauma Rehabilitation, 8,* 86–87.

Millen, F. J. (1966). Post-traumatic neurosis in industry. *Industrial Medical Surgery, 35,* 929–935.

Miller, T. R., Cohen, M.A., & Wiersma, B. (1996). *Victim Costs and Consequences: A New Look. National Institute ofJustice Research Report,* Washington, D.C.: U. S. Dept. of Justice.

Mirzaei, S., Knoll, P., Keck, A., Priether, B., Gutierrez, E., & Umek, H. (2001). Regional cerebral blood flow in patients suffering from posttraumatic stress disorder. *Neuropsychobiology, 43,* 260–264.

Myslobodky, M. S., Glicksohn, J. Singer, J., Stern, M., Bar-Ziv, J., Friedland, N., & Bleich, A. (1995). Changes in brain anatomy in patients with posttraumatic stress disorder: A pilot magnetic resonance imaging study. *Psychiatry Research, 58,* 259–264.

Neria, Y., Solomon, Z., & Dekel, R. (1998). An eighteen year follow up study of Israeli prisoners of war and combat veterans. *Journal of Nervous an Mental Diseases, 186,* 174–182.

Norris, F. H. (1992). Epidemiology of trauma: Frequency and impact of different potentially traumatic events on different demographic groups. *Journal of Consulting and Clinical Psychology, 60,* 409–418.

Ornitz, E. M. & Pynoos, R. S. (1989). Startle modulation in children with posttraumatic stress disorder. *American Journal of Psychiatry, 146,* 866–870.

Orsillo, S. M., Heimberg, R. G., Juster, H. R. (1996). Social phobia and PTSD in Vietnam veterans. *Journal of Traumatic Stress, 9,* 235–252.

Oscar-Berman, M. & Bardenhagen, F. (1998). Nonhuman primate models of memory dysfunction in neurodegenerative disease: Contributions from comparative neuropsychology. In A. Troster (Ed.) *Memory in Neurodegenerative Disease,* New York: Cambridge Un iv. Press, 3–20.

Paris, J. (2000). Predisposition, personality traits, and posttraumatic stress disorder. *Harvard Review of Psychiatry, 8,* 175–183.

Pfefferbaum, B. (1997). Posttraumatic stress disorder in children: A review of the past 10 years. *Journal of the American Academy of Child and Adolescent Psychiatry, 36* (11), 1503–1511.

Pitman, R. K., Orr, S. P., & Forgue, D. F. (1987). Psychological assessment of posttraumatic stress disorder imagery in Vietnam combat veterans. *Archives of General Psychiatry, 44,* 970–975.

Prigerson, H. G., Maciejewski, P. K., & Rosenheck, R. A. (2001). Combat trauma: Trauma with highest risk of delayed onset and unresolved posttraumatic stress disorder symptoms, unemployment, and abuse among men, *Journal of Mental Disease, 189* (2), 99–108.

Rahe, R. H. (1995) Stress and psychiatry. In H. I. Kaplan & B.J. Sadock (Eds.) *Comprehensive Textbook of Psychiatry, 6th ed.* Baltimore: Williams and Wilkins, 1545–1559.

Rainey, J. M., Aleem, A., & Ortiz, A. (1987). Laboratory procedure for the inducement of flashbacks. *American Journal of Psychiatry, 144,* 1317–1319.

Regehr, C., Goldberg, G., Glancy, G. D., & Knott. (2002). Posttraumatic symptoms and disability in paramedics. *Canadian Journal of Psychiatry, 47,* 953–958.

Reinherz, H. Z., Giaconia, R. M., Lefkowitz, E. S., Pakiz, B., Frost, A.K. (1993). Prevalence of psychiatric disorders in a community population of older adolescents. *Journal of the American Academy of Child and Adolescent Psychiatry, 32,* 369–377.

Resnick, H., Kilpatrick, D. G., Danksy, B., et al. (1993). Preva lence of civilian trauma and posttraumatic stress disorder in a representative national sample of women. *Journal of Clinical and Consulting Psychiatry, 61,* 984–991.

Roberts, G. I., Lawrence, J. M., Williams, G. M., & Raphael, B. (1998). The impact of domestic violence on women's mental health. *Australian New Zealand Journal of Public Health, 22,* 796–801.

Rutter, M. (1989). Pathways from child to adult life. *Journal of Child Psychology and Psychiatry, 30,* 23–51.

Sachinvala, N., Von Scotti, H., McGuire, M., Fairbanks, L., Bakst, K,. McGuire, M., & Brown, N. (2000). Memory, attention, function, and mood among patients with chronic posttraumatic stress disorder. *Journal of Nervous and Mental Disease, 188,* (12), 818–823.

Sapolsky, R. M. (2000). Glucocorticoids and hippocampal atrophy in neuropsychiatric disorders. *Archives of General Psychiatry, 57,* 925–935.

Sbordone, R. J. & Liter, J. C. (1995). Mild traumatic brain injury does not produce post- traumatic stress disorder. *Brain Injury, 9,* 405–412.

Sbordone, R. J. & Saul, R. E. (2000). Neuropsychology for health care professionals and attorneys, 2nd Ed. Boca Raton, FL: CRC Press.

Scheflin, A. & Brown, D. (1996). Repressed memory of dissociative amnesia. What the science says. *Journal of psychiatry and Law, 24,* 143–188.

Schlenger, W. E., Kulka, R. A., Fairbank, J. A., Hough, R. L., Jordan, B. K., & Marmar, C. R. (1992). The prevalence of posttraumatic stress disorder in the Vietnam generation: a multimethod multisource assessment of psychiatric disorder, *Journal of Traumatic Stress, 5,* 333–363

Schnurr, P. P., Friedman, M. J. & Rosenberg, S. D. (1993). Preliminary MMPI scores as predictors of combat-related PTSD symptoms. *American Journal of Psychiatry, 150,* 479–483.

Sedat, S. & Stein, D. J. (2000). Trauma and posttraumatic stress disorder in women: a review. *International Clinical Psychopharmacology, 15(3),* 525–533.

Shalev, A. Y. (1999). Psychophysiological expression of risk factors for PTSD. In R. Yehuda (Ed.) *Risk Factors for Posttraumatic Stress Disorder.* Washington, D.C.: American Psychiatric Press, 143–161.

Shalev, A.Y., Orr, S. P., & Peri, T. (1992). Physiological response to loud tones in Israeli patients with post-traumatic stress disorder. *Archives of General Psychiatry, 49,* 870–875.

Shalev, A.Y., Orr, S. P. & Pitman, R. K. (1993). Psychophysiologic assessment of traumatic imagery in Israeli civilian patients with posttraumatic stress disorder. *American Journal of Psychiatry, 150,* 620–624.

Shalev, A. Y., Bonne, O. & Eth, S., (1996). Treatment of posttraumatic stress disorder: a review. *Psychosomatic Medicine 58,* 165–182.

Shalev, A.Y., Peri, T., Canetti, L. & Schreiber, S. (1996). Predictors of PTSD in injured trauma survivors: A prospective study. *American Journal of Psychiatry, 153,* 219–255.

Shapiro, F., (1989). Eye movement desensitization: a new treatment for posttraumatic stress disorder. *Journal of Behavioral and Experimental Psychiatry. 20,* 211–217.

Shin, L. M., McNally, R. J., Kosslyn, S. M., Thomson, Rauch, S. L., Alpert, N. M., Metzger, L. J., (1999). Regional cerebral blood flow during script-imagery in childhood sexual abuse-related PTSD: A PET investigation. *American Journal of Psychiatry, 156,* 575–584.

Shore, J. H., Vollmer, W. M., & Tatum, E. L. (1989). Community patterns of posttraumatic stress disorders. *Journal of Nervous and Mental Disease, 177,* 681–685.

Solomon, S. D., & Davidson, J. R. T. (1997). Trauma: Prevalence, impairment, service use, and cost. *Journal of Clinical Psychiatry, 58* (suppl 9), 5–11.

Solomon, Z., & Mikulincer, M. (1992). Aftermaths of combat stress reactions: A three-year study. *British Journal of Clinical Psychology, 31,* 21–32.

Southwick, S. M., Krystal, J. H. & Morgan, A. (1993). Abnormal noradrenergic function in posttraumatic stress disorder. *Archives of General Psychiatry, 50,* 266–274.

Sparr, L. F. (1995). Post-traumatic stress disorder: Does it exist? Neurologic Clinics, *13,* 413–429.

Spitzer, R.L., Williams, J. B., Gibbon, M., & First, M. B. (1990). *Structured Clinical Interview for DSM-III-R.* Washington, D.C.: American Psychiatric Press.

Stuss, D. T. & Benson, D. F. (1986). *The Frontal Lobes.* New York: Raven Press.

Sutker, P. B., Allain, A. N., Jr., Winstead, D. K. (1993). Psychopathology and psychiatric diagnoses of World War II Pacific Theater prisoner of war survivors and combat veterans. *American Journal of Psychiatry, 150,* 240–245.

Symth, L. D. (1999). *Clinician's manual for The Cognitive-Behavioral Treatment of Post Traumatic Stress Disorder and Other Anxiety Disorders (2nd ed.).* Baltimore, Md: RTR.

Uddo, M. J.,Vasterling, J. J.,Bailey, K.,& Sutker, P. B. (1993). Memory and attention in combat-related post-traumatic stress disorder (PTSD). *Journal of Psychopathology and Behavioral Assessment, 15,* 43–52.

Van der Kolk, B. A. (1997). The *psychobiology* of posttraumatic stress disorder. *Journal of Clinical Psychiatry, 58,* 16–24.

Van der Kolk, B. A. & Van der Hart, O, (1989). Pierce Janet and the breakdown of adaptation in psychological trauma. *American Journal of Psychiatry, 146,* 1530–1540.

Wakefield, J. C. & Spitzer, R. L. (2002). Lowered estimates—but of what? *Archives of General Psychiatry, 59,* 129-130.

Warden, D. L., Labbate, L. A., Salazar, A. M., Nelson, R., Sheley, E., Staudenmeier, J., & Martin, E. (1997). Post-traumatic stress disorder in patients with traumatic brain injury with amnesia for the event. *The Journal Neuropsychiatry and Clinical Neurosciences, 9,* 18–22.

Watson, C. G., Juba, M. P., & Manifold, V. (1991). The PTSD interview: Rationale, description, reliability and concurrent validity of a DSM-III based technique. *Journal of Clinical Psychology, 47,* 179–188.

Weine, S. M., Becker, D. E., Levy, K. N., Edell, W. S., & McGlashan, T. H. (1997). Childhood trauma histories in adolescent inpatients. *Journal of Traumatic Stress, 10,* 281–298.

Wolfe, J. (1994). Applying the neuropsychology of memory disorder. In L. S. Cermak (Ed.), *Neuropsychological Explorations of Memory and Cognition: Essays in Honor of Nelson Butters* (pp. 285–293). New York: Plenum Press.

Wolfe, J.& Charney, D. S. (1991), Use of neuropsychological assessment in posttraumatic stress disorder. *Psychological Assessment, 3,* 573–580.

Wolfe, J. & Schlesinger, L. K. (1997). Performance of PTSD patients on standard tests of memory: Implications for trauma. In Yehuda, R. & McFarlane, A. C. (Eds.). *Psychobiology of Posttraumatic Stress Disorder. Annals of the* New York Academy of Sciences, Vol, 821, New York: New York Academy of Sciences, 208–218.

Wunderlich, J. (1998). Comorbidity patterns in adolescents and young adults with suicide attempts. *European Archives of Psychiatry and Clinical Neuroscience, 248,* 87–95.

Yehuda, R. & Southwick, E. L. (1991). Hypothalamic pituitary-adrenal dysfunction in posttraumatic stress disorder. *Biological Psychiatry, 30,* 1031–1048.

Yehuda, R., Southwick, S. M., & Mason, J. W. (1990), Interactions of the hypothalamic- pituitary adrenal axis and the catecholaminergic system of the stress disorder. In E. L. Giller (Ed.). *Biological Assessment and Treatment of PTSD.* Washington, D.C.: American Psychiatric Press.

Yehuda, R., Kahana, B., & Binder-Byrnes, K. (1995). Cortisol excretion in holocaust survivors with posttraumatic stress disorder. *American Journal of Psychiatry, J 52,* 982–986.

Yehuda, R., Keefe, R. S. E., Harvey, P. D., Levengood, R. A., Gerber, D. .K., Geni, J., Slever, L. J. (1995). Learning and memory in combat veterans with posttraumatic stress disorder. *American Journal of Psychiatry, 152,* 137–139.

Yellowless, P. M. & Kaushik, A. N. (1994). A case-control study of the sequelae of childhood sexual assault in adult psychiatric patients. *Medical Journal of Australia, 160,* 408–411.

Zaidi, L. Y. & Foy, D. W. (1994). Childhood abuse and combat-related PTSD. *Journal of Traumatic Stress, 7,* 33–42.

Zatzick, D. F., Weiss, D. S., Marmar, C. R., Metzher, T. J., Wells, K., Golding, J. M., Stewart, A., Schlenger, W. E., & Browner, W. S. (1997). Posttraumatic stress disorder and functioning and quality of life outcomes in female Vietnam veterans. *Military Medicine, 162(10),* 661–665.

Zubieta, J., Chinitz, J. A., Lombardi, V., Fig, L. M., Cameron, O. G., & Leberzon, I. (1999). Medial frontal cortex involvement in PTSD symptoms: A SPECT study. *Journal of Psychiatric Research,* 259–264.

20

The Prediction of Occupational Disability Related to Depressive and Anxiety Disorders

William H. Gnam

INTRODUCTION

Disability related to mental disorders has attained an unprecedented international prominence. With the publication of the Global Burden of Disease Study, a common metric for comparing the global burden of disparate health conditions was established, and the relative burden of mental disorders was revealed (Murray & Lopez, 1996). The Global Burden of Disease Study startled the international health community by finding that neuropsychiatric disorders as a group were the third leading cause of lost healthy years of life, and the foremost cause of disability. Mental disorders comprise four of the ten leading individual causes of disability throughout the world. By the year 2020, mental disorders and substance abuse are projected to account for 15% of the global disease burden (Murray, Lopez, & Jamison, 1994) Unipolar depression will emerge globally as the second leading cause of disability, behind ischemic heart disease.

Although the Global Burden of Disease Study had the most significant impact, other international studies have also found that mental disorders impose a formidable burden on society (Ustun et al., 1999). Cost-of-illness analyses have complemented disease burden studies by demonstrating that the social costs of mental disorders within developed countries are enormous, with a substantial proportion of the costs attributable to lost productivity arising from disability and premature mortality (Rice, Hodgson, & Kopstein, 1985; Rice, Kelman, & Miller, 1992).

As the scientific findings related to disease burden were being disseminated, policies for those disabled by mental disorders were being integrated into the larger policy framework for all disabled persons. Two countries enshrined civil rights for persons with disabilities, and granted these rights equally to those disabled by mental disorders. In the United States, the Americans with Disability Act of 1990 (U.S.Public Law 101–336, 1990) mandated that persons with major role restrictions due to health

DOI: 10.1007/978-0-387-28919-9_20, © 2009 Springer Science+Business Media, LLC

conditions be provided with access to employment, public services and accommodations (including transportation and telecommunications) equal to that of those without health-related limitations. In 1995, India passed the Persons with Disabilities Act (India, 1996), which assured that regional and local governments would provide disabled persons, including those disabled by mental illness and mental retardation, with free education, a quota of employment opportunities, as well as preventative and early detection services. In the international policy arena, the International Mental Health Task Force from the outset participated in the development of the World Health Organization's International Classification of Functioning, Disability, and Health, ensuring that mental disorders and disability were fully represented within the conceptual framework, definition, and measurement of health and disability (Kennedy, 2003).

In the United States, recognition of the disease burden imposed by mental disorders has motivated an extensive program of health care intervention research, whose objectives have been to increase the detection rates of mental disorders, and improve treatment quality (Gilbody, Whitty, Grimshaw, & Thomas, 2003). Unfortunately, no comparable attention and resource investment has been made to improve the identification and reduction of the disability related to mental disorders. The fact that diagnosis and clinical factors are poor predictors of functional outcomes highlights the need for greater investment in mental disability research. A recent review and discussion of the mental disability management literature concluded that no coherent and minimally adequate corpus of research exists to inform practices (Goldner et al., 2004; Gnam, 2004).

The prediction and early recognition of mental disability represent core objectives of disability management. However, to date there have been no syntheses of disability prediction research to provide guidance to clinicians and disability managers, and to inform research agendas. The objective of this chapter is to summarize and critique the state of knowledge related to the prediction of occupational disability arising from depressive and anxiety disorders. The disorders considered are major depressive disorder, dysthymic disorder, generalized anxiety disorder, panic disorder, agoraphobia, social phobia, and simple phobia. Post-traumatic stress disorder is not included here, but is discussed elsewhere in this volume. Depressive and anxiety disorders are the most common psychiatric conditions encountered in clinical practice among individuals who are employed or who have had meaningful labor market experience. To make this review tractable, we have excluded the literature relating non-specific psychological stress to disability, and we do not consider the determinants of disability duration, sickness absence, or return to work.

For the purposes of this review, occupational disability is broadly defined to represent a range of problems in functioning that includes impairments, activity limitations, and role restrictions (World Health Organization, 2001). Our approach is to review a range of factors—clinical and contextual—and evaluate the degree to which they predict the occupational disability associated with depressive and anxiety disorders. The analytic challenge inherent in this exercise is to distinguish the prediction of occupational disability from the risk of having a disorder itself. Socioeconomic status, for example, is a well-known risk factor for having a disorder (Robins & Regier, 1991; Kessler, Foster, Saunders, & Stang, 1995), but its relevance for those who have a mental disorder in predicting occupational disability is less clear.

We have assumed throughout this survey that the occupational disability arising from a mental disorder can be considered independently from having the disorder itself. Some readers may question this assumption, particularly in view of the revisions reflected in the Diagnostic and Statistical Manual of Mental Disorders, 4th edition (American Psychiatric Association, 1994), which increasingly emphasize the diagnostic criterion for several disorders of clinically significant impairment or distress. Three considerations suggest that the disability arising from mental disorders is not synonymous with the diagnosis. First, most studies which have examined mental disability have documented a wide variation in the degree of occupational disability among persons with a mental disorder, even after controlling for disorder severity. Second, the International Classification of Diseases (ICD), 10th edition (World Health Organization, 1992), has taken an approach to disability that explicitly differs with the DSM-IV: impairment and disability are not diagnostic criteria, but are included in the descriptions of the disorders. In clinical systems adhering to the ICD classifications, this implies that we should not expect a tight concordance between diagnosis and disability. Third, the assumption that disorder and disability are synonymous itself imposes a reductionism that is at odds with most conceptual frameworks for disability (World Health Organization, 2001)—frameworks which emphasize the importance of multiple levels of determinants extending well beyond clinical parameters.

The organization of this chapter is as follows. First, the strengths and weaknesses of the study designs used in the literature will be considered. In Section III, the recent epidemiology of depressive and anxiety disorders is briefly discussed. Section IV surveys the evidence supporting individual mental disorders, comorbid mental disorders, co-occurring physical disorders, and occupational, socioeconomic, and sociodemographic factors as predictors of mental occupational disability. Section V discusses the implications of the prediction literature for early detection and screening, and Section VI concludes.

LEVELS OF EVIDENCE

In examining the predictors of occupational disability related to depressive and anxiety disorders, we have relied on two types of evidence. Most of the studies surveyed below were cross-sectional, and based on large epidemiological or clinical samples. Cross-sectional studies typically compare disability measures in groups with and without various clinical, sociodemographic, occupational, and socioeconomic factors. Many of these studies attempt to isolate the predictive power of the factor of interest (e.g., a particular disorder) by controlling for the potential confounding factors such as age, gender, and comorbidity. However, some potential confounders will remain unknown or unmeasured. Cross-sectional studies in isolation cannot define the temporal relationship between the outcome and the predictor. For example, it not known whether socioeconomic status should be considered as a predictor of mental disability, as a consequence of disability, or as part of a bidirectional relationship.

Longitudinal studies involve repeated interviews and assessments with the same individuals over time. Longitudinal studies can examine the relationship between various factors and the evolution of disability in a manner that more clearly establishes temporal sequence. Still, longitudinal studies cannot fully control for confounding. Compared with cross-sectional data, the collection and analysis of longitudinal data are significantly more complex. Given the added effort and expense of collecting repeated measures, longitudinal studies are far less abundant than cross-sectional ones.

Another limitation of existing research is that disability measures are based predominantly on the self-report of the respondent. The self-report disability measures in the literature include subjective role impairment, absenteeism, lost productive time while at work ("presenteeism"), days spent in bed due to disability, cut-down days, short or long-term absence from work, and self-reports based upon standardized disability scales. These measures could be biased if persons with mental disorders provide overly pessimistic appraisals of their functioning. While there is some evidence to suggest that this bias may be significant (Coyne & Gotlib, 1983), the issue is far from settled.

EPIDEMIOLOGY

Recent population-based surveys in several developed countries have established that depressive and anxiety disorders are common and at least as prevalent as many chronic physical health conditions. The 1992 National Comorbidity Survey (NCS) in the United States found that 12-month prevalence of major depressive disorder in respondents aged 15–54 years was 10.3% (Standard error (SE): 0.6%). The 12-month prevalence of any anxiety disorder was 17.2% (SE: 0.7%) (Kessler et al., 1994). These prevalences and comparable figures from the earlier Epidemiological Catchment Area (ECA) study have been criticized for including a substantial proportion of false-postives—respondents classified as cases that were clinically insignificant (Regier et al., 1998; Narrow, Rae, Robins, & Regier, 2002).

In fact, the prevalences estimated in later surveys have been uniformly lower than those reported in the NCS. For example, the 2002 Canadian Community Health Survey cycle 1.2, a population—based survey of approximately 30,000 household residents, reported a 12-month prevalence of major depression of 4.5% (Statistics Canada, 2003). The range of 12-month prevalences for depressive and anxiety disorders reported in Canada (Statistics Canada, 2003), Australia (Andrews, Henderson, & Hall, 2001), the Netherlands (Bijl, Ravelli, & van Zessen, 1998), and six European countries (Alonso et al., 2004b) are as follows: major depressive disorder, 3.9–5.8%; dysthymic disorder, 1.1–2.3%; generalized anxiety disorder: 1.0–2.6%; panic disorder: 0.8–2.2%; agoraphobia (without panic), 0.4–1.6%; social phobia, 1.2–4.8%; simple phobia, 3.5–7.1%. The competing explanations for the wide variation in international prevalence estimates–variations in diagnostic instruments, differences in stigma and somatization, or genuine differences in prevalence—are still debated (Patten, 2003). Despite the controversy, few would dispute the important implications of the prevalence estimates for health service utilization. There is considerable evidence suggesting that the prevalence of mental disorders is significantly higher among patients in primary care (and other health settings) than in general populations (Katon et al., 1986; Ormel et al., 1994). Mental disabilities related to anxiety and depressive disorders are common clinical issues which are not confined to specialty mental health care settings.

PREDICTORS

Individual Mental Disorders

The most persuasive evidence that depressive and anxiety disorders contribute significantly to disability comes from several longitudinal clinical studies, which have consistently demonstrated that symptom severity and level of disability show synchronous change (Von Korff, Ormel, Katon, & Lin, 1992; Ormel et al., 1993; Judd et al., 2000): the presence of disability covaries with symptom severity. Most of these studies have focused on depressive disorders, but more limited evidence suggests that synchrony also exists for anxiety disorders (Ormel et al., 1993). While several studies relied upon self-report measures of disability, some included clinician ratings of disability and functioning. These studies are important because they help to clarify the meaning of the associations between mental disorders and disability found in the analyses of cross-sectional epidemiological data, and provide more confidence that mental disorders can legitimately be viewed as predictors of occupational disability.

Since 1990 virtually every population-based epidemiological survey of mental disorders has found strong associations between specific mood and anxiety disorders and various measures of disability, including self-reported work loss, work cut-back days, and role impairments. These studies are summarized in Table 1. The specific depressive and anxiety disorders associated with occupational disability include major depression, dysthymia, agoraphobia, panic disorder, social phobia, generalized anxiety disorder (GAD), and simple phobia (Kessler & Frank, 1997; Bijl & Ravelli, 2000; Lim, Sanderson, & Andrews, 2000; Kessler, Greenberg, Mickelson, Meneades, & Wang, 2001; Kessler et al., 2003a; Kessler, Ormel, Demler, & Stang, 2003b; Alonso et al., 2004a). While all of these disorders have at least one study supporting an association, the strongest associations with occupational disability are generally found with major depression and panic disorder.

Many of these studies made minimal attempts to control for contextual and other clinical factors. Notably, some of the earlier studies did not control for the disabling effects of co-occurring chronic physical health problems, implying that their results likely overestimate the extent of disability attributable to mental disorders. Several studies also failed to control for mental disorder comorbidity, and accordingly their results cannot be interpreted as the unique contribution of individual disorders to disability. From a methodological perspective, the two strongest studies represented in the Table are Bilj & Revelli (2000), and Alonso et al. (2004). These two studies found strong associations between disability and major depression, dysthymia, panic, simple phobia, and social phobia, weaker associations with agoraphobia, and contradictory evidence for GAD.

Epidemiological and clinical studies provide little evidence that subtypes of disorder have differential occupational disability consequences. The possible exception is atypical major depression, defined by those who meet criteria for the diagnosis of major depressive disorder that also features hypersomnia and hyperphagia. Based upon the U.S. National Comorbidity Survey data, Matza et al. (2000) reported that atypical major depression is associated with a higher burden disability days (Matza, Revicki, Davidson, & Stewart, 2003). While intriguing, it should be noted that the investigators did not control for the higher rates of comorbid psychiatric disorders

TABLE 1. Population-based Studies of Occupational Disability Related to Depressive and Anxiety Disorders (Based on Surveys Since 1990)

Survey (Country, year) sample size	Study N Age span	Work disability measure(s)	Disorders (strength of association[a])	Other factors controlled
OMHS[b] (Ontario, 1990) N = 9953	Goering et al. (1996) N = 8116 (15–64 yrs)	Main Activity Limitation	Affective Only (S) Anxiety Only (S)	None
	Dewa & Lin (2000) N = 4225 (18–54 yrs)	Work Loss Days, Work Cut-back Days	Affective Only (NA) Anxiety Only (S)	Occupational Grouping, 20 Physical Disorders
National Comorbidity Survey (USA, 1992) N = 8098	Kessler & Frank (1997) N = 4091 (15–54 yrs)	Work Loss Days, Work Cut-back Days	Major Depression (S) Dysthymia (NA) GAD (S) Panic Disorder (S) Simple Phobia (S) Social Phobia (S) Affective-Anxiety (S)	None
	Kessler et al. (2003) N = 5877[c] (15–54 yrs)	Work Loss Days	Major Depression (S) Dysthymia (S) Panic Disorder (S) Agoraphobia (S) Social phobia (S) Simple phobia (S) GAD (S)	Age, Sex, Education, Employment Status
NEMESIS[d] (Netherlands, 1996) N = 7147	Bilj & Ravelli (2000) N = 7076 (18–64 yrs)	Disability Days, Days Ill in Bed	Major Depression (S) Dysthymia (S) Panic Disorder (S) Agoraphobia (M) Social Phobia (M) Simple Phobia (M) GAD (S) OCD (M)	Age, Gender, Education, Income, Urbanicity, Any Physical Disorder
MIDUS[e] (USA, 1997) N = 3,032	Kessler et al. (2001) N = 2,074 (25–54 yrs)	Work Impairment Days	Mood Disorder (S) Panic Disorder (S) GAD (M)	Age, Gender, Education, 8 Physical Disorders
National Survey of Mental Health and Well-Being, (Australia, 1997) N = 10,641	Lim et al. (2000) N = 4,579 (18+ yrs)	Work Loss Days, Work Impairment Days	Major Depression (S) Dysthymia (NA) Panic Disorder (NA) Agoraphobia (NA) Social Phobia (NA) GAD (S) Affective-Anxiety (S)	Impairment Days Attributed to Physical Disorders
NCS-R[f] (USA, 2002) N = 9,090	Kessler et al. (2004) N = 5,564 (18+ yrs)	WHO-DAS[g], Sheehan Disability Scale	Major Depression (S)	None

TABLE 1. *(cont.)*

Survey (Country, year) sample size	Study N Age span	Work disability measure(s)	Disorders (strength of association[a])	Other factors controlled
ESEMeD[h] (Spain, France, Germany, Italy Netherlands, Belgium, 2003) N = 21,425	Alonso et al. (2004) N = 5489 (18+ yrs)	Work Loss Days (WHO-DAS II[i])	Major Depression (S) Dysthymia (S) Agoraphobia (NA) Social Phobia (S) GAD (NA) Specific Phobia (S) Panic Disorder (S)	Age, Sex, 5 Physical Disorders

[a]Bracketed abbreviations: NA: no association; S: strong association; M: moderate association.
[b]Ontario Mental Health Supplement
[c]Respondents had one of four chronic physical disorders
[d]Netherlands Mental Health Survey and Incidence Study
[e]Midlife Development in the United States Survey
[f]National Comorbidity Survey Replication
[g]World Health Organization Disablement Assessment Scale
[h]WHO Disablement Scale version 2

found in respondents with atypical major depression. Higher comorbidity rates, as discussed in the following section, could explain the increase in disability reported.

While the results of clinical studies (longitudinal and cross-sectional) are consistent with the epidemiological results, they additionally provide some preliminary evidence that different disorders exert unique patterns of disabling effects. The study illustrating this most clearly is Spitzer et al. (1995), who in a cross-sectional study of 1000 primary care clinic patients found that mood disorders exerted impairment across several domains of functioning, including social and role functioning, while anxiety disorders exerted stronger social impairment (Spitzer et al., 1995). Ormel et al. in the WHO Collaborative Study on Psychological Problems in General Health Care found that agoraphobia and somatization disorder did not exert a unique effect on occupational role dysfunction, once controls for psychiatric comorbidity were made (Ormel et al., 1994).

Comorbid Mental Disorders

Clinical and epidemiological studies have repeatedly demonstrated that persons with one mental disorder have high rates of additional comorbid mental disorders. Some critics have argued that psychiatric comorbidity is an artifact of the classification systems, which have focused almost exclusively on the phenomenology of mental conditions at the expense of theoretical foundations.

Comorbidity rates have been high internationally: 54% in the ECA Study; 56% in the National Comorbidity Survey; 45% in the Netherlands Mental Health Survey and Incidence Study; and 40% in the Australian National Survey of Mental Health and Well-Being. A robust finding accross several surveys is that persons with comorbid psychiatric conditions are at significantly greater risk for occupational disability. Kessler and Frank (1997) found that the highest work disability days were reported by individuals with concurrent anxiety, affective and substance use disorders. Comorbid anxiety and affective disorders represented the next most disabling combination. In a replication of the NCS in Ontario, Canada, Goering (1996) reported that individuals with comorbid mental disorders were more disabled than those with single disorder categories, with half of the comorbid group having anxiety and affective disorders. Bilj et al. (2000) found in descriptive analyses that respondents with comorbid psychiatric diagnoses reported dramatic elevations in the numbers of disability days, and days ill in bed. Andrews et al. (2002) provide evidence of a linear trend suggesting that the degree of occupational disability increases with the number of comorbid psychiatric conditions. Self-reported disability measured by work-loss days increased significantly with the number of mental disorders in the ESEMeD survey of six European nations. The findings from population-based samples have generally been replicated in clinical samples (Olfson et al., 1997).

Although the mechanisms behind the strong association between comorbidity and disability are unknown, the conclusion for the purposes of prediction is clear: individuals with comorbid mental disorders have a dramatically elevated risk of occupational disability. The implications of psychiatric comorbidity for early detection and research are considered respectively in Sections V and VI.

Co-occurring Physical Disorders

In both clinical and epidemiological samples, mental disorders have been found to co-occur with chronic physical disorders at rates far greater than what is predicted by chance. Depressive disorders have been associated with asthma, low back problems, gastrointestinal disorders, vascular disorders, brain injury, migraine headaches, cancer, sinusitis, and chronic emphysema/bronchitis (Wells, Golding, & Burnam, 1988; Patten, 1999; Patten, 2001) but in epidemiological samples no consistent association with diabetes or arthritis has been found. Major depression has been variably associated with hypertension (Wells et al., 1988; Patten, 1999). Anxiety disorders have been associated with arthritis, heart disease, hypertension, diabetes, and gastrointestinal conditions (Patten, 2001).

The mechanisms leading to these associations are generally unclear, but are likely to vary by specific physical disorder. Longitudinal studies defining the temporal evolution of these co-occurrences are clearly needed (Patten, 1999). Irrespective of the underlying mechanisms, the available evidence suggests that co-occurring physical and mental disorders have serious disability implications. The Medical Outcomes Study, a longitudinal study of health plan enrollees in the United States, found that mental disorders (predominantly mood and anxiety disorders) were at least as disabling as chronic medical conditions, and that patients with a co-occurring physical and mental disorder had significant increments in their disability (Wells et al., 1989). In an important study focused primarily on occupational disability, Kessler (2003) found that working NCS respondents with hypertension, arthritis, asthma, and ulcers reported increases in role impairment days compared to healthy respondents (Kessler et al., 2003b). The surprising result was that most of the increases were attributable to those respondents who had a co-existing mental disorder. Kessler's findings arose from population-based data, and have important implications for lost productivity and screening. The analysis was confined to the four most common chronic physical disorders in the survey (asthma, hypertension, ulcers, and arthritis), and an important goal for future research is to conduct similar analyses among workers for other (less prevalent) chronic health conditions.

Occupation

Clinical guidelines for evaluating psychiatric disability emphasize the importance of adjudicating impairment in the context of the patient's occupation and job requirements. Unfortunately, quantitative research has to date made limited contributions to defining the significance of occupation to mental disability.

There is some evidence that mental disorders are more prevalent in certain occupational clusters. Kessler and Frank (1997) found that workers in professional, managerial-administrative, and crafts occupations reported the lowest prevalence of psychiatric disorder, while clerical and sales workers, labourers, operatives and kindred workers had the highest (Kessler et al., 1997). Similar results were reported by Dewa and Lin (Dewa & Lin, 2000). As both studies analyzed cross-sectional data, the interpretation of occupational clustering is unclear. Occupation could influence the development of mental disorders are possible, but persons vulnerable to develop mental disorders could also plausibly select certain occupations.

Only two studies have examined whether the effects of mental disorders on disability (measured by work days lost) are similar across all occupations. Kessler and Frank (1997) found no differences between work loss days attributed to mental disorders, while effects on work cutback were greater among professional workers, certain clerical and sales workers, and janitors than those in other occupations (Kessler et al., 1997). Due to the large number of occupational clusters, Kessler and Frank's analysis may have lacked the requisite statistical power to detect real but modest differences in occupational disability. Lim et al. (Lim et al., 2000) did not detect any differences in work loss or work cutback days by occupational status, based upon a classification of five occupational categories (managers, professionals, tradespersons, clerical, and laborers). Lim suggested that a given disorder type is associated with similar levels of impairment, regardless of occupational status. However, this conclusion seems premature: in addition to limitations in statistical power, the occupational clusters employed in these studies may not represent the most meaningful classifications for the purposes of defining risk factors and predictors of disability. Research in this area lacks a conceptual framework to more systematically define occupational groupings.

Work Environment and Organization

In the broad literature that relates the organizational and psychosocial aspects of work to health, there is almost no research that directly addresses mental disability. Most of the extant literature relates psychosocial aspects of work to mental disorders through the well-known job strain model of Karasek and Theorell (Karasek & Theorell, 1990). According to the model, job strain occurs in jobs characterized by the combination of high psychological workload and low decision latitude.

Job strain has been identified by studies in several countries (Kauppinen-Toropainen & Hanninen, 1981; Braun & Hollander, 1988; Statistics Canada, 2003) as a risk factor for the development of mental disorders (relative risk of 1.5 or greater), but none of these studies focused on mental disability. Job strain predicted short-term sickness absence due to mental disorder in the longitudinal Whitehall II study of English civil servants (Fletcher, 1988; Stansfeld, Rael, Head, Shipley, & Marmot, 1997) aged 35–55 years, and high work social support and high skill discretion were protective against short spells of sickness absence. The implications of these findings for mental disability are unclear. Sickness absence is generally conceptualized as a complex phenomenon determined by numerous factors beyond disability. Moreover, many workers with mental disorders remain on the job despite experiencing disability, suggesting that sickness absence may be a biased and incomplete proxy for occupational disability.

Subjective experiences of workplace stress have been associated with low work satisfaction and high rates of minor psychological symptoms, but no studies have convincingly associated this with worker disability (Fletcher, 1988). The only published study that specifically relates the psychosocial aspects of work to mental disability was the longitudinal 6-year study of 15,348 Finnish employees (Appelberg, Romanov, Heikkila, Honkasalo, & Koskenvuo, 1996), who focused on the disability effects of interpersonal conflict at work and home. The investigators found that interpersonal conflict at work predicted mental disability, but only among women who simultaneously reported marital conflict (relative risk: 2.54). However, mental disability was measured only by the rates of long-term disability pension grants, a measure that is insensitive to less severe and persistent disability states.

Socioeconomic Status

Although we know that socioeconomic status and social position are important correlates of general health and longevity, there is a paucity of evidence relating socioeconomic status to mental disability. The Whitehall II study established that employment grade represents a significant risk factor for psychiatric disorder and sickness absence (Stansfeld, North, White, & Marmot, 1995; Stansfeld et al., 1997). However, as argued previously, that neither mental disorder nor sickness absences are appropriate proxy measures for disability. The only study that examines socioeconomic status and social position as independent risk factors for psychiatric disability is Melzer et al. (Melzer, Fryers, Jenkins, Brugha, & McWilliams, 2003), who performed an analysis of the cross-sectional data from the 1993 household survey of psychiatric morbidity in Great Britain. The investigators found that being a lone parent, having a severe lack of social support, and lower education were all associated with an elevated risk of psychiatric disability. Occupational social class was not an independent risk factor for psychiatric disablement. These findings clearly require additional corroboration based upon data from other countries.

Sociodemographic Factors

Marital status and urbanicity have been examined through multivariate analyses in only one cross-sectional study, which found no significant association with occupational disability (Bijl et al., 2000). The relationship between age and mental disability has not been systematically evaluated in the current literature. In multivariate analyses of cross-sectional data, one study reported lower rates of disability in the age range 25–34 years (Kessler et al., 2001), while another found the opposite effect among respondents in the same age group (Alonso et al., 2004a). In the absence of more hypothesis-driven research specifically considering age trends and effects, it is difficult to interpret these results.

Few published studies of mental disability have examined whether the impact of mental disorders on disability is modified or predicted by gender. Nonetheless, there are compelling reasons to suspect that gender may play an important role in the light of well-known sex differences in disorder prevalence and help-seeking (Piccinelli & Wilkinson, 2000). In a study of British civil servants aged 20–35 years, Jenkins (1985) found a larger effect of minor psychiatric morbidity on sickness absence in men than in women (Jenkins, 1985). Using longitudinal data from 3695 employed respondents to the first two waves of the NEMESIS survey described above, major depressive disorder, dysthymia, and simple phobia were predictive of subsequent sickness absence in men, but for women none of the DSM-IIIR anxiety or mood disorders was related to subsequent sickness absence (Laitinen-Krispijn & Bijl, 2000). Sandanger and Nygard (2000), by contrast, found in a small random sample of Norwegians that women who had a psychiatric disorder were 1.7 times more likely than men to have a sickness absence (Sandanger, Nygard, Brage, & Tellnes, 2000). However, the results from the cross-sectional European Study of the Epidemiology of Mental Disorders (ESEMeD) project, which more directly measured disability, suggest that gender exerted no independent effect on work disability measured by work-loss days, after controlling for age, psychiatric disorder, and several chronic physical health problems (Alonso et al., 2004a). Thus, the existing literature offers a contradictory perspective: there is little direct evidence to support gender effects, yet the gender differences in sickness absence could plausibly be related to gender differences in disability.

IMPLICATIONS FOR SCREENING AND EARLY DETECTION

For clinicians, the implications of this survey are threefold. First, the existing corpus of relevant research consistently indicates that several mood and anxiety disorders are predictors of mental disability. Second, the co-existence of mental disorders is common, and indicates an elevated risk of occupational disability. Third, the presence of severe or unusual occupational disability in a patient with a chronic physical disorder should prompt a careful search for co-existing mental disorders.

For broader population screening, the survey suggests that screening instruments should focus primarily on diagnostic screening that is broad enough to include most mood and anxiety disorders, as well as screening questions to detect chronic physical conditions. The implications for the targeting of screening are more tentative and limited, reflecting the paucity of our knowledge concerning contextual predictors. Workers at elevated risk for mood and anxiety disorders could be targeted for screening, but practical barriers as well as confidentiality and fairness concerns may deter employers from adopting this approach. Nonetheless, general employee screening and chronic disease management may have a role in human resource management, particularly if clinical and cost-effectiveness studies indicate that such interventions reduce human suffering, and enhance productivity (Pignone et al., 2002). Diagnostic screening for mental disorders could also be considered for persons with chronic physical disorders, although the same issues related to practicality, fairness and confidentiality apply. Injured workers treated through compensation systems are perhaps the most feasible population in which broad mental disorder screening could be implemented.

CONCLUSIONS

The most obvious conclusion to be drawn from this survey is that our knowledge of the contextual factors contributing to mental disability is minimal, but that our knowledge of clinical factors is only modestly better. One of the challenges to reduce the global burden of mental disability will be to create and fund an adequate research agenda that focuses on mental disability and disability management in a manner that is independent from traditional health provision research. Given the need to understand temporal sequence, the most important research design to advance mental disability research will be prospective longitudinal cohort studies. The survey also suggests that measuring and analyzing psychiatric comorbidity and physical-mental comorbidity will be essential elements of studies which focus on contextual factors, given their importance as predictors and determinants.

Longitudinal studies are expensive and time-consuming to complete, but researchers can take some comfort in the fact that numerous questions relevant to mental disability could begin to be addressed by analyses of existing data sources. The deficits in our knowledge may be daunting, but it should be recalled that they appeared even more daunting 15 years ago, and yet some progress has been achieved.

REFERENCES

Alonso, J., Angermeyer, M. C., Bernert, S., Bruffaerts, R., Brugha, T. S., Bryson, H. et al. (2004a). Disability and quality of life impact of mental disorders in Europe: results from the European Study of the Epidemiology of Mental Disorders (ESEMeD) project. *Acta Psychiatr Scand Suppl*, 38–46.

Alonso, J., Angermeyer, M. C., Bernert, S., Bruffaerts, R., Brugha, T. S., Bryson, H. et al. (2004b). Prevalence of mental disorders in Europe: results from the European Study of the Epidemiology of Mental Disorders (ESEMeD) project. *Acta Psychiatr Scand Suppl*, 21–27.

American Psychiatric Association (1994). *Diagnostic and Statistical Manual of Mental Disorders, 4th Edition*. Washington, DC: American Psychiatric Association.

Andrews, G., Henderson, S., & Hall, W. (2001). Prevalence, comorbidity, disability and service utilisation. Overview of the Australian National Mental Health Survey. [see comment][erratum appears in Br J Psychiatry 2001 Dec;179:561–2]. *British Journal of Psychiatry, 178*, 145–153.

Appelberg, K., Romanov, K., Heikkila, K., Honkasalo, M. L., & Koskenvuo, M. (1996). Interpersonal conflict as a predictor of work disability: a follow-up study of 15,348 Finnish employees. *J Psychosom Res, 40*, 157–167.

Bijl, R. V. & Ravelli, A. (2000). Current and residual functional disability associated with psychopathology: findings from the Netherlands Mental Health Survey and Incidence Study (NEMESIS). *Psychological Medicine, 30*, 657–668.

Bijl, R. V., Ravelli, A., & van Zessen, G. (1998). Prevalence of psychiatric disorder in the general population: results of The Netherlands Mental Health Survey and Incidence Study (NEMESIS). *Soc Psychiatry Psychiatr Epidemiol, 33*, 587–595.

Braun, S. & Hollander, R. B. (1988). Work and depression among women in the Federal Republic of Germany. *Women Health, 14*, 3–26.

Coyne, J. C. & Gotlib, I. H. (1983). The role of cognition in depression: a critical appraisal. *Psychol Bull, 94*, 472–505.

Dewa, C. S. & Lin, E. (2000). Chronic physical illness, psychiatric disorder and disability in the workplace. *Social Science & Medicine, 51*, 41–50.

Fletcher, B. (1988). The Epidemiology of Occupational Stress. In C.L.Cooper & R. Payne (Eds.), *Causes, Coping and Consequences of Stress at Work*, Toronto and New York: Wiley.

Gilbody, S., Whitty, P., Grimshaw, J., & Thomas, R. (2003). Educational and organizational interventions to improve the management of depression in primary care: a systematic review. *JAMA, 289*, 3145–3151.

Gnam, W. H. (2004). Researcher Response: Disability Management, Return to Work and Treatment. In Toronto: Canadian Institutes for Health Research.

Goldner, E., Bilsker, D., Gilbert, J., Myette, L., Corbiere, M., & Dewa, C. S. (2004). Discussion paper: Disability Management, Return to Work and Treatment. In Toronto: Canadian Institutes for Health Research.

India, No. 1. o. 1. (1996). The Persons with Disabilities (Equal Opportunites, Protection of Rights and Full Participation) Act, 1995.

Jenkins, R. (1985). Minor psychiatric morbidity in employed young men and women and its contribution to sickness absence. *Br J Ind Med, 42,* 147–154.

Judd, L. L., Akiskal, H. S., Zeller, P. J., Paulus, M., Leon, A. C., Maser, J. D. et al. (2000). Psychosocial disability during the long-term course of unipolar major depressive disorder. *Arch Gen Psychiatry, 57,* 375–380.

Karasek, R. & Theorell, T. (1990). *Healthy Work: Stress, Productivity, and the Reconstruction of Working Life.* New York: Basic Books.

Katon, W., Vitaliano, P. P., Russo, J., Cormier, L., Anderson, K., & Jones, M. (1986). Panic disorder: epidemiology in primary care. *J Fam Pract, 23,* 233–239.

Kauppinen-Toropainen, K. & Hanninen, V. (1981). *Job demands and job content: effects on job dissatisfaction and stress* Helsinki: Department of Psychology, Institute of Occupational Health.

Kennedy, C. (2003). Functioning and disability associated with mental disorders: the evolution since ICIDH. *Disability & Rehabilitation, 25,* 611–619.

Kessler, R. C., Berglund, P., Demler, O., Jin, R., Koretz, D., Merikangas, K. R. et al. (2003a). The epidemiology of major depressive disorder: results from the National Comorbidity Survey Replication (NCS-R). *JAMA, 289,* 3095–3105.

Kessler, R. C., Foster, C. L., Saunders, W. B., & Stang, P. E. (1995). Social consequences of psychiatric disorders, I: Educational attainment. *Am J Psychiatry, 152,* 1026–1032.

Kessler, R. C. & Frank, R. G. (1997). The impact of psychiatric disorders on work loss days. *Psychological Medicine, 27,* 861–873.

Kessler, R. C., Greenberg, P. E., Mickelson, K. D., Meneades, L. M., & Wang, P. S. (2001). The effects of chronic medical conditions on work loss and work cutback. *J Occup Environ Med, 43,* 218–225.

Kessler, R. C., McGonagle, K. A., Zhao, S., Nelson, C. B., Hughes, M., Eshleman, S. et al. (1994). Lifetime and 12-month prevalence of DSM-III-R psychiatric disorders in the United States. Results from the National Comorbidity Survey. *Arch Gen Psychiatry, 51,* 8–19.

Kessler, R. C., Ormel, J., Demler, O., & Stang, P. E. (2003b). Comorbid mental disorders account for the role impairment of commonly occurring chronic physical disorders: results from the National Comorbidity Survey. *Journal of Occupational & Environmental Medicine, 45,* 1257–1266.

Laitinen-Krispijn, S. & Bijl, R. V. (2000). Mental disorders and employee sickness absence: the NEMESIS study. Netherlands Mental Health Survey and Incidence Study. *Social Psychiatry & Psychiatric Epidemiology, 35,* 71–77.

Lim, D., Sanderson, K., & Andrews, G. (2000). Lost productivity among full-time workers with mental disorders. *J Ment Health Policy Econ, 3,* 139–146.

Matza, L. S., Revicki, D. A., Davidson, J. R., & Stewart, J. W. (2003). Depression with atypical features in the National Comorbidity Survey: classification, description, and consequences. *Archives of General Psychiatry, 60,* 817–826.

Melzer, D., Fryers, T., Jenkins, R., Brugha, T., & McWilliams, B. (2003). Social position and the common mental disorders with disability: estimates from the National Psychiatric Survey of Great Britain. *Social Psychiatry & Psychiatric Epidemiology, 38,* 238–243.

Murray, C. J. & Lopez, A. D. (1996). *The Global Burden of Disease: A Comprehensive Assessment of Mortality and Disability from Diseases, Injuries, and Risk Factors in 1990 and Projected to 2020.* Cambridge, MA.: Harvard University Press.

Murray, C. J., Lopez, A. D., & Jamison, D. T. (1994). The global burden of disease in 1990: summary results, sensitivity analysis and future directions. *Bull World Health Organ, 72,* 495–509.

Narrow, W. E., Rae, D. S., Robins, L. N., & Regier, D. A. (2002). Revised prevalence estimates of mental disorders in the United States: using a clinical significance criterion to reconcile 2 surveys' estimates. *Arch Gen Psychiatry, 59,* 115–123.

Olfson, M., Fireman, B., Weissman, M. M., Leon, A. C., Sheehan, D. V., Kathol, R. G. et al. (1997). Mental disorders and disability among patients in a primary care group practice. [see comment]. *American Journal of Psychiatry, 154,* 1734–1740.

Ormel, J., Von Korff, M., van den, B. W., Katon, W., Brilman, E., & Oldehinkel, T. (1993). Depression, anxiety, and social disability show synchrony of change in primary care patients. *Am J Public Health, 83,* 385–390.

Ormel, J., VonKorff, M., Ustun, T. B., Pini, S., Korten, A., & Oldehinkel, T. (1994). Common mental disorders and disability across cultures. Results from the WHO Collaborative Study on Psychological Problems in General Health Care. *JAMA, 272,* 1741–1748.

Patten, S. B. (1999). Long-term medical conditions and major depression in the Canadian population. *Can J Psychiatry, 44,* 151–157.

Patten, S. B. (2001). Long-term medical conditions and major depression in a Canadian population study at waves 1 and 2. *J Affect Disord , 63,* 35–41.

Patten, S. B. (2003). International differences in major depression prevalence: what do they mean? *J Clin Epidemiol, 56,* 711–716.

Piccinelli, M. & Wilkinson, G. (2000). Gender differences in depression. Critical review. *Br J Psychiatry, 177,* 486–492.

Pignone, M. P., Gaynes, B. N., Rushton, J. L., Burchell, C. M., Orleans, C. T., Mulrow, C. D. et al. (2002). Screening for depression in adults: a summary of the evidence for the U.S. Preventive Services Task Force. *Ann Intern Med, 136,* 765–776.

Regier, D. A., Kaelber, C. T., Rae, D. S., Farmer, M. E., Knauper, B., Kessler, R. C. et al. (1998). Limitations of diagnostic criteria and assessment instruments for mental disorders. Implications for research and policy. *Arch Gen Psychiatry, 55,* 109–115.

Rice, D. P., Hodgson, T. A., & Kopstein, A. N. (1985). The economic costs of illness: a replication and update. *Health Care Financ Rev, 7,* 61–80.

Rice, D. P., Kelman, S., & Miller, L. S. (1992). The economic burden of mental illness. *Hosp Community Psychiatry, 43,* 1227–1232.

Robins, L. N. & Regier, D. A. (1991). *Psychiatric Disorders in America: The Epidemiologic Catchment Area Study.* New York: Free Press.

Sandanger, I., Nygard, J. F., Brage, S., & Tellnes, G. (2000). Relation between health problems and sickness absence: gender and age differences—a comparison of low-back pain, psychiatric disorders, and injuries. *Scandinavian Journal of Public Health, 28,* 244–252.

Spitzer, R. L., Kroenke, K., Linzer, M., Hahn, S. R., Williams, J. B., deGruy, F. V., III et al. (1995). Health-related quality of life in primary care patients with mental disorders. Results from the PRIME-MD 1000 Study. *JAMA, 274,* 1511–1517.

Stansfeld, S. A., North, F. M., White, I., & Marmot, M. G. (1995). Work characteristics and psychiatric disorder in civil servants in London. *J Epidemiol Community Health, 49,* 48–53.

Stansfeld, S. A., Rael, E. G., Head, J., Shipley, M., & Marmot, M. (1997). Social support and psychiatric sickness absence: a prospective study of British civil servants. *Psychological Medicine, 27,* 35–48.

Statistics Canada (2003). *CCHS—Mental health and well-being* (Rep. No. Catalogue no. 82–617-XIE).

U.S.Public Law 101–336. (1990). Americans with Disability Act of 1990.

Ustun, T. B., Rehm, J., Chatterji, S., Saxena, S., Trotter, R., Room, R. et al. (1999). Multiple-informant ranking of the disabling effects of different health conditions in 14 countries. WHO/NIH Joint Project CAR Study Group. *Lancet, 354,* 111–115.

Von Korff, M., Ormel, J., Katon, W., & Lin, E. H. (1992). Disability and depression among high utilizers of health care. A longitudinal analysis. *Arch Gen Psychiatry, 49,* 91–100.

Wells, K. B., Golding, J. M., & Burnam, M. A. (1988). Psychiatric disorder in a sample of the general population with and without chronic medical conditions. *Am J Psychiatry, 145,* 976–981.

Wells, K. B., Stewart, A., Hays, R. D., Burnam, M. A., Rogers, W., Daniels, M. et al. (1989). The functioning and well-being of depressed patients. Results from the Medical Outcomes Study. *JAMA, 262,* 914–919.

World Health Organization (1992). *International Statistical Classification of Diseases and Related Problems, 10th edition.* Geneva: World Health Organization.

World Health Organization (2001). *International Classification of Functioning, Disability, and Health.* Geneva: World Health Organization.

III

APPLICATION OF DISABILITY PREDICTION IN COMPENSATION, HEALTH CARE, AND OCCUPATIONAL CONTEXTS

21

Secondary Prevention in Health-Care and Occupational Settings in Musculoskeletal Conditions Focusing on Low Back Pain

Chris J. Main, Ceri J. Phillips, and Paul J. Watson

INTRODUCTION

It has been estimated that there is an annual population prevalence of back pain of 16,500,000; with 4,000,000 consulting their GeneralPractitioner (GP), and 1,600,000 attending hospital out-patient departments. Health-care consulting is only part of the total costs involved. This is illustrated in Table 1. A major element of this burden results from the indirect costs associated with lost productivity. Within the UK, musculoskeletal problems account for over 22% of claimants on incapacity benefit, but the problem is accentuated due to the fact that while many go on to this register very few leave—3,000 people go on to the incapacity benefit scheme every week but only 300 ever return to work. It is known that in the UK the total cost of back pain amounts to over £12 billion—equivalent to 22% of UK healthcare expenditure; 2.5 million people have back pain every day of the year; that nearly 119 million working days are lost each year due to back problems; that 12.5% of unemployed people give back pain as the reason for not working; that 80% of people with back pain on incapacity benefit at 6 months are likely to be on benefit at 5 years; and, that chronic pain accounts for 4.6 million GP consultations—equivalent to 793 GPs. The social costs include incapacity benefits for those unable to work, payments associated with injuries, benefits paid to those who cannot access work because of a history of back pain and additional payments which may accrue as a result of entitlement to these benefits.

The economic burden of musculoskeletal conditions represents up to 2.5% of the GNP of western countries. The move from tertiary rehabilitation towards secondary prevention, in both health-care and occupational settings offers a tremendous opportunity to integrate the latest understanding about the prevention of chronicity

DOI: 10.1007/978-0-387-28919-9_21, © 2009 Springer Science+Business Media, LLC

TABLE 1. Estimated Costs of Back pain in the U.K. in 1998

Total National Health Services (NHS) costs	£845, million
Private health-care costs	£310, million
Social security benefits	£3,600, million
Sickness absence	£1,350–3500, million
Total	£6–8.2 billion

Source: Adapted from Waddell (2004) p. 413, Table 19.4.

into a systems approach focusing on obstacles to recovery. In this chapter we should like to address some recent initiatives in the U.K. which have attempted to address the problem.

MODELS OF PAIN, ILLNESS, AND DISABILITY

A complex chain of events links perception of part of the body as painful and the development of chronic disability. Although the process is multi-factorial and not fully understood, a number of key processes seem to be involved. Physical therapy is based on a biomedical understanding of incapacity. The patient's report of pain leads to a pain-focused clinical history with a clinical examination. It has long been considered that chronic pain can only be understood within a biopsychosocial framework, but it is now clear that psychological factors are important at an early stage.

Pain is a symptom, not a sign, and therefore is multiply determined. In specific instances there may be a clear and specific indication for manipulation but the dysfunction needs to be understood within a wider model such as the biopsychosocial model of pain and disability (Waddell 2004). At the heart of the biospychosocial model is the assumption of an on-going sensation that is nociceptive in nature or which is perceived by the sufferer as being painful. The patients' cognitions (i.e., what they think and understand about this sensation) will influence their emotional reaction to it. The behaviour demonstrated by the individual at any point in time will be a product of their beliefs and the emotional response to the pain and may in turn be influenced (reinforced or modulated) by the social environment in which the behaviour takes place. The model offers a radically different way of understanding the nature of pain-associated incapacity.

THE EMERGENCE OF SECONDARY PREVENTION

It would seem that further success in primary prevention, whether in terms of education about lifting and posture, or in terms of ergonomic redesign of the physical demands of work, is unlikely. Such initiatives may have decreased the likelihood specifically of workplace accidents, but they seem to have been unsuccessful in stemming the rise in back-associated disability. A clear focus on the psychological concomitants of pain and disability does appear however to have had some success with chronic pain patients (Morley, Eccleston & Williams, 1999). The logic of trying to prevent some of the "recoverable" disability seems irresistible. As Linton and van Tulder (2000) have pointed out, there are some ambiguities in the term "secondary prevention", but it generally refers to prevention of chronic incapacity in patients who are not yet chronically incapacitated. There is also epidemiological and economic support for such an endeavour. Since back pain is both common and recurrent, prevention of *disabling* back pain would appear to be a much more realistic target in primary prevention.

The identification of rapidly increasing costs of pain-associated disability has stimulated redirection of the primary focus of clinical activity from treatment to prevention. It has been shown that costs of subsequent episodes of low back pain are more costly than new episodes, and that the burden of work-associated sickness costs is a consequence of chronic sufferers (Watson et al., 1998). Early intervention, however, requires a system for identification of those potentially at risk of chronicity. The term "risk" is, though, used in a number of different ways, and so before consideration of possible targets for prevention, a degree of conceptual clarification is necessary.

RISKS, FLAGS, AND OBSTACLES TO RECOVERY

From Risks to Obstacles

Concepts of risk have usually been based on identification of factors associated with poor outcome, but there are different types of predictors of outcome, and not all are potential targets for intervention. *Epidemiological* studies are primarily descriptive, rather than explanatory and are population based. Statistically significant associations may serve as a foundation for major clinical initiatives (such as immunization) or social policy decisions involving the re-direction of resources, but such risk factors are usually not sufficiently powerful to be useful for decision making on an individual basis. The *Clinical* perspective on risk tends to focus primarily on factors associated with healthcare outcome. Although clinical studies are more narrowly focused than epidemiological investigations, and therefore provide a better basis for clinical intervention, the incorporation of demographic and educational factors (for example) may be helpful in targeting certain groups but they may not provide particular therapeutic targets or assist in the design of the preventative intervention. *Occupational* risk factors which tend to be wide-ranging may be very different from clinical risk factors but may equally be of little help in the targeting or design of preventative interventions. It may be helpful to base prevention not solely on risk as such, but to focus attention on *obstacles to recovery.*

The Concept of "Red Flags"

In the field of back pain, the concept of risk has been examined in terms of "flags". Waddell (1998) as part of an assessment strategy for patients presenting with back pain, recommends an initial diagnostic triage into simple back pain, nerve root pain or serious spinal pathology. The signs and symptoms considered indicative of possible spinal pathology or of the need for an urgent surgical evaluation became known as "Red flags". These "risk factors" for serious pathology or disease became incorporated into screening tools recommended for use in primary care by clinicians to identify those patients in whom an urgent specialist opinion was indicated.

Assessment of these risk factors were included within several new sets of clinical guidelines for the management of acute low back pain (CSAG, 1994; ACHPR, 1994).

Yellow Flags

The increasing costs of chronic incapacity, despite advances in technological medicine, stimulated the search for other solutions to the problem of low back disability. In New Zealand, increasing costs of chronic non-specific low back pain became an unmanageable burden. This fuelled a new initiative designed to complement a slightly modified set of acute back pain management guidelines with a psychosocial assessment system designed systematically to address the psychosocial risk factors which had been shown in the scientific literature to be predictive of chronicity (Kendall et al., 1997). The stated purpose of assessment of Yellow flags was to:

- Provide a method for screening for psychosocial factors
- Provide a systematic approach to the assessment of psychosocial factors
- Suggest better strategies for better management for those with back pain who appear at a higher risk of chronicity.

They included a specific focus on a number of key psychological factors:

- Belief that back pain is harmful or severely disabling
- Fear-avoidance behaviour patterns with reduced activity levels
- Tendency to low mood and withdrawal from social interaction
- Expectation that passive treatments rather than active participation will help.

The above factors were integrated into an assessment system, which included a screening questionnaire, interview guidelines and recommendations for early behavioural management in individuals with low back pain. It can be seen that there are clear *preventative* components within the management guidelines.It is important to note also that the Yellow flags were developed not only from a clinical perspective but also from an occupational perspective, and consisted of both psychological and socio-occupational risk factors.

More recently, a structured interview approach, the Initial Assessment Questionnaire (IAQ), has been developed using a "stem-and-leaf" approach based on the original Yellow Flags (Main & Watson (2003). It has been used as the basis for training staff in the elicitation and management of health-related and work-related concerns (i.e., Yellow and Blue Flags). Each of the seven sections consists of a stem question, a rationale for asking the question, a series of supplementary questions (should a problem have been identified) and intervention guidelines.

An example of one of the sections is shown in Table 2.

A Cautionary Note: Distinguishing Yellow from Orange Flags

Yellow flags should be thought of as aspects of *normal* psychological processes, but they have sometimes been confused with psychiatric disorder, such as major mental illness or major personality disorder, including illicit drug use and ongoing forensic involvement. Such factors have been termed *Orange Flags* and have been defined only in so far as they might be mistaken for Yellow Flags. The major orange flags are shown in Table 3. Orange flags can be thought of as the psychiatric equivalent of

TABLE 2. Example of Stem Question, with Rationale, and Supplementary Questions (Main & Watson, 2003)

Stem Question

If someone has had pain for a period of time, they usually have their own ideas of the cause. I know you're not a doctor, but what do YOU think is the cause?

Rationale

The patients' ideas about the onset and ongoing cause of their pain will influence the credence they give to the physiotherapist's interpretation. If patients remain convinced that they have one thing (e.g., "a slipped disc"), and the physiotherapist tells them another (e.g., a soft tissue strain), there will be a lack of concordance about the usefulness of the treatment. This question also attempts to explore patients' worries that they have not been fully investigated. Issues about not having had an X-ray, scan, or consultant opinion may come up in this section. The aim is to get the patient to air these fears and for the physiotherapist to allay them once the "depth" of the belief is ascertained.

Supplementary Questions

- Do you believe that the pain itself is harming or disabling you?
- Do you believe that you are going to have to get rid of ALL pain before you get back to work?
- Do you think that increasing activity or getting back to work is going to make your pain WORSE?
- Do you find yourself worrying in case your pain becomes progressively worse?
- Do you find yourself becoming generally more aware or concerned about symptoms in your body?
- Do you believe it is possible to control pain?
- Do you believe you can do much yourself or it is just a matter of the passage of time or the help that others can give you?

Intervention

If there are unhelpful beliefs about back pain, these must be countered by giving information about the course of back pain, the known causes, the lack of a need for further investigation if a full clinical examination has been conducted. (Note: the clinical examination is part of the process of challenging unhelpful beliefs). This may be supplemented by giving written information such as educational material. However, educational materials which gives only messages regarding the anatomy of the spine but does not tell people to keep active is unhelpful. The patient's understanding should be checked to ensure that it has indeed reduced and not heightened fears. As a general rule, ask yourself "what information do I need to give this person to allow them to move forward to seeing increasing activity as a helpful way to manage their problem".

Red flags in that they require specialist assessment /referral and render the individual unsuitable (at that time) for a straightforward biopsychosocial approach.

EARLY BIOPSYCHOSOCIAL MANAGEMENT IN PRACTICE

During the last decade, there have been a number of initiatives addressing various aspects of secondary intervention in low back pain. These include government guide-

TABLE 3. Orange Flags

- *Active* psychiatric disorder
- Major personality disorder
  - o Illicit drug use
  - o Current forensic involvement

• = Major communication problems.

TABLE 4. RCT of Biopsychosocial Management in Acute LBP (Hay 2004) Program Structure

- Hands-off biopsychosocial management (including re-activation) vs "manipulative therapy" ("hands-on")
- Located in community (primary-care)
- Early "stepped-care" (3–6 treatment sessions)
- Ca 80% (follow up). of 400 patients at 1 year
- Structured assessment, including psychometrics
- Training to competency
- Independent and blinded evaluation and follow up.

Elements of Training in "Hands-Off" Arm of Trial
- Biopsychosocial model of pain and disability
- Observational skills
- Problem analysis of cases
- Communication skills (role-play)
- Techniques for enabling self-disclosure
- Dealing with distressed and angry patients
- Efficient time and information management

lines on clinical and occupational management, patient-focused educational materials and awareness raising media initiatives (summarized in Waddell, 2004, pp 415–416). Treatment trials have tended to focus on specific types of biomedical or biomechanical treatments. Psychosocial parameters have seldom specifically been addressed except in so far as such parameters have been incorporated into selection or as predictors of outcome. Recently, however (Hay, 2004), a prospective randomised early intervention trial has been undertaken with the specific objective of comparing and contrasting a primarily biomechanical "hands-on" physiotherapeutic approach with a biopsychosocial physiotherapeutic approach based on the stem-and-leaf approach in the context of reactivation. The key elements of the program are summarized in Table 4.

At this time, the results are not as yet fully analysed, but the *preliminary* results indicate:

- Both treatments reduce disability
- Biopsychosocial approach is acceptable to patients
- Comparable reduction in disability at follow up.
- But
  - Biopsychosocial patients required fewer treatments
  - Biopsychosocial patients had lower health-care usage in the subsequent year

Analysis is ongoing on predictors, and possible "patient-treatment matching" is being investigated.

THE OCCUPATIONAL PERSPECTIVE

Traditionally, clinical rehabilitation had focused primarily on clinical outcomes, with relatively little attention directed specifically at work, and, although designed originally for a case-management system, the original Yellow Flags focused primarily on perceptions of health. It became clear, however, that implicit within the Yellow

TABLE 5. Work Organizational Factors Most Clearly Associated with Occupational Stress in Musculoskeletal Disorders

High demand and low control
Time pressure/monotonous work
Lack of job satisfaction
Unsupportive management style
Low social support from colleagues
High perceived workload

Flag initiative was the possibility of a range of different solutions, involving both health-care providers and occupational personnel. It was decided that insufficient attention had been given to specific occupational factors and it was decided, therefore, to subdivide the yellow flags into clinical yellow flags and occupationally focused blue flags, (Main & Burton, 1998; Burton & Main, 1998).

Blue Flags

The Blue flags have their origins in the work-related stress literature. The nature of work-related stress has been a major focus of research. It can be viewed in terms of characteristics of the working environment, in terms of physiologically related stress or as a consequence of interaction between individuals and their environment. Some of the more important factors are job demands, job content, job control, social interactions, role ambiguity and conflict, job future ambiguity, technology issues and organizational/ management issues including management style (Carayon & Lim, 1999). The available evidence provides most support for influence of the factors shown in Table 5 (Bongers et al., 1993; Vingaard & Nachemson, 2000), and it has been suggested that workers' reactions to psychosocial aspects of work may be more important than the actual aspects themselves (Davis & Heaney, 2000), with reported stress acting as an intermediary (Bongers et al., 1993; Shamansky, 2000).

These perceived features of work, generally associated with higher rates of symptoms, ill-health and work loss have been termed *Blue Flags* which, in the context of injury, may delay recovery, or constitute a major obstacle to it; and for those at work, may be major contributory factors to sub-optimal performance or "presenteeism." It should be emphasised that blue flags incorporate not only issues related to the perception of job characteristics such as job demand, but also to the perception of social interactions (whether with management or fellow-workers).

Summary of the Key Psychological Obstacles

The obstacles generally associated with failure to return to work are those associated with the individuals' perception of back pain, perceptions of work and the workplace (i.e., yellow and blue flags). Clinical perceptions predicting poor return to work and persistent incapacity include low mood (Magni et al., 1994; Main et al., 1992), beliefs about pain and injury (De Good & Shutty, 1992; Linton, 2000; Marhold et al., 2002; Vlaeyen et al., 2000) and preoccupation with somatic symptoms (Symonds et al., 1996). Occupational perceptions include job related issues such as job satisfaction, and perceptions about work safety (Cats-Baril and Frymoyer 1991; Fishbain et al.,

1997, 1999; Hazard et al., 1996; Main & Burton, 2000), although these refer, of course, to the patients' current employment and are not directly relevant in those who are unemployed.

From a work retention or work rehabilitation perspective, however, a further distinction has been made between two types of occupational risk factors: those concerning the perception of work (*Blue flags*) and organizational obstacles to recovery, comprising objective work characteristics and conditions of employment (*Black flags*) (Main & Burton 1998, 2000).

Black Flags: Social and Economic Obstacles to Return-to-Work

There may be formidable obstacles presented by the wage compensation-benefit system, conditions of employment and social policy (Main & Burton, 2000). To this can be added demographic factors, particularly the age, general health and co-morbidities of the individual when they initially absent from work (Bloch & Prinz, 2001). In the UK, those medically certified to be unable to work will, in all probability be in receipt of available benefits and movement from these into work is extremely low (Rowlinson & Berthoud, 1996). Some back pain sufferers may be symptomatic, but considered fit enough for some type of work and receive only benefits associated with unemployment (Job Seekers Allowance—JSA). Those who do not qualify for either of these benefits because of insufficient contributions may qualify for basic income support (IS). From the recipient's point of view, incapacity benefit is the more preferable because it is paid at a higher rate and allows access to other benefits. It might be expected from this that those on incapacity benefits (IB) would be less likely to return to work.

Black Flags are *not* a matter of perception, and affect all workers equally. They include both nationally established policy concerning conditions of employment and sickness policy, and working conditions specific to a particular organization.

There are also content-specific aspects of work, which characterize certain types of job, and which are associated with higher rates of illness, injury or work loss. These features of work, following injury, may require a higher level of working capacity for successful work retention. After certain types of injury, such jobs may be specifically contraindicated and therefore constitute an absolute obstacle to return-to-work.

Obstacles to Recovery or Opportunities for Change?

At the core of the "flag" construct is a conceptual shift from risks (many of which may be immutable) to *obstacles to recovery*, which may be individual clinical factors, perceptions of work or organization, and in turn require a range of solutions from individual clinical interventions and work re-integration strategies to fundamental redesign of the individual/organization interface. Unnecessary low back pain disability is unhelpful to both employer and worker. It should be noticed in this context, however, that the term *obstacles to recovery* does not necessary imply a complete resolution of symptoms, and should be understood as shorthand for *obstacles to recovery/optimal function* or viewed from a slightly different perspective as *obstacles to engagement in the recovery process.*

Salford-Bristol Back Pain Project : Returning the Chronically Unemployed with Low Back Pain to Employment (Watson et al., 2004)

It has been suggested that, in unemployed people with back pain, the chances of ever returning to work decreases with the passage of time. According to Waddell (1992), by the time someone has been off work for two years they are unlikely ever to return to work. There are a number of possible reasons for this. Those who lose their employment are more likely to suffer from mental health problems (Weich & Lewis, 1998), have lower life expectancy (Nylen et al., 2001) and have increased consultation rates for physical complaints (Kraut et al., 2000). The unemployed with back pain, however, face a number of additional problems specifically to do with work.

- They may become progressively less fit through inactivity.
- Their vocational skills may become outdated.
- They may not be able to identify suitable, sustainable employment.
- "Rehabilitation" programmes usually do not include job-seeking and vocational advice
- There may be prejudice from employers against people with back pain.
- There may be an adverse social climate, hostile to employees with back pain.

As a consequence, the unemployed person with back pain risks social exclusion and is presented with the twin problem of gaining access not only to clinical rehabilitation but also to vocational rehabilitation.

The Salford-Bristol study was based on a previous study by the authors and reported elsewhere (Main & Watson, 1995). It was established as an occupationally oriented pain management (rehabilitation) program for long-term unemployed people with low back pain as the declared reason for unemployment (Watson et al, 2004). Although a relatively small scale, and not a randomized control trial (RCT), the program was innovative in its attempt specifically to address yellow, blue and black flags. To permit the assessment of generalizability of findings, the project was conducted partly in Salford and partly in Bristol. The 86 subjects were referred by State Disability Employment Advisors (DEAs) or Personal Advisors (PAs) (civil servants)—who in general, interview and assess people with disabilities to advise them on returning to work. The subjects had a mean duration of unemployment of 40.8 months (+/− 36.3) and a mean duration of low back pain of 98.9 months (+/− 107.3). They underwent an occupationally oriented pain management rehabilitation program, comprising 12 half-days spread over 6 weeks, with up to an additional 3 hours of additional vocational focused advice, given on an individual basis. The subjects were followed up at 6 months to determine work status. At 6 months follow-up, 38.4% of all (86) participants or 39.3% of fluent English speakers were in paid employment. Of those who returned to work, none returned to their previous employer, 18 (21%) returned to the same type of job but with a different employer, and 15 (17.4%) were employed in different jobs with different employers. Comparable results were obtained in the Salford and Bristol cohorts. There were no systematic differences in the presenting characteristics of those who did and those who did not return to work, although those with negative outcomes at 6 months had a longer duration of unemployment and had higher initial scores for depression and somatic anxiety.

There were 48 subjects (56%) who were out of work for less than 2 years; 22 of these were working at 6 months follow up, and 38 (44%) were out of work for longer than 2 years, of whom 16 were working at follow up. Return to work rates were not statistically different, and subjects in each group were equally likely to return to work. Although the study demonstrated that positive progress is associated with shorter duration of unemployment, it showed also that even some of the long term unemployed could be rehabilitated into work.

LINKING HEALTH AND WORK: THE WELSH INITIATIVE

The *Yellow* Flag initiative has been important in two major ways:

- First, in promulgation of a "systems approach", involving all key stakeholders, in addressing issues of clinical and occupational rehabilitation, with emphasis on the need for better clinical-occupational interfaces
- Second, in attempting to identify and reduce risk factors for chronic incapacity, whether in health-care or in occupational settings.

The need for "joined-up" thinking was implied in a recent influential report (H.S.E., 2002) highlighting three principle reasons for a long-term occupational strategy:

- To stop people from being made ill by work;
- To help people who are ill return to work;
- To improve work opportunities for people currently not in employment due to ill health or disability.

There are also costs to employers which include wage compensation and lost production for those who are employed. The report also emphasized the pluralistic nature of the problems and their solutions, with a need for concerted, concentrated, multi-factorial, multi-dimensional and multi-agency approaches to target collective efforts on the areas that need it most. The role of partnership working was also highlighted, involving government, local authorities, individuals, large and small employers, trade unions and health professionals. In fact, during the previous year (2001), following a recommendation from the Welsh Assembly Government (WAG) and the U.K. Department for Work & Pensions (DWP), a new initiative, the Wales Health Work Partnership (WHWP) was established to conduct feasibility studies into the impact of ill-health and social exclusion on work as a basis from which to develop new approaches to work rehabilitation and work retention. The major report (Main et al., 2004) offers a new analysis of the problems of health and work as derived principally from a Consensus Conference of key stakeholders and from a survey of employers. The primary focus of the report is on musculoskeletal disorders, and back pain in particular (although the impact of stress on work was also identified).

Key Components of the Wales Health-Work Partnership (WHWP) Report

The Costs of Health-Related Work Absence in Wales

In Wales, over 34% of adults report long-term limiting illness that affects their normal daily activities; 30% report back pain and there are more than 110 million pain days each year within the Principality. The debilitating impact of musculoskeletal conditions on quality of life, relative to other conditions and diseases, was also highlighted. Prolonged unemployment can result in additional health problems. Those who lose their employment are more likely to suffer from mental health problems

(Janlert, 1997; Kposowa, 2001; Weich & Lewis, 1998) and have lower life expectancy (Marikainen & Valkonen, 1996, Morris et al., 1994, Nylen et al., 2001; Kraut et al., 2000). Mason et al. have reported increased consultation rates for physical complaints and even report more back pain (Kraut et al., 2000; Mason, 1994). These data illustrate the potential public health concerns associated with not rehabilitating back pain sufferers into work. In addition, the chance of ever returning to work after a period of absence from low back pain reduces over time (Waddell, 1987; Waddell, 1992).

The Costs of Absenteeism

In the U.K., the annual cost of absenteeism has been estimated at over 1% of the G.D.P. (Chatterji & Tilley, 2002) but it is known that health risk factors and disease also adversely affect worker productivity (Burton et al., 1999) and it has been estimated that 3–11 hours per week in terms of productivity is lost to employers. Perhaps unsurprisingly, mental illness such as depression has a powerful influence on absenteeism, but job performance is also affected. It has been shown that depressed workers are seven times more likely to have poor job performance than non-depressed workers. The authors concluded "because of presenteeism, previous reports of absenteeism may represent only a fraction of the cost of depression in the workplace" (Druss et al., 2000). Specific studies have examined the influence of physical disease on absenteeism. In another study sponsored by the Employers Health Coalition of Tampa, Florida, based on a 1999 analysis of seventeen diseases, researchers found that lost productivity due to presenteeism was on average 7.5. times greater than productivity due to absenteeism. For some conditions—notably allergies, arthritis, heart disease, migraine, and neck/back/spine pain—the ratio was 15 to 1; 20 to 1 or even approaching 30 to 1(Employers' Health Coalition, 2000).

The Additional Challenge of "Presenteeism" or Sub-Optimal Performance

Ill-health is a burden not only to individuals and society but also to employers. The costs of work absence or absenteeism have long been recognized. It has been suggested that the principal causes of absenteeism can be classified into five main categories: personal illness, family issues, personal needs, entitlement mentality and reported stress (Woo et al., 1999; Atchiler and Motta (1994). Health promotion programs have been advocated as a way of addressing absenteeism (Aldana and Pronk, 1994).

Conclusions from Consensus Conference

A wide range of perspectives emerged from the conference. For convenience, these are summarised under a number of headings.

The Influence of Health on Work

- There was general consensus that work had a positive effect on the health of people and other aspects associated with their quality of life.
- The adverse psychological effects of being unemployed were highlighted, especially with regard to anxiety and lack of self-esteem, since society places a high value on the type of work that a person does.

- There was, however, a much wider set of potentially negative influences of health related problems on work:
    - Key issues identified included practical access to work, problems within work and postural tolerance.
    - It was considered that care needed to be taken to avoid arriving at premature "judgements" about the individuals concerned and their role in the development of unnecessary levels of incapacity.
    - It was suggested that employers should attempt to take greater responsibility in the management of sickness absence, adopting a much more pro-active approach.
    - Employers need to be educated so as to enable workers with musculoskeletal problems to take more frequent breaks, engage in lighter duties and switch tasks and responsibilities with other workers. It was considered that specific workplace assessments might be beneficial, although these could be politically sensitive.

Factors Leading to Sickness Absence

- Factors leading to sickness absence included organizational policies and practices as well as individual factors. Ranges of "external" influences (medical, economic, personal and social) were identified.
- It was recommended that there needed to be a clear focus both on work-retention and on re-integration into work.
- A great majority of people receiving Incapacity benefits are affected by minor or moderate health complaints such as musculoskeletal conditions, mental health problems and cardio-respiratory conditions which are amenable to effective management facilitating return to the world of work.

Identification of Those at Risk of Long-Term Sickness and Disability

- A range of individual factors—work-related and non health-related environmental factors were identified.
- Reference was made to the difficulties in screening workers at relatively high risk.
- It was noted that, although a vast array of potentially useful evidence is currently available to inform policymaking, at the level of the individual organization the relative dearth of relevant information is a matter of some concern.

Identification of Relevant Skills and Knowledge Base for Work Retention and Reintegration

- Key skills required included ergonomic/workplace assessment, and specific clinical assessments with more general competencies in problem analysis, communication skills and knowledge of benefits and entitlements.
- The importance of increasing employers' knowledge of the benefit system, and improving the interface between clinical and occupational rehabilitation facilities was highlighted.

- An important aspect of work retention is assessment of personal issues which may be affecting workplace performance and health and a role for a third party, as an "honest broker" facilitating communication among all relevant stakeholders was identified.
- Lack of knowledge of job availability might adversely affect retention or resettlement.
- The importance of integrated or "joined-up" approaches was again stressed, with fundamental system changes needed to facilitate rather than hinder return to work.

The Survey of Employers

As part of the larger initiative, a range of employers in Wales were surveyed to obtain baseline data relating to the extent of the sickness absence problem, and to identify issues which employers considered to be of importance in tackling the problem. A sampling frame was constructed to identify employers located in North Wales, West Wales and South Wales, and to further identify at least one public service organization, one large employer (>100 employees) and identify smaller employers via the Welsh Development Agency regional offices. A questionnaire, based on the 3rd European Survey on Working Conditions (Paoli & Merle, 2000), was piloted in three organizations, amended slightly, and then the final version mailed to 44 companies, stratified (as described above) to represent the communities of Wales. Twenty-seven companies of those approached completed the questionnaire satisfactorily and returned it. They represented a total workforce of 82,500 employees, with a range of 20–>12,000.

The survey yielded information on the nature, size and type of the organization, and characteristics of the workforce, with organizations classified in terms of their core activity, into:

- Heavy manufacturing (n=3)
- Light manufacturing (n=5)
- Public service providers (including healthcare, policing, probation, social services and housing associations) (n=13)
- Other service industries (heterogeneous) (n=6).

The skills base of the employees was broken down into

- Professional (27%)
- Managerial (15%)
- Skilled manual (16%)
- Skilled non-manual (21%)
- Partly skilled (15%)
- Unskilled (6%)

The data were further broken down to ascertain the spread of employee skills within each organization. Working arrangements were appraised in terms of type of contract, hours of work, turnover and recruitment rates and working days lost due to sickness absence.

Further discussion of the findings and their implications are presented in the final project report. The principal recommendations are shown in Table 7.

TABLE 6. Major Findings of Wales Employers' Survey

- It was estimated that 7.84 working days were lost per employee per year (3.6% of total working days assuming that there are 215 working days per year), which translates into over 12.5 million working days lost in Wales per annum through sickness absence—assuming a working population of 1.6 million.
- The sickness absence 'hot-spots' amongst sections of the workforce, were different for each type of organization. In heavy manufacturing, partly skilled employees accounted for 80% of days lost; in light manufacturing unskilled workers accounted for 75% of days lost; in public services providers, professionals accounted for 36% of days lost; while in other service industries skilled non-manual workers accounted for 41% of days lost.
- In terms of longer sickness absence, 7% of employees had been off work for 2 consecutive weeks or more due to sickness absence, although in public services 19% of employees were longer-term absentees. Nursing staff had the highest rates of sickness absence in the health services, with particular problems relating to reported stress in staff working in mental health services. Among operators and technicians, musculoskeletal problems were identified as the major contributory factor. In the heavy manufacturing sector, reported stress-induced mental health problems were cited as a major cause of sickness absence. Manual and partly skilled workers were also reported to have higher rates of sickness absence than other sections of the workforce.
- Although 22 organizations had a return to work policy, there was considerable variation between organisations. Health care providers were unanimous with their concerns relating to sickness absence and its impact on their ability to provide excellent patient care, but were unhappy with their current systems of dealing with sickness absence. The majority were reviewing and implementing new schemes to tackle the issues, with particular emphasis being focused on monitoring and reporting of sickness absence and regular communication with staff. The biggest concern amongst social work providers and other service providers was the prevalence of reported stress related psychological illness. There was also a great deal of concern about managing the issue of sickness absence, especially the conflict between manager and employee. Light manufacturing employers were concerned about the cost burden of sickness absence in terms of statutory sick pay and work related absence or accidents, which led to claims on employee's liability insurance.
- There was general concern about the role of the GP in the process of sickness absence management, with a perception that a major conflict of interest existed and the need for greater liaison between GPs and employers in the management of sickness absence, rehabilitation and return-to-work was emphasised.
- It was generally agreed that the current system of dealing with sickness absence was at best inadequate or else non-existent. A need for greater understanding of the causes of sickness absence was called for so that it could be managed more effectively.

CONCLUSIONS AND RECOMMENDATIONS

Health care and social systems are slow to change and the power of underlying models of illness in directing the focus of attention needs to be recognized. The advent of evidence-based medicine has enabled a critical examination of the basis from which our therapeutic efforts are developed. In terms of prevention *per se*, there are many interesting new challenges, but they require reconsideration of our fundamental assumptions, not only regarding the objectives for intervention, but also the type of interventions.

The concept of prevention, within the field of musculoskeletal disorders, has developed mainly from a clinical perspective. We need to expand our role in terms of a "systems" perspective. As clinicians, however, we need to re-examine our range of competencies in the light of such new challenges. There needs to be a focus on skills rather than just professional accreditation. We may need to expand our clinically derived concepts of prevention; as well as broaden our skills and develop closer and more effective liaison with other agencies. This must, however, be carried out within an evidence-based framework. We need to develop and validate a new

TABLE 7. Conclusions from Consensus Meeting: Priorities for Consideration in Wales

1. A comparison of possible approaches to "case-management" or "case-co-ordination" in specific localities in Wales; linking both health-economic and occupational perspectives.
2. Detailed analysis of the impact of presenteeism on the development of work absence and entry into benefits, including a systematic review of literature and a series of case studies (in conjunction with employers and the DWP) in particular organizations and industries.
3. Development of instruments and profiles to measure people's desire to return to work; and sub-optimal performance (presenteeism).
4. Investigation of the causes of sickness absence is urgently needed.
5. Development of an awareness program for GPs and other primary care professionals and employers in relation to the employment/health interface.
6. Development of a 'community framework' for the management and organization of work retention and rehabilitation schemes, involving key stakeholders from within local communities at the employment-health interface.
7. Identification of competencies (and training), including communication skills, needed for work retention and work rehabilitation required for both the health-care and occupational sectors.
8. Investigation of ways of increasing awareness among employers of the need for a "joined-up" approach to work retention and rehabilitation.
9. A systematic review of the literature relating to the efficacy of interventions for people at risk of long-term sickness was recommended, but this in fact is already being undertaken by the DWP.
10. A replication of the *Working Backs Scotland* initiative in Wales.

generation of customized measurement instruments designed to identify possible targets for intervention and highlight potential obstacles to progress and, thus, facilitate competent decision making. The success of any such initiative can only be measured against relevant process and outcome measures relevant for the particular clinical or occupational context. Much work remains to be done.

Tackling Yellow and Blue Flags in the Workplace

Traditionally sickness and absence management has used absenteeism through ill-health as the principle index of impact of health on work. Occupational health strategy has been directed at sickness and disability management, whether employing in-house occupational health or "outsourcing" as in the recent U.K. government policy initiatives. It would appear, however, that "reported stress" has now overtaken musculoskeletal disorders as the major reason for sick-certified work loss. The importance of tackling "reported stress" has been declared a priority by the H.S.E.

Evaluation of the specific contribution of work-related factors, as opposed to other personal factors, however, is not as yet clear, but it would seem probable at this juncture that we are witnessing a phenomenon which has psychological, social and occupational components, and, as such, will require a much broader understanding of the relationship between health and work than is currently held. New imaginative solutions, involving collaborative arrangements among all key stakeholders, would seem to be required.

Tackling Black Flags

Black flags, however, also can be viewed in terms of *opportunities for change*. Thus, in order to facilitate optimal adaptation to work for individuals with low back symptoms, it may be necessary to develop new types of partnership between employers and their workforce, recognizing the worker as a human resource rather than an economic burden. Removal of obstacles to recovery (or to optimal function), as viewed from a sickness/disability perspective, may be assisted by positive organizational initiatives designed to enhance resilience and assist work-life balance.

REFERENCES

AHCPR (1994). *Acute low back pain problems in adults. Clinical practice guidelines no 14.* Rockville, MD: Agency for Health Care Policy and Research, US Dept. of Health and Human Services.

Altchiler, L., & Motta, R. (1994). Effects of aerobic and non-aerobic exercise on anxiety, absenteeism and job satisfaction. *Journal of Clinical Psychology, 50,* 829–840.

Aldana, S.G., & Pronk, N.P. (2001). Health promotion programs, modifiable health risks and employee absenteeism. *Journal of Occupational and Environmental Medicine, 43,* 36–46.

Bloch, F.S., & Prins, R. (2001). *Who Returns to Work and Why?* International Social Security Series (ISSA). New Brunswick: Transaction Publishers.

Bongers, P.M., de Winter, C.R., Kompier, M.A.J., & Hildebrandt, V.H. (1993). Psychosocial factors at work and musculoskeletal disease. *Scandinavian Journal of Work and Environmental Health, 19,* 297–312.

Burton, A.K. & Main, C.J. (2000). Obstacles to Recovery from Work-related Musculoskeletal Disorders. In W. Karwowski (Ed.) *International Encyclopaedia of Ergonomics and Human Factors,* p 1542–1544. London: Taylor and Francis.

Burton, W.N., Conti, D.J., Chen, C.Y., Schultz, A.B., & Edington, D.W. (1999). The role of health risk factors and disease on worker productivity. *Journal of Occupational and Environmental Medicine, 41,* 863–877.

Burton, W.N., Chen, C.Y., Schultz, A.B., & Edington, D.W. (1998). The economic costs associated with body mass index in a workplace. *Journal of Occupational and Environmental Medicine, 40,* 786–792.

Carayon, P. & Lim, S-Y. (1999). Psychosocial work factors. In W. Karwowski & W. Marras (Eds.) *The Occupational Ergonomic Handbook,* Chap 15, p 275–283.

Cats-Baril, W.L. & Frymoyer, J.W. (1991). Identifying patients at risk of becoming disabled because of low-back pain. The Vermont Rehabilitation Engineering Center predictive model. *Spine, 16,* 605–607.

Chatterji, M., & Tilley, C.J. (2002). Sickness, absenteeism, presenteeism and sick pay. *Oxford Economic Papers, 54,* 669–687.

CSAG (1994). The Clinical Standards Advisory Group on Back Pain. London: HMSO.

Davis, K.G., & Heaney, C.A. (2000). The relationship between psychosocial work characteristics and low back pain: underlying methodological issues. *Clinical Biomechanics, 15,* 389–406.

DeGood, D.E., & Shutty, M.S. (1992). Assessment of pain beliefs, coping and self efficacy. In D.C. Turk DC & R. Melzack (Eds.), *Handbook of Pain Assessment.* New York: Guildford Press.

Druss, B.G., Rosenheck, R.A., & Sledge, W.H. (2000). Health and disability costs of depression in a major U.S. Corporation. *American Journal of Psychiatry, 157,* 1274–1278.

Employer's Health Coalition (2000). *Healthy People/Productivity Community Survey,* 1999. (Restricted access).

Fishbain, D.A., Cutler, R.B., Rosomoff, H.L., Khalil, T., & Steele-Rosomoff, R. (1999). Prediction of "intent", "discrepancy with intent", and "discrepancy with nonintent" for the patient with chronic pain to return to work after treatment at a pain facility. *Clinical Journal of Pain, 15,* 141–50.

Fishbain, D.A., Cutler, R.B., Rosomoff, H.L., Khalil, T., & Steele-Rosomoff, R. (1997). Impact of chronic pain patients' job perception variables on actual return to work. *Clinical Journal of Pain, 13,* 197–206.

Hay, E.M. (2004). *Implementing Pain Management—a Primary Care perspective.* Paper presented to the Annual Scientific meeting of the Pain Society, Manchester U.K.

Hazard, R.G., Haugh, L.D., Reid, S. Preble, J.B., & MacDonald, L. (1996). Early prediction of chronic disability after occupational low back injury. *Spine, 21,* 945–51.

H.S.E. (2002) SECURING HEALTH TOGETHER: A long-term occupational strategy for England, Scotland and Wales. Health and Safety Executive. London.

Janlert, U. (1997). Unemployment as a disease and diseases of the unemployed. *Scandinavian Journal of Work and Environmental Health, 23,* 379–389.

Kendall, N.A.S., Linton, S.J., & Main, C.J. (1997). *Guide to assessing psychosocial yellow flags in acute low back pain: risk factors for long term disability and work loss.* Wellington, N.Z.: Accident Rehabilitation and Compensation Insurance Corporation of New Zealand and the National Health Committee.

Kposowa, A.J. (2001). Unemployment and suicide: a cohort analysis of social factors predicting suicide in the US National Longitudinal Mortality Study. *Psychological Medicine, 31,* 127–138.

Kraut, A., Mustard, C., Wald, R., & Tate, R. (2000). Unemployment and healthcare utilization. *Scandinavian Journal of Work Environment And Health, 26,* 169–177.

Linton, S.J. (2000). A review of psychological risk factors in back and neck pain. *Spine, 25,* 1148–1156;

Linton S.J. and van Tulder M.W. (2000) Preventative interventions for Back pain and Neck Pain. In A. Nachemson & E Jonsson (Eds.), *Neck Pain and Back Pain: The Scientific Evidence of Causes, Diagnoses and Treatment,* Chap 6, p 127–147. Philadelphia: Lippincott Williams and Wilkins.

Magni, G., Moreschi, C., Rigatti-Luchini, S., & Merskey, H. (1994). Prospective Study on the relationship between depression symptoms and chronic musculoskeletal pain. *Pain, 56,* 289–297.

Main, C.J. & Burton, A.K. (1998). Pain mechanisms. In R McCaig & M. Harrington (Eds.), *The Changing Nature of Occupational Health,* Chap 12, p 233–254. Sudbury, Suffolk: Health and Safety Executive Books.

Main, C.J. & Burton, A.K. (2000). Economic and occupational influences on pain and disability. In C.J. Main & C.C. Spanswick (Eds), *Pain Management: An Interdisciplinary Approach,* Chap. 4: pp 63–87. Edinburgh: Churchill Livingstone.

Main, C.J., Phillips, C., Farr, A., & Thomas, A. (2004). *Health and Work: Minimising the problems of musculoskeletal pain.* Report of the Wales Health Work Partnership. Welsh Assembly Government

Main, C.J., & Watson, P.J. (1995). Screening for patients at risk of developing chronic incapacity. *Journal of Occupational Rehabilitation, 5,* 207–217.

Main, C.J., & Watson, P.J. (2002). The distressed and angry low back pain (LBP) patient. In L. Gifford (Ed) *Topical Issues in Pain.* Vol.3., p 175–200. CNS Press, Falmouth.

Main, C.J., Wood, P.L.R., Hollis, S., Spanswick, C.C., & Waddell, G. (1992). The distress risk assessment method: A simple classification to identify the risk of poor outcome. *Spine, 17,* 42–52.

Marhold, C., Linton, S.J., & Melin, L. (2002). Identification of obstacles for chronic pain patients to return to work: Evaluation of a questionnaire. *Journal of Occupational Rehabilitation, 12,* 65–75.

Martikainen, P.T., & Valkonen, T. (1996). Excess mortality of unemployed men and women during a period of rapidly increasing employment. *The Lancet, 348,* 909–912.

Morley, S., Eccleston, C., & Williams, A. (1999). Systematic review and meta-analysis of randomized controlled trials of cognitive behaviour therapy and behaviour therapy for chronic pain in adults excluding headache. *Pain, 80,* 1–13.

Morris, J.K., Cook, D.G., & Shaper, G. (1994). Loss of employment and mortality. *British Medical Journal, 308,* 1135–1139.

Nylen, L., Voss, M., & Floderus, B. (2001). Mortality among women and men relative to unemployment, part-time work, overtime work, and extra work: a study based on data from the Swedish twins registry. *Occupational and Environmental Medicine, 58,* 52–57.

Paoli, P., & Merlie, D. (2000). *Third European Survey on Working Conditions.* European Foundation for the improvement of living and working conditions, Dublin

Rowlingson, K., & Berthoud, R. (1996). *Disability benefits and employment. Department of Social Security Research Report no. 54.* London: HMSO.

Shamansky, S.L. (2000). Editorial: Presenteeism or When Being There is Not Being There. *Public Health Nursing, 19,* 79–80.

Symonds, T.L., Burton, A.K., Tillotson, K.M., & Main, C.J. (1996). Do attitudes and beliefs influence work loss due to low back trouble?*Occupational .Medicine, 46,* 25–32.

Vingard, E., & Nachemson, A. (2000). Work related influences on neck and low back pain. In A. Nachemson & E. Jonsson (Eds), *Neck Pain and Back Pain: The Scientific Evidence of Causes, Diagnosis and Treatment.* Philadelphia: Lippincott Williams and Wilkins.

Vlaeyen, J.W.S., & Linton, S.J. (2000). Fear avoidance and its' consequence in chronic musculoskeletal pain: State of the art. *Pain, 85,* 317–332.

Waddell, G. (1987). A New Clinical Model for the Treatment of Low-Back Pain. *Spine, 12,* 632–644.

Waddell, G. (1992). Biopsychosocial analysis of low back pain. *Baillieres' Clinical Rheumatology, 6,* 523–557.

Waddell, G. (1998). *The Back Pain Revolution*. Edinburgh: Churchill-Livingstone.

Waddell G. (2004). *The Back Pain Revolution (2nd Ed.)*. Edinburgh: Churchill-Livingstone.

Watson, P.J., Main, C.J., Gales, T., Waddell, G., &Purcell-Jones, G. (1998). Medically certified work loss, recurrence and cost of wages compensation for back pain: a follow-up study of the working population of Jersey. *British Journal of Rheumatology, 37*, 82–86.

Watson, P.J., Booker, C.K., Moores, L., & Main, C.J. (2004). Returning the chronically unemployed with low back pain to employment. *European Journal of Pain, 8*:359–369.

Weich, S., & Lewis, G. (1998). Poverty, unemployment and common mental disorders: a population based cohort study. *British Medical Journal, 317*, 115–119.

Woo, M., Yap, A.K., Oh, T.G., & Long, F.Y. (1999). The relationship between reported stress and absenteeism. *Singapore Medical Journal, 40*, 1–12.

22

Biopsychosocial Factors in Complex Claims for Disability Compensation

Issues and Recommendations

Les Kertay and Thomas M. Pendergrass

INTRODUCTION

As used in the current text, the conditions covered under the rubrics "high risk", "complex", and "biopsychosocial" disabilities include a very broad range of potentially impairing physical and psychological diagnoses. Included are any conditions in which the subjective experience of pain, fatigue, mood disturbance, and neurocognitive impairment outstrip the underlying medical findings that might serve to explain them. Many of the conditions under consideration have been referred to in the literature as "functional somatic syndromes" (Barsky & Borus, 1999), while others have referred to them as "invisible" or "ambiguous" impairments (e.g., Mitchell, 2000). We would argue that all illness is biopsychosocial, in which the impact on functional capacity results from the interaction of the direct physical effects of a condition (the "biology"), the individual's attitudes and perceptions (the "psychology"), and the individual's social context (the "sociology").

The interaction of biological, psychological, and sociological factors is perhaps nowhere more evident than when an individual makes a claim for monetary compensation for disability based on a condition that by definition involves a substantial element of subjective evaluation, both on the part of the claimant and on the part of his or her treating providers. Just as we have said that all illness is biopsychosocial, it is our view that all claims for income protection compensation based on illness or injury are prototypically biopsychosocial. Seen in this way, the more "subjective" conditions that are the subject of the present volume are simply a subset of all potentially impairing conditions. By extension, the approach to evaluating, treating, and compensating these conditions is not essentially different from the approach that is applied to any condition. For all situations in which disability is an active or potential issue, the early identification and evaluation of psychosocial factors, in addition to

DOI: 10.1007/978-0-387-28919-9_22, © 2009 Springer Science+Business Media, LLC

the medical impairment itself, is an important step in determining outcomes for both the claimant and the insurer. In addition, early interventions that take psychosocial factors into account are more likely to result in positive outcomes. Finally, we note that, once a claim for disability is made, the compensation system itself becomes part of the social context, and the nature of the interactions between the claimant, his or her treating providers, and the insurer becomes part of the mix in determining the ultimate outcome for the individual who is ill or disabled.

Considered elsewhere in the volume are the broad conceptual, methodological, and clinical issues that can be used to develop an understanding of these conditions and their impact on the lives of people afflicted with them. We have been asked to discuss these conditions as they interface with compensation systems, particularly private disability insurance, and that discussion is the goal of the present chapter. In this chapter we will discuss (a) the scope and impact of the biopsychosocial conditions on compensation systems, and the inherent difficulties posed by the potential differences between the clinical and the contractual perspectives; (b) the additional challenges that become part of the clinical picture when a claim for disability compensation is filed, including concerns related to motivation, documentation, time, and impact on the therapeutic relationship; (c) medicolegal issues that arise in the context of claims for disability compensation, including terminology, standards of proof, privacy, and potential involvement in the legal system; and (d) potential pitfalls in the interaction between patients, their providers, and the insuring entity. Finally, we offer recommendations for practices that will minimize the problems inherent in claims for disability compensation and maximize positive outcomes for the patient. In doing so, we offer our thoughts based on research in the field, our experience as clinicians who have been involved in the evaluation and treatment of patients impaired by complex biopsychosocial conditions, and as psychologists who have worked as consultants to private and public disability insurers.

SCOPE AND IMPACT

That the present volume is being written is testimony to the extensive degree to which biopsychosocial factors impact on impairment and disability. As to the impact on private compensation plans, we are aware of no statistics, and no methodology, that enable us to differentiate the costs associated with psychosocial factors as compared to more easily measured "medical/biological" factors. That said, it is instructive to examine the prevalence of, and the costs associated with, conditions in which the degree of impairment is ambiguous and potentially difficult to assess. Psychiatric conditions, chronic pain, chronic fatigue, and "sensitivity syndromes" are among those most frequently mentioned in the context of such discussion, and these are considered briefly below.

Considering first the impact of psychiatric conditions, data have been published by the American Psychological Association (APA, 2002), indicating that an estimated 15–18% of the US population meets criteria for a diagnosable mental disorder, a number that climbs to 25% of patients in primary care medical practice. Up to 50–70% of visits to primary care physicians are said to involve complaints associated with psychological factors, either directly or indirectly. The largest single diagnostic criteria among these patients is unipolar depression. It is estimated that Major Depressive

Disorder annually costs $23 billion in lost work days. In a 3-year study of a large corporation, individuals with major depression were found to be 4 times more likely to take disability days from work when compared to non-depressed workers. In other data, the leading cause of non-fatal disease burden in 1990 was attributed to unipolar depression, accounting for 13.2% of cases and 7.2% of healthy years of life lost (Murray & Lopez, 1997).

As substantial as is the impact associated with unipolar major depressive disorder, it has been estimated that "minor depression" may account for as much as 51% more disability days than major depression. Considered even more broadly, as many as 60% of lost work days were associated with psychological factors in the corporate study mentioned above (APA, 2002). This finding points to the need to consider psychological and social factors in all claims for disability, regardless of the primary diagnosis for which the claim is presented. Moreover, in a study that examined role impairment from the four most commonly occurring physical disorders (hypertension, arthritis, asthma, and ulcers) in a nationally representative household survey of 5877 respondents, while all four physical disorders were associated with role impairment, analyses showed that these impairments were almost entirely confined to those cases with comorbid mental disorders (Kessler, Ormel, Demler, & Stang, 2003). This study is but one example of many in the literature that demonstrates the critical need to consider psychiatric comorbidity in the evaluation, treatment, and compensation of individuals claiming disability.

In the conditions that have been called "functional somatic syndromes," the interaction of psychosocial factors and physical symptoms is emphasized as is the problem of what Barsky (1979), Barsky & Borus (1999), and others have termed the "medicalization" of otherwise benign or non-medical factors. These concerns have also been variously expressed in relation to specific disorders with extensive psychosocial features, such as Chronic Fatigue Syndrome (Afari & Buchwald, 2003; Coetzer, Lockyer, Schorn, & Boshoff, 2000, 2001; Deale, Chalder, & Wessely, 1998; Jason, Richman, Friedberg, Wagner, Taylor, & Jordan 1997; Johnson, 1998; Wessely, 1997), Fibromyalgia (Coetzer et al., 2000, 2001; Gervais, Russell, Green, & Allen, 2001; Katon, Sullivan, & Walker, 2001; Winfield, 1997, 2000), and chronic pain more generally (Dersh, Gatchel, Polatin, & Mayer, 2002; Fishbain, Cutler, Rosomoff, & Rosomoff, 1997; Fishbain, Cutler, Rosomoff, Khalil, & Steele-Rosomoff, 1997; Gatchel, Polatin, & Mayer, 1995; Hart, Wade, & Martelli, 2003; MacFarlane, Stroud, Thorn, Jensen, & Boothby, 2000). In addition, for a more general discussion of psychosocial factors in disability, see Gatchel & Gardea (1999), Hadjistavropoulos & Bieling (2001), Khan, Khan, Harelezak, Tu, & Kroenke (2003), and William & Martin (2002).

Given the uncertainties involved in evaluating conditions in which there are few or no clear physical findings, it is important to consider risk factors that have been shown to contribute to outcome. Few would argue against the idea that recovering and return to work are in the best interests of both the claimant and the insurer (see for example, Hoaken & Sishta, 1988). In this regard, there are a number of risk factors that have been associated with potential for return to work. Though the relevant professional literature is vast and a full discussion beyond the scope of this chapter, based on the authors' review there are five factors that are repeatedly associated with potential for rehabilitation. First, and generally found to account for the largest proportion of variance, is the presence of physical findings related to a definable medical impairment. While physical findings are the best predictor of disability duration, the next four factors that typically are found to account for a substantial proportion of variance in return-to-work potential are all part of the psychosocial context in which the impairment exists. These are (a) the claimant's attitude toward disability and return to work; (b) the treating provider's attitude toward disability and return to work; (c) the claimant's perception of workplace support; and (d) the availability of compensation during the period of work absence.*

Given the extensive role played by psychosocial factors in impairment and disability, it is critical that those who treat, evaluate, or insure disability monitor the psychosocial factors involved in the claim in addition to the more clearly demonstrable clinical findings. In the conditions that in this volume are referred to as biopsychosocial disabilities, the psychosocial factors are even more critical in that there are sometimes few, if any, physical findings. In particular, it is the psychosocial factors that will need attention if there is to be an early identification of the risk that a claim will become chronic, and intervention to help ameliorate that possibility.

MEDICOLEGAL ISSUES IN DISABILITY COMPENSATION CLAIMS

The biopsychosocial conditions pose differing problems depending on the perspective from which they are approached. From a clinical perspective, the issues center on whether the condition can be accurately diagnosed, the extent to which it can be adequately differentiated from other conditions, and whether and to what extent it can be treated. From a rehabilitative perspective, the issues involve interventions that will increase functionality and/or accommodations that might be needed to make enhanced functioning possible. Both clinicians and rehabilitation specialists need to be able to accurately assess the impact of the condition on an individual's functioning across multiple life domains including work. Such assessment also involves considering the individual's motivations, emotional reserves, and social context, any and all of which will impact on the success of treatment and rehabilitation.

These perspectives are relevant to the clinical evaluation of a claim for disability compensation, but from the perspective of the disability insurer there are additional issues that must be addressed. Communication must be established with the treating clinicians and rehabilitation specialists, in order that the treating providers can provide information needed by the disability insurer in verifying the presence and extent of the medical impairment that is the basis of the disability claim. The clinician and rehabilitation specialist, who are used to working within their own professional language and settings, can be thrust into a medicolegal arena with which they are poorly

*With regard to the fourth factor, despite some controversy it has generally been shown across a number of contexts that the availability of compensation is associated with longer duration of disability (Hadjistavropoulos, 1999; Rohling, Binder, & Langhinrichsen-Rohling, 1995). That said, it is important to note that the data do not necessarily reflect causation, in the authors' opinion. Of course, as is often argued it may be that the availability of compensation is one reason some claimants remain on claim longer than necessary. However, it may also be that some individuals with legitimate impairments remain in the workplace longer than is medically advisable, because compensation is *not* available to them. Both conditions could account for the correlations found in the literature, and it seems to the authors likely that both are part of the equation. Additional research would be required to develop a model of causation.

prepared to cope, and about which they have little training (Barron, 2001). Even if a medical impairment is clearly established, the associated functional limitations and the restrictions from activity must be compared to occupational demands, in order to determine that the claimant cannot perform the duties of his or her occupation. Finally, the disparity between the claimant's functional capacity and the demands of his or her job must be compared to the specific contractual requirements, which vary depending on the type of compensation system (government, private disability, workers' compensation, etc.), as well as the specific contractual definitions to be applied (Barron, 2001; Hadjistavropoulos & Bieling, 2001; Mitchell, 2000). Specifically, even once it is established that a medical impairment exists, the question of disability is whether the claim is compensable, and this is a contractual rather than a clinical issue.

In the course of communicating with a disability insurer, the clinician often encounters unfamiliar terminology, or unfamiliar applications of otherwise known terms. Chief among these are the terms "impairment," "disability," "limitation," and "restriction." Though there are some differences in the use of these terms depending on the context,* the most critical distinction to be made is that "disability" should not be confused with "impairment." Generally speaking, "disability" is an administrative term that refers to an individual's inability to (or difficulty in) performing certain activities, such as work. "Impairment," on the other hand, is a medical term that can be defined as a loss of physiologic function or anatomic structure (AMA Guides, 2000; Creighton, 2001). Thus, disability is a broad term that incorporates impairment, but that also addresses factors other than medical that nevertheless contribute to problems in functioning. They include such issues as general health status, other physical abilities, mental and psychological capacities, and social context (Barron, 2001).

Within the description of impairment, a "limitation" is an internal constraint on functional capacity; i.e., a "limitation" is an activity or function that the individual either cannot perform, or would have significant difficulty performing. A "restriction," on the other hand, is an activity or function that the individual should not perform, generally because to do so might be harmful to the individual or to others. For example, an individual's impairment might be characterized by limited eyesight, on the basis of which he or she would likely be restricted from driving or performing dangerous activities for which eyesight is required.

An additional distinction to be made involves the relationship between a diagnosis and impairment as defined by limitations and restrictions. The important point is that a diagnosis does not necessarily mean that the individual is functionally impaired, as would for example be the case for an individual who met criteria for Major Depressive Disorder at one point, but who is currently well-treated and stable. Finally, just as diagnosis does not automatically translate to impairment, the presence

*In fact, some of the confusion arises from precisely the fact that there are variations on the use of these terms depending on the context. "Impairment" and "disability" have meanings that differ administratively, and that have been interpreted differently in the courts, depending for example on whether they are being applied in the context of ERISA-governed (Employee Retirement Income Security Act) private disability claims, non-ERISA claims, SSA (Social Security Administration) claims, or claims for accommodations governed by the ADA. While a comprehensive discussion of these contexts is beyond the scope of the chapter, the reader is strongly advised to assure that they understand the terms as they are being applied in the specific context in which they are involved.

of impairment does not automatically translate into disability in a particular area. For example, a defined impairment might involve restrictions and/or limitations, but those restrictions and limitations may not preclude the individual's performance of his/her occupational duties. In more concrete terms, an individual may have a back condition that limits the ability to lift, restricting him/her from lifting more than 15 lbs.; but if the job is sedentary and never requires the activity, then the impairment may not be a disability as determined by the relevant contract. Even an impairment that precludes some, but not all of the individual's occupational duties, might not meet the definition of disability as set forth in a particular contract (Barron, 2001; Hadjistavropoulos & Bieling, 2001; Mitchell, 2000).

Broadly speaking, the clinician involved in a process of disability determination, whether by choice as an independent examiner or by default as a treater who has been asked to complete a disability form, finds him/her self in a forensic, rather than a clinical, role. With this change in role comes the requirement for additional objectivity, which can in some circumstances and with some patients be difficult, at times impossible, and at times possible but therapeutically unwise. As a result, additional ethical considerations come into play in a number of areas. Second, the clinician who generally is in a position to take a patient's word for a description of symptoms and motivation, will now need to address symptom validity in some formal way (Fishbain, Cutler, Rosomoff, & Rosomoff, 1999; Gervais et al., 2001; Mittenberg, Patton, Canyock, & Condit, 2002; Reynolds, 1998). Finally, the clinician will find him/her self interpreting the patient's presentation, symptoms, diagnosis, and impairment within the context of a body of contractual language and legal precedents, perhaps unfamiliar to the clinician and almost certainly unfamiliar to the patient.

RELATING TO THE INSURER

The Decision to Support a Claim for Disability

When a patient requests that the treating provider consider supporting a claim for disability, not only is the therapeutic context altered but both the patient and the clinician are making a major commitment of time and energy. Often neither is aware of what may be involved. For the clinician, it will be necessary to clearly establish a primary diagnosis, to identify and describe impairment, and to document the findings in such a way that the insurer is helped to establish disability under the applicable policy provisions. In the course of this process, the clinician will be asked to provide information in a form that may be unfamiliar, as discussed above.

Even before attempting to evaluate the claimant's impairment, the clinician, in concert with the claimant will need to address the question, "Is it in the patient's best interest to support this claim?" A number of considerations will impact this decision. Mainly, it will be important to consider the potential impact on the clinician-patient relationship. In particular, the additional time and effort needed to document the claim may be difficult for the clinician to provide, may take away time from therapeutic interaction, and may strain the working therapeutic relationship.

It is worth noting that the therapeutic relationship will be affected whether the clinician does, or does not, agree to support the disability claim. If the clinician agrees to support a patient in their claim of disability, the additional demands placed on the clinician will impact the therapeutic relationship and the time available for patient care. If, on the other hand, the clinician chooses not to support the patient's request for disability certification, there will still be an impact on the clinician-patient relationship. The clinician may decide not to support the claim because clinical support is lacking, because the clinician desires to avoid medicolegal involvement, or because the clinician is unwilling to accommodate the additional demands on time and other resources. Whatever the reason, the clinician's decision not to support a disability claim may serve to strain the relationship with a patient who perceives himself as disabled and expects the clinician to act as an advocate for that belief.

Regardless of the clinician's decision, we recommend that the issues be thoroughly discussed with the patient. If the clinician decides not to support the claim, the reasons for the decision will need to be clearly explained to the patient, and it may be helpful to refer the patient for a second opinion or independent assessment. Such a referral provides an independent, collateral assessment and avoids the problem of the treating clinician being in a conflict of interest or a dual relationship, while allowing the clinician to continue treatment and to act as an advocate for the patient's best interests.

Competence to Assess Functional Capacity

One of the reasons for taking the time to consider carefully whether or not to support a patient's claim for disability is that the relationship between treating provider and patient differs from the relationship between objective evaluator and an examinee. Once it is determined that there is no clinical reason that the evaluation should not be undertaken, it then is important to determine if the clinician is *qualified* to do so. Clearly addressing this issue helps prevent potential pitfalls in professional, ethical, and legal areas.

From an ethical standpoint, the major professional associations maintain current ethical codes, and these will address issues related to scope of practice, competence, multiple (dual) relationships, and other areas of potential concern. There may also be available specialty guidelines available, such as the Specialty Guidelines for the Forensic Psychologists (American Psychological Association, 1991). Review of these codes and similar guidelines can assist the clinician in making sound decisions. Even if a clinician is ethically qualified, and assuming the clinician is qualified by training and/or experience, he or she still may not be qualified in the legal setting under their professional license. Licensed professional counselors and marriage and family therapists may not, for example, be able legally to provide a diagnosis. Further, for some clinicians practice may be limited to certain clinical areas such as marriage counseling or family therapy. Depending on jurisdiction, psychologists may not be allowed to testify to issues of permanency, causation, and maximum medical improvement, as these issues are seen to be areas of medical opinion (see, Selby v. Highways Inc., Supreme Court of TN, Special Workers' Compensation Appeals Panel, Nashville, 5/15/2003. Heilbrun (2001) contains an excellent discussion of ethical, legal, and treatment considerations for the interested reader.

Assuming the clinician is competent to make the evaluation in general terms, there remains the question of whether, in this particular instance, the clinician is capable of being objective in his/her evaluation. As the treating clinician, it may be difficult, and inherently conflictual, to become an advocate for disability determination especially if the clinician also attempts to assume or may be placed in the role of "expert" in the case (Greenberg & Shuman 1997, Greenberg & Gould 2001, and Strausburger et al. 1997). The critical concern centers on advocacy. Specifically, the treating clinician focuses on helping the patient deal with the implication of a medical disorder or state. Trust, development of a therapeutic relationship, and reliance on observation and self-report of symptoms and functioning are fundamental to this process. In short, the treating clinician most often takes the patient at his/her word. By contrast, the insuring body will approach a claim of disability with a greater need to evaluate, and will expect a more in-depth analysis and objective support for diagnosis and functional status. The role of the treating clinician may be further complicated if he or she advocates for disability as a means to relieve the social and emotional impact of the medical disorder, rather than as a result of a medical necessity based on the condition itself (McDonald, 2003). It is one thing to recommend time off in order to regroup or rest, but another to state that the individual is incapable of working due to a medical condition.

In many cases, even when the clinician believes the patient to be impaired, it may be advantageous for the treating clinician who has been asked to comment on impairment and disability to refer the patient to an independent evaluator for a second opinion. This avoids any question of dual relationship or potentially inappropriate advocacy, and sidesteps potential interference with the therapeutic relationship. Whether or not to undertake this step is a matter to be determined between the treating clinician and the patient, based on the patient's best interests.

Should the clinician elect instead to perform the evaluation, the key will be a thorough, well-supported, and objective analysis. While a discussion of the specific steps are outside the scope of this chapter, recommendations for conducting disability evaluations are available in a number of contexts. Barron (2001) provides an excellent overview of disability certification, decision making process, evaluation methods and practical points on disability evaluation and certification. He clarifies the role of the physician in disability determination as follows: "The family physician may be asked to complete a disability form by a patient, an insurance carrier, the workers' compensation board or other disability system. Each system defines disability according to its own needs and regulations, but the definitions typically lack specific criteria, thus precluding accurate determinations. It is also important to realize that an administrative law judge or other adjudicator assumes the role of decision maker in the process, rather than the family physician. In this situation, physicians will be typically asked to render a medical opinion to aid in the decision-making process, but will not assume a major role in the final determination" (p.1580). For a related discussion of similar issues, as well as specific recommendations regarding the evaluation of fatigue-related impairment, see also Coetzer et al (2000; 2001). For a discussion of these issues as they apply to the evaluation of impairment by the disability insurer, see Hadjistavropoulos (1999; 2001) and MacLeod, LaChapelle, & Pfeifer (2001).

Communicating with the Insurer

The information requirements of a disability insurer, whether public or private, often differ significantly from those of clinical practice. The insurer will request a formal and well-documented diagnosis, a clear and through description of functional limitations, and objective support for any restrictions and limitations reported. They may also request assessment or office notes to support and clarify the nature and extent of disability. While some of the communication with the insuring entity may seem foreign and outside the usual scope of the treater/patient relationship, the clinician can maximize benefit to the patient and minimize misunderstanding by knowing what is expected, and by communicating clearly within those expectations.

It is important for the clinician to keep in mind that a formal diagnosis suggests impairment, but does not necessarily infer disability. It is also important to keep in mind that the diagnosis must be formally documented, and is expected to adhere to known criteria that are accepted in the relevant professional field. Price (2001) and McDonald (2003), for example, provide excellent discussions of the necessity of a carefully formulated diagnosis as it applies to claims involving mental and emotional injuries. They point out that the general intent of the American's with Disabilities Act (ADA) regulations (and, we would add, many and perhaps most private disability contracts) imply that only disorders meeting specific diagnostic criteria, as defined in the Diagnostic and Statistical Manual of Mental Disorders, meet the definitions of covered mental impairments. McDonald cites several court rulings supporting this position. In Paleologos v. Rehabilitation Consultants, Inc., 990 (N.D. Ga. 1998), for example, the plaintiff was treated for work related stress, anxiety and depression. The Paleologos court emphasized the need for a formalized diagnosis. The court opined that stress and depression could qualify as impairments, but they must be the result of a documented mental disorder and that conclusory, self-report statements did not clearly or convincingly establish such impairment.

In addition to a diagnostic formulation, the thoughtful and thorough health care provider can greatly assist the disability determination process by providing fully articulated clinical data related to functional capacities. Price (2001) outlines for example the critical elements of clinical information in employment litigation as related to psychological injury claims. We suggest that the recommendations also have broader applicability and there are marked similarities in the development of information for disability determination. Price notes that critical elements include the following:

- Formalized DSM-IV-TR or ICD-9 or ICD-10 diagnoses stated in concise clinical terms, outlining how the diagnostic criteria are met.
- Subjective v. objective development of diagnostic data: Self-report data may be strengthened by the addition of strong behavioral observation and formalized mental status or similar measure, such as the Mini-Mental Status Examination, symptom specific inventories, objective psychological or medical testing, and symptom validity testing or discussion.
- Treatment issues: When the level of treatment intensity is consistent with the reported severity of the claimed disabling disorder, the credibility of the claim is enhanced. Infrequent appointments, vague treatment plans, low medication dosages, and inadequate medication trials do not lend support to the claim. Finally, outcome measures can be helpful documentation when clearly applied (Wiger & Solberg, 2001).
- Collateral Support: The clinical data may be further strengthened by collateral support consisting of documented information from family, co-workers, or other reliable sources.

- Pre-disability functioning: It is also important to provide some description or support for premorbid functioning. Such data must be carefully evaluated for the possibility of overstatement of premorbid function and potential minimizing of psychosocial factors, since self-reported medical history is often distorted (Barsky, 2002).

Perhaps the most important recommendation for communicating with a disability insurer is to focus on functional capacities, both those preserved and those impaired. While it is essential to reach a specific diagnosis that is well articulated in terms of diagnostic criteria as a baseline for the disability analysis, it is equally important to describe the nature and extent of any functional limitations associated with the primary (and secondary) diagnosis. This may be achieved by use of a variety of standardized and non-standardized evaluation methodologies. At a minimum, clinical interview and behavioral observations are the cornerstone of adequate biopsychosocial evaluation of impairment. In our opinion, formal mental status examination should be a part of any evaluation involving a disability claim, and the clinical records of any provider who plans to support the claim of a patient are necessary. Additional formal psychological and/or neurocognitive testing, performed in the office or by referral, are also appropriate in many cases in which cognitive complaints are claimed to impair functioning. Physical capacities can be measured by formal Functional Capacities Evaluation (FCE), or other methodology appropriate to the discipline of the clinician.

Finally, whether the claim is physical, mental, or comorbid it is important that test data and clinical measurements apply to "real world" disability issues; i.e., they should have adequate ecological validity. It is important to note that the presence of deficits on formal assessment measures does not necessarily predict or suggest disability. Bennett and Raymond (2003), for example, emphasize the importance of ecological validity and the necessity of strong behavioral observations in assessing neuropsychological functioning, and in our opinion their suggestions also have broader application. They note, "...the present authors believe that test scores and behavioral observations are both critically important. Nevertheless, neuropsychologists need to obtain not only test scores, but also observe how the patient approaches and performs each task that contributes to the specific test score. If a person obtains a normal score, but achieves this score in a manner that would never be successful in their ADLs, then the person is still disabled with respect to the cognitive ability being assessed."

Responding to Inquiries

The decision to certify disability will increase requests for information by the insuring body. We have already noted that disability determination is a multifactorial process, mediated by contractual language and based on medical proof. Treating providers cannot assume that their statements proclaiming an individual to be disabled will be accepted at face value. The insurer will request adequate, thorough and credible documentation to support any contention of disability. This assists the adjudicator and medical or psychological consultants in making fair and appropriate determinations as well as allowing for assessment of any claims which appear to be over-stated or inappropriate and outside of the parameters of the contractual language. Careful analysis of adequate information is needed to make a thoughtful, thorough, and fair determination (Hadjistavropoulos & Bieling, 2001).

The insurer will routinely request that all clinical data, assessment and progress notes be submitted in support of the disability claim. They may also request specific forms, such as attending physician's statements, mental status questionnaires or psychiatric/physical functional capacity evaluations that identify specific data related to diagnosis, symptoms, and functional levels. Dates of service and service codes may also be requested to assess treatment consistency and to correlate the reported treatment with the data reported in progress notes. The insurer may also request clarification of psychosocial issues, historical data for the determination of pre-existing disorders, or information to clarify treatment focus. If disability status is in the patient's best clinical interest, the treating provider would do well to assist in developing a thorough, well articulated and comprehensive information data base at the outset. Such a data base minimizes subsequent requests for additional information, solidifies and emphasizes the patient's diagnosis and any associated limitations, and minimizes any appearance of inconsistency of clinical presentation and treatment with reported levels of distress.

Requests for additional information should not be viewed as a challenge to the insured's credibility or to the treating provider's expertise. It should more realistically be viewed as a request for information to further develop an otherwise inadequate data set or to provide clarification on specific issues and questions that have specific implications for contractual eligibility. Most claims will be assigned to a specific claim representative and/or clinical reviewer. If requests for information are received, it would serve the treating provider and the patient best to directly communicate with the claim representative or reviewer, to develop a cooperative working relationship whenever possible, and to clarify any concerns or expectations rather than to avoid contact, become defensive, or assume an ardent advocacy role.

A final concern to be addressed involves the decision to submit complete office notes vs. narratives or other supplemental information. Typically, the insurer will request the complete record and will find contemporaneous notes more helpful than a retrospective reconstruction. That said, providing information is a mutual decision on the part of the patient and provider, made in the context the current HIPAA (Health Insurance Portability and Accountability Act) or other relevant regulations related to privacy. The patient is the ultimate decision maker in the release of information, but the certifying clinician will be responsible for providing data adequate to make a clear disability determination. If a narrative is to be provided rather than the original notes, the summary should be comprehensive, should address the primary and secondary diagnoses that are within the provider's expertise, and should describe functional limitations with supportive behavioral description and other relevant clinical information. The summary may be further clarified by the provision of medical data such as testing results or data summaries, dates of service and service codes to indicate the frequency and intensity of treatment. Treatment plans, especially as they relate to a focus on increased functionality, also provide supportive data. In the end, assuming (a) that the patient is impaired, (b) that the clinician has determined that it is in the patient's best interests to support a claim for disability, and (c) that the clinician has determined that it is appropriate to offer that support, then it is the communication with the insurer that will provide the basis for the insurer's ability to make a full, fair, and thorough evaluation of the claim.

CONCLUSIONS AND RECOMMENDATIONS

In conclusion, we offer some general recommendations regarding the evaluation of disability claims, based on our own experience and the work of other authors. In doing so, we echo some of the recommendations first offered by Hadjistavropoulus (1999; & Bieling, 2001), Mitchell (2000), Barron (2001), Coetzer et al. (2001), and others. First and foremost, it is important to recognize that the question of whether a medical impairment becomes a disability is biopsychosocial. In other words, it is a function of psychosocial issues in addition to the relevant medical concerns. Attention to the role of the individual's life circumstances, workplace issues, attitudes toward work and toward disabilty, motivation to resume improved functioning, and other risk factors need to be considered in evaluating a claim for disabilty. The issue is not whether to doubt nor to advocate the individual's claim of being disabled, but to appropriately and adequately assess all the relevant factors.

Second, return to work, or at a minimum return to a higher level of functioning, should be a focus for all parties involved. Health professionals can do more to encourage compensated and other insured patients to return to work, as there is little room for doubt across multiple areas of study that it is in the best interests of individuals to remain as productive as possible within whatever limitations they might have. The health care provider, in partnership with other involved parties, can play a critical role in developing a return to work plan. Employers in turn can do more to address workplace dissatisfaction and other issues that contribute to the experience of disability, and to minimize barriers to returning employees to work in a reasonable, graduated manner that makes accommodations where needed and where possible. They can do more to resolve competing self-interests and ambivalence regarding return to work, and they can avoid creating iatrogenic disability by using recommendations for disability claim as a means of managing difficult employees. Most importantly, employers can do more to become active partners in helping their employees return to work. Finally, insurers can do more to create collaborative relationships with claimants, with treating providers, and with employers. The goals are to minimize polarized interactions that tend to entrench positions or create "sides," and to maximize the potential for all parties to work together to support the claimant financially when medically and contractually appropriate, and to facilitate a return to better functioning as soon as is possible given the specific circumstances.

Third, more can be done to ensure diagnostic accuracy, a focus on functionality in evaluating impairment, and clear communication between the treating or evaluating providers and the insurers. Clinicians can focus on a thorough assessment that leads to an accurate and fully specified diagnosis, and they can address functional limitations clearly and precisely even in conditions where the condition is more difficult to define. Insurers can better define their expectations regarding documentation on the one hand, while on the other hand holding clinicians accountable for accurate and well-defined diagnoses and, wherever possible, treatment plans that contain a focus on improved functionality.

Finally, all participants in the disability process can do more to acknowledge and manage bias where it exists. As Hadjistavropoulus and Bieling (2001) wrote, "One may be tempted to assume that the parties involved, whether it is the claimant or the insurance company, are entirely motivated by economic factors. That is, one may assume that the goal of the insurance company is to reduce the amount of claims paid out, whereas the goal of the claimant is to maximize monies received" (p. 54). The authors argue that this scenario is unlikely on the part of the insurance company, because false claim denial undermines confidence in the company and can lead to substantial adverse legal and financial consequences. They also point out that claimants are unlikely to be motivated entirely by economics, as they generally would be better compensated for meaningful work. The keys to managing bias are to work cooperatively wherever possible, to evaluate credibility and motivation and to encourage treating clinicians to do so as well, and to be cognizant of the ethical issues in evaluating disability claimants.

In the end, we argue that all disability claims must be given a thorough evaluation of each relevant issue, including the psychosocial context. We acknowledge that, from the perspective of risk management, treatment, and rehabilitation, the conditions that are the subject of this volume can often benefit from early identification and intervention. To that extent, complex biopsychosocial disabilities can be seen to differ from other medical impairments. However, from the perspective of evaluating for insurance compensation based on disability, claims based on ambiguous or more subjective conditions do not require an approach that differs methodologically from any other claim. In fact, fairness requires that each claim be managed similarly, with respect to evaluation of functional impairment as it applies to the relevant contractual context. A full, fair, and objective evaluation is the best assurance that any claim for disability is appropriately considered. The understanding of disability claims becomes progressively more complex and difficult as the associated clinical conditions become more ambiguous and less clearly defined by verifiable medical evidence, but ultimately the approach to evaluating impairment and disability follows the same methodological principles.

ACKNOWLEDGMENTS: The authors wish to acknowledge the contribution of Bob Anfield, MD, JD in reviewing, commenting on, and encouraging this project. The opinions expressed in this chapter are based on literature review and on the personal and professional experience of the authors. They are not intended to represent the policy or official position of their employer, UnumProvident Corporation.

REFERENCES

Afari, N., & Buchwald, D. (2003). Chronic fatigue syndrome: a review. *American Journal Psychiatry, 160* (2), 221–236.

American Medical Association (2000). *Guides for the evaluation of permanent impairment* (5th ed.). Chicago: AMA Press.

Committee on Ethical Guidelines for Forensic Psychologists (1991). Specialty guidelines for forensic psychologists. *Law and Human Behavior, 15*(6), 655–665.

APA. (2002). *The costs of failing to provide appropriate mental health care.* Retrieved 8/5/2003, 2003, from http://www.apa.org/practice/failing.html.

Barron, B. A. (2001). Disability certifications in adult workers: A practical approach. *American Family Physician, 64*, 1579–1586.

Barsky, A. J. (2002). Forgetting, fabricating, and telescoping: the instability of the medical history. *Archives of Internal Medicine, 162*(9), 981–984.

Barsky, A. J., 3rd. (1979). Patients who amplify bodily sensations. *Ann Intern Med, 91*(1), 63–70.

Barsky, A. J., & Borus, J. F. (1999). Functional somatic syndromes. *Annals of Internal Medicine, 130*(11), 910–921.

Coetzer, P., Lockyer, I., Schorn, D., & Boshoff, L. (2000). Quantitative disability evaluation of syndromes presenting with chronic fatigue. *South African Medical Journal, 90*(10 Pt 2), 1034–1052.

Coetzer, P., Lockyer, I., Schorn, D., & Boshoff, L. (2001). Assessing impairment and disability for syndromes presenting with chronic fatigue. *Journal of Insurance Medicine, 33*(2), 170–182.

Creighton, M (2001). Mental disabilities under the Americans with Disabilities Act. *In*: J. J. McDonald & F. B. Kulick (Eds.), *Mental and Emotional Injuries in Employment Litigation* (2nd ed., pp. 72–116). Washington, DC: The Bureau of National Affairs.

Deale, A., Chalder, T., & Wessely, S. (1998). Illness beliefs and treatment outcome in chronic fatigue syndrome. *Journal Psychosomatic Research, 45*(1 Spec No), 77–83.

Dersh, J., Gatchel, R. J., Polatin, P., & Mayer, T. (2002). Prevalence of psychiatric disorders in patients with chronic work-related musculoskeletal pain disability. *Journal of Occupational and Environmental Medicine, 44*(5), 459–468.

Fishbain, D. A., Cutler, R., Rosomoff, H. L., & Rosomoff, R. S. (1997). Chronic pain-associated depression: antecedent or consequence of chronic pain? A review. *Clinical Journal of Pain, 13*(2), 116–137.

Fishbain, D. A., Cutler, R., Rosomoff, H. L., & Rosomoff, R. S. (1999). Chronic pain disability exaggeration/malingering and submaximal effort research. *Clinical Journal of Pain, 15*(4), 244–274.

Fishbain, D. A., Cutler, R. B., Rosomoff, H. L., Khalil, T., & Steele-Rosomoff, R. (1997). Impact of chronic pain patients' job perception variables on actual return to work. *Clinical Journal of Pain, 13*(3), 197–206.

Gatchel, R. J., & Gardea, M. A. (1999). Psychosocial issues: their importance in predicting disability, response to treatment, and search for compensation. *Neurologic Clinics, 17*(1), 149–166.

Gatchel, R. J., Polatin, P. B., & Mayer, T. G. (1995). The dominant role of psychosocial risk factors in the development of chronic low back pain disability. *Spine, 20*(24), 2702–2709.

Gelfand, S. G. (2002). The pitfalls of opioids for chronic nonmalignant pain of central origin. *Medscape Rheumatology, 4 (1)*. Retrieved from http://www.medscape.com/viewarticle/425468.

Gervais, R. O., Russell, A. S., Green, P., Allen, L. M., 3rd, Ferrari, R., & Pieschl, S. D. (2001). Effort testing in patients with fibromyalgia and disability incentives. *Journal of Rheumatology, 28*(8), 1892–1899.

Hadjistavropoulos, T. (1999). Chronic pain on trial: The influence of litigation and compensation on chronic pain syndromes. In A. R. Block, E. F. Kremer & E. Fernandez (Eds.), *Handbook of Pain Syndromes: Biopsychosocial Perspectives* (pp. 59–76). Mahwah, New Jersey: Lawrence Erlbaum Associates.

Hadjistavropoulos, T., & Bieling, P. (2001). File review consultation in the adjudication of mental health and chronic pain disability claims. *Consulting Psychology Journal: Practice & Research, 53*(1), 52–63.

Hart, R. P., Wade, J. B., & Martelli, M. F. (2003). Cognitive impairment in patients with chronic pain: the significance of stress. *Current Pain Headache Report, 7*(2), 116–126.

Heilbrun, K. (2001). *Principles of foresic mental health assessment: Perspectives in law & psychology, Vol. 12*. New York: Kluver Academic/Plenum Publishers.

Hoaken, N. H., & Sishta, S. K. (1988). *Insurability of the psychiatrically ill or those with a past history of psychiatric disorder: The position of the Canadian Psychiatric Association*. Retrieved July 3, 2003, from http://www.cpa-apc.org

Jason, L. A., Richman, J. A., Friedberg, F., Wagner, L., Taylor, R., & Jordan, K. M. (1997). Politics, science, and the emergence of a new disease. The case of chronic fatigue syndrome. *American Psychologist, 52*(9), 973–983.

Johnson, S. K. (1998). The biopsychosocial model and chronic fatigue syndrome. *American Psychologist, 53*(9), 1080–1082.

Katon, W., Sullivan, M., & Walker, E. (2001). Medical symptoms without identified pathology: relationship to psychiatric disorders, childhood and adult trauma, and personality traits. *Annals of Internal Medicine, 134*(9 Pt 2), 917–925.

Kessler, R. C., Ormel, J., Demler, O., & Stang, P. E. (2003). Comorbid mental disorders account for the role impairment of commonly occurring chronic physical disorders: results from the National Comorbidity Survey. *Journal of Occupational and Environmental Medicine, 45*(12), 1257–1266.

Khan, A. A., Khan, A., Harezlak, J., Tu, W., & Kroenke, K. (2003). Somatic symptoms in primary care: etiology and outcome. *Psychosomatics, 44*(6), 471–478.

MacFarlane, G. J., Morris, S., Hunt, I. M., Benjamin, S., McBeth, J., Papagerorgiou, A. C., et al. (1999). Chronic widespread pain in the community: The influence of psychological symptoms and mental disorder on healthcare seeking behavior. *Journal of Rheumatology, 26*(2), 413–419.

MacLeod, F. K., LaChapelle, D. L., Hadjistavropoulos, T., & Pfeifer, J. E. (2001). The effect of disability claimants' coping styles on judgments of pain, disability, and compensation: A vignette study. *Rehabilitation Psychology* (Vol. 46, pp. 417–435). US: American Psychological Assn/Educational Publishing Foundation, US, http:\\www.apa.org.

Mitchell, K. (2000, October, 2000). The dance of the invisible impairments: Chronic pain syndromes & the disability insurer. *American Society of Chronic Pain Newsletter.*

Mittenberg, W., Patton, C., Canyock, E. M., & Condit, D. C. (2002). Base rates of malingering and symptom exaggeration. *Journal of Clinical and Experimental Neuropsychoogyl, 24*(8), 1094–1102.

Murray, C. L. J., & Lopez, A. D. (1997). Global mortality, disability and the contribution of risk factors: Global Burden of Disease Study. *Lancet, 349*, 1436–1342.

Price, D. R. (2001). Clinical evaluation and case formulation of mental and emotional injury claims. In J. J. McDonald & F. B. Kulick (Eds.), *Mental and Emotional Injuries in Employment Litigation* (2nd ed., pp. 72–116). Washington, DC: The Bureau of National Affairs.

Reynolds, C. R. (1998). Common sense, clinicians, and actuarialism in the detection of malingering during head injury litigation. In C. R. Reynolds (Ed.), *Detection of malingering during head injury litigation.* (pp. 261–286). New York, NY, US: Plenum Press, New York, NY, US.

Rohling, M. L., Binder, L. M., & Langhinrichsen-Rohling, J. (1995). Money matters: A meta-analytic review of the association between financial compensation and the experience and treatment of chronic pain. *Health Psychology, 14*(6), 537–547.

Stroud, M. W., Thorn, B. E., Jensen, M. P., & Boothby, J. L. (2000). The relation between pain beliefs, negative thoughts, and psychosocial functioning in chronic pain patients. *Pain, 84*(2–3), 347–352.

Strausberger, L. H., Gutheil, T. G., & Brodsky, A. (1997). On wearing two hats: Role conflict in serving as both psychotherapist and expert witness. *American Journal of Psychiatry, 154*, 448–456.

Wessely, S. (1997). Chronic fatigue syndrome: a 20th century illness? *Scandinavian Journal of Work and Environmental Health, 23 Suppl 3*, 17–34.

Williams, M. A., & Martin, M. Y. (2002). Symptoms, signs, and ill-defined conditions. In S. B. Johnson, N. W. Perry, JR & R. H. Rozensky (Eds.), *Handbook of clinical health psychology: Volume 1. Medical disorders and behavioral applications.* (pp. 533–553). Washington, DC, US: American Psychological Association, Washington, DC, US.

Winfield, J. B. (1997). Fibromyalgia: what's next? *Arthritis Care and Research, 10*(4), 219–221.

Winfield, J. B. (2000). Psychological determinants of fibromyalgia and related syndromes. *Current Review of Pain, 4*(4), 276–286.

23

Secondary Gains and Losses in the Medicolegal Setting

Jeffrey Dersh, Peter Polatin, Gordon Leeman, and Robert Gatchel

Freud first proposed the concept of secondary gain, which he described as "... interpersonal or social advantage attained by the patient as a consequence of ... illness" (Freud, 1917). This is to be differentiated from primary gain, an intrapsychic phenomenon by which anxiety is reduced through an unconscious defensive operation resulting in symptoms of a physical illness. Blindness or limb paralysis for which a medical etiology cannot be demonstrated are examples of symptoms of illness mediated by primary gain. Ultimately, the psychiatric diagnosis of "hysteria," a somatoform conversion disorder, may be made in these patients.

Secondary gain was often conceptualized as a result of the symptoms created by primary gain mechanisms. Patients' need to alleviate guilt or conflict was expressed in the physical symptoms (primary gain).They were then able to avoid certain activities or to receive supports from their environment that would otherwise not be forthcoming (secondary gain). Both of these were considered by Freud to be unconscious processes (i.e., beyond awareness and volition). It should be noted that Freud did not link secondary gain exclusively to primary gain. Instead, he noted that secondary gain factors are consequences of "real" injuries or illness, as well as neurotic (i.e., psychological) illness, such as a phobia. Note that secondary gain is a perpetuating factor rather than a precipitant of illness.

Freud's description of an injured worker (Freud, 1917, 1966) vividly describes his ideas about secondary gain, as well as their continued relevance:

> A capable working-man, who earns his living, is crippled by an accident in the course of his occupation. The injured man can no longer work, but eventually he obtains a small disablement pension, and he learns how to exploit his mutilation by begging... If you could put an end to his injury you would make him, to begin with, without means of subsistence; the question would arise of whether he was still capable of taking up his earlier work again. What corresponds in the case of neuroses to a secondary exploitation like this of an illness may be described as the secondary gain from illness (p. 384, 1966).

DOI: 10.1007/978-0-387-28919-9_23, © 2009 Springer Science+Business Media, LLC

In more recent years, secondary gain has taken on a life of its own outside the traditional psychoanalytic arena (Fishbain, 1994; Leeman, Polatin, Gatchel, & Kishino, 2000). As early as 1976, Finneson (1976) observed that the term secondary gain "has developed increasing use and has generally referred to the financial rewards associated with disability". In turn, the presence of potential financial rewards is often equated with conscious malingering (Fishbain, 1994; Gatchel, Adams, Polatin, & Kishino, 2002; Leeman et al., 2000). The suspicion that arises in the clinician interferes with treatment and development of empathy. The secondary gain issues are then often used as an excuse for treatment failures.

MALINGERING

The term malingering, as it is typically understood, is pejorative and suggestive of criminality, or at least poor moral character. The American Psychiatric Association (American Psychiatric Association Task Force on DSM-IV., 1994) defines malingering as "the intentional production of false or grossly exaggerated physical or psychological symptoms, motivated by external incentives such as avoiding military duty, avoiding work, obtaining financial compensation, evading criminal prosecution, or obtaining drugs" (p. 683; APA, 1994). The APA does not classify malingering as a psychiatric disorder. In medicolegal contexts (including workers' compensation situations), there appears to be a widespread, implicit assumption that: *secondary gain = desire for financial compensation = probable malingering*. But, as noted by Fishbain and colleagues (Fishbain, Rosomoff, Cutler, & Rosomoff, 1995), "If all patients in a medical facility and/or all chronic pain patients were examined for alleged secondary gains, few patients should appear to be free of secondary gains" (p. 7). Can all of these patients be malingerers? Multiple sources of evidence suggest not. For example, King (King, 1994) quoted from the Social Security Administrations's Commission on the evaluation of pain "that there are simply not very many malingerers in the Social Security disability applicant population" (p. 279).

Our observations (Leeman et al., 2000), as well as those of other investigators [e.g., (Aronoff & Livengood, 2003)], in working with these populations of patients have led us to similar conclusions (i.e., that secondary gains are the rule not the exception, but that few patients are malingerers). Malingerers often have a sociopathic background of deviant and maladaptive behavior, whereas the vast majority of patients have been fairly normal prior to their injuries or illnesses, although not all experts agree that there is a strong correlation between malingering and sociopathy [e.g., (Clark, 1997)]. Rogers (Rogers, 1997) proposes an alternate adaptational model of malingering in which many types of individuals malinger when they perceive the assessment or treatment as adversarial and, after applying a cost-benefit analysis, they consider malingering the best means of achieving their goals. Nevertheless, malingerers typically pursue their agendas (e.g., disability claims) with a single-minded purpose, while keeping the rest of their lives in order. Patients who are not malingering will have difficulties in multiple aspects of their lives beyond their illness and disability, including family, finances, and transportation. Malingerers will be noncompliant with treatment, although they will attend all appointments (e.g., disability evaluations) which have the purpose of validating their claims (Leeman et al., 2000). It has been suggested that the label malingering be reserved for that small subset of patients who deliberately exploit others in order to get rewards (Robinson, Rondinelli, Scheer, & Weinstein, 1997).

There is additional support for this perspective on malingering. Fishbain and colleagues (Fishbain, Cutler, Rosomoff, & Rosomoff, 1999) extensively reviewed the literature and determined that between 1.25% and 10.4% of chronic pain patients are probable malingerers. They also reviewed attempts to identify disability exaggeration, malingering, and submaximal effort in the research literature. Despite the unfortunate use of the terms malingering and disability exaggeration as synonyms, their review was exceptional. They found a lack of empirical support for almost all methods to detect these phenomena, with the possible exception of isokinetic testing. They concluded that pain physicians should desist from believing that malingering can be conclusively identified in some way. Hutchinson (2000) also highlighted the difficulty of ascertaining the prevalence of malingering because, by definition, successfully malingering individuals go undetected. Accurate incidence rates are also difficult to determine because it overlaps with a host of everyday lying behaviors such as calling in sick for work when not ill, and making excuses to avoid social functions (Cunnien, 1997).

Another useful aspect of their review is attention to the concept of "gradations" of malingering, depending on the degree of self-deception (Ensalada, 2000; Fishbain et al., 1999; Garner, 1965; Rogers, 1997; Travin & Protter, 1984). We agree that there probably are gradations of malingering, but choose not to invoke the concept of self-deception in defining these gradations. In our conceptualization, a "pure" malingerer is not ill, injured, or in pain, but consciously presents symptoms consistent with injury, illness, or pain. Therefore, a "pure" malingerer does not have an agenda of improving health and function, because there is no real health decrement. A "partial" malingerer is consciously exaggerating existing illness, injury, or pain, but also has an agenda of improving health and function. A non-malingerer does not consciously feign or exaggerate any symptoms. It is our belief that many patients may fall in the category of partial malingering. However, we think it is useful to use the term malingering only for the "pure" malingerer because of the antipathy toward the patient that is associated with the term malingering. In our conceptualization, if at least one of the patient's agendas is improved health and function, they can be worked with productively, and without use of the term malingering.

FACTITIOUS DISORDER

The "intentional production of false or grossly exaggerated physical symptoms" is not limited to malingerers. When such symptoms are *internally* (versus externally; see above) motivated, the psychiatric diagnosis of factitious disorder is given (APA, 1994). In a factitious disorder, the internal (or intrapsychic) motivation for the behavior is to assume the sick role (presumably due to unmet needs to be cared for). Such patients have significant psychopathology (often borderline personality disorder) driving their relentless pursuit of frequently invasive medical procedures (Hutchinson, 2000). Factitious disorder is difficult to diagnose because the clinician must determine conscious production of symptoms, based upon unconscious motives, in an uncooperative patient (Cunnien, 1997).They are difficult to treat because their behavior is mostly driven by primary gain (Hutchinson, 2000), making it difficult or irrelevant to define or resolve secondary gain needs. In fact, resolution is not what they seek. When confronted, they will simply move on to another hospital, emergency room, or clinician and start all over again (Leeman et al., 2000). Fortunately, factitious disorder has been found to be an uncommon condition (Cunnien, 1997; Hutchinson, 2000), although accurate epidemiologic data are unavailable, because deception is an integral part of this disorder (Wise & Ford, 1999).

COMPENSATION AND LITIGATION NEUROSIS

Compensation and litigation issues have been found to be associated with illnesses being treated within a medicolegal context. The terms "compensation neurosis" and "litigation neurosis" have been popularized to describe the conscious or unconscious tendency of some individuals who are faced with secondary financial gain to amplify their symptoms (e.g., Allaz et al., 1998; Bellamy, 1997; Fishbain et al., 1995; Robinson et al., 1997). Compensation and litigation issues undoubtedly play an important role in the medicolegal treatment context. Indeed, numerous studies have found that injured workers with various types of medical conditions display a poorer response to treatment than do patients who are similar from a medical standpoint, but whose injuries are not work-related (Myerson, McGarvey, Henderson, & Hakim, 1994; Rainville, Sobel, Hartigan, & Wright, 1997; Robinson et al., 1997).

Financial issues play an important role in this phenomenon. Loeser and colleagues (Loeser, Henderlite, & Conrad, 1995) evaluated the effect of the wage replacement ratio (the ratio between an individual's workers' compensation income and the income received at the job of injury) on injury claims. They found that, as this wage replacement ratio increases, the frequency and duration of workers' compensation claims increases as well. In a country with no compensation system, Lithuania, patients with whiplash syndrome after an automobile accident were followed for 1-3 years. The incidence of chronic neck pain and headache was not significantly different from that found in a control group of age and gender matched uninjured individuals (Schrader et al., 1996).

However, conflicting findings have also been reported in the literature. For example, in Switzerland, Allaz and colleagues (Allaz et al., 1998) found that pain patients labeled "litigation neurosis" by their physicians were no more likely than those not labeled in this way to actually be involved in legal action or a claim for disability benefits. Even the wage-replacement findings can be challenged. In a military setting, the "compensation incentive" (similar to wage-replacement ratio) was calculated for those undergoing lumbar disc surgery. Although compensation incentive was linked to increased claims for disability, the results were confounded by base pay, with those who received less pay more likely to seek disability claims (Young, Shaffrey, Laws, & Lovell, 1997).

Perhaps most importantly, it has been noted that resolution of compensation or litigation issues does not result in decreased disability for many patients (Bellamy, 1997; Fishbain et al., 1995; Hutchinson, 2000). Fishbain and colleagues (1995) provided evidence from multiple studies that "some or most" chronic pain patients are *not* "cured by verdict." The failure of verdict to cure has been attributed to several factors. It has been argued that if the patient recovers fully, the perpetrator of injury upon them, as they perceive it, gets off without being punished .(Bellamy, 1997). Patients may also not recover because they fear to do so would be an admission of fraud and also because they may feel a need to defend their disability against the possible withdrawal of benefits should the case be re-examined (Bellamy, 1997). Fishbain and colleagues (1995) describe well the inconsistent results in the literature and possible reasons for these findings. Further, their review of the literature does not provide evidence that the poorer prognosis for patients being seen in a medicolegal context is directly related to financial secondary gain.

Other investigators have offered additional explanations for conflicting results in this area of research. It has been suggested, for example, that litigation and compensation neurosis are inadequate terminology for a poorly identified psychiatric morbidity (depression, personality disorders), or may reflect difficulty in the physician-patient relationship in the presence of a psychiatric morbidity (Allaz et al., 1998). Other investigators have pointed to various contextual issues as part of the explanation for less successful outcomes with work-related injuries, such as the nature of compensation laws, pre- and post-injury workplace factors, the local socioeconomic environment, and mixed messages from physicians, independent medical examiners, case managers, claims adjustors, employers, and attorneys (Robinson et al., 1997). It has also been noted that money has symbolic importance and, as such, is a powerful psychological motivator, often permitting revenge or punishment in a socially acceptable fashion. For example, it may be a victory over an authority figure (e.g., an employer) symbolized by money that the injured litigant seeks, not mere compensation itself (Cunnien, 1997).

Bellamy (1997) provides perhaps the most incisive explanation of compensation neurosis. He argues that it arises out of several societal factors, including the bureaucratic role of "gatekeeper" that has been thrust upon physicians against their will, the adversarial nature of pursuing a disability or personal injury claim (which places the patient in the position of needing to escalate symptomatology whenever challenged or reexamined), and a system that provides financial reward for illness or injury. The result of these factors is "social iatrogenesis" for disease production by well-intentioned social programs, disturbances in the physician-patient relationship (resulting in a nocebo effect instead of the usual placebo effect), somatization, and rationalization of symptoms. Bellamy states that:

> Population surveys show musculoskeletal symptoms to be extraordinarily common... In the noncompensation situation, such sensations usually are dismissed as not worthy of medical attention. That those situations become defined as cause for worry and evidence of the probable existence of tissue injury in compensation systems should not be a surprise... The rationalization process is easy to reconstruct. The patient asks himself or herself whether the symptoms existed before the accident. The answer for the claimant is no. Then the accident must have caused the symptoms in question. In a sense, the accident has caused the constellation of symptoms being experienced. But the accident did not directly cause the symptoms. It is the availability of and seductive appeal of the benefits that accrue from displays of illness behavior, combined with suggestion, somatization, and rationalization, that is the probable etiologic agent. The concept of learned pain behavior (operant pain) works well here also (Bellamy, 1997, p. 100).

DISORDERS OF SIMULATION

Hutchinson (2000) introduces the concept of "disorders of simulation" to refer to instances in which the patient exaggerates symptoms of illness. These disorders, which he estimates occur in approximately 5–10% of patients in his forensic practice, include malingering, factitious disorder, and "compensation neurosis" (although he believes that this latter term is misleading). Hutchinson argues that most patients being seen in medicolegal contexts are not malingering and do not suffer from factitious disorder. Instead, most simulating patients are best conceptualized as having compensation neurosis and fall somewhere in the "gray area" between these two extremes. The term simulation refers to the behavioral act of symptom creation, exaggeration, or misattribution with a clear intentional or volitional component.

Hutchinson (2000) proposes that almost all of these patients are exaggerating symptoms and disability to some extent, whether consciously or unconsciously. He further proposes that this group of patients can be subdivided into different syndromal patterns of simulation, based on patterns of behavior, motivational factors, and personality features. He then takes the fairly radical step of formulating these syndromes as disorders of simulation, akin to psychiatric disorders, but not recognized by the formal psychiatric community (except for factitious disorder). Hutchinson proposes diagnostic criteria for these three disorders, based on behavioral patterns, level of interpersonal functioning, and personality disorders. He contends that simulation is always an interpersonal phenomenon (it requires an audience), and that all of these patients have a personality disorder or other significant personality disturbance. He suggests that the reason symptoms frequently do not resolve post-litigation or at case settlement is because the compensation in compensation neurosis is a psychodynamic factor and may refer to gratification of dependency needs, expression of revenge, passive-aggressive discharge of anger, and other such motivations instead of or in addition to simple avarice (Hutchinson, 2001).

Hutchinson's (2000) ideas are novel, complex, and psychodynamically informed. Although Hutchinson (2000) primarily writes for the forensic evaluator in medicolegal contexts, his ideas and concepts also have great practical relevance for the clinician.

SYMPTOM MAGNIFICATION SYNDROME AND CHRONIC DISABILITY SYNDROME

Thoughtful observers have advocated abandonment of the terms compensation and litigation neurosis. They note that it is an unflattering diagnosis in that it implies malingering on the part of a claimant. Consequently, these terms are used polemically by defense attorneys and other advocates of insurance companies (Robinson et al., 1997). The term "symptom magnification syndrome" may be a less pejorative way to describe patients who display a self-destructive, socially reinforced behavioral pattern (with a volitional component) consisting of reports or displays of symptoms which function to control the life circumstances of the sufferer (Matheson, 1991). When the volitional component is absent, it may be more appropriate to use the term "chronic disability syndrome," (Strang, 1985) which refers to a set of dysfunctional attitudes and beliefs which develop over time as an injured worker adapts to disability

(Robinson et al., 1997), resulting in significant life disruption, including a marked restriction in functional activities (Aronoff & Livengood, 2003). This term is consistent with the observation that the relationship of most injured workers to the compensation system is one of dependence, rather than one of exploitation (Robinson et al., 1997). Patients with chronic disability syndrome have a "disability conviction," which is a belief that, because of chronic illness, one is unable to meet occupational demands and domestic, family, and social responsibilities, and unable to engage in avocational and recreational activities (Aronoff & Livengood, 2003). This syndrome is so common in patients with longstanding pain that the term "chronic pain syndrome" was introduced. Patients exhibiting chronic disability syndrome (including chronic pain syndrome) typically display a wide range of abnormal illness behaviors.

ABNORMAL ILLNESS BEHAVIORS

The chronic disability syndrome is not limited to dysfunctional attitudes and beliefs (i.e., disability conviction), but also describes several behavioral patterns that, as a whole, have been termed abnormal illness behavior. The general term "illness behavior" was introduced by Mechanic (1962) as the ways in which given symptoms may be perceived, evaluated, and acted (or not acted) upon by different kinds of persons. Illness, subjectively experienced by the individual based on both cultural factors and unique individual biographies, must be differentiated from disease, which is the actual pathological alteration in biological structure or function (Kleinman, 1988). Illness behavior typically elicits caregiving responses from others (Stuart & Noyes, 1999). Illness behavior also allows the individual to become a patient, and thus to adopt the "sick role" (Parsons, 1964, 1978). The sick role, a socially sanctioned (and physician-approved) role, describes a set of obligations and privileges that accrue to an ill person. Obligations of the sick role include accepting that it is undesirable, recognizing an obligation to cooperate with others to achieve health, and utilizing the services of those regarded by society as competent to diagnose and treat the illness. Privileges include a lack of responsibility for the symptoms and illness (i.e., not malingering), a right to receive care, and exemption from normal obligations (Parsons, 1964, 1978), which can also be viewed as secondary gains (Pilowsky, 1997).

Normal illness behavior describes behavioral responses that are appropriate and adaptive (Pilowsky, 1997) and, therefore, consistent with the sick role. Abnormal illness behavior, then, is the persistence of an inappropriate or maladaptive mode of perceiving, evaluating, and acting (or not acting) in relation to individuals' symptoms or state of health (Pilowsky, 1969) In other words, it is an excessive concern with somatic symptoms and inappropriate treatment-seeking in patients who are motivated by fear of severe disease or by the potential rewards of the sick role (Pilowsky, 1993). Abnormal illness behavior is therefore a violation of the socially sanctioned sick role.

Blackwell and Gutmann (1987) describe the prototypical abnormal chronic illness behaviors of disability claimants:

- Disability disproportionate to detectable disease.
- Seeking of disease validation by a physician who will place an acceptable somatic label on their condition.

- Placing responsibility on the physician for treatment outcomes.
- Attitudes of victimization, resentment toward those believed to be responsible for the injury (e.g., a supervisor), and a sense of entitlement to be cared for and compensated.
- Avoidance of healthy roles due to lack of skills, excessive expectations, or fear of failure because it reduces the anxiety associated with inadequate performance of such roles.
- Adoption of the sick role due to environmental rewards from family, friends, physicians, or social entitlement programs.
- Interpersonal behaviors to sustain the sick role, such as complaints, demands, threats, and hostility, which are designed to cause the physician to feel guilty; or helplessness and excessive compliance, which are designed to evoke caretaking.

Additional, related abnormal illness behaviors are also germane to our focus on secondary gain issues. These include somatization, symptom magnification, exaggerated suffering (or pain) behaviors, and delayed recovery. These expressions of illness may take on a communication function and may direct attention away from other issues (Stuart & Noyes, 1999). The clinician must be adept at understanding when this communication is operational, and what its purpose may be, in order to treat it appropriately (Leeman et al., 2000). It should be noted that abnormal illness behavior is not always reflective of secondary gain issues. Abnormal illness behaviors can also be the result of traditional psychiatric disorders, high levels of generalized psychological distress (Guo, Kuroki, & Koizumi, 2001), environmental reinforcers, and/or idiosyncratic responses to actual physical pathology. However, secondary gain issues should be considered when these behavioral patterns are observed. Stuart and Noyes (1999) point out that abnormal illness behaviors often result in interpersonal interactions that culminate in rejection by spouses, family members, and health care providers.

Somatization is the communication of personal and interpersonal problems in a physical idiom of distress and pattern of behavior that emphasizes the seeking of medical help (Kleinman, 1988). Features suggestive of somatization include multiple symptoms in different organ systems, symptoms in excess of objective findings, a chronic course, presence of a psychiatric disorder or generalized psychological distress, a history of extensive diagnostic testing, and rejection of previous physicians (Servan-Schreiber, Kolb, & Tabas, 1999). Anything from a muscle twitch to a delayed bowel movement assumes catastrophic significance to the patient. In fact, this overly focused way of thinking has been described as a "cognitive distortion" (Lefebvre, 1998) and is commonly seen in chronic pain, depression and other long-standing illnesses (Lewinsohn, Steinmetz, Larson, & Franklin, 1990). Pilowsky, who is the most prolific champion of the concept of abnormal illness behavior, considers somatization to be its core feature (Pilowsky, 1997).

Symptom magnification is the exaggeration of, and excessive focus on, physical symptoms that actually have only minor clinical significance. It is commonly associated with somatization, although it actually represents a separate behavioral phenomenon (Leeman et al., 2000). An example of such pathological behavior has been described by Waddell in patients with chronic low back pain (the so-called "Waddell's signs;" (Waddell, McCulloch, Kummel, & Venner, 1980)) and, more recently, in patients with chronic cervical pain (Sobel, Sollenberger, Robinson, Polatin, & Gatchel, 2000). Unfortunately, the terms "functional overlay" and "non-organic" have been used to describe these behaviors, contributing to the tendency of medicolegal evaluators to interpret the presence of such behaviors as evidence of psychiatric illness, simulated incapacity and/or conscious malingering (Leeman et al., 2000; Main & Spanswick, 1995). Such an interpretation was not intended by Waddell, and has never been scientifically established (Main & Spanswick, 1995). Main and Waddell (Main & Waddell, 1998) recently revisited the "Waddell's signs" and determined that these signs should not be used in isolation to indicate malingering or voluntary magnification of symptoms (Main & Waddell, 1998). In fact, research has suggested that non-organic behaviors are much more likely to be associated with psychological distress than malingering (e.g., Sobel et al., 2000). Main and Spanswick (1995) propose the term "behavioral signs and symptoms" as a less pejorative way to describe non-organic behaviors.

Exaggerated suffering (or pain) behaviors are exhibited for the purpose of calling attention to suffering. Fordyce (Fordyce, 1976) was the first to apply the learning model of operant conditioning, in which all overt behaviors are significantly influenced by their consequences, to pain behaviors. Pain behaviors include groaning, contortions of the face and body, guarding, rigidity, limping, rubbing parts of the body, crying for help, soliciting medications, asking for physical assistance, employing unnecessary assistive devices (e.g., splints, canes) and excessive inactivity (Fordyce, 1976). Reinforcement of such behaviors and other abnormal illness behaviors (e.g., positive attention from a spouse), whether intentional or not, typically increases their frequency. A lack of reinforcement, on the other hand, or reinforcement of "well" behaviors, should result in decreased pain behaviors. It should be noted that it is often difficult to identify exaggerated pain behaviors since these behaviors can be caused by relevant tissue damage or irritation (Sanders, 2002).

Finally, *delayed recovery*, discussed in detail by Headley (Headley, 1989), has a multifactorial etiology extending beyond actual physical pathology. Nevertheless, it represents either abnormally extended or inexplicable disability and should therefore trigger an exploration for secondary gain issues, psychiatric illness, and/or disorders of simulation (Tracy, 1972).

SECONDARY GAIN: CURRENT THEORETICAL AND RESEARCH PERSPECTIVES

Sophisticated observers are aware that secondary gain rarely equals malingering or factitious disorder (Ferrari & Kwan, 2001; Fishbain, 1994; Leeman et al., 2000). Furthermore, such observers understand that relatively few patients with medicolegal issues (including chronic pain patients) are malingerers or suffering from factitious disorder (e.g., (Fishbain et al., 1999; Hutchinson, 2000). As a result, several groups of investigators have attempted to clarify the concept of secondary gain and associated concepts (Ferrari & Kwan, 2001; Fishbain, 1994; Fishbain et al., 1995; Gatchel et al., 2002; Leeman et al., 2000). However, this information does not appear to be widely disseminated among clinicians (or the courts). This unfortunate set of circumstances may, in part, be due to unresolved theoretical issues. Whatever the reason, it

TABLE 1. Secondary Gains

Internal

1. Gratification of preexisting unresolved dependency strivings or affiliation needs.
2. Gratification of preexisting unresolved revengeful strivings (e.g., revenge directed toward insurance carriers or adjustors who gave patient a hard time; revenge directed toward spouse / partner who was perceived as not living up to his or her responsibilities in the relationship).
3. An attempt to elicit care-giving, sympathy, and concern from family and friends.
4. Family anger because of patient's disability may increase patient resentment and determination to get his or her due to prove entitlement.
5. Obtaining one's entitlement for years of struggling, dutiful attention to responsibilities, and a "much-earned" recompense.
6. Ability to withdraw from unpleasant or unsatisfactory life roles, activities, and responsibilities, including those of "breadwinner," spouse, and parent.
7. Adoption of "sick role" allows the patient to communicate and relate to others in a new, socially sanctioned manner.
8. Converting a socially unacceptable disability (psychological disorder) to a socially acceptable disability (injury or disease).
9. Displacing the blame for one's failures from oneself to an apparently disabling illness beyond one's control.
10. Maintenance of status in family.
11. Holding a spouse/partner in a marriage/relationship.
12. Avoiding sex.
13. Contraception.
14. Obtaining drugs.
15. Denial of the randomness of events.

External

1. Obtaining financial awards associated with disability.
   a. Wage replacement (short- and long-term disability, social security disability insurance, workers' compensation benefits).
   b. Settlement (disability- or impairment-based).
   c. Disability-based debt protection (e.g., credit cards, mortgage, auto loan).
   d. Subsidized child and family care, housing, and food.
2. Protection from legal and other obligations (e.g., child support payments, court appearances, parole or probation demands).
3. Job manipulation (e.g., promotion or transfer, handling personnel or work adjustment difficulties, prevention of lay-off or termination).
4. Vocational retraining and skills upgrade.

is essential that the clinician consider secondary gains whenever the symptom magnification (or disability) syndrome, abnormal illness behaviors, and/or disorders of simulation are recognized.

Table 1 contains a list of secondary gains culled from three sources (Ferrari & Kwan, 2001; Fishbain, 1994; Leeman et al., 2000). We have separated secondary gains into two categories—internal and external. Internal secondary gains are "psychologically" motivated (i.e., satisfy psychological needs or resolve psychological conflicts), whereas external secondary gains are typically associated with monetary gain, avoidance of debt or other legal obligation, vocational manipulation, or job redirection through vocational retraining .(Leeman et al., 2000). This list is not intended to be exhaustive. Further, the internal/external distinction is somewhat artificial (e.g., the pursuit of financial gain may serve to punish others). It is used here for illustrative purposes. Finally, it should be noted that not all secondary gains apply to each individual patient. Personality characteristics, relationship dynamics, conscious and unconscious motivations, reinforcers, and other factors determine which particular secondary gains may apply to a particular patient.

The concept of reinforcement is important to discuss at this point. Lists of secondary gains and reinforcers often overlap to a great degree. For example, financial gain is often considered both a secondary gain and a reinforcer. The distinction between these two related concepts is the object of focus. When examining secondary gain, the focus is on the individual (e.g., a motivation for financial gain). In contrast, when considering reinforcement, the focus is on factors exterior to the individual (e.g., actual financial gain).

Secondary gains and behaviors resulting from them (e.g., decreasing activity, lying down) result in environmental consequences. These consequences can either increase the pursuit of secondary gains and resulting behaviors (reinforcement) or decrease them (extinction or punishment). For example, a solicitous spouse may (unwittingly) reinforce pain behavior (e.g., grimacing) by paying more attention to the patient when these behaviors are displayed. On the other hand, in a well-run treatment facility, the patient will not be provided with additional attention when displaying pain behaviors. Instead, he or she will receive greater attention for "well" behaviors such as vocalizing a decrease in pain level or displaying an improved range of motion. As described earlier, Fordyce (1976) was the first to apply such operant conditioning principles to pain management, and treatment of chronic pain now routinely incorporates these principles. Several points about operant reinforcement are relevant to our discussion. First, for a particular patient, secondary gains and resulting behaviors may or may not be reinforced, resulting in either an increase or decrease in such gains and behaviors. Second, awareness by the clinician of the reinforcers of secondary gains and resulting behaviors will help in understanding an individual patient's motivations and actions. Finally, this information may be useful in increasing a patient's motivation for improved health and function.

The Work of Fishbain

Fishbain (Allaz et al., 1998; Fishbain, 1994; Fishbain et al., 1999; Fishbain et al., 1995) has been one of the most prolific and thoughtful writers to address the concept of secondary gain. Approaching this concept from a psychodynamic perspective, he has struggled with the issue of conscious vs. unconscious processes in secondary gain. Apparently tied to the psychodynamic origin of the term secondary gain, and also concerned about the "abuse" of this term, he has proposed that secondary gain be used to refer to "any behavior that results in acceptable or legitimate interpersonal advantage that can be shown to have an unconscious motivation" (1994; p. 271). Because this definition is impossible to objectively evaluate or operationally define, he proposes the term "secondary gain behaviors or perceptions" to refer to patient and nonpatient behaviors or perceptions that appear as if the individual is seeking some form of gain. Fishbain (1994) argues that these behaviors or perceptions would be obvious to the examiner, thus resulting in a definition that can be operationalized. Finally, he concludes that splitting the definition of secondary gain in this way would clarify the role of reinforcers in secondary gain. Reinforcers would then be the rewards for secondary gain behaviors or perceptions.

Fishbain's writings (1994,1995,1999) are essential reading for those interested in the concept of secondary gain. In our view, however, his determination to limit this term to unconscious processes has resulted in mental gymnastics and new terms (e.g., secondary gain behaviors and perceptions) that appear to further obfuscate the issue, rather than clarify it. In addition, this term does not appear to lend itself more easily to operational definition, which appears to be Fishbain's reason for introducing it. Finally, it does not appear that his new term has "caught on" since it was introduced in 1994. We could find no reference to it in the MEDLINE or PSYCHINFO databases.

Other Criticisms of Fishbain's Perspective

Others have criticized Fishbain's position, especially his strong focus on the conscious/unconscious dichotomy. For example, King (1994) disagrees with Fishbain's (1994) statement that "If patients respond to secondary gain issues in a conscious manner, then this behavior approaches the behavior in Munchausen's syndrome (i.e., factitious disorder) or malingering, or both". King further notes that it is questionable whether financial compensation issues can truly be out of any person's consciousness. In reference to Fishbain (1994), Gallagher (1994) states "Terms such as *unfulfilled dependency needs* or *unconscious motivation* are difficult to define operationally, and may encourage the very thing that Dr. Fishbain derides, over-inference" (p. 277).

Fishbain's approach also does not appear to take into account the fact that many Freudian psychodynamic concepts (e.g., repetition compulsion) have changed considerably over the years, reflecting theoretical advances. In addition, many psychodynamic terms have been "co-opted" by others, defined somewhat differently, and then "repackaged" and popularized using the new definition. This appears to be what has happened with the term secondary gain. In our opinion, it is more important to prevent (or perhaps rescue) the concept of secondary gain from being equated with malingering for financial compensation than it is to squabble over whether the construct of secondary gain does or does not include conscious mental processes.

The most impressive contemporary ideas regarding secondary gain that we have located are from a group of Canadian investigators: Ferrari, Kwan, and Friel. They have written a series of four articles thoroughly addressing the concept of secondary gain and related issues (Ferrari & Kwan, 2001; Ferrari, Kwan, & Friel, 2001; Kwan, Ferrari, & Friel, 2001; Kwan & Friel, 2002). These authors (Ferrari & Kwan, 2001) suggest that an incident (work injury, accident, infection, or other perceived injury) becomes a convenient focus of attention for the person and significant others and is "socially sanctioned as a no-fault entry into the sick role... the benefits of the sick role are multiple, referred to as secondary gains (pp. 77–78)."

These authors address the conscious/unconscious dichotomy by invoking the Freudian concept of the preconscious (just beneath awareness and easily brought to awareness). Although rooted in psychoanalytic theory, these authors also consider recent findings from the cognitive psychology literature (e.g., the concept of automaticity) to describe preconscious processes (Ferrari et al., 2001).

SECONDARY LOSSES

Building on Fishbain's work, and originally the work of Biernoff (1946), Ferrari and Kwan (2001) and others (Gatchel et al., 2002) have observed that there are also losses

TABLE 2. Secondary Losses

1. Economic loss.
2. Loss of meaningfully relating to society through work.
3. Loss of work social relationships.
4. Loss of social support network.
5. Loss of meaningful and enjoyable family roles and activities.
6. Loss of recreational activities.
7. Loss of respect from family and friends.
8. Negative sanctions from family.
9. Loss of community approval.
10. Loss of respect from those in helping professions (e.g., physicians).
11. New role not comfortable and not well defined.
12. Social stigma of being chronically disabled.
13. Guilt over disability.
14. Communications of distress become unclear.

associated with illness and disability, such as decreased income and inability to fulfill previously enjoyable activities. These losses are consequences of significant primary losses (good health and normal physical functioning)(Gatchel et al., 2002). These losses, which have been termed secondary losses, infiltrate virtually all domains of life in the ill or disabled individual, including autonomy, social relationships, financial stability, employment and familial roles, self-esteem, and even general worldview (Gatchel et al., 2002). Furthermore, the cascading losses that can occur with chronic illness often exact a substantial emotional toll on its sufferers (Gatchel et al., 2002). For obvious reasons then, secondary losses typically outweigh secondary gains, resulting in the person striving to regain health and function. However, it has also been noted that, despite these losses, the gains sometimes become the underlying motive of the illness behavior. Fishbain (1994) views this phenomenon as a conceptual challenge to the model of secondary gain. The common secondary losses associated with the sick role are presented in Table 2 (adapted from Fishbain, 1994).

To our knowledge, the issue of why secondary gain can be more motivating than secondary losses has not been discussed in the literature. It is our belief that there is often an effort to recoup secondary losses that ironically results in striving toward secondary gain. At some level, the patient thinks that "I've lost so much that I deserve something back." This is particularly noticeable when the individual becomes preoccupied with thoughts about the unfairness of his or her illness. The belief that the illness is some sort of punishment, whether delivered by a deity ("Why is God punishing me?") or by an employer ("My boss had it out for me"), can also be a contributing factor. The result is often a sense of entitlement and a belief that increased illness behavior will eventually "pay off," with the hope that the unfairness will be redressed or the offending party punished. The final outcome is further entrenchment in the sick role and preoccupation with secondary gain issues.

TERTIARY GAIN AND LOSS

Kwan and colleagues (2001) also consider the issues of tertiary gains and losses. As noted by several investigators (Dansak, 1973; Fishbain, 1994), tertiary gains are those sought or attained from a patient's illness by someone other than the patient, usually a family member. Fishbain (1994) describes the tertiary gains originating from the

TABLE 3. Tertiary Gains

Family Member Caretaker

1. Gratification of altruistic needs.
2. Desired change in role as a result of the illness (e.g., may solve family role conflict, such as who will be the "breadwinner").
3. Means of making the ill person develop a dependency on the caregiver, thus elevating the role of that caregiver in the relationship.
4. Gain sympathy from social network over the ill family member.
5. Decrease family tension and keep family together (e.g., conflicts over how to parent a child may decrease as the caretaker takes on more responsibilities related to parenting).
6. Resolve marital difficulties (e.g., conflicts over power in the relationship).
7. Financial gain.

Professional Caretaker

1. Gratification of altruistic needs.
2. Admiration and respect from patients or their support groups.
3. Gratification of one's need (or sense of righteousness) to level the playing field against powerful entities (e.g., the workers' compensation insurance company).
4. Establish one's position as compassionate and "pro-patient".
5. Gaining one's entitlement (fame and fortune) for years of struggling and dutiful attention to responsibilities.
6. Withdraw from (or simply avoid) unpleasant or potentially litigious situations that may result from confronting the patient with a diagnosis or treatment the patient and his/her community might reject.
7. Means to excuse oneself from the effortful position of intellectual honesty.
8. Means to attack one's professional detractors.
9. Gratification of pre-existing unresolved revengeful strivings wherein one's hostility towards the world is expressed through rebelling against established scientific facts.
10. Validating one's own illness of the same type.
11. Financial rewards associated with increased client pool.

patient's significant other or family. For example, the spouse of a patient may gain sympathy from family and friends over the ill family member. Kwan and colleagues (Kwan et al., 2001) broaden the discussion of tertiary gain by arguing that it arises out of the social construct of the caregiver role, thus broadening the concept beyond family members to health care workers, legal professionals, social workers, and religious community members. For example, a physician may benefit from the financial rewards associated with an increased number of patients. Recognized tertiary gains (adapted from Fishbain et al., 1994; Kwan et al., 2001) are presented in Table 3.

Tertiary loss is a concept proposed and described by Kwan and colleagues (Kwan et al., 2001). It is defined as the limitation or loss experienced by an individual other than the patient, yet is linked to the patient's illness. For example, financial difficulties may be experienced by the patient's family. Tertiary losses are listed in Table 4.

ECONOMY OF GAINS AND LOSSES

Awareness of secondary gains and losses, as well as tertiary gains and losses, assists in understanding a patient's behavior. As first proposed by Bayer (1985), and

TABLE 4. Tertiary Losses

Family Member Caregiver

1. Increased responsibilities (i.e., both at home, and perhaps having to work in place of the ill individual to maintain the family income).
2. Emotional effect of experiencing the suffering of a loved one.
3. Disturbance or discord (emotional or physical) within the relationship (e.g., loss of enjoyable shared activities, diminished sexual relationship).
4. Guilt created by the ill individual, which obligates the caregiver to remain in an already undesirable relationship.
5. Stigmatization of the family member in association with the ill individual.
6. Financial hardship.

Professional Caregiver

1. Being viewed by one's colleagues or others as dishonorable, feeling one is literally disabling the patient.
2. Feeling one may be ignoring one's duty to society, by directing a patient to the more appropriate diagnosis and treatment, even if the patient does not wish those.

elaborated on by Fishbain (1994), patient behavior can be thought of in terms of an *economy of gains and losses*. Fishbain presents this as the theoretical problem of understanding how, when balanced against secondary losses, secondary gains can reinforce the continuation of complaints. He again invokes unconscious processes to explain this phenomenon. Kwan and Friel (Kwan & Friel, 2002) approach the economy of gains and losses differently. While arguing that psychological issues are prominent, they suggest that these issues may be unconscious, preconscious, or conscious. They also highlight the importance of social factors in understanding why some patients seek secondary gain despite significant secondary losses. They argue that the sick role offers a solution to the patient's problem by changing a socially unacceptable psychological disorder to a socially acceptable disability. Thus, they assume that many who assume the sick role are primarily psychologically distressed, but unwilling (or unable) to acknowledge this due to existing social stigma against mental illness. One difficulty with this formulation is that the sick role is not limited to "physical" illness, but also applies to "psychological" illness. In fact, Freud did not limit the concept of secondary gain to those with physical illnesses (or conversion reactions), but instead applied it to neurotic (i.e., psychological) illness in general.

Kwan and colleagues (Kwan et al., 2001) also explore what they describe as the parallel *economy of tertiary gains and losses*. Here, the economy applies to the caretaker, whether family member, doctor, or other interested party. Like the economy described above, losses are usually more motivating than gains, resulting in a pursuit of improved health. However, as above, in a minority of cases, gains outweigh losses, resulting in the caretaker encouraging (i.e., reinforcing) continued disability in the patient.

It is our contention that awareness of possible secondary gains and losses, as well as possible tertiary gains or losses, is indispensable in the effective management of illnesses in a medicolegal context, and may also be valuable in the management of chronic illness in general whenever abnormal or excessive illness behaviors are observed or suspected. This is frequently the case with chronic pain patients.

SECONDARY GAIN: A CLINICAL PERSPECTIVE

Various perspectives can be brought to bear on the issues of gain and loss. The professional who is evaluating a patient in a medicolegal context will be very interested in issues of conscious versus unconscious processes (or the legal concepts of volitional versus involuntary and intentional versus unintentional), the presence (or absence) of psychiatric disorders in understanding symptomatology, the presence (or absence) of malingering, and the degree of conscious exaggeration or feigning. Those engaged in this type of endeavor will likely turn to references that focus on forensic issues (e.g., (Ensalada, 2000; Fishbain et al., 1999; Hutchinson, 2000; Rogers, 1997). Other investigators will be interested in understanding gain and loss issues from a diagnostic and nosological perspective, either the existing DSM or ICD systems, or perhaps a new diagnostic system. Interested readers are directed to several sources (e.g., Aronoff & Livengood, 2003; Ensalada, 2000; Fishbain et al., 1995; Hutchinson, 2000; Rief & Hiller, 1999). In this chapter, we approach gain and loss issues from a clinical perspective. We focus on how to identify these issues and how to deal with them therapeutically. Further, we describe situations in which clinical management of secondary gain issues does not lead to good therapeutic outcomes, with the goal of understanding these situations and how to respond to them effectively.

Theoretical and research efforts directed toward increased understanding of the economies of secondary and tertiary gains and losses appears to be the logical next step. Further pursuit of the conscious/unconscious dichotomy seems unnecessary from a pragmatic perspective. Of course, this issue is important in legal proceedings and may also be important clinically in helping to identify the small minority of patients who are malingerers or suffer from factitious disorder. For most patients seen in a medicolegal context, however, the following should be apparent:

- The term secondary gain is here to stay.
- Secondary gain issues are prominent factors in illness, particularly chronic illness and illness being evaluated and treated in a medicolegal context.
- Secondary gain issues are rarely suggestive of "pure" malingering or factitious disorder.
- Disability/illness exaggeration is frequently associated with secondary gain, and can often be inferred from abnormal illness behavior.
- Conscious, unconscious, and preconscious processes are involved in secondary and tertiary gain.
- Unconscious and conscious processes are better conceptualized from a dimensional perspective, rather than a dichotomous one.
- When conscious processes are primary, the patient may conceal secondary gains from others (resulting in hidden agendas). On the other hand, the patient may be quite open and transparent about his or her agendas.
- All chronic illnesses (physical and psychiatric) involve secondary gains and losses, as well as tertiary gains and losses.
- In almost all cases, there are multiple gains and losses, resulting in multiple agendas.
- Understanding the gain and loss issues (the secondary and tertiary economies) will lead to the most effective management of these patients.

- Operant conditioning (reinforcement) principles will often be effective in altering this economy in a positive direction.
- However, these economies cannot be understood in a purely mechanistic, operant conditioning, or rational manner.
- Psychodynamic and sociocultural factors are also important factors to be considered in understanding gain and loss issues.

For each individual, gains and losses are not usually of equal importance, and therefore, not equally motivating. Further the importance of particular gains and losses may change over time for the same individual.

CONCLUSIONS: CAN SECONDARY GAINS/LOSSES BE MANAGED?

Unfortunately, understanding and applying these principles does not always result in increased health and decreased disability. This is likely due to several factors. First, the relevant gains and losses may be difficult for the clinician to identify. Unless the patient is fully conscious of the gain, and completely honest with the clinician, inference is required. The process of inference is complicated given the large number of potential gains and losses, and is made even more difficult when it involves unconscious processes or when the patient has conscious hidden agendas. Further, if gain and loss issues are successfully identified, there is no guarantee that they can be influenced or managed by the clinician. Reinforcement contingencies in the patient's environment may have more of an impact than the clinician's interventions.

We have previously outlined a method for identifying and managing secondary gain issues in chronic pain patients (Leeman et al., 2000). This clinical model is summarized in Table 5. We made the conscious/unconscious dichotomy a non-issue by arguing that secondary gain involves both conscious and unconscious processes. We assumed that both conscious and unconscious secondary gain issues could be identified and, if identified, managed. We identified several behavioral patterns (i.e., abnormal illness behaviors) that suggest the presence of secondary gain issues, including somatization, symptom magnification, pain behaviors, and delayed recovery. We have found that our model of managing secondary gain to be a good complement to the functional restoration rehabilitation model (Mayer & Gatchel, 1988), which focuses on increasing function rather than ameliorating symptoms, with the assumption that subjective illness and disability will change only when there is an improvement in functional level. The large majority of our chronically disabled, workers' compensation pain patients have demonstrated good long-term outcomes in terms of work return and retention, case closure, decreased health utilization, and decreased pain (Mayer et al., 1985; Mayer et al., 1987).

However, this model has not proven to be effective with all patients. We believe that there are several reasons for this. Our previous model (Leeman et al., 2000) emphasized the importance of the disability case manager and, therefore, external secondary gain. In working with this model, we have observed that we overlooked several important issues about which the disability case manager should be informed. We also have noted that we did not adequately explore internal secondary gain issues. These issues can be evaluated and managed most effectively by a clinician trained in clinical psychology or psychiatry, particularly by a clinician well-versed in a variety of psychotherapeutic orientations (i.e., cognitive-behavioral,

TABLE 5. Techniques for Managing Secondary Gain

1. Establish trust and rapport.
   a. Be the expert—become well-versed in the jurisdictional aspects of the patient's case and communicate this expertise in understandable terminology.
   b. Clearly communicate the goals of further treatment—success should be defined with improved function and return to as normal a life as possible (not as a cure).
   c. Be a source of logistical and social support
   d. Be a patient advocate—for example, by providing clear documentation to assist the patient in resolving a claim.
   e. Demand something back—i.e., compliance in treatment, pursuit of previously defined goals, acceptance of a medical endpoint
2. Involve a disability case manager—i.e., a trained medical professional who fully understands the vocational and disability aspects of medical illness.
3. Contain financial secondary gain.
   a. Follow the money and do the math—analyze current, potential, or perceived sources of disability-based income—this typically points to return to work as the better financial option and dispels illusions about a "pot of gold" at the end of the disability rainbow.
   b. Distinguish "impairment" from "disability.
      i. A patient whose case falls under an impairment based system (e.g., workers' compensation) needs to know that the monetary reward will have little to do with his or her functional abilities and pain and that, therefore, progress toward recovery will have no impact on the impairment assessment.
      ii. A patient whose case falls under a disability based system (e.g, Social Security Disability Insurance) may be compensated differently depending on type of job previously held and previous wages; in addition, professional opinions about work capacity, pain and suffering may be taken into account. The patient needs to understand the previously mentioned treatment contract ("demand something back").
   c. Medical documentation in exchange for medical compliance.
   d. The "pain behavior" talk—the patient must know that his or her pain level is being documented in the medical record, therefore the patient must eliminate exaggerated behaviors because they accomplish nothing and may be interpreted negatively as conscious symptom exaggeration and, therefore, malingering.
4. Incorporate vocational planning—which includes vocational exploration, deciding upon a specific vocational plan, implementing this plan, and following up with the patient over the next six to twelve months.
5. Employ multimodal disability management—an interdisciplinary treatment model is essential and must address psychosocial issues of importance to the patient (e.g., anxiety, depression, and anger; family issues; stress-management).

psychodynamic, interpersonal, and family/systems). The most important lesson we have learned is the importance of collaboratively utilizing both a skilled disability case manager and a skilled psychologist or psychiatrist in effectively managing secondary gain issues, preferably in the context of an interdisciplinary team approach to treatment.

REFERENCES

Allaz, A. F., Vannotti, M., Desmeules, J., Piguet, V., Celik, Y., Pyroth, O., et al. (1998). Use of the label "litigation neurosis" in patients with somatoform pain disorder. *General Hospital Psychiatry, 20*(2), 91–97.

American Psychiatric Association Task Force on DSM-IV. (1994). *Diagnostic and Statistical Manual of Mental Disorders : DSM-IV* (4th ed.). Washington, DC: American Psychiatric Association.

Aronoff, G. M., & Livengood, J. M. (2003). Pain: psychiatric aspects of impairment and disability. *Current Pain and Headache Reports, 7*(2), 105–115.

Bayer, T. L. (1985). Weaving a tangled web: the psychology of deception and self deception in psychogenic pain. *Social Science Medicine, 20*(5), 517–527.

Bellamy, R. (1997). Compensation neurosis:Financial reward for illness as nocebo. *Clinical Orthopaedics and Related Research, 336*, 94–106.

Biernoff, J. (1946). Traumatic neurosis of industry. *Industrial Medicine and Surgery, 15*, 109–112.

Blackwell, B., & Gutmann, M. (1987). The management of chronic illness behavior. In S. McHugh & M. Vallis (Eds.), *Illness Behavior* (pp. 401–408). New York: Plenum Publishing.

Clark, C. R. (1997). Sociopathy, malingering, and defensiveness. In R. Rogers (Ed.), *Clinical Assesment of Malingering and Deception* (2nd ed., pp. 68–84). New York: The Guilford Press.

Cunnien, A. (1997). Psychiatric and medical syndromes associated with deception. In R. Rogers (Ed.), *Clinical Assessment of Malingering and Deception* (2nd ed., pp. 23–46): Guilford Press.

Dansak, D. A. (1973). On the tertiary gain of illness. *Comprehensive Psychiatry, 14*(6), 523–534.

Ensalada, L. H. (2000). The importance of illness behavior in disability management. *Occupational Medicine, 15*(4), 739–754, iv.

Ferrari, R., & Kwan, O. (2001). The no-fault flavor of disability syndromes. *Medical Hypotheses, 56*(1), 77–84.

Ferrari, R., Kwan, O., & Friel, J. (2001). Cognitive theory and illness behavior in disability syndromes. *Medical Hypotheses, 57*(1), 68–75.

Finneson, B. (1976). Modulating effect of secondary gain on the low back syndrome. *Advances in Pain Research and Therapy, 1*, 949–952.

Fishbain, D. A. (1994). Secondary gain concept: Definition problems and its abuse in medical practice. *American Pain Society Journal, 3*(4), 264–273.

Fishbain, D. A., Cutler, R., Rosomoff, H. L., & Rosomoff, R. S. (1999). Chronic pain disability exaggeration/malingering and submaximal effort research. *Clinical Journal of Pain, 15*(4), 244–274.

Fishbain, D. A., Rosomoff, H. L., Cutler, R. B., & Rosomoff, R. S. (1995). Secondary gain concept: a review of the scientific evidence. *Clinical Journal of Pain, 11*(1), 6–21.

Fordyce, W. E. (1976). *Behavioral methods for chronic pain and illness*. Saint Louis: Mosby.

Freud, S. (1917). *Introductory Lectures on Psychoanalysis*. London: Hogarth Press(1959).

Freud, S. (1966). *The Complete Introductory Lectures on Psychoanalysis* (J. Strachey, Trans.). New York: W.W. Norton & Company.

Gallagher, R. (1994). Secondary gain in pain medicine: Let us stick with biobehavioral data. *American Pain Society Journal, 3*(4), 274–278.

Garner, H. H. (1965). Malingering. *Illinois Medical Journal, 128*(3), 318–319.

Gatchel, R. J., Adams, L., Polatin, P. B., & Kishino, N. D. (2002). Secondary loss and pain-associated disability: theoretical overview and treatment implications. *Journal of Occupational Rehabilitation, 12*(2), 99–110.

Guo, Y., Kuroki, T., & Koizumi, S. (2001). Abnormal illness behavior of patients with functional somatic symptoms: relation to psychiatric disorders. *General Hospital Psychiatry, 23*(4), 223–229.

Headley, B. (1989). Delayed recovery: Taking another look. *Journal of Rehabilitation*, 61–67.

Hutchinson, G. L. (2000). *Disorders of simulation : malingering, factitious disorders, and compensation neurosis*. Madison, Conn.: Psychosocial Press.

King, S. (1994). Concept of secondary gain: How valid is it? *American Pain Society Journal, 3*(4), 279–281.

Kleinman, A. (1988). *The illness narratives : suffering, healing, and the human condition*. New York: Basic Books.

Kwan, O., Ferrari, R., & Friel, J. (2001). Tertiary gain and disability syndromes. *Medical Hypotheses, 57*(4), 459–464.

Kwan, O., & Friel, J. (2002). Clinical relevance of the sick role and secondary gain in the treatment of disability syndromes. *Medical Hypotheses, 59*(2), 129–134.

Leeman, G., Polatin, P. B., Gatchel, R. J., & Kishino, N. D. (2000). Managing secondary gain in patients with pain-associated disability: A clinical perspective. *The Journal of Workers Compensation, 9*(4), 25–43.

Lefebvre, M. (1998). Cognitive distortion and cognitive errors in depressed psychiatric and low back pain patients. *Journal of Consulting and Clinical Psychology, 49*, 517–525.

Lewinsohn, P., Steinmetz, J., Larson, D., & Franklin, J. (1990). Depression related conditions: Antecedents or consequences. *Journal of Abnormal Psychology, 90*, 213–219.

Loeser, J. D., Henderlite, S. E., & Conrad, D. A. (1995). Incentive effects of workers' compensation benefits: a literature synthesis. *Medical Care Research and Review, 52*(1), 34–59.

Main, C. J., & Spanswick, C. C. (1995). 'Functional overlay', and illness behaviour in chronic pain: distress or malingering? Conceptual difficulties in medico-legal assessment of personal injury claims. *Journal of Psychosomatic Research, 39*(6), 737–753.

Main, C. J., & Waddell, G. (1998). Behavioral responses to examination. A reappraisal of the interpretation of "nonorganic signs". *Spine, 23*(21), 2367–2371.

Matheson, L. N. (1991). Symptom magnification syndrome: Part 1: Description and definition. *Industrial Rehabilitation, 4* (1).

Mayer, T. G., & Gatchel, R. J. (1988). *Functional restoration for spinal disorders : the sports medicine approach*. Philadelphia: Lea & Febiger.

Mayer, T. G., Gatchel, R. J., Kishino, N., Keeley, J., Capra, P., Mayer, H., et al. (1985). Objective assessment of spine function following industrial injury. A prospective study with comparison group and one-year follow-up. *Spine, 10*(6), 482–493.

Mayer, T. G., Gatchel, R. J., Mayer, H., Kishino, N. D., Keeley, J., & Mooney, V. (1987). A prospective two-year study of functional restoration in industrial low back injury. An objective assessment procedure. *Journal of American Medical Association, 258*(13), 1763–1767.

Mechanic, D. (1962). The concept of illness behavior. *Journal of Chronic Disease, 15*, 189–194.

Myerson, M., McGarvey, W., Henderson, M., & Hakim, J. (1994). Morbidity after crush injuries to the foot. *Journal of Orthopaedic Trauma, 8*(4), 343–349.

Parsons, T. (1964). *Social Structure and Personality*. London: Collier-Macmillan.

Parsons, T. (1978). Action Theory and the Human Condition. New York: Free Press.

Pilowsky, I. (1969). Abnormal illness behavior. *British Journal of Medical Psychology, 42*, 347–351.

Pilowsky, I. (1993). Aspects of abnormal illness behaviour. *Psychotherapy and Psychosomatics, 60*, 62–74.

Pilowsky, I. (1997). *Abnormal illness behaviour*. Chichester ; New York: John Wiley & Sons.

Rainville, J., Sobel, J. B., Hartigan, C., & Wright, A. (1997). The effect of compensation involvement on the reporting of pain and disability by patients referred for rehabilitation of chronic low back pain. *Spine, 22*(17), 2016–2024.

Rief, W., & Hiller, W. (1999). Toward empirically based criteria for the classification of somatoform disorders. *Journal of Psychosomatic Research, 46*(6), 507–518.

Robinson, J. P., Rondinelli, R. D., Scheer, S. J., & Weinstein, S. M. (1997). Industrial rehabilitation medicine. 1. Why is industrial rehabilitation medicine unique? *Archives of Physical and Medical Rehabilitation, 78*(3 Suppl), S3–9.

Rogers, R. (1997). *Clinical assessment of malingering and deception* (2nd ed.). New York: Guilford Press.

Sanders, S. H. (2002). Operant conditioning with chronic pain: Back to basics. In R. J. Gatchel & D. C. Turk (Eds.), *Psychological Approaches to Pain Management: A Practitioner's Handbook* (pp. 128–137). New York: The Guilford Press.

Schrader, H., Obelieniene, D., Bovim, G., Surkiene, D., Mickeviciene, D., Miseviciene, I., et al. (1996). Natural evolution of late whiplash syndrome outside the medicolegal context. *Lancet, 347*(9010), 1207–1211.

Servan-Schreiber, D., Kolb, R., & Tabas, G. (1999). The somatizing patient. *Primary Care, 26*(2), 225–242.

Sobel, J. B., Sollenberger, P., Robinson, R., Polatin, P. B., & Gatchel, R. J. (2000). Cervical nonorganic signs: a new clinical tool to assess abnormal illness behavior in neck pain patients: a pilot study. *Archives of Physical and Medical Rehabilitation, 81*(2), 170–175.

Strang, J. P. (1985). The chronic disability syndrome. In G. M. Aronoff (Ed.), *Evaluation and Treatment of Chronic Pain* (pp. 603–623). Baltimore: Urban and Schwarzenberg.

Stuart, S., & Noyes, R., Jr. (1999). Attachment and interpersonal communication in somatization. *Psychosomatics, 40*(1), 34–43.

Tracy, G. (1972). Prolonged disability after compensable injury. *Medical Journal of Australia, 2*, 1305–1307.

Travin, S., & Protter, B. (1984). Malingering and malingering-like behavior: Some clinical and conceptual issues. *Psychiatric Quarterly, 56*(3), 189–197.

Waddell, G., McCulloch, J., Kummel, E., & Venner, R. (1980). Non-organic physical signs in low back pain. *Spine, 5*, 117–125.

Wise, M. G., & Ford, C. V. (1999). Factitious disorders. *Primary Care, 26*(2), 315–326.

Young, J. N., Shaffrey, C. I., Laws, E. R., Jr., & Lovell, L. R. (1997). Lumbar disc surgery in a fixed compensation population: a model for influence of secondary gain on surgical outcome. *Surgical Neurology, 48*(6), 552–558; discussion 558–559.

24

Evidence-Informed Best Practices for Injured Workers at Risk for Disability at the Subacute Stage

Secondary Prevention

Izabela Z. Schultz, Joan Crook, and Alanna Winter

INTRODUCTION

The development of evidence-based clinical guidelines for musculoskeletal pain disabilities has been driven by their high prevalence in working populations and the desire to prevent the growing economic pressures arising from the costs of health care, loss of productivity and disability benefits. Low back pain is the third leading cause of disability in persons under age 45 (Meyer & Gatchel, 1988) and the focus of most studies on early identification and prevention of musculoskeletal pain disabilities.

Low back musculoskeletal injuries pose a formidable health care problem for injured workers, industries and compensation systems. The lifetime prevalence of low back pain ranges from 60–90 percent, with an annual incidence of 5 percent (Spitzer et al, 1987). A small proportion of acute low back injuries progress to disability and chronicity, but these cases pose a significant economic, social and personal burden (Webster & Snook, 1990; Volinn et al, 1997; Spitzer et al, 1987; Hashemi et al, 1997; Williams et al, 1987). The human and financial costs of low back pain are staggering. Van Tulder (1995) estimates these costs to be 1.7% of the gross national product of a developed country. Annual productivity losses for the US workforce, due to back pain, have been estimated at $28 billion (Maetzel & Li, 2002; Rizzo, Abbott & Berger, 1998), comparable to other disorders such as heart disease, depression, diabetes and headache.

Despite economic pressures and the proliferation of research on musculoskeletal pain, specifically low back pain, a review of early intervention studies indicates that the current research literature is not yet methodologically ready for meta-analyses. It

DOI: 10.1007/978-0-387-28919-9_24, © 2009 Springer Science+Business Media, LLC

is almost equally challenging to perform a systematic review of the literature. This is due to the limited number of studies that met the methodological criteria set coupled with a wide range of methodological discrepancies across studies (Crook, et al., 2002).

At the same time, however, significant clinical advances have been made in the understanding of the medical management of acute and subacute back pain episodes as seen in the initiation and promulgation of clinical guidelines (Bigos et al., 1994; Boden & Swanson, 1998; Rosen & Hofberg, 1998). Nevertheless, very few integrative evidence-based practice guidelines have been developed for early intervention and secondary prevention of back pain occupational disability encompassing *both* clinical and occupational interventions (Waddell & Burton, 2001). Consistent with the biopsychosocial model of pain-related disability (Schultz et al., 2000 & 2002) and the new paradigm for the management of occupational back pain (Loisel, et al, 2001; Waddell & Burton, 2001), multi-system, interdisciplinary interventions integrating both clinical and occupational components, have shown the most promising outcomes thus far. Yet, no effective knowledge transfer has occurred. No evidence informed guidelines have been developed for systems mandated to manage and prevent occupational pain disability, particularly world wide workers' compensation and long-term disability insurance systems. Moreover, no such guidelines focusing specifically on workers at elevated risk for disability, who contribute the most to health and economic losses associated with the inability to work, have been published. This void persists, despite a proliferation of studies on risk factors for disability (Crook et al, 2002) and emerging research attempts at early intervention with this small group of workers. As a result, many early identification and intervention programs and approaches of unclear efficacy currently exist in the clinical and case management practices implemented in health care and compensation systems, as well as in the workplace.

This chapter attempts to bridge the gap between early intervention research literature and practices in early intervention and secondary prevention of occupational back pain disability in clinical, occupational and compensation contexts. It aims to set the ground for the development of evidence-informed and effective clinical, occupational and case management practices, particularly with those workers who are at heightened risk for chronicity. It also identifies methodological barriers to the integration of knowledge in this area and recommends future directions for both research and practice.

BARRIERS TO KNOWLEDGE TRANSFER IN EARLY INTERVENTION WITH BACK PAIN DISABILITY

Despite the strongly articulated need for effectiveness and efficacy studies of early intervention with high risk back injured workers, no comprehensive and empirically supported model of such an intervention exists in the literature. Further, no controlled trials of this type of intervention can be found in the literature. In the absence of such data, the authors of this chapter reviewed the growing literature on "best practices" and emerging consensus-based guidelines for the clinical and occupational management of acute and subacute back pain (Bigos et al., 1994; Black et al., 2000; Boden

& Swanson, 1998; Brooker et al., 1998; Rosen & Hofberg, 1998; Waddell & Burton, 2001), together with the body of evidence-based studies of early interventions pertinent to workers at risk for chronic back pain disability.

Currently, the literature on early intervention with workers at high risk for back pain disability, in general, does not offer any unified conceptual intervention model. The studies typically investigate either specific components for intervention modalities of interest or offer a "package" approach with implementation of multiple interventions, either in a phase-like or simultaneous fashion. Very few studies offer an integrated clinical and occupational intervention approach, and if so, they do not necessarily focus on workers identified as high risk for disability (Loisel, 1994, 1997 & 2000; Karjalainen et al., 2000). Moreover, none of the studies directly tackled the issue of the role a compensation system, such as workers' compensation or long term disability insurance carriers, can play in early intervention and prevention, even though the classic ecological system-based approach was postulated by Loisel (2001).

A review of the pertinent intervention literature identified multiple methodological barriers to the integration and generalizability of findings, the validity of research evidence and, ultimately, the transfer of knowledge and development of research informed practice guidelines.

Research Participants

Reviewed studies included the following types of research participants: general population, either in primary care or in specialized clinical settings; compensated injured workers, also accessed in different settings; and individuals at high risk (versus low risk) for chronic disability.

In addition, interventions have been tried with individuals who had a range of diverse musculoskeletal conditions including upper extremity and back pain, rather than only specifically and precisely defined low back pain. The impact of the heterogeneity of the research samples on generalizability of findings is unknown. So far, the frequently assumed notion that all musculoskeletal pain conditions can be managed, or prevented, using similar approaches has never been fully empirically validated and so caution is urged in generalizing.

Finally, definitions of "acute," "subacute," and "chronic" differed across studies and thus samples of individuals in different stages of disability were utilized in the research literature on early intervention, again limiting generalizability.

Study Design and Comparison Group

As the purpose of this review was to develop evidence informed intervention guidelines, primarily randomized controlled trials (RCTs) were selected from the literature and supplemented by recent literature reviews of evidence and emerging clinical guidelines (Bigos et al., 1994; Black et al., 2000; Boden & Swanson, 1998; Rosen & Hofberg, 1998; Waddell & Burton, 2001, Brodie et al., 1998). Notably, since most studies published in the field were not RCTs, a large number of non-randomized case and qualitative studies using samples of convenience were seen. In the reviewed RCTs, comparison groups using "usual" or "traditional" care were utilized, with one study using a placebo group.

Standardization of Intervention

Problems with the standardization of interventions are inherent in applied clinical research, particularly if psychosocial interventions, "real-life" settings and multiple service providers are utilized. Attempts at standardization range from manualized treatment protocols, such as those designed for cognitive-behavioral therapy, to general guidelines and orientation provided to the clinicians conducting interventions. Wide ranging differences in measures to monitor the consistency, or to periodically "re-calibrate" interventions were noted. Generally, limited data were provided on the methods applied to ensure standardization. Therefore, it is difficult to ascertain to what degree the outcomes of the studies have been potentially affected by insufficient standardization.

The more multifaceted the intervention, and the more systems involved, the more variability is likely to be introduced into the intervention. Thus replication of the most promising, interdisciplinary and conceptually-driven system-based interventions is likely to suffer. Differing contexts of intervention (e.g., clinics, workplaces and workers' compensation settings) constitute yet another source of variability.

Measurement of Outcomes

Another major barrier in the evaluation of the effectiveness of intervention RCTs are differences in outcome measurement. The outcome variables include: return to work, both short-term and long-term, with no uniform or standardized time intervals used; variously defined duration of disability (Dasinger & Deegan, 1999; Maetzel & Li, 2002); recurrence of disability; costs of disability benefits; health care costs and healthcare utilization (Maetzel & Li, 2002).

As empirically supported models of disability prediction differ depending on the set outcome criterion (Crook et al., 2002), likely so do intervention models. Therefore, an intervention showing a positive impact on immediate return to work may not necessarily have a positive impact on duration of disability costs or recurrence.

System-Based Barriers

In addition to the methodological problems limiting reproducibility, validity of evidence and generalizability of findings, which are making meta-analytic studies difficult, and systematic analysis of the literature problematic, there are also multiple system-based barriers to the transfer of knowledge to the systems seeking it. These barriers include the organizational characteristics of the system(s) that intend(s) to implement the knowledge, in this case early intervention guidelines. The necessary interaction of four key systems: the worker, the health care system, workers' compensation (or health/disability insurance system) and the employer, complicates the matter. This is due to inherent ideological, legal, organizational, cultural, communication-based and human resource-based differences among these systems in how new knowledge can be accommodated and effectively utilized to advance early intervention and prevention of work disability in "at risk" workers.

KEY DIMENSIONS OF EARLY INTERVENTION

Our review of current early intervention literature focusing on workers with subacute pain-related back disability revealed the following key themes and dimensions in effective early interventions:

1. multimodal and multidisciplinary intervention model;
2. coordination among the stakeholders;
3. appropriate and early timing of intervention;
4. focus on intense treatment;
5. evidence-supported primary care

Multimodal and Multidisciplinary Intervention Model

There is moderate evidence in the literature that a combination of optimum clinical management, a rehabilitation program and organizational interventions designed to assist the worker with back pain to return to work is more effective than single elements alone (Burton, Waddell et al., 1999). Of particular importance is the integration of the clinical management of back pain with an occupational intervention to ensure sustained return to work and disability prevention (Loisel et al., 2001). The involvement of all key stakeholders i.e., the worker, the health care system, the employer, and the workers' compensation system is particularly recommended (Loisel et al., 2001).

Generally, the most effective case management approach for early intervention with a back injured workers is one that utilizes many different components. As recommended by Frank et al (2002), an intervention should include a quota-based physical activity program, ergonomic adjustment, and comprehensive case review. The evidence indicates that a multidisciplinary biopsychosocial rehabilitation program applied at the subacute stage including a workplace visit or some form of more comprehensive occupational intervention facilitates return to work, lessens sick time and perceived disability in working age adults (Karjalainen et al., 2003, Linstrom at al., Loisel et al., 1997, Frank et al., 2000). A recent study by Gatchel et al. (2003) demonstrated the effectiveness of an interdisciplinary team approach which included psychology, physical therapy, and case management, guided by a supervising nurse-physician team, with patients identified as being at high risk of disability.

> BEST PRACTICE 1: *Multimodal and multidisciplinary interventions designed to assist workers with back pain to return-to-work are more effective than single elements alone.*

> BEST PRACTICE 2: *A multidisciplinary biopsychosocial rehabilitation program with workplace visits or more comprehensive occupational intervention facilitates return-to-work, lessens sick leaves and subjective disability in working age adults at the subacute stage.*

> BEST PRACTICE 3: *The optimal early intervention program for patients at high risk for disability involves an interdisciplinary team consisting of*

psychology, physical therapy, and case management coordinated by a supervising nurse-physician team.

Coordination among the Stakeholders

At the subacute stage, injured workers, care providers, employers, labor unions, and payers need to work in concert in order for the recommended solution to be effectively applied (Frank et al., 2000). According to Loisel et al (2001), workers' disability is influenced by the stakeholders' actions and attitudes, and by interactions occurring among the stakeholders. Therefore, an effective early intervention requires coordinated efforts among the stakeholders, to address pertinent clinical and occupational barriers to return to work and to facilitate employment.

BEST PRACTICE 4: *Interaction and coordination among the multiple stakeholders is critical to the success of any return-to-work program.*

Appropriate and Early Timing of the Intervention

A review of the evidence indicates that the subacute stage of back pain constitutes the "golden hour" for early intervention (Loisel et al., 2001, Frank et al., 2000). Frank and colleagues (2000) argued that at four weeks after the onset of back injury, clinicians become concerned about the failure to recover and the risk of long-term disability and chronicity. The number of lost time cases drops quickly over the first month and then stabilizes. Notably, cases that are off work longer than a month are more amenable to treatment to reduce subsequent disability than cases seen earlier (Frank et al., 2000). Elders et al. (2000) argued that starting interventions too early is needless due to the self-limiting effect of lower back pain.

After an initial four week period, intensive physiotherapy, particularly supervised exercise instruction with ergonomic intervention at the work site, is more likely to be successful in preventing long-term disability and promoting timely return to work than the same measures applied earlier (Frank et al., 2000).

BEST PRACTICE 5: *The time at which intensive interventions are more likely to be effective and promote timely return-to-work is at the beginning of the subacute stage (4–6 weeks).*

Focus on Intense Treatment

The literature suggests that at the subacute stage, it may be less important what kind of treatment is given, so long as an intensive intervention is applied that is designed specifically to get the worker back on the job (Frank et al., 2000; Burton et al., 1998).

BEST PRACTICE 6: *Intense and focused efforts to get workers with back pain back to work at the subacute stage, before disability and sickness absence become protracted, are likely to be most effective.*

Evidence-Based Medical Care

Primary care plays a pivotal role in preventing disability arising from low back pain. In a study completed by McGuirk et al. (2001) general practitioners were trained to manage patients at the acute-subacute stages of a low back episode. Dealing with the patients' fears and misconceptions was emphasized as well as providing confident explanations and empowering the patient to resume or restore the normal activities of daily living through simple exercises and graded activity. The initial results from evidence-based care were found to be marginally better than those from good usual care, but in the long-term evidence-based care achieved clinically and statistically significant gains with fewer patients requiring continuing care and remaining in pain (McGuirk et al., 2001). In addition, patients seem to benefit from maintaining activity as normal as possible, compared to inactivity and bed rest. The study suggested that information and fear reduction should also be offered systematically and consistently by the general practitioner. The physician's attempt to reduce the fear of 'doing something wrong' to the back may be even more important than the physical components of intervention (McGuirk, et al., 2001).

A recent Finnish study clearly demonstrated that for patients with subacute low back pain, a mini early intervention by a team consisting of a physician and physiotherapist, involving clinical examination, information, reassurance, support, and simple advice reduced daily symptoms and work absenteeism and improved adaptation to pain and treatment satisfaction. With this type of early intervention, the workplace visit did not incrementally improve the outcomes (Karjalainen, Malmivaara, Mutanen, Roine, Hurri & Pohjolainen, 2004).

> Best Practice 7: *Providing evidence-based care to primary care patients with back pain is effective in reducing the numbers of patients moving on to chronicity.*

> Best Practice 8: *Early examination, information, support, simple advice and reassurance by the physician/physiotherapist about the benign nature of non-specific back pain and the importance of maintaining activity as normal as possible is likely to assuage fears and facilitate return-to-work.*

SPECIFIC COMPONENTS OF EARLY INTERVENTION WITH BACK INJURED WORKERS

In addition to the key dimensions of early intervention, current research literature provides support for the implementation of specific components of early intervention with back injured workers. These components include the following:

1. Case management
2. Coordination between primary care physician and workers' compensation
3. Modified work programs
4. Return to normal activities
5. Exercise and physical restoration
6. Education
7. Cognitive-behavioral therapy and problem solving
8. Phone call support

Case Management

In keeping with the theme of integration and coordination of services and interactions among the stakeholders, the instrumental role of case management in facilitating return to work is critical.

A recent study revealed that nurses trained in the workplace accommodation process recommended more changes to the work environment, including workstation layout, computer-related improvements, furnishings, accessories, and lifting/carrying aids than untrained nurses. These changes appeared to facilitate return to work. Untrained nurses generally limited recommendations to light duty and lifting restrictions. Evidence indicates that nurses trained in the workplace accommodation process, promote and practice behaviors that may improve return-to-work outcomes (Lincoln, et al., 2002).

Case management and clinical direction provided to interdisciplinary early intervention teams by a nurse-physician team, were also found to be critical components of an effective early functional restoration program designed for patients at high risk for disability (Gatchel et al., 2003).

> BEST PRACTICE 9: *Training nurse advisors in modifying workplace ergonomic risk factors as a component of the workplace accommodation process results in a greater number and diversity of worksite accommodations recommended and implemented, and may improve return-to-work outcomes in injured workers.*

> BEST PRACTICE 10: *Clinical case management is a critical component of an interdisciplinary functional restoration program for high risk patients, reducing work disability and demonstrating substantial economic benefits to the payees.*

Coordination between Treating Physician and Workers' Compensation Medical Team

The coordination of healthcare between a treating physician and workers' compensation medical team was examined by Rossignol and colleagues (2000). Workers' compensation medical staff saw the worker immediately after the worker's name was given to the team to receive clinical evaluation. Medical staff made a diagnosis by considering three aspects: medical, psychosocial, and occupational. Then they established an evidence-based action plan with the worker in accordance with clinical guidelines for the management of subacute back pain. The conclusions and recommendations were explained to the worker and a summary was sent to the treating physician. Subsequently, the workers' compensation medical team provided assistance to the treating physician with finding and scheduling diagnostic and therapeutic procedures as appropriate. Nurses made weekly phone calls to the worker (standardized) and followed-up the worker's questions and problems presented each week. This type of coordinated medical care was shown to be effective.

In conclusion, coordination among the workers' compensation medical team, treating physician and the worker yields the most positive effects. Furthermore, contact between workers' compensation medical teams and treating physicians to facilitate referrals and services, can also reduce unnecessary health care services and costs (Rossignol et al., 2000).

> Best Practice 11: *Coordination among the worker, the treating physician and the workers' compensation medical team is effective in returning back injured workers to work faster in subacute stage.*

> Best Practice 12: *The therapeutic results for workers with back pain could be improved by implementing the clinical practice guidelines with primary care physicians without delaying the return to work.*

Modified Work Programs

The evidence from the literature indicates that modified work programs facilitate return-to-work for temporarily and permanently disabled workers. Injured workers who are offered modified work return to work about twice as often as those who are not. Similarly, modified work programs cut the number of lost work days in half and are cost effective. In their review, Weir and Nielson (2001) noted however that there is inadequate evidence to determine what particular aspects of modified work programs are helpful.

Modified work includes light duty, work trials, job accommodation, supported employment, and graded work exposure (Krause et al., 1998; Tate et al., 1999). A study by Yassi et al. (1995) demonstrated the effectiveness of work rehabilitation and job modification in an early intervention program for hospital nurses. It is also indicated that worker's active participation has been instrumental in successful modified work programs (Loisel et al., 1998, 2001).

> Best Practice 13: *The temporary provision of lighter or modified duties facilitates return-to-work and reduces time off work.*

> Best Practice 14: *The worker's active participation is instrumental in effective modified work programs.*

Return to Normal Activities

Patients with back pain need to return to normal activities as soon as possible but they are often afraid that movement or activity may be harmful. Clinical examination, information, reassurance and encouragement, provided in a manner designed to reduce fears, and to engage in physical activity as normally as possible, was effective in reducing sick leave (Hagen et al., 2000; Indahl et al., 1998; Moffett et al., 1999). In addition, Indahl et al. (1998) argued that "light normal activity may help restore normal function" (p. 2629).

> Best Practice 15: *Workers with subacute back pain need to be encouraged to return to normal activities including work activities as soon as possible.*

Notably, however a recent Cochrane review, indicates that the advice to stay physically active may not be as effective if implemented as a single treatment (Hagen et al.,

2002). Caution therefore applies to the central assumption of clinical guidelines for subacute back pain that the sole focus on encouraging return to normal activities in high risk patients is sufficient in preventing disability.

Exercise and Physical Restoration

Many studies have demonstrated that exercise is an effective element in return to work programs. Lindstrom's (1992) graded physical activity programs were shown to significantly reduce long term sick leave, especially in male patients. The patients in the graded activity program learned that it was safe to move while regaining function. The patients with subacute, nonspecific, mechanical low back pain who participated in the graded activity program regained occupational function faster than did the patients in the control group, who were given only traditional care (Lindstrom, 1992).

The efficiency of medical exercise therapy and conventional physiotherapy in patients between 8 weeks and 52 weeks following back injury as compared to self-exercise, as measured by costs for days on sick leave, was demonstrated in a study by Torstensen at al, 1998.

In addition, interdisciplinary, team-based functional restoration programs designed for patients at high risk of disability have been found to be both cost-effective and useful in reducing disability (Gatchel et al., 2003).

> BEST PRACTICE 16: *Patients with subacute back pain who participate in graded physical activity regain work function faster.*

> BEST PRACTICE 17: *Those subacute patients with low back pain who are at risk for disability benefit from an interdisciplinary functional restoration program.*

Education

The literature indicates that education alone is a relatively weak intervention. The traditional model involving biomedical information and advice based on spinal anatomy, biomechanics and an injury model is largely ineffective (Burton et al., 1999).

On the other hand, specific information and advice, designed to overcome fear avoidance beliefs about physical activity, and promote self responsibility and self care can produce positive shifts in beliefs and reduce disability. As concluded by Burton et al. (1999), "...carefully selected and presented information and advice, in line with current management guidelines, can have a positive effect on patients' beliefs and clinical outcomes (p. 2490)." Providing the worker with an educational booklet, whose purpose is to change beliefs and behaviors and not simply present factual information, (e.g., The Back Book), greatly improves beliefs targeting fear avoidance and encouraging physical activity (Burton, et al., 1999).

Educational experts advise that a coordinated approach in which physicians and therapists all give the same information and advice and use educational material to reinforce that message will have the most powerful effect. This has been demonstrated through the long-term effectiveness of early mini-intervention by a team of a physiatrist and physiotherapist, in which information, reassurance and simple advice was provided to subacute low back injured workers (Karjalainen, Malmivaara,

Mutanen, Roine, Hurri & Pohjolainen, 2004). This approach showed the best outcomes among patients with a high perceived risk of not recovering.

> BEST PRACTICE 18: *Carefully selected information and advice, designed to overcome fear avoidance beliefs about physical activity and promote self responsibility and self-care is effective in reducing disability.*

> BEST PRACTICE 19: *A coordinated approach in which all care providers give the same advice and use educational materials to reinforce that message will have the most powerful effect.*

Cognitive-Behavior Therapy and Problem Solving

The cognitive-behavior approach to therapy emphasizes the role of beliefs, thoughts or cognitive appraisals, self control, coping and problem-solving skills as crucial variables producing therapeutic change. Linton and Andersson (2002) demonstrated that a cognitive-behavior group intervention at the subacute stage of musculoskeletal pain disability can lower the risk of a long term disability developing. Sessions were organized to activate participants and promote coping through the development of problem solving skills, relaxation, activity scheduling, and communication skills. The participants in the cognitive behavior therapy group had fewer days off work and consumed smaller amounts of health care. This has important implications because it demonstrates that chronic problems can be prevented by providing self-help oriented intervention (Linton & Andersson, 2002; Moore et al., 2000).

Marhold et al. (2001) used a "cognitive-behavioral return to work program" focused on coping skills and return to work. Participants were taught to apply pain coping skills to various occupational risk factors at their workplace. Recent research on an effective interdisciplinary functional restoration approach to early intervention targeting persons at risk for disability also involved a psychological component using a cognitive-behavioral approach (Gatchel et al., 2003).

In a review paper, Raine et al. (2002) summarized that "research in secondary and primary care shows that cognitive behavior therapy and behavior therapy helps patients with back pain" (p. 1085).

> BEST PRACTICE 20: *The cognitive-behavioral approach that emphasizes the role of beliefs, thoughts or cognitive appraisals, self help, coping and problem solving skills is reported to be effective in early intervention.*

Problem solving counseling is located within the literature on cognitive-behavior therapy (Meichenbaum, 1995; Meichenbaum & Turk, 1987). It consists of stages designed to meet the following goals: (a) problem orientation: to nurture identification of problems, as well as strengths, thus fostering a shift from negative emotions and thoughts (e.g., feelings of helplessness, hopelessness, and demoralization) that hinder problem-solving to a positive sense of resourcefulness; (b) problem definition: to help identify realistic goals or desired outcomes for problem-solving; (c) generation of alternatives: to help generate and evaluate a wide range of alternative courses of action (both direct coping efforts for aspects that can be changed and emotionally palliative coping efforts for aspects that cannot) while developing and using social supports; (d) decision-making: to help evaluate the possible consequences of available alternative solutions and select the most effective and feasible ones for the short and long term; (e) solution implementation, verification, and relapse prevention: to help assess the outcome of the chosen solutions, take credit for changes, identify high-risk situations, and handle relapses or setbacks (Meichenbaum, 1992).

Research evidence indicates that problem-solving counseling improves psychosocial adjustment for those who are not well adjusted to their illness, who live alone, infrequently use problem-solving coping skills, or frequently use avoidance coping methods (Roberts, et al., 1995).

> BEST PRACTICE 21: *Problem-solving with the active participation of the worker, related to physical, psychosocial, occupational, health care and workers' compensation-based barriers to return-to-work is suggested to be effective.*

Phone Call Support

Instrumental or social support has been advocated as a method to improve coping and psychosocial adjustment to illness by Broadhead et al. (1983), Hornby et al. (1997) and Roberts et al. (1995).

> BEST PRACTICE 22: *Brief, five minute clinician initiated telephone calls once every two weeks with emphasis on active listening, offering supportive and encouraging comments and without probing were effective for those who were not well adjusted to their illness but used problem solving coping.*

COMPENSATION CONTEXT AND BEST PRACTICES

Knowledge transfer involving the development of evidence-informed best practice guidelines has traditionally been aimed at clinicians working in health care or rehabilitation settings. However, without support for the guidelines by system-based stakeholders such as workers' compensation or long term disability companies mandated to provide and pay for the care of the insured working population, wide scope implementation at the regional or national level is impossible.

The implementation of evidence-informed guidelines tends to falter at the intersection between a clinical setting and compensation setting, yet very few studies recognize and investigate this. As early as 1995, having a workers' compensation claim was identified as one of the key predictors of work disability (Gatchel et al., 1995). Likewise, a recent study demonstrated that the workers' compensation system's and employer's response to the low back injury claim constitutes one of the key predictors of duration and costs of disability, and not as much of the actual return to work, in the subacute stage (Schultz et al., 2002, 2004).

The process of implementing clinical guidelines, particularly those pertaining to a disability that does not conform to the "black and white" biomedical model is highly politicized and requires an integrated biopsychosocial approach. Organizational characteristics of the compensation system need to be recognized. These systematic characteristics are likely to serve as barriers to knowledge transfer and the implementation of guidelines. They include but are not limited to, the following factors:

1. Preference for biomedical, psychiatric, or insurance/forensic models as compared to a biopsychosocial model in conceptualization and management of injury, diagnosis, rehabilitation, return to work, and prevention (Schultz et al., 2000).
2. Preference for a medico-legal approach to service provision with focus on entitlement, causality, determination, and compensability rather than rehabilitation (Schultz et al., 2003); focus on litigation and identification of "secondary gain" and suboptimal motivation tend to create an adversarial service climate and prolong disability due to the lost capacity to intervene early, before chronicity sets in.
3. Risk for disability identification systems are non-existent, based on internal system-produced consensus or, at best, are based on the multi-color flag system, originally developed for New Zealand's workers' compensation system by Steven Linton and supported in the literature by Main and Spanswick (2000); none of the flagging-based risk identification systems has actually been empirically validated as a whole.
4. Vocational rehabilitation and return to work efforts are often initiated too late in the process, well past the 4-6 week "window of opportunity" after the injury, when chronicity has already set in and an adversarial relationship with the insurer has already developed.
5. The worker's role is to be passive recipient of services ("a claimant") rather than an active participant of the activation and return to work process.
6. Compensation systems, by virtue of their mandate, policies and business model of service delivery (as compared to a clinical model), focus more on "claim management" rather than the true interdisciplinary case management necessary for the success of early intervention programs.
7. Self-contained nature of insurance systems, with limited interaction/collaboration with other system-based stakeholders, particularly in the early life of a claim.

In this context, the main tenets of the early intervention guidelines may be difficult for compensation systems to fulfill. Notably, they require the worker's active participation, a coordinated approach by all stakeholders, identification of workers at risk for disability during the subacute stage, and setting up interdisciplinary case management teams interacting with the worker, primary care physician, employer and clinicians involved in physical restoration and activation. A working alliance must be established between the compensation system-based case management team in order for the intervention to be effective. Yet, the medico-legal and malingering detection focus, being a component of the traditional culture of such organizations, detracts from establishing such working relationships and often contributes to chronicity.

Only in an environment which actually promotes a worker's motivation to recover and return to work, are the guidelines for early intervention likely to be successfully implemented. Only in such a context can reassurance and reduction of worker's fears related to pain and work be accomplished. Only in this type of situation can practical goals for change and a focus on the barriers to return to work and problem areas be identified and worked on, with the active participation of the worker, employer and the health care practitioners in an integrative clinical and occupational approach. As a result, promotion of function, physical activation and job accommodation/modification, will more likely be successfully pursued and addressed.

CONCLUSIONS

The guidelines proposed in this chapter are of a "working" and "living" variety, as opposed to a fixed record of recommendations based on current knowledge. As more knowledge develops, these guidelines will require constant revisions, updates and overhauls.

The state of knowledge in early intervention research in musculoskeletal pain disability currently does not allow for development of evidence-validated or even evidence-supported recommendations in all pertinent areas. Specifically, more research is needed at the systemic and organizational level, which has been, with few exceptions, largely outside of the clinical researchers' scope of interest, yet postulated as critically important (Loisel, 2001). Also, more randomized controlled trials of interventions conducted with compensated workers are needed due to the uniqueness of this population, and the context in which disability occurs. Different algorithms and predictive, evidence-based actuarial formulas need to be developed and applied with workers at the subacute stage, to identify those who are at high risk for disability. Various outcome measures which operationalize disability in different ways, such as return to work, duration of disability, compensation and healthcare utilization, should be defined, standardized, and explored to establish the effectiveness and cost effectiveness of early risk identification and early intervention. Appropriate predictive and intervention models should be selected and investigated for different purposes as there is no single model that fits all applications.

Multi-stakeholder interaction and integration of clinical and occupation intervention approaches appear to be the most challenging component of the guidelines from the implementation perspective. This area would likely benefit from some exploratory, qualitative research to develop conceptual models, which are currently limited. Traditional, individual-oriented clinical research needs to be expanded to encompass the knowledge of systems, from organizational psychology and organizational behavior perspectives.

The cognitive-behavioral approach found to be most promising in early intervention will need to continue its expansion from the clinical laboratory and its application by psychologists, to wide-range case management applications with workers at risk for disability. Any, or almost any, dimension of early intervention can be conceptualized and operationalized as aiming at a change of cognitions: workers' expectations of recovery and return to work, perceptions and beliefs regarding disability and rehabilitation, perceptions of employer's and compensation system's reactions to the injury and belief about the threat of their job/employment posed by their injury (Schultz et al., 2002, 2004). At the same time, changes in employer's beliefs, perceptions and attitudes towards the workers and changes in the compensation system's beliefs, perceptions and attitudes, are likely to contribute to a successful outcome as well.

The methodological issues related to the standardization of interventions face an inherent conflict. On one hand, clinician-led interventions focused on an individual, have traditionally achieved the highest levels of standardization, albeit not without difficulties. On the other hand, multi-model, multi-system and multi-disciplinary interventions hold the most promise in early intervention research. Yet, these types of complex interventions are the most difficult to standardize.

Due to the paucity of RCTs in early intervention research, particularly with compensated workers, the limited scope of valid evidence, and research generalizability problems, the guidelines presented in this chapter can best be called "evidence-informed" as opposed to "validated" or even "supported." They constitute a direction in which to move at a time when more research is being undertaken.

ACKNOWLEDGMENTS: The authors wish to thank the Workers' Compensation Board of British Columbia for the provision of funding for this chapter through a research grant (A Prospective Study of the Effectiveness of Early Intervention with High Risk Low Back Injured Workers). We also would like to express our appreciation for the special assistance provided by the librarians at the Workers' Compensation Library in Richmond, British Columbia.

REFERENCES

Bigos, S., Bowyer, O., Braen, G., et al. (1994). *Acute low back problems in adults.* Clinical Practice Guideline, Quick Reference Guide Number 14. Rockville, MD: U.S. Department of Health and Human Service, Agency for Health Care Policy and Research, AHCPR Pub. No 95-0643.

Black, C., Cheung, L., Cooper, J., Curson-Prue, S., Doupe, L., Guirguis, S., Haines, T., Hawkins, L., Helmka, S., Holness L., Levitsky, M., Liss, G., Malcolm, B., Painvin, C., and Wills, M. (2001). *Injury/Illness And Return To Work/Function: A Practical Guide For Physicians.*

Boden, S.D., & Swanson, A.L. (1998). As assessment of the early management of spine problems and appropriateness of diagnostic imaging utilization. *Physical Medicine and Rehabilitation Clinics of North America, 9*(2), 411–417.

Brooker, A., Clarke, J., Sinclair, S., Pennick, S., & Hogg-Johnson, S. (2000). Effective disability management and return-to-work practices. In: T. Sullivan (Ed), *Injury And The New World Of Work.* Vancouver: UBC Press.

Burton, A.K., Waddell, G., Tillotson, K.M., & Summerton, N. (1999). Information and advice to patients with back pain can have a positive effect: A randomized controlled trial of a novel educational booklet in primary care. *Spine, 24,* 2484–91.

Cooper, J.E., Tate, R.B., Yassi, A. (1998). Components of initial and residual disability after back injury in nurses. *Spine, 23,* 2118–22.

Crook, J., Milner, R., Schultz, I.Z., & Stringer, B. (2002). Determinants of occupational disability following a low back injury: A critical review of the literature. *Journal of Occupational Rehabilitation, 12,* 277–295.

Crook, J., & Moldofsky, H. (1996). The clinical course of musculoskeletal pain in empirically derived groupings of injured workers. *Pain, 67,* 427–33.

Dasinger, L.K., Krause, N., Thompson, P.J., Brand, R.J., & Rudolph, L. (2001). Doctor proactive communication, return-to-work recommendation, and duration of disability after a workers' compensation low back injury. *Journal of Occupational and Environmental Medicine, 43,* 515–25.

Ehrmann-Feldman, D., Rossignol, M., & Abenhaim, L. (1996). Physician referral to physical therapy in a cohort of workers compensated for low back pain. *Physical Therapy, 76,* 150–157.

Elders, L.A.M., van der Beek, A.J., & Burdorf, A. (2000). Return to work after sickness absence due to back disorders—a systematic review on intervention strategies. *International Archives of Occupational and Environment Health, 73,* 339–48.

Emmons, K.M., & Rollnick, S. (2001). Motivational interviewing in health care settings opportunities and limitations. *American Journal of Preventive Medicine, 20,* 68–74.

Feuerstein, M., & Thebarge, R.W. (1991). Perceptions of disability and occupational stress as discriminatory of work disability in patients with chronic pain. *Journal of Occupational Rehabilitation, 1*, 185–95.

Fisher, R., & Ury, W. (1991). *Getting To Yes*. New York: Penguin Books.

Frank, J., Sinclair, S., Hogg-Johnson, S., Shannon, H., Bombardier, C., Beaton, D. et al. (1998). Preventing disability from work-related low-back pain. *Canadian Medical Association Journal, 158*, 1625–31.

Frank, J., Yassi, A., Stock, S., Guzmán, J., Clarke, J., Friesen, M. et al., (Eds) (2000). *Work-Ready: Return-to-Work approaches for people with soft-tissue injuries*. Toronto, Ontario: Institute for Work & Health.

Frank, J.W., Brooker, A., DeMaio, S.E., Kerr, M.S., Maetzel, A., Shannon, H.S. et al., (1996). Disability resulting from occupational low back pain: Part II: What do we know about secondary prevention? A review of the scientific evidence on prevention after disability begins. *Spine, 21*, 2918–29.

Friesen, M.N., Yassi, A., & Cooper, J. (2001). Return-to-work: The importance of human interactions and organizational structures. *Work, 17*, 11–22.

Gatchel, R.J., Polatin, P.B., Noe, C., Gardea, M., Pulliam, C., & Thompson, J. (2003). Treatment- and cost-effectiveness of early intervention for acute low-back pain patients: A one-year prospective study. *Journal of Occupational Rehabilitation, 13*(1), 1–9.

Hagen, M.E., Erikson, H.R., & Ursin, H. (2000). Does early intervention with a light mobilization program reduce long-term sick leave for low back pain? *Spine, 25*, 1973–76.

Hagen, K.B., Hilde, G., Jamtvedt, G. & Winnem, M.F. (2002). The Cochran Review of advice to stay active as a single treatment for low back pain and sciatica. *Spine, 27*(16), 1736–1741.

Hashemi, L., Webster, B.S., Clancy, E.A., & Volinn, E. (1997). Length of disability and cost of workers' compensation low back pain claims. *Journal of Occupational and Environmental Medicine, 39*, 937–45.

Hoxby, H., Roberts, J., Brown, G. B., Pallister, R., Gafni, A., and Streiner, D. (1997). *Telephone Nursing Support: Let's Talk*.

Indahl, A., Haldorsen, E.H., Holm, S., Reikerås, O., & Ursin, H. (1998). Five-year follow-up study of a controlled clinical trial using light mobilization and an informative approach to low back pain. *Spine, 23*, 2625–30.

Indahl, A., Velund, L., & Reikeraas, O. (1995). Good prognosis for low back pain when left untampered: A randomized clinical trial. *Spine, 20*, 473–77.

Jensen, M.P. (2001). Motivating the pain patient for behavioral change. In: J. D. Loeser, S. H. Butler, C. R. Chapman, & D. C. Turk, (Eds.) *Bonica's Management of Pain*. 3rd ed. Philadelphia: Lippincott, Williams & Wilkins.

Karasek, R., Kawakami, N., Brisson, C., Houtman, I., Bongers, P., & Amick, B. (1998). The Job Content Questionnaire (JCQ): An instrument for internationally comparative assessments of psychosocial job characteristics. *Journal of Occupational Health Psychology, 3*, 322.

Karjalainen, K., Malmivaara, A., Mutanen, P., Roine, R., Hurri, H. & Pohjolainen, T. (2004). Mini-intervention for Subacute Low Back Pain: Two-year follow-up and modifiers of effectiveness. *29*, 1069–1076.

Karjalainen, K., Malmivaara, A., Pohjolainen, T., Hurri, H., Mutanen, P., Rissanen, P. et al., (2003). Mini-intervention for subacute low back pain: A randomized controlled trial. *Spine, 28*, 535–541.

Karjalainen, K., Malmivaara, A., van Tulder, M., et al., (2000). Multidisciplinary biopsychosocial rehabilitation for subacute low back pain among working age adults (*Cochrane Review*). 2000. Oxford, Update Software.

Krause, N., Dasinger, L.K., &Neuhasuer, F. (1998). Modified work and return to work: A review of the literature. *Journal of Occupational Rehabilitation, 8*, 113–39.

Lewicki, R.J., Litever, J.A., Saunders, D.M., & Minton, J.W. (1993). *Negotiation: Readings, Exercises and Cases*. 2nd ed. Boston: Irwin.

Lindström, I., Öhlund, C., Eek, C., Wallin, L., Peterson, L., Fordyce, W. E. et al., (1992). The effect of graded activity on patients with subacute low back pain: A randomized prospective clinical study with an operant-conditioning behavioral approach. *Physical Therapy, 72*, 279–93.

Lindström, I., Öhlund, C., Eek, C., Wallin, L., Peterson, L., & Nachemson, A. (1992). Mobility, strength, and fitness after a graded activity program for patients with subacute low back pain: A randomized prospective clinical study with a behavioral therapy approach. *Spine, 17*, 641–52.

Linton, S.J., & Andersson, T. (2000). Can chronic disability be prevented?: A randomized trial of a cognitive-behavior intervention and two forms of information for patients with spinal pain. *Spine, 25*, 2825–31.

Linton, S.J., & Bradley, L.A. (1996). Strategies for the prevention of chronic pain. In: R.J. Gatchel & D.C. Turk (Eds.), *Psychological Approaches to Pain Management: A Practititoner's Handbook*. New York: Guildford.

Loisel, P., Abenhaim, L., Durand, P., Esdaile, J.M., Suissa, S., Gosselin, L. et al., (1997). A population-based, randomized clinical trial on back pain management. *Spine, 22*, 2911–18.

Loisel, P., Durand, M., Berthelette, D., Vézina, N., Baril, R., Gagnon, D. et al., (2001). Disability prevention: New paradigm for the management of occupational back pain. *Disability Management and Health Outcomes, 9*, 351–60.

Loisel, P., Durand, P., Abenhaim, L., Gosselin, L., Simart, R., Turcotte, J. et al., (1994). Management of occupational back pain: The Sherbrooke model. Results of a pilot and feasibility study. *Occupational and Environmental Medicine, 51*, 597–602.

Loisel, P., Gosselin, L., Durand, P., Lemaire, J., Poitras, S., Abenhaim, L. (2001). Implementation of a participatory ergonomics program in the rehabilitation of workers suffering from subacute back pain. *Applied Ergonomics, 32*, 53–60.

Loisel, P., Poitras, S., Lemaire, J., Durand, P., Southièse, A., & Abenhaim, L. (1998). Is work status of low back pain patients best described by an automated device or by a questionnaire? *Spine, 23*, 1588–94.

Maetzl, A., & Li, L. (2002). The economic burden of low back pain: A review of studies published between 1996 and 2001. *Best Practice & Research Clinical Rhematology, 16*(1), 23–30.

Main, C.J., & Spanswick, C.C. (2000). *Pain Management: An Interdisciplinary Approach*. New York: Churchill Livingstone.

Marhold, C., Linton, S.J., & Melin, L. (2001). A cognitive-behavioral return-to-work program: Effects on pain patients with a history of long-term versus short-term sick leave. *Pain, 91*, 155–63.

McGuirk, B., King, W., Govind, J., Lowry, J., Bogduk, N. (2001). Safety, efficacy, and cost effectiveness of evidence-based guidelines for the management of acute low back pain in primary care. *Spine, 26*, 2615–22.

Meichenbaum, D., & Turk, D.C. (1987). *Facilitating Treatment Adherence: A Practitioner's Guidebook*. New York: Plenum Press.

Miller, W.R., & Rollnick, S. (2002). *Motivational Interviewing*. New York: Guildford Press.

Moffett, J.K., Torgerson, D., Bell-Syer, S., Jackson, D., Llewlyn-Phillips, H., Frrin, A. et al., (1999). Randomised controlled trial of exercise for low back pain: Clinical outcomes, costs, and preferences. *British Medical Journal, 319*, 277–83.

Moore, J.E., Von Korff, M., Cherkin, D., Saunders, K., & Lorig, K. (2000). A randomized trial of cognitive-behavioral program for enhancing back pain self care in a primary care setting. *Pain, 88*, 145–53.

Nielson, W.R., & Weir, R. (2001). Biopsychosocial approaches to the treatment of chronic pain. *The Clinical Journal of Pain, 17*, S114–S127.

Prochaska, J.O., & Diclemente, C.C. (1982). Transtheoretical therapy: Toward a more integrative model of change. *Psychotherapy: Theory, Research, and Practice, 19*, 276–88.

Raine, R., Haines, A., Sensky, T., Hutchings, A., Larkin, K., & Black, N. (2002). Systematic review of mental health intervention for patients common somatic symptoms: Can research evidence from secondary care be extrapolated to primary care? *British Medical Journal, 325*, 1082–1085.

Roberts, J., Browne, G.B., Streiner, D., Gafni, A., Pallister, R., Hoxby, H. et al., (1995). Problem-solving counselling or phone-call support for outpatients with chronic illness: Effective for whom? *The Canadian Journal of Nursing Research, 27*, 111–37.

Roland, M., Waddell, G., Moffett, J.K., Burton, K., & Main, C. (2002). *The Back Book*. 2nd ed. Norwich, UK: TSO (The Stationery Office.

Rollnick, S., & Bell, A. (1991). Brief motivational interviewing for use by the nonspecialist. In: W.R. Miller & S. Rollnick (Eds.), *Motivational Interviewing*. New York: The Guilford Press.

Rollnick ,S., Heather, N., & Bell, A. (1992). Negotating behavior change in medical settings: The development of brief motivational interviewing. *Journal of Mental Health, 1*, 25–37.

Rollnick, S., Mason, P., & Butler, C. (2000). *Health Behavior Change: A Guide For Practitioners*. New York: Churchill Livingstone.

Rosen, N.B., Hoffberg, H.J. (1998). Conservative management of low back pain. *Physical Medicine and Rehabilitation Clinics of North America, 9*(2), 435–472.

Rossignol, M., Abenhaim, L., Séguin, P., Neveu, A., Collet, J., Ducruet, T. et al., (2000). Coordination of primary health care for back pain: A randomized controlled trial. *Spine, 25,* 251–59.

Schultz, I. Z. (2001). *Research Report on the Validation of Risk-for-Disability Questionnaire.* Workers' Compensation Board of British Columbia.

Schultz, I.Z., Crook, J., Fraser, K., & Joy, P.W. (2000). Models of diagnosis and rehabilitation in musculoskeletal pain-related occupational disability. *Journal of Occupational Rehabilitation, 10,* 271–93.

Schultz, I. Z., Crook, J., Meloche, G., Berkowitz, J., Milner, R., Joy, P., Zuberbier, O. A., and Meloche, W. (submitted). Psychological factors predictive of occupational low back disability: Towards development of a return to work model.

Schultz, I.Z, Crook, J.M., Berkowitz, J., Meloche, G.R., Milner, R., Zuberbier, O.A. et al., (2002). Biopsychosocial multivariate predictive model of occupational low back disability. *Spine, 27,* 2720–2725.

Slaiku, K.A.(1996). *When Push Comes to Shove: A Practical Guide to Mediating Disputes.* San Francisco: Jossey-Bass.

Spitzer, W.O., LeBlanc, F.E., Dupuis, M. (1987). Scientific approach to the assessment and management of activity-related spinal disorders: A monograph for clinicians. Report of the Quebec Task Force on spinal disorders. *Spine, 12,* S1–S59.

Tate, R.B., Yassi, A., Cooper, J. (1999). Predictors of time loss after back injury in nurses. *Spine, 24,* 1930–1935.

The Medical Research Council of Canada, The Natural Sciences and Engineering Research Council of Canada, and The Social Sciences and Humanities Research Council of Canada (1997). *Code of ethical conduct for research involving humans.*

Torstensen, T.A., Ljunggren,,A.E., Meen, H.D., Mowinckel, P. & af Geijerstam, P.T. (1998). Efficiency and costs of medical exercise therapy, conventional physiotherapy and self-exercise in patients with chronic low back pain. *Spine, 23,* 2616–2624

Ury, W.C. (1993). *Getting Past No: Negotiating With Difficult People.* New York: Bantam Books.

van Tulder, M.W., Koes, B.W., & Bouter, L.M. (1995). A cost-of-illness study of back pain in the Netherlands. *Pain,* 62, 233–40.

Volinn, E., Van Koevering, D., & Loeser, J.D. (1991). Back sprain in industry: The role of socioeconomic factors in chronicity. *Spine, 16,* 542–48.

Von Korff, M. (1994). Studying the natural history of back pain. *Spine, 19,* 2041S–6S.

Waddell, G., & Burton, A.K. (2001). Occupational health guidelines for the management of low back pain at work: Evidence review. *Occupational Medicine, 51,* 124–35.

Waddell, G., McCulloch, J.A., Kummel, E., & Venner, R.M. (1980). Nonorganic physical signs in low-back pain. *Spine, 5,* 117–25.

Ware Jr., J.E, & Sherbourne, C.D. (1992). The MOS 36-item short-form health survey (SF-36) 1. Conceptual framework and item selection.*Medical Care, 30,* 473–83.

Webster, B.S., & Snook, S.H. (1990). The cost of compensable low back pain. *Journal of Occupational Medicine, 32,* 13–15.

Williams, D.A., Feuerstein, M., Durbin, D., & Pezzullo, J. (1998). Health care and indemnity costs across the natural history of disability in occupational low back pain. *Spine 23*(21), 2329–2336.

Yassi, A., Tate, R., Cooper, J.E., Snow, C., Vallentyne, S., & Khoker, J.B. (1995). Early intervention for back injured nurses at a large Canadian tertiary hospital: An evaluation of the effectiveness and cost benefits of a two year pilot project. *Occupational Medicine, 45,* 209–14.

IV

EARLY INTERVENTION WITH AT-RISK GROUPS

25

Early Interventions for "At Risk" Patients with Spinal Pain

Steven James Linton

While identifying patients at risk for developing persistent spinal pain and disability is important, providing an effective intervention is crucial. Indeed, the central question after identification is "How do we prevent this problem from becoming chronic?" Without effective remedies, early identification is relatively meaningless. Thus, early identification has little inherent worth if it is not tied to action. However, developing effective early interventions has been a difficult challenge that has received too little attention. Still, some progress has been made and various researchers have developed programs and scientifically tested them.

The purpose of this chapter is to describe the development of preventive interventions for "at risk" patients suffering back pain with special emphasis on the program developed in our clinic in Sweden. The approach we have worked on incorporates early identification as well as interventions that may be used at the first visit as well as for those clearly deemed as "at risk" for developing disability. Moreover, we have focused on interventions that health-care providers can master and use, for example, in primary care settings.

PSYCHOLOGICAL RISK FACTORS DESERVE PSYCHOLOGICAL INTERVENTIONS

Psychological factors are powerful risk factors linked to the development of persistent disability. Even though psychological factors are often found to be potent risk factors, most treatments offered to patients early on are nevertheless medical in nature. Consequently, patients displaying such psychological risk factors seem to deserve an intervention that addresses these. Let us examine this idea more closely.

Although many factors may be related to the development of disability, psychological factors appear to be particularly relevant. Other chapters in this book cogently show that a host of factors are related to the development of persistent pain and disability. These involve medical or biological factors such as ishias pain, and

DOI: 10.1007/978-0-387-28919-9_25, © 2009 Springer Science+Business Media, LLC

sensitization, in addition to previous history of treatment (Nachemson & Jonsson, 2000). Furthermore, the work environment is important both in terms of physical work (Westgaard & Winkel, 2002; Wickström & Pentti, 1998) and in terms of psychosocial factors such as stress, control and demands (Hoogendoorn, van Poppel, Bongers, Koes, & Bouter, 2000; Linton, 2001). Social factors akin to educational level, income, race, family situation are complex, but certainly may also influence the development of a pain problem (Nachemson & Jonsson, 2000; Waddell, Aylward, & Sawney, 2002). However, psychological factors have been found to have a clear relationship to the development of persistent pain (Gatchel, 1996; Gatchel, Polatin, & Kinney, 1995; Linton, 2000a; Pincus, Burton, Vogel, & Field, 2002; Pulliam & Gatchel, 2002; Schultz et al., 2002). Moreover, psychological factors are integrally related to the transition from acute to chronic pain (Linton, 2002b). Thus, psychological factors seem to be of great importance for the understanding of the development of chronic disability.

There is considerable logic in providing a psychologically oriented intervention for a problem characterized by psychological aspects. For example, providing a psychological intervention would help to match the treatment to the patient's unique needs. Further, the identification of psychological factors might provide guides for defining intervention targets and barriers to recovery. Finally, the identification of psychological factors might also enhance the development of interventions by providing insight into the mechanisms that are maintaining the problem. For example, if depressed mood were identified, appropriate measures might be taken.

Although it would seem logical to employ psychologically oriented interventions, this seldom happens in the current health-care system. For a variety of reasons, most health care units fail to identify psychosocial factors let alone implement an early psychologically oriented intervention (Armstrong, McDonough, & Baxter, 2003). Consider the fact that although psychological factors are often present, it is still common to only provide medical treatments (Vingård et al., 2002). This appears to be related to an approach of providing "more of the same" if a treatment is not successful. In other words, as the problem progresses towards chronic disability, there is a tendency to prescribe more of the same therapies tried early on. Consequently, the "dose" of the treatment is increased rather than viewing the progression as a risk situation that needs to be tackled in an alternative way. However, if psychological factors are catalyzing the problem towards chronicity, these treatments may be ineffective because they do not address the problem. Unfortunately, before the clinician realizes that this "normal" treatment is not successful, the problem may well be on the way to a persistent disability. In order to be successful then, changes in the system of health care may need to be taken in order to implement an alternative that can address psychological aspects of the problem.

Early intervention that addresses psychological issues involves early assessment followed by appropriate interventions. Because musculoskeletal pain is a natural part of life and most people will recover with self-help procedures (Waddell, 1998), there is a need to gear the intervention to the patient's needs. Fortunately, most patients do not develop long-term disability. However, the minority of patients who do develop disability, consume a majority of the resources available (Nachemson & Jonsson, 2000; Waddell, 1998). Thus, it is important to identify those who are at risk of developing long-term disability so that appropriate interventions can be initiated. It is also logical that more resources might be used for "at risk" patients since they have greater need. Likewise, it is logical that patients at low risk will not need as intricate interventions. Nevertheless, some "preventive" measures might be initiated even at the first visit. Following the reasoning above these would need to be simple measures that I would suggest are similar to good practice ideals.

With the above background, let us now turn to the issue of implementing an early, preventive intervention program into practice with an eye on effectiveness. This involves developing a procedure for identifying patients at risk of developing long-term disability as well as interventions appropriate for the problem and point in time (Linton, 2002a).

EARLY IDENTIFICATION

Before an early, preventive intervention may be implemented, candidates need to be properly identified. Because programs strive to match the intervention to the patient's needs, an assessment of risk factors is considered a prerequisite. It is not enough to simply establish that a patient appears to be "at risk"(Waddell, Burton, & Main, 2003). Instead, an evaluation of which factors maybe catalyzing the development is necessary to determine an appropriate intervention. How then, might this be achieved in a busy clinical setting.

In clinical practice, early identification often involves screening procedures. Screening is a rough assessment to narrow down the number of patients who need to be assessed in more detail (Sheridan & Winogrond, 1987). The purpose of psychosocial screening procedure for people with (sub) acute back pain problems is essentially threefold. First, it offers a rough estimation of the risk the patient runs of developing long-term disability. This is useful, for instance, in deciding the amount of treatment suitable. Second, it focuses attention on the patient's specific problem areas and is helpful in establishing goals. Third, it provides information about possible mechanisms and thus aids in matching the patient with the appropriate intervention. Identifying goals and possible mechanisms is of special value because the psychosocial aspects may be integrated with the medical findings. Accordingly, a screening procedure that can guide the initial assessment to those at risk and that can help focus on the most important psychological risk factors is beneficial. A number of instruments are available (Waddell et al., 2003); however, we have developed a special instrument for clinical use that provides an estimate of risk as well as information that is beneficial in developing an intervention strategy.

THE ÖREBRO MUSCULOSKELETAL PAIN SCREENING QUESTIONNAIRE

The Örebro Musculoskeletal Pain Screening Questionnaire was developed as a tool for clinicians in the early identification of people at risk of developing long-term problems (Boersma & Linton, 2002; Linton & Halldén, 1998). The questionnaire contains 25 items covering a range of psychosocial variables that are related to long-term disability such as work related variables, coping, function, stress, mood, and fear-avoidance beliefs. It provides an overall score from which risk may be judged as well as ratings on separate items. Usually the scores are divided into high risk (definitely need to attend to this case), medium risk (may need special attention, continue to observe progress), and low risk (expect to get better). Several studies have shown the questionnaire to be reliable and valid (Ektor-Andersen, Örbaek, Ingvarsson, & Kullendorff, 2002; Hurley, Dusoir, McDonough, Moore, & Baxter, 2001; Hurley et al., 2000; Linton & Boersma, 2003). In the clinic, the risk estimate is but one part of the procedure. Indeed, we use the instrument to engage the patient, identify targets, and build a potential intervention.

Providing Feedback

A notable part of screening is providing the patient with proper feedback. Typically, people are curious to know what the result of the screening is particularly when they have invested the time and effort to complete a questionnaire. Thus, the patient may

TABLE 1. An Overview of the Items in the Örebro Musculoskeletal Pain Screening Questionnaire

Question	Variable Name
1. What year were you born?	Age
2. Are you a man/woman?	Gender
3. Were you born in Sweden (country of study)?	Nationality
4. What is your current employment status?	Employed
5. Where do you have pain	Pain site
6. How many days of work have your missed (sick leave) because of pain during the past 12 months?	Sick leave
7. How long have you had your current pain problem?	Pain duration
8. Is your work heavy or monotonous?	Heavy work
9. How would you rate the pain you have had during the past week?	Current pain
10. In the past 3 months, on the average, how intense was your pain?	Average pain
11. How often would you say that you have experienced pain episodes, on the average during the past 3 months?	Pain frequency
12. Based on all the things you do to cope, or deal with your pain, on an average day, how much are you able to decrease it?	Coping
13. How tense or anxious have you felt in the past week?	Stress
14. How much have you been bothered by feeling depressed in the past week?	Depression
15. In your view, how large is the risk that your current pain may become persistent?	Expected outcome
16. In your estimation, what are the chances that you will be able to work in 6 months?	Expected outcome
17. If you take into consideration your work routines, management, salary, promotion possibilities, and workmates, how satisfied are you with your job?	Job satisfaction
18. Physical activity makes my pain worse.	Fear-Avoidance Belief
19. An increase in pain is an indication that I should stop what I am doing until the pain decreases.	Fear-Avoidance Belief
20. I should not do my normal work with my present pain.	Fear-Avoidance Belief
21. I can do light work for an hour.	Function: work
22. I can walk for an hour.	Function: walk
23. I can do ordinary household chores.	Function: household work
24. I can do the weekly shopping.	Function: shopping
25. I can sleep at night.	Function: sleep

be concerned about their pain problem as well as the results of the assessment. To counteract this anxiety, a clear explanation is necessary that includes concrete information about how the patient may actively participate in treatment and prevention.

Providing feedback also represents an excellent opportunity to develop rapport with the patient, provide educational information and promote self-help behaviors. In giving feedback on the screening questionnaire results, an overview should be provided. A short summary that stresses the usefulness of the information, underscores some positive results, and leads into detailed questions (see below) is ordinarily done at the beginning of the meeting. A final summary is provided at the end of the session. Although professionals often discuss patients in terms of "risk levels", I recommend avoiding this word, as it is often misunderstood. For patients, "risk" is often a dichotomous concept that indicates either a "normal" score or the terrible certainty of developing chronic disability. Instead, the discussion might focus on consequences of the pain and how the problem might best be dealt with to avoid future problems.

Listening is an imperative aspect. Remember that we are collecting information and the individual patient is in a position to provide us with key features.

Identifying Target Behaviors

Screening seems to make sense only if it promotes a more effective way of proceeding with the case. Identification *per se* has no certain value. Indeed, using psychological screening to simply *identify* patients at risk would seem to be a waste of important information. Certainly going a step further and using the information to develop ideas about goals for intervention as well as factors maintaining the problem would utilize the information more wisely and enhance the assessment. After all, the promise of screening is to appropriate resources to those patients most likely to benefit from them. To utilize the screening material attention may be turned to possible targets for intervention as well as probable maintaining factors that in turn would help in tailoring the intervention to the individual's actual needs.

To identify targets in the clinical situation we recommend using the answers to individual items on The Örebro Musculoskeletal Pain Screening Questionnaire as a basis for a discussion with the patient. After reinforcing positive behaviors, we ask open-ended questions about items that have atypical responses. Areas of concern such as a high score on a fear-avoidance or depression item can in this way be identified and assessed. For example we may ask: "I see that you have rated your mood with an 8, could you tell me more about this?" This creates an opportunity to assess and understand the patient's beliefs about their problem and probable recovery.

As we proceed through the various items on the questionnaire, a picture should begin to emerge concerning potential targets. The patient's conception of the problem should become clearer. Moreover, barriers to recovery e.g. workplace factors or fear, should become apparent. The patient's goals typically also come to the forefront. In short, the patient and practitioner develop a shared understanding of the problem and what the focus of the treatment should be on.

A preliminary analysis may be conducted in order to generate hypotheses about factors causing or maintaining the problem. This characteristically involves combining items on the questionnaire to get a picture of antecedents, behaviors, thoughts and beliefs, as well as consequences. For example, anticipated problems for a return to work may be enhanced by fear-avoidance beliefs. Specifically, the patient may believe that her/his work is harmful and should be avoided until after full physical recovery. Or, fear-avoidance beliefs may be pertinent even though some activities, say, walking are not affected, while others, such as household chores are affected. An attempt to identify why the patient can walk, but not do household chores could proceed, as the patient may believe that certain movements (bending, twisting, lifting) are harmful. Thus, the screening setting offers an opportunity for initiating an analysis of factors that maintain the problem.

Communication: Planning for Treatment

Perhaps the most central aspect of screening is that it provides an opportunity for clear communication. To engage patients in early interventions, communication seems essential for providing an understanding of the problem and its treatment. The time pressures of the clinic make this a true challenge, but research indicates that poor communication contributes to the development of problems. Bear in mind that a recent study of chronic pain patients revealed that only 32% could provide an accurate cause of their problem, while 20% gave a cause that did not coincide with their actual diagnosis, while the remaining 48% could not report the cause at all (Geisser & Roth, 1998). Consider further that patients come to the clinic with expectations about the course of the problem and treatment and these are relatively powerful predictors of future disability ()(Linton & Halldén, 1998; Waddell, Newton, Henderson, Somerville, & Main, 1993).

By making the most of the discussion with the patient concerning their answers provided on the screening questionnaire, we may enhance communication. Indeed, one goal is to establish a shared understanding of the problem and its character. Once this is accomplished, potential interventions may emerge and be discussed. We may also evaluate the patient's interest in the various options for interventions available. For example, we may ask an open-ended question regarding how mood might be dealt with. At this point we may need to employ our own problem solving skills to make decisions with the patient on what might be done and how we should proceed. Having established a shared understanding of the cause of the problem and the targets for intervention, it should be easier to establish an alliance with the patient to enhance cooperation. Although back and neck pain often remits undramatically, certain action may be warranted. Frequently, this action will involve relatively simple measures such as information or further assessment. It may also involve advice, education or skills training. Fortunately, many patients may not need additional treatment as information and advice may be sufficient to enhance their own self-care skills.

EARLY PREVENTIVE INTERVENTIONS

Providing effective early interventions that will help prevent future disability is an eminent goal for the health-care system. In this section, two different situations that are typical in primary care will be discussed in terms of the options available for intervention. In the first situation we will deal with a patient seeking care for an acute episode with relatively low risk. This provides an example of a concise, but cogent intervention that likens "good practice" and may long-term decrease disability. In the second situation a patient identified as "at risk" for developing long-term disability will be considered. This provides a basis for presenting many of the options available for early, preventive interventions for neck and back pain.

First Consultation

Although there is an excellent chance for "full" recovery, the very first consultation for a back pain problem nevertheless presents a unique opportunity to promote healthy attitudes and self-help measures. Certainly, many of the attitudes and beliefs patients develop are related to encounters with health-care providers. In addition, good communication is necessary to engage the patient as modern interventions invariably involve "self-help" efforts such as exercising, practicing relaxation or taking medications on a specific schedule.

To understand why the patients are seeking help, consider the fact that they are quite concerned that their pain is the result of a serious injury (Von Korff et al., 1998). As a result, most guidelines recommend providing such patients with reassurance and clear advice about how to continue their daily activities (Koes, van Tulder, Ostelo, Burton, & Waddell, 2001; Main & Spanswick, 2000; Nachemson & Jonsson, 2000). Indeed, treatment "style" is related to outcome for low back pain patients (Von Korff, Barlow, Cherkin, & Deyo, 1994). In this study, those doctors with a style featuring frequent recommendations for bed rest and analgesics as needed had patients with significantly more disability at follow-up than did doctors clearly communicating the need for self-care strategies. Furthermore, a recent review found that while advice for bed rest was counterproductive, advice to remain active despite the pain produced a significantly better long term result with regard to pain and disability (Waddell, Feder, & Lewis, 1997). Consequently, the first consultation may be an excellent opportunity for sowing the seeds of self-management rather than those of disability development.

In our clinic, we developed a relatively simple program for patients seeking care very early on. The program features an appropriate physical examination, good communication, and the clear message that self-management is necessary. We trained doctors and physical therapists to conduct a physical examination to assess possible "red flags" and to provide feedback. Moreover, these professionals reinforced functional and well behaviors and underscored the importance of maintaining everyday activities and maintaining/returning to work. In a randomized controlled study, 198 patients received either the early program described above or treatment as usual in primary care. Usual treatment was monitored and characteristically consisted of advice to rest as needed as well as analgesics. For patients with no previous history of back pain, sick leave records indicated that there were dramatic differences between the groups. Patients in the early treatment condition as compared to treatment as usual had significantly less dysfunction and less sick leave one year later and the risk for developing chronic disability was reduced by eight fold (Linton, Hellsing, & Andersson, 1993).

However, there may be problems implementing such early interventions where the quality of administration and compliance to follow the guidelines are serious issues. Some studies that have provided early, guideline-based care have only demonstrated limited effects (Hagen, Hilde, Jamtvedt, & Winnem, 2002; Smith, McMurray, & Disler, 2002). As an illustration, occupational physicians were provided with guidelines for an early intervention, but results one year later showed no significant benefit as compared to a group receiving usual primary care (Verbeek, van der Weide, & van Dijk, 2002). Physicians' poor compliance with the program was one reason given to explain the results. Consider also a case-control study where guideline-based management was compared to usual treatment in primary care settings in Australia (McGurik, King, Govind, Lowry, & Bogduk, 2001). Patients with less than 12 weeks of pain were treated in the respective clinics and then followed for one year. Thus, the study highlights the implementation of the guidelines into usual practice routines. Although some important significant differences were noted at the follow-ups favoring the guideline based treatment, the main results showed that both groups improved dramatically with low rates of recurrence suggesting that the guideline based treatment had less effect than expected. A recent Cochrane review also suggests that advice to stay active, one of the central guideline recommendations, may not be effective as a single treatment (Hagen et al., 2002). The skill with which the guidelines are applied appears to be important for successful implementation. Indeed, dealing with psychosocial variables and providing clear advice requires considerable skill that many professionals may not have obtained during their education. Finding the recommendations and interpreting them is a first step. Yet, we found that physical therapists tended to identify more than twice as many risk factors than are supported by the evidence (Overmeer, Linton, & Boersma, in press). Moreover, a survey from Britain showed that clinical guidelines were seldom employed (Armstrong et al., 2003); instead professionals tend to employ the methods learned during their basic education (Turner & Whitfield, 1997). Consequently, while early interventions may provide considerable effects when applied properly, this is not always the case. It appears that the way in which the guidelines are employed is a key factor to success. I suggest that some failures are accounted for by a simple lack of employing the methods at all, while others are accounted for by a failure to properly pinpoint the psychosocial risk factors.

In the very early stages then, preventive methods, e.g. a part of the ordinary clinical routine, may be relatively easy to administer, have simple content and involve a minimum of time. With proper compliance and administration this may enhance results, although the final judgment on this awaits additional clinical trials. However, as the patient's problem develops toward a persistent state of disability, so too does the extent of the prophylactic intervention required. While good communication and specific recommendations may be valuable methods for first visits, more elaborate techniques as well as the need for other professionals may become necessary as the problem progresses.

Interventions for At Risk Patients

Once a patient has been identified as clearly risking the development of persistent disability, the issue becomes how to intervene to prevent this from happening. In our setting in Sweden, two alternatives are recommended. The first involves offering a rather broad cognitive-behavioral group intervention designed to address psychological risk factors, while the other involves an individualized approach based on a behavioral analysis.

Cognitive-Behavioral Groups (CBT)

Although psychological factors are believed to be central in the development of persistent disability, there have been surprisingly few attempts to apply psychological interventions. Yet, if psychological processes enhance or catalyze the development of disability, then psychological techniques might be useful. In order to provide such a secondary preventive intervention, a program was developed in our clinic that builds on experiences from earlier programs provided for chronic pain patients (Compas, Haaga, Keefe, Leitenberg, & Williams, 1998; Linton, 2000b; Morley, Eccleston, & Williams, 1999; van Tulder et al., 2000). However, we paid close attention to the risk factors identified in the screening assessment described above. As a result, the content focuses on the *prevention of persistent pain and disability* and not simply pain treatment. The intervention is provided in groups of 6 to 10 people and encompasses six, two-hour sessions.

The CBT intervention is geared to help each participant develop her/his own coping program. We ask participants to learn, and apply all the skills presented during the course so that a tailored program that bests suits each person's needs is developed. Naturally, from a provider's point of view, we hope to prevent pain related disability, and the need for health-care services, as well as to improve quality of life. Because back pain is recurrent in nature, we do not attempt to eliminate all back pain, but rather to decrease recurrences and reduce their impact.

Sessions are organized to activate participants and promote coping. Each session begins with a short review of homework assignments. Subsequently, the therapist introduces the topic for the session and provides information for a maximum of 15 minutes. Issues concerning how one might control pain intensity, participate in activities, or problems encountered with work or leisure are examples of topics. Participants work with a case description where they are asked to solve problems concerning the case. This allows participants to analyze the "case" and compare it with their own situation. Solutions are presented in the group and discussed. Subsequently, the therapist introduces new coping skills and participants practice them. These includ pain control measures such as relaxation and distraction. However, most skills are oriented towards activity and function. These range from problem solving skills, graded activity, to social and stress management skills. Homework assignments are then made and these are tailored to the participant's needs. Every participant is asked to apply all of the skills learned in their everyday life to evaluate their use. Finally, the session is reviewed underscoring what the participants have learned and strengths and weaknesses of the session are discussed. During the course of the group meeting, participants develop their own personal coping program based on the techniques they believed are most effective for their problem.

Strategies for Behavioral Change

Changing cognitions, emotions and behaviors is central to self-management, but how might it be achieved? Our CBT course is designed to help participants actively alter current cognitions and behaviors. For example, beliefs about the relationship between pain and activity ("*The more I do, the more it will hurt*") or beliefs about stress ("*I must do everything asked of me and exactly on time*") may need to be revised. Likewise, behaviors may need to be changed e.g. increasing activity levels or being able to say "no" to certain demands. Our program employs several strategies to promote such changes.

First, the program engages the participant. Learning by doing is emphasized. Therefore, much of the session consists of practicing new skills and working with the cognitions and emotions surrounding them. Even for discussions, *every* participant is asked individually to provide input. Above all, each person is given the mission of developing his or her own personal coping program. Second, restricted amounts of information are used to prime behavioral changes. Thus, this part of the session is used to model appropriate behaviors as well as to challenge common beliefs. A third strategy is behavioral tests. For patients we conceptualize this as learning through experience. Thus, we ask patients to "test" each skill they learn to assess its possible value for them. This is one basis participants employ for the selection of skills to be included in their personal coping program.

Problem solving is a fourth strategy. This skill is honed in a special problem-based learning module, and it is employed whenever patients describe a "problem" or hindrance. Fifth, the group leader is taught to shape new thoughts and behaviors by reinforcing successive approximations of good coping behavior. Positive reinforcement such as in the form of encouragement is contingently provided when participants correctly approximate a goal behavior. Thus, gradual change is encouraged.

A sixth method is to enhance each patient's self-efficacy, that is, the patient's belief that he/she can impact on the pain and its course. This is a logical goal since many patients have low self-efficacy levels and do not believe that they can change their health behavior. For example, we might ask a person who has successfully completed a homework assignment (e.g. practiced relaxation and decreased pain) to tell the entire group how he/she has accomplished this, to share the "secret" of their success.

Finally, enjoyment is used to enhance learning, engagement, maintenance and pleasure. It is an important strategy to ensure that every participant feels good about his/her accomplishments. People should have the opportunity to laugh and to receive social support. Thus, encouragement is contingently delivered in a rich schedule and humor is used to provide a good learning atmosphere.

EFFECTIVENESS

Although psychologically oriented preventive methods are relatively new, several evaluations have been reported. For example, Von Korff reported the results of one of the first studies where groups were used to help patients specifically deal with psychological aspects of the trouble in the hope of preventing future problems (Von Korff et al., 1998). The intervention was based on lay-led groups for arthritic pain and focused on self-care (von Korff, 1999). An evaluation was conducted on 255 patients about 8 weeks after a primary care visit for back pain and participants were randomized to the cognitive-behavioral group or a control group. At the one-year follow-up the cognitive-behavioral group had significantly reduced worry and disability relative to the treatment as usual control. Participants in the lay-led group also had a significantly more positive view toward self-care, but there was no significant difference with regard to pain intensity or medication use. Similar results have been reported in two other investigations using similar methods (Moore, Von Korff, Cherkin, Saunders, & Lorig, 2000; Saunders, Von Korff, Pruitt, & Moore, 1999).

We have tested the CBT program described above in four randomized controlled trials. The first test of utility compared this approach to treatment as usual (Linton & Andersson, 2000). Participants suffered from musculoskeletal pain, perceived that they had a risk of developing a chronic problem, but had not been off work more than 3 months during the past year. We randomised 243 people fulfilling the criteria to one of three groups. The first two groups received usual treatment plus self-help information on dealing with back pain. The third group received the cognitive-behavioral group intervention described above. Results at the one-year follow-up indicated a preventive effect. All three groups reported some improvements, e.g. reduced pain intensity. However, the risk for a long-term sick absence was nine fold lower for the cognitive-behavioral intervention group than for the groups receiving information. The CBT intervention also produced a significant decrease in perceived risk, as well as significantly fewer physician and physical therapy visits in contrast to the comparison groups. Thus, long-term disability and health-care use was "prevented" in the cognitive-behavioral group.

The second test was similar to the first, but focused on a very early intervention in a group of non-patients from the general population (Linton & Ryberg, 2001). The 253 participants reported four or more episodes of relatively intense spinal pain during the preceding year, but had not been off work more than 30 days. Participants were randomly assigned to the cognitive-behavioral group or a treatment as usual comparison group. At the one-year follow-up results showed that the cognitive-behavioral group, relative to the comparison group, had significantly better outcomes on fear-avoidance, number of pain-free days, and amount of sick leave. In fact, the risk for long-term sick leave during the follow-up was three times lower in the cognitive-behavioral group than in the treatment as usual comparison group.

Return to work skills were combined with the CBT group in a third test designed for patients off work because of their pain (Marhold, Linton, & Melin, 2001). In brief, the results demonstrated that participants on short-term sick leave (mean 3 months) had significantly less absenteeism at the one-year follow-up relative to a treatment as usual control group.

Finally, the fourth test focused on incorporating the cognitive-behavioral groups into a primary care setting (Linton, Boersma, Jansson, Svärd, & Botvalde, Accepted for publication). Since physical therapy is a frequent treatment for back pain we were interested in whether the psychological and physical therapy modules might be combined. The physical therapy methods employed were of a preventive nature and based primarily on exercise. Random assignment of the 185 patients was to either a standardized, guideline-based, treatment as usual, or to a cognitive-behavioral group (alone), or to the combination of a cognitive-behavioral group and physical therapy. The results showed that for work absenteeism the two groups receiving cognitive-behavioral interventions had fewer days off work for back pain during the 12-month follow-up than did the guideline-based treatment as usual group. The risk for developing long-term sick disability leave was more than five-fold higher in the guideline-based treatment as usual group than the other two groups receiving the cognitive-behavioral intervention. Thus, there is some evidence that employing a psychologically oriented intervention may help prevent future disability.

Individualized Intervention

Another intervention option is to develop a tailored program for the patient based on a behavioral assessment. Some patients, for example, may have specific problems not properly dealt with in the CBT groups. Moreover, in some settings it may be difficult to organize groups or patients who may wish to have individual attention. The main advantage is the design of a treatment plan directly based on the findings in the assessment. As a result, the intervention could be highly effective. Depending on the results of the assessment, the various treatment plans could be quite different. Indeed, they could incorporate any number of methods. However, this might also be a disadvantage as it would be difficult to maintain competency in a large number of methods and it might also lead to "drift" toward more medically oriented procedures even though the focus is designed to be on psychological factors.

An example may set the stage for understanding the individualized approach. A relatively common problem encountered in patients with back pain at risk for developing persistent problems is "fear-avoidance" (Boersma & Linton, in press). Typically, the patient scores high on fear-avoidance beliefs measures and low on measures of function. If additional assessment reveals that pain related fear is associated with the low function, treatment should probably address this issue. One issue in the early stages of such a problem is the control of pain intensity. Analgesics and non-pharmacological methods may help the patient to reduce the pain and thereby also reduce the fear and functional difficulties. Unfortunately, the problem has often developed beyond the acute stage and more psychologically oriented treatment may be needed. We suggest considering either graded activity (Lindström et al., 1992; Linton, 1993) or exposure treatment (Vlaeyen, de Jong, Geilen, Heuts, & van Breukelen, 2001). Graded activity appears to be helpful and may be employed to help patients gain confidence in increasing their activity and mobility levels. By bringing the patient into contact with feared movements, it may also reduce the fear. Incorporating the fear-avoidance model into graded activity appears to improve outcome for such patients (George, Fritz, Bialosky, & Donald, 2003). In this study, standard physical therapy was compared to a fear-avoidance-based physical therapy utilizing information, encouragement and graded activity training in a randomized clinical trial. Results showed that patients with high levels of pain related fear had significantly less disability when receiving the fear-avoidance-based graded activity as compared to regular treatment.

A novel treatment for patients with very high levels of pain related fear and avoidance behavior has been recently developed (Vlaeyen et al., 2001). This method employs an exposure technique where the patient is gradually and systematically exposed to a hierarchy of movements in order to reduce the fear. Thus, it is similar to exposure methods widely used in the treatment of phobias (Davison & Neale, 1998). Although much work remains to be done, some first studies of this technique have shown real promise ()(Boersma et al., in press; Linton, Overmeer, Janson, Vlaeyen, & de Jong, 2002; Vlaeyen et al., 2001; Vlaeyen, de Jong, Geilen, Heuts, & van Breukelen, submitted). For example, we treated six patients with high levels of fear and avoidance in a multiple baseline design and could show dramatic improvements in fear and function (Boersma et al., in press). While exposure training has yet to be tested as an early, preventive measure, research does indicates that fear-avoidance beliefs are not only present, but also good predictors of future problems, even at the acute stage of the problem (Buer & Linton, 2002; Fritz & George, 2002; Fritz, George, & Delitto, 2001; Linton, Buer, Vlaeyen, & Hellsing, 2000; Sieben, Vlaeyen, Tuerlinckx, & Portegijs, 2002; Sinclair, Hogg-Johnson, Mondloch, & Shields, 1997) Thus, it is reasonable to suspect that exposure training early on might be beneficial for patients with high levels of fear, more work needs to be done along these lines. In sum, individualized interventions might be tailored to the patient's needs and therefore produce effective results.

CONCLUSIONS

Psychological factors are important determinants of the development of persistent disability including being off work. Consequently, psychological risk factors may have an important role to play in identifying patients who are at risk of developing long-term pain and disability problems. Indeed, research to date shows that it is possible to identify such patients with satisfactory levels of accuracy.

Because psychological factors are involved in the development of long-term pain and disability, early psychological interventions are warranted. Indeed, psychological techniques aimed at alleviating the psychological processes catalyzing the development of the problem would logically seem to be of value. Some techniques have been developed and tested. For those seeking care for the first time, guidelines have been developed that stress reassurance and recommendations such as to remain active. Results suggest that these may reduce the problem and help prevent long-term disability. However, problems in proper administration and compliance are considerable and sometimes appear to reduce greatly the effects of the intervention.

Preventive interventions based on psychological methods have also been developed for those who are clearly at risk for developing a disability. One particular approach has been the use of CBT in a group format. Several randomized, controlled studies indicate that this may be a particularly useful method. However, more work is needed and barriers to implementation need to be crossed. Individualized interventions have also been tested with in-vivo exposure being one clear example. Early results are promising, but more work is needed. Further, individualized approaches also have the disadvantage of greater cost.

The promise of preventing typical, annoying back pain from becoming a persistent pain and disability problem is an attractive one. Although we have just gotten started, considerable progress has been made. Early identification has been enhanced. Psychologically oriented preventive interventions have been developed on the individual and group level. Several key studies have shown that this approach may well reduce disability and improve the quality of life for patients. However, it is far too early to declare victory. More work is direly needed to develop better our assessment tools as well as our treatment methods. Further work is also needed to test the interventions worth in scientifically sound investigations. Finally, the knowledge at hand must be properly implemented into practice. When this is accomplished, we may expect a considerable improvement in results.

REFERENCES

Armstrong, M. P., McDonough, S., & Baxter, G. (2003). Clinical guidelines versus clinical practice in the management of low back pain. *International Journal of Clinical Practice, 57*(1), 9–13.

Boersma, K., & Linton, S. J. (2002). Early assessment of psychological factors: The Örebro Screening Questionnaire for Pain. In S. J. Linton (Ed.), *New avenues for the prevention of pain* (Vol. 1, pp. 205–213). Amsterdam: Elsevier.

Boersma, K., & Linton, S. J. (in press). Screening to identify patients at risk: Profiles of psychological risk factors for early intervention. *Clinical Journal of Pain.*

Boersma, K., Linton, S. J., Overmeer, T., Janson, M., Vlaeyen, J. W. S., & de Jong, J. (in press). Lowering fear-avoidance and enhancing function through exposure in vivo: A multiple baseline study across six patients with back pain. *Pain.*

Buer, N., & Linton, S. J. (2002). Fear-avoidance beliefs and catastrophizing—occurrence and risk factor in back pain and ADL in the general population. *Pain, 99*(3), 485–491.

Compas, B. E., Haaga, D. A. F., Keefe, F. J., Leitenberg, H., & Williams, D. A. (1998). A sampling of empirically supported psychological treatments from health psychology: Smoking, chronic pain, cancer, and bulimia nervosa. *Journal of Consulting and Clinical Psychology, 66*, 89–112.

Davison, G. C., & Neale, J. M. (1998). *Abnormal psychology* (Seventh ed.). New York: John Wiley & Sons, Inc.

Ektor-Andersen, J., Örbaek, P., Ingvarsson, E., & Kullendorff, M. (2002). *Prediction of vocational dysfunction due to muskuloskeletal symptoms by screening for psychosocial factors at the social insurance office.* Paper presented at the 10th World Congress on Pain, San Diego, CA.

Fritz, J. M., & George, S. Z. (2002). Identifying psychosocial variables in patients with acute work-related low back pain: The importance of fear-avoidance beliefs. *Physical Therapy, 82*(10), 973–983.

Fritz, J. M., George, S. Z., & Delitto, A. (2001). The role of fear-avoidance beliefs in acute low back pain: relationships with current and future disability and work status. *Pain, 94*, 7–15.

Gatchel, R. J. (1996). Psychological disorders and chronic pain: Cause and effect relationships. In R. J. Gatchel & D. C. Turk (Eds.), *Psychological approaches to pain management: A practitioner's handbook* (Vol. 1, pp. 33-54). New York: Guilford Press.

Gatchel, R. J., Polatin, P. B., & Kinney, R. K. (1995). Predicting outcome of chronic back pain using clinical predictors of psychopathology: a prospective analysis. *Health Psychology, 14*(5), 415–420.

Geisser, M. E., & Roth, R. S. (1998). Knowledge of and agreement with chronic pain diagnosis: Relation to affective distres, pain beliefs and coping, pain intensity, and disability. *Journal of Occupational Rehabilitation, 8*(1), 73–88.

George, S. Z., Fritz, J. M., Bialosky, J. E., & Donald, D. A. (2003). The effect of a fear-avoidance-based physical therapy intervention for patients with acute low back pain: Results of a randomized clinical trial. *Spine, 28*(23), 2551–2560.

Hagen, K. B., Hilde, G., Jamtvedt, G., & Winnem, M. F. (2002). The Cochran Review of advice to stay active as a single treatment for low back pain and sciatica. *Spine, 27*(16), 1736–1741.

Hoogendoorn, W. E., van Poppel, M. N. M., Bongers, P. M., Koes, B. W., & Bouter, L. M. (2000). Systematic review of psychosocial factors at work and in the personal situation as risk factors for back pain. *Spine, 25*(16), 2114–2125.

Hurley, D., Dusoir, T., McDonough, S., Moore, A., & Baxter, G. (2001). How effective is the Acute Low Back Pain Screening Questionnaire for predicting 1-year follow-up in patients with low back pain? *The Clinical Journal of Pain, 17*, 256–263.

Hurley, D., Dusoir, T., McDonough, S., Moore, A., Linton, S. J., & Baxter, G. (2000). Biopsychosocial screening questionnaire for patients with low back pain: Preliminary report of utility in physiotherapy practice in Northern Ireland. *Clinical Journal of Pain, 16*(3), 214–228.

Koes, B. W., van Tulder, M. W., Ostelo, R., Burton, A. K., & Waddell, G. (2001). Clinical guidelines for the management of low back pain in primary care. *Spine, 26*(22), 2504–2514.

Lindström, I., Öhlund, C., Eek, C., Wallin, L., Peterson, L. E., Fordyce, W. E., & Nachemson, A. L. (1992). The effect of graded activity on patients with subacute low back pain: A randomized prospective clinical study with an operant-conditioning behavioral approach. *Physical Therapy, 72*, 279–293.

Linton, S. J. (1993). *Psychological interventions for patients with chronic back pain.* Geneva: World Health Organization.

Linton, S. J. (2000a). Psychologic risk factors for neck and back pain. In A. Nachemson & E. Jonsson (Eds.), *Neck and back pain: The scientific evidence of causes, diagnosis, and treatment* (pp. 57–78). Philadelphia: Lippincott Williams & Wilkins.

Linton, S. J. (2000b). Utility of cognitive-behavioral psychological treatments. In A. Nachemson & E. Jonsson (Eds.), *Neck and back pain: The scientific evidence of causes, diagnosis, and treatment* (pp. 361–381). Philadelphia: Lippincott Williams & Wilkins.

Linton, S. J. (2001). Occupational psychological factors increase the risk for back pain: A systematic review. *Journal of Occupational Rehabilitation, 11*(1), 53–66.

Linton, S. J. (2002a). A cognitive-behavioral approach to the prevention of chronic back pain. In R. J. Gatchel & D. C. Turk (Eds.), *Psychological approaches to pain management* (Second ed., pp. 317–333). New York: Guildford Publications, Inc.

Linton, S. J. (2002b). Why does chronic pain develop? A behavioral approach. In S. J. Linton (Ed.), *New avenues for the prevention of chronic musculoskeletal pain and disability* (pp. 67–82). Amsterdam: Elsevier Science.

Linton, S. J., & Andersson, T. (2000). Can chronic disability be prevented? A randomized trial of a cognitive-behavior intervention and two forms of information for patients with spinal pain. *Spine, 25*(21), 2825–2831.

Linton, S. J., & Boersma, K. (2003). Early identification of patients at risk of developing a persistent back problem: The predictive validity of the Örebro Musculoskeletal Pain Questionnaire. *The Clinical Journal of Pain.*

Linton, S. J., Boersma, K., Jansson, M., Svärd, L., & Botvalde, M. (Accepted for publication). The effects of cognitive-behavioral and physical therapy preventive interventions on pain related sick leave: A randomized controlled trial. *Clinical Journal of Pain.*

Linton, S. J., Buer, N., Vlaeyen, J., & Hellsing, A. L. (2000). Are fear-avoidance beliefs related to a new episode of back pain? A prospective study. *Psychology and Health, 14*, 1051–1059.

Linton, S. J., & Halldén, K. (1998). Can we screen for problematic back pain? A screening questionnaire for predicting outcome in acute and subacute back pain. *The Clinical Journal of Pain, 14*(3), 209–215.

Linton, S. J., Hellsing, A. L., & Andersson, D. (1993). A controlled study of the effects of an early intervention on acute musculoskeletal pain problems. *Pain, 54*, 353–359.

Linton, S. J., Overmeer, T., Janson, M., Vlaeyen, J. W. S., & de Jong, J. R. (2002). Graded in-vivo exposure treatment for fear-avoidant pain patients with function disability: A case study. *Cognitive Behavior Therapy, 31*(2), 49–58.

Linton, S. J., & Ryberg, M. (2001). A cognitive-behavioral group intervention as prevention for persistent neck and back pain in a non-patient population: A randomized controlled trial. *Pain, 90*, 83–90.

Main, C. J., & Spanswick, C. C. (2000). *Pain management: An interdisciplinary approach.* Edinburgh: Churchill Livingstone.

Marhold, C., Linton, S. J., & Melin, L. (2001). Cognitive behavioral return-to-work program: effects on pain patients with a history of long-term versus short-term sick leave. *Pain, 91*, 155–163.

McGurik, B., King, W., Govind, J., Lowry, J., & Bogduk, N. (2001). Safety, efficacy, and cost effectivenss of evidence-based guidelines for the management of acute low back pain in primary care. *Spine, 26*(23), 2615–2622.

Moore, J. E., Von Korff, M., Cherkin, D., Saunders, K., & Lorig, K. (2000). A randomized trial of a cognitive-behavioral program for enhancing back pain self care in a primary care setting. *Pain, 88*, 145–153.

Morley, S., Eccleston, C., & Williams, A. (1999). Systematic review and meta-analysis of randomised controlled trials of cognitive behaviour therapy and behaviour therapy for chronic pain in adults, excluding headache. *Pain, 80*(1–2), 1–13.

Nachemson, A., & Jonsson, E. (Eds.). (2000). *Neck and back pain: The scientific evidence of causes, diagnosis, and treatment.* Philadelphia: Lippincott Williams & Wilkins.

Overmeer, T., Linton, S. J., & Boersma, K. (in press). Do physical therapists recognise established risk factors? Swedish physical therapists' evaluation in comparison to guidelines. *Spine.*

Pincus, T., Burton, A. K., Vogel, S., & Field, A. P. (2002). A systematic review of psychological factors as predictors of chronicity/disability in prospective cohorts of low back pain. *Spine, 27*(5), E109.120.

Pulliam, C. B., & Gatchel, R. J. (2002). Employing risk factors for screening of chronic pain disability. In S. J. Linton (Ed.), *New avenues for the prevention of chronic musculoskeletal pain and disability* (pp. 183–204). Amsterdam: Elsevier Science.

Saunders, K. W., Von Korff, M., Pruitt, S. D., & Moore, J. E. (1999). Prediction of physician visits and prescription medicine use for back pain. *Pain, 83*(2), 369–377.

Schultz, I. Z., Crook, J. M., Berkowitz, J., Meloche, G. R., Milner, R., Zuberbier, O. A., & Meloche, W. (2002). Biopsychosocial multivariate predictive model of occupational low back disability. *Spine, 27*(23), 2720–2725.

Sheridan, D. P., & Winogrond, I. R. (1987). *The preventive approach to patient care* (first ed.). Amsterdam: Elsevier.

Sieben, J. M., Vlaeyen, J. W. S., Tuerlinckx, S., & Portegijs, P. J. M. (2002). Pain-related fear in acute low back pain: The first two weeks of a new episode. *European Journal of Pain, 6*, 229–237.

Sinclair, S. J., Hogg-Johnson, s., Mondloch, M. V., & Shields, S. A. (1997). The effectiveness of an early active intervention program for workers with soft-tissue injuries. *Spine, 22*(24), 2919–2931.

Smith, D., McMurray, N., & Disler, P. (2002). Early intervention for acute back injury: Can we finally develop an evidence-based approach? *Clinical Rehabilitation, 16*, 1–11.

Turner, P., & Whitfield, T. A. (1997). Physiotherapists' use of evidence-based practice: A cross-national study. *Physiotherapy Research International, 2*, 17–29.

Waddell, G. (1998). *The back pain revolution*. Edinburgh: Churchill Livingstone.

Waddell, G., Aylward, M., & Sawney, P. (2002). *Back pain, incapacity for work and social security benefits: An international literature review and analysis*. London: The Royal Society of Medicine Press.

Waddell, G., Burton, A. K., & Main, C. J. (2003). *Screening to identify people at risk of long-term incapacity for work: A conceptual and scientific review*. London: Royal Society of Medicine Press.

Waddell, G., Feder, G., & Lewis, M. (1997). Systematic reviews of bed rest and advice to stay active for acute low back pain. *British Journal of General Practice, 47*, 647–652.

Waddell, G., Newton, M., Henderson, I., Somerville, D., & Main, C. J. (1993). A Fear-Avoidance Beliefs Questionnaire (FABQ) and the role of fear-avoidance beliefs in chronic low back pain and disability. *Pain, 52*, 157–168.

van Tulder, M. W., Ostelo, R., Vlaeyen, J. W. S., Linton, S. J., Morely, S. J., & Assendelft, W. J. J. (2000). Behavioral treatment for chronic low back pain: A systematic review within the framework of the Cochrane Back Review Group. *Spine, 25*(20), 2688–2699.

Verbeek, J. H., van der Weide, W. E., & van Dijk, F. J. (2002). Early occupational health management of patients with back pain: A randomized controlled trial. *Spine, 27*(17), 1844–1851.

Westgaard, R. H., & Winkel, J. (2002). On occupational ergonomic risk factors for musculoskeletal disorders and related intervention practice. In S. J. Linton (Ed.), *New avenues for the prevention of chronic musculoskeletal pain and disability* (Vol. 1, pp. 143–164). Amsterdam: Elsevier Science.

Wickström, G. J., & Pentti, J. (1998). Occupational factors affecting sick leave attributed to low-back pain. *Scandinavian Journal of Work and Environmental Health, 24* (2), 145–152.

Vingård, E., Mortimer, M., Wiktorin, C., Pernold, G., Fredriksson, K., Németh, G., & Alfredsson, L. (2002). Seeking care for low back pain in the general population. *Spine, 27* (19), 2159–2165.

Vlaeyen, J. W. S., de Jong, J., Geilen, M., Heuts, P. H. T. G., & van Breukelen, G. (2001). Graded exposure in vivo in the treatment of pain-related fear: A replicated single-case experimental design in four patients with chronic low back pain. *Behavior Research and Therapy, 39*, 151–166.

Vlaeyen, J. W. S., de Jong, J., Geilen, M., Heuts, P. H. T. G., & van Breukelen, G. (submitted). The treatment of fear of movement/(re)injury in chronic low back pain: Exposure in vivo versus graded activity. A replicated single-case experimental cross-over design.

von Korff, M. (1999). Pain management in primary care: An individualized stepped/care approach. In R. J. Gatchel & D. C. Turk (Eds.), *Psychosocial factors in pain* (1 ed., pp. 360–373). New York: Guilford Press.

Von Korff, M., Barlow, W., Cherkin, D., & Deyo, R. A. (1994). Effects of practice style in managing back pain. *Annals of Internal Medicine, 121*(3), 187–195.

Von Korff, M., Moore, J. E., Lorig, K., Cherkin, D. C., Saunders, K., González, V. M., Laurent, D., Rutter, C., & Comite, F. (1998). A randomized trial of a lay-led self-management group intervention for back pain patients in primary care. *Spine, 23*, 2608–2615.

26

Working with the Employer

The Sherbrooke Model

Patrick Loisel and Marie-José Durand

INTRODUCTION

Occupational back pain is a widespread, self-limited and recurring health problem that impairs workplace productivity. Although 90% of acute low back pain sufferers spontaneously return to pre-injury activity tolerance within one to three months (Philips and Grant, 1991), 5% to 7% develop long-term disability and are responsible for the majority of the costs related to this disorder (Spitzer et al., 1987). Besides high societal costs (Volinn et al., 1991; Hashemi et al., 1998; Murphy and Courtney, 2000), this persistent pain experience has also been associated with long work absence (Rossignol et al., 1988; Walsh et al., 1992; Lawrence et al., 1998) and poor health and functional outcomes (Makela et al., 1993; Cassidy et al., 1998).

When non-specific back pain prevents an individual from working for one month, the situation can no longer be viewed as an illness/disease problem but must be seen as a disability problem. The causes of disability encompass more than the original injury/disease producing event. Return to work will not depend on the resolution of a benign condition but rather on diverse psychosocial and occupational factors which contribute to disability. Consequently, the task before health professionals is not curing a pain condition, but rather focusing on the rehabilitation of an individual who is at risk for losing their social role of worker. Hence, disability, especially work disability, must be seen as different from the original disorder having initiated the disability (Loisel et al., 2001). This suggests that the traditional disease-focused treatment paradigm should be replaced by a disability prevention paradigm to avoid prolonged disability (Loisel et al., 2001).

Recent evidence has demonstrated that disability from musculoskeletal disorders is a multifactorial problem due not only to the causal disorder, workers' global characteristics (physical and mental) and environmental factors such as the workplace, the healthcare system, the compensation system and the interactions between all stakeholders in the disability problem (Frank et al., 1998; Loisel et al., 2001). It

DOI: 10.1007/978-0-387-28919-9_26, © 2009 Springer Science+Business Media, LLC

has been emphasized that workplace factors can influence absenteeism and it has been argued that the workplace itself could be used as a rehabilitation setting (Fordyce, 1994). Although workplace demands have been associated with back pain, few workplace intervention studies, aimed at facilitating the return to work of injured workers before chronicity, have been undertaken.

This chapter will focus on the importance of centralizing work rehabilitation in the workplace. More precisely, we will describe the Sherbrooke Model, an integrated program directed at both the worker and the workplace, and its effectiveness.

THE SHERBROOKE MODEL

Background

The Sherbrooke Model was developed following the recommendations of the Quebec Task Force on Spinal Disorders in the Workplace. The Task Force proposed focusing on early detection and evidence-based interventions in order to prevent prolonged work disability (Spitzer et al., 1987). Based on a comprehensive literature review indicating the ineffectiveness of single modality treatments, the Quebec Task Force suggested that employing a host of rehabilitation procedures to address the causes of pain related disability might be clinically as well as cost-effective (Spitzer, 1987). More specifically, they recommended implementing the following interventions: 1) advice of a medical specialist after seven weeks of absence from work, 2) active treatment after eight weeks and if no improvement, 3) early vocational rehabilitation and ergonomic intervention. Further evidence of the effectiveness of a multidisciplinary rehabilitation program came from Mayer et al. (1985). These investigators claimed that a rehabilitation program using physical fitness and work simulation/hardening along with a cognitive–behavioral approach was effective in reducing pain-related disability. The rehabilitation program, however, was delivered in a clinical setting with little or no attention paid to the individual's work environment.

Additionally, the findings of Wiesel et al. (1984) indicated that a standardized medical approach with the collaboration of practicing physicians and unbiased medical monitoring was effective in a large industrial settlement in reducing the duration of absence from work, the number of surgical interventions, and the financial costs. Furthermore, other studies (Bigos et al., 1986; Bigos et al., 1991) have found a close relationship between back pain and job satisfaction but, unfortunately, no practical implications were presented.

Description of the Sherbrooke Model

The Sherbrooke Model was designed to meet certain objectives: a back pain management program based on evidence, available to a population of workers, compatible with provincial law, and linking clinical and occupational interventions. The Sherbrooke Model proposes an integrated approach, directed at both the worker and the workplace, using different evidence-based interventions to be implemented following a progressive and graded schedule.

The interventions included in this model of management had as a principal aim the early identification of workers at risk of prolonged disability (four weeks of absence from regular work) and their return to regular work. A work rehabilitation process, graded to match the improvement of the worker's capacities with a progressive augmentation of work demands, was utilized. Additionally, a simultaneous ergonomic intervention was undertaken to permanently reduce excessive work demands (Loisel et al., 1994). Workers were recruited in the back pain clinic at the 4th week of absence from work in an effort to avoid unnecessary efforts and costs arising from the high proportion of workers that return to work before four weeks.

As illustrated in Figure 1, the Sherbrooke Model is composed of three integrated steps: an occupational intervention, a clinical intervention and an early rehabilitation. Occupational interventions, initiated after six weeks of absence from work, include visits to an occupational medicine physician and a participatory ergonomics intervention. This latter intervention includes the workers' active involvement in ergonomic knowledge and procedures. Implementation is conducted with the support of the workplace, the supervisors and the managers in order to improve working conditions (Nagamachi, 1995). Participatory ergonomics involves several steps. It begins with clarification of the nature of the worker's tasks using descriptions made separately by the employer and the worker. Then, the work tasks are observed by the ergonomist, generally in the presence of the injured worker. Data are collected on the work process, characteristics of other jobs linked to the tasks involved, features of equipment used and design of the workplace, loads handled, precision, quality, quantity handled, pace of the job, postural requirements, and environmental characteristics of the job. After these observations are gathered, an "ergonomic diagnosis" is made with regards to the back, with recommendations for job modifications discussed and proposed to the employer. The employer is at liberty to implement these ergonomic recommendations or not.

After eight weeks of absence from regular work, parallel to the ergonomic intervention, the clinical intervention is introduced. This intervention consists of a clinical examination by a back pain medical specialist to exclude a possible serious underlying condition (red flags). In absence of such a serious condition, workers are directed to a back school. The back school includes back education, coaching, practice of appropriate exercises and counseling for daily life activities one hour per day for a four weeks period.

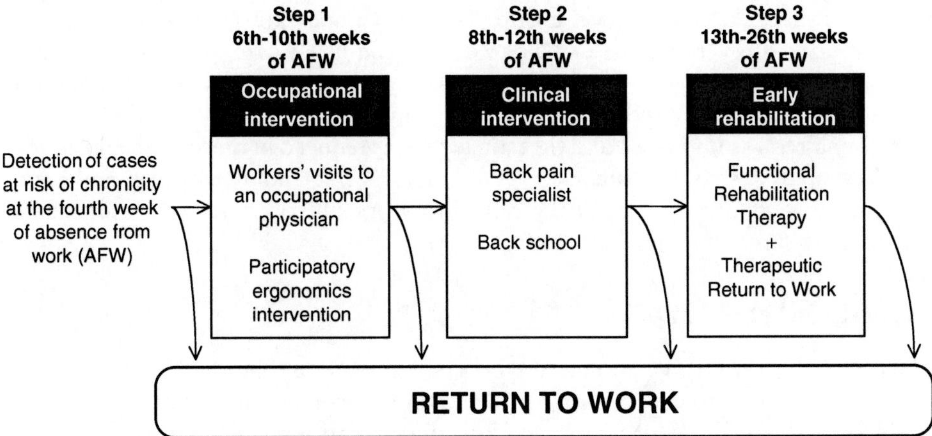

Figure 1. The Sherbrooke Model (*Source:* Loisel et al. [2003]. Reproduced by permission of Lippincott Williams and Wilkins)

If return to work does not occur after this relatively light clinical intervention the rehabilitation intervention is initiated at 12 weeks absence from work. This intervention includes two successive activities: functional rehabilitation therapy and therapeutic return to work. Functional rehabilitation therapy (FRT) is a modified Mayer's intervention consisting of fitness development and work conditioning associated with a cognitive-behavioral approach. This intervention is carried out by a multidisciplinary team of health care providers. It allows the development of the global condition of the worker with focus on improvement of the specific skills and endurance required by the worker's tasks. More realistic expectations concerning the back condition and pain management skills are taught. The FRT is followed by the Therapeutic return to work (TRW). This innovative intervention progressively centralizes the rehabilitation in the workplace, at the worker's regular job. Time spent in the clinical setting is progressively replaced by time on the job with reduced duties. An agreement is made between the team's occupational therapist and the worker's supervisor as to what partial duties are expected from the worker, with the worker often being placed in a supernumerary position or helping a coworker to do partial tasks of the job. Tasks are then progressively augmented until full job demands are fulfilled (Durand et al., 2001).

Effectiveness (Loisel et al., 1997)

The Sherbrooke model was evaluated through a population-based, randomized clinical trial (RCT). One hundred and thirty workers from 31 eligible workplaces in the Sherbrooke area, absent from work for more than four weeks for back pain, were randomized in one of four treatment groups: 1) usual care, 2) clinical/rehabilitation intervention (back school, functional rehabilitation therapy and therapeutic return to work), 3) occupational intervention (on-site ergonomic intervention and occupational medicine), and 4) the Sherbrooke model intervention (a combination of the last two). The clinical intervention group was eligible only for steps 2 and 3 of the model, the occupational intervention group was eligible only for step 1, and the Sherbrooke model group was eligible for all interventions of the model. The Sherbrooke model group returned workers to their regular work 2.41 ($p < 0.01$) times faster than the usual care intervention group. The most important effect came from the occupational intervention that, compared with the usual care intervention group, reduced by 1.9 times ($p < 0.01$), the duration of absence from work. In addition, functional status, measured by the Sickness Impact Profile (SIP) and the Oswestry questionnaire, was improved and the pain level was reduced in the Sherbrooke model group compared with the usual care group. One specific and innovative finding was that the most significant part of the return to work outcome was the result of the workplace intervention.

Costs (Loisel et al., 2002)

The costs related to the back injured workers' treatment at one year follow-up were higher in the standard care group ($7 133) than in the experimental groups (respectively $6 458, $6 529, $6 515 for the clinical, occupational and Sherbrooke Model groups) and much higher in the 5.4 following years ($16 384 compared to $3 586, $6 291 and $545). The highest total consequence of disease costs at the mean 6.4 year follow-up were found in the standard care group ($23 517) and the lowest in the Sherbrooke model group ($7 060). The clinical (−$2 250) and Sherbrooke model groups (−$2 348) were not cost-beneficial during the first year following the intervention compared to the standard care group (negative cost), with the occupational group moderately cost-beneficial ($220). Over the course of the total follow-up period (mean 6.4 years) all experimental interventions were cost-beneficial with savings in the Sherbrooke model group ($18 585) moderately higher than those in the clinical ($16 176) and the occupational ($16 827) groups. During the total follow-up period, the mean number of days on full benefits (DFB) due to back pain was the highest in the standard care group with a mean of 418.3 days, while it was the lowest in the Sherbrooke model group with a mean of 125.6 days. The clinical and occupational groups had means of 178.7 and 228.0 DFB due to back pain, respectively.

These results indicate that the experimental interventions did not save costs in the first year (active management period) but saved major costs in long-term follow-up. The Sherbrooke model group was the most cost-beneficial at the mean 6.4 years follow-up with a mean savings of $18 585 per worker. Thus, experimental interventions were effective to prevent long-term disability and were cost-effective. Additional costs due to the Sherbrooke Model interventions ($3291) can be considered as an investment since $16 457 of disease consequence costs was saved six years later compared to usual care. In other words, each dollar invested in the Sherbrooke Model helped to save approximately five dollars six years later. In sum, this fully integrated disability prevention model for occupational back pain allowed a quicker return to work, savings to the compensation system, and improvement in quality of life.

Evidence Emerging from the Sherbrooke Model

The Sherbrooke Model study was the first RCT to evaluate an integrated intervention aimed at both improving the worker condition and lowering workplace demands. In a previous RCT, Lindstrom et al. (1992) also shifted the rehabilitation process into the workplace but did not modify work demands. The Sherbrooke Model has demonstrated that bringing to the disabled worker an early, coherent and organized evaluation and case management, delivered by an independent multidisciplinary team in close coordination with the worker, the employer, the union (when applicable) and the insurer is more effective for return to work and quality of life improvement than usual management. Reassuring explanations and a link with the workplace seem to be key issues for a success in return to work (Loisel et al., 2003).

The Sherbrooke Model directly addressed the disability problem rather than the disease. Despite the availability of numerous treatments from various therapists, no single approach has been proven more effective than the others. When back pain does not resolve, disability occurs, leading to prolonged absence from work. Knowing that 90% of back pain resolves spontaneously, the Sherbrooke model targets the population at most risk of long term disability, that is workers with subacute and chronic back pain. The early detection of these "at risk workers" allows prevention of disability by initiating the right intervention at the right time. In doing so, unnecessary treatments and large amounts of money can be saved.

The primary aim of the Sherbrooke model is returning workers to their regular work, rather than the cure of a disease. In other words, it is directed at the disability rather than the disease, targeting causes of disability rather than causes of disease. As the determinants of disability are many and generally different from the cause of the disorder, the solution should be different and correspond more to a person-environment (ecological) model rather than the so-called traditional medical model (Engel, 1977; Bronfenbrenner, 1979; Dobren, 1994). Recently, authors have used the image of flags of various colors to describe these models. Red flags are medical and identify the symptoms and signs of a serious disease. Other flags are non medical and tied more to the person-environment model: yellow flags signify psycho-social factors (e.g.: fears, inappropriate beliefs about back pain), blue flags represent negative perceptions of work factors (e.g.: lack of job satisfaction, poor social support by colleagues, perceived time pressure) and black flags objective work characteristics (e.g.: postures at work, number of working hour, rates of pay) (Main, 2002). By its comprehensive approach to the patient/worker and the workplace, the Sherbrooke model is able to detect these diverse flags: the possible red flags are detected by the back pain medical specialist (step 2), the yellow and blue flags are dealt with during the clinical interventions (steps 2 and 3) and the blue and black flags are addressed during the workplace intervention (step 1). Also, the coordination between stakeholders brought by the interdisciplinary team members allows for continuous reassurance, activity promotion and restoration and appropriate job changes finally leading to return to regular work.

In the Sherbrooke Model, the usual bipartite healthcare encounter, healthcare provider-patient, becomes a four-player team: patient/worker, work rehabilitation interdisciplinary team, employer, and attending physician. All of them agree to make efforts to attain a common aim: return to work. Moreover, as disability is associated with multifactorial causes, it is essential to have a multidisciplinary team of health care providers in order to address the full scope of the problem. The professionals of the team bring their complementary skills and common values to the common purpose of return to work and they know that they share amongst themselves, and with the other stakeholders' part of the responsibility for success or failure of the return to work process. All these collaborative efforts might be demanding and daunting but are rewarded through the empowerment of all parties whose joint efforts are necessary for a successful return to work.

In order to attain this aim, employers' involvement (and also unions' when present) is a key issue. One might think that most employers would be reluctant to participate in such an approach. However, our experience is that employers are often compliant with this approach, although convincing an employer to adopt the model may be challenging in some occasions. First, employers are more and more aware of the direct and indirect costs related to work disability and may be subjected in some jurisdictions to important financial penalties for a poor track-record in disability prevention. Second, the lack of a skilled employee may lead to production problems. Finally, when appropriately explained, the comprehensive return to work program often makes sense to the employer who is helped in the rehabilitation process by a skilled interdisciplinary team. They may also benefit from ergonomic recommendations that do not involve major costs, may improve work organization and even productivity.

A new approach, the therapeutic return to work (TRW), was developed and tested throughout the Sherbrooke Model. One fundamental characteristic of the TRW is that it is situated in the workplace instead of a clinical setting, as is more usually the case in work rehabilitation interventions (Durand et al., 1998). The workplace is not considered to be a potentially harmful place, but rather a rehabilitation setting, insofar as it is appropriately controlled by the rehabilitation team in close collaboration with the employer. Progressively, the hours, duties and performance expectations of a job are increased until the worker is ready for regular full duties. Workers receive education and pain management that are directly applied to their work situation. The use of the natural working environment facilitates the knowledge transfer. Being exposed to the regular work tasks, the worker could decrease his/her fear avoidance behavior towards pain and work and could also progressively increase physical capacities. Progressive exposure to work requires close supervision from the rehabilitation team in order to plan the graded treatment and assure the security of the worker in his/her workplace. By itself, the TRW has demonstrated a high return to work success (Durand et al., 2001).

Another innovation of the Sherbrooke Model is the introduction of the use of participatory ergonomics in a rehabilitation context. Ergonomic interventions have been principally used to prevent work injuries and disorders. However, as shown in the Sherbrooke Model, this kind of intervention can be used to reduce disability and facilitate return to work for low back pain workers because reduction of occupational risk factors addresses disability determinants (blue flags). The ergonomist can reduce workplace risk factors either by decreasing work demands, modifying work organization or routine or addressing work relationship problems with colleagues and the employer. The evaluation of the implementation of participatory ergonomics in the Sherbrooke Model study, revealed the risk factors targeted by the ergonomic solutions proposed for job task improvement were mainly posture, excessive use of strength, safety hazards, and the environment (Loisel et al., 2001). Solutions were aimed at various areas such as equipment, job site lay-out, task content, work organization, and education/training. The perceptions of employer representatives, union representatives, and injured workers of the participating workplaces regarding participatory ergonomics were assessed through a questionnaire. The results showed that about half of the ergonomic recommendations were implemented according to the perception of the participants, with substantial agreement between respondents. The relatively large number of solutions implemented suggests that they could have been associated with quicker return to regular work as observed in workers that received the ergonomic intervention compared to those that did not received it. Besides promoting a quicker and safer return to work by modifying work demands, the increased awareness of back pain risk factors in the workplace following the participatory ergonomics program and the benefit to coworkers working at the same jobsite might also have had a potential beneficial impact on the primary prevention of back pain. Recent studies have shown that primary and secondary prevention are not independent but that appropriate actions in one of these sectors may positively impact the other. Thus, both may be viewed on a continuum of prevention of pain in the workplace and its consequences (Yassi et al., 2003).

Implementation of the Sherbrooke Model

In order to apply the Sherbrooke Model to a general population, a regional division (Montérégie) of Quebec's Public Health supported a task force under the first author's responsibility. The Sherbrooke Model was adapted for use in a larger uncontrolled community setting to not only comply with the most recent evidence, but also to be offered to a general community using the usual rules of referral of disabled workers in the province of Quebec by a Workers' Compensation Board (WCB) caseworker. This allowed the development of the PREVICAP program (PREVention of work handiCAP) that is now under evaluation. The PREVICAP program is a hospital-based work rehabilitation program offered to workers absent from work at the chronic stage of musculoskeletal disorders. It involves an interdisciplinary team (general practitioner, occupational therapist, physical educator, psychologist, ergonomist, and team coordinator) and includes two major steps: a disability determination, usually followed by a work rehabilitation intervention. The disability determination step was not described in the Sherbrooke model even though it was informally carried out by the multidisciplinary clinical team involved in the trial. In the PREVICAP program, the disability determination utilizes the results of the Work Disability Diagnostic Interview (WoDDI) to make recommendations for patient management (Durand et al., 2002). The WoDDI is composed of open-ended questions inquiring into physical, psychosocial, occupational and administrative factors, collated into an interview form used at the first encounter with the disabled worker. It enables clinicians to develop a rehabilitation plan and focus on disability resolution in patients absent from work due to a musculoskeletal disorder (Durand et al., 2002). As in the Sherbrooke Model, the subsequent intervention step is the Therapeutic return to work (TRW) that involves a progressive return to work process linked to an ergonomic intervention (Loisel et al., 1994; Durand et al., 1998; Loisel et al., 2003). The PREVICAP program takes into account present scientific evidence to bring empowerment to the patient/worker through progressive return to work. The process avoids evaluations and decisions taken far from the workplace context and reality. It ensures that the fearful worker is not submitted to contradictory explanations and decisions but conversely empowers the worker by restoring progressively his own capability of returning to a productive working life, in spite of some residual pain. It is accomplished through the close collaboration of the employer with the WCB caseworker, bringing appropriate education and help to these stakeholders (Loisel and Durand, 2003).

An attempt at dissemination of the PREVICAP program in the province of Québec was undertaken through the Réseau en re réadaptation au travial de Québec (RRTQ), a consortium of work rehabilitation centers located in most area of funding (Loisel et al., 2003). However, cessation of funding from the Québec WCB has limited this dissemination.

CONCLUSION

The process of returning a disabled worker to work presents numerous challenges to the employees, employers, health care providers, and insurers. It is essential that all parties work together to achieve the common goal of safe and durable return to work. During the last decades, evidence has emerged from several quality studies that suggests the need for shifting the rehabilitation process directly into the workplace. Evidence has shown that graded and controlled return to regular work for back pain sufferers may contribute to improvements in the workplace and workers' health. The implementation of such programs must be specifically tailored to the needs and context (legal, social, and cultural) of the communities they serve. Extended careful implementation of such programs would allow vast savings to employers, insurers and pension plans as well as improvement of the quality of life of workers disabled due to musculoskeletal disorders.

REFERENCES

Bigos, S. J., Spengler, D. M., Martin, N. A., Zeh, J., Fisher, L. & Nachemson, A. (1986). Back injuries in industry: a retrospective study. III. Employee-related factors. *Spine, 11*: 252–6.

Bigos, S. J., Battie, M. C., Spengler, D. M., Fisher, L. D., Fordyce, W. E., Hansson, T. H., Nachemson, A. L. & Wortley, M. D. (1991). A prospective study of work perceptions and psychosocial factors affecting the report of back injury. *Spine, 16*: 1–6.

Bronfenbrenner, U. (1979). *The ecology of human development: Experiments by nature and design.* Massachusetts: Harvard University press.

Cassidy, J. D., Carroll, L. J. & Cote, P. (1998). The Saskatchewan health and back pain survey. The prevalence of low back pain and related disability in Saskatchewan adults. *Spine, 23*: 1860–6.

Dobren, A. A. (1994). An ecologically oriented conceptual model of vocational rehabilitation of people with acquired midcareer disabilities. *Rehabilitation Counseling Bulletin, 37*: 215–228.

Durand, M. J., Loisel, P. & Durand, P. (1998). Le retour thérapeutique au travail comme une intervention de réadaptation centralisée dans le milieu de travail: description et fondements théoriques. *La revue canadienne d'ergothérapie, 65*: 72–80.

Durand, M. J., Loisel, P. & Durand, P. (2001). Therapeutic Return to Work: rehabilitation in the workplace. *Work: A Journal of Prevention, Assessment and Rehabilitation, 17*: 57–63.

Durand, M.-J., Loisel, P., Hong, Q. & Charpentier, N. (2002). Helping clinicians in work disability prevention: The Work Disability Diagnosis Interview. *Journal of Occupational Rehabilitation, 12*: 191–204.

Engel, G. L. (1977). The need for a new medical model: a challenge for biomedicine. *Science, 196*: 129–136.

Fordyce, W. E. (1994). *Back pain in the workplace. Management of disability in non specific conditions.* Seattle: IASP Press.

Frank, J., Sinclair, S., Hogg-Johnson, S., Shannon, H., Bombardier, C., Beaton, D. & Cole, D. (1998). Preventing disability from work-related low-back pain—New evidence gives new hope—If we can just get all the players onside. *CMAJ, 158*: 1625–1631.

Hashemi, L., Webster, B. S., Clancy, E. A. & Courtney, T. K. (1998). Length of disability and cost of work-related musculoskeletal disorders of the upper extremity. *Journal of Occupational and Environmental Medicine, 40*: 261–269.

Lawrence, R. C., Helmick, C. G., Arnett, F. C., Deyo, R. A., Felson, D. T., Giannini, E. H., Heyse, S. P., Hirsch, R., Hochberg, M. C., Hunder, G. G., Liang, M. H., Pillemer, S. R., Steen, V. D. & Wolfe, F. (1998). Estimates of the prevalence of arthritis and selected musculoskeletal disorders in the United States. *Arthritis and Rheumatism, 41*: 778–99.

Lindstrom, I., Ohlund, C., Eek, C., Wallin, L., Peterson, L., Fordyce, W. E. & Nachemson, A. L. (1992). The effect of graded activity on patients with subacute low back pain: a randomized prospective clinical study with an operant-conditioning behavioral approach. *Physical Therapy, 72*: 279–293.

Loisel, P., Durand, P., Abenhaim, L., Gosselin, L., Simard, R., Turcotte, J. & Esdaile, J. M. (1994). Management of occupational back pain: the Sherbrooke model. Results of a pilot and feasibility study. *Occupational & Environmental Medicine, 51*: 597–602.

Loisel, P., Abenhaim, L., Durand, P., Esdaile, J. M., Suissa, S., Gosselin, L., Simard, R., Turcotte, J. & Lemaire, J. (1997). A population-based, randomized clinical trial on back pain management. *Spine, 22*: 2911–8.

Loisel, P., Durand, M. J., Berthelette, D., Vezina, N., Baril, R., Gagnon, D., Lariviere, C. & Tremblay, C. (2001). Disability prevention—New paradigm for the management of occupational back pain. *Disease Management & Health Outcomes, 9*: 351–360.

Loisel, P., Gosselin, L., Durand, P., Lemaire, J., Poitras, S. & Abenhaim, L. (2001). Implementation of a participatory ergonomics program in the rehabilitation of workers suffering from subacute back pain. *Applied Ergonomics, 32*: 53–60.

Loisel, P., Lemaire, J., Poitras, S., Durand, M. J., Champagne, F., Stock, S., Diallo, B. & Tremblay, C. (2002). Cost-benefit and cost-effectiveness analysis of a disability prevention model for back pain management : a six-year follow up study. *Occupational and Environmental Medicine, 59*: 807–815.

Loisel, P. & Durand, M.-J. (2003). Worker accomodation, clinical intervention and return to work. In T. Sullivan & J. Frank (Eds.), *Preventing and managing disability at work*. London, ON: Taylor & Francis.

Loisel, P., Durand, M. J., Diallo, B., Vachon, B., Charpentier, N. & Labelle, J. (2003). From evidence to community practice in work rehabilitation: the Quebec experience. *Clinical Journal of Pain, 19*: 105–113.

Main, C. J. (2002). Concepts of treatment and prevention in musculoskeletal disorders. In S. J. Linton (Eds.), *New avenues for the prevention of chronic musculoskeletal pain and disability (pp.47–63)*. Armsterdam: Elsevier. *12*.

Makela, M., Heliovaara, M., Sievers, K., Knekt, P., Maatela, J. & Aromaa, A. (1993). Musculoskeletal disorders as determinants of disability in Finns aged 30 years or more. *Journal of Clinical Epidemiology, 46*: 549–59.

Mayer, T. G., Gatchel, R. J., Kishino, N., Keeley, J., Capra, P., Mayer, H., Barnett, J. & Mooney, V. (1985). Objective assessment of spine function following industrial injury. A prospective study with comparison group and one-year follow-up. *Spine, 10*: 482–93.

Murphy, P. L. & Courtney, T. K. (2000). Low back pain disability: Relative costs by antecedent and industry group. *American Journal of Industrial Medicine, 37*: 558–571.

Nagamachi, M. (1995). Requisites and Practices of Participatory Ergonomics. *International Journal of Industrial Ergonomics, 15*: 371–377.

Philips, H. C. & Grant, L. (1991). The evolution of chronic back pain problems: a longitudinal study. *Behaviour Research & Therapy, 29*: 435–41.

Rossignol, M., Suissa, S. & Abenhaim, L. (1988). Working disability due to occupational back pain: three-year follow-up of 2,300 compensated workers in Quebec. *Journal of Occupational Medicine, 30*: 502–5.

Spitzer, W. O. (1987). State of science 1986: quality of life and functional status as target variables for research. *Journal of Chronic Diseases, 40*: 465–71.

Spitzer, W. O., LeBlanc, F. E., Dupuis, M., Abenhaim, L., Bélanger, A. Y., Bloch, R., Bombardier, C., Cruess, R. L., Drouin, G., Duval-Hesler, N., Laflamme, J., Lamoureux, G., Nachemson, A., Pagé, J. J., Rossignol, M., Salmi, L. R., Salois-Arsenault, S., Suissa, S. & Wood-Dauphiné, S. (1987). Scientific approach to the assessment and management of activity-related spinal disorders. A monograph for clinicians. Report of the Quebec Task Force on Spinal Disorders. *Spine, 12*: S1–59.

Volinn, E., Van Koevering, D. & Loeser, J. D. (1991). Back sprain in industry. The role of socioeconomic factors in chronicity. *Spine, 16*: 542–8.

Walsh, K., Cruddas, M. & Coggon, D. (1992). Low back pain in eight areas of Britain. *Journal of Epidemiology and Community Health, 46*: 227–30.

Wiesel, S. W., Feffer, H. L. & Rothman, R. H. (1984). Industrial low-back pain. A prospective evaluation of a standardized diagnostic and treatment protocol. *Spine, 9*: 199–203.

Yassi, A., Ostry, A. & Spiegel, J. (2003). Injury Prevention and Return to Work: Breaking Down the Solitudes. In T. Sullivan & J. Frank (Eds.), *Preventing and managing disability at work*. London, ON: Taylor & Francis.

27

An Early Screening and Intervention Model for Acute and Subacute Low Back Pain

John P. Garofalo, Robert J. Gatchel, Nancy Kishino, and Alan M. Strizak

Low back pain (LBP) is one of the most common causes of disability. Volinn (1997) identified seven epidemiological investigations conducted in Belgium, Germany, Great Britain and Sweden that reported on the point prevalence of LBP. By weighting the percentages by the sample size, and then aggregating across studies, it was found that the rates of LBP in these countries averages approximately 34%. This is almost twice that reported in surveys conducted in less developed countries. Also, as Mayer and Gatchel (1988) had originally reviewed, it is the number one cause of disability of persons under age 45. Over this age, it is the third leading cause of disability, becoming progressively less of a factor during later years when function and productivity become of less concern than survival. It should also be noted that back-related disorders represent the most prevalent source of disability in the U.S. military (Feuerstein, Berkowitz & Peck, 1997). Indeed, in the U.S, of all the occupational musculoskeletal disorders, the most research attention to date has been dedicated to LBP disability, because this is the most expensive benign condition in industrialized countries (Volinn, 1997). It has been estimated that, in any one year, about 3–4% of the population in all industrialized countries has a temporarily disabling LBP episode, and that more than 1% of the working age population is "totally and permanently disabled" by this problem. From a financial point of view, it is one of the most costly problems in the North American workplace (Krause & Ragland, 1994). An even more startling trend is the disproportionate increase in LBP disability as measured against population growth. For example, Frymoyer and Cats-Baril (1991) had earlier reported LBP disability increasing at a rate 14 times the population-growth from1957 to 1976. This trend is continuing to this day.

The critical nature of occupational musculoskeletal disorders such as LBP is further highlighted by the fact that, in 1998, the National Institutes of Health requested

DOI: 10.1007/978-0-387-28919-9_27, © 2009 Springer Science+Business Media, LLC

the National Academy of Sciences/National Research Council to convene a panel of experts to carefully examine some major questions raised by the U.S. Congress concerning occupational musculoskeletal disorders (2001). One of the important issues raised by Congress was: "Does the research literature reveal any specific guidance to prevent the development of chronic conditions?" As further evidence of the growing worldwide concern about musculoskeletal disorders such as LBP, the World Health Organization convened an inaugural consensus meeting in April 1998 (1998). During this conference, a large number of representatives of international scientific journals and societies discussed the significant problem of occupational musculoskeletal disorders and the patient-burden on society that they have created. Major concerns raised included the following: back pain is the second leading cause of sick leave; and there is an anticipation that 25% of healthcare expenditures in developing countries will be spent on musculoskeletal-related care by the year 2010. This recognition prompted a proposal to declare the years 2000-2010 as the "Decade of the Bone and Joint System."

A need for early prevention of chronic LBP is further highlighted by additional epidemiological studies that continue to show that LBP is a serious problem resulting in immeasurable emotional suffering, work loss and high cost (Crombie, Croft, Linton, LeResche & Von Korff, 1999). There is now a call for early intervention methods to prevent acute and subacute LBP from becoming a chronic disability problem (Linton, 2002; National Research Council, 2001). Our early intervention research was based upon a number of suggestions by leading experts in the field that, in order to decrease the high cost of chronic musculoskeletal disability, there is a great need for better identifying patients at the acute and subacute phase who would benefit from such early intervention (Hazard, 1995; Linton, 2002; Linton & Bradley, 1996).

There are benefits and disadvantages to the various earlier predictive models that have empirically examined risk factors to disability. Accurate and convincing risk assessments may motivate acutely and subacutely injured patients to participate in risk management and prevention programs (Krause, Frank, Dasinger, Sullivan & Sinclair, 2001; Linton & Hallden, 1998; Mondloch, Cole & Frank, 2001). Evaluation of risk is intended to promote aggressive intervention on those at greatest risk, and is a necessary condition for major interventions. It is likely that many of these same variables affect life quality and this has fueled the growing investigation to identify potential patient characteristics and other variables that contribute to increased vulnerability to disability and to overall quality of life in patients with back pain. While research has begun to catch up with these trends, early interventions remain an understudied approach and the investigation of their efficacy is important in several aspects of public health. The predictive models of disabling chronic LBP developed in the past have generally justified their development as representing the blueprints for an aggressive intervention tailored to the salient factors of the model (Frymoyer, 1992).

Lemstra and Olszynski (2003) compared the effectiveness of different approaches in the management of Worker's Compensation injury claims: 1) occupational management; 2) early intervention; and 3) standard care. Using a retrospective design, the investigators compared the number of injury claims, the duration of disability, and the costs of disability between one company with access to standard care and a comparable company with access to an early intervention program. In a second arm of the study, the investigators prospectively evaluated the benefits of a company changing from a standard care program to an occupational management program, which involved both primary and secondary strategies. In terms of the primary prevention approach, the company made available worker-rotation scheduling, reduced lifting, and ergonomic changes in responsibilities. The early intervention program was designed to provide quick rehabilitation services to recently injured workers that involved intensive physical therapy and work-hardening programs. Finally, standard care programs involved receiving the traditional medical approaches as well as being placed on waiting lists for physical therapy. The investigators found that the occupational management program resulted in lower injury claims, a shorter duration for injury, and smaller costs than either the early intervention program or standard care. The early intervention program that was heavily weighted in addressing the physical needs of the patient faired the worse, suggesting that while rapid delivery of care is important, the nature of the intervention itself bears more heavily on reducing occupational-related injury disability.

Not all studies evaluating the benefits of early intervention programs for pain patients have found them to be beneficial. Sinclair and colleagues (1997) followed 1,600 workers unable to work due to soft-tissue musculoskeletal problems and compared those actively attending an early exercise and education program. The program was sponsored by a regional worker's compensation board, and closely adhered to a sports-medicine model in which functional conditioning and fitness achievement was emphasized. It was hypothesized that those regularly attending this program would receive compensation benefits for less time and would have fewer subsequent periods of receiving compensation. However, participation in the program only revealed non-significant differences between attendees and non-attendees in terms of functional status, health-related quality of life, and pain reports. The investigators noted that these findings did need to be interpreted in the context that this was a quasi-experimental design. In addition, baseline data were collected two weeks after the treatment program had already begun. Thus, overall, investigators testing the efficacy of early interventions have met mixed results. In spite of the growing recognition and support for such early intervention, few studies have systematically tailored their interventions around the most important risk factors that have been identified. This "state of affairs" was the impetus for initiating our clinical research program in this area.

REVIEW OF INITIAL STUDIES

In this section, a series of projects funded by the National Institutes of Health will be reviewed that have made significant advances in the development of early intervention programs. The major goal of our initial project was to identify predictors of when acute and subacute LBP occurrences were likely to develop into chronic disability problems. The results of that initial project clearly isolated some significant psychosocial risk factors that successfully predicted the development of chronicity during a one-year follow-up. Using a receiver-operator characteristic (ROC) curve analysis, which was based on the probabilities estimated from the logistic regression model developed on the large cohort of patients evaluated during that project, a statistical algorithm was developed that could be used to identify (with a

90.7% accuracy rate) "high risk" acute/subacute LBP patients who were prime candidates for early intervention in order to prevent chronicity. Subsequently, as an extension of these important findings, a second project involved the assessment of a large cohort of acute/subacute LBP patients in order to screen out those patients who were at high risk for developing chronicity (using the aforementioned ROC algorithm). These high-risk patients were then randomly assigned to one of two groups: an early intervention group or a non-intervention group. During the next year, routine three-month follow-up evaluations were then conducted in order to assess important long-term socioeconomic outcomes, such as return-to-work, healthcare utilization rates, medication use rates, etc. It was hypothesized that early intervention at the acute and subacute stage would prevent the development of chronic disability. It should also be noted that, as a replication of the previous grant project results, the non-intervention group was compared to a demographically-matched cohort of initially assessed acute/subacute LBP patients who did not display the "high risk" profile. It was hypothesized that the high-risk non-intervention group patients would demonstrate higher rates of chronic disability at one year relative to the low or "not-at-risk" profile patients.

Mental Health Results

An initial study emanating from our research further characterized those patients who were classified as high risk or low risk, based upon our classification algorithm (Pulliam, Gatchel & Gardea, 2001). Results clearly revealed mental health differences between these two groups. The high-risk patients were found to have lower scores on positive temperament (i.e., less energy, enthusiasm and optimism when undertaking projects) as measured on the Schedule for Nonadaptive and Adaptive Personality (Clark, 1993), greater reliance on an avoidance coping strategy as assessed on the Ways of Coping Questionnaire-Revised (Vitaliano, Russo, Carr, Maiuro & Becker, 1985), and a greater prevalence of a DSM-IV Axis I Disorder. These findings, therefore, again highlight the fact that our identified high-risk patients have a stronger potential for psychosocial factors that may contribute to chronic mental and physical health disability if not managed in a timely fashion. Moreover, a just-completed analysis of a larger cohort of patients from this project (and not just those who participated in the early intervention component of the study) has indicated that the high-risk subjects had a higher prevalence of Mood Disorders, Anxiety Disorders, Somatoform/Pain Disorders, Substance Abuse/Dependence Disorders, and Co-morbid Axis I and Axis II Disorders.

Socioeconomic Outcome Results

Our results also clearly indicated that early intervention at the acute/subacute stage of LBP significantly reduced the prevalence of chronic disability, relative to those high-risk acute/subacute LBP patients who did not receive such early intervention (Gatchel et al., 2003). Table 1 summarizes the outcome data that displayed significant differences among groups in the anticipated directions. As can be seen in this Table, the major hypotheses of this study were confirmed: the high-risk acute/subacute LBP patients who received early intervention (the HR-I group) displayed significantly fewer

TABLE 1. Long-Term Outcome Results at 12-Month Follow-Up

Outcome Measure	HR-I (n = 22)	HR-NI (n = 48)	LR (n = 54)	*p* Value
Percentage return-to-work at follow-up*	91	69	87	.027
Average number of healthcare visits regardless of reason**	25.6	28.8	12.4	.004
Average number of healthcare visits related to LBP **	17.0	27.3	9.3	.004
Average number of disability days due to back pain**	38.2	102.4	20.8	.001
Average of self-rated most "intense pain" at 12-month follow-up (0–100 scale)**	46.4	67.3	44.8	.001
Average of self-rated pain over last 3 months (0–100 scale)**	26.8	43.1	25.7	.001
Percentage currently taking narcotic analgesics*	27.3	43.8	18.5	.020
Percentage currently taking psychotropic medication*	4.5	16.7	1.9	.019

*Chi-square analysis **ANOVA

indices of chronic pain disability on a wide range of work, healthcare utilization, medication use and self-reported pain variables, relative to the high-risk acute/subacute LBP patients who did not receive such early intervention (the HR-NI group). Relative to the HR-NI group, the HR-I group was much more likely to have returned to work (odds ratio = 4.55), less likely to be currently taking narcotic analgesics (odds ratio = 0.44), and also less likely to be taking psychotropic medication (odds ratio = 0.24). In addition, the HR-NI group also displayed significantly more symptoms of chronic pain disability on these variables relative to the initially low-risk acute/subacute LBP patients (the LR group).

Cost-Comparison Savings Results

The cost-comparison savings data from this study were also quite impressive. Using unit cost multipliers obtained from the Bureau of Labor Statistics for compensation costs due to disability days (2002), from the *Medical Fees in the United States 2002* (2002) for healthcare costs, and the *Drug Topics Red Book 2002* (2002) for medication costs, we were able to calculate the average costs per patient associated with healthcare visits related to LBP, narcotic analgesic and psychotropic medications, and work disability days/lost wages. Table 2 lists these costs associated with the HR-I and HR-NI groups. As can be seen, the average overall costs per patient over the one-year follow-up period (even taking into account the $3,885/patient cost of the early intervention for the HR-I group) was significantly higher for the

TABLE 2. Cost-Comparison Results (Average Cost Per Patient/YEAR)

Cost Variable	HR-I (n = 22)	HR-NI (n = 48)
Healthcare visits related to LBP	$1,670	$2,677
Narcotic analgesic medication	$70	$160
Psychotropic medication	$24	$55
Work disability days/lost wages	$7,072	$18,951
Early intervention program	$3,885	NA
Totals	$12,721	$21,843

HR-NI group. An independent *t* test found this difference to be statistically significant (p <.05, two-tailed).

Overall Results

These above results, obviously, have major implications in terms of decreasing emotional distress and producing socioeconomic cost-savings for this prevalent disability problem. It should also be noted that another interesting finding from this study was that, even in the early intervention group, some problems were encountered by certain patients when they were ready to return to work. Preliminary evaluations indicated that there were often workplace factors that presented significant obstacles for some of these patients to immediately return-to-work when they are ready to do so. Indeed, a growing body of literature suggests the importance of taking into account such potential obstacles in order to most expeditiously return patients back to work.

For these preliminary evaluations, two patient assessments were conducted, using the Obstacles to Return-to-Work Questionnaire (ORQ, Marhold, Linton & Melin, 2002) and the Liberty Mutual Disability Risk Questionnaire. The preliminary results we obtained have now prompted us to more systematically evaluate these potential obstacles to work return within the context of our already-developed and successful biopsychosocial assessment-treatment protocol. Therefore, we are now in the process of evaluating a three-component biopsychosocial model of early intervention, which includes the following (Figure 1):

- The identification of high-risk status by use of our empirically-supported statistical algorithm.
- The administration of our empirically-supported successful early intervention program for these high-risk patients.

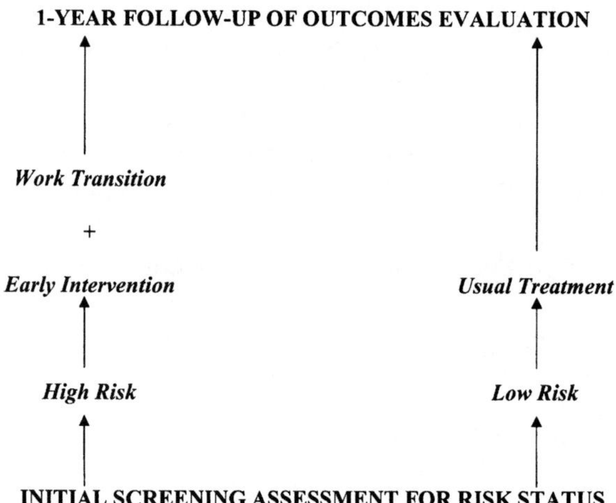

Figure 1. Three-Stage Biopsychosocial Approach to Early Screening and Intervention for Aute/Subacute Low Back Pain

- The introduction of a back-to-work transition component in order to directly modify any potential work force obstacles that may prevent the most expeditious return-to-work.

It is hypothesized that the latter work-transition component will be the "final piece of the puzzle" of this overall biopsychosocial model of early intervention developed to maximize early work return and the prevention of chronicity in high-risk acute/subacute LBP patients. We are also conducting this translational biopsychosocial research in partnership with the largest workers' compensation insurance company in the U.S. (Liberty Mutual). Not all the acute/subacute LBP patients used in the previous project were workers' compensation cases, which are usually the most difficult to treat because of potential secondary gain issues (Beals, 1984; Hammonds, Brena & Unikel, 1978; Rainville, Sobel, Hartigan & Wright, 1997). A significant addition to our present research program is the use of only the more difficult and recalcitrant workers' compensation population.

OBSTACLES TO RETURN-TO-WORK CONNECTED WITH THE WORKPLACE

As we have discussed, the consideration of potential obstacles to work return will be important in any comprehensive early intervention program. Indeed, there is general agreement in the scientific literature that the more time off from work substantially decreases the likelihood of successful return-to-work (Hildebrandt, Pfingsten, Saur & Jansen, 1997). Waddell (1996) reported that the probability of return-to-work after 2 months of not working is 70%; after 5 months is 50%; after 12 months is 30%; and at 2 years is 10%. In spite of these statistics, Marhold and associates (2002) have pointed out that the assessment of obstacles to return-to-work connected with the workplace is a relatively undeveloped field. However, there has been some recent research to demonstrate that psychosocial workplace factors are often associated with the development of persistent and chronic musculoskeletal disability. For example, Hoogendoorn and colleagues (2000) reported strong evidence that lack of social support at work, as well as job satisfaction, were risk factors for the development of persistent LBP. A number of studies (Himmelstein et al., 1995; Linton, 2001; National Research Council, 2001; Pransky et al., 2000) have also found that work-related psychosocial factors are associated with more persistent musculoskeletal disability disorders such as LBP. In fact, van Der Giezen and colleagues (2000) have found that psychosocial aspects of work have a larger impact on return-to-work than more physical requirements of the job. Furthermore, Teasell and Bombardier (2001) have also found a moderate amount of evidence for the significance of two employment-related factors that predict chronic pain disability: lack of availability of modified work and work autonomy at the workplace.

Clinical care that follows a traditional medical management model may fail to properly address workplace ergonomic and psychosocial factors that have been shown to be risk factors for low back disability (National Research Council, 2001; Shaw, Feuerstein, Haufler, Berkowitz & Lopez, 2001). Therefore, restoring occupational function to pre-injury levels may require that intervention efforts integrate workplace accommodation with clinical care. Both physicians and injured workers report that facilitating communication and resolving conflicts among patients, providers, and employers is a critical component of case management (Brines, Salazar, Graham, Pergola & Connon, 1999; Pergola, Salazar, Graham & Brines, 1999).

Workplace Accommodation Research

A review of empirical studies of workplace accommodation, including modified or temporary alternate duty, graded work exposure, and work trials, has shown that return-to-work rates are doubled among injured workers offered such options (Krause, Dasinger & Neuhauser, 1998), and that accommodated work reduces the number of lost work days by 50%. Companies that report proactive return-to-work programs, and create an environment where employees participate in problem-solving and decision making within company operations, have been shown to experience fewer injury claims (Habeck, Hunt & Vantol, 1998; Habeck, Leahy, Hunt, Chan & Welch, 1991; Habeck, Scully, Vantol & Hunt, 1998). In 1980, the American Biltrite Company (400 workers) instituted a sensitivity training program for management that focused on early reporting of musculoskeletal pain, positive acceptance and empathy for affected workers, and providing modified duty work. The program resulted in a 50% reduction in claims with lost work time and a ten-fold decrease in workers' compensation costs for low back disorders (Fitzler & Berger, 1982,1983). Another study (Wood, 1987) provided hospital managers with training that emphasized frequent communications with employees (every 10 days), communicating a positive message ('Your job is waiting for you'), and providing modified duty work assignments. This program resulted in a 5-fold reduction in low back claims exceeding 125 days lost work time. Finally, a pilot intervention study (Mclellan, Pransky & Shaw, 2001) evaluated the impact of a brief training program tailored for work supervisors to reinforce proactive and supportive responses to work-related musculoskeletal symptoms and injuries among employees (e.g., implement accommodations whenever possible, increase sensitivity to possible work-related discomfort, facilitate communication, etc.). It was found that this pilot study resulted in decreases in lost work time among workers. McLellan and colleagues (2001) concluded that these results warrant future controlled trials to further confirm this effect.

After the initial treatment of symptoms, employers may disagree with returning employees, and with their physicians, on the perceived need for modified or alternate duty or physical accommodations. Among workers with occupational LBP and greater than four weeks' work absence, only one-half are offered modifications to their original jobs, and only one-half of employers provide special equipment needs requested by workers or physicians (Strunin & Boden, 2000). Among workers with disabilities, reasonable accommodation is the most common area of dispute between employees and their employers (Huang, Berkowitz, Feuerstein & Peck, 1998). Although corporate policies and procedures appear to impact disability rates, there have only recently been attempts to examine these policies from the perspective of workers (Mclellan et al., 2001). The success of a modified duty transition requires the joint cooperation and agreement of the worker, treating physician, and employer.

One preliminary study that most closely approximates an attempt to provide some form of work transition for subacute LBP workers in order to prevent prolonged disability was conducted by Loisel and colleagues (1997). In a randomized clinical trial, subjects who had been absent from work for more than four weeks due to LBP were assigned to one of four groups: usual care; clinical intervention; occupational intervention; or full intervention (a combination of the last two). One-year follow-up evaluations were conducted. It was found that the full intervention group returned to work faster (odds ratio = 2.41) than the usual care group, as well as faster than the other two groups. These investigators, therefore, concluded that there needs to be a close association between clinical care and occupational intervention/transition in order to impede the progression toward chronic LBP disability. Marhold and colleagues (2001) have also reported the importance of such an integrated approach with chronic musculoskeletal pain patients. Although all of these studies suggest the importance of a combined intervention approach, none of these studies has evaluated such treatment approaches for *acute/subacute* LBP. We are currently evaluating this important issue.

Assessing Return-to-Work Obstacles

As a result of the above studies, there has been an increased interest in developing assessment instruments to evaluate and potentially modify obstacles to return-to-work connected with the workplace, although these measures are still in the early stages of development. (Marhold et al., 2002). Marhold and colleagues have developed a questionnaire for the identification of obstacles for pain patients to return-to-work (the Obstacles to Return-to-Work Questionnaire, or ORQ). Various scales on the ORQ have significantly predicted sick leave in a cohort of 154 patients with musculoskeletal pain, and correctly classified 79% of these patients.

Liberty Mutual is also very interested in this issue, and has developed its own questionnaire for evaluating potential obstacles for return-to-work in workers' compensation patients ("Liberty Mutual Disability Risk Questionnaire"). In a Liberty Mutual study of 600 workers with acute and subacute occupational LBP, the Disability Risk Questionnaire has shown that longer disability duration is predicted by a number of scale items, including: physical job demands, shorter job tenure, negative responses of supervisors, pain ratings, pain avoidance beliefs, poor patient expectations for recovery, and clinician ratings of functional limitation, depression, and anticipated recovery time (Shaw, Pransky, Fitzgerald, Patterson & Winters, 2002). Such data, again, suggest that a patient's perceptions and beliefs about work and returning to work (i.e., psychosocial variables) may be significant factors that can hinder actual recovery.

We have used both of these questionnaires in a preliminary, retrospective study of the high-risk acute/subacute LBP patients who participated in our most recently completed project. The results of that pilot study (in which a structured telephone interview was used to administer the questionnaires) indicated that many of the patients in our early intervention program could have returned to work much earlier if they had not encountered some significant workplace obstacles to return-to-work. For example, on the Liberty Mutual Disability Risk Questionnaire, it was found that a patient who did not return-to-work immediately after she was ready, but delayed and initiated vocational retraining, reported to be *not* satisfied about the following workplace variables, relative to those who did promptly return: the employer's lack of attempts to communicate with her after the injury; the perception that her boss blamed her for the injury; and there were no job accommodations made to help deal with her injury, even though her doctor ordered some work changes. This post-injury non-satisfaction was present even though this patient reported complete job satisfaction *before* her injury on the "Work Satisfaction" scale of the ORQ! Even though these were pilot, retrospective evaluations not collected for all patients, such results provide additional important preliminary data to suggest that one must effectively modify these potential obstacles of work return in order to maximize the early intervention program for high-risk acute/subacute LBP patients, and to thus further prevent the development of chronic disability. Such data are also in keeping with the results of the Marhold et al. study (2002) of the importance of a patient's perception of workplace variables that present potentially formidable obstacles to expeditious work return.

SUMMARY AND CONCLUSIONS

As discussed in this Chapter, chronic LBP is one of the most common causes of disability in industrialized countries today. It represents a growing, worldwide concern because of its great economic cost, the emotional suffering it causes, and its still growing prevalence. This has prompted calls for early prevention methods to deter the further increase in chronic LBP. In response to this need, we have conducted a series of studies that have been reviewed, starting with an initial study that developed a statistical algorithm to identify acute/subacute LBP patients who were at risk for developing chronic disability; an early intervention program successfully used with these high risk acute/subacute LBP patients; and now a study introducing a work transition component in order to transition these patients back to work more easily and quickly. What future clinical research issues should now be pursued? A number readily come to mind, as will be elucidated next.

One important question is whether we can better tailor the early intervention/work transition program for each specific patient. That is to say, rather than to automatically assume that "one size fits all," there may be ways to better individualize such a program. Although, overall, the approach is already yielding high return-to-work rates, perhaps rates of early work return and other socioeconomics can be better maximized. Also, some patients may require a lesser "dose" of early intervention, relative to others, which may result in even greater cost savings.

Associated with the above is the issue that, even though low-risk patients as a group require little in the way of early intervention, there may be some who can benefit from it in terms of socioeconomic outcomes. We should not automatically exclude these patients. Some may benefit and yield health care cost savings. Relatedly, there may potentially be even greater cost savings if such early intervention could be implemented in the actual workplace. This would possibly eliminate the major problem of work transition after being away from the workplace.

Another important issue for further future investigation is whether there are specific job descriptions/industries for which such an approach is more or less efficacious. To date, little work has been conducted to evaluate how generalizable our initial results are to the wide range of job requirements and environments. Finally, can this same early risk evaluation and intervention approach be successfully used with other musculoskeletal pain disability problems, such as upper extremity disorders (which are now reaching epidemic proportions)? We are currently evaluating the use of this approach with temporomandibular disorders, with some initial promising results (Epker, Gatchel & Ellis, 1999). A next important step will be the development of similar approaches with other musculoskeletal disorders.

In conclusion, we are on the brink of putting all of the "pieces of the puzzle" together in terms of early risk assessment and intervention with acute/subacute LBP patients in order to prevent chronicity. This success should now stimulate other investigators to continue on this road of finally solving this very prevalent problem of chronic pain disability.

Acknowledgments: The research for this chapter was supported in part by Grants No. 3R01 MH046452, 2K02 MH1107, and 5R01 DE010713 from the National Institutes of Health and Grant No. DAMD17-03-1-0055 from the Department of Defense.

REFERENCES

Beals, R. (1984). Compensation and recovery from injury. *Western Journal of Medicine, 140*, 233–237.

Brines, J., Salazar, M. K., Graham, K. Y., Pergola, T. & Connon, C. (1999). Injured workers' perceptions of case management services. A descriptive study. *AAOHN Journal, 47*(8), 355–364.

Bureau of Labor Statistics. (2002). 2002, from http://data.bls.gov/surveymost

Clark, L. (1993). *Schedule for Nonadaptive and Adaptive Personality (SNAP)*. Minneapolis: University of Minneapolis Press.

Crombie, I. K., Croft, P. R., Linton, S. J., LeResche, L. & Von Korff, M. (1999). *Epidemiology of Pain* (Vol. I). Seattle: IASP Press.

Drug Topics Redbook 2000. (2002). Montvale, NJ: Thompson Medical Economics.

Epker, J. T., Gatchel, R. J. & Ellis, E. (1999). An accurate model for predicting TMD chronicity: Practical applications in clinical settings. *Journal of the American Dental Association, 130*, 1470–1475.

Feuerstein, M., Berkowitz, S. M. & Peck, C. A. (1997). Musculoskeletal related disability in U.S. Army personnel: Prevalence, gender, and military occupational specialties. *Journal of Occupational and Environmental Medicine, 39*, 68–78.

Fitzler, S. L. & Berger, R. A. (1982). Attitudinal change: The Chelsea Back Program. *Occupational Health and Safety, 52*, 52–54.

Fitzler, S. L. & Berger, R. A. (1983). Chelsea Back Program: One year later. *Occupational Health and Safety, 52*, 52–54.

Frymoyer, J. & Cats-Baril, W. (1991). An overview of the incidence and costs of low back pain. *Orthopedic Clinics of North America, 22*(2), 263–271.

Frymoyer, J. W. (1992). Predicting disability from low back pain. *Clinical Orthopaedics & Related Research, 279*, 101–109.

Gatchel, R. J., Polatin, P. B., Noe, C. E., Gardea, M. A., Pulliam, C. & Thompson, J. (2003). Treatment- and cost-effectiveness of early intervention for acute low back pain patients: A one-year prospective study. *Journal of Occupational Rehabilitation, 13*, 1–9.

Habeck, R. V., Hunt, H. A. & VanTol, B. (1998). Workplace factors associated with preventing and managing work disability. *Rehabilitation Counseling Bulletin, 42*, 98–143.

Habeck, R. V., Leahy, M. J., Hunt, H. A., Chan, F. & Welch, E. M. (1991). Employer factors related to workers' compensation claims and disability management. *Rehabilitation Counseling Bulletin, 34*, 210–226.

Habeck, R. V., Scully, S. M., VanTol, B. & Hunt, H. A. (1998). Successful employer strategies for preventing and managing disability. *Rehabilitation Counseling Bulletin, 42*, 144–160.

Hammonds, W., Brena, S. & Unikel, I. (1978). Compensation for work-related injuries and rehabilitation of patients with chronic pain. *Southern Medical Journal, 71*(6), 664–666.

Hazard, R. G. (1995). Spine update: Functional restoration. *Spine, 20*, 2345–2348.

Hildebrandt, J., Pfingsten, M., Saur, P. & Jansen, J. (1997). Prediction of success from a multidisciplinary treatment program for chronic low back pain. *Spine, 22*, 990–1001.

Himmelstein, J. S., Feuerstein, M., Stanek, E. J., Koyamatsu, K., Pransky, G. S., Morgan, W., et al. (1995). Work-related upper extremity disorders and work disability—Clinical and psychosocial presentation. *Journal of Occupational and Environmental Medicine, 37*(11), 1278–1286.

Hoogendoorn, W. E., van Poppel, M. N. M., Bongers, P. M., Koes, B. W. & Bouter, L. M. (2000). Systematic review of psychosocial factors at work and in the personal situation as risk factors for back pain. *Spine, 25*, 2114–2125.

Huang, G. D., Berkowitz, S. M., Feuerstein, M. & Peck, C. A. (1998). Occupational upper-extremity-related disability: Demographic, physical, and psychosocial factors. *Military Medicine, 163*, 552–558.

Krause, N., Dasinger, L. K. & Neuhauser, F. (1998). Modified work and return to work: A review of the literature. *Journal of Occupational Rehabilitation, 8*, 113–140.

Krause, N., Frank, J. W., Dasinger, L. K., Sullivan, T. & Sinclair, S. J. (2001). Determinants of duration of disability and return to work after work-related injury and illness: Challenges for future research. *American Journal of Industrial Medicine, 40*, 464–484.

Krause, N. & Ragland, D. R. (1994). Occupational disability due to low back pain: A new interdisciplinary classification used in a phase model of disability. *Spine, 19*, 1011–1020.

Lemstra, M. & Olszynski, W. P. (2003). The effectiveness of standard care, early intervention, and occupational management in worker's compensation claims. *Spine, 28*, 299–304.

Linton, S. J. (2001). Occupational psychological factors increase the risk for back pain: A systematic review. *Journal of Occupational Rehabilitation, 11*(1), 53–66.

Linton, S. J. (2002). A cognitive-behavioral approach to the prevention of chronic back pain. In D. C. Turk & R. J. Gatchel (Eds.), *Psychological Approaches to Pain Management: A Practitioner's Handbook* (2nd ed.). New York: Guilford.

Linton, S. J. & Bradley, L. A. (1996). Strategies for the prevention of chronic pain. In R. J. Gatchel & D. C. Turk (Eds.), *Psychological Approaches to Pain Management: A Practitioner's Handbook*. New York: Guilford Publications, Inc.

Linton, S. J. & Hallden, K. (1998). Can we screen for problematic back pain? A screening questionnaire for predicting outcome in acute and subacute back pain. *Clinical Journal of Pain, 14*, 209–215.

Loisel, P., Abenhaim, L., Durand, P., Esdaile, J. M., Suissa, S., Gosselin, L., et al. (1997). A population-based, randomized clinical trial on back-pain management. *Spine, 22*(24), 2911–2918.

Marhold, C., Linton, S. J. & Melin, L. (2001). A cognitive-behavioral return-to-work program: Effects on pain patients with a history of long-term versus short-term sick leave. *Pain, 91*, 155–163.

Marhold, C., Linton, S. J. & Melin, L. (2002). Identification of obstacles for chronic pain patients to return to work: Evaluation of a questionnaire. *Journal of Occupational Rehabilitation, 12*, 65–76.

Mayer, T. G. & Gatchel, R. J. (1988). *Functional Restoration for Spinal Disorders: The Sports Medicine Approach*. Philadelphia: Lea & Febiger.

McLellan, R. K., Pransky, G. & Shaw, W. S. (2001). Disability management training for supervisors: A pilot inventory program. *Journal of Occupational Rehabilitation, 11*, 33–42.

Medical Fees in the United States 2000. (2002). Los Angeles: Practice Management Information Corporation.

Mondloch, M. V., Cole, D. C. & Frank, J. W. (2001). Does how you do depend on how you think you'll do? A systematic review of the evidence for a relation between patients' recovery expectations and health outcomes. *Canadian Medical Association Journal, 165*(10), 174–179.

National Research Council. (2001). *Musculoskeletal Disorders and the Workplace: Low Back and Upper Extremities*. Washington, D.C.: National Academy Press.

Pergola, T., Salazar, M. K., Graham, K. Y. & Brines, J. (1999). Case management services for injured workers: Providers' perspectives. *AAOHN Journal, 47*(9), 397–404.

Pransky, G. S., Benjamin, K., Hill-Fotouhi, C., Himmelstein, J., Fletcher, K. E., Katz, J. N., et al. (2000). Outcomes in work-related upper extremity and low back injuries: Results of a retrospective study. *American Journal of Industrial Medicine, 37*, 400–409.

Pulliam, C., Gatchel, R. J. & Gardea, M. A. (2001). Psychosocial differences in high risk versus low risk acute low back pain differences. *Journal of Occupational Rehabilitation, 11*, 43–52.

Rainville, J., Sobel, J., Hartigan, C. & Wright, A. (1997). The effect of compensation involvement of the reporting of pain and disability by patients referred for rehabilitation of chronic low back pain. *Spine, 22*(17), 2016–2024.

Shaw, W. S., Feuerstein, M., Haufler, A. J., Berkowitz, S. M. & Lopez, M. S. (2001). Working with low back pain: Problem-solving orientation and function. *Pain, 93*, 129–137.

Shaw, W. S., Pransky, G. S., Fitzgerald, T. E., Patterson, W. & Winters, T. (2002). *Returning to work after acute occupational low back pain: A multiple site study of prognosis.* Montreal: Montreal International Forum V for Primary Care Research on Low Back Pain.

Sinclair, S., Hogg-Johnson, S., Mondloch, M. & Shields, S. (1997). The effective of an early active intervention program for workers with soft tissue injuries: The early claimant cohort study. *Spine, 22*, 2919–2931.

Strunin, L. & Boden, L. I. (2000). Paths of Reentry: Employment experiences of injured workers. *American Journal of Industrial Medicine, 38*, 373–384.

Teasell, R. W. & Bombardier, C. (2001). Employment-related factors in chronic pain and chronic pain disability. *Clinical Journal of Pain, December 2001 supplement*, S39–S45.

van Der Giezen, A. M., Bouter, L. M. & Nijhuis, F. J. N. (2000). Prediction of return-to-work of low back pain patients sick listed for 3–4 months. *Pain, 87*, 285–294.

Vitaliano, P., Russo, J., Carr, J., Maiuro, R. & Becker, J. (1985). The ways of coping checklist: Revision and psychometric properties. *Multivariate Behavioral Research, 20*, 3–26.

Volinn, E. (1997). The epidemiology of low back pain in the rest of the world: A review of surveys in low- and middle-income countries. *Spine, 22*, 1747–1754.

Waddell, G. (1996). Low back pain: A 20th Century health care enigma. Spine, 21, 2820–2825. *Spine, 21*, 2820–2825.

Wood, D. J. (1987). Design and evaluation of a back injury prevention program within a geriatric hospital. *Spine, 12*, 77–82.

World Health Organization. (1998). Bone and joint decade 2000–2010. *ACTA Orthopaedics Scandinavia, 69*, 219–220.

28

The CtdMAP^{TM} Intervention Program© for Musculoskeletal Disorders

J. Mark Melhorn and Larry K. Wilkinson

THE MESSAGE

The National Academy of Sciences study found that musculoskeletal disorders of the back and arm are an important national health problem with over 1,000,000 workers missing time from their job each year, at a cost of over $50 billion a year (National Academy of Sciences, 1999). When one takes indirect costs such as reduced productivity, loss of customers due to errors made by replacement workers and regulatory compliance into account, estimates place the total yearly cost of all workplace injuries at well over $1 trillion or 10 percent of United States Gross Domestic Product (Melhorn, 2002b). Debates regarding causation and subsequent financial responsibility have delayed the opportunity to provide effective intervention and prevention in the workplace for musculoskeletal disorders. Effective prevention of musculoskeletal disorders (MSDs) in the workplace (illnesses) through active intervention is not only possible, but results in significant cost savings for the employer while reducing the physical and psychosocial disability experienced by the individual employee.

MSDs management refers to a collaborative process in which employers, healthcare providers and employees work together as members of a multi-disciplinary team to make the best possible options and services available to the employee. This collaboration includes assessing employee needs, planning and implementing intervention, healthcare treatment when appropriate, providing return to work options, coordinating services, monitoring and evaluating processes, and effective communication between team members. Although MSDs management systems can vary greatly in scope and design, the critical element is the use of an individual and job risk assessment instrument.

The benefits of MSDs management can include lower costs due to fewer MSDs, decreased absenteeism, reduced workers' compensation premiums, reduced

DOI: 10.1007/978-0-387-28919-9_28, © 2009 Springer Science+Business Media, LLC

TABLE 1. Prevention Program Savings by Employer Type

Employer type	Savings/Dollar spent	Total employees	Dollars saved
Doctor	80	12	$10,000
Medical clinic	86	120	$120,000
Plastic	92	245	$810,000
Construction	121	8	$100,000
Legal	125	212	$400,000
Hospital	130	957	$1,000,000
Petroleum	145	6,200	$2,420,000
Plastic	185	2,100	$1,250,000
Elevator	212	378	$1,000,000
Education	214	891	$600,000
Grocery	216	1,700	$500,000
Aircraft	257	2,120	$1,300,000
Energy	288	10,000	$3,250,000
Aircraft	285	8,000	$2,300,000
Energy	288	10,000	$3,250,000
Salt	312	756	$1,100,000
Aircraft	390	6,000	$5,000,000
Aircraft	475	11,000	$2,420,000
Aircraft	Indirect	11,000	$13,500,000

Source: Reprinted by permission. © MAP Managers, Inc.

disability, increased productivity, and higher product quality (Gough, 1985; McKenzie, Storment, & VanHoom, 1985; Lapore, Olson, & Tomer, 1984; LaBar, 1994; LaBar, 1989; GAO, 1997). The benefit to cost ratio (dollars saved per dollar spent) provides insight into the successfulness of MSDs programs. If a MSDs management program saved $100 dollars for every dollar spent, the benefit to cost ratio would be 100. Table 1 lists the dollars saved per dollar spent (benefit to cost ratio), total number of employees and the total dollars saved for different types of employers in a one year period who used the CtdMAP™ Intervention Program®.

INTRODUCTION

In 1975, the National Center for Health Statistics Interview Survey estimated that 16 million upper extremity injuries occur yearly and these injuries result in 16 million days lost from work (Kelsey, Pastides, & Kreiger, 1980). These numbers continue despite the 1986 National Institute for Occupational Safety and Health (NIOSH) national strategy for the prevention of work-related diseases and injuries (Melhorn, 1997c). After much debate, there is still little agreement on the three controversial aspects of cumulative trauma disorders (CTDs) and musculoskeletal disorders (MSDs): 1) appropriate definition for work-related musculoskeletal pain; 2) the best ergonomic and epidemiologic model for CTDs/MSDs; and, 3) the specific exposure relationships of the individual as they relate to the activities in the workplace. There is, however, common agreement on the need for reduction of CTDs/MSDs in the workplace. In 1997, direct health care costs were over $418 billion, and lower range estimates for indirect costs were over $837 billion for a total cost of $1.25 trillion (Brady et al., 1997).

As the costs for CTDs have risen there has been an effort to redefine the term CTDs by using the term MSDs (Melhorn, 1998d). Musculoskeletal pain is defined as any pain that may involve the muscles, nerves, tendons, ligaments, bones or joints. The United States government and other organizations have described MSDs pain as any musculoskeletal pain that an individual believes is associated with activities performed at work. For the pain to be considered as work compensable, state governments have legislated a variety of work contribution requirements (United States Bureau of Labor Statistics, 1996).

The need for screening and prevention for CTDs/MSDs is documented by many groups including publications by Gordon, Blair, and Fine (1995), *Repetitive Motion Disorders of the Upper Extremity,* and Rosenstock (United States Department of Health and Human Services, 1997) *Musculoskeletal Disorders and Workplace Factors, A Critical Review of Epidemiologic Evidence for Work-Related Musculoskeletal Disorders of the Neck, Upper Extremity, and Low Back.* Gordon, Blair, and Fine (1995) recommended screening for cumulative trauma disorders and state that "workers with physically demanding jobs should undergo careful screening to disqualify those with unacceptable intrinsic risk factors, and a program of continuing physical conditioning should be required. In addition, it should be recognized that after 10 to 20 years, a worker should be transferred to a less demanding task. The belief that any worker can do any job until age 65, which is a premise of much workers' compensation policy and labor union rhetoric, is not realistic (p. 12)." Rosenstock (United States Department of Health and Human Services, 1997) recommends prevention and states: "The National Institute for Occupational Safety and Health (NIOSH) concludes that a large body of credible epidemiologic research exists that shows a consistent relationship between MSDs and certain physical factors. NIOSH will continue to address these inherently preventable disorders (p. 7)."

As important as diagnosis and treatment are for the restoration of the worker to the workplace, the NIOSH cannot, except administratively, address the larger scope of CTDs/MSDs. To control this increasing workplace problem, health professionals and employers alike must direct their attention to prevention of CTDs/MSDs. Traditional approaches to injury reduction in the workplace have focused heavily on ergonomics and methods of effecting change through manipulation of the physical environment (Hackman & Oldham, 1980; Nordin & Franklin, 1989; Grandjean, 1980). Beyond ergonomics and education, medical consultation broadens the scope of intervention to include active surveillance of the worker population by means of health screens, clinical examinations and when indicated early referral for conservative management. A physician knowledgeable about CTDs/MSDs and familiar with risks within the workplace is able to treat and rehabilitate injuries optimally for both the worker and the employer (Melhorn, 1996c; Melhorn, 1998g).

Occupational illness results from any abnormal condition or disorder (other than one resulting from an occupational injury) caused by exposure to a factor(s) associated with employment (United States Bureau of Labor Statistics, 1997). This category is often referred to as cumulative trauma disorders (CTDs), repetitive strain injury (RSI), repetitive motion disorder (RMD) or chronic overuse syndrome. Unfortunately, these descriptive terms are often considered medical illnesses or commonly described as injuries, which only adds to the confusion. These terms are not medical diagnoses but descriptive terms or labels for individuals that experience pain in the workplace.

ETIOLOGY OF MUSCULOSKELETAL DISORDERS

Many healthcare providers believe the etiology of musculoskeletal disorders is multifactorial but choose to focus on the things they can evaluate and change (medical conditions) rather than the things they cannot change (age, gender, inherited health risk) or things they do not typically treat (workplace conditions). Thus, some healthcare providers believe it is the individual's medical history that largely determines if he or she will develop a musculoskeletal disorder. Similarly, ergonomists, also fully aware of the multifactorial nature of musculoskeletal disorders, choose to focus on the things they can evaluate and change (workplace conditions) rather than those things they cannot change or things they cannot treat (medical conditions). The workplace, therefore, becomes their primary focus for understanding the causation of musculoskeletal disorders. Both groups have come to realize that there is a third factor influencing MSDs, commonly described as psychosocial or biosocial issues (Melhorn, 2003; Melhorn, 2002d; Melhorn, 2002c).

UNDERSTANDING RISK

For a CTDs/MSDs to occur two elements are required: an individual and a job. Each element is associated with unique risks. The bucket analogy can be helpful in providing an overview as to how these risks interact. Consider the individual body as a bucket with a faucet. Activities at work and home are like paint. As the activities increase, the amount of paint in the bucket increases. The capacity of the faucet is controlled by the individual's inherited health characteristics and psychosocial issues (learned behaviors). If too much paint is in the bucket or the faucet is too small, the paint will spill over. Likewise, if an individual's activity level is high and their learned behaviors are not adequate to accommodate this level of activity the chance of a CTDs/MSDs occurring is greater, as seen in Figure 1.

The paint (workplace stressors such as repetitions, force, postures, vibration, contract stress, and cold) can be modified or decreased by changes in the job, job activities, and management style. Changing the capacity of the faucet can be more challenging, as changing one's inherited health risk is very difficult. It is more realistic to focus on changing an individual's physical capacity. Conditioning a body for activity in the workplace can be accomplished as effectively as for performance in sport. This conditioning can result in improved performance and decreased injuries. The development of musculoskeletal pain in the workplace can be predicted based on individual risk contributing 65 percent and job risk 35 percent (Melhorn, Wilkinson, & O'Malley, 2001b).

Figure 2 suggests the impact ergonomic intervention could have, while Figure 3 suggests the impact that could result from medicine and psychosocial issues (learned behavior and biosocial issues). The best approach would likely result from combining the benefits obtained by ergonomics (the job) and medicine (the individual), requiring healthcare providers to be knowledgeable about musculoskeletal disorders and possess an understanding of the workplace.

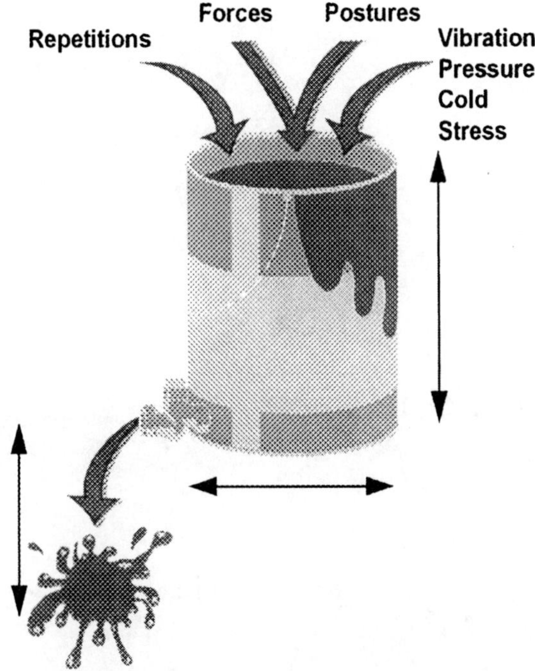

Figure 1. Individual Risk for CTDs/MSDs (*Source*: Reproduced with permission © MAP Managers, Inc.)

Individual Risk Factors

Individual risk factors include age, gender, inherited health characteristics, psychosocial issues (learned behaviors and biosocial issues), and nonworkplace activities (Melhorn, 1996b; Melhorn, 1996c; Melhorn, 1998g; Melhorn, 1998a). Furthermore, the experience of pain is influenced by the ability to tolerate discomfort (Melhorn, 2003). Tolerating discomfort is determined by three elements: 1) the level of biological stimulus (discomfort or pain), 2) existing psychological distress, and 3) current personal social stress (Colledge & Johnson, 2000).

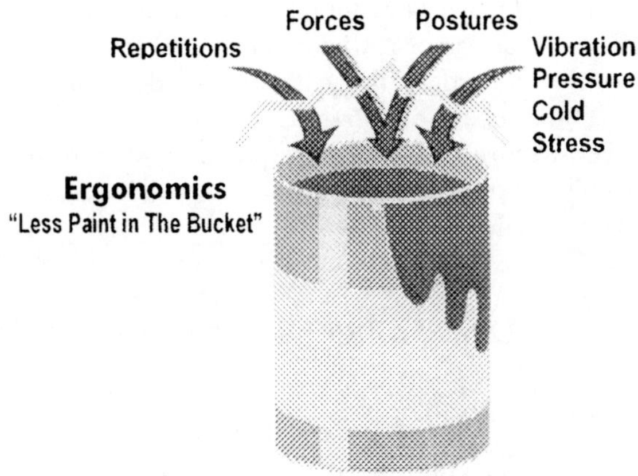

Figure 2. Ergonomics Perspective for CTDs/MSDs (*Source*: Reproduced with permission © MAP Managers, Inc.)

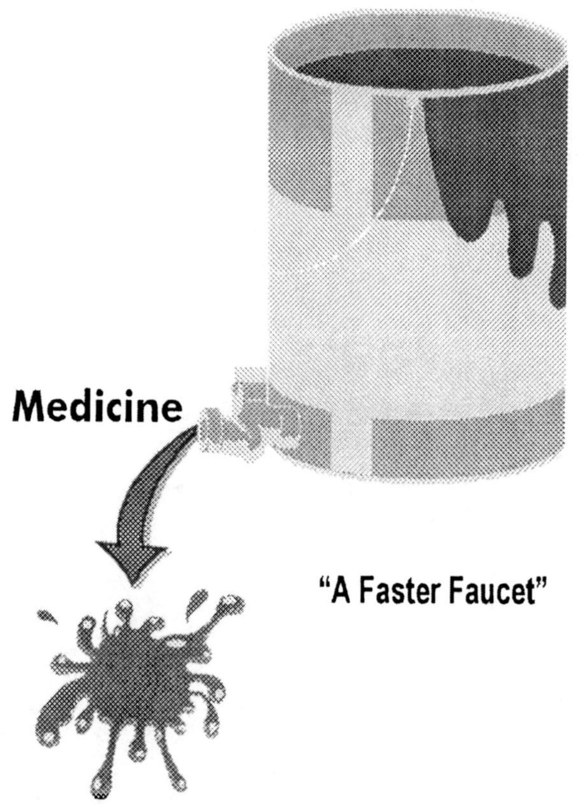

Figure 3. Medical Perspective for CTDs/MSDs (*Source*: Reproduced with permission © MAP Managers, Inc.)

Employer Risk Factors

Workplace risk factors include all aspects of the production process (the manufacturing of a product). As discussed above, individual risk factors contribute to, moderate, and buffer the demands of the workplace and thus affect an individual's development of MSDs. Workplace or employer risk factors can be placed into three broad categories that include job or task demands, organizational structure, and the physical work environment. Epidemiologically identified physical stressors associated with job activities include repetition—frequent or prolonged repetitive movements, force—forceful exertions, posture—awkward postures, vibration—local or segmental, temperatures—cold, contact stress and static muscle loads, unaccustomed activities, and combinations (Hales et al., 1996).

MUSCULOSKELETAL DISORDERS ERGONOMICS PROGRAM

Successful Ergonomic Programs

The development and implementation of an ergonomics program requires a team effort. The implementation of a successful ergonomics program can benefit the employer and employee by: 1) reducing the number and severity of work-related injuries and illnesses, 2) reducing employee turnover, 3) increasing productivity, 4) increasing product quality, and 5) increasing employee morale. These benefits result in lower costs due to fewer MSDs, decreased absenteeism, reduced disability, reduced workers compensation premiums, increased productivity and higher product quality (Gough, 1985; McKenzie et al., 1985; Lapore et al., 1984; LaBar, 1994; LaBar, 1989). The General Accounting Office (GAO, 1997) and NIOSH (Cohen, Gjessing, & Fine, 1997) list six critical elements necessary for a successful ergonomics intervention program in the workplace: 1) Management commitment (Hoffman, Jacbos, & Landy, 1995), 2) Employee involvement (Noro & Imada, 1991), 3) Risk assessment of individual and job (Melhorn, 2001), 4) Analysis of data and development of controls (Melhorn, Hales, & Kennedy, 1999a; Keyserling, Stetson, Silverstein, & Brouwer, 1993), 5) Training and education (Melhorn et al., 2001b), and 6) Traditional health care management (Melhorn, Wilkinson, & Riggs, 2001b).

Risk Assessment Instruments

Although the concept of MSD prevention is appealing, in practice some health care providers may have difficulties assessing individual and job risk factors. It is likely that appropriate effective, risk assessment instruments must meet certain criteria. They must possess reliability (test-retest reliability or reproducibility); internal consistency (the ability of a scale to measure a single coherent concept); validity (the instrument actually measures what it is purported to measure); and sensitivity or responsiveness to change (the instrument's ability to detect changes in clinical status) (Franzblau, Salerno, Armstrong, & Werner, 1997; Guyatt, Walter, & Norman, 1987; Guyatt, Kirshner, & Jaeschke, 1992; Amadio, 1993; Bergner & Rothman, 1987). Additionally, research has shown that disease specific instruments are usually more accurate and sensitive than general outcome instruments for measuring specific injuries or illnesses (Guyatt, Bombardier, & Tugwell, 1986; Dane et al., 2002).

The remainder of this chapter will discuss successful management of MSDs in the workplace using the CtdMAP™ Intervention Program® that assigns individual risk for upper extremities, lower extremities and the back. Individual risk is based on age, gender, inherited health characteristics, biosocial issues, learned behaviors and nonworkplace activities (Melhorn, 1996b; National Academy of Sciences, 1999; National Research Council, 1998; Melhorn et al., 2001b; Melhorn, 1996c; Melhorn, 1998g; Melhorn, 1998a). Job risk is based on input (raw materials), production (methods, materials, machines, environment, physical stressors [such as repetitions, force, postures, vibration, contact stress, and cold]) and output (finished product) (Melhorn, 1998b). Since MSDs require an individual to be employed, both individual and job risk assessments can be combined to produce a composite risk score, from 1 (low) to 7 (high), to assist in management protocols. Individual risk is assessed via 79 questions and 24 physical measures (Melhorn, 1996b), while job risk is evaluated by 85 questions and use of a modified rapid upper limb assessment instrument (Melhorn, 2001). Previous publications have documented reliability, internal consistency, validity, and sensitivity (Melhorn, 1996b; Melhorn, 1996a; Melhorn, 2002a; Melhorn, 1997a; Melhorn, Wilkinson, Gardner, Horst, & Silkey, 1999b; Melhorn, 1999b; Melhorn, 1998a; Melhorn, 1998e; Melhorn, 1998f; Melhorn, Wilkinson, & O'Malley, 2001a; Melhorn et al., 2001b).

THE EVIDENCE

Occupational Management of Current Employees

In 1998, an aircraft company modified their medical intervention protocol to include the use of the CtdMAP risk assessment instrument to assist in the decision of medical referral after retrospectively reviewing the previous two years workers' compensation records. A decision was made to address medical management of MSDs seen by health services. The foundation for this combined approach was supported in previous studies (Melhorn, 1994; Melhorn, 1996b; Melhorn, 1996a; Melhorn, 1997c; Melhorn, 1997d; Melhorn, 1998a; Melhorn, 1998c; Melhorn et al., 1999b).

A prospective study was developed with a specific decision tree for all employees that reported to health services with a recordable OSHA 200 MSD as seen in Figure 4. The company physician evaluated each employee using traditional health-care techniques and the completion of the risk assessment instrument. After completing the history and physical examination, the physician would review the current and previous individual risk score. If either individual risk score was above average (>4),

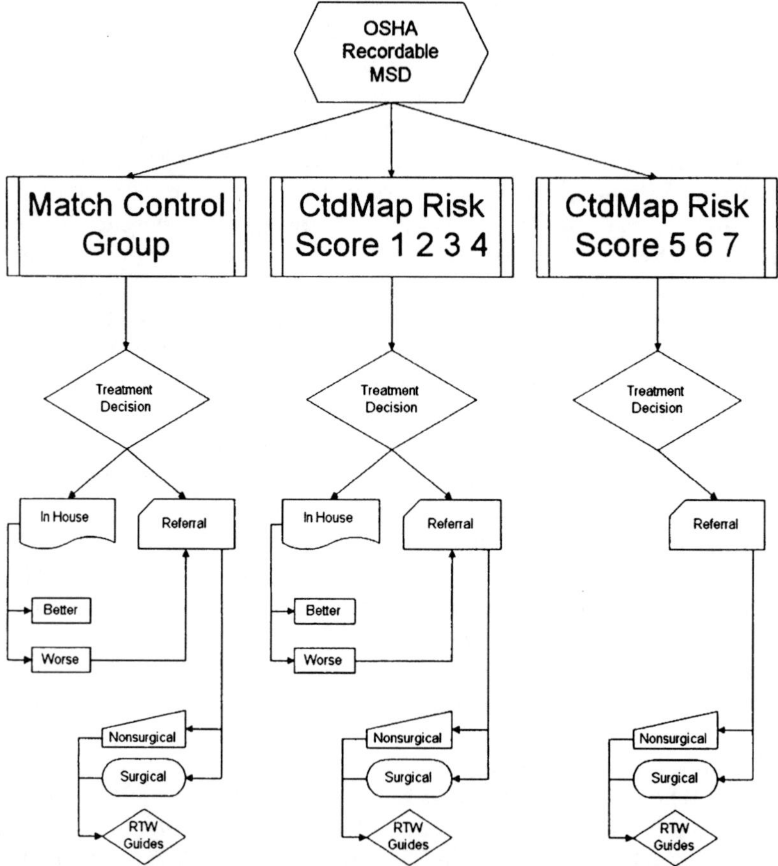

Figure 4. Algorithm for Intervention of OSHA Recordable CTDs/MSDs (*Source*: Reproduced with permission © MAP Managers, Inc.)

TABLE 2. Workers' Compensation Costs per Case by CtdMAP™ Risk Level

CtdMAP™risk level	Cost per case in (dollars)	Total costs in (dollars)
1	842	842
2	1211	9004
3	1794	21672
4	2479	32487
5	2609	88060
6	3142	22672
7	5126	69314
Mapped average	2468	433421
Matched average	3800	838704
Study group average	3134	636062
Company average	2691	

Source: Reprinted with permission © MAP Managers, Inc.

the employee was referred to a specialist for additional treatment. If the individual's risk score was below average or average (≤4) in-house medical care was provided.

Ten outcome measures were analyzed and reviewed (recordable case incidence rate, lost time case incidence rate, lost time day severity incidence rate, airplane production, costs of intervention program, estimated workers' compensation costs, number of operations, medical treatment and job activities or new tasks). Improvements in incidence rates and production occurred with reduction in costs, surgery and treatment as seen in Table 2. New tasks and onset of symptoms were reviewed. Over 70 percent of low risk individuals and none of the high-risk individuals had experienced a job change or new task in the previous 6 weeks prior to onset of symptoms. Conclusions: traditional medical management of MSDs can be enhanced by using a risk assessment instrument. Employer-estimated savings in direct workers' compensation costs were \$2.42 million and estimated indirect savings were more than \$13.5 million during the study with a benefit to cost ratio (or direct costs only) of over 398 percent for the program.

Observations: Individual risk scores of 6 and 7 did not require a change in job or a new task to trigger a MSDs event. As the individual risk score decreases the job requirements or task change could increase without risk of a MSD. The data suggests an individual to job risk ratio of 65 to 35 for predicting the likelihood of an individual developing a MSD. This ratio is currently being further evaluated to assist in better allocation of intervention funds in an effort to reduce risk and incidence.

MSDs Prevention in New Staff Modified by Job Requirements

In January of 1995, an aircraft company established a prospective MSDs risk management program for new staff. The MSDs intervention program was designed to integrate a traditional occupational medicine clinic (physician on site) and a risk assessment instrument for assigning risk and implementing intervention (Melhorn et al., 1999b). The MSDs intervention program was designed to prospectively evaluate each new employee for his or her individual risk of developing MSDs in the workplace and assist the physician in matching the employee to the most appropriate available job. The concept of best fit (the goal of ergonomics) was utilized in this practical situation. Since these employees were being hired for many different jobs,

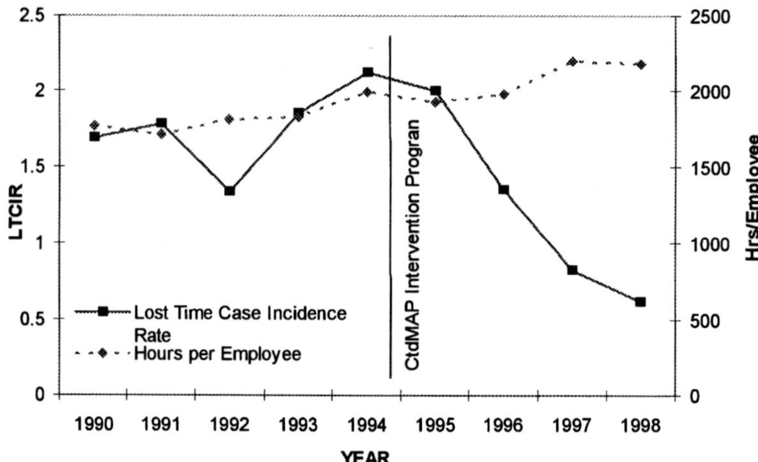

Figure 5. Lost Time Case Incidence Rate by Hours Worked per Employee Pre- and Post-CTD Intervention Program (*Source*: Reproduced with permission © MAP Managers, Inc.)

each job was risk assessed and an essential functions description was developed. The physician used an algorithm based on individual risk score and provided transitional work options, long-term work guides, education and exercise programs. Before job placement, individuals at higher risk were assigned to a period of transitional work.

Analysis of six outcome measures was reviewed (recordable case incidence rate, lost time case incidence rate, lost time day severity incidence rate, airplane production, costs of intervention program and estimated workers' compensation costs) as seen in Figure 5. All rates were converted to 200,000 hours worked per year to allow comparison with other publications. There was no significant change in recordable case incidence, a significant reduction in lost time and lost time day severity incidence rate and no change in airplane production. Risk intervention costs over 4 years were: $122,928 for 3152 assessments, $29,697 for 761 repeat assessments, $142,500 for transitional work (production loss), $2,028 for education and $7,485 for administration with a total of $304,470 or $76,118 per year which represented less than 0.06 percent of the employer's annual salary costs. Workers' compensation cost decreases per year were: 16 percent, 3 percent, 24 percent and 12 percent, while work hours increased 56 percent as seen in Figure 6. Employer-estimated savings in direct workers' compensation costs per year were $469,990, $678,337, $1,936,105 and $1,995,759 during a time when the total hours worked doubled with a benefit to cost ratio of over 390 percent for the program.

Conclusions: New hire MSDs management can be improved by including the risk associated with the future job activities. After a period of transitional work, most employees will not require permanent work guides. This will become increasingly important as the national workforce ages and more individuals with disabilities are employed. Observation: Only 11 of the 34 (29 percent) with risk scores of 7 required permanent restrictions as follows: vibratory or power tool was limited to 6 of 8 hours in time blocks of 1½ hours per 2 hours and repetitive motion tasks were limited to 6 of 8 hours in time blocks of 50 to 55 minutes per hour. This group represents less than 1 percent of the original high-risk group (risk scores 5 to 7, n = 761) and only 0.4 percent of the entire study group.

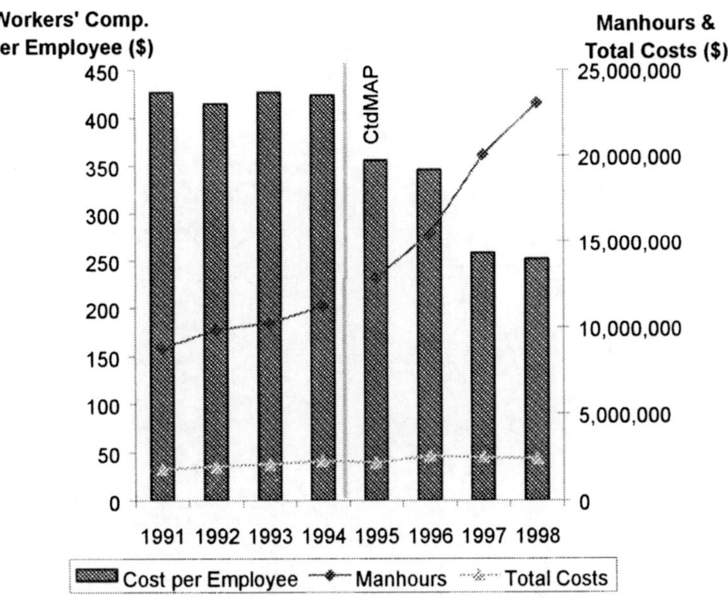

Figure 6. Study Company Workers' Compensation Per Employee (*Source*: Reproduced with permission © MAP Managers, Inc.)

MSDs Prevention for New Staff

A prospective study with historical data for comparison was completed for an aircraft manufacturer using an assessment instrument (Melhorn, 1996b; Melhorn & Wilkinson, 1996; Melhorn, 1997c; Melhorn, 1997d). During a two-year period, 1010 new employees were hired. The company elected to risk-assess individuals for the high risk job of sheet metal mechanic (n = 754) and not to risk assess individuals for the low risk job of administrative staff (n = 256) which served as the control group. After a conditional job offer, each individual was seen by the company physician for a functional capacity assessment, which included a traditional employment examination and laboratory testing. Risk assessment was provided for the high-risk job group only. The individual risk assessment scores were used to help the physician develop individual specific education and exercise programs as seen in Figure 7. Education included review of ergonomics in the workplace, proper lifting, body mechanics and early reporting of MSD symptoms and signs. Exercises included strengthening and flexibility programs to develop endurance, similar to the concept of spring training in baseball. Job matching was not a part of this study, as all individuals were hired for a specific job title. No intervention was provided for the control group.

Analysis of outcome measures showed a reduction in lost work hours from 3000 to 1000 and 1000 to 650 in years one and two compared to 780 to 782 and 782 to 791 in the control group. Over the two-year study period, the number of surgeries in the study group was reduced from 14 per 754 (1.9 percent) to 1 per 754 (0.1 percent) compared to the control group with 3 per 256 (1.1 percent) to 2 per 256 (0.78 percent).

Conclusions: Individuals bring a unique risk for the development of MSDs to the workplace. Although the job may act as a trigger event for a MSD, intervention should involve an approach that takes into account the individual. Interesting observations

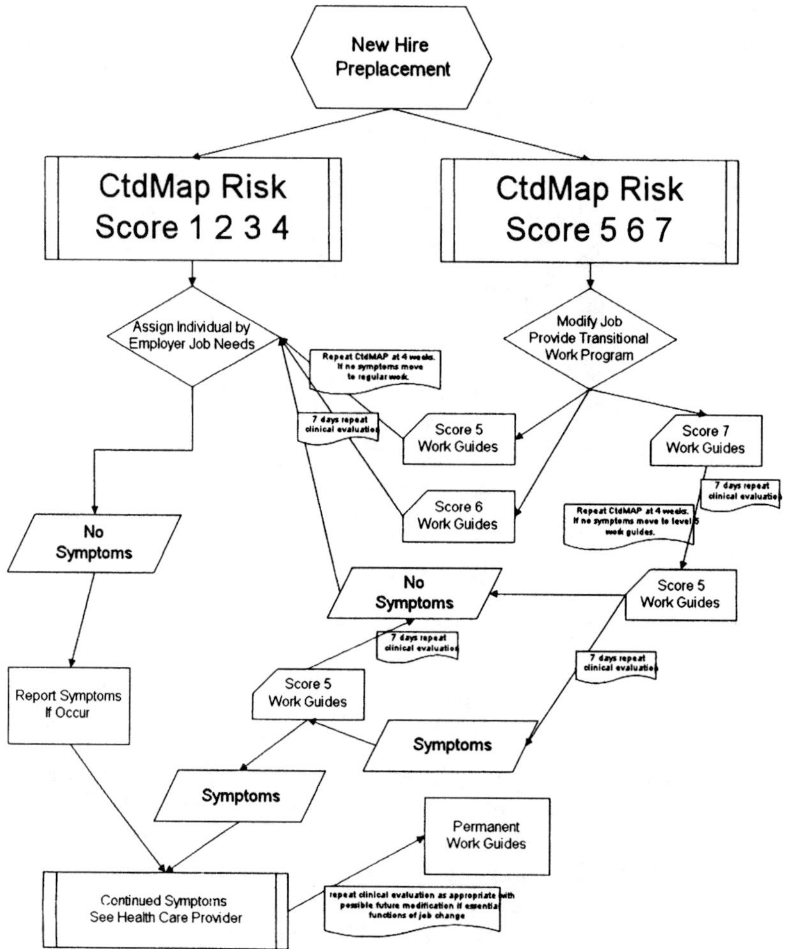

Figure 7. Algorithm for Intervention for New Staff by CtdMAP™ Risk Level. (*Source*: Reproduced with permission © MAP Managers, Inc.)

included a lower rate of surgery for individuals now performing the "high risk job," 0.1 percent versus 0.78 percent, and a lower lost work hours to employee ratio, 0.8 ratio versus 3.1. When considering the reduction in lost work hours and the direct costs of workers' compensation, the employer estimated savings of $1.8 million for the two year period with a benefit to cost ratio of over 257 for the program. The data seemed to suggest that additional benefits could be obtained by adding job risk evaluation to the new hire placement process.

Workplace Intervention Program

In a prospective study, a plastic products manufacturer wanted to improve their safety program by identifying individuals and jobs at risk (Melhorn, 1997c). All jobs were analyzed for workplace risk factors (methods, materials, machines, environment and physical stressors) and were prioritized for interventions based on job and individual risk. The ergonomics team (which consisted of an employee representative, supervisor, ergonomists, safety engineer, health nurse and physician) reviewed higher risk jobs (Melhorn et al., 1999a). Job modifications included administrative controls, work practice modification, personal protective equipment, retrofit engineering and informed purchasing. When new product lines were developed, workplace design was part of the initial consideration based on the benefits of previous job modifications and job risk reduction, as measured by the risk assessment instrument. Individual intervention included education, exercise and job training.

Quarterly analysis showed a reduction in the OSHA 200 incidence rate, lost time workday severity index and workers' compensation costs while production increased and rework decreased. Over a 24 month period, the combined composite risk score from the instrument for the company moved from 4.79 to 3.95. Conclusions: A risk assessment instrument can be used to identify job risk, to prioritize job modification by an ergonomic team and to identify individual risk for development of personalized intervention programs based on education, exercise and job training. This combined approach provided the employer with reduced costs of $234,000 for year one and $953,000 for year two when compared to the previous two years. The benefit to cost ratio was 185 for the intervention program without consideration of the increased production. Observations: Individual and job risk assessment resulted in effective distribution of limited funds that were available for this prevention program.

Tools and Ergonomic Program Design

A prospective study (Melhorn, 1996b) using the CtdMAP™ randomly sampled 212 workers out of an 8,000 member workforce who were assigned randomly to one of four primary factor groups: vibration-dampened rivet guns, standard rivet guns (control group), ergonomic training, and exercise training (Melhorn, 1996a). Risk assessment was performed at the start of the study and at 7 and 15 months. Ergonomics training included awareness of early warning signs of MSDs, methods for controlling risk factors, techniques to apply forces with less stress or strain, and correct posture and stance to improve balance and absorb forces. Exercise training included muscle relaxation and gentle stretching of muscles and tendons. Tools included vibration dampening rivet (recoilless) gun or standard rivet gun, training and practice using those tools, and conventional bucking bars. A study model was developed with results showing ergonomic training to be the only main factor that was statistically significant. Additional reduction of risk occurred with ergonomic training for the covariates of dominant hand, time spent in an awkward position, and number of standard rivets bucked. Exercise training demonstrated a risk reduction benefit for the covariates of dominant hand, number of parts routed, and number of parts ground. Vibration dampening riveting provided risk reduction for new employees but increased risk for current employees. Vibration dampening riveting increased the risk for the covariates of number of rivets bucked. Employees benefited from ergonomic training and exercise training with decreased symptoms; the employer estimated savings of $4 million with a benefit to cost ratio of 285.

Impact of Workplace Screening

A prospective study of the impact of workplace screening was undertaken in 1997 by a financial institution with 82 employees assigned to six branch offices. Data was collected for age, gender, job, branch local and study group (control or screened). The control group was made up of individual employees who received no information regarding the study or MSDs in the workplace. The study group was introduced to MSDs in the workplace by an office memo, employee management meetings, educational materials and a question and answer session over a four-week period followed by 40 of the employees being screened using an assessment instrument (screened group) (Melhorn, 1996b).

The screened group was further randomly divided into a group of 20 individuals who were informed of their risk assessment score and 20 who were not informed. Individuals were notified or informed of their individual risk level by letter and were given a follow-up interview. Education was provided to the informed group but no specific health interventions, workplace modification, or ergonomic programs were provided. Retrospective data was collected for the 5 years before the start of this study. During the study period, the employer experienced the usual first aid events and workplace injuries, but no OSHA 200 "F" injuries (MSDs). Conclusions: Employers may be concerned with workplace screening, however, this study suggests that the impact to the recordable rate may be minimal.

OSHA "Quick Fix" Ergonomic Intervention

A prospective study for evaluation of the CtdMAP^{TM} OSHA "Quick Fix" ergonomic intervention module was established with a fast food provider. Using the proposed 1999 ergonomic standards (NIOSH, 1999), a "Quick Fix" approach was developed using the CtdMAP^{TM} individual symptoms survey, the job activities form (completed by employee and employer), and the job ergonomics form. These four assessment instruments are combined to provide an incidence specific report the OSHA 200 recordable MSDs. The CtdMAP^{TM} I & E (injury and ergonomics) Report provides information on the individual (date of onset, current individual risk score, symptom complaints, body part for complaints), job risk, average risk for all individuals performed job with highest and lowest individual risk, ergonomic risk details as identified by the ergonomic standards, maximum hours and body part with exposure to possible physical stressors, an intervention form that includes options for identifying source of risk, preprinted suggestions, and options for workplace improvement. This form is then completed and the appropriate ergonomic workplace modifications provided with documentation on the I & E Report.

Over a 12 month period, 12 OSHA 200 recordable MSD events occurred in a workforce of 134 employees for an incidence rate of 8.95. This rate was consistent with the previous four years of 9.87, 8.43, 8.54, and 8.99 respectively for an average of 8.94. For each event, the four forms were completed and workplace modifications were provided. Time to complete the four forms was 60 minutes with an additional 20 minutes to review the job I & E Report, develop job modifications, and discuss the I & E Report with the employee.

SUMMARY

Successful management of occupational musculoskeletal problems goes beyond the traditional medical dimension. Despite the continuing debate on causation, current medical and epidemiological literature supports a relationship between activities and musculoskeletal pain. Reasonable management decisions can be made based on individual and job risk provided by assessment instruments (Melhorn, 1998a; Gordon et al., 1995; American College of Occupational and Environment Medicine, 1997; Day, 1988; Herington & Morse, 1995; Melhorn, 1997b). The dollar savings to the employer for musculoskeletal disorder interventions can be over 300 percent (Melhorn, 1999a; Melhorn, 1996a; Melhorn, 1998a; Melhorn, 1998f). Financial and legislative initiatives mandate prevention from a public health perspective (Baker, Melius, & Millar, 1988; NIOSH, 1999). Prevention by risk assessment currently provides another opportunity for reduction of the incidence and severity of work-related musculoskeletal disorders by allowing engineering controls to be applied in a prioritized approach, resulting in real solutions for the problems facing the American worker.

REFERENCES

Amadio, P. C. (1993). Outcomes measurements. *Journal of Bone and Joint Surgery, 75A*, 1583–1584.

American College of Occupational and Environment Medicine (1997). 1997 Labor Day checklist: ergonomic tips to prevent cumulative trauma. *American College of Occupational and Environment Medicine Conference, 9*, 1–2.

Baker, E. L., Melius, J. M., & Millar, J. D. (1988). Surveillance of occupational illness and injury in the United States: Current perspectives and future directions. *Journal of Public Health Policy, 9*, 198–221.

Bergner, M. & Rothman, M. L. (1987). Health status measures: an overview and guide for selection. *Annual Review of Public Health, 8*, 191–210.

Brady, W., Bass, J., Royce, M., Anstadt, G., Loeppke, R., & Leopold, R. (1997). Defining total corporate health and safety costs: Significance and impact. *Journal of Occupational and Environmental Medicine, 39*, 224–231.

Cohen, A. L., Gjessing, C. C., & Fine, L. J. (1997). *Elements of Ergonomics Programs. A Primer Based on Workplace Evaluations of Musculoskeletal Disorders.* (vols. Publication No. 97–117) Cincinnati, OH: U.S. Dept. of Health and Human Services, Public Health Services, Centers for Disease Control, National Institute for Occupational Safety and Health, DHHS (NIOSH).

Colledge, A. L. & Johnson, H. I. (2000). S.P.I.C.E.—a model for reducing the incidence and costs of occupationally entitled claims. *Occupational Medicine, 15*, 695–722, iii.

Dane, D., Feuerstein, M., Huang, G. D., Dimber, L., Ali, D., & Lincoln, A. (2002). Measurement properties of a self-reported index of ergonomic exposures for use in an office work environment. *Journal of Occupational and Environmental Medicine, 44*, 73–81.

Day, D. E. (1988). Preventive and return to work aspects of cumulative trauma disorders in the workplace. *Ergonomics Health, 1*, 1–22.

Franzblau, A., Salerno, D. F., Armstrong, T. J., & Werner, R. A. (1997). Test-retest reliability of an upper-extremity discomfort questionnaire in an industrial population. *Scandinavian Journal of Work and Environmental Health, 23*, 299–307.

GAO (1997). *Worker protection. Private sector ergonomics programs yield positive results.* Washington, DC: U.S. General Accounting Office, Report to Congressional Requesters. GAO/HEHS 97–163.

Gordon, S. L., Blair, S. J., & Fine, L. J. (1995). *Repetitive Motion Disorders of the Upper Extremity.* Rosemont, IL: American Academy of Orthopaedic Surgeons.

Gough, M. (1985). *Preventing illness and injury in the workplace.* Washington, DC: Office of Technology Assessment.

Grandjean, E. (1980). *Fitting the task to the man: an ergonomic approach.* (3rd ed.) London: Taylor and Francis.

Guyatt, G. H., Bombardier, C., & Tugwell, P. X. (1986). Measuring disease-specific quality of life in clinical trials. *Canadian Medical Association Journal, 134*, 889–895.

Guyatt, G. H., Kirshner, B., & Jaeschke, R. (1992). Measuring health status: What are the necessary measurement properties? *Journal of Clinical Epidemiology, 45*, 1341–1345.

Guyatt, G. H., Walter, S. D., & Norman, G. (1987). Measuring change over time: Assessing the usefulness of evaluative instruments. *Journal of Chronic Disability, 40,* 171–178.

Hackman, J. R. & Oldham, G. A. (1980). *Work redesign.* Reading, MA: Addison Wesley.

Hales, T. R. & Bernard, B. P. (1996). Epidemiology of work-related musculoskeletal disorders. *The Orthopedic Clinics of North America, 27,* 679–709.

Herington, T. N. & Morse, L. H. (1995). Cumulative trauma/repetitive motion injuries. In T.N. Herington & L. H. Morse (Eds.), *Occupational injuries evaluation, management, and prevention* (pp. 333–345). St. Louis: Mosby.

Hoffman, D. A., Jacbos, R., & Landy, F. (1995). High reliability process industries: Individual, micro, and macro organizational influences on safety performance. *Journal of Safety Research, 26,* 131–149.

Kelsey, J. L., Pastides, H., & Kreiger, N. (1980). *Upper extremity disorders: A survey of their frequency and cost in the United States.* St. Louis: CV Mosby.

Keyserling, W. M., Stetson, D. S., Silverstein, B. A., & Brouwer, M. L. (1993). A checklist for evaluating ergonomic risk factors associated with upper extremity cumulative trauma disorders. *Ergonomics, 36,* 807–831.

LaBar, G. (1989). Employee involvement yields improved safety record. *Occupational Hazards, 51,* 101–104.

LaBar, G. (1994). Safety at Saturn: A team effort. *Occupational Hazards, 56,* 41–44.

Lapore, B. A., Olson, C. N., & Tomer, G. M. (1984). The dollars and cents of occupational back injury prevention training. *Clinical Management, 4,* 38–40.

McKenzie, F., Storment, J., & VanHoom, P. (1985). A program for control of repetitive trauma disorders in a telecommunications manufacturing facility. *American Industrial Hygiene Associaiton Journal, 46,* 674–678.

Melhorn, J. M. (1994). Occupational injuries: the need for preventive strategies. *Kansas Medicine, 95,* 248–251.

Melhorn, J. M. (1996a). A prospective study for upper-extremity cumulative trauma disorders of workers in aircraft manufacturing. *Journal of Occupational and Environmental Medicine, 38,* 1264–1271.

Melhorn, J. M. (1996b). Cumulative trauma disorders: How to assess the risks. *Journal of Workers' Compensation, 5,* 19–33.

Melhorn, J. M. (1996c). Three types of carpal tunnel syndrome: the need for prevention. *Association for Repetitive Motion Syndromes News, 5,* 18–24.

Melhorn, J. M. (1997a). CTD in the Workplace: Treatment Outcomes. In *Seventeenth Annual Workers' Compensation and Occupational Medicine Seminar* (pp. 168–178). Boston, MA: Seak, Inc.

Melhorn, J. M. (1997b). CTD Solutions for the 90's: Prevention. In *Seventeenth Annual Workers' Compensation and Occupational Medicine Seminar* (17 ed., pp. 234–245). Boston, MA: Seak, Inc.

Melhorn, J. M. (1997c). Identification of Individuals at Risk for Developing CTD. In D.M.Spengler & J. P. Zeppieri (Eds.), *Workers' Compensation Case Management: A Multidisciplinary Perspective* (pp. 41–51). Rosemont, IL: American Academy of Orthopaedic Surgeons.

Melhorn, J. M. (1997d). Physician Support and Employer Options for Reducing Risk of CTD. In D.M.Spengler & J. P. Zeppieri (Eds.), *Workers' Compensation Case Management: A Multidisciplinary Perspective* (pp. 26–34). Rosemont, IL: American Academy of Orthopaedic Surgeons.

Melhorn, J. M. (1998a). Cumulative trauma disorders and repetitive strain injuries. The future. *Clinical Orthopedics, 351,* 107–126.

Melhorn, J. M. (1998b). Management of Work Related Upper Extremity Musculoskeletal Disorders. In *Kansas Case Managers Annual Meeting* (pp. 16–25). Wichita: Wesley Rehabilitation Hospital.

Melhorn, J. M. (1998c). Musculoskeletal Disorders Cumulative Trauma Disorders Risk: Individual and Employer Factors. In J.P.Zeppieri & D. M. Spengler (Eds.), *Workers' Compensation Case Management: A Multidisciplinary Perspective* (pp. 211–266). Rosemont, IL: American Academy of Orthopaedic Surgeons.

Melhorn, J. M. (1998d). Prevention of CTD in the Workplace. In *Workers' Comp Update 1998* (pp. 101–124). Walnut Creek, CA: Council on Education in Management.

Melhorn, J. M. (1998e). Reduction of Musculoskeletal Disorders Cumulative Trauma Disorders in the Workplace: A How to Manual. In J.P.Zeppieri & D. M. Spengler (Eds.), *Workers' Compensation Case Management: A Multidisciplinary Perspective* (pp. 267–286). Rosemont, IL: American Academy of Orthopaedic Surgeons.

Melhorn, J. M. (1998f). The Future of Musculoskeletal Disorders (Cumulative Trauma Disorders and Repetitive Strain Injuries) in the Workplace—Application of an Intervention Model. In T.G.Mayer, R. J. Gatchel, & P. B. Polatin (Eds.), *Occupational Musculoskeletal Disorders Function, Outcomes, and Evidence* (pp. 353–367). Philadelphia, PA: Lippincott, Williams & Wilkins.

Melhorn, J. M. (1998g). Understanding the types of carpal tunnel syndrome. *Journal of Workers' Compensation, 7,* 52–73.

Melhorn, J. M. (1999a). Occupational Orthopaedics the Future: A How to Manual. In J. M. Melhorn & J. P. Zeppieri (Eds.), *Workers' Compensation Case Management: A Multidisciplinary Perspective* (pp. 407–448). Rosemont, IL: American Academy of Orthopaedic Surgeons.

Melhorn, J. M. (1999b). The impact of workplace screening on the occurrence of cumulative trauma disorders and workers' compensation claims. *Journal of Occupational and Environmentat Medicine, 41,* 84–92.

Melhorn, J. M. (2001). Successful Management of Musculoskeletal Disorders by Identifying Risk. In *2001 Governor's Conference on Workers' Compensation and Occupational Health & Safety* (pp. 1–35). Helena, MT: Montana Department of Labor and Industry.

Melhorn, J. M. (2002a). CTD's: Assessment of Risk (Risk Assessment Applications in the Workplace). In J.Williams (Ed.), *Proceedings of McPherson College Science Symposium April 26–27, 1996* (pp. 161–166). McPherson, KS: McPherson College.

Melhorn, J. M. (2002b). Occupational Orthopaedics: Raising public awareness. *American Journal of Orthopedics, XXXI,* 441–442.

Melhorn, J. M. (2002c). Successful Management of Musculoskeletal Disorders in the Workplace Using Risk and Ergonomics. In *Twenty-second Annual National Workers' Compensation and Occupational Medicine Seminar* (pp. 247–300). Falmouth, MA: Seak, Inc.

Melhorn, J. M. (2002d). The Etiology and History of Cumulative Trauma Disorders (CTDs) and Musculoskeletal Pain (MSP) in the Workplace. In R.J.Harrison (Ed.), *16th Annual Scientific Session* (pp. 135–157). Chicago, IL: American Academy of Disability Evaluating Physicians.

Melhorn, J. M. (2003). Upper Extremities: Return to Work Issues. In J.M.Melhorn & D. M. Spengler (Eds.), *Occupational Orthopaedics and Workers' Compensation: A Multidisciplinary Perspective* (pp. 256–285). Rosemont, IL.: American Academy of Orthopaedic Surgeons.

Melhorn, J. M., Hales, T. R., & Kennedy, E. M. (1999a). Biomechanics and Ergonomics of the Upper Extremity. In T.G.Mayer, R. J. Gatchel, & P. B. Polatin (Eds.), *Occupational Musculoskeletal Disorders Function, Outcomes, and Evidence* (pp. 111–141). Philadelphia, PA: Lippincott, Williams & Wilkins.

Melhorn, J. M. & Wilkinson, L. K. (1996). *CTD Solutions for the 90's: A Comprehensive Guide to Managing CTD in the Workplace.* Wichita, KS: Via Christi Health Systems.

Melhorn, J. M., Wilkinson, L. K., Gardner, P., Horst, W. D., & Silkey, B. (1999b). An outcomes study of an occupational medicine intervention program for the reduction of musculoskeletal disorders and cumulative trauma disorders in the workplace. *Journal of Occupational and Environmental Medicine, 41,* 833–846.

Melhorn, J. M., Wilkinson, L. K., & O'Malley, M. D. (2001a). Musculoskeletal Pain: Management by Individual Risk. In *American Industrial Hygiene Conference & Exposition Embracing Change EHIS 2001* (pp. 107–108). New Orleans, LA: American Industrial Hygiene Association.

Melhorn, J. M., Wilkinson, L. K., & O'Malley, M. D. (2001b). Successful management of musculoskeletal disorders. *Journal of Human Ecological Risk Assessment, 7,* 1801–1810.

Melhorn, J. M., Wilkinson, L. K., & Riggs, J. D. (2001b). Management of musculoskeletal pain in the workplace. *Journal of Occupational and Environmental Medicine, 43,* 83–93.

National Academy of Sciences (1999). *Work Related Musculoskeletal Disorders: Report, Workshop Summary, and Workshop Papers.* Washington, DC: National Academy of Sciences, National Research Council, Institute of Medicine.

National Research Council (1998). *Work-Related Musculoskeletal Disorders: A Review of the Evidence.* Washington, DC: National Academy Press.

NIOSH (1999). *Working Draft of a Proposed Ergonomic Program Standards.* (March 99At www.osha-slc.gov/SLTC/ergonomics/ergoreg.html ed.) Washington, DC: Occupational Safety and Health Administration.

Nordin, M. & Franklin, V. H. (1989). Evaluation of the workplace: An introduction. *Clinical Orthopedics,* 85–88.

Noro, K. & Imada, A. S. (1991). *Participatory ergonomics*. Bristol, PA: Taylor & Francis, Inc.

United States Bureau of Labor Statistics (1996). *Survey of Occupational Injuries and Illnesses in 1994*. Washington, DC: United States Government Printing Office.

United States Bureau of Labor Statistics (1997). *Occupational Injuries and Illnesses: Counts, Rates, and Characteristics, 1994*. (April 1997 ed.) (vols. Bulletin 2485) Washington, DC: United States Government Printing Office.

United States Department of Health and Human Services (1997). *Musculoskeletal Disorders and Workplace Factors. A Critical Review of Epidemiologic Evidence for Work-Related Musculoskeletal Disorders of the Neck, Upper Extremity, and Low Back*. (vols. DHHS 97–141) Cincinnati, OH: National Institute for Occupational Safety and Health.

V

WHERE ARE WE NOW AND WHERE ARE WE HEADED?

29

Research and Practice Directions in Risk for Disability Prediction and Early Intervention

Izabela Z. Schultz and Robert J. Gatchel

INTRODUCTION

Both traditional medical models, including the biomedical model and the psychiatric model, have failed to explain and arrest the expansion of the occupational disability epidemic (Schultz et al., 2000). A new generation of disabilities, including musculoskeletal pain, mild traumatic brain injuries, Posttraumatic Stress Disorder and other poorly medically understood conditions continue to challenge scientists, clinicians, health care, compensation and legal systems, as well as the economy in general. These conditions appear to be best conceptualized, ameliorated and prevented using an integrated biopsychosocial model and, therefore, may best be called "biopsychosocial" disabilities, in defiance of the Cartesian mind-body dichotomy. The Panel on Musculoskeletal Disorders and the Workplace of the National Research Council and Institute of Medicine (2001) aptly stipulated that: "Because workplace disorders and individual risk and outcomes are inextricably bound, musculoskeletal disorders should be approached in the context of the whole person rather than focusing on body regions in isolation" (p. 9). This comment appears to apply well to all biopsychosocial disabilities, as our book clearly demonstrates.

With the expansion of the human and economic impact of biopsychosocial disabilities in all Western countries comes the need to develop new scientific, clinical, service, administrative and legal paradigms to detect them early and intervene effectively. The detection process requires the construction of models of prediction of occupational disability which will allow for identification of those individuals who are at risk for disability and who require early intervention. As it happens, only a minority of individuals who sustain a trauma or injury go on to develop chronicity, yet they disproportionately contribute to rising health care, compensation and litigation costs, as well as to productivity losses.

DOI: 10.1007/978-0-387-28919-9_29, © 2009 Springer Science+Business Media, LLC

How ready are we, in basic and clinical research and practice, to develop and apply such early prediction models for different biopsychosocial disabilities to aid identification and early intervention with individuals at risk for disability? Can we cut through the politicization of these conditions and the unending debate over what is objective and what is subjective, with evidence? How can we assist health care, compensation, disability administration and legal systems to avert the escalation of the epidemic of biopsychosocial disabilities and develop evidence-based, fair and equitable practices for persons with these disabilities? Can we bridge the clinical, occupational and case-management interventions by multiple stakeholders to prevent work disability? This book attempts to answer many of these questions, at the conceptual, methodological, clinical and service levels, both from global and condition-specific perspectives. This chapter will discuss some of the common themes articulated or implied by the book's contributors in the areas of concepts, measurement, prediction of disability, early intervention and clinical applications. At the same time, the unresolved issues and barriers to integration and transfer of knowledge will be highlighted. From this review, future research and practice directions will be drawn.

CONCEPTUAL ISSUES IN DISABILITY PREDICTION AND EARLY INTERVENTION

As articulated by the authors of earlier chapters, many fundamental conceptual, research and clinical problems inherent in the early prediction of, and early intervention with, people at risk for disability are arising. The reasons for this stem from a lack of scientific and clinical consensus, ambiguity and diverse diagnostic perspectives on the very conditions in question. Particularly, various definitions of conditions such as chronic pain, fibromyalgia, activity-related stress disorders, whiplash, Posttraumatic Stress Disorder (PTSD), and Mild Traumatic Brain Injury (MTBI) exist in the literature. Even in cases where prescriptive definitions are developed by an established clinical authority such as the Diagnostic and Statistical Manual of Mental Disorders (DSM-IV, 1994 and DSM-IV-TR, 2000), the diagnostic underpinnings, for example in PTSD, can or perhaps should be challenged (Bowman, this book).

Evidently, if the very conditions under study are ill defined, the body of knowledge arising from clinical observations or individual research studies is difficult to integrate and effective transfer of knowledge can be limited. However, on a positive note, it appears that a definitional consensus has been emerging but, in many instances, has not yet been articulated well enough to be translated into consistent research and clinical practices. Some of the most "definitionally challenged" areas appear to be related to research on posttraumatic psychological and neuropsychological conditions such as PTSD and MTBI, despite the proliferation of both clinical and forensic research. In these areas, most of the research focuses on which individuals are most likely to develop a disorder/condition, in keeping with the biological and psychological vulnerability hypothesis, rather than on which individuals already diagnosed with the condition are likely to develop disability (risk for disorder versus risk for disability).

The social construction and relativistic nature of the concept of disability, including occupational disability, constitutes another conceptual challenge, together with controversies around the relationship between measurable impairment and actual disability (Bickenbach, Chatterji, Badley & Ustin, 1999; Franche, Frank & Krause, this book; Melhorn, chapter 1 this book; Schultz, this book; Tate & Pledger, 2003; Wright & McGeary, this book). The definition of disability, depending on the context, appears to be a "moving target" paradigm and stakeholder perspective within which it is defined.

The U.S. Department of Education (2000) emphasized the differences between the new and traditional paradigms in disability and rehabilitation in the following way: "The old paradigm which was reductive to medical condition has presented disability as the result of a deficit in an individual that precludes him/her from performing functions and activities ... the new paradigm is integrative and holistic and focuses on the whole person functioning in an environmental context" (p. 9).

The multiple dimensions of occupational disability also make operationalization difficult. Such dimensions, in addition to physical ability aspects, also include psychological dimensions: cognitive ability, emotional control, interpersonal skills and stress resilience, as well as mobility (Koch & Samra, this book; Guilmette, this book). There is no single, uniformly accepted definition of work disability but rather there are numerous research and practice-oriented operationalizations arising from different social and legal perspectives. This also contributes to difficulties with knowledge integration, particularly in the case of biopsychosocial disabilities characterized by the interaction between physical and psychosocial dimensions.

The literature on biopsychosocial disabilities is replete with arguments for or against "subjectivity" or "objectivity" of biopsychosocial conditions. This appears to be a reflection of the different philosophical, ideological and political perspectives of these conditions. The ongoing controversy in this regard likely reflects an anachronistic Cartesian mind-body dualism and contributes a rather unhelpful polemic that does not lead to the advancement of science and practice in early detection and prevention of occupational disability. Remarkably, most of this book's contributors do not advocate the usefulness of the "subjective-objective" dichotomy. Moreover, throughout the history of medicine, conditions initially attributable to purely "subjective" causes have been found, usually through technological advances, to be explainable by ever-expanding lists of "objective" causes (i.e., various biomedical markers of increasing levels of complexity and sophistication in measurement).

Yet another factor complicating the conceptualization of the prediction of occupational disability is the existence of disparate constructs of disability and return to work interventions, with different underlying Biomedical, Psychiatric, Insurance, Labor-Relations, and Biopsychosocial Models (Schultz et al., 2000). Moreover, stage models of disability, from Cause through Disability to Decision (Franche & Krause, 2002; Wright & McGeary, this book) have added a critically important temporal dimension, often ignored in research and practice, that allows for the diversification of prognostic factors depending on the stage post injury and anchoring early interventions accordingly (Krause et al, 2001).

With different models of disability, interesting sets of relationships between models of disability and models of early intervention have developed:

- Early intervention models based on empirically derived biopsychosocial disability models (Gatchel, this volume; Linton, this volume)
- Early intervention/disability prevention models based on biopsychosocial concepts of disability, which combine occupational and clinical dimensions,

without specifically identifying those at risk though targeting those in at-risk stages of disability (Loisel & Durand, this volume)

- Early intervention models not based on any clearly articulated predictive models but rather on the researchers' consensus (not published in this volume).

Generally, future research is required in the area of developing and selecting the right predictive models for the right purpose at the right time. Clearly, despite attempts at "flagging" early claims of disability as "high risk," attempted by various compensation systems, there is no universal prediction model that applies to all phases of disabilities, conditions and contexts, and no such model is ever anticipated to be developed.

MEASUREMENT AND RESEARCH ISSUES

In reviewing the most current research and scientific trends in the prediction of disability in biopsychosocial conditions, a steady progression from a *clinical* to *actuarial* approach is seen. Using an actuarial approach, the predictors are quantified and combined following a set of empirically supported rules whereas, in clinical approaches to prediction, practitioners use their own subjective judgments with respect to predictors and outcomes in the process known as prognosis (Lanyon & Goodstein, 1997). In application of the actuarial prediction of occupational disability, based on current research, it is now possible for each of the obtained predictors to be given a quantitative weight. Subsequently, these predictors can be combined utilizing a "best fitting" actuarial model.

Recent studies on early identification of individuals at risk for occupational disability have advanced to a point whereby actuarial formulae can be used to determine an individual person's probability of return to work, duration of disability or costs. Due to the need for large and fairly homogeneous sample sizes, the research in this field to date has been limited to musculoskeletal pain conditions, particularly back pain (Gatchel, et al., 2003, this book; Linton, this book; Marhold, Linton & Melin, 2002; Schultz et al. submitted paper). It is anticipated that research on other conditions will follow this lead. Indeed, the superiority of the actuarial approach, as compared to a clinician's own predictions, has been consistently demonstrated over the last 50 years in the general clinical literature (Garb, 1994; Grove, et al., 2000; Kleinmuntz, 1990; Meehl, 1954, 1965). Though it is unlikely that empirically based actuarial prediction rules will be able to totally replace clinical judgment in individual cases, augmentation of clinical decision-making on future occupational disability is of critical importance for prognosis and intervention purposes (Groth-Marnat, 2003).

At this time, except for selected musculoskeletal conditions, occupational disability predictions for other conditions of interest in this book can be made primarily using a clinical prognostic approach, though in a manner augmented by emerging research evidence not yet captured by an actuarial formula. Future research on the development of occupational disability prediction formulas for different conditions, contexts, populations, purposes and stages after the injury is anticipated to continue accelerate, fuelled by demands of healthcare and compensation systems.

The stage of accumulation of research evidence and its readiness for integration is often demonstrated by meta-analytic studies. Such studies are lacking in the area of prediction and early intervention with occupational disabilities. Systematic reviews of the literature have been primarily emerging in the musculoskeletal pain area (Crook et al., 2002; Turner, Franklin & Turk, 2000), showing that only a minority of studies meet the set methodological criteria for the reviews. There is a danger that, in the absence of a more substantial body of research on conditions other than back pain, future prediction and early risk identification and intervention models will be primarily based on the back pain literature which dominates the field.

One of the factors limiting validity and generalizability of current and emerging predictive models of disability is the lack of a clear definition of outcome (Krause et al., 2001). The definition varies depending on the particular perspective and stakeholder. Patients, families, employers, health care providers, insurance and compensation system and vocational specialists have their own preferred outcomes (Polatin, Robinson & Garofalo, this volume). Should it be quality of life, treatment satisfaction, return-to-work, resolution of litigation, etc.? Even the most common definition of occupational disability (i.e., return to work status), is not uniformly defined. Studies differ with respect to such characteristics of return to work as: time/timing, sustained vs. non-sustained employment, same vs. different position, same vs. different employer, hours of work, types of responsibilities, compensation, job accommodations, job satisfaction and stability of employment over time (Polatin, Robinson & Garofalo, this volume). Of course, assessment of occupational outcomes is often functionally-based. This can also be problematic due to the need for inclusion of both physical and psychosocial functions, the still difficult to capture role motivation plays in function-oriented assessment and the difficulty assessing generic work capability as opposed to specific job functions (Polatin, Robinson & Garofalo, this book).

The generalizability of research on early prediction of occupational disability has also been adversely affected by population sampling issues. As pointed out by others (Polatin, Robinson, & Garofalo, this book, Crook et al., 2002), these issues include the following: not having all individuals with a given condition captured in the sample; focusing on only those who received medical help rather than all of those with a condition; and limiting study samples to small clinical samples, often those which are called "samples of convenience."

Because the optimal research paradigm in prediction of occupational disability and early intervention is biopsychosocial, a multi-method, multi-respondent and multi-system approach to research is of critical importance. Yet such research is labor intensive, costly and requires the collaboration of multiple stakeholders who may have conflicting interests. It requires combining an individual clinical approach with an occupational and system-based approach. When accomplished, however, it yields the most promising outcomes (e.g., Gatchel, this volume; Loisel et al., 2002, Loisel & Durand, this volume; Schultz et al., 2002).

Last, but not least, research on occupational disability, particularly in the context of predictors of disability and early intervention, must, overtly or covertly, tackle the issue of motivation to work and motivation to cope. The Readiness for Return to Work Model (Franche & Krause, 2002) implies that two sets of dimensions of change facilitate understanding of the complex interrelationships among the injured worker, health care provider, the workplace and the insurer. The first principle is related to duration and stage of disability, and the second key principle involves the concepts of decisional balance, self-efficacy and change processes (Franche & Krause, 2002;

Wright & MeGeary, this volume). The Readiness for Return to Work Model is based on Prochaska's (Prochaska & DiClemente, 1983) concept of stages of change and its subsequent applications in changing health behaviors. Only recently this stage-based concept of readiness for behavioral change has been applied to return to work of workers with musculoskeletal injuries (Schultz, 2003—research proposal for early intervention).

Motivation to return to work can also be conceptualized using social learning theory. Particularly, the significance of expectations of outcome was postulated by Bandura (1996), in combination with expectations of efficacy, in predicting a person's ability to achieve desired outcomes. Return to work following injury is one such outcome, as argued by Roessler (1988,1989). According to the instrumental theory of motivation, "action results when an outcome, i.e., returning to work, is perceived as both probable and beneficial" (Roessler, 1989, p. 14). McDaniel's expansion of the Valence, Instrumentality and Expectation Theory assumes that motivation is a function of expectations, understood as a person's chances of achieving a desirable outcome and the utility (value) of the outcome divided by costs of performing such action (McDaniel, 1976). Therefore, in the context of occupational disability, it can be argued that the worker's motivation to return to work following an injury may be a function of expectations of recovery and the value placed on work/employment, balanced by personal costs such as pain (Schultz et al., 2004). The significance of expectations of recovery in predicting return to work of individuals with musculoskeletal pain conditions has been demonstrated in several studies (Cole et al., 2002; Sandstrom & Esbjornsson, 1986; Schultz et al., 2002, Schultz et al., 2004). More research on validation of social learning theories in the return to work context is likely to be of assistance in its further application to disability prediction purposes.

Motivation to return to work (or remain off work) is also often conceptualized as a balance between the secondary losses and secondary gains of the individual following compensable injury (Dersh et al, this volume). The impetus behind research in this area has come from the Forensic (or Insurance) Model of Disability and an interest in motivational phenomena such as malingering, exaggeration and symptom magnification. As we have indicated earlier in the book, we have found that our interdisciplinary model of managing secondary gain issues (including somatization, symptom magnification, pain behaviors, and delayed recovery) is a good complement to our functional restoration rehabilitation model, and does not have to negate the possibility of therapeutic improvement.

Despite the existence of a vast literature on secondary gains, very few studies have focused on secondary losses, and even fewer on how individuals balance secondary losses and gains to make return to work decisions and sustain employment following injury, often while coping with residual symptoms. Moreover, despite their likely predictive importance, the secondary losses and gains have not been operationalized well enough in occupational disability research to be included in empirically-derived biopsychosocial models of prediction of disability. Clearly, the difficulty researchers and clinicians have in defining, operationalizing and measuring human motivation has been translated into difficulties in consistently recognizing this important construct in predictive modeling of occupational disability and early intervention with high risk individuals.

COMMON THEMES IN PREDICTION OF DISABILITY

There appears to be a consensus in the current literature on occupational disability that the Western world is facing a disability epidemic with far-reaching economic consequences (Melhorn, Lazarovic and Roehl, this volume). In particular, there is a proliferation of musculoskeletal and psychological or neuropsychological disabilities which challenge the traditional biomedically-based healthcare, compensation and employment systems in industrialized countries. The need for a biopsychosocial paradigm in managing and combating this epidemic has been well recognized by clinicians and researchers. Yet, it has not translated into new public awareness, policy development and the administrative structures and service delivery models that reflect the biopsychosocial construction of such disabilities. Likewise, the need for early identification and intervention with those individuals at the highest risk for occupational disability has been well recognized among clinicians and researchers. Notwithstanding recent multi-color, risk-flagging systems (Main & Spanswick, 2000; Main, Phillips & Watson, this book), this need has not translated into practice.

Commonly, the failure of individuals at risk for disability to return to work following injury or trauma is seen by all of the players involved- the worker, employer, health care system and compensation system- as a "lose-lose solution". Yet, the translation of empirical research to date, with its predictive models, actuarial formulas for risk stratification and emerging early intervention programs, into multi-system and multi-player practice is in its very early stages. Expansion of research on predictors of disability, above and beyond epidemiological predictors of disorder, will likely lead to wider-scale applications of findings in secondary prevention and early intervention programs. Though the focus on prediction of disability, rather than on the disorder, is becoming more prevalent in the area of musculoskeletal pain conditions, studies on psychological or neuropsychological conditions appears to be still dominated by research into individual risk/vulnerability factors for developing the condition. This appears to be particularly evident in the current research literature on PTSD and other posttraumatic conditions as well as depression.

Another key common theme across the spectrum of disorders and disabilities discussed in this book is the consensus that biological markers and impairment alone do not predict disability. The correlation between impairment and disability is often low or non-existent. Biopsychosocial models including individual, workplace, health care-related, compensation-related and other social contextual factors appear to explain the variance in occupational disability best and much more accurately than traditional biomedical and demographic factors.

The severity of trauma or injury also does not seem to have a direct bearing on disability outcomes. Rather, it is the *perception* of trauma, injury and their sequelae that has been consistently shown to be a predictor of disability, together with the ability to cope with adverse consequences of trauma or injury. Psychological factors have been clearly demonstrated to play a pivotal role in the transition to chronicity, among most of the biopsychosocial conditions discussed in this book. Among the psychological factors predictive of disability, cognitions (including perceptions, beliefs and expectations of recovery and return to work) appear to best explain the difference between those who cope adaptively and return to employment and those who do not. The research on psychological factors in occupational disability appears to be shifting from the psychopathology model to the study of individual differences in cognitions (and behaviors) in interaction with the context of injury and recovery: the health care, compensation and workplace system.

A promising model for predicting disability and designing early intervention programs for workers at high risk for disability is the ecological conceptual model. This model involves both *mezosystems* (i.e., organizational characteristics), and *macrosystems* of healthcare, compensation systems, workplace culture, law and economy (MacKenzie et al., 1988; Loisel et al, 2002). The integration of the ecological approach to early intervention, particularly emphasizing the workplace, with the individual, clinical approach is likely to be the research paradigm that actually leads to change in disability outcomes. The evidence for validation of this new paradigm has already been emerging and demonstrating long-term (as opposed to short-term) outcomes in musculoskeletal disability (Waddell & Burton, 2001; Durand & Loisel, 2001; Gatchel, this book; Linton, this book; 2001; Loisel et al., 2002; Loisel & Durand, this book).

Blending with macrosystems, involving compensation for disability, and individual motivation to cope, recover and return to work, are compensation and litigation factors. The literature has been consistently demonstrating that the duration of compensated disability has been longer than the duration of non-compensated disability, with an associated increase in costs. At the same time, however, the disability would not typically end with a favorable court verdict and suitable compensation (Leeman, Polatin, Gatchel & Kishino, 2000; Rainville, Sobel, Hartigan & Wright, 1997). Multiple factors are likely at play mediating the relationship between compensation and the medico-legal context of disability on one hand and disability outcomes on the other. Such factors may include the involvement of multiple systemic stakeholders with uncoordinated or poorly coordinated policies, practices and actions; the availability of treatment and rehabilitation that otherwise would not be within reach; the medicalization or overpathologization of otherwise benign conditions; and the adversarial nature of the disability legitimization process, together with individual motivational and coping factors involving the balance of secondary losses and gains.

EMERGING THEMES IN EARLY INTERVENTION

As discussed in an earlier chapter in this text (Garofalo, Gatchel, Kishino & Strizak), we are on the verge of developing a comprehensive early intervention program for acute and subacute low back pain (ALBP and SLBP), between 0 and 10 weeks following injury. Hopefully, a similar paradigm can be used for other biopsychosocial disabilities. Basically, a number of important steps were taken in this process, as delineated below. It should be noted that all of this clinical research was supported by grants from the National Institutes of Health.

- The major goal of an initial grant project in this series was to identify predictors of when ALBP/SLPB occurrences were likely to develop into chronic disability problems. The results of that initial project clearly isolated some significant psychosocial risk factors that successfully predicted the development of chronicity during a one-year follow-up. Using a receiver-operator characteristic (ROC) curve analysis, which was based on the probabilities estimated from the logistic regression model developed on the large cohort of patients evaluated during that project, a statistical algorithm was developed that could be used to identify (with a 90.7% accuracy rate) "high risk" ALBP/SLBP patients who were prime candidates for early intervention in order to prevent chronicity.

- As an extension of these important findings, the second funded grant project involved the assessment of a large cohort of ALBP/SLBP patients in order to screen out those patients who were at high risk for developing chronicity (using the aforementioned algorithm). These high-risk patients were then randomly assigned to one of two groups: an early intervention group or a non-intervention group. During the next year, routine three-month follow-up evaluations were then conducted in order to assess important long-term socioeconomic outcomes, such as return-to-work, healthcare utilization rates, and medication use rates. It was hypothesized that early intervention at the acute stage would prevent the development of chronic disability. It should also be noted that, as a replication of the previous grant project results, the non-intervention group was compared to a demographically-matched cohort of initially assessed ALBP/SLBP patients who did not display the "high risk" profile. It was hypothesized that the high-risk non-intervention group patients would demonstrate higher rates of chronic disability at one year relative to the low or "not-at-risk" profile patients.

An initial study emanating from this project further characterized those patients who were classified as high risk or low risk, based upon our classification algorithm. Results clearly revealed additional mental health differences between these two groups. The high-risk patients were found to have lower scores on positive temperament (i.e., less energy, enthusiasm and optimism when undertaking projects) as measured on the Schedule for Nonadaptive and Adaptive Personality (Clark, 1993), greater reliance on an avoidance coping strategy as assessed on the Ways of Coping Questionnaire-Revised (Vitaliano, Russo, Carr, Maiuro & Becker, 1985), and a greater prevalence of a DSM-IV Axis I Disorder. These findings, therefore, again highlight the fact that our identified high-risk patients have a stronger potential for psychosocial factors that may contribute to chronic mental and physical health disability if not managed in a timely fashion. Moreover, a just-completed analysis of a larger cohort of patients from this project (and not just those who participated in the early intervention component of the study) has indicated that the high-risk subjects had a higher prevalence of Mood Disorders, Anxiety Disorders, Somatoform/Pain Disorders, Substance Abuse/Dependence Disorders, and Co-morbid Axis I and Axis II Disorders.

The early intervention approach evaluated in this just-completed grant project was based upon a number of suggestions by leading experts in the field that, in order to decrease the high cost of chronic musculoskeletal disability, there is a great need for better identifying patients at the acute phase who would benefit from such early intervention (Hazard, 1995; Linton, 2002; Linton & Bradley, 1996). Moreover, early detection and intervention in order to prevent chronic disorders was recognized as a high priority research area (Human Capital Initiative Coordinating Committee, 1996). As noted earlier, with the realization that work-related musculoskeletal disorders are a major socioeconomic problem in the United States, a series of questions posed by the U.S. Congress prompted the National Institutes of Health to request the National Research Council to examine ways of reducing this problem of work-related musculoskeletal disorders. This resulted in a publication, which, as one of its conclusions, highlighted the importance of early intervention in order to reduce the development of chronic disability (National Research Council, 2001).

The results of this just-completed grant project clearly indicated that early intervention at the acute stage of LBP significantly reduced the prevalence of chronic disability, relative to those high-risk ALBP/SLBP patients who did not receive such early intervention (Gatchel et al., 2003). The major hypotheses of this study were confirmed: the high-risk ALBP/SLBP patients who received early intervention (the HR-I group) displayed significantly fewer indices of chronic pain disability on a wide range of work, healthcare utilization, medication use and self-reported pain variables, relative to the high-risk ALBP/SLBP patients who did not receive such early intervention (the HR-NI group). Relative to the HR-NI group, the HR-I group was much more likely to have returned to work (odds ratio = 4.55), less likely to be currently taking narcotic analgesics (odds ratio = 0.44), and also less likely to be taking psychotropic medication (odds ratio = 0.24). In addition, the HR-NI group also displayed significantly more symptoms of chronic pain disability on these variables relative to the initially low-risk ALBP/SLBP patients (the LR group).

The cost-comparison savings data from this study were also quite impressive. Using unit cost multipliers obtained from the Bureau of Labor Statistics for compensation costs due to disability days (Bureau of Labor Statistics, 2002), from the *Medical Fees in the United States 2002* (Medical Fees in the United States 2000, 2002) for healthcare costs, and the *Drug Topics Red Book 2002* (Drug Topics Redbook 2000, 2002) for medication costs, we were able to calculate the average costs per patient associated with healthcare visits related to LBP, narcotic analgesic and psychotropic medications, and work disability days/lost wages.

- Another interesting finding from this study (although it was not a specific aim of the grant project) was that, even in the early intervention group, some problems were encountered by certain patients when they were ready to return-to-work. As reviewed earlier, preliminary evaluations indicated that there were often workplace factors that presented significant obstacles for some of these patients to immediately return-to-work when they are ready to do so. Indeed, a growing body of literature suggests the importance of taking into account such potential obstacles in order to most expeditiously return patients back to work.

For these preliminary evaluations, two patient assessments were conducted, using Linton's Örebro Risk for Disability Questionnaire and the Liberty Mutual Disability Risk Questionnaire. The preliminary results we obtained have now prompted us to more systematically evaluate these potential obstacles to work return within the context of our already-developed and successful biopsychosocial assessment-treatment protocol for high-risk ALBP/SLBP patients. This will represent a three-component biopsychosocial model of early intervention, which includes the following:

1. The identification of high-risk status by use of our empirically-supported statistical algorithm (actuarial formula).

2. The administration of our empirically-supported successful early intervention program for these high-risk patients.
3. The introduction of a back-to-work transition component in order to directly modify potential work force obstacles that may prevent the most expeditious return-to-work.

It is hypothesized that the latter work-transition component will be the "final piece of the puzzle" of this overall biopsychosocial model of early intervention developed to maximize early work return and the prevention of chronicity in high-risk ALBP/SLBP patients.

In conclusion, future work with other biopsychosocial disabilities should use a similar research-oriented paradigm as reviewed above. The major components consist of the following:

- Early screening for disability risk; development of actuarial formulas for identifying patients at high risk for chronicity
- Early intervention during the critical time window (acute stage)
- The use of a biopsychosocial, interdisciplinary intervention model; combining clinical and occupational intervention, with multiple players involved. Functional restoration, combined with cognitive-behavioral approaches are effective
- Workplace factors and job accommodation are key factors that also need to be considered, with workplace transition being the final missing piece of the puzzle in the complete rehabilitation process.

There is currently limited quantitative research beyond low back pain. Similar models need to be developed for other disabilities.

CLINICAL APPLICATION ISSUES

The currently developing actuarial models of prediction of occupational disability, risk identification and early intervention programs for those at risk are intended for two applications:

1. Large scale system-wide applications by insurance, compensation and health care systems aimed at flagging those individuals who require differential early intervention and case management
2. Individual clinical prognosis of occupational outcomes by clinicians: physicians, psychologists, physiotherapists, nurses, occupational therapists and vocational rehabilitation consultants, often in the interdisciplinary service context.

The challenges in translating empirically-based models to system-wide applications are multiple and caution needs to be exercised as the population on which the model was constructed may not demographically and clinically match the population for which it is being applied. The administrative system and purpose of the original model might also not match the one in which the model originated. Many newly developed models may have narrow applications (e.g. workers' compensation claimants only in the subacute stage post injury in a non-litigious workers' compensation system) and should not be automatically generalizable to other systems. The evaluation of the validity, with particular emphasis on specificity-sensitivity issues, of emerging models for applications other than the original research purpose will likely constitute a challenge for researchers in the upcoming decade.

Despite the labor-intensiveness of studies on predictive actuarial formulas and limitations of the existing models, even small improvements in the system's ability to detect those at risk for disability and intervene with them before chronicity sets in are of critical importance, both clinically and economically. This is particularly evident when reviewing long term health care-cost-offset data and savings arising from the application of the early intervention models (Gatchel, et al., 2003, Gatchel, this book; Loisel et al., 2002; Loisel & Durand, this book).

When applying group-based outcome prediction formulas to individuals, several caveats apply as well. As Groth-Marnat aptly stipulates: "A further difficulty with a purely actuarial approach is that development of both test reliability and validity, as well as actuarial formulas, requires conceiving the world as stable and static. For such approaches to be useful, the implicit assumption is that neither people nor criteria change" (Groth-Marnat, 2003, p.30). However, retreating to the sole focus on subjective clinical judgment about work prognosis and identification of those who are at risk for disability, is not an option clinically, ethically, economically and legally.

The inferences offered by actuarial approaches need to be integrated with data and inferences which can be collected through the use of clinical methods. It is anticipated that future computer-assisted analysis of clinical assessment/examination data will be increasingly capable of providing actuarial predictions (i.e., Garb, 2000). This approach will be of particular assistance to clinicians working with complex biopsychosocial disabilities in the contentious medico-legal environment of compensation and litigation. The enhanced application of research-based models and actuarial formulas for prognosis purposes in the medico-legal context will likely serve to increase the scientific standard of clinical assessments, objectifying them and making them more forensically defensible. In the United States, such assessments would, more likely than clinician-judgment based assessments, meet court standards for admissibility of scientific evidence arising from *Daubert* challenges.

Cutting through the politicization of occupational disability with scientific evidence in the form of empirically based predictive models and risk identification formulas is the foremost task for next couple of decades. In the absence of a substantial accumulation of evidence, the polarization of views on where the "blame for disability" lies, within the individuals or within their environment, will needlessly continue, and the unhelpful battle between the biopsychosocial and forensic/insurance models of disability will continue to wage. The development of evidence-based guidelines, to supplement the emerging consensus-based best practices, for early intervention with individuals at high risk of disability, starting with musculoskeletal pain disabilities where several thousand studies on predictors of disability have already been published, appear to be of primary significance to combat not only the disability epidemic but also the politicization of this epidemic.

Are the major stakeholders in disability ready for the new evidence-supported, biopsychosocial paradigm for detection and intervention with individuals at high risk for disability? Even though all players, including the worker, employer, health care system and the compensation system appear to agree on the need for such a paradigm, each one of them faces major challenges to such a paradigm's application. The importance of capturing psychosocial predictors of disability, implicated in most predictive models, is one of the challenges. Both health care and compensation/insurance systems traditionally based on the biomedical model share discomfort in systematically collecting, recognizing and accounting for psychosocial variables in their data collection systems. Psychosocial factors as predictors of disabilities continue to be somewhat of an officially unspoken topic in compensation and insurance systems, where such factors are recognized at the individual claim decision level and affect disability entitlement decisions; yet no actual data on psychological factors is collected by systems in general. At the same time, the wealth of demographic and medical facts routinely collected in the administrative databases is of limited use for disability prediction purposes (Schultz et al., 2002). When questioned on this apparent double standard, the insurance companies often cite fear of being accused of discrimination against individuals with psychosocial problems and possible legal challenges arising from risk for disability identification.

Notably, in the absence of the effective transfer of knowledge from studies on prediction of disability and risk identification to practice, case management and entitlement decision practices of many insurance/compensation systems are based on biomedical models and "psychosocial factors" continue to be commonly reduced to secondary gain and malingering. To challenge this position, even though the existing body of knowledge on biopsychosocial predictors of disability and risk identification does not consistently meet the *Daubert* legal standard, particularly in less-researched and less-prevalent conditions, the legal defensibility of claim determinations based on empirical evidence to date is undoubtedly higher than what current claim practices entail.

Another key stakeholder in disability, the employer, also has major potential for effecting changes in occupational disability rates (Loisel et al., 2002; Loisel & Durand, this book), the employer is likewise not provided with any published evidence-based best practices that can be applied to tackle some of the early risk factors prior to progression of disability, in a secondary prevention format, and to facilitate the safe, timely and durable return to work. Despite legislative advances such as the Americans with Disabilities Act in the United States, and the Employment Equity Act in Canada, employers are often left to their own resources with respect to effective and proactive disability management practices, and particularly job accommodation, of critical importance in early intervention with high risk injured workers. The transfer of knowledge on such effective workplace based practices from research studies to employers will continue to be a future challenge for those involved in occupational disability prevention and intervention.

It appears that even though employers in Western countries have made major progress in attracting, accommodating and maintaining workers with *physical* disabilities, workplace-based practices (and likely attitudes) toward workers with *biopsychosocial* disabilities are lagging behind. This is particularly evident in the areas of "invisible disabilities" without a clearly identifiable medical cause, such as pain-related and psychological disabilities. The development of evidence-informed guidelines for job accommodation, despite significant research support for it in the case of biopsychosocial disabilities (Krause et al., 2001; Crook et al., 2002), and assisting employers with their implementation is critically needed. Employers typically reflect the views of the public at large and therefore, just like health care and compensation systems, adhere to the traditional medical model in their conceptualization of disability. A lack of awareness and distrust of the psychosocial factors at play in the workplace that promote disability and a failure to intervene with them will, therefore, inevitably follow.

In order to assist employers with bridging the chasm between clinical treatment and durable return to work, organizational and rehabilitation psychology require integration of their efforts to form a united research front with occupational medicine, physical medicine and rehabilitation, as well as rehabilitation therapies. Such integrated clinical research evidence could then be transferred to the employers through best business administration/human resource management practices, workers' compensation (or insurance companies') prevention and disability management policies, and clinical input of occupational physicians, nurses, psychologists, therapists and vocational consultants.

CONCLUSIONS

In conclusion, many biopsychosocial issues need to be taken into account, as we have just reviewed in this chapter. This makes for a daunting task in which new methodologies and theoretical models will need to keep pace with the accumulating research literature. An interdisciplinary, biopsychosocial approach will need to be utilized to take into account individual factors, the work environment, social/cultural variables, health care system issues, and the economy in general in order to overcome the current epidemic of biopsychosocial disabilities we are facing today, and which threatens to continue to grow in the future if left unchecked. Although this appears to be an enormous undertaking, as reviewed through this text, significant advances are being made. Persistence in these efforts is now greatly needed. A recent quote provided at the 2004 Joint Annual Meeting of the American and Canadian Pain Societies in Vancouver, British Columbia, provides us with an excellent motivational message to continue to pursue our enormous tasks in the future.

> *"Dream No Small Dreams for They May Have No Power to Move the Hearts of Men."*
>
> GOETHE

REFERENCES

Americans With Disabilities Act of 1990, *42 U.S.C.A. § 12101 et seq.* (West 1993).

American Medical Association (2001). *Guides for the evaluation of permanent impairment* (5th ed.). Chicago: AMA Press.

American Medical Association (1993). *Guides for the evaluation of permanent impairment* (4th ed.). Chicago: AMA Press.

Bandura, A. (1986). *Social foundations of thought and action.* Englewood Cliffs, NJ: Prentice-Hall.

Beck, K., A., & Schultz, I. Z. (2000). *Translating psychological impairment into occupational disability ratings: A decision making model* (Research report). Vancouver, British Columbia: Workers' Compensation Board of British Columbia.

Bickenbach, J.E., Chatterji, S., Badley, E.M., & Ustin, T.B. (1999). Models of disablement, universalism and the international classification of impairments, disabilities and handicaps. *Social Science and Medicine, 48,* 1173–1187.

Bowman, M. (2004). The role of individual factors in predicting Posttraumatic Stress Disorder. In I.Z. Schultz and R. Gatchel (Eds.) *Complex Occupational Disability Claims: Biopsychosocial Approach to Early Risk Identification and Intervention. New York: Kluwer.*

Bureau of Labor Statistics. (2002). 2002, from http://data.bls.gov/surveymost

Clark, L. (1993). *Schedule for Nonadaptive and Adaptive Personality (SNAP)*. Minneapolis: University of Minneapolis Press.

Cole, D.C., Mondloch, M.V., Hogg-Johnson, S. (2002). Listening to injured workers: How recovery expectations predict outcomes—a prospective study. *Canadian Medical Association Journal, 166*(6), 749–754.

Crook, J., Milner, R., Schultz, I. Z., & Stringer, B. (2002). Determinants of occupational disability following a low back injury: A critical review of the literature. *Journal of Occupational Rehabilitation, 12*(4), 277–295.

Drug Topics Redbook 2000. (2002). Montvale, NJ: Thompson Medical Economics.

Dersh, J., Polatin, P., Leeman, G., & Gatchel, R. (2004). Secondary gains and losses in the medicolegal setting. In I. Z. Schultz and R. Gatchel (Eds.) *Complex Occupational Disability Claims: Biopsychosocial Approach to Early Risk Identification and Intervention.* New York: Springer.

Durand, M. & Loisel, P. (2001). Therapeutic return to work: Rehabilitation in the workplace. *Work, 17*, 57–63.

Franche, R., Frank, J., & Krause, N. (2004). Predictive factors and models of occupational disability. In I. Z. Schultz and R. Gatchel (Eds.) *Complex Occupational Disability Claims: Biopsychosocial Approach to Early Risk Identification and Intervention.* New York: Springer.

Franche, R., & Krause, N. (2002). Readiness for Return to Work following injury or illness: Conceptualizing the interpersonal impact of health care, workplace, and insurance factors. *Journal of Occupational Rehabilitation, 12*(4), 233–256.

Garb, H.N. (1994). Toward a second generation of statistical prediction rules in psychodiagnostics and personality assessment. *Computers In Human Behavior, 10*, 377–394.

Garb, H.N. (2000). Computers will become increasingly important for psychological assessment: Not that there's anything wrong with that. *Psychological Assessment, 12*, 31–39.

Gatchel, R. J., Polatin, P. B., Noe, C. E., Gardea, M. A., Pulliam, C. & Thompson, J. (2003). Treatment- and cost-effectiveness of early intervention for acute low back pain patients: A one-year prospective study. *Journal of Occupational Rehabilitation, 13*, 1–9.

Gatchel, R.J., Polatin, P.B., Noe, C., Gardea, M., Pulliam, C., & Thompson, J. (2003). Treatment- and cost-effectiveness of early intervention for acute low-back pain patients: A one-year prospective study. *Journal of Occupational Rehabilitation, 13*(1), 1–9.

Groth-Marnat, G. (2003). *Handbook of Psychological Assessment (4th ed.)*. New York: John Wiley & Sons, Inc.

Grove, W.M., Zald, D.H., Lebow, B.S., Snitz, B.E., & Nelson, C. (2000). Clinical versus mechanical prediction: A metanalysis. *Psychological Assessment, 12*, 19–30.

Guilmette, T.J. (2004). Prediction of vocational functioning from neuropsychological data. In I.Z Schultz and R. Gatchel (Eds.) *Complex Occupational Disability Claims: Biopsychosocial Approach to Early Risk Identification and Intervention.* New York: Springer.

Hazard, R. G. (1995). Spine update: Functional restoration. *Spine, 20*, 2345–2348.

Human Capital Initiative Coordinating Committee. (1996). *Doing the Right Thing: A Research Plan for Healthy Living.* Washington: American Psychological Association.

Kleinmuntz, B. (1990). Why we still use our heads instead of formulas: Toward an integrative approach. *Psychological Bulletin, 107*, 296–310.

Koch, W.J. & Samra, J. (2004). Posttraumatic Stress Disability after motor vehicle accidents: Impact on productivity and employment. In I. Z. Schultz and R. Gatchel (Eds.) *Complex Occupational Disability Claims: Biopsychosocial Approach to Early Risk Identification and Intervention.* New York: Springer.

Krause, N., Frank, J.W., Sullivan, T.J., Dasinger, L.K., & Sinclair, S.J. (2001). Determinants of duration of disability and return to work after work-related injury and illness: Challenges for future research. Invited Paper for Special Issue of *American Journal of Industrial Medicine, 40*, 464–484.

Lanyon, R.I., & Goodstein, L.D. (1997). *Personality Assessment (3rd ed.)*. New York: John Wiley & Sons, Inc.

Leeman, G., Polatin, P., Gatchel, R. & Kishino, N. (2000). Managing secondary gain in patients with pain-associated disability: A clinical perspective. *Journal of Workers Compensation, 9*, 25–44.

Linton, S.J. (2000). A review of psychological risk factors in back and neck pain. *Spine, 25*, 1148–1156.

Linton, S. J. (2002). A cognitive-behavioral approach to the prevention of chronic back pain. In D. C. Turk & R. J. Gatchel (Eds.), *Psychological Approaches to Pain Management: A Practitioner's Handbook* (2nd ed.). New York: Guilford.

Linton, S.J. (2004). Early interventions for "at-risk" patients with spinal pain. In I.Z. Schultz and R. Gatchel (Eds.) *Complex Occupational Disability Claims: Biopsychosocial Approach to Early Risk Identification and Intervention.* New York: Springer.

Linton, S. J. & Bradley, L. A. (1996). Strategies for the prevention of chronic pain. In R. J. Gatchel & D. C. Turk (Eds.), *Psychological Approaches to Pain Management: A Practitioner's Handbook.* New York: Guilford Publications, Inc.

Loisel, P., & Durand, M. (2004). Working with the employer: The Sherbrooke Model. In I.Z. Schultz and R. Gatchel (Eds.) *Complex Occupational Disability Claims: Biopsychosocial Approach to Early Risk Identification and Intervention.* New York: Springer.

Loisel, P., Lemaire, J., Poitras, S., Durand, M., Champagne, F., Stock, S., Diallo, B., & Tremblay, C. (2002). Cost-benefit and cost-effectiveness analysis of a disability prevention model for back pain management: A six year follow up study. *Occupational and Environmental Medicine, 59,* 807–815.

MacKenzie, E.J., Morris, J.A., Jurkovich, G.J., Yasui, Y., Cushing, B.M., Burgess, A.R., DeLateur, B.J., McAndrew, M.P., & Swiontkowski, M.F. (1998). Return to work following injury: The role of economic, social, and job-related factors. *American Journal of Public Health, 88*(11), 1630–1637.

Main, C.J., Spanswick, C.C. (2000). *Pain Management: An interdisciplinary approach.* Edinburgh: Churchill Livingstone.

Marhold, C., Linton, S.J., & Melin, L. (2002). Identification of obstacles for chronic pain patients to return to work: Evaluation of a questionnaire. *Journal of Occupational Rehabilitation, 12*(2), 65–75.

McDaniel, J. (1976). *Physical disability and human behavior.* New York: Pergamon. Medical Fees in the United States 2000. (2002). Los Angeles: Practice Management Information Corporation.

Meehl, P.E. (1954). *Clinical versus statistical prediction: Theoretical analysis and a review of the evidence.* Minneapolis: University of Minnesota Press.

Meehl, P.E. (1965). Seer over sign: The first good example. *Journal of Experimental Research in Personality, 1,* 27–32.

Melhorn, J.M., Lazarovic, J., & Roehl, W.K. (2004). Do we have a disability epidemic? In I.Z. Schultz and R. Gatchel (Eds.) *Complex Occupational Disability Claims: Biopsychosocial Approach to Early Risk Identification and Intervention.* New York: Springer.

National Research Council. (2001). *Musculoskeletal Disorders and the Workplace: Low Back and Upper Extremities.* Washington, D.C.: National Academy Press.

Panel on Musculoskeletal Disorders and the Workplace, Commission on Behavioral and Social Sciences and Education, National Research Council and Institute of Medicine (2001). *Musculoskeletal Disorders and the Workplace: Low Back and Upper Extremities.* Washington, DC: National Academy Press.

Polatin, P., Robinson, R.C., & Garofalo, J.P. (2004). Outcome measures. In I.Z. Schultz and R. Gatchel (Eds.). *Complex Occupational Disability Claims: Biopsychosocial Approach to Early Risk Identification and Intervention.* New York: Springer.

Prochaska, J.O., & DiClemente, C.C. (1983). Stages and processes of self-change of smoking: Toward an integrative model of change. *Journal of Consulting and Clinical Psychology, 51*(3), 390–395.

Rainville, J., Sobel, J., Hartigan, C. & Wright, A. (1997). The effect of compensation involvement of the reporting of pain and disability by patients referred for rehabilitation of chronic low back pain. *Spine, 22*(17), 2016–2024.

Roessler, R.T. (1988). A conceptual basis for return to work interventions. *Rehabilitation Counseling Bulletin, 32,* 99–107.

Roessler, R.T. (1989). Motivational factors influencing return to work. *Journal of Applied Rehabilitation Counseling, 20*(2), 14–17.

Sandstrom, J., & Esbjornsson, E. (1986). Return to work after rehabilitation: The significance of the patient's own prediction. *Scandinavian Journal of Rehabilitation Medicine, 18,* 29–33.

Schultz, I. Z. (2000). *Translating psychological impairment into occupational disability* (Research report). Vancouver, British Columbia: Workers' Compensation Board of British Columbia.

Schultz, I. Z. (2003). The relationship between psychological impairment and occupational disability. In I. Z. Schultz, & D. O. Brady (Eds.), *Psychological Injuries at Trial.* Chicago: American Bar Association.

Schultz, I.Z. (2004). Impairment and occupational disability in research and practice. In I.Z. Schultz and R. Gatchel (Eds.) *Complex Occupational Disability Claims: Biopsychosocial Approach to Early Risk Identification and Intervention.* New York: Springer.

Schultz, I. Z., Crook, J., Fraser, K., & Joy, P. W. (2000). Models of diagnosis and rehabilitation in musculoskeletal pain-related occupational disability. *Journal of Occupational Rehabilitation, 10*(4), 271–293.

Schultz, I. Z., Crook, J., Meloche, G. R., Berkowitz, J., Milner, R., Zuberbier, O. A., Meloche, W. (2004). Psychosocial factors predictive of occupational low back disability: Towards development of a return to work model. *Pain, 107,* 77–85.

Schultz, I.Z., Crook, J., Berkowitz, J., Milner, R., & Meloche, G.R. (submitted). Predicting Return to Work After Low Back Injury Using the Risk for Occupational Disability Instrument: A Validation Study.

Schultz, I., Crook, J., Milner, R., Berkowitz, J., Meloche, G. (2002). Use of Administrative Databases for the Multivariate Prediction of Occupational Disability: A feasibility assessment. *The Journal of Workers Compensation, 12*(1), 43–55.

Tate, D.G., & Pledger, C. (2003). An integrative conceptual framework of disability: New directions for research. *American Psychologist, 58*(4), 289–295.

Turner, J.A., Franklin, G., & Turk, D.C. (2000). Predictors of chronic disability in injured workers: A systematic literature synthesis. *American Journal of Industrial Medicine, 38,* 707–722.

U.S. Department of Education, Office of Special Education and Rehabilitation Services, National Institute on Disability and Rehabilitation Research (2000). *Long range plan: 1999–2003.* Washington, DC: Author

Vitaliano, P., Russo, J., Carr, J., Maiuro, R. & Becker, J. (1985). The ways of coping checklist: Revision and psychometric properties. *Multivariate Behavioral Research, 20,* 3–26.

Waddell, G. & Burton, A.K. (2001). Occupational health guidelines for the management of low back pain at work: Evidence review. *Occupational Medicine, 51*(2), 124–135.

Wright, A.R., & McGeary, D.D. (2004). Musculoskeletal Injury: A three-stage continuum from cause to disability to decision. In I.Z. Schultz and R. Gatchel (Eds.) *Complex Occupational Disability Claims: Biopsychosocial Approach to Early Risk Identification and Intervention.* New York: Springer.

Index

C

D

E

F

N

O

S

T

U

V

W

Y

CPSIA information can be obtained at www.ICGtesting.com
Printed in the USA
LVOW070450270412

279386LV00003B/11/P